THE TALMUD AND RABBINIC LITERATURE

This volume guides beginning students of rabbinic literature through the range of historical-interpretive and culture-critical issues that contemporary scholars use when studying rabbinic texts. The editors, themselves well-known interpreters of rabbinic literature, have gathered an international collection of scholars to support students' initial steps in confronting the enormous and complex rabbinic corpus. Unlike other introductions to rabbinic writings, the present volume includes approaches shaped by anthropology, gender studies, oral-traditional studies, classics, and folklore studies.

Charlotte Elisheva Fonrobert is the author of *Menstrual Purity: Rabbinic and Christian Reconstructions of Biblical Gender* (2000), which won the Salo Baron Prize for a best first book in Jewish Studies of that year and was one of three finalists for the National Jewish Book Award.

Martin S. Jaffee is the author of *Torah in the Mouth: Writing and Oral Tradition in Palestinian Judaism, 200 B.C.E–400 C.E.* (2001); *Early Judaism: Religious Worlds of the First Judaic Millennium* (2nd ed., 2006); and several volumes of rabbinic translation and commentary. He is currently coeditor of the *AJS Review*.

CAMBRIDGE COMPANIONS TO RELIGION
This is a series of companions to major topics and key figures in
theology and religious studies. Each volume contains specially
commissioned chapters by international scholars that provide an
accessible and stimulating introduction to the subject for new readers
and nonspecialists.

Continued after the Index

THE CAMBRIDGE COMPANION TO

THE TALMUD AND RABBINIC LITERATURE

Edited by Charlotte Elisheva Fonrobert
Stanford University

Martin S. Jaffee
University of Washington

CAMBRIDGE
UNIVERSITY PRESS

CAMBRIDGE UNIVERSITY PRESS
Cambridge, New York, Melbourne, Madrid, Cape Town, Singapore, São Paulo

Cambridge University Press
32 Avenue of the Americas, New York, NY 10013-2473, USA

www.cambridge.org
Information on this title: www.cambridge.org/9780521843904

First published 2007

Printed in the United States of America

A catalog record for this publication is available from the British Library.

Library of Congress Cataloging in Publication Data

The Cambridge companion to the Talmud and rabbinic literature / edited by Charlotte
Elisheva Fonrobert, Martin S. Jaffee.
    p. cm. – (Cambridge companions to religion)
Includes bibliographical references and index.
ISBN-13: 978-0-521-84390-4 (hardback)
ISBN-13: 978-0-521-60508-3 (pbk.)
    1. Talmud – Criticism, interpretation, etc.   2. Rabbinical literature –
History and criticism.   3. Jewish law – History – To 1500.   I. Fonrobert, Charlotte
Elisheva.   II. Jaffee, Martin S.   III. Title.   IV. Series.
BM504.C36   2007
296.1'206–dc21   2006022821

ISBN   978-0-521-84390-4 hardback
ISBN   978-0-521-60508-3 paperback

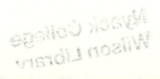

Contents

Contributors

Elizabeth Shanks Alexander is Assistant Professor in the Department of Religious Studies at the University of Virginia. Her research interests include the oral character of rabbinic texts. She has just begun work on the development of gender in rabbinic law.

Daniel Boyarin is the Hermann P. and Sophia Taubman Professor of Talmudic Culture in the Departments of Near Eastern Studies and Rhetoric, University of California at Berkeley. His interests include the relationship between Judaism and Christianity in Late Antiquity, as well as conceptions of sexuality in Late Antique culture.

Shaye J. D. Cohen is Littauer Professor of Hebrew Language and Literature at Harvard University. He is interested in the history of Jewish identity and has just begun work on a history of rabbinic law.

Yaakov Elman is Professor of Judaic Studies at Yeshiva University. His interests include the intellectual and cultural history of Late Antiquity and the history of biblical exegesis.

Charlotte Elisheva Fonrobert is Associate Professor of Religious Studies at Stanford University. She teaches the history and culture of rabbinic Judaism and studies the dynamics of gender in rabbinic culture, in particular rabbinic thinking about the human body, as well as rabbinic conceptions of space in connection with formations of Jewish identity.

Steven D. Fraade is the Mark Taper Professor of the History of Judaism at Yale University. He teaches the history and literature of Late Second Temple and early rabbinic Judaism.

Isaiah Gafni is the Sol Rosenbloom Professor of Jewish History at the Hebrew University of Jerusalem and Chair of the Mandel Institute of Jewish Studies. His areas of recent research include rabbinic Judaism and rabbinic portrayals of the past as expressions of self-identity, frameworks, and authority structures of the Jewish community in Late Antiquity, as well as the Jewish Diaspora and its links with the Land of Israel in Second Temple and post-Temple times.

Galit Hasan-Rokem is the Max and Margarethe Grunwald Professor of Folklore, Department of Hebrew Literature and the Jewish and Comparative Folklore Program, Mandel Institute for Jewish Studies, Hebrew University of Jerusalem. Her areas of specialization include hermeneutical and comparative aspects of folk literary production, especially in classical rabbinic culture, as well as Proverbs and riddles.

Christine Hayes is the Robert F. and Patricia R. Weis Professor of Religious Studies in Classical Judaica in the Department of Religious Studies at Yale University. She has written about the relationship between the Palestinian and the Babylonian Talmud, as well as Jewish perceptions of non-Jews in Late Antique Jewish literature.

Catherine Hezser is Professor of Rabbinic Judaism in the Department of the Study of Religions at the University of London. Her research centers on the social history of Jews in Late Antique Roman Palestine, particular in the context of early Greco-Roman and early Christian society.

Martin S. Jaffee is Professor of Comparative Religion at the Henry M. Jackson School of International Studies, University of Washington in Seattle. His research interests include the relationship between orality and textuality in rabbinic literature, as well as the relationship among Judaism, Christianity, and Islam.

Jeffrey L. Rubenstein is Professor of Hebrew and Judaic Studies in the Skirball Department of Hebrew and Judaic Studies at New York University. His interests include rabbinic stories, the history of Jewish law, the culture of the Babylonian Talmud, and Jewish ethics.

Jonathan Wyn Schofer is Assistant Professor of Comparative Ethics at the Harvard Divinity School. His research centers on rabbinic ethics and self-cultivation.

Seth Schwartz is the Gerson D. Cohen Professor of Rabbinic Culture and Professor of History at The Jewish Theological Seminary. He has written about the influence of Roman imperialism on the political, social, and economic developments of Jewish life in late ancient Palestine.

Michael D. Swartz is Professor of Hebrew and Religious Studies at the Ohio State University. He has written on Jewish mysticism, magic, liturgy, and ritual in Late Antiquity.

Acknowledgments

The editors wish, first and foremost, to thank Ms. Phyllis Berk, of Howard Berk Associates, who took extraordinary pains to edit a very complex manuscript and prepare it for press. Her patience and good humor always encouraged us to propose improvements as they suggested themselves to us; and her eagle eye for consistency in citation and transliteration have spared us many embarrassments. Needless to say, any remaining inconsistencies in the final product are the sole responsibility of the editors. We also owe a great debt of thanks to Ms. Claire Sufrin, a doctoral student at Stanford University, for invaluable assistance in preparing the glossary and the index.

Professor Fonrobert, in particular, would like to thank the Stanford Humanities Center for the research fellowship in 2004–05, which enabled her to do a significant portion of the preparatory work for this volume and to absorb many costs involved with preparing the manuscript for submission to the Press.

For his part, Professor Jaffee wishes to thank three individuals without whom his contribution to this volume would certainly have suffered. First, he acknowledges his wife and closest friend, Charla Soriano Jaffee, whose companionship and moral support have afforded him the security and peace of mind to pursue this and other projects. Secondly, he gladly acknowledges a great debt to his Talmud study-partner, Dr. Shlomo Goldberg of Seattle. Their friendship, renewed each dawn in the study of Mishnah and each Sabbath in the study of Talmud, has taught Professor Jaffee what it means to study Torah with one's entire being, from the critical intellect to the mysterious symbolic representations that bubble up from the subconscious mind. Finally, during the entire span of this project, Professor Jaffee has benefited enormously from the daily study of a page of Talmud (*daf yomi shi'ur*) conducted by Rabbi Moshe Kletenik of Seattle's Congregation Bikur Cholim-Machzikay Hadas. Professor Jaffee's training in rabbinic studies has taken place exclusively in the academic milieu of historical-literary criticism. Therefore, it has been a revelation to witness the breadth of textual knowledge, acuteness of literary analysis, and encyclopedic mastery of the entire tradition of medieval and modern Talmudic exegesis commanded by an exemplary contemporary *talmid ḥakham*, as embodied in the person of Rabbi Kletenik.

Charlotte Elisheva Fonrobert
Stanford University
Palo Alto, CA

Martin S. Jaffee
University of Washington
Seattle, WA

R'osh Ḥodesh Tevet, the Eighth Light of Hanukkah, 5767
December 22, 2006

Brief Time Line of Rabbinic Literature

Late Second Temple Period (ca. 200 B.C.E.–70 C.E.)

200: Temple-state of Judaea passes from Egyptian Ptolemaic to Syrian Seleucid control.

ca.180: The scribe Yeshua b. Sira describes the Temple cult administered by the High Priest, Simon (Wisdom of ben Sira 50: 1ff.). This Simon is probably the figure recalled in Mishnah Avot 1:2 as Shimon the Righteous, "a remnant of the Great Assembly," the first named figure in the post-biblical period identified as a tradent of Torah received from Moses at Sinai.

167–152: The Maccabean uprising against the Seleucids and consolidation of Hasmonean rule

152–63: Hasmonean Dynasty

ca. 152–140: The anonymous author of the "Halakhic Letter" (found among the Dead Sea Scrolls: 4QMMT) refers to disputes regarding cultic purity ascribed in the Mishnah (Yadayim 4:6–7) to the Sadducees and Pharisees.

134–104: Reign of John Hyrcanus

Emergence of Pharisees as proponents of "traditions (*paradoseis*) not written in the Torah of Moses" (Josephus, Antiquities 13)

103–67: Reigns of Alexander Jannaeus and Alexandra Salome

Composer of the Qumran Pesher Nahum refers to Pharisaic opponents as *dorshei ḥalakot* ("seekers of smooth things"), a possible punning reference to *halakhot* derived from proto-rabbinic midrashic hermeneutics.

63 B.C.E.–70 C.E.: Herodian Period

63: Pompey intervenes in a Hasmonean dynastic controversy and Rome incorporates Palestine as a province.

37–34: Herod rules Palestine as Jewish king and begins massive renovation of the Jerusalem Temple.

32 C.E.: Roman procuratorial administration sentences Jesus of Nazareth to execution by crucifixion for political crimes.

ca. 50–70 C.E.: Earliest Gospel traditions refer to Pharisees as guardians of "traditions" (*paradoseis*).

66–73: Palestinian Jews wage war against Rome.

Early Rabbinic ("Tannaitic") Period (ca. 70–220)

70–90: Depopulation of Judaea and shift of Jewish settlement to Galilee

ca. 80–130: Postwar Jewish leadership, centered in Yavneh, formulates and gathers traditional teachings ascribed to pre-70 sages "beginning with Hillel and Shammai" (T. Eduyot 1:1).

115–117: Suppression of Diaspora Jews' uprising against Rome and obliteration of Alexandrian Jewry

132–135: Bar Kokhba rebellion and Hadrianic repression of Galilean Jewry encourages migrations of early rabbinic sages to Parthian Empire.

ca. 140–200: Consolidation of Patriarchate under the Gamalian dynasty

ca. 180–220: Rabbinic traditions trace the origins of the Patriarchate back to the first-century B.C.E. Pharisee Hillel the Elder (e.g., M. Hagigah 2:2, T. Pesahim 4:1-2).

ca. 200–220: Rabbi Yehudah ha-Nasi, administering Jewish affairs from his patriarchal seat in Sepphoris, sponsors the promulgation of the Mishnah, a curriculum of memorized literary traditions designed for the training of rabbinic disciples.

Middle Rabbinic ("Amoraic") Period (ca. 220–500)

ca. 200–220: Patriarchate of Rabban Shimon b. Rabbi Yehudah ha-Nasi ca. 220–250: The anonymous introduction to Mishnah Avot (1:1–2:8) provides a transmissional chain linking Torah received at Sinai to the patriarchal line, which now includes Hillel and Rabban Yohanan b. Zakkai and culminates in the traditions of Rabban Shimon b. Rabbi Yehudah ha-Nasi, the patriarchal scion of Sepphoris.

ca. 220: Rav (Abba Arikha) and Mar Shmuel establish rabbinic presence in Parthian Empire.

226: Shapur I becomes first king of Sasanian Empire in Babylonia.

ca. 220–350: Compilation by anonymous Galilean editors of extra-mishnaic "tannnaitic" traditions into mnemonically structured compositions. The Tosefta ("Supplement") is organized in terms of the structure of the Mishnah, while works of scriptural exegesis (*midrash*) are organized in tandem with scriptural verses.

ca. 250: Galilean sages in the circle of Rabbi Yohanan b. Nappaha circulate earliest traditions that the Oral Torah received at Sinai is "embedded in the Mishnah" (e.g., Y. Peah 2:6).

313: Roman Emperor Constantine issues Edict of Milan, establishing Christianity as a tolerated religious sect in Roman Empire.

ca. 220–425: Galilean amoraic traditions and tannaitic antecedents are gathered for circulation with the Mishnah as a focused curriculum. The Talmud Yerushalmi represents a version of this curriculum as transmitted primarily in Tiberias.

ca. 320–425: Byzantine Palestine becomes a center of Christian pilgrimage as the "Holy Land."

360–363: Emperor Julian sponsors efforts to rebuild the Jerusalem Temple, but his death interrupts the project.

ca. 300–500: Galilean amoraic traditions are compiled into a series of accompaniments to the books of the Torah (e.g., Genesis Rabbah) and key liturgical scrolls, such as Lamentations (Lamentations Rabbah) and Koheleth (Koheleth Rabbah).

425: Palestinian Patriarch Gamaliel VI dies and no successor is appointed.

ca. 220–500: Babylonian sages, centered in such towns as Sura, Pumbeditha, Nehardea, Huzal, and Mehoza, develop, formulate, and amplify traditions of learning (*gemara*) to accompany memorization and analysis of the Mishnah and other tannaitic materials.

Late Rabbinic ("Savoraic"-"Stammaitic") Period (ca. 550–620)

553: Emperor Justinian attacks the rabbinic *deuterosis* ("oral tradition").

500–600: Compilation of Palestinian midrashic anthologies, such as Pesikta de-Rav Kahana, Pesikta Rabbati, Midrash Tanhuma

ca. 600: Savoraic tradents have organized amoraic traditions from Babylonia and Palestine into coherently plotted critical discourses (*sugyot*) to accompany mishnaic tractates.

620: Completion of the Babylonian Talmud: A final redactional voice (the "Stam") enhances the Savoraic gemara with hermeneutical cues and synthesizing discussion that serve as interpretive supplements. The earliest manuscript fragments of the ninth century correspond to extant medieval manuscripts of the Babyblonian Talmud.

Early Geonic Period (ca. 620–800)

620: Beginning of Islamic conquests in Mesopotamia and North Africa.

661: Umayyad Dynasty established, with capital in Damascus

750: Abbasid Dynasty establishes Baghdad as its capital

750–800: Geonic heads of Suran and Pumbedithan rabbinical academies relocate to Baghdad. The Babylonian Talmud is the chief curriculum and the source of legal tradition for administering the Jewish *ahl al-dhimma* on behalf of the Caliph.

Glossary

'aggadah: nonlegal rabbinic teachings, often appearing in the form of commentary on the narrative portion of biblical text (*midrash 'aggadah*).

'Amora'im: literally, "expounders." These are rabbinic sages, living from the middle of the third to the early sixth centuries in both Palestine and Babylonia, who appear throughout the Talmud, commenting on the discussions of the Tanna'im found in the Mishnah and the Tosefta.

'am ha'arez: literally, "people of the land." In rabbinic usage it tends to convey a perjorative evaluation of the majority of Jews who are uneducated in or resistant to rabbinic customs.

baraita'/baraitot: literally, "external." A baraita' is a tannaitic legal ruling, regarded as part of the Oral Torah that was not included in the Mishnah. Baraitot are often cited in the Talmud as evidence for or against amoraic interpretations of the Mishnah.

bet midrash: rabbinic study group or disciple circle, later institutionalized as study house.

Dead Sea Scrolls: a collection of more than 800 fragmentary documents of the Late Second Temple period discovered in several caves near Qumran on the shore of the Dead Sea. The scrolls include biblical texts, commentaries known as *pesharim*, previously unknown works such as the Temple Scroll and Genesis Apocryphon, and other documents. The first Dead Sea Scrolls were discovered in 1947.

Diaspora: settlements of Jews outside the Land of Israel.

Essenes: a Second Temple pietist and sectarian group, known for being particularly strict in the observance of the commandments. Many scholars believe that the Essenes bore some connection to the Dead Sea sect at Qumran.

Great Assembly: a legendary body of sages listed in the opening paragraph of Mishnah Avot as one link in a chain transmitting the teachings of Torah from the rabbis to Moses.

Ḥakham/Ḥakhamim: rabbinic term for a sage, cognate to the Greek *philosophos* or *didaskalos*.

halakhah/halakhot: literally, "the procedure (for fulfilling a biblical commandment)." This is the general term for rabbinic law. Halakhah addresses religious and ritual matters as well as civil and criminal law. The seeds of halakhah are found in the Hebrew Bible and developed by the rabbis in the Talmud and other documents. Legal commentary on the Bible is known as *midrash halakhah.*

Ḥaver/Ḥaverim: rabbinic term for an associate or colleague in the circle of masters and disciples (*bet midrash*),

masekhet/masekhtot: a tractate or subtopic within one of the orders (*sedarim*) of the Mishnah or Talmud.

Masoretic Text: the "official" version of the Hebrew Bible. Between the seventh and tenth centuries C.E., a group of scholars known as the Masoretes standardized the text's spelling, cantillation, vowels, and accents. Direct ancestors of the Masoretic Texts are attested in many biblical manuscripts found among the Dead Sea Scrolls.

midrash/midrashim: the rabbinic mode of biblical commentary, composed in both Palestine and Babylonia by both Tanna'im and 'Amora'im. Rabbinic midrash comments on either legal or narrative portions of the biblical text (*midrash halakhah* and *midrash aggadah*, respectively). Palestinian *midrash* can be found in various collections (e.g., Genesis Rabbah or Pesikta de-Rav Kahana). Both Palestinian and Babylonian midrash appear in the Talmud.

mikveh: a ritual bath, used for rites of purification from various sorts of uncleanness that would limit a person's access to the Temple and its sacrificial forms of cleansing. In post-Temple rabbinic Judaism, it is used most commonly at set times during a woman's menstrual cycle.

min/minim: within the Talmud, the term referring to Jews who hold legal or theological views that place them beyond the rabbinic pale. In any given context, references to *minim* might include believers in the messiahship of Jesus, Sadducees, Boethusians, Zealots, and Samaritans. As depicted in the Talmud, *minim* are often quite familiar with the scriptural text but dispute rabbinic interpretations.

Mishnah: the earliest collection of tannaitic traditions, organized into six orders and sixty-three tractates. The contents are mostly legal in nature. According to rabbinic tradition, Rabbi Yehudah ha-Nasi (early third century C.E.) is responsible for the compilation of the Mishnah.

mitzvah/mitzvot: literally, "commandment." The term describes a scriptural law or, in some cases, rituals prescribed by sages (e.g., the lighting of lights on Hanukkah). The rabbis believed the mitzvot were commanded by God to the Jewish people (and, in the case of the seven Noahide commandments, to all humankind).

pesher/pesharim: running commentaries to the books of the Prophets and Psalms, found among the Dead Sea Scrolls and characterized by a distinct eschatological bent. Pesher is a direct antecedent of rabbinic *midrash*.

Pharisees: a dominant group of Second Temple Jews, from which some early rabbinic sages likely descended.

Sadducees: a group of Second Temple priestly families who appear in rabbinic literature as opponents of halakhic rulings of early sages.

Samaritans: natives of Samaria traditionally opposed to the Judaean Jewish community of the Late Second Temple and early rabbinic periods. Their customs are often disparaged in rabbinic texts as examples of religious error or intentional deviation from rabbinic halakhic norms. Accordingly, rabbinic halakhah defines Samaritans as Jews in some contexts and as non-Jews in others.

Savora'im: a hypothetical group of rabbinic scholars falling chronologically between the 'Amora'im and the Stamma'im, often believed to have a crucial role in the editing of talmudic *sugyot* in the century or so prior to 620 C.E.

seder/sedarim: literally, "order." The six major legal divisions of the Mishnah, the Tosefta, and the Talmudim.

Shekhinah: a name for God's presence, usually associated with God's feminine characteristics.

Shema: Deuteronomy 6:4–9, when recited as part of the liturgy.

Stamma'im: the anonymous sages who, perhaps around 600 C.E., edited the Babylonian Talmud by collecting and reworking earlier traditions. The *Stam* is the interpretive voice of these anonymous editors.

sugya': the characteristic literary unit of the Talmud exploring some legal or homiletic issue through the voices of disputing or interacting parties. A *sugya'* can be as brief as a few lines of discourse or, in contrast, extend over a folio page or more of the printed Talmud.

talmid ḥakaham/talmidei ḥakhamim: rabbinic term for a disciple(s).

Talmud: literally meaning "study." The Talmud is a lengthy commentary on the Mishnah composed in Hebrew and Aramaic. The earlier edition, most likely redacted in Tiberias in the late fourth and/or early fifth centuries C.E., is known as the Jerusalem or Palestinian Talmud (*Talmud Yerushalmi*). The later and larger edition, redacted in Persia in as-yet poorly understood stages between the late fifth and late eighth centuries C.E., is known as the Babylonian Talmud (*Talmud Bavli*). Like the Mishnah, the Talmud is organized into orders (*sedarim*) and within the orders into tractates (*masekhot*).

Tanna'im: literally, "repeaters" (i.e., of orally transmitted teachings). According to Talmudic chronology, the period of the Tanna'im begins with the remnants of the Men of the Great Assembly, presumably around the time of Ezra, and continues through the generation of Rabbi Yehudah ha-Nasi. They are responsible for the traditions included in the Mishnah, Tosefta, and other early rabbinic literature.

Torah: the first five books of the Hebrew Bible (the Pentateuch). It is also a generic term for all authoritative religious teaching, for example, "Moses received Torah from Sinai" (M. Avot 1:1).

Torah she-be'al peh: literally, "the oral Torah." This is the all-inclusive term for traditional rabbinic teaching as it is found in the Mishnah and Talmuds. According to rabbinic tradition, it was taught orally by God to Moses on Sinai and transmitted in an unbroken link of masters and disciples to the talmudic masters.

Torah she-bikhtav: literally "the written Torah." Broadly, this refers to the canonical Scriptures of the Hebrew Bible, although the paradigmatic work of "Written Torah" is the scroll of the Five Books of Moses.

Tosefta: one of the early tannaitic compilations of rabbinic literature (dating to the third century). Understood by most scholars to be a supplementary commentary on the Mishnah, it is also largely legal. The circumstances and purpose of its compilation are unknown, although it is traditionally ascribed to Rabbi Hiyya bar Abba.

Abbreviations

BAR:	*Biblical Archeology Review*
DSD:	*Dead Sea Discoveries*
FJB:	*Frankfurter Judaistische Beiträge*
HTR:	*Harvard Theological Review*
HUCA:	*Hebrew Union College Annual*
IEJ:	*Israel Exploration Journal*
JAOS:	*Journal of the American Oriental Society*
JBL:	*Journal of Biblical Literature*
JHS:	*Journal of the History of Sexuality*
JJS:	*Journal of Jewish Studies*
JQR:	*Jewish Quarterly Review*
JSHL:	*Jerusalem Studies in Hebrew Literature*
JSJ:	*Journal for the Study of Judaism in the Persian, Hellenistic, and Roman Periods*
NJPS:	*Tanakh: The Holy Scriptures. The New JPS Translation According to the Traditional Hebrew Text*
PAAJR:	*Proceedings of the American Academy for Jewish Research*
PWCJS:	*Proceedings of the World Congress of Jewish Studies*
SZ:	*Sifre Zuta*
ZSS:	*Zeitschrift der Savigny Stiftung für Rechtsgeschichte*

THE CAMBRIDGE COMPANION TO

THE TALMUD AND RABBINIC LITERATURE

Introduction: The Talmud, Rabbinic Literature, and Jewish Culture

The Babylonian Talmud (Hebr. *Talmud Bavli*) is without doubt the most prominent text of rabbinic Judaism's traditional literature. Indeed, the simple phrase "the Talmud says" often stands as a kind of shorthand for any teaching found anywhere in the vast rabbinic corpus surviving from Late Antiquity. Among Jews, of course, the Talmud has been revered, studied, and commented upon over and over again for more than a millennium. But preoccupation – even obsession – with the Talmud has extended at times beyond the borders of traditional rabbinic communities as well. Christian theologians and historians have on occasion viewed the Talmud, much more than the Hebrew Bible itself, as encapsulating the spiritual and intellectual core of Judaism.

This interest has not always had benign results; it has, at times, turned the Talmud into a target of polemics and even violence. Repeated burnings of the Talmud and its associated writings by Christian authorities in medieval Europe were meant to destroy the intellectual sustenance of Judaism. In modern times, the Talmud has become a target even of Jews: Many secularized Jews of the post-Enlightenment period ridiculed its "primitive" religious worldview; reformers of Judaism sought to move behind it, as it were, to restore the Bible (or certain interpretations of it) as the normative source of Jewish belief; while Zionist Jews, concerned with restoring a vital Jewish culture in the ancient Jewish homeland, belittled the "diasporic" culture of "sterile" learning embodied by the Babylonian Talmud.

It is not the task of this book to rehearse the remarkable history of theological and political attacks on the Talmud. Rather, it aims to address readers for whom the Talmud, and the larger body of rabbinic literature of which it stands as a kind of emblem, is not a threatening presence but, by contrast, a complex cultural puzzle inviting solutions of the vast range of interpretive approaches developed in the contemporary humanities. The Christian and Jewish polemicists, for whom the rabbinic literature represented the "essence" of what they objected to in

Judaism generally, were blind to literary and cultural dimensions of the literature that, from the perspective of cultural studies and comparative religion, render it immensely interesting.

Unlike most texts in the Western literary and religious canons, for example, and in contrast to later medieval Jewish literature, the texts of the rabbinic canon were not produced by an "author" or by one particular group of authors, unless one considers generations of sages extending at least six centuries to be a coherent group of authors. As a partial consequence of having no authors, rabbinic literature is also difficult to locate clearly in space and time beyond the routine banalities of encyclopedia definitions (e.g., "Middle East, first seven centuries C.E."). There is virtually no passage in the rabbinic corpus of which we can confidently state that "it was written in such and such a year, in such and such a place, by such and such an individual." At best, individual passages of rabbinic literature can be dated, on the basis of redactional-critical and tradition-critical criteria, in a merely relative sense. This permits critics to distinguish between earlier and later layers of text within the roughly six centuries of its accumulation and growth, but rarely permits firmer dating in terms of decades or calendar years.

To complicate matters, most texts have a prehistory as orally circulated texts, and may have been edited orally. So we must reckon with an unspecified gestation period separating the text preserved in a medieval manuscript of the Talmud from the milieu of oral transmission in which it found its earliest expression. One of the few traits of the Talmud and other rabbinic writings that appear to be useful for dating the texts is the rabbinic habit of stating laws and other teachings in the names of specific sages and teachers. For the first century of modern talmudic studies, many assumed that securing the dates in which a specific teacher flourished would enable historians to date the composition of his teachings. But it is precisely the "nonauthored" character of rabbinic literature that prevents us from assuming with any degree of historical certainty that Rabbi Akiva or any other rabbinic figure cited in the talmudic discussions "really" said what is attributed to him. Indeed, for most rabbinic sages, we do not have external historical or biographical references, nor do we have extensive internal biographies. In the best case, we know as much about such major rabbinic authorities as Hillel, Rabban Gamaliel, Rabbi Akiva, or Rav as we do about the historical Jesus. Often less. The fragmentary biographical or, rather, hagiographical accounts remaining to us are often in conflict with parallel sources in different contexts, making it extremely difficult to describe any individual sage as a historical figure.

Finally, the literary processes that produced the surviving copies of most rabbinic texts are entirely unclear. We know next to nothing about the last generation(s) of sages who edited the vast quantities of textual material and gave it the approximate shape in which the manuscripts have come down to us. Those who produced the texts successfully blurred the historical traces of their production. This is not to say that there are not various theories that scholars have advanced over the last century. Yet the gap of several centuries between the assumed redaction of the talmudic and other rabbinic texts and the first actual manuscripts is hard to bridge with any meaningful historiographic account.

THE CONCEPT "RABBINIC LITERATURE"

These texts then defy easy classification, and they fit traditional or Western categories of genre, such as law code, encyclopedia, or even "literature" only with great difficulty, if at all. Indeed, the term "rabbinic literature" itself is a creation of the modern, historical study of the Jewish religious and cultural tradition. It would have been unintelligible to the producers of these writings.

In the first place, the adjective "rabbinic," employed to distinguish one Jewish group from another, has a medieval, not a Late Antique, genealogy. It would have had no resonance in the community of sages prior to the rise of Islam and the subsequent emergence of polemical exchanges between self-proclaimed "rabbanite" and "karaite" Jewish authors. What contemporary scholars call "rabbinic literature" was known to medieval "rabbanites" as an inheritance of tradition bequeathed to them by an ancient lineage of teachers, as the Talmud has it, *rabbanan*, "our Masters." While many of these originating teachers bore the honorific title of "rabbi" (my master/teacher), this title in and of itself implied nothing about the social identity of its bearer.

At the same time, many figures cited as authoritative masters of "rabbinic" tradition did not have the title of rabbi. And as archaeologists have learned, the term "rabbi" could designate a landlord or a patron as well as teacher. During the centuries in which the sages' traditions were gaining classical form, their transmitters did not view themselves as "the rabbis." The teachers who form the collective voice of rabbinic literature identified as *ḥakhamim* ("sages," cognate to the Greek *philosophos* or *didaskalos*), *ḥaverim* ("associates" or "colleagues"), or *talmidei ḥakhamim* ("disciples"). They constituted themselves as a distinctive group within the larger Jewish community and often took note – at times with dismay and at others with a certain kind of elitist pride – of the ways in which their patterns of life differed from those customary among other Jews.

The sages developed various strategies of representing other Jews, but one prominent strategy was to claim the term "Israel" for themselves and those who lived by their values and laws, while others were depicted as ignorant (the so-called *'ammei ha'arez* and the Samaritans [*kutim*]) or sectarian (e.g., *minim* and Saducees [*zedukim*]). At the same time, they believed that the rules by which they lived were the patrimony of all Jews, even if the Jews themselves rejected that patrimony. To that end, they presented themselves as continuers of ancient tradition, rather than as innovative sectarians.

Secondly, as self-conscious "traditionalists," these sages would not have asserted that the texts issuing from their study circles represented their own rabbinic views and interests. The "rabbinic literature" for them had its origin in the revelation at Mount Sinai, not in the rabbinic study circles or schools. Pre-Islamic Jewish sages knew of two kinds of authoritative texts. There was the revealed text of Scripture, disclosed to Moses, and of the later prophets, and stored carefully in hand-copied scrolls. It was often called *Torah she-bikhtav* ("written Torah") to distinguish it from the second sort of text. In the rabbinic conception, this second type of text was just as deeply rooted in the revelation at Mt. Sinai. But it had been transmitted in face-to-face oral instruction in an unbroken line of tradition. As one of the most famous and oft-quoted texts has it: "Moses received Torah from Sinai and handed it down to Joshua, and Joshua to the elders, and the elders to the prophets, and the prophets down to Men of the 'Great Assembly'" (Mishnah Avot 1:1). Torah here designates tradition as a whole, and in particular tradition as the rabbis gave shape to it. The second type of text, then, that emerged from this concept of tradition, was called *Torah she-be'al peh* ("oral/memorized Torah"). No one could claim to have "written" or "composed" texts of Oral Torah since they represented the voice of tradition rather than the opinions of authors. At best, certain sages were credited by their descendants as having "gathered" or "arranged" earlier traditions into compilations in order to facilitate study and application.

So the producers of "rabbinic literature" saw their knowledge as "Torah" rather than as specifically rabbinic tradition and did not advance any claim of authorial responsibility to the works scholars ascribe to them. Indeed, they would not have had the slightest conception that the texts they taught were "literature." And here we need to problematize this half of our title as well. The academic study of literature is grounded in the early modern humanist conviction that the study of great, classic texts could connect contemporaries to the intellectual, moral, and imaginative worlds of those who produced them. Literature was considered to be the written record of the magnificent products of original human minds. When the German-Jewish founders of research in rabbinic literature named their topic, they too meant to develop tools that would disclose the secrets of the minds of the authors of the rabbinic writings, the key to their originality as founders of a unique Jewish culture. They wanted to make the riches of rabbinic writings available for comparison with other great "national literatures," from the Greek and Latin classics to the emerging vernacular poetry, fiction, and science of the modern European peoples. Well and good. But for the groups among whom the writings known as "rabbinic literature" emerged, it was inconceivable to compare any Torah – written or oral – to anything so mundane as human creativity in communicating law, lore, and, indeed, laughs by means of the written word. Careful readers will find plenty of law, lore, legend, and (even, on occasion) laughs in the pages of rabbinic texts, but those who preserved this material included it because it was Torah, not because they hoped to express themselves in an engaging or unique way.

All this being said – and it will be said again in other forms at numerous points in this book – we are stuck with the term "rabbinic literature" to describe the writings (which are not authored) produced by Jewish teachers (who were not yet "the rabbis") that became, by the High Middle Ages, the literary patrimony of virtually all the Jewries of Christian Europe and the Islamic Middle East (though it was not recognized by them as anything resembling "literature"). Conventions die hard, especially convenient ones, and the existence of rabbinic literature is an important one for anyone studying the history of Judaism and its cultural offspring in modernity. As long as we remember that the term is a useful fiction that reflects the cultural assumptions unique to European modernity, it will serve us in communicating about our topic.

THE MAIN TEXTS OF RABBINIC LITERATURE

The foundation of the rabbinic literary tradition is embodied in the Mishnah ("repeated/memorized tradition") and the Tosefta ("supplement"). Composed in elegant Hebrew, and containing the fundamental legal traditions of the earliest generations of rabbinic teachers (viz., the *Tanna'im*, that is, "repeaters of early tradition-texts"), the Mishnah and the Tosefta have traditionally been considered as separate works reflecting diverse selections from a prior oral tradition. However, their contents and structures so deeply interpenetrate and wind around each other that is has become increasingly difficult to untangle their many knots of connectedness. Medieval scholars normally viewed the Tosefta as a companion to the Mishnah that covered similar ground in its own idiosyncratic way. Among modern scholars the tendency has been to see the Mishnah as the core document and the Tosefta as a kind of rambling commentary. Both are primarily legal in focus, divided like ancient law codes into major topics (*sedarim*, "orders") and subtopics (*masekhot*, "treatises"). The rabbinic tradition itself ascribes the editing of the Mishnah to the Palestinian patriarch Rabbi Yehudah Ha-Nasi, whose work would have occurred in the northern Galilean town of Sepphoris in the early third century C.E. Responsibility for the compilation of the Tosefta is at times ascribed to a younger colleague, Rabbi Hiyya bar Abba. But, in fact, there is little historical or literary evidence to link either text directly to its reputed compiler.

All later rabbinic compilations share the essential anonymity of the redaction of the Mishnah and the Tosefta. Usually ascribed to the late third and early fourth centuries C.E. is a series of compositions of an exegetical character that use books of the Hebrew Bible as their principle of editorial organization. Differing dramatically in style, content, and preoccupations, they nevertheless share with one another and the Mishnah and Tosefta a common language – post-biblical, aramaicized Hebrew – and a common attribution to the Tanna'im, as well as a common universe of rabbinic law (*halakhah*). They are collectively referred to under the generic title *midrash* ("scriptural commentary"), and more specifically as *tannaitic* or *halakhic midrashim*. As running commentaries, they focus primarily on the legal portions of the last four scrolls of the Torah, Exodus through Deuteronomy. The midrash to Exodus has been preserved in two primary recensions, the *Mekhilta de-Rabbi Ishmael* ("the Interpretive Canon of the Tradition of Rabbi Ishmael") and the *Mekhilta de-Rabbi Shimon ben Yohai.* The midrash on Leviticus is known as the *Sifra de-vei Rav* ("the Book of the Master's School"), without specifying the name of a particular sage. Finally, independent midrashic collections associated with Numbers and Deuteronomy are preserved under the common title *Sifrei* ("the Books") and *Sifrei Zuta'* ("the Smaller Books"). Most historians of rabbinic literature agree that these appear to have been compiled in Palestine under Roman hegemony, prior to the ascendancy of Constantine. Often, scholars speak of tannaitic literature when referring to the body of texts from the Mishnah to these later midrashic compilations. At times, they also extrapolate from the literature and apply the term "tannaitic" to the period as a whole, as a period in Jewish historiography.

The reign of Constantine, which resulted in the rise of Christianity to the rank of a dominant state religion, corresponds to an important demarcation in the rabbinic literature. The tannaitic literature discussed so far was most probably compiled, in at least preliminary form, at a time prior to that watershed era; the core material of all rabbinic compositions thereafter is ascribed to a later group of sages referred to as *'Amora'im* ("explainers of tannaitic tradition"). The names of amoraic figures from the middle third to the early sixth centuries fill the surviving pages of rabbinic works produced from the fourth century and beyond in both Palestine and Mesopotamia. Amoraic traditions regarding the text and meaning of the halakhic traditions of the Mishnah and the Tosefta form the basis of the talmudic compilations that stem from Byzantine Palestine and Sasanian Babylonia. We shall say more about them momentarily. Similarly, the great tradition of scriptural commentary begun in tannaitic compilations underwent dramatic enhancement of content, form, and genre under amoraic hands.

The literary work of the 'Amora'im is both continuous with and an innovation upon the textual canons produced among the Tanna'im. At the linguistic level, amoraic texts continue to use the post-biblical Hebrew preferred by the Tanna'im, but their texts incorporate Hebrew into a broader literary language that includes various local dialects of Aramaic. There are also continuities and innovations at the level of genre and overall models of textual coherence. Tannaitic tradition yielded, on the one hand, the Mishnah and the Tosefta, that is, highly formulaic, self-enclosed legal texts of a rather arcane sort. It yielded, on the other, scriptural commentaries of a generally line-by-line, expository character. In contrast, the literary work of the 'Amora'im ranged more widely.

Let's begin with the area of biblical commentary. Belonging properly to the Byzantine world of Palestine from the fourth through the sixth century C.E. is a series of midrashic compilations arranged for study in conjunction with pentateuchal and non-pentateuchal Scriptures. Unlike the tannaitic midrashic compilations, those of the Palestinian 'Amora'im tend to be less concerned with the legal implications of the Scriptures than with historical and theological topics. They also experiment with new formal arrangements.

Some, like *Genesis Rabbah* ("the great Genesis commentary"), a vast commentary that treats virtually every verse of Genesis, continue a kind of line-by-line exegetical pattern pioneered by the Tanna'im. But most, such as *Leviticus Rabbah* on Leviticus, focus upon only a few key words of each Sabbath biblical lection, supplementing them with long series of overlapping interpretive discourses. Others, most notably *Song of Songs Rabbah*, *Lamentations Rabbah*, and *Pesikta de-Rav Kahana* ("Sections From Rav Kahana"), are compendia of midrashim devoted to fast days or festivals of the liturgical year. Many of these, along with *Deuteronomy Rabbah*, introduce their exegetical discourses with rhetorical compositions – *petihta'ot* – that suggest an origin, or perhaps a suggested application, in instructional sermons or lectures. Other well-known Palestinian midrashic works, such as *Pesikta Rabbati* and *Midrash Tanhuma*, seem to stem from the later post-amoraic schools of Byzantine Palestine, although their discourses are filled with well-known amoraic figures.

One of the compilations that has best resisted all efforts to locate it in space, time, and literary genre is the companion to Mishnah Avot itself, *Avot de-Rabbi Nathan*. In form and style it is very much like a tractate of the Tosefta, intertwining its own versions of the mishnaic tractate with additions and amplifications in the names of tannaitic masters known from the Mishnah. But *Avot de-Rabbi Nathan*, of which two independent versions exist, has never circulated within the boundaries of the Tosefta. Moreover, there is still little firm scholarly consensus on the time and place of its compilation, with some critics regarding it as a Palestinian work compiled by the end of the fourth century and others detecting influences from such later texts as the Babylonian Talmud itself.

Palestinian 'Amora'im produced an enormous quantity of biblical commentary, but as the example of *Avot de-Rabbi Nathan* already demonstrates, midrashic composition hardly exhausts the range of literary activity in the last centuries of the Byzantine domination. Indeed, the most characteristic work of rabbinic culture is a pair of commentaries on, or highly structured discussions of, the Mishnah. Both works are identified as *Talmud* ("study," "curriculum"), the term that eventually became a virtual synonym for rabbinic literature as a whole. Like amoraic midrashic works, they are composed in various mixtures of Hebrew and local Aramaic. The earlier of these, most likely edited in Tiberias in the Galilee, is nevertheless often called the "Jerusalem Talmud" (*Talmud Yerushalmi*) in the early medieval commentary literature, where it is also referred to as "Talmud of the Land of Israel," or "Talmud of the West." The title of Jerusalem Talmud, in which Jerusalem has to be understood as a synecdoche for the Land of Israel rather than as an actual place of origin, has gained predominance in Hebrew literature, both traditional and academic. European languages, on the other hand, often refer to this Talmud as the "Palestinian Talmud," after the name of the Roman imperial province instituted by Hadrian, *Syria Palaestina*.

It is thought to have been redacted in the latter quarter of the fourth century C.E. or perhaps the first quarter of the fifth century, even though we do not have any historical information to make a precise dating possible.

We have already, at the very beginning of this essay, discussed its younger but much larger and more complex counterpart, the Babylonian Talmud, compiled in rabbinic academies in Persia under the Sasanian Empire (early third through early seventh century C.E.). Early medieval authorities refer to it as "our Talmud." Again, due to the lack of historical information, the approximate date of the edition or redaction of this work can only be established hypothetically. Thus, scholars have dated this process anywhere from the end of the fifth century C.E. to the early seventh century C.E., while most assume that the individual tractates may have been edited independently, each in its own time.

While the Talmud Bavli is filled with the names of Palestinian and Babylonian sages, a crucial literary trait distinguishes it from both the Talmud Yerushalmi and virtually all other amoraic compilations. Orchestrating and commenting upon the various amoraic discussions, there lurks an anonymous redactional "voice" that guides students through complex passages, points out contradictions, adds crucial bits of information, and in sundry other ways serves as a kind of disembodied textual teacher. Traditional medieval rabbinic historiography refers to this voice as that of the *Savora'im* ("Critical Editors"). These are the hypothetical compilers of the amoraic tradition into coherent Mishnah commentaries. Presumably these anonymous compilers – called *Stamma'im* by some contemporary scholars – are the true creators of the Babylonian Talmud in its present form.

It is worth emphasizing here that the Babylonian rabbinic communities did not produce independent midrashic compilations, as the Palestinian rabbinic schools did. Rather, the stammaitic editors of the Bavli worked the entirety of received rabbinic scriptural commentary into their commentary on the Mishnah. Thus, it served as a kind of *summa* of the entirety of the rabbinic Oral Torah – *mishnah* and *midrash*, *halakhah* and *'aggadah*, combined into a single "encyclopedia" of knowledge that subsumed all other textualities within its own corpus. Largely because of the influence of Baghdadi rabbinic leaders in the eighth century C.E. and later, the Babylonian Talmud came to enjoy the high status we noted at the beginning of this Introduction. It is the most widely disseminated and revered rabbinic work, and the one that was and is studied most in rabbinic academies and schools. It includes not only acute discussions of mishnaic and other ancient legal sources, but also vast collections of midrashic tradition of both Palestinian and Babylonian venues.

THE GOALS OF THE PRESENT VOLUME

The modern study of Judaism began with the study of rabbinic literature in the new contexts of the nineteenth-century German university. Most of the key texts of rabbinic literature have existed in European translations for well over a century now. Nevertheless, in spite of all this interpretive work, the texts remain difficult to access for outsiders to rabbinic culture. Their language, rhetoric, hermeneutic, and logic is often highly encoded and requires a significant amount of training – linguistic, philological, and historical – for one to acquire the skill of decoding them in any meaningful way. Further, a section of text may appear in different edited shapes in two or more compilations of rabbinic texts, making even the question of boundaries between texts extremely complicated. Even within one corpus, within the Talmud for instance, textual sections may appear and reappear, not always verbatim, in several contexts. Centuries of transmission subsequently added to the continued emendation or revision of textual traditions in one corpus due to what might have been considered to be a more authoritative version in another corpus.

In addition to the influence of institutional religious concerns in the past, the structure of modern academic disciplines has also led to rabbinic literature being traditionally dealt with in isolation from other fields in the humanities. Scholars in departments of Semitic literature, for instance, focused on solving difficult textual-philological questions in talmudic exegesis by comparative studies of the languages spoken by communities among whom the sages lived. But such focus on linguistic detail, important as it is, left unexplained the literary "forest" within which the "trees" of the rabbinic lexicon were planted.

One might have expected greater interest in such a forest on the part of scholars engaged in the historical and cultural studies of rabbinic literature. But here, too, pressures in the nineteenth- and early-twentieth-century European and North American academy to produce a "usable," or "noble" model of Jewish history encouraged the isolation of the study of rabbinic texts from the cultural world of Late Antiquity that nourished them. This is only in part due to the dearth of specific or explicit historical anchors within the texts themselves. To consider rabbinic literature as just one cultural phenomenon among others in the world of Late Antiquity, some feared, might call into question the position of the sages in emerging narratives of Jewish history as the sole legitimate inheritors of biblical tradition. A predominant scholarly practice has therefore been to locate rabbinic textual practices somewhere on the Jewish trajectory from Bible to the Talmud and beyond, but not synchronically as products of the Late Antique religious and intellectual world.

For these reasons, the individual chapters in this volume will not repeat what most introductions to rabbinic literature have done, namely, primarily describe and analyze the individual compilations of rabbinic texts. There is no lack of excellent handbooks for students at various levels. Such an approach does not render the unique character of rabbinic texts and textual practices any more accessible to a serious conversation with scholars and students of other textual, intellectual, or religious traditions. Rather, to set the stage, the first part of this collection of essays addresses various ideological, social, and political conditions that shaped rabbinic textual production. Martin Jaffee discusses the collective and even collectivist nature of the composition of rabbinic literature and analyzes its denial of authorial creativity, not as an accident but as the expression of an ideology of "anonymity" that served the large conception of rabbinic tradition as "Oral Torah." Continuing this point, Elizabeth Shanks Alexander analyzes the relationship between orality and textuality in rabbinic literature and thus throws some critical light on the rather diverse conceptions of "orality" contained within rabbinic narratives about the transmission of rabbinic traditions. The next two essays in this section examine conditions external to the literature itself. Often, these conditions are only allusively assumed in the texts, and must be drawn into an explicit picture by means of sociological or anthropological analyses. This is particularly true of Jeffrey L. Rubenstein's essay on the social and institutional settings of rabbinic literature, prominently the rabbinic academy (*bet midrash*). The character of the rabbinic academy, in whatever forms it may have existed in talmudic times, must be studied not only or even principally by collecting descriptions of its operations in talmudic texts; but the rhetoric and structure of the texts themselves, shifting over time, constitute its their own sort of evidence about the ethos of study that shaped these institutions. Finally, the historian Seth Schwartz examines the influence of the two imperial contexts within which rabbinic texts took shape, namely, the Roman and the Persian Empires. He carefully elaborates on how the political and social conditions of Jewish life in separate empires shaped rabbinic textual creativity in distinctive ways.

The second, and longest, section of our volume will address the various cultural and literary forms of the rabbinic corpus, whether that concerns rabbinic hermeneutics (*midrash*), rabbinic notions of law and legal composition, or the folkloric dimensions of rabbinic texts. The essays in this section identify textual practices peculiar to rabbinic literature and explore their connections to other textual modes in the Late Antique world. Steven Fraade elucidates rabbinic scriptural exegetical practices by contextualizing them within the antecedent exegetical practices of the Hellenistic period, as refracted in the writings of Jewish groups in Alexandria and Qumran. Shaye Cohen turns to the legal orientation of rabbinic texts and explores both the continuities of mishnaic law with earlier (mostly Second Temple period) Jewish legal traditions, as well as the ways in which the ideological concerns of the rabbinic sages transform inherited traditions in the unique but characteristic directions embodied in the Mishnah. Turning from the substance of legal tradition to its literary form, Catherine Hezser proceeds more synchronically and discusses comparatively the character of legal codification in Roman and Byzantine law (e.g., Justinian's "Digest") and in rabbinic compositions, particularly those of a Byzantine-Palestinian provenance, such as the Yerushalmi. Parallel to her essay, Yaacov Elman discusses some of his own pioneering work documenting ways in which the legal traditions of the Babylonian Talmud are impacted at various points by the Pahlavi legal tradition and larger cultural patterns of the Zoroastrian Sasanian Empire. The last two essays in this section are devoted to rabbinic textual practices that are often neglected in classical rabbinic scholarship, since they have wrongly been considered to be marginal to the rabbinic world. Michael Swartz's essay exposes the ways in which the relatively few visionary texts scattered throughout the central rabbinic compilations – concerning, in particular, the divine throne world and other domains of cosmic reality – resonate with broader Jewish and non-Jewish traditions on these themes. And finally, Galit Hasan-Rokem demonstrates that although rabbinic literature is generally considered to stem from an elite of highly trained teachers and students of the traditions of Oral Torah, it is in fact not only embedded in but also draws from "folk tradition." Her contribution explores several examples of multilingual and multilevel wordplay and punning in the Byzantine-Palestinian compilations in particular, demonstrating, among other things, that rabbinic sages can be viewed as a "folk society" of sorts.

The last section of this volume most fully addresses rabbinic literature as a cultural production that actively interacts with specific stimulae to affect or even critique its own cultural ethos. Here, we have assembled a number of essays that analyze important cultural tensions and their (sometimes tentative) solutions in rabbinic literature. While these essays are devoted to issues that are at the core of the rabbinic literary enterprise, they also demonstrate with special clarity the ways in which recent scholarship in rabbinics resonates with conversations in the humanities elsewhere.

Christine Hayes's essay discusses the rabbinic depiction of "the social other" – namely, other Jews and non-Jews whose domains circumscribed the perimeter of the rabbinic social world. Since rabbinic culture at no point accepted a fully separatist, sectarian, or monastic conception of the ideal rabbinic society, it had of necessity to define a precarious path between separatism and integration regarding the many "others" with whom members of rabbinic society were forced to interact on a daily basis. Hayes's essay analyzes the dynamics in the representations of the diverse others who populate the landscape of rabbinic literary discourse, and thus makes it possible to bring rabbinic cultural material to bear upon the larger cross-cultural questions represented by diverse modes of "othering."

Charlotte Elisheva Fonrobert's essay is devoted, in a sense, to what may be seen as the ultimate "rabbinic other," describing various ways in which the opposition of male and female gender operates within rabbinic literature. First, she explains how rabbinic metaphors for the female body reveal the construction of women's bodies as objects of exclusively male halakhic analysis. Secondly, she explores a contemporary theoretical issue in gender studies – the relation of gender to biological sex – through a study of rabbinic attempts to categorize the *androginos* – the person born with both male and female genitalia. Is the androginos a male or a female? Fonrobert analyzes rabbinic efforts to answer this question through the application of halakhic criteria. Her discussion reveals in bold outline how thoroughly halakhic discourse is structured by usually unstated assumptions about gender.

Moving into quite a different area, Isaiah Gafni's essay provides a critical assessment of rabbinic understandings of the past. Rabbinic texts are notorious for refusing to provide historiographical accounts at least in any way comparable to the conventions accepted by ancient historians such as Josephus (and his predecessors and successors). However, scattered throughout various rabbinic compilations can be found references to historical events, such as the Maccabean struggle, the Roman-Jewish wars, or the destruction of the Temple. Gafni demonstrates how talmudic texts develop their own techniques of representing and remembering the past, quite distinct from contemporary Roman and Roman-Christian practices, and explains ways in which these forms of historical memory cohere with the large intellectual and religious goals of the sages.

If the tension between the rabbinic "self" and its various social, somatic, and gendered "others" forms a major preoccupation of rabbinic texts, we should not be surprised, in light of recent ethical reflections associated with Emmanuel Levinas, to find obsession with "the other" playing a central role in forming rabbinic ethical attitudes. Jonathan Schofer, a leading theorist of rabbinic ethics, offers in the present volume a study of a significant number of rabbinic texts devoted to the problem of the formation of the self. Here, Schofer explores how the self itself can be objectivized as an other, especially in the effort to expunge "bad desires" from the self. He does so by offering a fresh reading of the rabbinic concept of the "bad urge" (*yeẓer ha-ra*ʿ), demonstrating how the very construction of rabbinic ethical texts and compilations offers models for actively suppressing the "otherness" of the bad urge so that the "self" modeled by the sage and his Torah can assert its dominance.

The volume concludes with Daniel Boyarin's final reflection on the way in which the texts of rabbinic tradition both reflect and actively engage the project of reducing or negotiating diverse tensions alive in the cultures of their producers. Focusing on the Babylonian Talmud as his main source, Boyarin highlights fundamental tensions regarding the value of rational argument to achieve truth. Drawing upon recent advances in the analysis of the anonymous editorial stratum of the Talmud (the *Stam*), Boyarin finds hidden and previously unsuspected connections between irrationalist theological tendencies in later Syrian Christianity in the Sasanian Empire and the Stam's reworking of amoraic and tannatic narratives in order to highlight either the independence of halakhic deliberation from divine influence or the inscrutability of divine judgment to human understanding. Boyarin thus shows how this hidden Christian connection to the Bavli's final editors helps to explain the "hellenization" of rabbinic Judaism in Babylonia despite the surrounding Persian-Sasanian-Zoroastrian cultural milieu.

The corpus of rabbinic literature is vast, often likened by its students to an ocean. It is impossible to do justice to the complexities and beauties of this literature in one small volume of essays. The best that we hope to accomplish is to provide some guidance to the variety of Late Antique Mediterranean and Mesopotamian cultural currents that swirl through the rabbinic text and account for its characteristic ripples and eddies. The result, we hope, will be one more useful navigation tool in guiding scholarship in rabbinic texts into the harbors of the humanistic disciplines.

Part I

The Conditions of Rabbinic Literary Activity

1 Rabbinic Authorship as a Collective Enterprise

MARTIN S. JAFFEE

ALL THAT WRITING — AND NO WRITERS? THE PUZZLE OF RABBINIC AUTHORSHIP

Rabbinic literature of Late Antiquity certainly had its audience. But can it be said to have had authors? From the perspective of the rabbinic tradition itself, the axiomatic answer is, of course, "no." A half millennium of tradition, the Mishnah tells us, links the moment at which "Moses received Torah from Sinai" to the teachings of the Men of the Great Assembly who, in the shadow of Persian hegemony, "said three things: be cautious in judgment, raise up many disciples, and build a fence for the Torah" (M. Avot 1:1).

In the rabbinic view, formulations of collective rabbinic wisdom, such as those ascribed to the Men of the Great Assembly, are "said," "received" or "heard," and "transmitted." But they are not "authored." Not any more than a rhythmic refrain, stemming out of seventeenth-century West African tribal dance, that – transplanted with its enslaved bearers to the cotton fields of the American South – adopts the musical scale of Scotch-Irish reels and emerges in 1938 as a chord progression supporting this recorded confession of a Robert Johnson:

> I went down to the crossroad, fell down on my knees;
> I went down to the crossroad, fell down on my knees;
> asked the Lord above "Have mercy now, save poor Bob if you
> please."[1]

In point of fact, despite Robert Johnson's immersion in the traditional African American musical idioms that worked their way through his soul (and the souls of many others) to become the blues, he exercised a good deal more sovereign authorship of his chords and his lyrics than any given rabbinic sage might have enjoyed in controlling the way his own performances of traditional Jewish wisdom might be remembered and transmitted.

How, then – deprived of the comfortable convention of "authorship" – shall we think of the diverse social, cultural, and imaginative processes that produced the resolutely anonymous and collectivist literature that lies at the very foundations of everything that eventually became the core of the rabbinic library? I will not offer a definitive answer to this question, which is the central issue of this essay. Barring a discovery of ancient rabbinic writings on the order of the Dead Sea Scrolls, we can say very little about the processes that transformed rabbinic tradition from the oral-performative milieu of the Roman or Sasanian rabbinic discipleship circle (*bet midrash*) into the manuscript copies of the Mishnah, Tosefta, two Talmuds, and scores of midrashic collections that survived the Middle Ages.

What I shall offer, by way of small consolation, are a few cautious contributions toward thinking about rabbinic authorship. These are, in order of appearance: 1) some theoretical reflection on the concept of authorship that many of us bring to our study of rabbinic literature; 2) discussion of the way rabbinic sages themselves seem to have understood their participation in literary activities, such as formulating and editing texts; 3) description of some basic compositional features of rabbinic writings; and finally 4) a proposal about how such considerations may help us to think more concretely about rabbinic textual authorship.

AUTHORSHIP IN A COLLECTIVE MODE

The first question that needs asking is a bit obvious: What sorts of assumptions about the act of writing are packed into our common-sense views of literary authorship? If we become aware of them, is it possible that the puzzle of rabbinic authorship might appear more manageable? It's a fair question. In order to answer it, let me pose another: What distinctions do we commonly draw, in our least reflective moments, between, say, a writer and a typist? Or between an author and a scribe?

Most of us, I dare say, would probably offer something like this. Writers and authors are the creative individuals who produce letters, novels, scholarly essays, poems, newspaper editorials, and so forth. By some magic they transform the contents of their mental life into written texts. Typists and scribes, in contrast, are the more or less mindless drones who package the creative texts of others, when necessary, into a form ready for communication to some audience or other. That audience might consist of a single individual, as when a secretary types a business letter composed by an executive to communicate with another colleague. Or the audience might be a mass readership, such as those who obediently wait in impossible lines to purchase the autobiographical musings of libidinally incontinent former presidents and other cultural luminaries. Whatever the case may be, the creative process proceeds, as it were, downhill: from the creative mind of the author "in the beginning," to his or her written representation of the mental creation, to the multiplication and distribution of the text by industrious copyists, and from there to you, the reader. At each successive stage in the chain, literary creativity diminishes, even though other sorts of creativity – for example, production of the written text as a physical object and its marketing as an item in a commercial exchange – may take over.

If I've presumed correctly in the previous paragraph, permit me to let you down gently at the very beginning. A good deal of literary theory in the last several decades poses serious questions about the absolute creativity of authors and the relative passivity of those who edit, copy, and otherwise disseminate their texts. Some have suggested, in particular, that the production of literary texts involves creative writing and rewriting through the entire chain of command, from the so-called authorial imagination down to those who produce the forms of texts that will actually find their way into readers' hands. "Authorship," for such theorists, is not confined to a single, originating mind, but is rather a complex social process. The final product – the "literary work" – is a collective creation, the expression of a culture that works itself through the minds of the various individuals whose labor produced the text.[2] From this perspective, we rarely appreciate that the creative process issuing in a modern novel is not utterly different from the series of experiments with cultural heritage that yields one of Robert Johnson's blues tunes – or, for that matter, a tractate of the Mishnah.

Recent literary theorists, in fact, observe that the trickle-down model of individual literary authorship I rehearsed a moment ago has more than a little to do with the history of communications media and the idea of authorship under the conditions of capitalistic market-driven economies. It describes something real, as far as it goes, but doesn't tell us much about what literary processes were like in the vast ages between the development of written communication systems some three millennia ago and, roughly, the fifteenth century C.E., when literature moved from the handmade to the mass-produced page pretty much for good (or for better and worse). To the contrary. For many, many centuries in the history of writing – in civilizations as diverse as ancient Egypt, Mesopotamia, India, and China – the producers of written texts rarely drew fast distinctions between the "creative" authors and "passive" copyists among them.[3]

This is particularly true in that specific literary marketing niche called "world scriptures." Texts as totally unrelated in their contents and cultural origins as, for example, the Memphite Theology (Egypt, ca. third millennium B.C.E.), the Enuma Elish (in its neo-Babylonian forms, ca. 500 B.C.E.), the Vedas (India, ca. 1500 B.C.E.), the Torah (Mesopotamia, ca. 450 B.C.E.), the Tipitaka (in its Pali translation, Sri Lanka, first century B.C.E.), the I Ching (China, ca. 1000 B.C.E.), the Quran (Arabia, 650 C.E.), and countless others shared only one thing in common – their advertising campaigns. That is, none were promoted as the creation of single, identifiable, human authors. They all were somehow "delivered" (by the gods, *a certain* god, the *only* God, or, in the case of the Vedas and other Hindu and Buddhist classics, no one in particular) into the hands of human elites (usually male: scribes, prophets, kings, or priests) for safekeeping, proper copying, usually memorization, and, ultimately, veneration. There *were* no creative human beings involved at all, as far as the preservers of such texts were concerned. The creative moment happened in a time long ago, well before humanly measured time, and in a place far away, a domain no living person could ever enter except, perhaps, in visions.

Of course, as academic children of Spinoza's naturalistic historicism, we have our difficulties with stories about texts that drop down from Heaven or get channeled through the cosmic spheres to our front door. For us, texts of any kind are produced by real people in historical time. If pseudonymous scribes choose to deflect attention from their own creativity by honoring fictitious deities or cosmic alignments as the true sources of their writing, they must have their reasons. Part of any historical understanding of their work is, in fact, explaining what specific social, cultural, or ideological agenda may have shaped their claim to have had nothing to do with creating the texts they created. These real people are "authors," even if they worked collaboratively and didn't sign their work. And that is why, in the next section of this essay, we'll take a quick look at how the sages of rabbinic literature made oblique references to their own intervention in the creation of texts that "just happened." But even if we stretch our concept of authorship well beyond our usual habits, we will not get to the original quill that brought ink to parchment in the creation of a single line of rabbinic writing. Yet we may still have something to say about how rabbinic sages and scribes went about producing the texts they refused to acknowledge as their own work.

AUTHORSHIP BY ANY OTHER NAME: RABBINIC
REPRESENTATIONS OF LITERARY CREATIVITY

If you've followed me this far, you'll be in a position to appreciate the complexity of defining the kind of authorship that produced rabbinic literature. In the first place, rabbinic sages were well aware that not every book of religious interest came, like the Torah itself, "from Heaven." They did, in fact, know very well that individual authors occasionally wrote books. Not only did rabbinic sages know about revered pagan poets and fabulists like Homer and Aesop (although sages hadn't any use for them), but they also treasured their own homegrown list of best-selling authors: post-Mosaic prophets like Joshua, David, Solomon, Ezekiel, and so forth. They respected some recent Jewish authors, such as Yeshua b. Sira (ca. 180 B.C.E.), the author of a book of wise sayings widely cited in the Talmud Bavli in particular with almost scriptural authority. And even if they may never have heard of Philo of Alexandria, the first-century C.E. Jewish *homme de lettres* who composed in Greek philosophical genres, they would surely have known of Jews who wrote books in Greek under their own names. Despite these available models, however, the rabbinic sages quite obviously refused to make use of them.

This refusal of responsibility for authorship begins at the smallest literary level: the brief saying, judgment, or ruling. Most of these sayings, whether they are cited as the words of a specific sage or as the view of the anonymous collectivity of "sages," are produced by following a few very common, rigid formulas. Among the most common is the following: *X says (or said) + a declarative sentence.* Alternatively, we commonly find this: *A declarative sentence + the words of X.* There are surely hundreds of examples of this way of formulating material in the Mishnah alone. Very few of them pretend that the sage who reports the statement actually composed or invented it by stuffing his knowledge through such a stereotypical stylistic meat grinder.

Here is a typical example, plucked utterly at random from a tractate of the Mishnah (M. Berakhot 4:3):

> *Rabban Gamliel says: Each day a person should pray eighteen
> benedictions.*

You can see how this statement follows the formula. You can also see why it is not likely that Rabban Gamliel actually invented or wrote this line of text. Consider this: Here, Rabban Gamliel (we know of two of them, and this one, the grandson of the first, lived in the late first century C.E.) reports about a prayer text (the "18 benedictions") that the rabbis believed originated in its broad outlines with the Men of the Great Assembly five hundred years earlier. The substance of his teaching is that all who are obliged to recite this prayer should recite it in its entirety.

Can Rabban Gamliel have authored this opinion in the sense of thinking it up all by himself? Someone, we should imagine, in the half millennium separating the Great Assembly from Rabban Gamliel, would have made (or challenged) this rather obvious point! Rather, he is merely the latest one to pass it on, at best its transmitter ("tradent," in academese), not its creator or author. Who actually first said the words: "Each day a person should pray eighteen benedictions"? I don't suppose we'll ever have any idea. The best I can propose is that someone (or some group?) responsible for formulating rabbinic legal knowledge believed that a recent authority, such as Rabban Gamliel, was an appropriate tradent of such a statement because he had subscribed to it himself.[4]

Now, in rabbinic culture, to be a tradent of tradition is an honored role. The authority of the tradent is deemed crucial in the transmission of knowledge. It is often acknowledged – especially in the Babylonian Talmud – that a particular sage transmitted a text "in accord with the conception of" (*'aliba' de-*) his Master, Rabbi So-and-So (e.g., B. Berakhot 3a, the first of countless examples of this formula). But this is not a claim for creative authorship on the part of Rabbi So-and-So, who, so to speak, got the statement going through the tradition. Rather, it only assigns responsibility to the transmitting sage for *preserving the integrity of the received version as received from an authoritative teacher*. This is the point of the famous self-representation of the first-century C.E. Rabbi Eliezer b. Hyrcanus: "I never said a thing I didn't hear from my Master" (B. Sukkah 28a; cf. T. Yevamot 3:4). It is echoed in the frequently cited dictum that "a person is obliged to recite in the formulation of his Master" (M. Eduyot 1:3) or the equally widespread reminder to "report a statement in the name of the one who taught it" (M. Avot 6:6).

The sages' reluctance to claim literary originality for their own teachings is matched by yet another hesitation. They deny any innovative intent in their efforts to bring together synopses of traditions representing the views of a variety of teachers. In describing pioneering forms of literary creativity, such as the original gathering of the traditions of Oral Torah into the distant ancestors of mishnaic and talmudic tractates, compilations of midrashic exegesis, and so forth, rabbinic memory is satisfied with a few sketchy metaphors. None of them adds up to ancient or modern conceptions of creative, individual authorship – or even the more subtle presence of editorial literary shaping. The great Rabbi Akiva (who was martyred ca. 135 C.E.), for example, is recalled as making important contributions to the curriculum of rabbinic learning. But the descriptions of his method leave much concerning his literary procedures in doubt. Thus:

> [In his compilation of early tannaitic traditions] what was Rabbi Akiva like? He was like a laborer who took up his basket and went out. Finding wheat, he put it in. Finding barley, he put it in. Finding spelt, he put it in. Finding lentils, he put them in. Upon arriving at his home he sorted (*mevarer*) the wheat on its own, the barley on its own, the beans on their own, and the lentils on their own. Thus did Rabbi Akiva proceed as he made the entire Torah into links upon links (*taba'ot taba'ot*)[5] [of thematically organized tradition]. (*Avot de-Rabbi Nathan* A:18, 34a)

The dominant image here of the sage's traditions is one of so many found objects. Rabbi Akiva simply arranges them into their natural, self-evident categories on the basis of the affinity of species to one another, like beads of knowledge on a string organized by color, shape, or texture.

According to this picture, nothing in the tradition is changed or shaped by editing it into categories. We are, moreover, given little guidance in interpreting the way in which the metaphorical harvest may be interpreted as an editorial or literary process. Are wheat and spelt distinct legal topics? If so, Rabbi Akiva's activity might be imagined as composing legal compendia on specific themes. Are wheat and spelt metaphors for literary genres? Then, perhaps, Rabbi Akiva is laying the literary foundations for distinctions between *mishnah* and *midrash*? Are they kinds of produce to the contrary, metaphors for the mnemonic labor of organizing memorized traditions in terms of formal stylistic traits, wheat with wheat and spelt with spelt? Perhaps. But we cannot know.

Shorn of the homey agricultural metaphors, the same ambiguity plagues other contexts as well, where, as noted, the responsibility of the gatherer of traditions is simply to preserve them as received. We learn further of Rabbi Akiva's literary activity as a process of "preparing (*hitkin*)[6] interpretations, legal traditions, and stories" (Y. Shekalim 5:1, 48c) or "arranging (*misader*) legal traditions for his disciples" (T. Zabim 1:5). Similarly, with regard to Rabbi Yehudah ha-Nasi, usually assumed to have edited the extant text of the Mishnah, a relatively late description of his activity is that he "prepared" the Mishnah (*matnytyn ma'n takyn? Rabbi*: B. Yevamot 64b). But more commonly, he is said to have "repeated" or "taught" the text in a specific version (*shanah*:

e.g., Y. Bava Batra 8:6, 16b; B. Bava Batra 131a; Y. Bava Metzia 4:1, 9c; B. Bava Metzia 44a; Y. Kiddushin 3:14, 64c; B. Gittin 29a; B. Yevamot 50a). "Repetition" is hardly a vivid metaphor for literary interventionism (although it might indeed attempt to obscure it, but that's another question). In any case, such descriptions reveal little about the kinds of literary sources used by Rabbi Akiva or Rabbi Yehudah ha-Nasi in their work.

Were the sources altered for transmission? Did the "preparers" and "repeaters" work from written texts or from memory? Is the "Mishnah" in question in these settings the canonical *Mishnah* (refered to in the Talmud Bavli as "our Mishnah," *mishnatenu* or *matnytyn*) that forms the textual spine of the discourse of the Yerushalmi and the Bavli? Or is the term *mishnah* – or, in the ubiquitous Aramaic form, *matnyta'* – merely a synonym for the entirety of the "Repeated Tradition," that is, the Oral Torah as a whole? The answer is hardly clear for the case of Rabbi Akiva. And with regard to Rabbi Yehudah ha-Nasi, the extent of his creative interference with previous tradition remains a matter of conjecture, depending upon one's own hunches about what is likely to have been the case.[7]

The one clear thing is that rabbinic ambiguity about the methods of literary tradition transmission is contrasted, in the rabbinic historical imagination, against a far superior, normative, and, alas, vanished clarity. Sages of the second century C.E. and later recalled a "golden age" of tradition, prior to their own day, when all disciples transmitted the words of their teachers with none of their own added inflections. But, alas, those days ended in the time of the disciples of Hillel and Shammai (ca. first century B.C.E.–first century C.E.), who "did not serve their masters appropriately" (T. Sanhedrin 7:1; Y. Sanhedrin 1:6, 19c; B. Sanhedrin 88b). The chaos introduced into the system by incompetent discipleship was made only more acute with the destruction of the Temple in 70 C.E. The postwar foundation of discipleship training in the obscure coastal small city of Yavneh, under the directorship of Rabban Yohanan b. Zakkai (e.g., B. Gittin 56b), is recalled in early rabbinic texts as an attempt to reconstruct traditions for proper preservation and transmission (T. Eduyot 1:1–2). There are different versions of tradition afoot, the sages admit. But the task is to minimize innovation and discord by preserving intact exactly what one has received. Accordingly, "anonymous passages of the Mishnah [transmit the tradition according to] Rabbi Meir, anonymous passages of the Tosefta [transmit according to] Rabbi Nehemiah, anonymous passages of Sifra are Rabbi Yehudah, anonymous passages of Sifre [transmit according to] Rabbi Shimon. And all accord with the conception of (*'aliba' de-*) Rabbi Akiva [who taught each of these masters]" (B. Sanhedrin 86a). The chaos of each disciple teaching his own version of tradition is overcome by the establishment of canonical compilations of tradition, each one linked to an authoritative source, all stemming ultimately from Rabbi Akiva.

The ambiguity regarding the actual practices by which sages reviewed, collated, and revised traditions for disciplined circulation remains consistent even into the most recent layers of the Babylonian Talmud's depiction of the literary processes engaged in by its own authorities. In the few instances where sages ascribe to specific figures some literary function that contemporary humanists might recognize as "authorial," it is not entirely clear what that function may have been or how that work is reflected in the extant forms of the Talmud. Rav Ashi (Babylonia, early fifth century c.e.), for example, is credited with producing a first and then a second *mahadura'* of his teachings (B. Bava Batra 157a). Perhaps, as some modern scholars have surmised, it was a kind of proto-Talmud. But it is entirely unclear from the Talmud's description whether these acts of literary shaping should be regarded as formal literary "recensions" (a more print-informed rendering of *mahadura'*)[8] or, simply, a master teacher's occasional summary of a cycle of his lessons (as a recent dictionary urges).[9] The fact that this very dictionary lists "a round of drinks" as within the semantic range of *mahadura'* suggests that we have to do more with a lesson cycle than an act analogous to the editing of a lecture series.

To summarize the rabbinic view of rabbinic authorship: As far as human authorship is concerned, there are no Yeshua b. Siras or Philos in the rabbinic literary world. Rabbis would not admit to writing formative texts for the ages out of the resources of their own imaginations until the ninth century c.e., when political and cultural exigencies drew Rabbi Sa'adia b. Yosef of Baghdad out of the shell of anonymity to confront Muslim philosophers and dissident Jewish Karaites in his own literary voice. As producers of literary works, the sages of Late Antiquity, by contrast, imagine themselves at most as shapers of what already exists in tradition. They are not authors but repeaters (*Tanna'im*) and "explainers" (*'Amora'im*); they do not invent, they merely transmit.

In light of this rabbinic reticence to take responsibility for their own literary work, we might expect the sages to follow the venerable model of other great scribal communities of Israelite antiquity – that is, to ascribe the whole of their literary canon to the creative work of a deity delivering his oracles to selected human ears, either by direct dictation (e.g., Moses) or by indirect inspiration (e.g., Ezra). This option, too, the sages avoided.

While some rabbinic teachers of the mid–third century C.E. onward claim for their oral *tradition* an originating point in an historical moment of revelation – Sinai – the *texts* in which the tradition is carried make no claim to a literary debut on a mountaintop scriptorium. God may have taught the tradition of Oral Torah to Moses, and all that (B. Eruvin 54b; see E. Alexander's contribution to this volume for details). But nowhere in rabbinic writings of antiquity do we find anyone claiming that Moses wrote it down for safekeeping.

In fact, at least one ancient sage, Rabbi Yehudah bar Shalom, is remembered as holding just the opposite. In response to Moses' request that God write down the oral tradition for Israel, Rabbi Yehudah reports the Creator's unambiguous refusal: "Let them have the Scripture in writing. But the Repeated Tradition (*mishnah*), homiletics (*midrash*), and dialectics (*talmud*) shall remain in the mouth" (Midrash Tanhuma, *Ki Tisa'*, 17; cf. Pesikta Rabbati 14b; Midrash Tanhuma-Buber, *Vayera'* 44b). Moses surely copied down the Written Torah as God had dictated it to him, but God permitted nothing of the kind to happen with the Oral Torah. At the very most, "many legal traditions (*halakhot*) were stated (*ne'emeru*) to Moses on Sinai, and all of them are embedded in the *mishnah*"[10] (Y. Peah 2:6, 17a and parallels). So the creators of rabbinic literature not only denied any creative role for themselves in the composition of their texts; they also denied a creative role to God. Whatever he might have said to Moses is incorporated into the texts of oral tradition, but one cannot distinguish them from those that were taught afterward. The texts, we continue to observe, "just happened."

MODES OF COLLECTIVE AUTHORSHIP IN RABBINIC COMPILATIONS

Well, no literature extending to thousands of manuscript pages and including dozens of sophisticated literary and rhetorical genres just happens, does it? If the sages' descriptions of their own literary labors tell us little about how the composers of rabbinic writings worked, the only other option is to look at what they did and try to figure it out. Our problem in the remainder of this essay, therefore, is to point to certain typical literary aspects of rabbinic texts from antiquity. We'll use these literary traits in an effort to imagine how these writings took shape in the specific forms they eventually embody. Our basic approach will be to focus on three interconnected but theoretically distinct, types of compositional work that seem to underlie the kinds of texts preserved in rabbinic culture. In an earlier reflection on the topic of rabbinic writing, without claiming any particular originality, I called these the "lemmatic," the "intermediate," and the "documentary" level of textual composition.[11] For the sake of convenience, let's continue to use them.

Lemmatic Composition

The first and most basic literary process is the composition of *lemmata*. This is the plural form of a Greek word, *lemma*, that can mean "argument." The Latin, *sententia*, which can mean "opinion," is a close cognate of the Greek. Literary scholars of the Greco-Roman classics often use the term *lemma* to refer to the smallest whole unit of a literary text – the small group of sentences that convey a coherent thought. Historians of rabbinic literature have come to use it as well. So we ask: What sorts of conventions govern the making of lemmata in rabbinic writings?[12]

The most fundamental dimension of rabbinic textual authorship, from this perspective, is the mastery of a certain kind of communal diction capable of funneling vast topical and thematic content into an astonishingly small range of stylistic formulas. Among the most common of these formulas is the juxtaposition of different lemmata to simulate discussion and disputative argument among specific sages. By way of illustration, let's view the earlier tradition ascribed to Rabban Gamliel in its present mishnaic context:

> *Rabban Gamaliel says: Each day a person should pray eighteen benedictions.*
>
> *Rabbi Joshua says: An abbreviated version of the eighteen.*
>
> *Rabbi Akiva says: If he's fluent in his prayers, let him pray eighteen; but if not, an abbreviated version of the eighteen.* (M. Berakhot 4:3)

We saw earlier that Rabban Gamaliel is not represented as the "author" of the tradition stated in his name. Similarly here, none of the parties to this discussion is represented as either the author or composer of his own statement or of the entire piece of tradition. Rather, the three sages' utterances are artfully linked together by an anonymous literary voice to produce what might be termed an abstract rendering of a possible conversation.

What literary capacities on the part of rabbinic tradents make such a composition possible? In the beginning, so to speak, is the abstract "dispute form," a literary device invented by no one in particular, but publicly available to be drawn upon by any composer needing a convenient form for storing diverse sorts of content. In the present instance (there is more than one kind of dispute form, but let's leave that for another time), the form is something like this:

> X says: A
>
> Y says: C (the opposite)
>
> Z says: B (something in between)

That is, the sort of dispute represented at M. Berakhot 4:3 contains two extreme opinions followed by a mediating opinion. This package can, of course, contain virtually any literary content, just as a 6½-ounce tin might contain anything from Bumblebee Tuna in Spring Water to Friskies Beef & Liver Dinner. In the present instance, an editor (or an editorial committee – how will we ever know?) has drawn from a variety of perspectives on the recitation of the eighteen benedictions. No sage doubts the tradition that Jewish prayer consists of eighteen benedictions. But sages know of a number of positions regarding whether or not their content is as fixed as their number. Can each benediction be abbreviated in some way? The resulting composition of the dispute elegantly packages the views into clearly defined legal lemmata, illustrating the appropriate parameters of received opinion and a reasonable resolution.

Intermediate Compositions: The "Microforms"

The fundamental building blocks of virtually any rabbinic composition of Late Antiquity are larger aggregations of lemmatic compositions such as these, employing a rather impressive palette of traditional patterns of formulation. An influential scholar, Peter Schaefer, has proposed the term "microform" to identify such literary compositions.[13] The conventions of organizing these aggregations involve what I call the "intermediate" focus of critical attention. That is, in this case, our gaze is focused on literary units larger than, for example, the dispute, but smaller than an entire document. This is, admittedly, a pretty wide target, allowing the critic lots of room to experiment with different ways of defining basic literary compositions within a document, and explaining the logic that brings them into literary relationships. It is a procedure as old as early medieval commentaries on rabbinic literature. And no contemporary scholar with any wisdom would think of attempting it today without first studying as many classical attempts as possible.

The main concern in the study of intermediate literary units and their microforms is to identify the principle of coherence that accounts for the received composition of subunits into something like a complete literary statement. There is nothing mystical about this principle of coherence. We find it by examining the style and substance of the lemmata of the intermediate unit in relationship to one another and to the whole of which each is one part.[14]

A very simple example of the composition of an intermediate unit of tradition is available in the eighth chapter of M. Berakhot. This chapter consists of a series of disputes between two ancient rabbinic schools, the School of Shammai and the School of Hillel.[15] What links them all together, beyond the names of the disputants, is the fact that each dispute concerns some aspect of law governing the Sabbath meal. That is, the principle of coherence that unifies diverse lemmata into a cogent intermediate composition is simply, in this case, the development of a single legal theme. In the current example, the editor(s) of M. Berakhot have helped us to isolate this principle by introducing the whole series as follows: "These issues distinguish the School of Shammai from the School of Hillel regarding the meal" (M. Berakhot 8:1). Mishnaic editors are not always this accommodating, and no one has yet explained why they choose to disclose their principles of coherence in one context while concealing them in another. But in most cases, hard critical work will usually yield some insight into the editorial logic that underlies a given formulation of rabbinic tradition. And when mishnaic editors fail to perform this service, you can be sure that the editors of the Talmud will take up the task.

Take a look, for example, at the Bavli's approach to M. Shabbat 7:2. This passage offers a list of thirty-nine discrete actions introduced by the phrase "The primary acts of labor are forty minus one." The Mishnah itself offers no comment on the relation of the listed items to one another or the logic of their arrangement in the specific sequence in which they currently appear. It is the Bavli's discussions of this list, at B. Shabbat 49b and, more extensively, at B. Shabbat 73a–74b, that unpacks the deeper editorial logic of the Mishnah's formulation:

> Another time [some disciples] were sitting in study and a question arose regarding this tradition that we transmit [in the Mishnah]:
>> *The primary acts of labor are forty minus one* –
>>> to what do they correspond?
> Said to them Rabbi Haninah b. Hama: They correspond to the work of constructing the Wilderness Tabernacle....[16]

As an oral tradition teaches:

> One is obliged [to bring an offering in atonement for an
> unwitting violation of the Sabbath] only for labors that recall
> those employed in the construction of the Wilderness Tabernacle.
>
> They sowed seeds [to produce plants for use as dyes: Rashi], so
> you shall not sow. They harvested [the plants yielding these dyes],
> so you shall not harvest.
>
> They lifted boards from the ground to a wagon, so you shall
> not bring objects from the public to the private domain.
>
> They lowered boards from the wagon to the ground, so you
> shall not bring from the private to the public domain.
>
> They brought objects from one wagon to another wagon, so
> you shall not bring from one private domain into another private
> domain. (B. Shabbat 49b)

Here, the Bavli suggests the broad logic that explains the list, leaving
to the student the labor of attempting to reconstruct the lines of correspondence linking each act of labor to its archetype in the construction
of the Tabernacle.

Now, the Talmud itself recognizes that this reading of the Mishnah's
prohibition against Sabbath labor is not without its problems. When the
Bavli again treats this theme (B. Shabbat 73a ff.), it notes, for example,
that such labors as winnowing, sorting, and sifting are difficult to distinguish. The authorities, Rava and Abaye, defend the Mishnah from
redundancy by pointing out that "any act done in the Tabernacle is
included, even though some are similar to each other" (B. Shabbat 73b–
74a). But even more importantly, the Talmud also points out that its
proposed explanation for the coherence of the Mishnah's list of labors is
not beyond critique, for this explanation itself poses some interpretive
difficulties.

Consider the sequence of labors with which M. Shabbat 7:2 begins –
"sowing, plowing, harvesting, binding sheaves, threshing, winnowing,
sorting, grinding, sifting, kneading, and baking." Here the Talmud observes: "Said Rav Papa: Has our tannaitic teacher abandoned the labors
connected to boiling dyes in the Tabernacle in order to mention baking?"
That is to say, if the sequence of labors is supposed to be connected to
the planting, harvesting, and cooking of herbs used to dye the skins
and cloths used in the Tabernacle, how does the act of baking (not to
mention sifting and kneading) make sense? Rav Papa answers his own
question: "Rather, our tannaitic teacher understands this list to describe
the sequential production of bread" (B. Shabbat 74b). Thus, the entire

paradigm of the Mishnah's logic is shifted, enabling the thirty-nine labors to be reconsidered as actions that correspond to the uniquely human forms of creativity: creation of bread, creation of clothing ("shearing wool, bleaching . . . tearing in order to sew two stitches"), the creation of books ("hunting the deer, slaughtering . . . cutting the hide . . . erasing in order to write two characters"), and the creation of shelter ("building, dismantling"). These are proscribed for Jews on the Sabbath, in imitation of God's rest from explicitly divine forms of world construction.[17]

Documentary Compositions: The Macroforms

We have seen rabbinic tradents using inherited formulas to compose lemmata on diverse topics. We have also seen that these lemmata are normally gathered together into intermediate units of tradition (microforms) that preserve and shape the lemmata in terms of some larger purpose: to collect material appropriate to a discrete legal or theological theme, for example. From time to time, and for reasons no one has satisfactorily supplied, certain circles of sages collected microforms of literary tradition into more ambitious compositions. These are what we mean by rabbinic "documentary compositions" – mishnaic or talmudic tractates, midrashic compilations, and the like. Roughly speaking, lemmata are to intermediate units as intermediate units are to documents. Just as an intermediate unit organizes its incorporated lemmata in service of some larger, cumulative purpose (thus imposing a kind of unity upon them), so documentary composition organizes the intermediate units and opens them up to broader ranges of meanings (simply because they are now gathered together and juxtaposed within a larger literary framework).

Peter Schaefer has given the name "macroforms" to such compositions (see n. 13). It is within this frame of analysis that literary scholars have been tempted to look most persistently for something like our modern "authors" or, at least, "editors" standing behind the received rabbinic macroforms. If, after all, there is a composition, does this not imply the existence of a composer or a collector/arranger? Perhaps. But the real issue in rabbinic literary studies, as Schaefer has put it, is whether or not the various compilations produced by the sages are in any profound way analogous to something as planned and self-conscious as a composition written by a single author. What are rabbinic microforms and what did the sages who compiled them think they were doing while on the job?

Over the past several decades, the most important answer to this question has been offered by the brilliant contemporary scholar Jacob Neusner. In a series of studies of virtually every rabbinic composition of Late Antiquity, Neusner proposed that the very essence of rabbinic literary creativity is to gather intermediate units of tradition into carefully plotted compositions (documents) that use received textual material to convey fresh propositions about topics crucial to rabbinic Judaism. In short, every rabbinic document, in his view, is supervised by an organizing literary hand that shapes every line in terms of some larger rhetorical, philosophical, legal, or theological program.[18] The most important thing about Neusner's proposal is that it is almost certainly wrong. But as historians of ideas well know, one error of a brilliant mind is often more useful than thousands of correct judgments by the rest of us. As a chorus of the "rest of us" has dutifully pointed out, mishnaic tractates, talmudic commentaries, and midrashic compilations are normally far messier in their construction than his analyses would allow.[19] Indeed, Peter Schäfer developed his theory of the rabbinic document as macroform, constantly undergoing literary reshaping within tradition, largely as a foil to Neusner's theory of the rabbinic document as cogent, methodical essay that reaches some sort of foreordained completion in accord with the intentions of an editorial mind. The result is that for the past three decades or so, academic scholars have been debating whether rabbinic compositions are, at one extreme, as carefully plotted as any novel, or at the other, nearly random collections of stuff that, to recall our earlier discussion of rabbinic theories of rabbinic texts, "just happened."

THE ANTHOLOGICAL MODEL OF RABBINIC LITERARY COMPOSITION

As is common when entertaining theoretical extremes, it is wise to consider a median position. Happily, in the past decade or so, such a position has begun to emerge. A number of scholars have pointed out that there is enough coherence in many rabbinic compilations to justify the postulate of some sort of governing plan that informs the collection of intermediate units into larger documentary wholes.[20] Yet, as many note, these wholes are just disjunctive enough in structure to caution us against subjecting them to hermeneutical torture in order to secure their editors' confession of harboring some sort of comprehensive urge to self-expression. Perhaps, then, it is possible to propose a way of acknowledging both observations by a small shift in perspective in thinking about the genres of rabbinic compilations.

It is in this spirit of compromise that some academic observers of the Neusner-Schäfer wars have proposed that the most apt literary analogy for most forms of rabbinic documentary composition is the anthology.[21] So long as we add a crucial proviso: Rabbinic anthologies must be distinguished from those composed in cultures – such as that of early modern Western Europe and its inheritors – ascribing sovereign integrity to authored literary works. Similarly, they should not be viewed – like the scriptural canons of ancient Judaism, Christianity, and Islam – as relatively immutable literary treasures. In distinction to both of these models, rabbinic compilations are anthologies whose compilers had no hesitations in altering the form and content of the anthologized materials. Lemmata, apparently, continued to be transmitted with the intention of leaving them "as told to the disciples by the Masters." But the larger collections of gathered material – thematically driven microforms, or even larger collections of the latter into diverse macroforms – were never perceived as "works" in their own right. They were, accordingly, malleable and adaptable to meet specific needs of local rabbinic communities.

It would seem that the intermediate traditions were viewed by their literary handlers as elements in a larger kaleidescope of tradition perceived as an authentic communal possession. The documentary compilation is a kind of freeze-frame of that tradition, temporarily stilled by the intervention of the compilational activity itself. But that activity was not conceived as the production of a finished "work." It was, at best, a "work in progress," finished only at the point – perhaps generations after the anthology had entered life as a physical object – at which the perceptions of its transmitters and users began to define the compilation as a text representing "tradition" itself, rather than the ad hoc storage place of tradition's remnants.

Precisely how consciously any of these kaleidescopic compilations was composed, or even the degree to which "composition" is an appropriate term for the literary wholes transmitted under specific titles, remains to be decided on a case-by-case basis. Speaking only impressionistically, it seems to me that mishnaic tractates routinely stand on the "highly composed" end of the spectrum – more "work" and less "progress." By contrast, their toseftan companions seem rather more loose in structure and "unfinished."[22] Similarly, the tractates of the Babylonian Talmud are, by and large, rather carefully worked over by several organizing hands, and are comparatively speaking far more "finished" than corresponding tractates of the Talmud Yerushalmi. The nearly incoherent Hekhalot corpus – upon which Schäfer honed his conception of microforms and macroforms – would stand close to the "uncomposed" pole in which the compilational process was conceived as an open-ended, agglutinative matter with no overall design other than that provided by the incorporated intermediate units. Finally, various midrashic compilations would fall at as-yet unspecified points in between.

The virtue of the anthological model is that it helps make sense of precisely those aspects of rabbinic documentary composition that reveal its collective dimension. The loosely knit anthology, composed of materials that retain a good deal of fluidity, is a particularly apt compositional convention for a culture like that of the rabbinic sages. As Elizabeth Alexander points out in the essay to follow this one, rabbinic culture cultivated a strong oral-performative tradition, as attested by the countless instances in which disciples and Masters are represented as engaging in discourse over a publicly recited text. At the same time, this oral-performative tradition intermeshed in numerous ways with scribal practices in which written texts were memorized and oral conventions of diction and formulation shaped what was written.[23]

The crucial point is to recognize that rabbinic anthologizing took place in the midst of a culture committed to preserving a living oral-performative tradition that intersected in numerous ways with the written word. It is still unclear how early the first written versions of midrashic compilations or of mishnaic or talmudic tractates were recorded. The Talmud itself (B. Gittin 60a) knows of nonlegal midrashic works in written form attested to the third or fourth century C.E. Perhaps, as many scholars insist, the Mishnah and the Babylonian Talmud were first recorded in written books only as late as the tenth or eleventh centuries.[24] But quibbles about the dating of the "first" written versions change nothing about the fundamental reality that the written collections of material were composed in deep interactive relationship to orally performed versions, just as orally mastered, memorized texts, would commonly be tailored for preservation in written documents.

The result is the typical rabbinic compilation wherever we find it: a convenient storage system for loosely formed intermediate literary units known widely from the oral-performative tradition. At the very moment that it transforms oral texts into fixed texts destined for rote mastery, this storage system sends its written versions back into the ether of oral transmission and performance. The anthologies that reflect the written pole of this process function both as mnemonic aids in the preservation of the material and as springboards for restoring textually fixed traditions to the aural/oral world of analysis and debate generated by the rabbinic discipleship curriculum. The written anthology serves, finally, as a point of departure for a return to orality, as the preserved text triggers other literary and conceptual associations drawn from previous experience in the aural/oral world of rabbinic instruction.

CONCLUSION: THE AUTHORS OF THE RABBINIC TEXTS

Let me, finally, take a minute to knit our various observations together in response to the central issue of rabbinic collective authorship. Seen from the perspective of their function in a larger system of information storage, rabbinic anthologies cannot be interpreted as analogues to authored works. They are not subtle attempts to convey a larger concept or argument to a reader. Indeed, if they were, we should judge them – in light of the history of how they were read in the Middle Ages – as colossal literary failures. Their composition is not explained by the desire to communicate an authorial mind to an audience of one or many. Rather, the gaps and fissures of the rabbinic anthological style – the ways in which various juxtaposed microforms often *fail* to cohere into elegant macroforms – seem designed to deflect attention from the written text outward toward a world of speech in which there are no documents, but much discourse. Rabbinic compositional style within the conventions of the anthology points to a literary culture in which the minds and intentions of authors are displaced by the interpretive experiments that emerge among people engaged in mutual discourse over the shared text. Does this last point leave us, in the end, with a bunch of authorless texts? Not at all! In fact, it constitutes the solution to the puzzle of rabbinic textual authorship. The completion of the process of collective rabbinic authorship lies not in the writing down of a document. Written textual composition is only the first moment in a larger authorial enterprise that is completed only, if at all, in the restoration of the written text to its oral-performance tradition. It is in the return of writing to speech that rabbinic texts achieve their literary purpose and gain their completion as "works" that are, of course, constantly being rewritten as they are studied and performed.

This essay began with the observation that the rabbinic texts of Late Antiquity certainly had an audience. We wondered whether it had authors. Now we can answer that question without much hesitation. In the writings of rabbinic Oral Torah, the author was – and is – the audience!

Notes

1. Robert Johnson's "Crossroad Blues" is cited from www.deltahaze.com/johnson/lyrics.html#kwb.
2. A very influential example of this theoretical position is Foucault 1984.
3. An important illustration, with wide-ranging examples, is offered by Roger Chartier, "The Text Between the Voice and the Book," in Raimonda Modiano, Leroy F. Searle, and Peter Shillingsburg, eds.,

VoiceTextHypertext: Emerging Practices in Textual Studies (Seattle: University of Washington Press, 2004), 54–71.

4. The best discussion of the meaning of attributions in rabbinic literature is that of Green 1978.

5. Saul Lieberman, a major mid-twentieth-century scholar of rabbinic literature, translated this word as "rings," and argued that "these rings seem to signify general rules." See "The Publication of the Mishnah," in Lieberman 1950, 95. A manuscript variant that might affect this interpretation is available in Solomon Schechter and Menahem Kister, eds., *Avoth De-Rabbi Nathan: Solomon Schechter Edition* (New York: Jewish Theological Seminary, 1977): *mtby'ot mtby'ot* (67 n. 4). This could be construed as "a series of formulae."

   As I was preparing this essay for publication, I learned that a prominent Israeli scholar, Shlomo Naeh, has proposed that this text refers to the mnemonic discipline of organizing traditions for memorization in the absence of a recourse to writing. His Hebrew article, "The Art of Memory: Structures of Memory and the Forms of Texts in Rabbinic Literature," appears in Zussman and Rozental 2005. See 567ff. for his discussion of our text.

6. The root *t-k-n* has a pre-rabbinic history as a description of literary activity, as in Ecclesiastes 12:9, where it describes the act of compiling or critically evaluating parables. Fishbane 1985, p. 32, points out that the usage in Ecclesiastes parallels the contemporary Hellenistic scribal term *diorthoun*, which corresponds to the sense of editing a written text. Such conceptions surely lie behind the rabbinic term *htkyn*, even if, as I suggest, the term is extended to refer to orally managed literary work.

7. See Hezser 2002. Some late-breaking news on this front comes from Yaakov Zussman, one of this generation's great Israeli scholars of rabbinic literature. In the volume dedicated to the memory of Prof. Urbach (see n. 5), Prof. Zussman offers an encyclopedic essay on the oral formulation of the Mishnah in particular, providing exhaustive documentation of the technical terms employed in rabbinic literature to describe oral-literary processes of creation, transmission, and editing texts, such as those in the Mishnah. I render the Hebrew title in English as "'Oral Torah' Means Just What It Says." See, in particular, 259–75 in Zussman and Rosental 2005.

8. Avraham Even-Shoshan, *Milon Even-Shoshan*, rev. ed. (2003), vol. 3, 898.

9. Michael Sokoloff, *A Dictionary of Jewish Babylonian Aramaic* (Ramat Gan: Bar-Ilan University Press, 2002), 644, s.v., *mhdwr'*.

10. I deliberately leave *mishnah* untranslated here, since it is not at all obvious that the redacted Mishnah ascribed to Rabbi Judah the Patriarch is the object. It is far more likely that the reference here is to the repeated oral tradition or Oral Torah in general, as at B. Eruvin 54b.

11. Jaffee 1999, 13ff. Here I build upon Neusner 1989.

12. For an accessible introduction to the formulaic analysis of rabbinic compositions, with specific reference to the Mishnah, you might consult Neusner 1980.

13. See Schäfer 1986a and 1989, 89–94. Jonathan Schofer makes use of this model in his contribution to the present volume as well.
14. A good recent model of such literary criticism is A. Tropper's analysis of the editing of the various subunits of Mishnah Avot in Tropper 2004b, 21–47.
15. An analysis of this chapter forms the core of an excellent introduction to the study of the Talmud, Neusner 1984.
16. For purposes of brevity, I omit the ensuing text that disputes this view and seeks to link the Mishnah's list of labors to other texts in the Torah. Italicized portions of this translation indicate that a tannaitic source is being cited by the Talmud.
17. For this discussion, I am indebted to Goldenberg 1987.
18. E.g., Neusner 1995b, 21–29 and throughout.
19. Goldenberg 2000, 3–12, offers excellent criticism. For my own two cents, see, Jaffee 1999.
20. See, for example, Milikowsky 1988 and Mandel 2000.
21. D. Stern 2004 offers particularly helpful discussions: Yaakov Elman, "Order, Sequence, and Selection: The Mishnah's Anthological Choices," 53–80; Eliezer Segal, "Anthological Dimensions of the Babylonian Talmud," 81–107; and David Stern, "Anthology and Polysemy in Classical Midrash," 108–42. Each of these first appeared in *Prooftexts: A Journal of Jewish Literary History* 17 (1997).
22. See M. Fox 1999.
23. E. S. Alexander 1999; Elman 1999; Fraade 1991 and 1999b; Jaffee 2005; Nelson 2005. Prof. Zussman (see n. 5) strenuously argues that writing played no role in either the prehistory of the formulation of the traditions now in the Mishnah in particular or in the composition and transmission of the final mishnaic text. He is undoubtedly correct in his basic claims that the Mishnah known to the Talmuds was studied only as a memorized, orally managed text. But he also ignores many ways in which rabbinic sages used the skills of writers in their formation of the mishnaic tradition.
24. Brody 1998, 156–61, and Elman 1999.

2 The Orality of Rabbinic Writing

ELIZABETH SHANKS ALEXANDER

Oral teaching and transmission of literary compositions of various degrees of textual fluidity played a prominent role in the shaping of rabbinic culture. Throughout the period leading up to the emergence of the rabbinic movement, both scribal and oral technologies were used in complementary fashion to transmit Jewish tradition. In certain ways, the rabbis were typical of their day in their reliance on oral transmissional techniques. It is noteworthy, however, that though other Jewish groups in antiquity had developed bodies of oral tradition, only the rabbis attributed significance to the fact that they transmitted tradition orally.[1] They alone claimed that the traditional teachings under their guardianship originated in an oral revelation, which had, ever since, been transmitted exclusively by word of mouth. The rabbis highlighted the oral aspect of their teachings by calling it "Oral Torah." For the rabbis, then, oral instruction was not merely a technology of transmission. Through the concept of Oral Torah (and its partner concept, Written Torah), technologies of transmission took on ideological coloration. This article seeks an understanding of what was at stake for the rabbis when they highlighted the oral, as opposed to written, modes of transmission used in the conveyance of their teachings.

As the rabbis understood the matter, God's revelation to Moses at Mt. Sinai had two components. The written revelation, or Written Torah, had a fixed literary form and was handed down in the form of the twenty-two books of the biblical canon. The oral revelation, or Oral Torah, was an interpretive supplement to the written scriptures. It was to be passed from teacher to student by word of mouth alone. Now, rabbinic literature does not contain anything close to a history of this oral tradition. Some texts do claim, however, that by the time the Oral Torah had reached the teachers and students of the Late Second Temple Period, it was in a state of disarray. The destruction of the Second Temple in Jerusalem in 70 C.E. additionally brought the loss of a center of great learning and scribal expertise. An early rabbinic tradition from the Tosefta tells of a gathering of sages shortly after 70 C.E. that was intended to counteract the loss of tradition:

> When the sages went into the Vineyard at Yavneh,[2] they said: The time will come when a man will seek a matter of Torah but he will not find it. He will seek a matter of the scribes, but he will not find it. . . .
>   They said: Let us begin with [the teachings] of Hillel and Shammai. (T. Eduyot 1:1)

This source describes the beginning of what eventually became a major cultural project for the rabbis: organizing, collating, and preserving for future posterity a body of received oral traditions. From the humble beginnings of collecting Hillel's and Shammai's traditions in the vineyard at Yavneh, the corpus of rabbinic literature as we have it today was eventually produced.

For modern students who wish to understand how the rabbis thought about the oral character of their teachings, it is helpful to look at rabbinic sources that describe the Written and Oral Torahs. These sources offer a glimpse into what the rabbis took to be the distinctive features of oral, as opposed to written, transmission.

ORAL TORAH: AN UNBROKEN CHAIN OF TRANSMISSION

A survey of sources reveals that the rabbis understood the oral character of the Oral Torah in (at least) two different ways. On the one hand, some rabbinic sources highlight the fact that the Oral Torah was passed on orally from Sinai to the rabbis in an unbroken chain of transmission. In these sources, the distinctive feature of Oral Torah is that it is conveyed by word of mouth and memorized. On the other hand, other sources focus on Oral Torah as teachings that are unfolded through intensive analysis, interrogation, and debate. In these sources, the orality of Oral Torah lies more in the oral instructional environment in which traditions are articulated. Surely, other sources could be found that offer other ways of understanding that which is oral about Oral Torah, but for heuristic purposes, I will offer a close reading of several sources in which these two distinctive views of the orality of Oral Torah are expressed.

A first set of sources proposes that there is a direct line of transmission in the conveyance of the oral traditions from Sinai. Oral Torah begins, and remains throughout the course of its transmission, a discrete and defined body of material, which each tradent is responsible for reproducing in a verbatim manner for the next recipient. Modern scholars of oral traditions would call this a "literary" conception of orality because it is associated with societies that have access to literary texts.[3] The so-called literary view of oral transmission views it as capable of reproducing tradition with the precision and fixity of written literary texts. In this view of oral transmission, the only difference between the Oral and the Written Torahs is the medium of their initial revelation and ongoing conveyance. Both sets of traditions are transmitted as discrete and finite bodies of material; they travel in tandem throughout the generations. The significant difference between them is that one set of traditions is fixed in writing and the other is fixed in memory and conveyed, without the aid of written versions, by word of mouth.

The famous teaching that begins the mishnaic tractate called "The Fathers" (Avot, ca. 220–250 C.E.) represents the transmission of Oral Torah in this fashion. The text there reads:

> Moses received the Torah from Sinai and transmitted it to Joshua, Joshua to the elders, and the elders to the prophets, and the prophets transmitted it to the Men of the Great Assembly.
> (M. Avot 1:1)

In this source, a discrete set of materials (Torah – presumably both Oral and Written) is handed down. Each of the tradents (Moses, Joshua, the elders, the prophets, and the Men of the Great Assembly) passes it on as received, giving the sense of an unbroken chain of continuity. One has no reason to doubt that the Torah received in the final stages of transmission (by the Men of the Great Assembly) is at all different from the Torah promulgated at its point of origin (Sinai).

A second source likewise understands Oral Torah to be a stable and clearly defined set of materials passed on intact from one tradent to another. Adding a new element, this source from the Babylonian Talmud describes a technology that makes possible accurate preservation of oral tradition:

> Our rabbis taught: How was the transmission of Mishnah (viz. "Repeated Tradition") organized? Moses learned from the mouth of the All-Powerful One; Aaron entered and Moses taught him his lesson; Aaron moved aside and sat down to the left of Moses; Aaron's sons entered and Moses taught them their lesson; the sons moved aside . . . ; the elders entered and Moses taught them their lesson; the elders moved aside; then the entire nation entered and Moses taught them their lesson. It thus followed that Aaron heard the lesson four times, his sons three times, the elders twice, and the entire nation once. At this stage Moses moved aside and Aaron

taught them his lesson; Aaron then moved aside and his sons taught them their lesson; the sons then moved aside and the elders taught them their lesson. Thus it turned out that everybody heard the lesson four times. (B. Eruvin 54b)

In this very complicated orchestration of shifting teachers and audiences, everyone succeeds in hearing the lesson four times. An early rabbinic sage, R. Eliezer, took this description of Moses' transmitting Oral Torah to be a precedent for his own time, asserting that all rabbinic teachings should be repeated four times in order to secure them properly in the memory.

The described sequence of teaching, however, suggests that tradition is preserved by more than just its four-time repetition. One part of the process of securing tradition involves direct teaching from teacher to disciple (e.g., Moses to Aaron). Another equally important part of the process involves establishing witnesses as the teacher transmits to others (e.g., Aaron listening in as Moses teaches his sons). One absorbs the tradition in part by having it conveyed directly, but equally importantly, by having it taught to others in one's presence. The importance of passively witnessing direct transmission between others, however, extends beyond the role it serves to secure the tradition in the memory of the witness. The presence of the witness(es) also ensures that the *material taught* remains the same from one lesson to the next. With Aaron present as witness, Moses cannot teach his sons, the elders, or the nation a different lesson. Once Moses leaves, the stakes become even higher because now transmission is in the hands of tradents who did not receive it directly from the All-Powerful One. As Aaron teaches, the witness who *did* hear directly from Moses ensures that Aaron's lesson will be commensurate with those of Moses. Likewise, when Aaron leaves, the presence of an audience who heard from Moses and Aaron ensures that Aaron's sons will not deviate from the correct tradition. And so on. This source, then, presents a very complex choreography between teachers and disciples, performers and audiences, that ensures the intact preservation of a discrete body of tradition. As with the source discussed previously (M. Avot 1:1), oral transmission is here represented as an unbroken chain. The Torah received at the end of a long chain of transmission should be the same as the Torah promulgated at the beginning. The brilliance of this talmudic source (B. Eruvin 54b) is that it offers a strategy for ensuring this outcome.

In this first set of sources, we might think of the Oral and Written Torahs as two discrete bodies of tradition received at the same time, transmitted in tandem, albeit in different media. By the Gaonic Period (ca. 700–1100), the Oral Torah was often characterized as an interpretive supplement to the Written Torah. When the sources presented here are read through the gaonic lens, these sources suggest that the interpretative sources of Oral Torah were fully developed at the time of Sinaitic revelation. As we will see shortly, not all rabbinic sources share the view that the Oral Torah was received as a discrete and finite set of traditions. Later controversies between the Rabbanites (early medieval inheritors of rabbinic tradition) and the Karaites (those who rejected the authority of the rabbinic tradition) made this view of Oral Torah particularly appealing to those who accepted the authority of rabbinic tradition. How better to defend the sacred status of rabbinic tradition than to say it originated at Sinai and from there was transmitted intact, as a discrete body of tradition?

ORAL TORAH: ACTUALIZING THE INTERPRETIVE POTENTIAL OF WRITTEN TORAH

A second set of sources acknowledges profound *discontinuities* between the original revelation at Mt. Sinai and the traditions articulated and transmitted by the rabbis. In these sources, the orality of Oral Torah would seem to have more to do with the dynamic encounter among sacred text, teacher, and student than with the stability of tradition enabled by technologies of memory. In these sources, Oral Torah is not represented as an interpretive supplement that originates at Sinai. Instead, Oral Torah is portrayed as *the actualization of interpretive possibilities already embedded within the text of the Written Torah.* Though the interpretive traditions articulated as Oral Torah are understood to be intrinsic to the Written Torah, they lie there dormant until activated by the teacher's encounter with text and student in the classroom.

A famous story in the Babylonian Talmud represents the Oral Torah as "heaps and heaps of laws" that will one day be interpreted out of the decorative flourishes that God attached to letters of the Torah at Sinai. The story retells the events of Sinaitic revelation, making an allowance for the dual revelation of both the Written and Oral Torahs:

> When Moses ascended on high he found the Holy One, blessed be He, engaged in attaching crownlets to the letters. He said to Him, "Lord of the Universe, why should you bother with this?" He answered, "There is a man who is destined to arise at the end of many generations, named Akiva ben Yosef, who will expound upon each crownlet heaps and heaps of laws." [Moses] said to him,

"Master of the Universe, show him to me." He replied, "Turn
around." Moses went and sat down behind the eighth row [of
students and listened to the discourse], but he could not understand what they were saying. His strength left him. But then they
came to a certain topic and the disciples said to [R. Akiva], "Rabbi,
how do you know it?" He replied, "It is a law given to Moses at
Sinai." And Moses was comforted. (B. Menahot 29b)

Though to Moses the crownlets may appear to be merely decorative, God
explains that for the great rabbinic scholar R. Akiva, they will hold great
interpretive potential. With his wisdom and insight, he will be able to
discern a number of additional laws that God intends to communicate
to his people.

I would argue that as one of the foundational scholars of the greatest
renown within the early rabbinic movement, R. Akiva in this source
metonymically stands in for the rabbinic movement at large. To say,
R. Akiva's teaching were intended by God at the original moment of
divine revelation, is to suggest implicitly that all rabbinic teaching has
its origin with God at Sinai. The story continues in a manner, however, that casts doubt on the conclusion that rabbinic teaching derives
from Sinai. Moses, who is intrigued that the revelation he is receiving
will be studied for generations to come, asks to see the great scholar at
work. In a fantastical journey through time that only God can engineer,
Moses turns around and finds himself in Rabbi Akiva's classroom. He
is gravely disappointed, however, when he realizes he can't follow the
conversation. Here is a remarkable admission on the part of the rabbis.
Even while positing that the Oral Torah is dependent on and derivative
of the Written Torah, this source also acknowledges a serious and real
gap between the two bodies of literature. So great are the differences
between the two that Moses, who himself received the Written Torah
from God and knew God's voice more intimately than any other human
being, cannot understand the plain sense of the rabbinic tradition as
taught by Rabbi Akiva. Only when Rabbi Akiva cites Moses our Master as the source of his teachings is Moses reassured of the connection
between his teaching and those of the rabbis. Though Moses is ultimately assuaged by Rabbi Akiva's comment to his students, one cannot
help but be shocked by this source's implicit admission that a gap exists
between the revelation Moses received and the later teachings of the
rabbis.

How are we to make sense of the orality of the Oral Torah in this
story? If the Oral Torah is given in a cryptic form, from which more fully
drawn-out teachings be articulated only later, it no longer makes

sense to think of its orality as lying in the unbroken series of face-to-face oral transmissions. In this depiction of Oral Torah, we do better to think of the orality of rabbinic tradition as linked to the dynamics of the classroom. It is there that Rabbi Akiva engages his students. In response to their questions he articulates the laws that are foreign to Moses, and also in response to their questions he affirms the origin of the traditions in Sinaitic revelation. The site of the classroom, then, with its dynamic interchange between teacher and student over the generative material of the sacred text symbolizes the oral aspect of Oral Torah. Orality here is not primarily a medium for transmission. Rather, it is a mode of engagement, one that is fluid and dynamic, and represented by the interaction between teacher and student as developed and amplified in the process of tradition.

A second source also suggests that the content of the Oral Torah was not received directly from the mouth of God at Sinai. Like the previous source, it situates the orality of the Oral Torah in an engaged analysis of the Written Torah. As mentioned, the interpretations of the Oral Torah are seen to be encoded by God in the Written Torah, but in *potential* form. Also as mentioned, vigorous engagement with the Written Torah is seen as the best way to retrieve or recover Oral Torah. In this source (*Seder Eliahu Zuta* 2, ca. 700–800) a rabbinic narrator responds to a heretically inclined interloculor who does not believe that the Oral Torah originates at Sinai. The narrator tells a parable in order to show how both Torahs do in fact come from Sinai:

> What is the difference between the Written and Oral Torahs? They told a parable. To what may the matter be compared? To a king of flesh and blood who had two servants. He loved them both with a perfect love. To one he gave a kab of wheat and a bundle of flax and to the other he gave a kab of wheat and a bundle of flax. What did the wise one do? He took the flax and wove it into a tablecloth. He took the wheat and made it into fine flour; he sifted it and he ground it. He kneaded it and he baked it. Then he placed it on the top of the table and spread over it the tablecloth. Then he left it for the king's return. The foolish among them did not do anything at all.
>
> After some days the king returned to his house and said: My sons, bring me what I gave you. One brought out the bread of fine flour upon the table with the tablecloth spread over it. The other brought out the wheat in a box and the bundle of flax upon it. Alas for his shame, alas for his disgrace.

The key to understanding how this parable elucidates the difference between the Written and Oral Torahs is to focus on the difference
between the wheat and flax in their raw state, on the one hand, and the
tablecloth and bread in their processed state, on the other. The foolish
servant receives the wheat and flax and sees them only for what they
are. He thinks that he appropriately "keeps" the goods of the king (i.e.,
God) when he leaves them untouched. By way of contrast, when the
wise servant encounters the raw materials (i.e., Written Torah), he sees
them for what they *could be*. He is not worried that he has to manipulate
them extensively in order for them to assume their more useful forms.
When the king returns, it is clear that one servant has greatly honored
the king, while the other has not. The parable seems to be saying, then,
that God *wants* his servants to engage the Written Torah actively. It
is interesting to note that as here and unlike in the first set of sources,
God does not dictate the contents of the Oral Torah directly to its human
recipients. It is clear, however, that God intends for the rabbinic community to do its interpretive work. Insofar as God gave Israel the raw
materials (Written Torah) and insofar as they bring more honor to God
when they are manipulated into processed form (Oral Torah), this source
suggests that God wants Israel to derive Oral Torah from Written Torah.
As previously, the orality of the Oral Torah must be understood to lie
in active intellectual engagement. While the source locates that activity
in the rabbinic classroom, this source offers the analogy of transforma-
tive labor (weaving, sifting, grinding, kneading, and baking). To perform
Oral Torah is to engage in an activity that leaves the raw materials of the
Written Torah in a different state. We must assume that the transforma-
tive labor of Oral Torah study includes intensive questioning, debate,
and discussion.

This second set of sources represents the orality of the Oral Torah
in a manner quite different from the first set. Here, Oral and Written
Torah differ not only in the medium of their revelation but also in their
degrees of relative fixity and fluidity. Whereas the words of the Written
Torah are fixed for eternity, the words of the Oral Torah are unfolded
in an ongoing manner through the vigorous engagement of student and
teacher with the foundational text of the Written Torah.

In sum, from the rabbinic sources that reflect on the relationship
between the Written and Oral Torahs we find both "literarily" and
"orally" inclined representations of Oral Torah. The first pair of sources
(M. Avot 1:1 and B. Eruvin 54b) represents Oral Torah as a discrete set
of traditions, dictated by God directly and transmitted with an almost
literary precision throughout the generations. By way of contrast, the

second pair of sources (B. Menahot. 29b and Seder Eliahu Zuta 2) represent Oral Torah as potential interpretations embedded within the Written Torah that remain dormant until activated by a teacher and student's vigorous engagement of the sacred text. The first representation is more "literary" in orientation insofar as the Oral Torah is characterized by a fixity that is generally associated with literate society and literary technologies of preserving text. The second representation is more "oral" in orientation insofar as it figures rabbinic tradition as fluid and flexible. Researchers have shown that oral societies tend to have a more fluid, flexible, and multiform understanding of textuality.[4] It is interesting that even though the rabbinic rhetoric stresses orality (it is, after all, the *Oral* Torah), the sources reveal *both* literary and oral ways of thinking about it.

A RHETORIC OF ORALITY AND WRITTEN TEXTS

This discussion of texts makes clear that though the rabbis found it ideologically useful to understand their traditions as *Oral* Torah, they sometimes thought about their traditions through a *literary* lens. We need not dig deeply into the corpus of rabbinic writings to find further evidence of tension between an idealized understanding of rabbinic tradition as oral and a realistic recognition that the rabbis were a highly literate society and used their literary tools in shaping their own rabbinic tradition.

The ideal that Oral Torah be transmitted in an exclusively oral fashion is preserved in a number of sources that proscribe the use of written texts in the teaching and transmission of rabbinic tradition. A source from the Talmud records three different versions of the ban:[5]

> R. Abba son of R. Hiyya b. Abba said in the name of R. Yohanan: Those who write down the words of *halakhot* [rabbinic legal teachings, i.e., Oral Torah] are likened to one who burns the Torah.
>   R. Yehudah son of Nahum, the declaimer of Resh Lakish expounded: . . . One may not recite oral teachings from a written document and one may not recite written teachings from memory.
>   The school of R. Ishmael taught: "Write for yourself *these words*" [Exodus 34:27]. *These words* [i.e., Written Torah] you may write, but you may not write *halakhot* [i.e., Oral Torah].
>   (B. Temurah 14b; cf. B. Gittin 60b; author's emphasis)

The first tradition related by R. Abba in the name of R. Yohanan makes clear the stakes attached to the medium of transmission. To write down the teachings of Oral Torah is no light matter. The deed is likened to burning the Torah! The second tradition related by R. Yehudah in the name of the translator of Resh Lakish explains that the ban is in fact twofold. Not only is one prohibited from teaching Oral Torah from a written exemplar, one is equally forbidden to teach Written Torah *without* a written exemplar. Apparently, the teachings of the Written and Oral Torahs are constituted by more than their verbal content. An equally essential component of these divine revelations would seem to be the *medium* of their transmission. The mode of transmission, it seems, is not merely incidental but central to the Torah's meaning.

It is interesting, however, that the very text that communicates the gravity of writing down rabbinic tradition also records instances in which highly respected scholars ignored the ban.

> Were not R. Yohanan and Resh Lakish accustomed to looking at a book of *aggadah* on the Sabbath?

R. Yohanan and Resh Lakish were the leading sages of their generation. In spite of the ban, they studied non legal rabbinic teachings from a written exemplar. The fact that R. Yohanan and Resh Lakish violate the stated cultural norms cannot be mere coincidence. These are the two sages from whose schools the aforementioned dictums originate. Recall that one version of the ban is transmitted in the name of R. Yohanan and another version is transmitted in the name of Resh Lakish's translator, a chief functionary in his academy. It appears that this source wishes to highlight the tension between reality and the stated cultural ideals. The text goes on to explain that this exception was permitted because of a fear that the traditions might be forgotten if not written down. While this is an acceptable justification for the aberrant act, one wonders why a text so committed to the stated norms would chose to "remember" and record it.

We find a similiar tension between the stated norms and actual practice represented elsewhere. A ban on writing rabbinic teachings is also recorded in the earlier of the two Talmuds, the Palestinian Talmud.

> R. Haggai in the name of R. Shmuel son of R. Isaac said: Words that were spoken orally, must be [taught] orally. Words that were spoken [*sic*] in writing must be [taught from] writing. (Y. Megillah 4:1, 64d)

Here, rabbinic practices of transmission are understood to be a way of imitating and perhaps even reenacting God's initial revelatory act.

Whatever God delivered in oral form must be preserved, taught, and studied in oral form; whatever God imparted in written form must be read from a written document. If one teaches in the same medium that God initially spoke (and it is interesting that the rabbis understood God as having *spoken* both orally and in writing!), then the Sinaitic revelation is experienced as an event not just of the distant past but also of the rabbinic present. Here we begin to gain some insight into the ideological force of the medium of transmission: It is important because it helps construct and sustain the notion of an ongoing revelation. When one teaches as God spoke, the force of Sinaitic revelation becomes more immediate and accessible.

In this source also the stated norms do not go uncontested. Here, however, it is the other half of the rule – the proscription not to perform the Written Torah from memory – that is violated. Stories are told about R. Meir who wrote out a scroll of Esther, and R. Ishamel b. Yose boasts that he is able to write out a whole Torah scroll from memory. Thus, even while these two sources (B. Temurah 14b and Y. Megillah 4:1, 64d) state the ideal norms of rabbinic society in an unambiguous manner, they also bring sufficient anecdotal evidence to indicate that the rules were not always observed and that such violations were not considered scandalous. One might postulate that what was important about the ban was not that it be strictly observed but that it be stated. This raises an obvious question: What is so special, distinctive, or significant about oral means of conveying tradition that the rabbis felt it important to identify their teachings as oral?

THE MODERN SCHOLARLY DEBATE ABOUT THE ORALITY OF RABBINIC LITERATURE

Modern scholars interested in understanding the ways in which oral teaching and study functioned in ancient rabbinic settings have inherited a puzzling body of conflicting evidence. On the one hand, a norm was expressed that rabbinic teachings should be transmitted orally. On the other hand, anecdotal evidence suggests that some sages preserved rabbinic teaching in written form. The conflicting evidence concerning the orality of rabbinic tradition extends beyond the materials discussed here. On the one hand, the texts of the rabbinic corpus leave palpable traces of an active oral life. The Mishnah is formulated in a manner that facilitates memorization (see n. 10). Much talmudic discourse is structured as if it were the record of a conversation among interloculars at the study house. Both the midrashic corpus and the Talmud use an oral rhetoric ("from whence do you say?" "what might I have said?" "I hear it to mean" ... and so forth) that gives the impression of having originated in a conversational setting. Evidence of this sort leads to the conclusion that rabbinic teachings *were* taught and transmitted orally. On the other hand, the literature reaches its current audience in written form.[6] There is a certain irony to the fact that the body of literature known as Oral Torah today fills the greater part of a wall of bookshelves. If Oral Torah really was composed, transmitted, and studied orally, how and why did it come to be preserved in written form?

PURIST UNDERSTANDINGS OF RABBINIC ORALITY

The question of how and when the texts of Oral Torah came to be written down has engaged academic scholars persistently since at least the nineteenth century. The inquiry has focused in particular on the Mishnah, a compendium of legal cases, whose compilation is attributed to Rabbi Yehudah ha-Nasi in 200–225 C.E. There are several reasons why the Mishnah in particular serves as a catalyst for discussion about the extent of orality and textuality in rabbinic literature. First, the Mishnah is the earliest extant collection of rabbinic teachings and it represents the rabbis' first (preserved) attempt at formal transmission. Some of the traditions preserved in the Mishnah clearly have pre-rabbinic origins. For scholars interested in recovering the long trajectory of oral transmission before the formalization of rabbinic teachings, the Mishnah is an excellent starting point. A second reason why so many inquiries into rabbinic practices of oral transmission focus on the Mishnah is that rabbinic sources themselves attest to a widespread practice of orally performing mishnaic texts. On a number of occasions, the Talmuds make reference to a public functionary in the rabbinic academies called the *Tanna*, literally "a repeater of traditions."[7] His job was to publically recite mishnaic texts in the academies. A third reason why the Mishnah attracts much attention on questions related to oral performance is what can loosely be called its "oral style." This feature of the text remains accessible and apparent to contemporary readers in spite of their distance from the original settings in which the text would have been composed and performed. The Mishnah employs numerous mnemonic techniques.[8] It often structures its discussion of cases using parallelism, and it organizes material topically, using both legal content or sages' names as an organizing principle. It also often lists items in groups of three or five.

It is, however, ironic that the Mishnah is also among the most literarily elegant of rabbinic texts. Its prose is simple and clear. If it is among the most orally transparent of rabbinic texts, it is also among the most literary in its refinement.

Scholars debating the question of how orality and textuality interact in the transmissional life of the Mishnah have generally framed the question as follows: "Was the Mishnah written down?"[9] The question proceeds from the expectation that the Mishnah, as a genre of Oral Torah, should have been composed and transmitted using exclusively oral means, but it also acknowledges the evidence that the Mishnah was available in written form. A standing assumption associated with this line of inquiry is that "real" oral transmission does not include the use of written texts. Scholars have generally found one way or another to circumscribe the role of written texts in the transmission of the Mishnah in order to restore the sense of a pure orality. For illustrative purposes, I will examine the work of three prominent scholars who have written and thought extensively about these matters.

J. N. Epstein takes the anecdotal evidence that mishnaic texts existed in written form during the rabbinic period at face value.[10] He argues, however, that the Tannaim recited the Mishnah in an exclusively oral manner. In the academy, all study of the Mishnah was to be done from memory.[11] Written exemplars of the text existed only to serve as a point of reference when questions arose concerning the correct version of the text.[12] The written version, then, established the authoritative and correct text, which the orally performed version in the academy made accessible for study and reflection. Epstein's theory has the merit of adequately explaining where the mishnaic texts that eventually emerged came from. They were the official versions that were kept "on file" for reference. It does seem, however, that the significance of orality is diminished in Epstein's model. For him, the orally performed version is a mere shadow or reflection of the official written version.

Following Epstein, Saul Lieberman accepts the anecdotal evidence for early written versions of the Mishnah. He understands the role of the written texts, however, to be exactly the opposite of that argued by Epstein. Whereas Epstein argues that the *written* versions were to be accepted as authoritative over the flaws of human memory, Lieberman argues that only the *oral* versions performed in the academy had authority. According to Lieberman, the written versions were used for personal reference only and had no official standing at all. A particular version of the text would be considered authoritative only when it was performed in the academy by an official Tanna who had memorized the sanctioned version of the text.[13] Lieberman's theory is interesting in that he reverses long-standing assumptions about writing versus orality. Whereas *writing* is usually assumed to confer fixity in a way that lends it authority, Lieberman argues that fixity was achieved orally and that authority was granted to only the *orally* performed version. This theory is attractive because it restores the centrality of the Mishnah's orality. It fails, however, to account fully for the emergence of the later written versions of the text. If the written personal notes were not authoritative, why would they have later become the basis for the written texts that *were* authoritative.

Writing after Epstein and Lieberman, Shmuel Safrai accepts their conclusions that during the rabbinic period, written versions of the Mishnah were available. He argues for a pure mishnaic orality by adopting what can be called a "serial approach." He suggests that *first* the rabbis used exclusively oral means of transmission; they composed, consolidated, and edited the text orally. Only later, after it achieved a stable identity as Oral Torah did the rabbis record it in writing. Safrai suggests that at this point, it no longer would have been problematic to write it down because there was no danger of it being confused with Written Torah.[14] His theory has the advantage of preserving an oral essence to the Mishnah in its origins, and it also explains how the current mishnaic texts came to be, but one wonders why the shift to writing was made.

Underlying each of these explanations of the data is the belief that written texts have no place in a transmissional process that is called "oral." Each of the three scholars discussed here circumscribes the role of written texts when characterizing the oral aspects of the Mishnah's transmission. Epstein argues that the official written version of the Mishnah had no role in the academy where it was recited by the Tannaim for study purposes. Lieberman argues that written versions of the Mishnah had no place in the academy because they were not officially sanctioned; they were used only for personal reference. Safrai preserves the orality of Oral Torah by arguing for a pure oral stage that *preceded* the emergence of the written version. In all cases, orality entails the exclusion of writing.

INTEGRATING WRITTEN TEXTS INTO ORALITY: A MODEL FROM CROSS-CULTURAL ORALITY STUDIES

A recent generation of rabbinics scholars has been influenced by research on oral tradition in cross-cultural settings. Working with data from a variety of cultural settings and historical periods, scholars of oral traditions have increasingly come to the conclusion that very rarely do oral and literary media operate in isolation from each other. Far more pervasive are situations in which oral and literary media interface with each other, with each influencing the way information conveyed in the other modality is encountered. The work of Ruth Finnegan is especially useful for an understanding of the interaction between writing and orality in rabbinic literature.

Finnegan discusses a phenomenon known as the "broadside" ballads, which reveals how completely intertwined written texts can become in the oral performative life of traditional material.[15] The broadside ballads received their name because they were distributed in sixteenth-century England in broadside form (large unfolded sheets of paper with large Gothic type). According to Finnegan, the large-scale printing was intended to facilitate "wide distribution and cheap sale."[16] On the face of it, the broadside ballads would seem to represent a written phenomenon. Their distribution, however, relied heavily on oral performance. Ballad singers went out to the fairs and markets of the towns and countryside and performed the ballads *orally* in order to attract interest and buyers. Even after the ballads were purchased in printed form, they continued to have an active oral life. Finnegan writes:

> After that it seems clear that the ballads often circulated orally, with people singing the currently popular ones, or adopting and adapting their own favorites – so that many ballads which started as printed broadside texts then circulated largely through oral means, subject to the variability and re-composition so common in oral literature.[17]

The ballads, then, benefited from wide distribution made possible by the printed form, but their distribution also relied heavily on the traditional venues of oral performance. Even the extent to which it is appropriate to speak of the ballads having originated in printed form is questionable. Though the printers employed writers to compose many original ballads, they also sent agents into the field to collect traditional songs from the folk. In such cases, the reduction to writing took an oral form that already existed in one area and made it available through print to oral performers in other areas.

Finnegan's work illustrates the falsehood of the traditional assumption that if writing is involved, then the fluidity associated with oral performance is compromised. She shows that the mere fact of writing a text down does not prevent the text from being orally appropriated and transformed. Even making a song available in printed format, where the same version is reproduced thousands of times, does not stop the adaptations that occur as the result of oral performance. Though the broadside ballads enjoyed the standardization and mass distribution made possible by print, the songs continued to circulate and be transformed by oral performance. The two modes of distribution – print and oral performance – did not operate in isolation from each other, but rather interacted in complex ways. What began as an oral form was transformed by writing, as standardized versions were created by printers. Even so, the salesmen and the populace continued to appropriate, adopt, and further distribute the printed versions through oral performance.

Although I have focused on Finnegan's work in great detail, the insight that orality and writing are not distinct phenomena is not hers alone. A whole network of scholars in the field of orality studies has made this same point in a variety of ways.[18] Exposure to the broad range of this work has helped scholars of rabbinics rethink the role of writing in the performance and study of rabbinic teachings. Rather than assuming that writing necessarily confers fixity and therefore must be disassociated from the oral life of the Mishnah and other rabbinic texts, scholars are increasingly finding evidence for the fact that writing played an integral part in the composition and transmission of the teachings of Oral Torah.

RABBINIC ORALITY AS THE SOCIAL ENACTMENT OF WRITTEN TEXTS

More than any other scholar in rabbinics, Martin Jaffee has used the insights from the field of orality studies to clarify the role of writing and the nature of orality in rabbinic literature. Jaffee's work has approached the matter from two different directions. First, certain aspects of his work examine instances in which the composition and/or study of specific texts involved both writing and oral performance. In this part of his work, he moves beyond the anecdotal evidence for the use of writing in rabbinic academic circles discussed earlier and complements it with evidence that is left in the traces of the literature itself. In one instance, Jaffee documents the interaction of writing and oral performance in Greco-Roman rhetorical exercises and uses it as a paradigm for postulating the existence of similar interactions between writing and oral performance among the rabbis.[19] Jaffee explains that in

Greco-Roman settings, students were instructed to transpose a written saying into a variety of different oral permutations. For example, they might be asked to formulate the saying using the subjunctive voice or present it as a direct or indirect quotation. While the oral transpositions conveyed essentially the same material as the original written saying, they differed in various incidental aspects of their presentation. Jaffee discovers a series of parallels to a mishnaic saying that would likewise seem to represent oral manipulations of a written prototype into different permutations. While the Mishnah and its parallels cover the same basic material, they differ in incidental details, like whether or not they list items in an ascending or descending order. On the basis of the fact that one of the parallel versions has fewer embellishments, he suggests that it may have been the original written version from which the others were orally adopted. In another instance, Jaffee identifies a "popular" song that he suggests enjoyed a second oral life as a part of the learned teachings recited among the rabbis.[20] The extant mishnaic text in which the song is preserved includes intermittent notes of commentary on the song. He suggests that these random interjections originated as scribal glosses to a written text. It is likely, then, that in the rabbinic circles the song was performed from a written prototype. These are just several of the analyses that Jaffee offers to show that writing was integral to the rabbinic academic enterprise.

The second major thrust of Jaffee's work is to account for the rabbinic discomfort with the written character of their teachings. Here, Jaffee offers an answer to a question raised earlier in this essay: What was it that the rabbis so valued in oral teaching that led them to insist that their corpus was the product of an exclusively oral pedagogical environment in spite of well-attested evidence to the contrary? As Jaffee understands the matter, the key difference between learning material orally and learning it from a written text is the mediating presence of a sage.[21] When a tradition is conveyed orally, a sage is present for the disciple in order to reinforce its spiritual meaning through his own behaviors. When the disciple sits by himself in front of the text, the true meaning of a teaching can easily be missed. The presence of a sage offers an embodied realization of the tradition through his exemplary action. Jaffee argues that rabbinic culture valued oral transmission because it recognized how central the relationship between sage and disciple was to perpetuating their culture. For him, rabbinic orality lives in the face-to-face encounter between sage and disciple. Even if such discussions sometimes took written texts as their point of departure, their oral nature was no by means diminished.

Steven Fraade offers another interesting way to think about the oral aspect of rabbinic literature. Fraade's model for how written texts interact with oral performance has much resonance with Finnegan's work on the broadside ballads. Just as she demonstrates that an originally oral form passed into written form only to be re-oralized, Fraade's work alerts us to the orality that lies both *behind* and *in front of* the extant rabbinic texts. Writing about the midrashic commentary Sifre Deuteronomy, Fraade exposes the ways in which rabbinic texts serve as a script for future oral performance. Specifically, he notes ways in which the midrashic juxtaposition of rabbinic commentary with scriptural text positions the disciple to reenact the reception of Torah (both Oral and Written) at Sinai. In a much-quoted formulation, Fraade proposes that we think of the extant rabbinic texts as "the literary face of an otherwise oral circulatory system of study and teaching."[22] Like the broadside ballads, the midrashic texts he discusses have their origins in oral performance prior to being recorded in written form. Unlike Safrai's model, however, where the reduction to writing marks the end of the fluid stage of the materials, Fraade's oral circulatory metaphor proposes that there is a second stage of "re-oralization." Here, the written text acts as a script, anticipating the questions and answers that the study will generate. Rather than thinking of the extant rabbinic texts as "*reports* of a transformation already completed," Fraade suggests we think of them as "part of the very *work* of that transformation."[23] According to Fraade, the rabbis did not intend for their texts to be passively received as the record of study already complete. Rather, it was hoped that performing the texts would be a catalyst for creating the ideal rabbinic society they imagined. In this way of thinking, rabbinic texts are not a literary by-product but an integral part of an (orally based) social process in progress. Here, the focus shifts from recovering an "original" orality to highlighting the oral afterlife engendered by rabbinic texts.

In the work of this latest group of researchers, orality need not preclude the use of written texts. Indeed, written texts prove to have an integral part in the cycles of oral teaching. For these scholars, orality need not be understood in a literal sense. The essence of rabbinic orality shifts to the face-to-face encounter between teacher and student and the active way in which this encounter brings a tradition of teaching to life. These researchers teach us to think of orality as the social enactment of the words on the page. For sages who were trying to craft a religious ethic and mold men of wisdom and virtue in the wake of great societal upheaval, this was a reason to value orality.

Notes

1. See Fraade 1999b, 42, and Jaffee 2001, generally, but see esp. vii, viii, 7, 9.
2. Yavneh (Jamnia) was a small town near the Mediterranean coast of Roman Palestine. Such sources as Babylonian Talmud Gittin 56b recall it as the location of a pioneering academy of Torah studied – the fabled "Vineyard of Yavneh" – founded by Rabban Yohanan b. Zakkai in the wake of the defeat of 66–73 C.E.
3. See, e.g., Ong 1982, 78–116, and Lord 2000, 99–138.
4. See Lord 2000, 99–123, and Ong 1982, 31–77.
5. Epstein argues that the ban originated in a liturgical setting and was initially intended to proscribe the recitation of rabbinic translation and interpretation of the Written Torah from written texts in the synagogue only. See Epstein 2000 (Hebrew), 697. Safrai, "Oral Torah," Safrai 1987, 45–46, makes a similar point.
6. Strack and Stemberger date the oldest rabbinic manuscripts to the twelfth and thirteenth centuries, though some Geniza fragments of Mishnah and Talmud may come from as early as the seventh, eighth, or ninth centuries. See Strack and Stemberger 1992, 157, 177, 199–202, 227–29.
7. Epstein elaborates on the various sources (both Jewish and non-Jewish) that allude to the Tanna. See Epstein 2000, 673–91. See also Saul Lieberman, "The Publication of the *Mishnah*," Lieberman 1994, 88–90.
8. See Neusner 1977, 1985, and 1987b. See also Faur 1990, and E. S. Alexander 2006, Chapter 1.
9. Another version of this question is: "What did the medieval authorities have to say about whether or not the Mishnah was written down?" Whereas Epstein, Lieberman, and Lewin argue that there were deep controversies among medieval sages about the matter, Abrahamson argues that there was no controversy at all among the medieval sages. See Epstein 2000, 693; Lieberman 1994, 84; Lewin 1921, xlvii–lxxi; and Abramson 1989, 27–52. See Brody 1998, 21–22, for a helpful summary of the history of the modern scholarly debate about the medievals.
10. Epstein 2000, 698–706, lists the anecdotal evidence for written versions of the Mishnah and other rabbinic documents. See also Safrai 1987, 73–74. As this volume was being prepared for press, I became aware of a major new discussion of this issue by the Israeli scholar Jacob Zussman, "'Oral Torah' Means Just That" (Hebrew), Zussman and Rozental 2005, 209–384. The essay attempts to prove that no written copies of the Mishnah existed in the rabbinic academies of Late Antiquity. While proving a negative is a precarious enterprise for a historian, Prof. Zussman does offer the most thorough collection of talmudic citations bearing upon the question of the oral transmission of rabbinic literature.
11. See Epstein 2000, 702, as well as 688–93.
12. See Epstein 2000, 698, 703.
13. "The Publication of the *Mishnah*," in Lieberman 1994.
14. Safrai 1987, 71–75.
15. Finnegan 1992, 162–66.

16. Ibid., 162
17. Ibid., 162–63
18. Stock 1983, Thomas 1992, and Calinescu 1993.
19. Jaffee 2001, 128–40.
20. Ibid., 103–6.
21. Ibid., 140–52.
22. Fraade 1991, 19.
23. Ibid., 74; emphasis in the original.

3 Social and Institutional Settings of Rabbinic Literature

JEFFREY L. RUBENSTEIN

Classical rabbinic literature was produced within rabbinic educational institutions, by the sages who taught and studied there, for the purpose of educating those who attended them. This much seems clear, though unfortunately, just about all specific historical details of this process are uncertain. Until recently, the consensus of scholars regarding the nature of the rabbinic schools of Late Antiquity was anachronistic. Throughout the Gaonic Period (ca. 700–1100 C.E.), rabbis studied in academies (*yeshivot*), which continued to be the dominant form of rabbinic organization during the Middle Ages and to the present day.[1] The term *yeshivah* indeed appears in the Mishnah and subsequent rabbinic works, and a few talmudic passages portray the rabbis in establishments that look like the Gaonic academy. Scholars therefore assumed that rabbis had founded academies in very early times, certainly in the tannaitic era and even during the Second Temple Period. However, the word *yeshivah* simply means "sitting" or "session," from the root *y-sh-b*, "to sit." That a rabbinic source describes the rabbis meeting in a session/sitting (*yeshivah*) to study Torah does not necessarily tell us anything about the forum in which they "sat." In principle, the rabbis could have held sessions in private homes, synagogues, courts, or anywhere they happened to be. In later times, the rabbis met in an academy, and thus the term came to refer not only to the study session but to the academy in which the session was held. But in earlier times, the nature of such sessions is an open question that can be answered only after careful study of the sources and their portrayals of rabbinic meetings.

Yet this task, too, is a tricky business due to the difficulties of deriving historical information from rabbinic sources – a problem already raised in the editors' Introduction to this volume. The sources themselves rarely provide descriptions of the schools or forums of learning. Where they do, the images tend to be exaggerated or utopian projections of rabbinic ideals, rather than realistic representations of contemporary situations. In many cases rabbinic sources project back upon earlier ages the conditions at the time the sources were formulated, which gives a distorted historical picture. For these reasons, rabbinic traditions must be evaluated very carefully and assessed in the widest possible framework. In all cases, the sources closest in time with the era they purport to describe must be given preference. For example, the Mishnah's descriptions of tannaitic conditions are far more reliable than the portrayal of tannaitic times found in the Talmuds. But even this principle can be difficult to apply. The Bavli contains traditions that span at least a 500-year period (200–700 C.E.). Most of these traditions cannot be dated with precision, so that we cannot determine whether a source pertains to the beginning of that period or the end. I have therefore cited numerous sources in the following discussion such that the reader can appreciate the problems of interpretation and judge for him/herself the proper conclusions to draw.

TANNAITIC PERIOD (70–220 C.E.)

Rabbinic schools of tannaitic times are more accurately characterized as "disciple circles" than academies.[2] There were no school buildings, hierarchies of positions, administrative bureaucracies, curricula, or requirements. Because study was oral, there was no need for books or libraries either. A few disciples gathered around a rabbinic master and learned traditions from him in his home or in some other private dwelling that could serve as a school. But such formal instruction in the memorization and interpretation of texts constituted only part of the educational experience. It was supplemented on a daily basis as students served their master as apprentices, observing his daily conduct and emulating his religious practice as he passed through a market, journeyed to various villages, performed his personal hygiene, or ate his meals. After years of learning, having reached a certain level of proficiency and perhaps (though not always) formal "ordination" from their master, disciples might leave their master and strike out independently, attempting to gather their own circles of disciples. If their master died, they would have to seek a new master elsewhere as there was no institutional framework to provide continuity or a replacement. As opposed to an academy, the disciple circle was not an institution in that there was no ongoing life or continuity of the group beyond the individual teacher.[3] The "school" was essentially the master himself.

The most common term for the forum for rabbinic study and education in tannaitic sources is the "study house" (*bet midrash* = house of study).[4] Unfortunately, it is very difficult to determine the particulars of the study house, including its structure, scope, and even the number of sages present. There are many reports such as: "R. Meir said: Once we were sitting in the study house before R. Akiva. We recited the Shema but did not say it out loud because of a [Roman] Quaestor who stood at the door" (T. Berakhot 2:13). Here, R. Meir and some other students were studying with their master, R. Akiva, during the time of Roman persecutions. But it is hard to judge the size or nature of this "study house." Similarly, "R.Yehudah said: Once R. Tarfon went to the study house on Friday night. They gave him a sheet and he held it [over him] with his two hands, and went out with it, on account of the rain" (T. Shabbat 5:13). It seems most likely that the study house was quite literally the private house of the master, or perhaps a specific room in his house designated for study – the word *bet* can also mean "room." One source mentions that "Once four elders were sitting in the gatehouse (*bet sha'ar*) of R. Yehoshua . . . discussing that which R. Akiva had taught them" (T. Berakhot 4:18). The gate-house was a small domicile located near the entrance of the property, perhaps occupied from time to time by a guard. It thus appears that rabbinic masters regularly met with small groups of disciples in houses or in specific rooms designated for study.

Even when the sources speak of somewhat larger assemblies – perhaps when several masters gathered together along with their disciples – the settings are typically the "upper story" of a house, probably the large house of an aristocrat who made an upstairs room available to the sages to meet. We find several descriptions such as the following: "R. Yehudah said: When we gathered in the upper story of the House of Nitze in Lod they perforated an eggshell and filled it with oil . . . and the elders were there" (T. Shabbat 2:5); and "It once happened that the sages entered the upper story of the House of Guryeh in Jericho and a heavenly voice went forth and said to them, 'There is a certain man among you here who is fit to be a prophet'" (T. Sotah 13:3). We are not told how many "elders" or "sages" were present, but the number appears to be rather small.[5] Similarly, the Mishnah and Tosefta often refer to two early rabbinic groups, the "House of Hillel" (*bet hillel*) and "House of Shammai" (*bet shammai*), which existed during temple times. Though sometimes portrayed as academies or full-fledged schools, these too were probably small-scale disciple circles that gathered around two important early masters, and the term "house" should be taken at face value. The gatherings of these "Houses" are also set in private domiciles: "These are among the rulings stated in the upper story of Hanania b. Hizkiah b. Goryon. When [the sages] went up to visit him they voted. The House of Shammai outnumbered the House of Hillel, and they decreed eighteen things on that day" (M. Shabbat 1:4). Though we have no solid information about this Hanania (nor about the Nitze or Guryeh families mentioned in the other sources), he was apparently an aristocrat who patronized the rabbis and opened his house to them. Here the Mishnah reports that at one of these gatherings, the disciples resolved a number of issues that had been disputed. Mishnah Avot exhorts, "Let your house be a meeting-house for sages" (M. Avot 1:4), which suggests that the sages met in private houses of those who were willing to make their spaces available.

Rabbis sometimes served as judges, and their disciples also learned as they assisted their masters in court. These were informal, voluntary courts rather than an official judicial system with real coercive power. The official courts were the Roman provincial system under the ultimate authority of the Roman governor.[6] Yet individuals who respected the sages and their knowledge could approach a rabbinic master to adjudicate disputes. And, of course, many Jews would turn to rabbis to rule on religious questions. There are also a few traditions that mention rabbinic courts enacting various amendments or adjustments to rabbinic law, for example, "Rabbi [Judah the Patriarch] and his court decreed that one may buy vegetables immediately after the close of the sabbatical year" (T. Sheviit 4:17). These traditions too – to the extent they are historical and not legendary – point to a rabbi with some of his associates and students who issued a ruling based on their own authority, not a formal, large-scale court with its own building and organization.

Because of its small scale, rabbinic study could take place in a variety of locations. Many rabbinic disciples were apprentices as much as students, serving their teachers in much the same way as servants served their masters – the word "rabbi" literally means "my master."[7] Students learned from observing their teachers' conduct day in and day out, in both mundane and religious activities, and often accompanied their masters when they traveled or visited other sages. Thus we find, "Once R. Tarfon was reclining in the shade of a dovecote on Sabbath afternoon. They brought a pail of cold water before him. He said to his students, 'He who drinks water to satisfy his thirst – what blessing does he recite [afterward]?' They said to him, 'Let the master teach us'" (T. Berakhot 4:16). R. Tarfon happens to be taking a rest on the Sabbath in a shady location and seizes the opportunity for an impromptu lesson concerning the appropriate blessing after drinking water. The climate in The Land of Israel is very hot for much of the year, and at times the coolest and most comfortable places were outside and in the shade. It makes good sense that rabbis and disciples met in groves, fields, and other such places.

It is possible that the study house of the family of the *nasi* (patri-arch), the dynasty of Rabban Gamaliel, was a school of a somewhat larger scale, especially toward the end of the tannaitic period. The vast wealth of the family and official (or semiofficial) Roman political recognition, coupled with their high status in the eyes of their fellow Jews, may have provided the necessary resources and prestige to create a quasi academy, that is, a school with a more developed organization and hierarchy. This assumption is complicated by the difficulty in determining when such political recognition was extended to the family and how substantive it was.[8] In one source, R. Eleazar b. Zadok reports: "Once we were sitting before Rabban Gamaliel in the study house in Lod. Zunan the overseer (*memuneh*) came and said, 'The time has come to burn the leaven'" (T. Pesahim 3:11). Was Zunan an official or functionary in the bureau-cracy of the school? Or was he simply a servant or employee of Rabban Gamaliel who came to advise the rabbis that the hour had arrived? That R. Judah the Patriarch succeeded in composing the Mishnah in an author-itative or canonical form that was accepted by all rabbis may imply that he led a type of school that included a number of sages and their dis-ciples. Once again we are frustrated by the lack of information in the sources.

In sum, the tannaitic rabbis were a loose network of like-minded sages dispersed throughout villages and towns of the Land of Israel. The leading rabbis organized "schools" at their homes, instructing small groups of disciples in a room or area designated for that purpose. From time to time, sages gathered together in the mansions or large houses of their supporters to discuss issues of importance. Disciples also accom-panied their masters both on travels and on their daily business. They learned by observation and imitation and from discussions held through-out the day. When masters served as judges, disciples assisted their mas-ters in the proceeding and deliberations.

AMORAIC PERIOD: THE LAND OF ISRAEL (220–425 C.E.)

The rabbinic social and organizational structure of amoraic times differs but slightly from that of the tannaitic era.[9] There is some evi-dence that more rabbis resided in the larger towns or cities of the Land of Israel, including Tiberias, Sepphoris, Caeserea, and Lod, rather than in smaller villages. The main location for rabbinic instruction continued to be the study house (*bet midrash*), and this remained a rather small-scale school, probably to be identified with the rabbi's house, where he met with a small group of disciples. In several amoraic sources, the study house is called after the master's name, for example: "R. Yohanan entered and expounded in the study house of Rabbi Benaya" (Y. Taanit 1:2, 64a). Another source refers to the *mezuzah* (doorpost amulet) of "the study house of R. Hanania" (Y. Megillah 4:12, 75c). We also have from this period the only unambiguous archaeological remains of a study house. An inscription on a lintel found in the Golan reads that "this is the study house (*bet midrash*) of R. Eliezer HaKappar."[10] But no identifiable structure was excavated with the lintel. The general lack of archaeological remains – or at least identifiable archaeological remains – of study houses suggests again that the rabbinic study house was indistinguishable from an ordinary house or building.

In addition to "study house," the Yerushalmi employs two other terms to designate forums of rabbinic study. Numerous sources describe rabbis teaching or expounding in the "assembly house" (Hebrew: *bet va'ad*; Aramaic: *be va'ada'*).[11] In most cases, this seems to be a synonym for the study house. There, rabbis study, teach, meet with other sages, and do all the things that they do in the study house. When once asked a difficult question that he could not answer, R. Eleazar responded, "You ask about the matter which the rabbis of the assembly house still need [to explain]" (Y. Bikkurim 1:8, 64d). That he refers to "rabbis of the assembly house" suggests that the assembly house was a common location for rabbinic meetings. In one story, Rabban Gamaliel instructs a student that "when I enter the assembly house tomorrow, stand up and ask about this law" (Y. Berakhot 4:1, 7d). Another story relates: "When R. Eleazar b. R. Shimon would enter the assembly house, Rabbi [Yehuda Ha-Nasi's] face would darken" (Y. Shabbat 10:5, 12c). Rabbi was afraid of his colleague's greater ability – a "dark face" expresses fear or concern.

The other term that appears in the Yerushalmi, albeit rarely, is "hall" or "great hall" (*sdar, sdara' rabba'*).[12] This, too, seems to be a synonym for study house, or perhaps a large private house made available to sages for gatherings. Rabbi Yonah once instructed, "Do not sit on the outer benches of the hall of Bar Ulla, because they are cold" (Y. Shabbat 4:2 [7a]). The benches, also mentioned in traditions about the assembly house, were those that the sages sat upon while studying. R. Mana relates that "I went up to the hall and heard Rav Huna say in the name of Rav..." followed by a law about fasting. R. Yose reportedly "ruled in the great hall" on one occasion (Y. Taanit 2:2, 65c). One of these great halls was evidently located in Tiberias (Y. Shabbat 6:2, 8a). Why the sages came to refer to the study house as the "hall" or "great hall" is not completely clear. But nothing suggests that the hall differed substantially from a study house.

One interesting change from the tannaitic era is the increasing rabbinic presence in the synagogue. Tannaitic sources rarely locate rabbis within the synagogue (although they do contain legislation on proper behavior within a synagogue and so forth). Synagogues were places for prayer, frequented by ordinary Jews, and led by aristocrats or prominent members of the local community. Study houses were places for study, occupied by rabbis and their disciples. During the amoraic period, as rabbis competed to become the religious leaders of all Jews and gradually became more influential among the people, they became more prominent in the synagogue. Many traditions depict rabbis preaching and expounding (*doresh*) in the synagogue, often before a lay audience. According to one story, a Babylonian immigrant to the Land of Israel found R. Berakhia "sitting and expounding in the synagogue," and after his sermon, R. Berakhia instructed the community that the Babylonian be given charity (Leviticus Rabbah, *'emor, par.* 32:7 [ed. Margoliot, 752–53]). R. Abbahu reports: "I was once passing by the synagogue of the Tarsians in Lod and I heard the voice of R. Samuel bar Nahman sitting and expounding…" followed by a beautiful homily (Leviticus Rabbah, *behukotai, par.* 35:12 [ed. Margoliot, 830–31]). Perhaps the strongest assertion of rabbinic authority over the synagogue is attributed to R. Yehoshua b. Levi: "Synagogues and study houses are for the sages and their students" (Y. Megillah 3:1, 74a). A few synagogue inscriptions have been found that mention rabbis among the donors to the construction of the synagogue.[13] In some cases, rabbis seem to have taught their students in synagogues: "R. Abbahu was sitting and teaching in the synagogue" (*kenishta'*) in Caeserea (Y. Berakhot 3:1, 6a). But this appears to have been somewhat exceptional. Sages would typically teach their own students in the study house and preach to commoners and lay folk in the synagogue.

Along with their increasing ties to the synagogue, the sages benefited from patriarchal patronage in receiving appointments to judicial and municipal positions during the third and fourth centuries. The patriarchs, the descendants of R. Yehudah Ha-Nasi, naturally had strong sympathies with other rabbis, and sometimes used their status and power to support the sages (along with their other aristocratic friends) in a variety of ways. According to one source, the villagers of Simonias asked Rabbi Yehudah Ha-Nasi to send them someone who could "expound and judge, serve as sexton and scribe, teach and fulfill all our needs," and the patriarch sent his student Levi b. Sisi (Y. Yevamot 12:6, 13a).[14] R. Yehudah

Nesi'ah (R. Yehudah Ha-Nasi's son) reportedly sent three sages to visit villages and appoint teachers of Torah and of oral law (Y. Hagigah 1:8, 76c = Y. Nedarim 10:10, 42b). Other sages were reportedly appointed judges, tax collectors, and community officials with varying responsibilities.[15] While these traditions are by no means historically reliable, it nevertheless appears that the sages gradually assumed a variety of positions encompassing different religious roles in synagogues and communities throughout Israel. But these positions were attained episodically and on an individual basis. There was no umbrella organization or coordinated institution of rabbinic judges and synagogue functionaries.

It is likely that toward the end of the amoraic period in the Land of Israel (ca. 350–425 C.E.) a small *yeshivah* or academy developed in one of the larger Galilean cities. That the last sages mentioned by name in the Yerushalmi lived around this period indicates that the Talmud was compiled then or shortly thereafter. The process of collecting, organizing, and editing a corpus of traditions suggests an institutional setting, such as an academy. Now throughout the Gaonic Period, a centralized academy was the seat of rabbinic leadership in the Land of Israel. The earliest "evidence" for the existence of this academy is the (probably legendary) Babylonian tradition that Mar Zutra II, a descendant of the exilarch, fled Babylonia in the early sixth century and came to the academy of the Land of Israel.[16] More solid evidence derives from a number of sources of the seventh and eighth centuries.[17] So it is possible that a small rabbinic academy formed at the end of the fourth century or in the early fifth century and was the precursor to the rabbinic academy of the Islamic era.

The rabbis of the amoraic period, like those of the tannaitic period, appear to have been a relatively small affiliation of scholars, a religious elite with loose ties both to other sages and to the general population of Jews in the Land of Israel. Indeed, the total number of sages was fairly small. According to Hanokh Albeck's count, about 48 rabbis from the first amoraic generation are mentioned in rabbinic sources (ca. 225–50); 47 from the second (ca. 250–80); 135 from the third (280–310); 82 from the fourth (310–40); and 45 from the fifth (340–75).[18] These numbers should be augmented by students, disciples, and other sages who were not mentioned in the extant documents. Nonetheless, the unimpressive total gives a sense of the size and scope of the sages, and suggests that whatever institutional structure existed, if any, must have been limited. The small number may have enhanced their shared ideology and group identity, but placed limits on the degree of institutionalization that could be achieved.

AMORAIC PERIOD: BABYLONIA (200–550 C.E.)

We know very little about the state of rabbinic Judaism in Babylonia during tannaitic times. More solid historical information is available for the amoraic period when students of Rabbi Yehudah Ha-Nasi brought the Mishnah to Babylonia in circa 220 and began to teach and disseminate rabbinic tradition among the Babylonian Jewish communities.[19] In their quest for authority and leadership, the rabbis had to grapple with the exilarch, who, like the patriarch, was sometimes a help and sometimes a hindrance.[20] The rise of rabbinic Judaism as the dominant form of Judaism in Babylonia was therefore a slow and gradual process.

The picture of rabbinic schools and social organization during the amoraic period in Babylonia is similar to that of the Land of Israel. Rabbinic study took place on a limited scale with individual rabbinic masters teaching small disciple circles in disparate towns and villages. The standard term for the place of study is *be rav*, the "master's house," which should be taken literally: Students or a group of sages met at the home of a certain rabbi. Thus, we find numerous reports such as the following: "Rav Huna, son of R. Yehoshua stated: I found the sages at the master's house (*be rav*) sitting and saying...and I said to them..." (B. Niddah 47a). Rav Huna relates to his contemporaries an earlier discussion with several rabbis that took place at an unidentified master's house. In many cases, the name of the master is given, for example: "Avimi learned [Tractate] Menahot at the house of Rav Hisda (*be rav hisda*)" (B. Menahot 7a). Rav Hisda's house was probably the place where Avimi regularly studied. Similarly, "Meremar said: I asked the rabbis of Rav Yosef's house (*be rav yosef*), Who recites the [Passover] Haggadah at Rav Yosef's house?" Here Meremar asked the students who studied with Rav Yosef about his practice on Passover.[21] Although the source can be interpreted in several ways, it probably implies that the students who studied with Rav Yosef also spent the holidays with him. They learned not only from their formal studies in school but also by observing his ritual practices in a variety of contexts.[22]

Because the amoraic disciple circle was a voluntary and informal arrangement, disciples were always free to seek out another master. According to one story:

> R. Yose b. Avin regularly studied before R. Yose of Yokrat. He left him and came before Rav Ashi....He [Rav Ashi] said to him, "Did you not regularly study before R. Yose of Yokrat?" He [R. Yose b Avin] said to him, "Yes." He said to him, "Why did you leave him and come here?" (B. Taanit 23b–24a).

R. Yose then explains that he left because his master treated his own son and daughter "without mercy," and he realized that he could expect the same sort of treatment. In this case, a disciple decides he would be better served by another teacher and simply abandons his former master for a different one. While Rav Ashi inquires why R. Yose b. Avin has joined his group, he does not seem surprised by such movements. Likewise, when a master died, the disciple would have no choice but to seek instruction elsewhere:

> Rav Huna bar Manoah, Rav Shmuel b. Idi and Rav Hiyya of Astunia regularly studied before Rava. When Rava died they came before Rav Papa. Whenever he recited a tradition before them and it did not make sense to them, they would signal one another. Rav Papa was embarrassed. (B. Taanit 9a–b)

When their master, Rava, dies, the students go to Rav Papa and join his disciple circle. They gesticulate to one another because their new master's teachings contradict what they had formerly been taught, which causes Rav Papa to feel that he is being mocked. Clearly, the source does not presuppose an academy or any such ongoing institution or it would state something like "When Rava died, Rav Papa took his place." Both of these traditions envision a small and loose association in which disciples were in principle free to study with the master they felt would most benefit them (assuming that that master would accept them as disciples) and to leave when they wished.

Like their counterparts in the Land of Israel, the Babylonian rabbis had a tenuous relationship with the synagogue. The synagogue was a communal institution led by local elites, which the sages slowly "rabbinized" over a long period. Though some rabbis prayed in synagogues regularly, it was not an important center of rabbinic study.[23] In fact, it seems that in Babylonia, the synagogue was less central to the general Jewish community than in the Land of Israel, therefore even less of a focus of rabbinic energy. A few traditions refer to study in the synagogue, for example: "Abaye said: At first I would recite traditions at home and pray in the synagogue. Now that I have heard that which [King] David said, 'O Lord, I love your temple abode' [Psalms 26:8], I recite traditions in the synagogue."[24] But such sentiments are few and far between.

Rabbis and their students also interacted with non-rabbis in a teaching forum that the Bavli calls a *pirka'*. This seems to have been a sermon or lecture delivered by a sage to a lay audience: Several such descriptions begin "Rabbi So-and-so expounded (*darash*) at the *pirka'*". (see e.g. B. Pesahim 50a). Some sources draw a distinction between that which should be taught at the *pirka'* and that which should be made known only to sages:

> Rav Huna bar Hinena inclined to expound it [= a leniency regarding the law of vows] at the *pirka'*. Rava said to him: "The teacher [of this Mishnah] concealed the law in order that they not treat vows lightly, and you mean to expound it at the *pirka'*?!"
> (B. Nedarim 23b)

Rava remonstrates that it is inappropriate to teach at a *pirka'*, a popular and public setting, a type of loophole by which vows can be annulled, as people will then not take their vows seriously. He does not dispute the law, only the appropriateness of expounding it at a *pirka'*. Similarly, another tradition relates: "When Rav taught his students he taught them [that the law follows] the opinion of R. Meir. But when Rav expounded at the *pirka'* he expounded [that the law follows] the opinion of R. Yehudah, on account of the common people (*'amei ha'arez*)" (B. Hullin 15a). In this case, R. Meir held the more lenient opinion and R. Yehudah the stricter view. Despite teaching his students in private that the law follows the lenient view, Rav taught the stricter position at the *pirka'* due to his concern that non-rabbis in attendance might not behave scrupulously and violate the law.

Unfortunately, the sources do not clarify where the *pirka'* took place, nor how many people were in attendance. There are also sources that portray the *pirka'* as a gathering that sages attended or at least were expected to attend. For example:

> Rav Avaya was sick and did not attend the *pirka'* of Rav Yosef. When he [Rav Avaya] entered the following day, Abaye wanted to reassure Rav Yosef [that Rav Avaya had a good reason for missing his *pirka'*.] He said to him, "Why did the Master [= you] not attend the *pirka'*?" He [Rav Avaya] said to him, "My heart was weak, and I was not able." (B. Kiddushin 28b)

Abaye was apparently worried that Rav Yosef would have been insulted had Rav Avaya simply decided not to attend his *pirka'* for no good reason. Abaye therefore made sure Rav Yosef understood that Rav Avaya failed to attend because he was ill, but meant no disrespect. I think it is possible that this and other such sources are compatible with the sources that present the *pirka'* as a popular assembly. It may be that the sage delivering the lecture to the popular audience nevertheless expected his colleagues or disciples to attend in order to honor him with their presence and witness his preaching abilities. Other sages, however, may have been reluctant to attend a popular talk where they might have been bored. But the truth is that we simply do not know as much as we would like about the nature of the *pirka'*.

Babylonian sages also served as judges, which provided another forum for the instruction of disciples and the propagation of rabbinic Judaism. The exilarch apparently appointed some sages as judges in the courts under his jurisdiction. In this capacity, the sages would have possessed the formal authority of the exilarchate, including the power to mete out fines and punishments that could be enforced. But in most cases, rabbinic courts were essentially a voluntary arrangement where those who respected the rabbis consulted them to resolve religious questions and civil disputes.[25] A good example of rabbinic study in a judicial setting is the following case report:

> A certain ass bit off the hand of a child. [The case] came before Rav Papa b. Shmuel. He said to them, "Go and assess [the value] of the four categories [of compensation required in cases of damage]."
> Rava said to him, "But we learned five categories!" He said to him, "I thought to exclude the depreciation." Abaye said to him, "But this was [a case of damage done by] an ass, and an ass pays only the depreciation." He [Rav Papa b. Shmuel] said to them, "Go and assess the value of the depreciation." (B. Bava Kamma 84a)

Rav Papa b. Shmuel's ruling is challenged by Rava and Abaye, who invoke other traditions that yield a different judgment, on the basis of which Rav Papa changes his decision. The case provides the occasion for the sages to engage in a detailed examination of the issue, which takes place at the court.

The court was an opportune, though not always ideal, locus for rabbinic instruction and debate. In one case, Rav Nahman became annoyed when his colleague Rava raised some pointed questions about his rulings and protested: "Did I not tell you that when I am sitting in judgment you should not say anything to me . . . that man is a renowned thief and I wish to penalize him" (B. Bava Kamma 96b). Rav Nahman's judgment may not have been in accord with rabbinic law, but he knew what he was doing. Other sages sometimes questioned a master's judgments, just as they questioned interpretations in private study. According to one report: "A certain man borrowed an axe from his fellow and it broke. [The case] came before Rav. He said to him, 'Go and pay him [the full value of] an axe.' Rav Kahana and Rav Asi said to Rav, 'Is that the law?' Rav was silent" (B. Bava Metzia 96b–97a). Of course, we have to imagine that a more complex discussion took place in which Rav Kahana and

Rav Asi explained their position and the basis for their dispute. In any event, Rav's silence suggests that he had no good reply to their claims. The Bavli proceeds to note that the law is that the man returns the broken axe and makes up the difference in price between a broken and functional axe.

THE SAVORAIC-STAMMAITIC PERIOD (550–800 C.E.)

The traditions incorporated into the Babylonian Talmud were compiled and reworked over the course of a lengthy period of time by generations of anonymous sages known as "Stamma'im" (*stam* = anonymous).[26] In contrast to the 'Amora'im, who attached their names to their traditions, the Stamma'im ceased preserving attributions. They dedicated themselves to the explanation, interpretation, and reworking of the amoraic traditions they inherited and constructed the *sugyot* (literary units) that comprise the talmudic text. The Stamma'im also reworked earlier *'aggadot*, including stories about the sages, and perhaps even composed some new narratives. But they reworked and told these stories in light of their own experience, projecting their own culture and situation upon the past.[27] Through these fictional narratives, we gain a window into the cultural world of the Stamma'im.

The rabbinic academy (*yeshivah* [Hebrew] or *metivta'* [Aramaic]), a permanent, ongoing institution, arose during stammaitic times.[28] Indeed, the development of rabbinic academies may have been a critical factor in the shift from amoraic to stammaitic times, that is, in the decision no longer to preserve attributions, as the introduction of new forms of social organization often entails significant cultural shifts. The stammaitic academy appears to have been a tightly organized, hierarchically structured body, led by the "Head of the Academy" (*rosh yeshivah* or *resh metivta'*). We cannot tell exactly how many sages studied there – the sources exaggerate the numbers – but there may have been fifty to a hundred full-time students of Torah and additional sages who attended intermittently.

The following passage from a fictional story about the Babylonian sage Rav Kahana and his visit to the academy of R. Yohanan in the Land of Israel offers a picture of the late Babylonian academy and illustrates how sages of later times projected their experience of that academy onto their descriptions of earlier ages (B. Bava Kamma 117a–b):

> The next day they seated him [Rav Kahana] in the first row [of sages]. He [R. Yohanan] said a tradition and he [Rav Kahana] did not object. He [R. Yohanan] said [another] tradition and he [Rav

Kahana] did not object. They seated him back through seven rows until he was in the last row. R. Yohanan said to Resh Laqish, "The lion you mentioned has become a fox."

... He [Rav Kahana] stood up on his feet. He said, "Let the master go back to the beginning."

He [R. Yohanan] said a tradition and he [Rav Kahana] objected [until] they placed him in the first row. He said a tradition and he objected. R. Yohanan was sitting on seven cushions. They removed a cushion from under him. He said a tradition and he objected to him, until they removed all the cushions from under him and he was sitting on the ground.

This academy is arranged hierarchically with the best students seated in the first row and the most inferior students at the back. Rav Kahana is initially seated among the superior students. When he cannot respond to the source under discussion, exhibiting an apparent lack of knowledge, he is relegated backward row by row. He no longer seems to be the "lion," the powerful master of talmudic debate, but a weak "fox," of mediocre talent. Subsequently, as Rav Kahana objects to every tradition, displaying his dialectical acumen, he is promoted row by row to the very front. R. Yohanan, the head of the academy, is depicted as sitting upon seven cushions or rugs, facing the assembly of sages, who were seated on the floor. The elevated seat is a sign of honor, befitting his status as leader of the academy, and so the story has him demoted when he proves unequal to his position.

The practice of seating aristocrats and leaders on a number of cushions was common in Persia, and appears to have been emulated in the Babylonian rabbinic academy.[29] Another story relates how the sages of the academy scrambled to find their places when the head of the academy entered. One sage who was slow "because of his weight, was trampling as he went," and was rebuked by his colleague, "Who is this one who tramples on the heads of the Holy People?"[30] Here, too, the sages of the academy seem to be sitting on the floor in designated places according to their status such that when the latecomer struggles to get to his seat, it appears that he treads on the heads of his colleagues.

These stories portray the formal study sessions in which the head of the academy led a discussion and analysis of certain traditions. The rest of the sages sit arrayed in designated places before him and attempt to participate in the discussion so as to display their acumen. Yet the sages also spent a great deal of time studying in private or in small groups, preparing the sources assigned for the larger study sessions.

The academy maintained ties with students, sages, and interested laymen who lived in distant towns and villages through an institution known as a *kallah*.[31] This was a periodic – some sources imply a semiannual[32] – gathering at the academy that lasted for several days and was devoted to the study of a designated tractate. Apparently, a tractate was assigned at each kallah for study at the following kallah. The visiting rabbis studied and prepared the tractate during their months at home and reviewed it with the head of the academy and other leading sages during the kallah. (Some sources mention the position of *resh kallah*, the "head" or "leader" of a kallah, which may refer to the teacher of a group of visiting students.)[33]

Talmudic sources portray the crowds at the kallah in hyperbolic fashion:

> When the rabbis departed from the school of Rav, twelve hundred rabbis remained. [When the rabbis departed] from the school of Rav Huna, eight hundred rabbis remained. Rav Huna expounded with thirteen speakers. When the rabbis would rise up [to depart] from the study sessions (*metivta'*) with Rav Huna and shake out their clothes, the dust would rise and cover the sun, and they would say in the West [Israel], "They arose from the study session of Rav Huna the Babylonian."
>
> When the rabbis rose [to depart] from the schools of Rabbah and Rav Yosef, four hundred rabbis remained, and they called themselves "orphans."
>
> When the rabbis departed from the school of Abaye – some say from the school of Rav Papa, and some say from the school of Rav Ashi – two hundred rabbis remained, and they called themselves "orphans among orphans." (B. Ketubot 106a)[34]

Here, too, the conditions of later, post-amoraic times have been projected back upon the leading sages of the amoraic period. The "departing rabbis" appear to be those who traveled to the academies for the kallah gathering. Supposedly, the gathering was so large when Rav Huna lectured that he required thirteen "speakers," that is, thirteen human loudspeakers, to repeat his words, shouting them out to the assembled multitude. And a multitude it was – of such proportions that the dust cloud, produced when these aspiring students stood up from the ground, was visible hundreds of miles away in the Land of Israel. The rabbis who "remained" after these massive departures were probably those who studied full time in the academy. They felt like "orphans," as though they had been abandoned by their family, when the visiting colleagues returned home. While these figures are clearly exaggerated, they never-theless suggest that a significant number of sages regularly journeyed to the academies for these periodic assemblies.

In sum, a survey of rabbinic forums for study from the Tannaitic through the Stammaitic Periods reveals increasing institutionalization. As the rabbis grew in influence and numbers, gradually attracting more followers and persuading their fellow Jews to follow their teachings, they created larger and more permanent schools. For reasons that are not completely clear, and may simply be a function of the rabbis reach-ing a "critical mass" of size and material support, the small disciple circles of earlier times became larger, well-established academies in the Stammaitic Period. These academies were the precursors of the great Gaonic rabbinic academies of the Islamic era.

Notes

1. Granted that the size, structure and nature of rabbinic academies changed over time, and Gaonic academies differed in many respects from contem-porary institutions.
2. Goodblatt 1975, 267, first used the term "disciple circle" in contrast to an "institutionalized school," i.e., an academy, in reference to rabbinic schools.
3. This notion of an institution is adapted from idem, 267.
4. For a comprehensive and historically reliable study of rabbinic schools in the Land of Israel in Late Antiquity, see Hezser 1997.
5. M. Yadaim 3:5 and 4:2 transmit statements attributed to R. Shimon b. Azzai that he received a tradition from seventy-two elders. This number, however, is typological. *Sifre Bamidbar, pis.* 124 (ed. Horovitz, p. 158) refers to thirty-eight sages who gathered in Yavneh, while the parallel in T. Mikvaot 7:11 mentions thirty-two elders in Lod.
6. See Seth Schwartz's essay in this volume and S. Schwartz 2001a, 111–12, 120–21.
7. On the history of the term "rabbi," see Hayim Lapin, "Rabbi," *The Anchor Bible Dictionary*, ed. David Noel Freeman (New York: Double-day, 1992), 5: 600–2.
8. On the status of the patriarchs in the Roman world, see Schwartz's essay to follow and S. Schwartz 2001a, 110–28, and 1999.
9. See Hezser 1997 and I. Levine 1989.
10. A photograph and transcription of the inscription can be found in Levine 1989, 29.
11. This term is attested in but three tannaitic sources: M. Avot 1:4, M. Sotah 9:15, and T. Megillah 3:5.
12. Michael Sokoloff, *A Dictionary of Jewish Palestinian Aramaic* (Ramat-Gan: Bar-Ilan University Press, 1990), 369.
13. Cohen 1981–82, 1–17. However, it is not clear that these "rabbis" match any mentioned in our rabbinic sources.

14. On the implications of this source concerning patriarchal authority, see Schwartz 2001a, 121–22.
15. Levine 1989, 137; Hezser 1997, 86–93.
16. The legend of Mar Zutra II is found in a chronology known as *Seder Olam Zuta*, published in Neubauer 1887–95, 2: 73–76.
17. See Gil 1992, 496–500, 653–57.
18. Albeck 1969, 669–81, cited in Levine 1989, 67.
19. The fundamental studies of rabbinic learning in Babylonia are Goodblatt 1975 and Gafni 1990. See, too, Neusner 1965–70.
20. On the exilarch, see Schwartz's essay in this volume.
21. That Rav Yosef was blind makes this a pressing question for the rabbis, as the blind are exempt from certain commandments.
22. An oft-quoted anecdote relates that Rav Kahana once hid under the bed of Rav, his teacher, in order to learn how Rav made love to his wife. When Rav rebuked him, "Kahana! Get out! This is not proper!" Rav Kahana replied, "This is a matter of Torah, and I need to learn it" (B. Berakhot 63a).
23. See Gafni 1990, 111–16; Neusner 1965–70, 2:273–74, 3:234–38, 4:149–51.
24. B. Megillah 26b. The Munich manuscript reads "Rava said" and concludes "I would only recite in the synagogue."
25. See Gafni 1982, 23–40.
26. On the Stamma'im, see Halivni 1986, 76–104, and the Introduction to this volume
27. See Rubenstein 1999.
28. See Rubenstein 2003, 16–38.
29. See Herman forthcoming, n. 33.
30. B. Yevamot 105b. However, there are some sources that suggest that sages sat on benches, not on the floor.
31. The etymology of this term is unclear. See Goodblatt 1975, 169–71; Gafni, 1990, 198–200.
32. For sources and discussion, see Goodblatt 1975, 165–70. Gaonic sources explicitly mention semiannual gatherings in Adar and Elul.
33. See, e.g., B. Bava Batra 22a and Goodblatt 1975, 156.
34. For manuscript variants, see Gafni 1990, 221. Some manuscripts add "R. Hiyya b. Abba said: I am among the leaders of the smaller *kallah* sessions [*reishe kalla*] of Rav Huna, and six hundred rabbis used to attend."

4 The Political Geography of Rabbinic Texts

SETH SCHWARTZ

It is impossible to draw any simple causal connections between the characteristics of the various rabbinic corpora and the political environments in which they were produced. There is no way to argue convincingly, for example, that the structure (as opposed to some of the content) of the Mishnah and Tosefta reflect in some discernible way the conditions of the High Roman imperial East, or that the Bavli owes its compendious, generically composite, character to the conditions of the Sasanian west.

One reason for this is the state of our knowledge: Even in the case of the Palestinian documents, whose Roman political context is in fact quite well known (Sasanian history, by contrast, is very poorly understood), we are nearly completely ignorant of the circumstances in which the texts were produced. Rabbinic literature itself identifies the editors of some of the texts but – apart from the fact that these identifications are questionable – it reports next to nothing about the ways the editors worked (we may contrast the abundant contemporary information about the production of the Theodosian Code).[1] In the cases of some of the midrash collections and the Bavli, even the approximate dating of redaction is highly controversial, and the datings of the other corpora are perhaps not as controversial as they should be.[2]

There are more profound reasons for our inconclusiveness: The relation between any literary artifact and the political, cultural, and social circumstances in which it was produced can only ever be oblique and complex, in any case certainly resistant to comprehensive description. But our inability to provide a full account does not absolve us from the responsibility for attempting a partial one. In what follows, I will provide such an account by investigating historiographically and historically a single question: What can be known about the political and social roles of the rabbis who produced the texts? This investigation is ramified; it involves considering the status and position of the Jews in the two great empires of the Late Antique Mediterranean world and the Middle East, the relations between the leaders, if any, of religious or national minorities and the state, and the extent to which such groups acculturated.[3] It also has profound implications for how we read the rabbinic texts themselves: If the rabbis constituted official or semi-official judicial or legal-consultative bureaucracies, then their law books (the rabbinic texts are not codes but study books) can be approached in much the same way as Roman legal texts like the Digest.[4] If, however, the rabbis were marginal figures, who aspired to authority and prestige they never achieved in Antiquity, then their texts are more closely comparable – though not precisely analogous – to the sectarian library of Qumran. We begin in Palestine.

WERE THE RABBIS "LEADERS"? A HISTORICAL RECONSTRUCTION

It is overwhelmingly unlikely that anything resembling a rabbinic class existed before the destruction of the Second Temple in 70 C.E. Josephus, our main historical source for this period, writes frequently of priests and members of the Herodian family, who, together with the Romans, constituted the leadership of pre-Destruction Jewish Palestine.[5] He writes somewhat less frequently of Pharisees, by the first century a religious organization negligible neither in size nor in importance.[6] But he mentions no rabbinic organization and indeed only one person, the Jerusalem Pharisee and rebel leader Simon ben Gamaliel, whom the rabbis themselves would later count among their forebears.[7] Prominent post-Destruction rabbis, like Yohanan ben Zakkai, Eliezer ben Hyrcanus, Tarfon, and Joshua ben Hananiah, were necessarily active before the Destruction, yet play no role in Josephus's narrative.

It is, furthermore, difficult to regard the post-Destruction rabbis as simply a renamed version of a pre-Destruction group. They clearly had some connection with the Pharisees, and many early rabbis were also *kohanim* (priests), but there were important differences, too. For example, the Pharisees seem to have valued unanimity and regarded tradition as absolutely binding, while the rabbis eventually (though the conscious validation of these features may have been the result of several centuries of development) came to value disagreement, dialectic, and an interrogative approach to tradition.[8] Also, there is some tendency in rabbinic legislation to disfavor priests, rendering any simple connection between rabbis and priests problematic. Perhaps even more striking was the difference in scale: According to Josephus, there were six thousand Pharisees before the Destruction and apparently an even larger number of priests, whereas after the Destruction, there were never more than several dozen rabbis alive at any one time.[9]

Rabbinic tradition itself preserves many stories about the rabbinic past. The first chapter of Mishnah Avot claims that the "Oral Torah" was given to Moses on Mount Sinai and then transmitted to the present (i.e., probably the third century C.E.) through an unbroken chain of religious authorities.[10] In this view, the existence of a discrete rabbinic organization is of little significance, while rabbinic tradition is presented as coextensive with Judaism and nothing more. Other sources, though, acknowledge the novelty if not of the rabbis' Torah, then at least of the rabbinic group. According to these stories, Rabban Yohanan ben Zakkai escaped from besieged Jerusalem and was allowed by Vespasian [sic] (Vespasian did not participate in the siege) to establish in the coastal town of Yavneh a new, or revived, High Court with himself as its head.[11] Rabban Yohanan's students, and their students in turn, constituted the core of the early rabbinic movement. Other stories, though, describe Rabban Gamaliel, apparently the son of the Jerusalem Pharisee Simon mentioned by Josephus (and grandson of the Pharisee Gamaliel who was, according to Acts of the Apostles, the teacher of the future apostle Paul), as leader of the nascent rabbinic movement.[12]

It seems unlikely that the earliest history of the rabbinic movement can be reconstructed. We may speculate that the rabbis whom later tradition assigned to the immediate post-Destruction period were the battered, drastically reduced remnant of the large pre-Destruction class of legal/religious functionaries, many of whom were probably priests and/or sectarians. To the extent that they began to coalesce into an organization within a few decades of 70, it was more likely from a sense of shared need for mutual support than in the pursuit of some grand, and under the circumstances grandly implausible, scheme to preserve Judaism in the absence of a Temple – an intention often anachronistically ascribed to them by modern scholars.[13]

Indeed, to the extent that some of these men preserved some residual prestige and influence after the Destruction, the failure of the Bar Kokhba rebellion in 135 would have dealt them and their followers an even more serious blow. The Jews as a whole were now numerically reduced and scattered, the rabbis' home district of Judaea was very largely depopulated, and Palestine was under direct Roman rule in a way that secured its political and economic stability but probably at the price of the nearly complete suppression of any tendency toward Jewish autonomy. Well into the third century, Palestine was to all appearances a more or less normal province of the Roman Empire: All power, and probably most prestige as well, was in the hands of the Roman governor and of collaborationist municipal elites, not experts in Torah interpretation. Presumably, some Jews continued to support the rabbis and somewhat larger numbers occasionally deferred to them and honored them, but it seems very unlikely that in this period they wielded much authority.[14]

The situation began to change around 200. Perhaps a general demographic and economic recovery now began to enable a limited reassertion of specifically Jewish culture, now concentrated in the cities and big villages of northern Palestine. At any rate, it is then, rabbinic sources imply, that rabbis began to settle in Tiberias, Sepphoris, Caesarea, and a few other towns; that they almost certainly began to constitute a distinctive group that came increasingly to form some part of the fabric of northern Palestinian life;[15] and that they acquired a leader, Rabbi Judah the Patriarch (Rabbi Yehudah Ha-Nasi), who was wealthy and not without influence even outside rabbinic circles. Rabbinic tradition itself, furthermore, regarded Rabbi Judah as the editor of the Mishnah. Whether this tradition is accurate or not, by the very fact of its existence, the Mishnah provides the earliest clear evidence for the emergence of a discrete and self-conscious rabbinic organization. However, some of the stories about the patriarch – for example, the accounts of his friendship with a Roman emperor – should be seen as anachronistic retrojections, reflecting the increasingly institutionalized and grand position of the patriarchs of the late third and fourth centuries.[16]

Indeed, by the middle and later third century, there is evidence, mainly but not exclusively from stories preserved in the Talmud Yerushalmi, of the growing importance of a quasi-autonomous patriarchal establishment. The timing of this development is probably not coincidental. The centralizing thrust of the Roman imperial center was weakened by chronic, though in the event temporary, instability and civil war, while the prestige and perhaps more to the point the finances of the emperors' main agents in the East, the city councils, faltered due to the near collapse of the economy.[17] The patriarchal dynasty and its retainers were not the only formerly peripheral eastern family to take advantage of imperial weakness.[18]

Many rabbinic sources concerning the third century, and many non-rabbinic sources written in the fourth, believed that the patriarchs possessed the partly official right to appoint judges and other agents, and such sources must be taken seriously. Rabbinic sources assume that in this period the rabbis became a distinctive component of a para-governmental legal and religious establishment (in the mid–third century the

Church Father Origen was already familiar with a fair amount of rabbinic lore);[19] but they also state that rabbis were not the sole beneficiaries of patriarchal largesse. The patriarchs also supported, patronized, and employed, both as judges and in other capacities, other prominent Jews whom the rabbis regarded as undeserving, appointed only because of their wealth; yet "those appointed for money" were also called "rabbi," wore the judicial gown (*stole*), and expected the deference of the masses (Y. Bikkurim 3.3, 65d).[20] It would not be absurd to speculate that the "rabbis" buried in catacomb 20 at Beth Shearim – provided, unusually, with Hebrew epitaphs but never mentioned in rabbinic literature – were patriarchal appointees of this type.[21]

The institutional strength of the patriarchal establishment was only strengthened after the conversion of the emperor Constantine to Christianity in 312, and probably reached its peak in the reigns of Theodosius I (379–95) and his son Arcadius (Augustus, 383–408), almost certainly because the patriarch enjoyed the personal patronage of the emperors. It was in this period, too, that the Talmud Yerushalmi reached completion, though under circumstances that are entirely unknown. In the course of the fourth century, the patriarchs gradually acquired official recognition as the leaders of the Jewish polity, senatorial rank, and in the 390s even the honorary praetorian prefecture. St. Jerome and the pagan orator Libanius of Antioch, writing in that decade, both report anecdotes demonstrating that the patriarch was more powerful, or more favored by the emperor, than the imperial governors of Second Palestine (the late imperial province that included the patriarchs' home city of Tiberias).[22] The patriarchs then enjoyed the right to collect taxes from the Jews; they and their judicial appointees (including but not limited to rabbis) were given official jurisdiction in matters of religious law – however that may have been defined. In general, the emperors by the 390s came to regard the Jews as constituting a legally recognized "church" (the Jews were Roman by nationality; even the most zealous emperors never took the step of identifying Roman citizenship with orthodox Christianity). Its clergy possessed privileges comparable to those of the Christian clergy, and just as Christian presbyters derived their authority from the ordination of their bishops, so too Jewish communal functionaries were thought to serve under the authority of the patriarch.[23] In Palestine at least, if we may trust Jerome, though not in the Diaspora, such local functionaries were sometimes of at least partly rabbinic character, notwithstanding the common, and not necessarily incorrect, modern view that in the fourth century, relations between the patriarchs and the rabbis deteriorated.

However, this situation came to a sudden and drastic end under Theodosius II (Augustus, 408–50). Soon after 425, the patriarchate ceased to exist, under unknown circumstances.[24] What became of the patriarchs' religious, judicial, and financial establishment after this date is wholly unknown. We may make several observations, though: Texts in the rabbinic tradition continued to be written in the fifth century and later – midrash collections and *piyyutim* (liturgical poetry), for example – but not a single name of a rabbi is known, unless we count the rabbinically oriented *payyetan* (liturgical poet) Yannai, who probably lived in the sixth century. This period is also the great period of synagogue construction, in both Palestine and the Diaspora – a fact that demonstrates the growing significance of the Torah and of Judaism in general in Jewish public life, but which provides little evidence for the ascendancy of rabbis in Jewish communal affairs, even in Palestine.[25]

HISTORIOGRAPHY AND THE QUESTION
OF RABBINIC LEADERSHIP

The previous account should not be regarded as the consensus of scholars in the field, not even in its broad outlines. Indeed, until the late 1960s, almost all historians believed that after the Destruction the rabbis led what was, in effect, an autonomous Jewish client state, without serious opposition; that this state went into decline after the conversion of Constantine (312); but that even then the rabbis' position was not seriously challenged. Only in the past generation have some historians begun to minimize the role of the rabbis, though there is still no agreement on the issue. The terms of the debate were basically set in the middle of the twentieth century by, on the one side, the work of the Zionist/ Israeli historian Gedalyah Alon (died 1950) and, on the other, that of the American historian of religions Erwin R. Goodenough and his follower Jacob Neusner. A brief discussion of this scholarship may help explain the failure of later scholars to agree on even the most basic questions about the history of the Jews after 70.

The Impact of Zionist Historiography

For older historians, most influentially Heinrich Graetz (1817–91), the national history of the Jews came to an end with the destruction of the Second Temple in 70 C.E., or at any rate with the failure of the Bar Kokhba rebellion in 135 – with perhaps a very brief and partial revival under Rabbi Yehudah Ha-Nasi and the Severan emperors around 200. Forever after, the Jews had only a "spiritual" history, and as spiritual leaders the rabbis had no meaningful competition.[26] The Jews also occasionally required the help of intermediaries between themselves and the state, and as in the medieval and modern periods it was secular grandees, the Palestinian patriarchs, and the Babylonian exilarchs, who played this role; but in the absence of politics, even these men were not quite leaders of the Jews in any conventional sense.

Zionist historians, who tended to scour the past for models of Jewish national autonomy in the Land of Israel, rejected this view. Most influentially, Gedalyah Alon (1902–50) argued, expanding the view of Ben Zion Dinur, that the Jews in Palestine continued to have a genuine national history long after the Destruction, perhaps even as late as the Arab Conquest around 634.[27] This implies the enduring existence of an institutionalized political leadership, which, in Alon's view, consisted of the patriarchate and the rabbinate (which Alon called the "Sanhedrin" – an entity almost unattested in rabbinic literature as a functioning judicial body after 70)[28] – separate but intimately connected institutions, whose relations continued, with varying degrees of harmony and tension, until the end of the patriarchate shortly before 430 C.E.[29] After this date, the Sanhedrin ruled unopposed, though the Palestinian Jewish community was by then in headlong decline.

But even in the view of Alon, who tended to emphasize rabbinic authority and influence because he regarded the rabbis as practically the distillation of the Jewish national will, there were periods when rabbinic hegemony was challenged: Local elites, whether or not they were subject to rabbinic influence, were always important. But by some time in the third century, they began to form part of the patriarchal clientele, side by side with the rabbis, with whom they now entered into open competition.[30] And yet even then, the very process of the "secularization" of the patriarchs "perhaps contributed to the preservation and confirmation of the popular character of the Sages."[31] This points to a fundamental tension in Alon's work, which his followers resolved by adopting a rabbinocentrism even more extreme than Alon's.[32] It should be added that even in Alon's less rabbinocentric moments, he supposed that the upper-class non-rabbinic leaders, whatever their legal authority and however "hellenized" they might have been, had little cultural impact. The rabbis always remained the true popular leadership of the Jews,[33] and the Jewish nation was unusually united in its devotion to the religious ideology that had formed it, and in its resistance, first political and later cultural, to Rome.

These views had a fateful impact on Alon's method of reading rabbinic texts – a method still influential in Israel today despite indications

that in other respects, the Alon school no longer holds the sway it once
did. If the rabbinic texts were basically unmediated statements of the
core religious ideology of a quite thoroughly unified Jewish nation, then
it follows that not only descriptive but even prescriptive texts must
be read as authoritative accounts of social reality. When, for example,
M. Bava Batra 1–2 lists public expenses incumbent on the citizen of
every Jewish town, we should read it not as rabbinic wishful thinking, nor even as law that might, like all laws, sometimes be evaded or
ignored, but as an account of how the finances of Jewish towns actually
did work. The rabbis, in this view, generally had no need for compul-
sion: As embodiments of Torah, their authority was accepted without
question, internalized by the Jews, and fully institutionalized.[34] Now,
rabbinic laws are frequently expressed in institutional terms. In tractates Sanhedrin and Makkot, the rabbis imagined fully developed court
systems – not informal judgment and arbitration – parallel to the fully
institutionalized temple cult and priesthood the rabbis legislated for in
the mishnaic orders of *Kodashim* ("Sanctified Offerings") and *Tohorot*
("Purifications"). But *stories* of rabbinic and patriarchal judgment and
legislation in Palestinian sources more often describe their heroes as
using moral suasion and force, and sometimes failing to impose their
will, than as benefiting from embedded institutional authority.[35] So,
the political theory underpinning the work of Alon and his followers –
Zionism as a movement of Jewish national renewal – affected their interpretation of both halakhic and non-halakhic texts, the point being that
Zionist historiography skewed interpretations of the historical record by
reading rabbinic representations of the past through the prism of Zionist
aspirations for the Jewish present and future.

Another fundamental characteristic of Alon's method of reading that
he shared with almost all historical scholarship before 1970 is the fact
that he was relatively uninterested in the rabbinic texts as texts. He paid
little – though not no – attention to such questions as how, when, and
why the texts were compiled and edited. Thus, he tended (and as usual,
what was merely a tendency for Alon, a careful and subtle historian,
became a basic principle for his followers) to regard rabbinic literature as
full collections of basically reliable raw material, from which a tolerably
full account of ancient Jewish life could be easily enough produced, as
ore is mined and then refined.

Reactions to Alon
Elements of Alon's view were challenged from many different quarters. Here we survey the two most influential of these responses, those

of the great scholar of Hellenistic Jewish art, E. R. Goodenough, and of the equally luminous student of the Greco-Roman matrix of rabbinic literature, Saul Lieberman.

Goodenough

E. R. Goodenough's criticism was implicit. He began by making a comprehensive collection of "Jewish" archaeological remains – including many items Goodenough alone regarded as Jewish – mainly from the first seven centuries c.e.[36] On the basis of his work he drew several conclusions. First of all, notwithstanding the common view, the Second Commandment did not prevent the post-Destruction – in contrast to the pre-Destruction – Jews from making extensive use of figurative artistic representation. Secondly, much of this ancient Jewish art was derived from unambiguously pagan sources. Third, while most Jews disavowed the standard pagan interpretations of these images, the images did have distinctly religious, not merely decorative, functions – a conclusion as true of the simplest nonfigurative ornamentation as it is of the most complex figurative assemblages. The character of the art itself implies that its religious meaning was profoundly hellenized, that the Jews understood Judaism as a kind of Greco-Roman mystery religion. The most coherent literary articulation of this hellenized Judaism was to be found in the works of Philo of Alexandria.[37]

This religion, shared in Goodenough's view by the vast majority of the Jews living under Roman rule, was very remote from the archaic, "semitic" Judaism of the rabbis – a view of the rabbis surprisingly close to Alon's. This assumption led to Goodenough's major conclusion, that the rabbis were neither the political nor the religious leaders of the Jews; in fact, they were little more than a marginal sect, with little or no constituency or influence. Rabbinic Judaism was just one religious option for post-Destruction Jews, and even in Palestine one that most Jews chose to reject. Goodenough had little to say about Mesopotamia, except for Dura Europus, not actually in Mesopotamia but an outpost of the Roman Empire on the west bank of the Euphrates.

While most critics praised Goodenough's collection of material for its comprehensiveness, the more speculative elements of his work were not well received. Even the most sympathetic critics, like Morton Smith, regarded Goodenough's method of "reading" individual pieces of iconography, which relied on introspection in a Jungian vein, as unacceptably subjective and arbitrary (as Goodenough himself came close to admitting), and were unconvinced by his hypothesis of a stable, empire-wide, hellenizing, mystical Judaism.[38]

There, however, the consensus about the significance of Good-enough's work ended. The Israeli scholars Michael Avi Yonah and E. E. Urbach, to take the most influential examples, reacted to Goodenough's arguments about the marginality of the rabbis by striving to produce rabbinizing readings of ancient Jewish iconography or, alternatively, by arguing that the art had no religious meaning and was therefore halakhi-cally inoffensive, and so a matter of indifference to, or even supported by, the rabbis.[39] Such reactions simultaneously acknowledged, if only tacitly, the force of Goodenough's argument and were meant to salvage the conventional assumption of rabbinic religious dominance, even in the Diaspora.

By contrast, Morton Smith argued that much, though not all, of Goodenough's art was religiously meaningful, though not necessarily in the ways he had thought. But whatever precisely the art might mean, Goodenough was certainly right to observe that there was nothing in rabbinic literature to prepare us for the sheer fact of its existence, an argument that made attempts like Urbach's, and much more recently S. Stern's, to defend the art in halakhic terms, moot;[40] the art does seem to demonstrate that the rabbis did not control the Jews, or to put it more subtly, that rabbinic Judaism did not serve as the Jews' sole or primary cultural or religious model. In Smith's view, this was not because the Jews as a group self-consciously opposed the rabbis. For Smith, more Jews were apathetic toward or ignorant of the rabbis' views than opposed them.

In sum, the scholarship of the middle of the twentieth century offered widely varying assessments of the rabbis' political status, in a way that eventually had a crucial impact on how rabbinic texts were read, since it matters profoundly for our understanding of the documents whether we view them, à la Alon, as the constitution of the Jewish nation or, à la Goodenough (though in a way first elaborated by Jacob Neusner, as will be seen), as the utopian writings of a sect, or as something in between.

Rather paradoxically, though, all agreed on the rabbis' isolation from the normative Greek culture of the High Roman imperial East. The reason this is paradoxical is that we would have expected politically powerful rabbis to have played the same role as intermediaries between their constituents and the Roman state as local elites did elsewhere in the empire – and concomitantly to have undergone the same sort of process of Romanization. But Alon and his followers regarded post-70 Palestinian Jews not primarily as Roman subjects, or after 212 (when the emperor Caracalla granted citizenship to almost all inhabitants of the empire) as citizens, but fundamentally as members of a separate nation, one that possessed fully functioning national institutions and a fully preserved national culture, both remarkably impervious, even after three disastrously failed revolts, to the integrative interventionism of the Roman state. Indeed, Alon believed that the patriarchs, not the rabbis, eventually did become romanized, but that in the process they lost their status as leaders of the Jews.

Lieberman and Cultural History

Concurrently, however, a different historiographical approach developed, which stressed the internal cultural diversity of the rabbinic movement, but in general its tendency toward acculturation. This approach was specifically American, its immediate source having been the two short books that Saul Lieberman published in English – his only books in the language – shortly after immigrating in 1940.[41] In fact, Lieberman seems to have been arguing for a fairly superficial rabbinic hellenization, which was a consequence of the rabbis' close connection with the (superficially hellenized) "common people." Indeed, the latters' life "is often mirrored in rabbinic literature with the simplicity of life itself " – a view Lieberman shared with Alon.[42] Lieberman's followers, though, partly under the impact of Goodenough's hypothesis of the Jews' profound religious hellenization, argued that the rabbis, too, were profoundly hellenized, and were comparable to Greek philosophers, orators, Roman jurists, and so on.[43]

What was characteristically American about the views of both Lieberman and his followers was that none bothered to consider the political background of rabbinic acculturation, with the result that much of this work (Lieberman's less so than his successors') reads like a rather sentimental celebration of Jewish-Roman symbiosis, as if the Jews were not the battered, suppressed remnant of a nation – sometimes resistant, sometimes accommodationist, sometimes apathetic, always dominated – but a group of voluntary, happily acculturating (but not too acculturating!) immigrants to a liberal state quite unlike imperial Rome.

History Challenged: The Intervention of Jacob Neusner

Jacob Neusner, shaped by the work of Morton Smith, Goodenough, and Lieberman, has left such an enormous mark in contemporary rabbinic historiography that it is often difficult to recall the shape of the field when he began to publish in the middle 1960s. In his earlier work, Neusner merged the approaches of Goodenough and Lieberman, in that he tended to regard the rabbis as having been at least at some periods politically and culturally marginal (but see the end of this section), but at the same time, like the Jews in general, significantly hellenized.[44] In the final analysis, though, it was the influence of Goodenough and of the New Testament scholar Rudolf Bultmann, the latter mediated through Morton Smith, that shaped Neusner's revolution in the study of rabbinics. Bultmann's work taught Neusner profound skepticism about the historicity of rabbinic texts – transformed through Smith's intermediation into a thoroughgoing hermeneutics of suspicion (one can find traces of this in earlier scholarship, especially Alon, but Neusner elevated it to a core theoretical principle) – and a methodological rigor unprecedented in rabbinic scholarship.[45] Neusner almost always rejected rabbinic historiographical and biographical stories, especially those about the Second Temple and early post-Destruction periods, as propagandistic fictions composed to serve the interests of later rabbis.[46] While Israeli scholars keenly sought to isolate the "historical kernel" even of the most obviously legendary tales, Neusner argued that any such kernel as may exist is in practice unrecoverable. Furthermore, even halakhic traditions are of little historical utility because they must be supposed to have been selected, revised sometimes beyond recognition, and often misattributed, by their tradents and the editors of the documents in which they are reported, to suit interests that can be reconstructed with difficulty, if at all. In sum, Neusner insisted on regarding the rabbinic documents not as archives or repositories of raw data but as texts seeking to create a fictive sense of reality for polemical purposes; he was the first historically inclined rabbinist to take seriously the role of the editors and the environments in which they worked in shaping the specific contents of the rabbinic documents. With Neusner, the mining operation came to a halt.

While such views might, if applied with flexibility, have yielded a more careful, critical, and minimalistic historiography than the Israeli followers of Alon were then producing, in fact Neusner's work tended mainly to confirm and institutionalize the distaste for political and social history already characteristic of American ancient Judaic scholarship. This was because in Neusner's reading, rabbinic texts provided evidence primarily for the history of rabbinic self-interest or, to put it differently, ideology, not for the history of the Jews. By the 1980s, Neusner himself had demonstratively and repeatedly rejected the legitimacy of talmudic history as an intellectual pursuit and was advocating instead a "history of religions" approach, which focused on taxonomizing and tracing changes in religious systems – in Neusner's parlance, "Judaisms" – that is, individual rabbinic texts, viewed synoptically.[47]

By this time, Neusner had partly abandoned the hermeneutics of suspicion he had inherited from Morton Smith; what he now designated a Judaism, he would previously have dismissed as an aggregation of rabbinic self-interest. Neusner still occasionally wrote on historical topics, usually in the course of working up sketchy, stereotype-laden accounts of the contexts of his "Judaisms." But these accounts were often wholly unaffected by Neusner's rigorously skeptical readings of the rabbinic texts themselves. Thus, in his book on the Judaism of the Talmud Yerushalmi, his account of the roles of the rabbis and patriarchs in third- and fourth-century Palestine differs from Alon's mainly in being less coherent.[48]

The Present

These two approaches, Alon's and Goodenough's/Neusner's, continue, with some changes, to dominate the field. As suggested, some signs are now palpable of a weakening of Alon's influence among the youngest scholars (e.g., A. Schremer 2003), but the mainstream of Israeli scholarship – A. Oppenheimer, D. Sperber, B. Z. Rosenfeld, Z. Safrai, J. Schwartz – largely perpetuates the great tradition.[49] Outside of Israel, though most of Neusner's students have followed their master in abandoning talmudic history, most historically oriented scholarship is firmly situated in the Neusnerian penumbra, because it does not assume the dominance of the rabbis and is skeptical about (though not invariably dismissive of) the historicity of rabbinic sources. In this loosely constituted group we may place L. Levine (though he works in Jerusalem), D. Goodblatt (the exceptional historian among Neusner's students), M. Goodman, S. Cohen, C. Hezser, S. Schwartz, and H. Lapin.[50]

A REMAINING HISTORIOGRAPHICAL ISSUE: RABBINIC JUDAISM IN THE CHRISTIAN ROMAN EMPIRE

The main works of rabbinic historiography tended to neglect the period that began with the Christian emperor Constantine's conquest of the East in 323. Alon's *History* devoted a few pages to the last three centuries of Roman rule in Palestine, and followed the standard account of them as a period of decline for the Jews. The two-volume history that Alon's students published in 1982–84 to fill this gap contains excellent discussions of archaeology, late Roman administration, and the gradual Christianization of Palestine, but makes little effort to describe the position of the later rabbis, or to account for the political or cultural contexts of the Yerushalmi, the pre-Islamic midrash collections, and the classical *piyyut*.[51]

Indeed, there is an abundant and ever-growing scholarship attempting to describe the impact of Christianity on the aggadic midrash (either it is implicitly responding to Christian claims or appropriating Christian ideas, or both)[52] and the *piyyut* (complex liturgical poetry, some of which features anti-Christian polemics). Indeed, the entire question of the direction of cultural influence in the piyyut requires clarification: While the literary genre as a whole seems an adaptation of a new style of Christian liturgical poetry whose prime examples are the *madrashe* of the fifth-century Syriac poet Jacob of Serugh, and the *kontakia* of the sixth-century Greek poet Romanos the Melode, it is also possible that the Christian writers borrowed the Jewish form.[53] There have also been some attempts to contextualize this material in a more general Late Antique setting.[54] Scholars of Late Antique Jewish magical texts, such as the *Sefer Ha-Razim*, the *Ḥarba de-Moshe*, and amulets discovered in archaeological excavations, have adopted similar methods.[55] But no one has yet attempted a complete political and social contextualization of any of these texts.

One reason for this is surely simply the nature of the evidence. While some of the midrashim and magical texts are filled with material evocative of the early Byzantine settings in which the works were composed, none of them contain historical tales about the fifth- and sixth-century rabbis (and magicians, if they were different from rabbis) who formulated the texts – their dealings with one another, with non-rabbinic Jews, with prominent Romans, and with other gentiles. It is just such tales that, when told in earlier rabbinic texts about rabbis of the second through fourth centuries, make even the most skeptical sort of historiography possible.

The Yerushalmi occupies a kind of intermediate position between the heavily contextualized high imperial texts and the uncontextualized Byzantine ones. The Talmud was probably redacted toward the end of the fourth century, but much of the material in it seems situated in the third and early fourth centuries (Sussman 1990b), and almost all the scholars mentioned here have made extensive use of this material in their accounts of Jewish Palestine in the second and third centuries. Furthermore, the later fourth and early fifth centuries were a kind of high point of Christian writing, and many of the Church Fathers of the time – Epiphanius, Jerome, and John Chrysostom, to mention only the best known – professed to be especially interested in their Jewish contemporaries. The Roman emperors, too, took a particular interest in the legal status of Jewish communities in the 390s (Linder 1987). All of this material plus archaeology may require careful and sophisticated study before justice can be done to the late-fourth-century setting of the Yerushalmi.

A REMAINING HISTORIOGRAPHICAL ISSUE: RABBINIC JUDAISM IN BABYLONIA

Not unsurprisingly, the historical study of the Talmud Bavli has tended *not* to serve as an ideological, methodological, and theoretical battleground.[56] The modern historiographical tradition on Babylonian Jewry in the Late Parthian and Sasanian Periods (ca. 200–650 C.E.) is in fact quite meager, especially if one excludes from consideration a growing body of recent work on "rabbinic culture" that fails to engage in a serious way with the rabbis' roles – or with their broader political or social environment – outside the *bet midrash/yeshivah* (a failure that does not necessarily invalidate such work a priori).

All historical or historicizing work on the Babylonian rabbis and their Talmud must confront the same problem – our comprehensive ignorance – and it is difficult to see how this problem may be overcome.[57] Practically the only extra-rabbinic evidence for the Jews in Babylonia, apart from some stray references – mostly to Jews in northern Mesopotamia, not Babylonia – in the works of Syriac Church Fathers, are several hundred earthenware vessels, probably from the Late Sasanian Period, containing spells written on their inner surfaces in ink, generally in Jewish Aramaic script and language. Residents of Nippur (an ancient town near the rabbinic center of Sura), not necessarily Jewish ones alone, buried these "magical bowls" under the floors of their houses in order to ward off or trap demons. Although the bowls are important for introducing us to a type of Jewish or part-Jewish religiosity somewhat different from that of the Bavli – and simultaneously for revealing the extent to which Babylonian Jewish magical practice had been rabbinized, in contrast to its Palestinian counterpart – they do little else to fill out the picture of Jewish life in Mesopotamia.

Still worse, the history of the Sasanian Empire is itself very poorly attested. While even in the absence of specific information we can form a fairly detailed impression of what cultural, social, and religious life was like, how comprehensively the state intervened, and what languages are likely to have been spoken in northern Palestinian towns like Caesarea or Sepphoris, their Babylonian counterparts – Sura, Mahoza, Pumbedita – are very obscure places indeed. There are, for instance, no Middle Persian literary texts, and very few nonliterary ones, that may be unproblematically dated to the Sasanian Period.[58] In sum, far more so than is the case for the Jews of Palestine, however obscure and controversial some of *their* history may be, the history of the Jews of Sasanian Babylonia, the role and status of their rabbis and exilarchs (the Babylonian counterparts to the patriarchs), and their relations to the Persian state and to the state priesthood (if any!) must all be wrested from a single text. In the case of Babylonia, there is, then, no escaping the fact that all historiography is necessarily primarily talmudic exegesis.

Exilarchs and Rabbis

Nevertheless, there is broad consensus on several crucial points.[59] It is generally thought that the Parthian Empire was very little centralized, that outside of its Iranian center it relied in part on alliances/ friendship/vassalage between the Parthian kings and local rulers (the older characterization of the Parthian Empire as "feudal" is no longer generally accepted). Jewish historians have supposed that in such conditions, the Jews, too, enjoyed extensive autonomy,[60] though this is not self-evident. It seems likely that it was primarily the rulers of states – geographical regions – who served as Parthian vassals; that the leaders of religious/ethnic minority communities did so, too, is possible but unknown. There seems little reason to believe that the Jews, however numerous they were, predominated demographically in any region of Mesopotamia; they were thus no more than a minority community, wherever they lived. Be this as it may, there is no unambiguous evidence until the very end of the Parthian Period for the existence in Jewish Mesopotamia of anything like exilarchs or rabbis.

Many scholars regard this point as confirmed by a story that Josephus (*Antiquities* 18.310–79) tells of two brothers, Anilaios and Asinaios, who around 40 C.E. established a short-lived Jewish or part-Jewish kingdom near the Babylonian town of Nehardea (modern scholars seem far more certain of the kingdom's "Jewishness" than Josephus's account warrants). Although this story is primarily a homily – no less so than the rabbinic "historical" tales discussed earlier – about the value of observing Jewish laws, for the brothers fell when they violated them and so lost divine support – all scholars have drawn extensive historical conclusions from it. Nehardea was later an important rabbinic center, but here it is the center of a principality ruled by two Jewish brigands who retained their popularity, if not God's favor, despite their neglect of Jewish law (they also had pious Jewish opponents). The story features no hint of any remotely rabbi- or exilarch-like figure.[61]

This began to change, according to the consensual view, toward the end of the Parthian Period. There had, to be sure, "always" been some men of Babylonian origin among the Palestinian rabbis, and probably also isolated individual rabbis living in or near Babylonia (and there would continue to be rabbinic movement back and forth between the two countries into the High Middle Ages). But by circa 220 C.E., some of the returnees – the most prominent among them, according to rabbinic sources, accepted without hesitation by more conservative scholars, having been Rav, a student of Rabbi Yehudah ha-Nasi – somehow quickly established a more or less institutionalized rabbinic presence in Babylonia.[62]

Almost all scholars regard Babylonian Jewry of the amoraic period (ca. 220–ca. 500) as having been significantly rabbinized. Even Neusner, who thought that the rabbis' cultural influence was limited, argued that they had real authority as state-recognized civil judges. Given the state of our knowledge, it is impossible to explain how this might have happened (if in fact it did), but it is striking that aside from Neusner, whose five-volume history of the Jews of Babylonia has as its central historical problem the institutionalization of the rabbinate, no scholars seem to have felt the need to try.

More controversial has been the role of the exilarchs. While it is agreed that they were in some sense the leaders of the Jewish community of Sasanian Babylonia, the Talmud has remarkably little to say about them. Nevertheless, many scholars have regarded them as standing at the pinnacle of a Jewish religious/political hierarchy, as the original (though at times unreliably compliant) source of the rabbis' judicial authority, as having been responsible for tax collection, and as having served as quasi-official intermediaries between the Jews and the Sasanian court, in which some of the incumbents enjoyed extremely high status. It has also been suggested that they ruled the Jews not only in Babylonia but throughout the Sasanian Empire.[63] But I. Gafni, who produced the most careful history of the Jews of Babylonia, dismissed every one of these claims: The Bavli never ascribes to the exilarchs anything like the right to appoint judges such as the Yerushalmi attributes to the later patriarchs; never describes the exilarchs as collecting taxes – not surprisingly since it seems unlikely that the Jews bore any corporate tax burden; and is surprisingly vague about the relations between the exilarchs and the state. All of this is so despite the fact that Babylonian Jewry was, institutionally speaking, heavily centralized, featuring little of the local communal self-determination characteristic of all Jewish settlements, including those in Palestinian towns and villages, in the Roman Empire. Gafni's views – however admirable their minimalism – have the disadvantage of leaving the role of the exilarchate very vague indeed.

In general, Gafni's work illustrates the limitations of the undertaking. His treatment of the talmudic sources is careful and critical, his account filled with novel, interesting, sometimes compelling observations. He apparently made every effort to track down relevant and potentially relevant extra-rabbinic information, despite the diminishing returns the effort indubitably yielded. (Yaakov Elman's potentially pioneering work, an example of which is included in this volume, comparing the Talmud with Zoroastrian legal texts, seems poised to yield impressive results, perhaps more relevant to explicating the cultural than the political or social context of the Talmud).[64] Yet it is hard to avoid the feeling that the task is impossible. In fact, Gafni's history is highly episodic and largely devoid of chronological specificity. As careful as his reading of the texts is, it is still often excessively positivistic, extracting accounts of entire historical episodes from single homiletical tales.[65] Even Gafni's most impressive and plausible conclusions – for example, about the relative weakness of the Babylonian Jewish local community (105–17) – are vulnerable to the criticism that we simply do not have enough information to be able to justify such a characterization over four centuries of Jewish life in Sasanian Babylonia.

Although it seems unlikely that there can ever be as rich an historiography of Jewish Babylonia as there is of Jewish Palestine, some progress, or at least change, may still be possible. Indeed, in his Jerusalem dissertation, "The Exilarch in the Sasanian Period," Geoffrey Herman provides a thoroughly revisionary account of this central topic, one aware of recent developments in Persian studies, little inclined toward a Moshe Beer–like phenomenological or institutional historical account of the exilarchate. His work is, in sum, a reexamination of the material, which is yielding a substantially messier, more complex, and more lifelike account, one that at least *sounds* like history.[66] The general picture, nevertheless, is one of uncertainty and controversy. The latter is paradoxically more pronounced in the case of post-70 Palestine, where the evidence is relatively abundant, than in Babylonia, where, outside of the talmudic text, it barely exists at all.

As unsatisfying as this conclusion may be, it is still of great importance to readers of rabbinic texts: Almost every careful reader assumes some sort of historical context, and this chapter may be taken as a warning to such readers against making excessively rigid contextual assumptions. We remain uncertain about the roles the formulators of the texts played in Late Antique Jewish, Roman, and Sasanian life and so can never be certain whether to read their laws as normative or aspirational, their stories as components of a subversive "hidden transcript" (in the phrase of James Scott) or as authoritative expressions of official ideology.

Notes

1. See Matthews 2000. See also Catherine Hezser and Martin Jaffee in this volume.
2. For basic discussion, see Strack and Stemberger 1992.
3. On the question of the acculturation of Babylonian teachers in particular, see Elman's essay in this volume.
4. See Catherine Hezser's essay in this volume for some results of this approach.
5. For the post-Herodian, pre-revolt period (4 B.C.E.–66 C.E.), see *Jewish War*, Book 2, and the *Jewish Antiquities*, Books 18–20; also, E. Gabba, "Social, Economic and Political History of Palestine 63 B.C.E.–70 C.E.," in Davies et al. 1999, Vol. 3, 94–167.
6. See in detail Mason 2001; for a more mainstream approach, Saldarini 2001.
7. See especially Josephus, *Autobiography*, 190–94. Cf. *Antiquities* 15.3: Pollio the Pharisee and his disciple, Samaias, mentioned in connection with Herod, may be identical to Avtalion and Shemaiah, or perhaps Shammai, who appear as links in the chain of tradition in M. Avot, Chapter 1.
8. For an illuminating recent discussion, see Boyarin 2004, 151–225. The current consensus on this point has been strongly influenced by Cohen 1984.
9. Josephus, *Antiquities* 17.42; on the number of rabbis, the relatively minimalistic view of Albeck 1969 is preferable to the alternatives, though even the maximalist view does not change the general picture; see discussion in L. I. Levine 1989.
10. See Elizabeth Alexander's essay in this volume.
11. See Avot de-Rabbi Nathan, version A, Chapter 4 (ed. S. Schechter, pp. 22–24); version B, Chapter 6 (Schechter, p. 19) = Midrash Mishle, ed. S. Buber, 79–80; B. Gittin 56a–b; Midrash Eikhah, parashah 1, 31.
12. See the sources discussed in S. Schwartz 1990, 200–8. The classic modern discussion is Alon 1952–61, Vol. 1, 219–73. On Alon, see the section devoted to him in this essay for more.
13. See Schwartz 2001a, 110–14.
14. This and much of what follows summarizes Schwartz 2001a, 103–61.
15. See H. Lapin, "Rabbis and Cities in Later Roman Palestine: The Literary Evidence," *JJS* 50 (1999), 187–207; and *Economy, Geography, and Provincial History in Later Roman Palestine*, Tübingen: Mohr Siebeck, 2001, 175–91.

16. On these stories, see most recently S. Cohen, "The Conversion of Anton-inus," in P. Schäfer, ed., *The Talmud Yerushalmi and Graeco-Roman Culture*, Vol. 1, Tübingen: Mohr Siebeck, 1998, 141–71.

17. See M. Whittow, "Ruling the Late Roman and Early Byzantine City: A Continuous History," *Past & Present* 129 (1990), 3–29; W. Liebeschuetz, "The End of the Ancient City," in J. Rich, ed., *The City in Late Antiquity*, London: Routledge, 1992, 1–49; C. Kelly, *Ruling the Later Roman Empire*, Cambridge, Mass.: Harvard University Press, 2004, 109–10.

18. See M. Goodman, "The Roman State and the Jewish Patriarch in the Third Century," in L. Levine, ed., *The Galilee in Late Antiquity*, New York: Jewish Theological Seminary, 1992, 127–39.

19. See, in general, N. de Lange, *Origen and the Jews: Studies in Jewish-Christian Relations in Third-Century Palestine*, Cambridge: Cambridge University Press, 1976. Sources about the patriarchs and their relations to the rabbis are discussed in L. I. Levine, "The Status of the Patriarch in the Third and Fourth Century: Sources and Methodology," *JJS* 47 (1996), 1–32.

20. See G. Alon, "Those Appointed for Money: On the History of the Various Juridical Authorities in Eretz-Israel in the Talmudic Period," *Jews, Judaism and the Classical World: Studies in Jewish History in the Time of the Second Temple and Talmud*, Jerusalem: Magnes Press, 1977, 15–57.

21. See Schwartz 2001a, 153–58; N. Avigad, *Beth Shearim*, Vol. 3, Jerusalem: IES-Mosad Bialik, 1971, 63–84, 177–87.

22. See H. Newman, "*Hieronymus vehayehudim*," Ph.D. diss., Hebrew University, 1997, 9–13.

23. See, in general, the laws codified in the Codex Theodosianus 16.8–9, discussed in A. Linder, *The Jews in Roman Imperial Legislation*, Detroit: Wayne State University Press, 1987, plus CTh 13.5.18 (= Linder #19) and 2.1.10 (= Linder #28).

24. See CTh 16.8.29 (= Linder #53).

25. See, in general, L. I. Levine 2000.

26. *Geschichte der Juden*, 4th ed., Vol. 4, Leipzig: Oskar Leiner, 1897, noting especially the introduction to the volume, 1–8.

27. See Dinur, *Yisra'el ba-golah*, Vol. 1, Tel Aviv: Mossad Bialik, 1958, 5–7 = *Israel and the Diaspora*, Philadelphia: Jewish Publication Society, 1969, 3–6; Alon, *Toldot hayehudim be'-erez yisra'el bi-tekufat ha-mishnah veha-talmud*, 2 vol., Tel Aviv: Ha-kibbutz Ha-me'uḥad, 1952–61, Introduction to Vol. 1 = *The Jews in Their Land in the Talmudic Age*, Cambridge, Mass.: Harvard University Press, 1989.

28. On the nonexistence of a Sanhedrin after 70, see Levine 1989, 76–83; D. Goodblatt, *The Monarchic Principle: Studies in Jewish Self-Government in Antiquity*, Tübingen: Mohr Siebeck, 1994, 232–76.

29. *The Jews in Their Land*, 725.

30. This is the main point of the fundamental article, "Those Appointed for Money," 374–435.

31. *Toldot*, 2.148; even more emphatically, *The Jews in Their Land*, 726.

32. Z. Safrai, *The Jewish Community in the Talmudic Period*, Jerusalem: Merkaz Shazar, 1995, 76–98.

33. An important later variant of this view is the hypothesis that certain types of rabbinic literature – usually the midrash collections but sometimes also the Targumim, but usually not the Talmudim – are "popular." See, for example, Galit Hasan-Rokem, *The Web of Life: Folklore in Rabbinic Literature* (Hebrew), Tel Aviv: Am Oved, 1996, 14, and her contribution to this volume.
34. See for example Alon, *Jews, Judaism*, 382–86.
35. See Schwartz 2001a, 103–28.
36. Goodenough 1953–67.
37. H. Wolfson 1947; Belkin 1940.
38. See M. Smith 1967.
39. Urbach, 1959, 149–65; 229–45; for Avi-Yonah, see Avi-Yonah 1981.
40. Y. S. Stern 1996.
41. Lieberman 1994 and 1950.
42. Lieberman 1994, 3.
43. Works following in Lieberman's footsteps include Cohen 1981, Fischel 1973, Goldin 1988, and Visotzky 1995. For a more detailed discussion of the post-Lieberman tendency to "normalize" the rabbis, see S. Schwartz 2001b.
44. Neusner 1963 and 1968.
45. Morton Smith's role in pushing Neusner in a Bultmannesque direction (first of all in *Development of a Legend: Studies on the Traditions concerning Yohanan ben Zakkai*, Leiden: Brill, 1970) is discussed in S. Schwartz, "Historiography on the Jews in the 'Talmudic Period,'" in M. Goodman, ed., *Oxford Handbook of Jewish Studies*, Oxford: Oxford University Press, 2002, 100–2. Bultmann in turn regarded Wellhausen as his most important predecessor – *The History of the Synoptic Tradition*, trans. J. Marsh, Oxford: Blackwell, 1972, 2 (first published, Göttingen: Vandenhoeck/Ruprecht, 1921); I am providing Neusner with a very different ancestry from that suggested by J. Pasto, "Who Owns the Jewish Past? Judaism, Judaisms and the Writing of Jewish History," Ph.D. diss., Cornell University, 1999, 365–68.
46. E.g., Neusner 1971b and 1973.
47. For an early, very mild version of the rejection of history, see Neusner 1981, 13, 22–24. For some examples of Neusner's "systemic" approach, that is, his translation of each discrete rabbinic text into a "Judaic system," or a "Judaism," prior to embedding it in the larger "matrix" of rabbinic Judaism, see Neusner 1986, Vol. 1, 79–89, and 1988, 9–15; more recently: Neusner 2000, 3–16.
48. Neusner 1983.
49. Oppenheimer 1991; Rosenfeld 1997; Safrai 1994a; J. Schwartz 1986 and 1991; Sperber 1974 and 1978.
50. Cohen 1999; Goodblatt 1980 and 1994; Goodman 1993; Hezser 1997; Lapin 2001; Levine 1989 and 2000; Schwartz 2001a.
51. Z. Baras 1982–84. And see now Kalmin and Schwartz 2003; Levine 2004.
52. For recent examples, see Hirshman 1996 and Boyarin 2004.
53. On the *piyyut* and Romanos, see classically Schirmann 1953.
54. See Yahalom 1999 and Schwartz 2001a, 240–74.

55. See, e.g., Harari, "Early Jewish Magic," Ph.D. diss., Hebrew University, 1998; Swartz 1996; the amulets are published by Naveh and Shaked 1985 and 1993.

56. This section has been greatly improved by my conversations with Richard Kalmin (Jewish Theological Seminary) and Geoffrey Herman (Hebrew University).

57. See, however, the remarkable efforts of Yaakov Elman, in this volume and elsewhere, to address this issue.

58. For a survey, see A. Perikhanian's article in Yarshater 1983, 627–31. See also Elman in this volume.

59. The most important synthetic or synthesizing histories of the Jews in rabbinic period Babylonia are Neusner 1965–70, Beer 1970, and Gafni 1990.

60. So, for example, Neusner 1965–70, 1:152–63; 2:95–96; implicitly Beer 1970, 27.

61. Neusner 1965–70, 1:50–54; cf. Gafni 1990, 62–64.

62. Neusner 1965–70, 2:111–15

63. The same basic view is shared by Neusner and Beer.

64. See, for now, Y. Elman, "Marriage and Marital Property in Rabbinic and Sasanian Law," in Hezser 2003, 227–76.

65. R. Kalmin, "Persian Persecution of the Jews: A Reconsideration of the Talmudic Evidence," in S. Shaked and A. Netzer forthcoming, volume 6. The same criticism may be applied to A. Schremer's rich but frustrating account of the Jewish family in Late Antique Jewish Mesopotamia, *Male and Female He Created Them: Jewish Marriage in the Late Second Temple, Mishnah and Talmud Periods,* Jerusalem: Merkaz Zalman Shazar, 2003.

66. See, in the meantime, Herman 1996.

Part II

The Genres of Rabbinic Literary Composition

5 Rabbinic *Midrash* and Ancient Jewish Biblical Interpretation

STEVEN D. FRAADE

In the last several decades, the quantity and variety of ancient Jewish literature that displays interpretive engagement with the Hebrew Bible has vastly increased, in large measure thanks to the ongoing publication of and scholarship on the Dead Sea Scrolls. While we might think of the Dead Sea Scrolls as representing the textual activity of a relatively small and short-lived sectarian community, the value of these discoveries have had much broader implications for the history of the texts of what was to become the Hebrew Bible and for their interpretation beyond the boundaries of this one community or movement and its time. The many biblical texts found among the Dead Sea Scrolls open a window onto the evolving state of scriptures in Jewish society more broadly, as does the discovery of many texts that would not find their way into the Jewish scriptural canon, yet which are not specifically "sectarian" and, therefore, can be assumed (and in some cases known) to have circulated much more broadly in Second Temple Jewish society and beyond. Thus, it is not just the quantity of texts of scriptural interpretation that has increased but the very parameters of what is understood to constitute the varieties of scriptural interpretation. Texts long known prior to the discovery of the Dead Sea Scrolls (generally transmitted through Christian channels and often in later Christian translations) are now appreciated as early works of Jewish scriptural interpretation, whereas previously, their value was thought to lie elsewhere (as history, philosophy, eschatology, etc.). In effect, a scholarly field of study of biblical interpretation has been created where either none previously existed or it only existed in the shadows of other scholarly preoccupations.

While the important implications of these developments for the study of rabbinic *midrash* should be apparent, they still need to be delineated and emphasized. Our earliest rabbinic midrashic collections date from the middle to late third century, even though they contain interpretive traditions, whether attributed or anonymous, that might be significantly older. Likewise, the social, cultural, and intellectual roots of

the rabbinic interpretation of the Hebrew Bible extend back certainly to the times and contexts of Late Second Temple Judaism. Nonetheless, there exists a chronological gap of about four hundred years between the last of the canonical biblical books (Daniel: ca. 165 B.C.E.) and the earliest rabbinic midrashic collections in their extant forms (ca. 250 C.E. at the earliest), and about a hundred and fifty years between the destruction of the Second Temple (and the last of Second Temple Jewish texts) and our earliest rabbinic midrashic collections. Were this chronological span not significant enough, it is difficult to assess just how broadly, deeply, or immediately the destruction of the Second Temple in 70 C.E. altered Jewish textual/discursive practices. Although the rabbis' most immediate intellectual and spiritual forebears were likely to have been the Pharisees, who are reported to have been "strict/exact interpreters of the Law,"[1] they have left us no surviving writings of any kind, let alone actual scriptural interpretations (except as these might have been transmitted through later rabbinic channels, are embedded in the apologetic accounts of Josephus, or are reflected indirectly in New Testament and Qumran polemics). Therefore, it is natural and inevitable, in seeking a better understanding of the forms, methods, and contents of early rabbinic midrash, to inquire as to their origins by comparing them with the extant Jewish writings of the Second Temple Period, especially for their lately expanded evidence of scriptural interpretation.

This search for the antecedents of rabbinic midrash has hardly been (nor could it be) hermeneutically innocent. Rather, like the search for the origins of New Testament traditions (much of which are similarly exegetical) in the Jewish literature of the Second Temple Period, this search, seemingly historical, is often no less ideological/theological. Since both early Christian and early rabbinic tradents, largely through their scriptural interpretations, claim for themselves to be the monolinear successors to and inheritors of the Hebrew Bible (Old Testament) and its covenantal promises, fulfilled or to be fulfilled through their line, study of the textual remains of Second Temple Judaism serves to provide the "missing links" to the later chains of Jewish or Christian tradition and authority. Thus, there is a tendency, in some scholarly quarters, for comparisons of early rabbinic midrash with its Jewish interpretive antecedents to stress continuities and similarities, while ignoring or downplaying discontinuities and dissimilarities (while, in other quarters, to react by doing just the opposite).[2] While such favoring of one over the other is a pitfall of any comparative exercise, it is particularly fraught in this case for the additional ideological freight that it must carry. Needless to say, in any comparison, similarity is meaningless

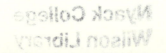

unless set against dissimilarity and vice versa; that is, the two are mutually instructive, and without either, comparison is impossible. Unfortunately, however, there is no simple formula for finding the right balance between the two, nor for quantifying and tallying the many points of concordance and discordance so as to declare triumphantly more continuity rather than less (or the opposite) to be the winner.

Nor are scholars always clear or consistent as to what precisely they are comparing between rabbinic scriptural interpretation and its antecedents: interpretive *traditions*; the interpretive *methods* by which those traditions are thought to have been exegetically derived; the formal *structures* by which they are textually embodied in our extant documents; the rhetorical *strategies* by which those documents seek performatively to engage (and transform) their audiences within particular socioreligious settings; or the underlying assumptions or claims to interpretive *authority* on behalf of the texts' authors/transmitters/studying communities?

Before proceeding, a further comparative difficulty must be acknowledged, even if it cannot be surmounted. While for rabbinic midrash the existence of a closed, fixed scriptural canon can be presumed, the same cannot be said for all varieties of Second Temple Judaism, as we now know well from the evidence of the Dead Sea Scrolls. That is, it is a matter of some uncertainty and debate (partly terminological) where the "inner-biblical" process of scriptural formation, through successive stages of revision, ends, and the "post-biblical" practice of scriptural interpretation begins, the line between them often not being clear, except perhaps through hindsight, which risks retrojection. Thus, what might appear as differences of interpretive form or method may be, at least in part, attributable not so much to the ideological stances or social settings of the respective interpretive communities as to the changing status of the scriptural texts themselves, although these factors are likely to have been intertwined. This is a question to which I will return later.

Finally, we must constantly remind ourselves of the partial, fragmentary nature of the comparative evidence before us. Almost all of Second Temple Jewish literature outside of the Dead Sea Scrolls has reached us through the hands of Christian transmission (in some cases, significantly Christianized). What was so preserved is likely to represent a particular *selection* of pre-rabbinic Jewish literature that appealed to the ideological/theological self-interests of Christian transmitters (e.g., more eschatological, less legal, materials). While the Dead Sea Scrolls, essentially a textual "time capsule," go a long way toward remedying this situation, much of their contents are preserved in very fragmentary form. It is a matter of dispute how much of what survives of those scrolls is particular to one relatively small community/movement, and how much is representative of a broader slice of Second Temple Jewish society, and if so, how much broader. Thus, a good dose of modesty is called for before claiming to have catalogued the varieties of Second Temple Judaism and their textual practices, or to have connected the dots between the Hebrew Bible and early rabbinic interpretation thereof. Much, if not most, of what falls between may simply be lost, leaving us unable, however much we might desire, to draw continuous lines of filiation.

In what follows, I will not provide a comprehensive survey of scriptural interpretation in pre-rabbinic times and contexts, in part since the scope of the present essay would not allow it and in part since this has been provided elsewhere.[3] Rather, I wish to highlight aspects of Second Temple scriptural interpretation that help to historically contextualize rabbinic midrash socially, culturally, and intellectually.

EXEGETICAL TRADITIONS AND CONTENTS

Even before the discovery and publication of the Dead Sea Scrolls, many interpretive traditions found in early rabbinic *midrash* were also to be found in antecedent Jewish writings (especially Philo, Josephus, the Apocrypha, and Pseudepigrapha, not to mention the New Testament). Works such as Louis Ginzberg's *Legends of the Jews*[4] wove together Jewish interpretations from pre-rabbinic and rabbinic writings (as well as from patristic, Islamic, and medieval Jewish exegetes) so as to assert the existence (or create the impression) of a deep and broad font of Jewish exegetical lore (and law), and of continuity between the rabbis and their pre-70 antecedents.

As the Dead Sea Scrolls became increasingly available, many more such shared interpretive traditions were uncovered (narrative as well as legal, but the emphasis was on the former), leading to the creation of a scholarly approach called "comparative midrash," in which "*midrash*" denoted scriptural interpretation in general, whether explicit or inferred, dating all the way back, not just to the closing of the Hebrew scriptural canon but inner-biblically into the later books of the Bible in their own reworking of earlier scriptural books or passages. One of the emphases of such studies was to claim that most of the interpretive methods and products of rabbinic midrash could now be found centuries earlier in the period either following or contemporaneous with the gradual closing of the biblical canon. Such studies sought to show not only that a wide variety of types of Jewish texts from a broad range of times and settings share many scriptural interpretations, but also that those shared interpretations revealed a shared "midrashic" approach to Scripture. From this perspective, some viewed rabbinic midrash as simply a late repository for interpretive traditions that had long and broadly circulated, proving that notwithstanding apparent differences in textual forms, religious beliefs, and practices, there were great exegetical affinities among the varieties of ancient Judaism (including rabbinic and Jewish-Christian). To give but one example of this approach:

> A corpus of methodological assumptions, as well as a good many specific interpretations, came to be shared even by the warring groups whose names and works we know from the end of this period. And it is this common inheritance – communicated orally, as suggested, perhaps through the instruction of children and/or the public reading and translation or exposition of Scripture – that is responsible for the common assumptions, and much common material, that we have seen to characterize the written sources that have survived from those early times.[5]

Needless to say, this approach tends to discount the formal and rhetorical differences between the textual practices by which these shared traditions are expressed in the textual corpora of different communities, so as to emphasize points of convergence rather than divergence. Similar traditions of interpretation need not require direct knowledge of or influence between the sources or their authors/communities, nor even that they drew on a shared reservoir (whether written or oral) of exegetical tradition. In some cases, it is possible that such similar interpretations were arrived at in total independence of one another, the products of similar responses to a shared scriptural barb, gap, or ambiguity, possibly informed by shared exegetical presuppositions about the interpretability of the divinely revealed scriptural text. This is not to deny the possibility, even likelihood, of borrowed or shared traditions, but rather to admit that in most specific cases, we simply do not know; that is, we cannot reconstruct the relation between scriptural interpretation and traditional filiation. Thus, for example, we have no way of knowing whether or to what extend the tannaitic sages had direct or indirect knowledge of the Dead Sea Scrolls, or whether Philo knew of the teachings of the Pharisees (and vice versa), notwithstanding points of shared (or disputed) scriptural interpretation.

In addition to the question of shared interpretive traditions, there is another aspect of comparing the contents of early rabbinic literature to its antecedents that has not received much attention: which parts of the Hebrew Bible receive exegetical attention. Our earliest rabbinic biblical commentaries (*Mekhilta, Sifra, Sifrei*) focus on the Pentateuch, with the exception of the Book of Genesis, even though they incorporate interpretations of verses from all of the Hebrew Bible. However, even within these collections, while there is in some cases greater concentration on legal sections of the Pentateuch (which may explain the absence of an early commentary to the Book of Genesis), narrative sections are hardly excluded, and in some collections constitute more than half of what is covered.[6] By contrast, Philo concentrates his exegetical attention on the Books of Genesis and Exodus, with much more on the former, while treating laws less exegetically. Josephus, in *Jewish Antiquities* 1–11, in retelling all of biblical history (and then extending it to his own time), deals with the legal parts of the Pentateuch much less systematically and continuously, saving them for a projected work that he apparently never wrote.[7] While the Dead Sea Scrolls provide ongoing running commentaries (*pesharim*, on which more in the next section) to the Books of the Prophets and Psalms, otherwise their exegetical energies are heavily focused on the Book of Genesis, especially its antediluvian and early patriarchal periods, but more through implicit interpretation and retelling than through formal commentary or explicit interpretation. Notwithstanding the importance of Sinai to the Qumran community's collective and covenantal self-understanding, we find (in contrast to early rabbinic midrash) hardly any direct exegetical engagement with biblical passages narrating the revelation at Mt. Sinai as a way of exegetically linking their revelatory self-understanding to that central scriptural event.[8]

In comparing the exegetical contents of early rabbinic midrash with its Second Temple antecedents, we need to be as attentive to those aspects that concord as to those that do not. However, in addition to considering discrete interpretive traditions, we need to look more broadly at which biblical books, or parts of books, attracted the interpretive attentions of different interpretive authors/communities (even if only at the editorial level of the extant texts). Presumably, such differences of scriptural focus do not simply reflect differences regarding what was considered to be canonically authoritative, but also which parts of shared scriptures were of particular significance to the rhetorical/ideological self-defining interests of the respective authors and their textual communities.

EXEGETICAL FORM AND FUNCTION

The explosion of evidence for scriptural interpretation among the varieties of pre-rabbinic Judaism has had, perhaps, the greatest impact on our realization of the great diversity of literary forms that such cultural activity could assume, defying the neat rubrics under which we had previously thought it could be sorted. Judging from early rabbinic midrash, it might appear that the commentary form of interpretation would have been the "natural" consequence of scriptural canonization. That is, canonization would have necessitated the literary-critical labor of "lemmatizing" – that is, formally defining the beginning and end of each scriptural verse (as in contemporary Bibles) – and providing an explanation of each scriptural lemma in turn. This might be imagined as the common practice, at least from the time of Ezra (Nehemiah 8:1–8), whether in synagogues or places of study: reading and explaining the scriptural verses in succession; alternating formally between scriptural words and their explication. The fact that among the very first of the Dead Sea Scrolls to be discovered and published were *pesharim* – Hebrew, sectarian, eschatological decodings of the prophetic books, in commentary form – confirmed, at least initially, that here lay direct antecedents to rabbinic midrash, with both *pesher* and midrash employing common methods otherwise employed in dream interpretation.[9] The scriptural commentaries long known among the allegorical treatises of Philo of Alexandria were also now given a renewed and more concentrated examination, both in the context of their Greek-speaking diasporan cultural context, and increasingly in the context of the history of Jewish scriptural interpretation. Although rabbinic midrash is distinct in many respects from these antecedents (as they are from one another), they provide important alternative models for scriptural commentary with which early rabbinic midrash can be fruitfully compared and contrasted. For example, while early rabbinic midrash shares with Philo's commentaries (but with important differences) the traits of multiple interpretations and dialogical (question and answer) rhetoric, it shares important exegetical terminology and methods with the pesharim.

In recent years, however, as more of the Dead Sea Scrolls have been published, it has become clear that most texts of scriptural interpretation at Qumran do *not* take the form of running commentary. As important as the *pesharim* are, they are hardly defining of the forms that scriptural interpretation takes in the Dead Sea Scrolls, both sectarian and nonsectarian. More commonly, the explicit citation and interpretation of isolated verses, or of a cluster of verses, is embedded in a hortatory, legal, thematic, or liturgical text that does not take the form of continuous scriptural commentary.[10] Most often, however, scriptural verses are paraphrased; that is, they are not explicitly cited at all, but are rather "retold," with varying degrees of expansion, reduction, reordering, and combination with other retold scriptural verses. While one effect of the "commentary" mode is to differentiate between scriptural text and its interpretation, the mode of scriptural paraphrase (in the absence of explicit scriptural citation) has the effect of blurring, if not effacing, the boundary line between the two. Writings that favor the latter mode have variously been termed "para-biblical" or "rewritten Bible."

These sorts of writings are by no means unique to the Dead Sea Scrolls, with several important such texts long known before the discovery of these scrolls, especially the Book of Jubilees, 1 Enoch 6–11; Josephus's *Jewish Antiquities* 1–11; and Pseudo-Philo's *Liber Antiquitatum Biblicarum*. However, with the discovery of the Dead Sea Scrolls, especially the *Genesis Apocryphon* and the *Temple Scroll* (and fragments of Jubilees and 1 Enoch in their original languages), interest was refocused on such writings as prime exempla of the "genre" (if it can be called that) of rewritten Bible, with sharpened focus on their exegetical aspects. More recently, with the publication of such Qumran texts as "Reworked Pentateuch" and a number of para-biblical prophetic works, whose paraphrastic interventions are more modest, the limits and usefulness of the rubric "rewritten Bible" has been called into question. Some of these texts seem closer to inner-biblical "revisions" than to post-biblical "rewritings," blurring the lines between biblical versions (such as the Septuagint and Samaritan Pentateuch) and rewritten Bible. While the term "rewritten Bible" might presume the status of a fixed, canonical Scripture prior to its "rewriting," such a presumption may be a retrojection from the Bible's subsequent acquisition of closed, canonical authority. Nor is it self-evident how such "rewritten" scriptures were understood by their "authors" or "audiences" to relate to what came to be the Hebrew Bible, for example, whether as interpretive complement or supplement, or as revelatory replacement or successor. Stated differently, did such "rewritten" texts share in or borrow from the authority of their antecedent scriptures, or did they seek to supplant or upstage them? Such works display a variety of strategies whereby their authors claim authority for their para-biblical creations, with pseudepigraphy being only one, which variety might be underappreciated once such a broad range of writings is subsumed under a single generic rubric. Furthermore, while it is important to differentiate between the commentary format of early rabbinic midrash – with its terminological differentiation between Scripture and its interpretation, and its explicit employment of hermeneutical methods – and the more implied nature of scriptural interpretation in "rewritten Bible" of the Second Temple period, it is important not to lose sight of their shared exegetical aspects.

The formal differences between early rabbinic midrash and its antecedents (as among them) are suggestive of broader and deeper differences in how their respective authors and audiences regarded Scripture as divine revelation (whether as a one-time past event or a continuous process), on the one hand, and their own roles as human receptors/ transmitters of scriptural revelation, on the other. With whom did interpretive authority reside, from whence did it derive, how was it transmitted, and how did it manifest itself discursively amidst the studying communities for whom the varied textual forms performatively functioned? It would be a serious mistake to discount the formal traits of each writing as mere literary detritus standing in the way of our constructing a disembodied meta-tradition of scriptural interpretation or of our uncovering a subterranean font of shared laws and legends.[11] Quite to the contrary, traditions are never communicated or engaged by their tradents apart from their ideologically freighted and socially formative rhetorical embodiments. The medium may not alone be the message, but it certainly contributes mightily to it. Of course, describing such formal differences is one thing; accounting for them is quite another.

One way that scholars have accounted for the differences between rewritten Bible of the Second Temple Period and early rabbinic midrashic commentary is to attribute them to chronological development. For example, since our earliest rabbinic collections, including *midrashim*, are some two to three hundred years later than the core Dead Sea Scrolls, they might reflect a later, more developed stage of Jewish exegetical practice. In particular, some time between the last of the Dead Sea Scrolls and the first extant rabbinic texts, the Hebrew biblical canon came to final closure. This would have encouraged a more "post-biblical" attitude to the biblical text and its authority. New teachings, whether legal or narrative, would now need to be explicitly anchored in the words of a fixed and closed biblical text, from which they would derive their authority, rather than presented in the form of para-biblical teachings deriving from pseudepigraphic attributions or charismatic claims to prophetic knowledge. However, while this progression in canonical scriptural status is a *necessary* precondition for rabbinic midrash, it is not alone a *sufficient* explanation of its differences from its antecedents.

Another (or additional) developmental explanation might be that the failed Jewish revolts of 70 and 135 C.E. would have discouraged the sort of actualized eschatological commentaries of the Qumran *pesharim* for a more transtemporal and eschatologically deferred commentary, as found in early rabbinic midrash. These events might also have discouraged reliance on prophetic/charismatic figures, or pseudepigraphic attributions, for singular interpretive authority, in favor of more collective groundings of interpretive authority. Finally, in the aftermath of Second Temple Period Jewish sectarianism, which according to the rabbis was the cause of the Temple's destruction, the rabbinic sages might have felt it necessary to turn from intercommunal diatribe to intra-rabbinic dialogue, from multiple "Judaisms," each claiming that it alone possessed the divinely authorized understanding of Scripture, to multiple scriptural interpretations within a common interpretive community.[12]

Such linear developmental explanations, while narratively satisfying, are reductive not only of the complexities of historical causation but also of the great variety of forms of scriptural interpretation found, often side by side, in Second Temple cultural contexts, especially at Qumran, as well as within early rabbinic literature, in both of which aspects of rewritten Bible and scriptural commentary can be found interpenetrating one another. For these linear explanations to work, we would have to presume that pharisaic (pre-70 C.E.) scriptural interpretation would have resembled in form that of the Dead Sea Scrolls (more rewritten Bible and less dialogical commentary) and that the remnants of the Dead Sea community (post-70 C.E.) would have changed their manner of scriptural interpretation in the direction of rabbinic midrash in response to the changed circumstances of scriptural canonicity in post-Destruction Judaea and Galilee. This assumes, as is reasonable, that the Pharisees were the closest antecedents to the rabbis and that there were significant numbers of sectarians identified with the Qumran community, but who lived elsewhere, who survived the Roman destruction of the Qumran central camp in 68 C.E. Of course, since neither of these groups has left us any writings, these assumptions can neither be proved nor falsified. Nevertheless, it seems to me doubtful that chronological development alone could account for the differences between Qumran and rabbinic interpretive stances and practices.

Rather, before seeking such reductivist developmental explanations, we need to ask (with varying emphases, depending on what particular sources allow us to discern): How does each form (or admixture of forms) of scriptural interpretation function in relation to its respective textual community's ideology of the chronology, theology, and anthropology of continuing divine revelation across history? That is, how does it correlate with the possible claim for a human role, whether by the community or its elites, in the process of ongoing revelatory teaching? How do the rhetorical forms of scriptural interpretation performatively shape or reinforce a self-understanding of privileged covenantal status vis-à-vis competing textual communities or learned elites, whether historical or fictive? How do the various rhetorical forms that scriptural interpretation assumes function pedagogically, or paideically, to transform their respective audiences into the kind of polity that might embody Torah in their very lives of collective textual/oral study and practice?

A CASE IN POINT: REUBEN AND BILHAH

For purposes of illustration, let us compare several exegetical treatments of an extremely brief, and hence enigmatic, scriptural narrative, as recounted in the Book of Genesis, following the account of Rachel's death and burial by Israel/Jacob (35:16–21): "While Israel stayed in that land, Reuben went and lay with Bilhah, his father's concubine; and Israel found out. Now the sons of Jacob were twelve in number" (35:22; *NJPS*).[13] The verse is most notable for what it does *not* say: What were the circumstances and motives that led Reuben (Jacob's eldest son, born to Leah) to "lie" with Bilhah (Rachel's maidservant and Jacob's concubine). How did Jacob learn of this act and what was his response? What were the consequences for Reuben of his deed, especially considering that the Torah expressly prohibits such sexual relations, with severe penalty (Leviticus 18:8, 20:11; Deuteronomy 23:1, 27:20). What is the relation of this seemingly eclipsed narrative to what precedes and succeeds it, especially in light of the Masoretic "punctuation," which combines in a single verse the statement of Reuben's deed with the introduction to the following enumeration of Jacob's twelve sons by four women?

Reuben's deed is not mentioned again until Jacob's deathbed "blessing" of Reuben in Genesis 49:3–4: "Reuben, you are my firstborn, / My might and first fruit of my vigor, / exceeding in rank / And exceeding in honor. / Unstable as water, you shall excel no longer; / for when you mounted your father's bed, / You brought disgrace – my couch he mounted!" (*NJPS*). Although this verse contains its share of difficulties, it clearly indicates that Reuben has lost much of his privilege as Jacob's first-born son as a consequence of his having "mounted [his] father's bed," presumably an allusion to his "lying" with Bilhah (perhaps too egregious to be referred to explicitly).[14] Reuben's adulterous deed, we are here told *twice*, was performed (whether actually or figuratively) on Jacob's bed, emphasizing all the more the brazenness of the act. However, Jacob's "blessing" of Reuben brings to mind Moses' no less enigmatic, but seemingly positive, blessing of the tribe of Reuben (though the subject could be understood to be Reuben the individual) just prior to Moses' death (Deuteronomy 33:6): "May Reuben live and not die, / Though few be his numbers" (*NJPS*).

The task of exegetically filling in the gaps within and between these verses begins (or continues) already inner-biblically, with 1 Chronicles 5:1–2, just prior to listing the sons of Reuben: "The sons of Reuben the first-born of Israel. (He was the first-born; but when he defiled his father's bed, his birthright was given to the sons of Joseph son of Israel, so he is not reckoned as first-born in the genealogy; though Judah became more powerful than his brothers and a leader came from him, yet the birthright belonged to Joseph.)" (*NJPS*). Thus, the principal consequence of Reuben's having "defiled his father's bed" is the forfeiture of his birthright as the firstborn son of Jacob (by Leah), that is, the double-portion inheritance, to Joseph (Genesis 48:5–6), Jacob's firstborn son by his favorite wife, Rachel (but the eleventh of twelve in birth order). Still, this inner-biblical interpretation opens as many questions as it resolves, not the least of which being that such a father's annulment of the birthright of his firstborn son in favor of the child of his favored wife is expressly prohibited in the law of Deuteronomy 21:15–17.

However much these verses intertextually shed light upon one another, they hardly furnish us with a narrative of what "took place" between Reuben and Bilhah, or consequently between Reuben and Jacob. For this we must turn to our earliest "retelling" of the story of Reuben and Bilhah, found in the Book of Jubilees (ca. 150 B.C.E.).[15] After retelling the story of Rachel's death and burial, it narrates a remarkably expanded and coherent version of Reuben's deed with Bilhah (33:1–9), undoubtedly drawing on earlier traditions and interpretive understandings of the previously cited biblical verses:

> Jacob went and lived to the south of the Tower of Eder Ephratah. He went to his father Isaac – he and his wife Leah – on the first of the tenth month. When Reuben saw Bilhah, Rachel's maid – his father's concubine – bathing in water in a private place, he loved her. At night he hid. He entered Bilhah's house at night and found her lying alone in her bed and sleeping in her tent. After he had lain with her, she awakened and saw that Reuben was lying with her in the bed. She uncovered the edge of her (clothing), took hold of him, shouted out, and realized that it was Reuben. She was ashamed because of him. Once she had released her grip on him, he ran away. She grieved terribly about this matter and told no one at

all. When Jacob came and looked for her, she said to him: "I am not pure for you because I am too contaminated for you, since Reuben defiled me and lay with me at night. I was sleeping and did not realize (it) until he uncovered the edge of my (garment) and lay with me." Jacob was very angry at Reuben because he had lain with Bilhah, since he had uncovered the covering of his father. Jacob did not approach her again because Reuben had defiled her. (*Jubilees*, trans. VanderKam, 218–20)

As is so characteristic of the Book of Jubilees, it uses this narrative as an opportunity to anticipate later Mosaic legislation (already recorded on heavenly tablets):

As for any man who uncovers the covering of his father – his act is indeed very bad and it is indeed despicable before the Lord. For this reason it is written and ordained on heavenly tablets that a man is not to lie with his father's wife and that he is not to uncover the covering of his father because it is impure. They are certainly to die together – the man who lies with his father's wife and the woman, too – because they have done something impure on the earth. There is to be nothing impure before our God within the nation that he has chosen as his own possession. Again it is written a second time: "Let the one who lies with his father's wife be cursed because he has uncovered his father's shame." All of the Lord's holy ones said: "So be it, so be it." Now you, Moses, order the Israelites to observe this command because it is a capital offense and it is an impure thing. To eternity there is no expiation to atone for the man who has done this; but he is to be put to death, to be killed, and to be stoned and uprooted from among the people of our God. For any man who commits it in Israel will not be allowed to live a single day on the earth because he is despicable and impure. (*Jubilees*, 33:9b–14, trans. VanderKam, 221–22)

To the extent that Jubilees appears to cite biblical verses, it does so by way of paraphrase and amalgamation, rather than direct citation and exegesis. Such a severe divine judgment of sexual intercourse between a man and his father's wife, deriving as it appears to in Jubilees from the negative example of Reuben, begs the question of why Scripture records no direct punishment of Reuben (or of Bilhah, but she is portrayed as having been the innocent and passive victim of Reuben's impulsive lust). Nevertheless, the legal elaboration of our retold narrative appears to allow no room for extenuating circumstances (nor for expiation and atonement), at least not for the male. Jubilees anticipates and answers this question directly:

> They are not to say: "Reuben was allowed to live and (have) forgiveness after he had lain with the concubine-wife of his father while she had a husband and her husband – his father Jacob – was alive." For the statute, the punishment, and the law had not been completely revealed to all but (only) in your time as a law of its particular time and as an eternal law for the history of eternity. There is no time when this law will be at an end nor is there any forgiveness for it; rather both of them are to be uprooted among the people. On the day on which they have done this they are to kill them. (Jubilees 33:15–17, trans. VanderKam, 222)

Although Reuben's deed was egregious and the law prohibiting it was in existence at the time, it had not yet been "completely revealed to all," for which reason Reuben was not punished with death, but was forgiven (presumably by God). However, from the time of the revelation at Mt. Sinai, and forever after, the law was to be eternal and uncompromisable, without the possibility of forgiveness. Reuben's deed, although not punished in his time, was to be a reminder to Israel of the grave consequences of such behavior:

> For all who commit it on the earth before the Lord are impure, something detestable, a blemish, and something contaminated. No sin is greater than the sexual impurity which they commit on the earth because Israel is a holy people for the Lord its God. It is the nation which he possesses; it is a priestly nation; it is a priestly kingdom; it is what he owns. No such impurity will be seen among the holy people. (*Jubilees*, trans. VanderKam, 223–24)[16]

While these passages fill in many details "missing" from the biblical narrative traces, providing a continuous narrative with its legal context and implications, notably absent is any indication of Reuben's own view of his deed once committed (except that he "flees the scene of the crime"). While Bilhah expresses her shame and Jacob expresses his anger, Reuben does not here express any regret or contrition. If he is pardoned, it is more on a "technicality" than in response to any expression of remorse or petition by him for forgiveness. Simply put, the aim of the storyteller here is to impress upon his audience how detestable to God is Reuben's deed, and to stress how, post-Sinai, Israel's covenantal identity as a holy people is tied to its complete avoidance of such acts of sexual depravity and impurity.

Equally noteworthy, however, is the form of rewritten Scripture, both narrative and legal and especially their intertwining, that our text takes. While it includes many scriptural allusions and undoubtedly incorporates traditions that derive from a long history of scriptural interpretation, it does not formally engage Scripture, nor rhetorically invite its readers/auditors to engage in questions of scriptural interpretation. Rather, it presents itself as an esoteric revelation, whose intended or assumed relation to Scripture is never made clear.

From all of pre-rabbinic Jewish literature, we only have one example, albeit very brief, of a direct commentary on the scriptural texts relating to Reuben and Bilhah. In a fragment from the Dead Sea Scrolls (4Q252 [*Commentary on Genesis*] IV, 3–7), employing the terminology of *pesher*, we find the following:

> The blessings of Jacob: "Reuben, you are my firstborn and the firstfruits of my strength, excelling in dignity and excelling in power. Unstable as water, you shall no longer excel. You went up unto your father's bed. Then you defiled it. On his bed he went up!" [Genesis 49:3–4a]. [*vac*] Its interpretation (*pishro*) is that he reproved him for when he slept with Bilhah his concubine.[17]

Although the verse cited contains several minor variants from the Masoretic text, its identity as a biblical verse is unmistakable. Jacob's "blessing" of Reuben is, rather, a reproof of Reuben for having slept with Bilhah. The unclear scriptural phrase "you went up unto your father's bed" is explained as referring to Reuben's sin of having "lain" with Bilhah (Genesis 35:22). Although we might say that one verse (Genesis 49:4) is explained in terms of another (Genesis 35:22), the *pesher* comment does not do so explicitly by citing the latter, only by decoding the former. Nor is there anything particularly ideological or sectarian in this comment, just a deictic statement of signification. Unlike the "rewritten Bible" of the Book of Jubilees, it formally cites the scriptural verse and provides its interpretive decoding, with the terminological marker *pishro* clearly differentiating between the two.

Turning now to one of our earliest rabbinic midrashic collections, the Sifrei to the Book of Deuteronomy (redacted around mid–third century C.E.), we find six sections dealing, whether directly or indirectly, with Reuben's sin with Bilhah.[18] They mostly emphasize Reuben's confession of and/or repentance for his deed, but fill in other aspects of the narrative as well. Unlike Jubilees, they appear less interested in the actual deed itself, but rather in Reuben's (and secondarily, Jacob's) response. While the midrashic commentary, like Jubilees, fills in "missing" narrative details, it does so structurally and rhetorically through exegetical engagement with the biblical verses, so noticeably missing in Jubilees. The first passage that we will examine appears in the context of commentary to Deuteronomy 6:4 (the opening verse of the *Shema*). The midrash portrays Jacob worrying that his twelve sons would not all prove worthy as covenantal inheritors, focusing in particular on Reuben:

> Similarly, Scripture says, "And it came to pass, while Israel stayed in that land, that Reuben went and lay with Bilhah, his father's concubine, and Israel heard of it" [Genesis 35:22]. When Jacob heard about it, he was shaken and said, "Woe is me! Perchance an unworthy one has appeared among my children." Forthwith, however, the Holy One informed him that Reuben had repented, as it is said, "Now the sons of Jacob were twelve" [Genesis 35:22]. Did we not know that they were twelve? Rather, this indicates that it was made known by the Holy One that Reuben had repented. Hence we learn that Reuben fasted all his days, as it is said, "And they sat down to eat bread" [Genesis 37:25]. Could one ever imagine that the brothers would sit down to eat bread without their eldest brother? [Yet he was in fact not with them on that occasion], thereby teaching you that he fasted all his days, until Moses came along and accepted him because of his repentance, as it is said, "Let Reuben live, and not die" [Deuteronomy 33:6]. . . . Hence it is said, "And Israel bowed down upon the bed's head" [Genesis 47:31]. Did he actually bow upon the bed's head? Rather, he gave thanks and praise to God that unworthy ones had not issued from him. Some say that "And Israel bowed down upon the bed's head" [means that he gave thanks] for Reuben's repentance.[19]

This passage displays characteristics of early rabbinic midrash not found, or at least not in combination, in pre-rabbinic forms of scriptural interpretation: dialogical (question and answer) rhetoric, multiple interpretations, and interpreting one verse through the juxtaposition and interpretation of others. The midrash attends to the unusual joining of three statements in a single verse: Reuben lay with Bilhah; Jacob heard of it; the sons of Jacob were twelve. As previously noted, the final juxtaposition is particularly strange, especially for its Masoretic punctuation, which essentially makes one verse of two. According to our midrash, this juxtaposition is taken to mean: Even after Reuben's brazen sexual sin and affront against his father, he was still counted among Jacob's twelve sons, a sign that he had repented (and had, presumably, been divinely forgiven).[20]

We are next told that the form of Reuben's penitence was lifelong fasting, as is exegetically derived from another scriptural incident, the sale of Joseph. In Genesis 37:21–22, Reuben convinces his brothers not to kill Joseph but to throw him alive into a pit. From 37:29, we learn that Reuben was absent when his brothers sold Joseph to the Ishmaelites, prior to which they ate together a meal, presumably without Reuben. The Bible is silent as to where Reuben had gone or for what purpose. The midrash assumes that the brothers would not normally have eaten without their eldest brother being present, from which it concludes that he must have been fasting. As a final proof that Reuben had repented, our midrash adduces Deuteronomy 33:6, Moses' blessing, which is understood to relate to Reuben the individual, rather than the tribe. Since the phrase "Let Reuben live, and not die" would seem to contain a redundancy, it is commonly glossed by the rabbis to mean "live *in this world*, and not die *in the world to come*," thereby signifying Moses' expectation or petition that Reuben's repentance would earn him eternal life in the world to come. Finally, among three interpretations of Jacob's bowing prior to his death at the head of his bed (Genesis 47:31), one is that he was giving thanks that the defilement of his bed by Reuben (Genesis 49:4; 1 Chronicles 5:1) had been rectified through Reuben's repentance.

Let us look at the Sifrei's commentary to Deuteronomy 33:6, Moses' blessing of Reuben. Among several interpretations of this verse we find the following:

> Another interpretation: "Let Reuben live" – because of his action in the matter of Joseph – "and not die" – because of his action in the matter of Bilhah. R. Hananiah ben Gamaliel says: Merit is never replaced by guilt, nor guilt by merit, except in the cases of Reuben and David. ... The Sages, however, say: Merit is never replaced by guilt, nor guilt by merit, but one receives a reward for (performance of) religious duties and punishment for transgressions. What then is the meaning of "Let Reuben live, and not die"? It indicates that Reuben repented. Rabban Simeon ben Gamaliel says: Reuben was saved from that sin and did not commit that deed. Is it possible that he who was to stand at the head of the Tribes on Mount Ebal and say, "Cursed be he that lieth with his father's wife" [Deuteronomy 27:20], would commit such a deed? What then does Scripture mean by "Because thou wentest up to thy father's bed" [Genesis 49:4]? He avenged his mother's shame.[21]

The midrash resolves the possible redundancy between "live" and "not die" by glossing the verse so that each refers to a different incident in Reuben's life. In so doing, it responds to the implied question of why Reuben was not punished with death for his egregious sin: His meritorious deed of saving Joseph's life counteracted the consequences of his sin with Bilhah. According to R. Hananiah ben Gamaliel, this would be one of only two exceptions (the other being David) to the rabbinic rule that merit does not cancel guilt, but that each receives its appropriate recompense. The "sages," however, in denying any such exceptions to the rule, must provide an alternative solution: that Reuben's repentance for his sin with Bilhah canceled (or lessened) its consequences, independently of his meritorious saving of Joseph's life. As we have seen, emphasis on Reuben's repentance for his sin with Bilhah is a recurring theme in the *Sifrei to Deuteronomy*, as throughout rabbinic literature. However, an altogether different and, in a sense, opposite solution is attributed to R. Simeon ben Gamaliel: that Reuben did *not* commit adultery with Bilhah (but only appeared to have done so). R. Simeon derives this from Moses' instructions to the tribes to perform a ritual of blessings and curses after entering the land and arriving at Mts. Gerizim and Ebal (Deuteronomy 27:11–26), according to which the tribe of Reuben is the first mentioned of the tribes to stand on Mt. Ebal and utter the "curses" (27:13), one of which is specifically against lying with one's father's wife (27:29). If so, then Reuben's mounting Bilhah's bed must be interpreted to refer to something other than sexual intercourse, since, to quote the Mishnah, "Whoever is suspected of something, may neither judge nor bear witness with respect to it" (M. Bekhorot 4:10, 5:4). The tradition here alluded to ("He avenged his mother's shame") is elsewhere articulated more fully as follows: While Rachel was alive, Leah, Reuben's mother, was aggrieved because Jacob kept Rachel's bed next to his. However, when Rachel died, Jacob moved the bed of Bilhah (Rachel's maidservant) next to his. Reuben, seeking to avenge his mother's "shame," removed or overturned Bilhah's bed and replaced it with Leah's. Thus, although Reuben may have acted improperly toward his father (or father's bed), his misdeed was not nearly as egregious as adultery, and was committed, understandably, out of sympathy for his mother's treatment by Jacob. It should be noted that this idea, that Reuben did *not* sin sexually with Bilhah, is unattested in pre-rabbinic sources.

We are left, both within the Sifrei's commentary and in rabbinic midrash more broadly, with two main approaches to Reuben's sin, which, while responding to identical scriptural difficulties and ambiguities, arrive at very different (if not contradictory) conclusions, in part by employing different intertextual scriptural traces:

1.　Reuben, through his acknowledgment of and repentance for his terrible sin with Bilhah, achieved forgiveness and, ultimately, eternal reward, serving thereby as a principal model of repentance for all.
2.　Reuben only appears to have sinned egregiously, not possibly having done that which Scripture seems to impute to him, but actually having acted sympathetically, thereby preserving his meritorious reputation, even if reduced by a much lesser wrong.

Compared to its Second Temple antecedents (limited as they are), the midrashic commentary is far less coherent in thematic and narrative terms and far more inclusive of a variety of interpretations. These two exegetical trajectories, already present in the Sifrei, one of our earliest rabbinic commentaries, highlight two of rabbinic Judaism's central teachings, especially in the aftermath of the destruction of the Second Temple: Human repentance and divine forgiveness are possible in the absence of sacrificial worship and priestly officiation; all of the "children of Israel," that is, all of the descendants of Jacob, are worthy bearers of that name and inheritors of the prophetic promises of redemption, both as individuals and as a covenantal polity.

From this small case study of interpretive texts on a single scriptural topic, it should be clear that early rabbinic midrash shares much with Second Temple antecedents in its interpretation of Scripture and in many of the exegetical traditions that it thereby incorporates. Of course, tracing direct lines of filiation among these traditions and accounting for their differences in terms of linear development is much more difficult (if not impossible) to accomplish, given the fragmentary nature of our extant evidence and our uncertainty regarding possible bridges between their respective tradents. However, aside from such similarities for which we cannot fully account, there are also significant differences between our Second Temple and early rabbinic sources, not only in content and emphasis but especially in their formal and rhetorical self-presentation. This is especially true with respect to the dialogical manner in which the rabbinic midrashic sources explicitly engage questions of scriptural meaning, and rhetorically draw their student auditors into that interpretive process, in this case with remarkably open-ended results. Not surprisingly, Louis Ginzberg, in producing a modern "rewritten Bible," incorporates a vast array of traditions concerning Reuben's sin and repentance, but homogenizes the particularities of their textual practices (not to mention their historical contexts), both between Second Temple and rabbinic sources and among the latter, so as to create the impression of a common tradition across historical time and social setting.[22]

CONCLUSION

In the end, we need not choose absolutely between developmental and morphological models of comparison, since the two are mutually conditioned. The structures and practices of both pre-rabbinic and rabbinic scriptural interpretation are hardly static over time, but undergo internal developments that should be viewed, at least in part, as correlates to broader changes in historical and cultural circumstances. Conversely, the very different discursive practices by which each textual community responds exegetically to those changing circumstances cannot be reduced simply to historical reflexes but should be viewed as correlates to each community's social structure and religious ideology, that is, how it is organized and understands itself, often in contradistinction to other groups (whether real or imagined), and always in relation to Israel's sacred history, both past and future. Precisely because these two sets of correlates are so deeply intertwined, it is often difficult, if not impossible, to isolate one from the other. For example, to what extent does the rabbinic favoring of dialogical scriptural commentary, in contrast to the more deictic forms of scriptural interpretation in "rewritten Bible" and Qumran *pesher*, reflect the decentered and oral rabbinic structures of rabbinic master–disciple study circles, the deferred eschatology of rabbinic Judaism in the aftermath of the destruction of the Second Temple and the failed Bar Kochba revolt, or the rise of scriptural commentary as a means of self-definition and self-justification within nascent Christianity? Need we choose among, or be limited to, these? Furthermore, even at a given place and time in each textual community's history, a variety of exegetical strategies and rhetorical formations must have coexisted in the contexts of varied pedagogical domains. For example, the textual practices required for the teaching of new members to textual communities would have been different from those required for the training of communal leaders or officiants. How each community employed Scripture in the context of worship would have been different from its employment in the context of study, even as these domains might have intersected and overlapped. As we have seen, homogenized constructs of "common tradition," linear models of progressive development, and reductive models of cultural historical determinism, while attractive for their simplicity, do not do justice to the complexity of our puzzle, many parts of which, of course, remain missing.

Notwithstanding the severe limitations imposed on such comparative ruminations by the partial and fragmentary nature of our extant sources, it should be manifestly clear that the relatively recent dramatic increase in the size and spectrum of the textual trove of ancient Jewish scriptural interpretation has exponentially enriched our ability to contextualize early rabbinic midrash – socially, culturally, and intellectually – within the continuous history of the Jewish exegetical engagement with the Hebrew Bible.

Notes

1. See Josephus, *Life* 191; *Jewish War* 1.110; 2.162. Cf. Acts 22:3; 26:5.
2. For references to earlier treatments along these lines, see Steven D. Fraade, "Looking for Legal Midrash," in Stone and Chazon 1998, p. 62 n. 7. For the most recent attempts to emphasize the similarities, rather than differences, between rabbinic *midrash* and Qumran interpretation, see Mandel 2001 and Schiffman 2005.
3. See, in particular, the essays collected in the following volumes: Mulder 1988; Sæbø 1996; Stone 1984.
4. Ginzberg, *Legends of the Jews* (trans. Henrietta Szold and Paul Radin, 7 vols., Philadelphia: Jewish Publication Society of America, 1913–38). It has now been reissued in a new edition with an excellent introduction by David Stern. See Ginzberg 2003. For the cultural-historical context and significance of Ginzberg's Legends, see Rebecca Schorsch, "The Making of a Legend: Louis Ginzberg's Legends of the Jews" (Ph.D. diss., University of Chicago, forthcoming).
5. Kugel 1990, p. 267.
6. Thus, their designation as *"midreshei halakhah"* (legal *midrashim*) is somewhat of a misnomer. For further discussion, see Fraade 1983, pp. 255–56 n. 21, 298.
7. See *Jewish Antiquities* 1.25, 192; 3.94, 143, 205, 218, 230, 257, 259; 4.198, 302; 20.268. Instead, in *Jewish Antiquities* 4, he digresses from his narrative history to present "these laws and this constitution (*politeia*) recorded in a book" by Moses (4.194) at his death, based mainly on the laws of Deuteronomy 12–26.
8. For a fuller discussion of this point, in comparison to early rabbinic *midrashim*, see Fraade, "Looking for Legal Midrash."
9. For a review, see T. H. Lim 2002, pp. 48–51.
10. For specifics, with further bibliography, see Fraade, "Looking for Legal Midrash"; and idem, "Looking for Narrative Midrash at Qumran."
11. See David Stern, "Introduction to the 2003 Edition," in Ginzberg 2003, esp. pp. xix, xxii.
12. See in particular, Cohen 1984.

13. For much fuller treatments of the variety of interpretations of this and related verses, see the following: Shinan 1983; Kugel 1995 and 1998, pp. 463–69; Rosen-Zvi 2006.

14. This is one of the unseemly biblical passages to be read but not translated (at least not in public), according to M. Megillah 4:10 and T. Megillah 3:35. Josephus (*Jewish Antiquities* 1.21.3, §343–44), in his retelling of biblical history, skips this incident altogether.

15. Another account is found in the Testament of Reuben 1:6–10, 3:11–15, 4:2–4, which while sharing several elements with Jubilees, has others that are distinctive. However, the dating and provenance of the Testaments of the Twelve Patriarchs are uncertain, which cannot, in their present form, be assigned to a Second Temple Jewish context.

16. For the association of sexual sin with moral impurity in the Book of Jubilees, see J. Klawans (2000), pp. 46–48 and C. Hayes (2002), p. 76, 245 n. 39.

17. For text and translation, see Brooke et al., Qumran Cave 4. XVII: Parabiblical Texts, Part 3, pp. 203–4.

18. See Sifrei Devarim 2, 31, 329, 347, 348, 355 (ed. Finkelstein, pp. 10, 52–53, 379, 404–5, 405, 420).

19. For the Hebrew text, see Sifrei Devarim, *Va-'ethanan*, pis. 31, to Deuteronomy 6:4 (ed. Finkelstein, pp. 52–53). The translation follows, with minor adjustments, *Sifre: A Tannaitic Commentary on the Book of Deuteronomy*, 57–78.

20. Compare Sifrei Devarim 2 (ed. Finkelstein, p. 10), where Jacob's silence upon hearing of Reuben's sin, and his delay until just prior to his death before reprimanding him, is explained in terms of Jacob's fear that by reprimanding Reuben immediately he would alienate him and send him running instead to his uncle Esau).

21. Sifrei Devarim 347, to Deuteronomy 33:6 (ed. Finkelstein, pp. 404–5).

22. See *Legends of the Jews*, 1:415–416; 2:12, 24, 36, 131, 137, 140–41, 190–92, 192; 3:58–59, 199, 220, 223, 232, 452–53, 455, 462; 4:360. Although, unlike Ginzberg, James Kugel gives considerable attention to the exegetical inner workings of post-biblical sources, his treatment of our subject is similar to Ginzberg's in his emphasis on a common tradition across time and context and his ahistorial blending of sources in disregard to their formal and rhetorical particularities.

6 The Judaean Legal Tradition and the *Halakhah* of the Mishnah

SHAYE J. D. COHEN

The subject of this essay is the prehistory of mishnaic law. Sixty-two of the sixty-three tractates of the Mishnah treat questions of *halakhah*, that is, law, practice, and ritual. When the Mishnah talks about blessings and tithes, Sabbath and festivals, marriage and divorce, torts (physical and financial damages) and contracts, slaughter and sacrifice, or purity and impurity, it devotes almost exclusive attention to the exposition of law, at great length and in great detail. Whence come all these laws and all these details?

The Mishnah itself is not interested in this question. The opening paragraphs of Mishnah Avot, the lone mishnaic tractate not devoted to legal matters, presents the theory of a rabbinic chain of tradition, stretching via master and disciple from Moses on Mt. Sinai to the mishnaic sages themselves:

> Moses received Torah at Sinai and transmitted it to Joshua; Joshua to the elders; the elders to the prophets; the prophets transmitted it to the Men of the Great Assembly.... Simeon the Righteous was one of the last of the Men of the Great Assembly.... Antigonus of Sokho received [Torah] from Simon the Righteous ... [four more links in the chain are given] ... Hillel and Shammai received [Torah] from them.... Rabban Yohanan ben Zakkai received [Torah] from Hillel and Shammai.... Rabban Yohanan ben Zakkai had five disciples: R. Eliezer b. Hyrcanus, R. Joshua b. Hannaniah [and three others].

The chain of rabbinic tradition links Moses to R. Eliezer and R. Joshua, who are cited frequently throughout the Mishnah.

Like Moses, the mishnaic sages teach and transmit "Torah." What exactly is meant by "Torah" is not clear. A minimal definition might be "rabbinic authority," so that Avot is saying that the mishnaic sages have the authority of Moses to teach and to issue legal decisions. They sit "on the seat of Moses" and teach "with authority" (Matthew 7:29 and 23:2).

In this conception, Moses will not necessarily have known all the details of mishnaic law, but his ignorance does not prevent the mishnaic sages from believing that they were working within a Mosaic framework. Or perhaps "Torah" here should be understood maximally: As the Talmud would later explain, "any teaching ever to be taught by a disciple before his master was already revealed to Moses at Mount Sinai" (Y. Peah 2:6, 17a, and parallels). In this conception, all of mishnaic law – indeed all of rabbinic law as explicated by the talmudic sages of Antiquity, and later by the interpreters and legal codifiers of the Middle Ages – was known to Moses. But whether minimal or maximal, the notion of Torah in Avot seems to adumbrate the talmudic idea of "the Oral Torah," according to which Moses at Mount Sinai received two Torahs from God, the Written Torah, what we call the Five Books of Moses, the Pentateuch, Genesis through Deuteronomy, and "the Oral Torah," which supplemented and explicated the Written Torah. According to various passages in the Talmud, the contents of the Mishnah derive from the Oral Torah.[1]

In contrast with the Talmud, the Mishnah itself nowhere advances the theory of the Oral Torah and, aside from the opening paragraphs of Avot, seldom calls itself "Torah" or associates itself with either Moses or Mount Sinai. A few passages attribute some specific laws to "Moses at Mount Sinai"; why just these laws are singled out for such attribution is not clear. Similarly, a few laws are attributed to specific historical moments (e.g., "at first they used to do *x*, later they did *y*") or are labeled "enactments" instituted by specific sages in response to specific conditions.[2] All of these scattered passages do not add up to much; if gathered together, they would equal in length one mishnaic chapter, perhaps two (the Mishnah contains 523 chapters). These bits and pieces are important for a study of the Mishnah's conception of its own history, but are of only marginal importance for our question.

What, then, are the origins of mishnaic law? I discuss here seven possible sources: 1) Scripture; 2) the legal traditions of the ancient world; 3) the common practice (or "common Judaism") of Jewish society; 4) the realia of Jewish institutions; 5) the teachings of priests; 6) the teachings of pietists and sectarians. In each of these first six cases, I seek extra-mishnaic evidence for mishnaic rulings and technical terms.[3] For the purposes of this essay, I ignore the Mishnah's attribution of specific rulings to various named authorities, and I ignore, too, the abundant evidence that the editor of the Mishnah has adopted and adapted pre-existing collections of material. I take all of the Mishnah as a single undifferentiated unit and, in my quest for the prehistory of mishnaic law, I look outside the Mishnah for attestation of rulings and terms found in the Mishnah. After treating those elements that entered the Mishnah from sources 1 through 6, I turn to 7) the contribution of the mishnaic sages themselves.

I. SCRIPTURE

The rabbinic sages, like all other Jews of Antiquity, understood the Bible to be timeless, eternally valid, and authoritative. Every detail of the text was significant, since the Bible is the record of divine speech. For knowledge of religious law and practice, they looked first and foremost to the Torah, the Five Books of Moses. Other Jews did the same: Pre-rabbinic writings of the Second Temple Period, such as *Jubilees*, the *Temple Scroll*, the *Covenant of Damascus*, and the essays of Philo of Alexandria, all relate to the Torah in different ways for different purposes, but all use the Torah, whether explicitly or implicitly, as the basis for their presentations of Jewish law.[4] One of the striking features of the Mishnah, however, is its relative independence from the Torah.

The Mishnah is neither a commentary on, nor a paraphrase of, the Torah. It does not, as a rule, cite the Torah or speak in biblical Hebrew. Nor is it organized along the lines of the Torah. But every so often, for reasons that are not very clear, the Mishnah departs from its usual practice and explicitly adduces Scripture, usually the Torah, in order to buttress a legal ruling. Here, for example, is M. Berakhot 1:3:

> The House of Shammai say: in the evening everyone should recline when they recite [the *Shema*], but in the morning they should stand up, as it says *when you lie down and when you rise up* [Deuteronomy 6:7]. But the House of Hillel say: everyone recites it in his own way, as it says *and when you walk by the way* [Deuteronomy 6:7]. Why then is it said *when you lie down and when you rise up*? At the hour that people lie down and at the hour that people usually rise up. (Author's emphasis.)

The Houses of Shammai and Hillel debate the proper posture required during the recitation of the *Shema*,[5] a question that depends on the proper exegesis of Deuteronomy 6:7, one of the verses of the *Shema*. The Shammaites say that the phrase *when you lie down and when you rise up* should be understood literally, so that in the evening one should recline when reciting the *Shema*, and in the morning one should stand.

The Hillelites, however, argue that the Torah intended to legislate not the posture of the reciter but the time of the recitation. The *Shema* is to be recited in the evening (*when you lie down*) and in the morning (*when you rise up*); as to posture, the reciter may stand or recline or adopt any other desired position. Here then is a good example of a simple legal debate anchored in simple scriptural exegesis; each side explains how its ruling is consonant with the demands of the Torah. Passages like this are relatively rare in the Mishnah, for the Mishnah on the whole is not interested in showing how its laws are to be attached to, or extracted from, the words of the Torah.[6]

Far more common than explicit citation of the Torah is implicit reference. *Jubilees* and the *Temple Scroll* paraphrase the laws of the Torah; some scholars have even argued that these two works are presenting themselves as the authentic Torah, the transcript of the real revelation of God to Moses. The Mishnah does not advance such claims about itself, nor does it paraphrase the Torah. And yet, some sections of the Mishnah stand in such close relationship with the Torah that barely a line of the former can be understood without knowledge of the relevant verses of the latter. These verses, although essential for understanding the text, are not quoted; the editor of the Mishnah assumes that the reader will supply what is missing.

A good example of this intertextual relationship between Mishnah and Torah is provided by M. Kilayim 8:1:

> It is forbidden to sow diverse kinds in a vineyard . . . and it is forbidden to make any use of them.
>
> It is forbidden to sow diverse kinds of seeds . . . but they are permitted as food, and all the more so [are they permitted] for use.
>
> Diverse kinds of garments are permitted in all respects; it is forbidden only to wear them.

The Torah prohibits *kilayim*, "diverse kinds," that is, the mixing of like with unlike, whether in a field, a vineyard, or a garment. The Mishnah juxtaposes the three prohibitions, but differentiates among them as to their severity. Mixed seed may be sown in neither vineyard nor field, but the product of mixed seed in a vineyard is forbidden to be eaten or used, whereas the product of mixed seed in a field is permitted to be eaten or used. In contrast, it is permitted to manufacture or to derive benefit from a garment made of wool and linen, but wearing it is forbidden. Why do these prohibitions differ so? The Mishnah does not explain, but the answer is obvious – so long as one knows the verses that stand behind the Mishnah. The prohibition of sowing two kinds of seed is expressed in identical language for both vineyard and field: *you shall not sow your field with diverse kinds of seed* (Leviticus 19:19) and *you shall not sow your vineyard with diverse kinds of seed* (Deuteronomy 22:9). But only with reference to the vineyard does the Torah add *else the crop ... and the yield of the vineyard may not be used* (Deuteronomy 22:9). Hence, concludes the Mishnah, the yield of mixed seed in a vineyard is prohibited from use, but not the yield of mixed seed in a field. Why the Torah should make such a distinction is not the Mishnah's concern. As to garments, the Torah says *you shall not put on cloth from a mixture of diverse kinds of material* (Leviticus 19:19) and *you shall not wear cloth combining wool and linen* (Deuteronomy 22:11). Hence, concludes the Mishnah, only wearing is prohibited; manufacture and profit are permitted. These mishnaic rulings cannot be understood without knowledge of the verses of the Torah that they tacitly interpret.

The Mishnah is filled with such examples. Like God in the world, the Torah in the Mishnah is Omnipresent yet Invisible (or, to be a little more accurate, almost Omnipresent and usually Invisible).[7] Are all of the laws of the Mishnah derived from the Torah like the two examples just cited? The Mishnah itself answers this question (M. Hagigah 1:8):

> The absolution of vows hovers in the air, for it has nothing [in the Torah] upon which to depend.
>
> The laws of the Sabbath, festal offerings and sacrilege – lo, they are like mountains hanging by a hair, for they are little Scripture but many laws.
>
> Civil laws, sacrifices, purities, impurities and prohibited marriages – they have something [in the Torah] on which to depend.

Some areas of law have a corpus of scriptural verses on which to depend. This Mishnah does not say that all of the mishnaic laws regarding civil matters, sacrifices, purities, impurities, and prohibited marriages in fact derive from Scripture; it says simply that the mishnaic laws in these areas have a basis in Scripture. Other areas of law, however, have little or no basis in Scripture. Whence come the laws regarding the absolution of vows, the Sabbath, festal offerings, and sacrilege? The Mishnah does not say.[8] The Talmud regularly tries to find a basis in the Written Torah for the laws of the Mishnah, occasionally arguing, as I discussed briefly, that they derive from the Oral Torah. This interpretive stance is theology, not history; it shows how the Talmud understands the Mishnah, but it does not necessarily give us usable historical information about the origins of the laws of the Mishnah. For that we need to look elsewhere.

2. THE LEGAL TRADITIONS OF THE ANCIENT WORLD

In some areas of law, notably civil law, marriage law, and documentary procedures, the Mishnah follows the legal traditions of the ancient Near East. There is nothing surprising about this; the "Covenant Code" of the Torah (Exodus 21–23) has numerous parallels and points of intersection with the great law codes of ancient Mesopotamia. The Mishnah does as well.[9] Here are three examples:

The Mishnah distinguishes between two classes of dowry property: *melog* (also vocalized *melug*) and "iron sheep" (*z'on barzel*). The husband has the right to use and profit from either type of property. The difference between them is that the husband is not liable for the value of the principal in the former (*melog*) but is liable for the value of the principal in the latter (iron sheep). If the husband divorces his wife, he must return her dowry to her; if the property has appreciated (or depreciated) in the interim, the profit (or loss) belongs to the wife if the dowry is melog, to the husband if the property is iron sheep (M. Yevamot 7:1). The word *melog* is not Hebrew but Akkadian, and is used to describe certain kinds of dowry property in documents as old as the second millennium B.C.E. Similarly, the term "iron sheep" to designate property of imperishable worth, guaranteed by the recipient to the owner, seems also to be of Mesopotamian origin. These terms do not appear in the Torah or in any pre-mishnaic Jewish document; we may presume that they survived in traditional scribal practice until they resurfaced in the Mishnah.[10]

Second example: "Double documents" have a long history in the ancient Near East. A scribe would write two copies of a document (e.g., a bill of sale) on the same sheet of parchment or papyrus, one above and one below with a space between them. The upper or "inner" copy would be rolled up, tied in place, and sealed; the lower or "outer" copy would be left open and available for inspection. If a dispute should arise about the wording of the contract, a court could open the upper, or inner, copy to verify the text. Two mishnaic passages refer to this scribal practice of "tying" a document (M. Gittin 8:9–10; Bava Batra 10:1–2). Several documents discovered in the Judaean desert were written in this manner, showing that this was standard scribal practice in Judaea in Roman times.[11] The practice is well attested in Ptolemaic Egypt, and has its origins in ancient Mesopotamia: A clay tablet bearing the inner text would be inserted into a clay envelope on which the outer text would be engraved.[12]

Third example: If a seller says "I am selling you a *kor*'s area of soil as measured by the rope," the piece of land involved must measure precisely one *kor's* area of soil. If it is greater, the buyer must return the excess; if it is less, the buyer may deduct the shortfall from his price. If, however, a seller says "I am selling you a *kor's* area of soil, whether less or more," according to M. Bava Batra 7:2 the actual amount of land transferred to the buyer does not have to equal one *kor* precisely and the price remains unaffected, so long as the deviation is within a given degree. The phrase "less or more" (or its equivalent) in land sale contracts appears in documents discovered in the Judaean desert, showing again that this was standard scribal practice in Judaea in Roman times. The phrase appears regularly in documents of Ptolemaic Egypt and has its origins in old Babylonian.[13]

In all these examples, the Mishnah does not even hint at the antiquity of its content. The institution of *melog* property, the practice of double documents, and the phrase "less or more" in land sale contracts all have a history of at least a millennium before the Mishnah. In material of this type, the Mishnah attests long-standing scribal tradition and practice.

These examples show that the Mishnah is, at least to some extent, a repository of legal traditions and procedures that reach back to ancient Mesopotamia. Whether the Mishnah also stands in a relationship with the legal traditions of the ancient Mediterranean world, notably Greece, the Hellenistic empires, and Rome, is much debated. Although the Mishnah was composed in a land that was in turn part of the Hellenistic empire of Egypt, the Hellenistic empire of Syria, and the Roman Empire, there is no clear sign that the legal systems of these empires contributed to the form or content of mishnaic law. It is easy to draw parallels and contrasts between mishnaic law and the law of the Hellenistic and Roman Empires, but it is not easy to determine influence or borrowing in either direction. Although the question remains open, surely it is a reasonable possibility that in some areas of law, notably civil law, marriage law, and documentary procedures, the Mishnah may have been influenced by the legal traditions of the Mediterranean, just as it was by the legal traditions of Mesopotamia.[14]

3. THE COMMON PRACTICE (OR "COMMON JUDAISM") OF JEWISH SOCIETY

The Mishnah's voice is prescriptive, not descriptive. It prescribes how things ought to be done; it does not describe how things actually are done.[15] However, as we have just seen, sometimes what the Mishnah prescribes was the actual practice of people in the ancient Near East long before the Mishnah itself was ever composed. In this section, we shall see that sometimes what the Mishnah prescribes was the actual practice of Jews even before the Mishnah itself was composed.

Since in the previous section I spoke about documentary practice, I continue that theme for a moment. The documents discovered in the Judaean desert reveal that most of the stipulations required by the rabbis for a marriage contract were, in fact, standard stipulations in Jewish marriage contracts; that the divorce formula required by the rabbis for a bill of divorce was in fact the standard formula in Jewish bills of divorce; and that clauses discussed by the Mishnah in connection with contracts for the sale of land were in fact standard clauses in such contracts.[16]

I turn now from the common Judaism of documents and civil law to the common Judaism of religious law. "Common Judaism" is an idea popularized by E. P. Sanders; this is the Judaism as lived by common people, that is, nonelites.[17] I draw my examples from the area of Sabbath practice.[18] Many different sources of the last centuries of the Second Temple Period describe, or purport to describe, how Jews actually observed the Sabbath, and these sources, for all of the inevitable difficulties involved in their interpretation, provide excellent data to compare with rabbinic Sabbath law. Here, for example, is a passage by Philo, the Jewish philosopher of Alexandria (first half of the first century C.E.). It is part of a polemic against the "extreme allegorists" (as they are usually known), Jews who contend that the laws of the Torah need not be observed so long as their "inner meaning" is respected. Among the laws that they do not observe are the laws of the Sabbath. Here is Philo (*On the Migration of Abraham* 91):

> It is quite true that the Seventh Day is meant to teach the power of the Unoriginate and the non-action of created beings. But let us not for this reason abrogate the laws laid down for its observance, and light fires or till the ground or carry loads or institute proceedings in court or act as jurors or demand the restoration of deposits or recover loans or do all else that we are permitted to do as well on days that are not festival seasons.

Even if, says Philo, we correctly understand that the purpose of the Sabbath is to teach us the immensity of God's power and the paltriness of our own, that is no excuse to ignore the provisions of Sabbath law. And what are the laws that we must not slight? Philo's list includes the following: a) not to light fires; b) not to till the ground; c) not to carry loads; d) not to institute proceedings in court or act as jurors; e) not to demand the restoration of deposits or the recovery of loans.

We may safely assume that Philo chose these five prohibitions because he believed them to be observed by everyone in the Alexandrian Jewish community, everyone, that is, except the "extreme allegorists" who were the targets of his polemic. We may also safely assume that these prohibitions were no less part of the common Judaism of Judaea as of Alexandria. These assumptions are confirmed by the testimony of Greek and Roman authors who comment that Jews do not a) light a fire or b) farm on the Sabbath. In addition, the emperor Augustus issued an edict guaranteeing the Jews the right to follow their ancestral laws; among these is the right not to be compelled to post bond (in a court) either on the Sabbath "or on the day of preparation for it, from the ninth hour." This edict coheres nicely with Philo's point d.[19] So, although Philo is an Alexandrian Jew writing in Greek, I am going to proceed on the assumption that his testimony is not so much Alexandrian as it is Jewish; that is, he could have written the same list of Sabbath prohibitions had he and his protagonists lived in Judaea – which, of course, they did not.[20]

Four of the five Philonic prohibitions appear in the Mishnah, but the contrasts between Philo and the Mishnah are just as great as the similarities. The prohibition of lighting a fire (a) is of course stated explicitly in Exodus 35:3; for the Mishnah, lighting a fire is one of the thirty-nine archetypal classes of labor prohibited on the Sabbath. Each class, in turn, subsumes a variety of labors that resemble it; this concept is unknown to Philo but is central to the Mishnah's conception of the Sabbath prohibitions, as I shall discuss. Tilling the ground (b) is also one of the Mishnah's thirty-nine archetypal labors, although this one does not have any scriptural support. The prohibition of carrying a burden (c), another of the Mishnah's archetypal labors, has scriptural support not from the Torah but from the Prophets (Jeremiah 17:21–22) and the Hagiographa (Nehemiah 13:15 and 13:19). The interesting point here is that Philo, like Jeremiah and Nehemiah, seems to understand the prohibition of carrying in terms of the labor involved in carrying a "burden," while the Mishnah ignores the concept of "burden" in order to redefine carrying in terms of transferring an object from one domain to another. This conception, too, is unknown to Philo, as I shall discuss.[21] The prohibition of judicial activity (d) appears in the Mishnah, but not as an archetypal labor, nor even as a subordinate labor. Rather, it appears as a *shevut*, a category of labor prohibited on the Sabbath not because it is considered "work" but because performing it will diminish the obligation to "rest" on the Sabbath day. As the Mishnah constructs things, *shevut* prohibitions are less severe than the prohibitions of archetypal labor and its extensions.[22] This distinction, too, is unknown to Philo.

Perhaps the most interesting item on Philo's list is the last (e), the prohibition of demanding the restoration of deposits or the recovery of loans. The Mishnah nowhere records such a prohibition, which has its closest analogues in the Book of Jubilees 50:8 and in the Qumran scrolls.[23] I can see two ways of explaining this lineup of sources. Perhaps Philo, in stating the prohibition of demanding the restoration of deposits or the recovery of loans, was following a pietistic strand of ancient Judaism; this prohibition was never part of the common Judaism of either Alexandria or Judaea. The first four items on his list were "common" or widely accepted, but this one was not. Why Philo chose to include it here, we do not know. Or perhaps this prohibition was part of the common Judaism of Alexandria and Judaea; on this point Philo, Jubilees, and the Qumran scrolls fairly represent Judaism as lived by the broad reaches of the Jewish population. The Mishnah, for whatever reason, simply did not record this prohibition. I do not know how to decide between these alternatives.

These are not the only Sabbath observances, of course, that made their way from "common Judaism" to the Mishnah. Others include the following: to light lamps before the onset of the Sabbath; not to walk more than a prescribed distance from one's home or from the city; to circumcise a baby boy on the eighth day even if that day be the Sabbath; not to engage in medical or healing activity.[24] No doubt there are many others.

4. THE REALIA OF JEWISH INSTITUTIONS

The Mishnah contains abundant legislation concerning the central institutions of the Israelite polity: the Temple, the high priesthood, the calendar, the Sanhedrin, and the king. I omit the synagogue from this list because in both Second Temple and mishnaic times, it was not yet a central institution. The rabbis imagine that they are in charge of all these institutions, that the Sanhedrin is a rabbinic operation, and that high priests and kings obey rabbinic instruction. These claims are, if not outright fantasy, much exaggerated.[25] And yet at least some of this material may preserve bona fide reminiscences of the Second Temple Period.

So, for example, the Mishnah states that just before and just after each Sabbath, three blasts of the *shofar* would be sounded in the Temple, "three blasts to make the people cease from labor, and three to separate between holy and profane." Josephus says almost exactly the same thing:

There was a place in the Temple, he says, "where one of the priests stood and gave a signal with a trumpet at the beginning of every seventh day, in the evening twilight, and also at the evening when the day was finished, in order to give notice to the people when they were to leave off work, and when they were to go to work again." A few years ago in the rubble of the Temple Mount, archaeologists discovered an inscription indicating the very spot where the priest once stood.[26]

Tractate Middot of the Mishnah gives a detailed description of the architecture and layout of the Temple, and tractate Tamid gives a detailed description of its daily operations. These two tractates, filled with nostalgia for "the good old days," combine accurate reminiscences of the Second Temple with revisionist history, wishful thinking, fantasies inspired by the last chapters of Ezekiel, and a blueprint for the messianic era. Separating these strands one from the other is not easy. But we may be sure that these tractates contain genuine historical reminiscences large and small. Among the latter is the Mishnah's reference to the glorious Temple gates donated by Nicanor of Alexandria, and the scarecrow (actually a scare-raven) on the roof of the Temple. The glorious gates are mentioned in Nicanor's epitaph, which was discovered in the nineteenth century; the scare-raven is mentioned by Josephus. Here, then, are two details that derive from the reality of the Second Temple.[27]

5. THE TEACHINGS OF THE PRIESTS

Well over half of the Mishnah concerns matters of interest to priests: the Temple, Temple rituals, sacrifices, offerings brought to the Temple, offerings given to priests, purity within the Temple, purity outside the Temple, impurity, purifications, and the like. We may safely assume that at least some of this material derives from priestly circles, whether in the Temple or outside it. These priestly circles may have even persisted after 70 C.E. In a few passages, the Mishnah takes notice of a "tribunal of priests" that dissents from, or of a priestly legal tradition that differs from, the rulings of the sages; these passages imply that a priestly legal identity persisted into mishnaic times (M. Shekalim 1:4, Ketubot 1:5, Rosh Hashanah 1:7, Eduyot 8:2). However, since the Torah itself devotes so much attention to priestly matters – modern scholars routinely identify two of the Torah's main sources as "P," the priestly document, and "H," the holiness code, which is closely related to P – even non-priests studied the priestly Torah as part of their intellectual curriculum. Furthermore, many modern scholars have argued that pietistic groups in the Late Second Temple Period affected priestly ways, behaving like priests even though they were not. If this is correct – the point has been much debated – the "priestly" material in the Mishnah may derive not from priests themselves but from lay groups acting like priests. So, it is hard to specify which rulings of the Mishnah derive from priestly circles, as opposed to pietistic circles. Nevertheless, I think it likely that such rulings are among the constitutive elements of the Mishnah.

A good candidate to be regarded as a priestly legacy in the Mishnah is the *mikveh*, or "immersion pool." The Torah states that a man with gonorrheal oozing can become pure if he washes his body *in living water* seven days after the oozing has stopped (Leviticus 15:13). A man who has experienced normal ejaculation may wash his entire body in water and become pure on the nightfall following his ejaculation (Leviticus 15:16). Similarly, a man being purified from the impurity of leprosy needs to wash his body in water (Leviticus 14:8–9). The Torah also states that *a spring or a cistern in which water is collected* is impervious to the impurity caused by the corpse of a creeping thing (Leviticus 11:36). From these meager scriptural foundations came the idea that a pool dug into bedrock, large enough for full-body immersion and filled with rain or spring water, could serve as surrogate "living water" so as to purify men[28] and objects from impurity caused by sexual discharge, leprosy, or other sources of impurity.[29]

The earliest such mikveh yet discovered is part of the Hasmonean palace complex at Jericho, to be dated to the second half of the second century B.C.E. Archaeologists in Israel have unearthed hundreds of additional *mikva'ot* dating from the last two centuries of the Second Temple Period and, after a gap in our documentation, from the third century C.E. and on.[30] The mikveh is a priestly, perhaps Hasmonean, invention. It appears first in a residence of the Hasmoneans, who of course were priests, and is frequently to be found in association with priests. Thus, mikvaot have been found in the houses of priests in Late Second Temple Jerusalem, near the entrances to the Jerusalem Temple, and at the settlement of Qumran, home to a group with a strong priestly self-definition and perhaps priestly origins. The appearance of the mikveh at Qumran is surprising since it is nowhere mentioned in the Qumran scrolls. In fact, the mikveh is absent from the entire literary record of the Second Temple Period. The oldest extant literary reference is in the Mishnah. If the schools, sects, and parties of the Second Temple Period debated one another about the efficacy and statutory requirements of the mikveh, neither Josephus nor the Qumran scrolls nor the New Testament nor any other text of the period documents it. This silence is particularly remarkable because archaeology shows that ancient Jews did indeed debate the requirements of the mikveh. For some Jews, a single deep immersion pool was all that was required; for others, however, a mikveh required a second, smaller "storage pool" (known as the *'oẓar*), which would, so we imagine, contain the actual "living" water (rainwater, we assume) that could be mixed with the regular water found in the large pool. The Mishnah endorses the two-pool system. In the absence of literary sources, we do not know exactly how either type of mikveh was filled and maintained, whether any specific group or school is to be associated with one mikveh type or another, or indeed what legal issues underlay the distinction between the two types.[31]

In any case, what is important for our purposes is that the mikveh is a legal innovation of the Late Second Temple Period, probably of priestly origin. The Mishnah devotes an entire tractate to the subject. Here is priestly Torah in the Mishnah.

6. THE TEACHINGS OF PIETISTS AND SECTARIANS

The pietists of the Second Temple Period also contributed to mishnaic law. Some of these pietists belonged to "sectarian" groups, that is, groups that separated themselves from society at large, declaring that they alone possessed the truth to which society at large aspired. Perhaps the most famous such group – perhaps the only such group in ancient Judaism – were the Jews of Qumran, the authors and readers of the Dead Sea Scrolls. Other pietists were not sectarians; whether alone or in groups, they simply affected a piety exceeding that of the average Jew. These pietists and sectarians, whose identification does not matter here, contributed to the Mishnah both positively and negatively. Positively, in the sense that some pietistic teachings entered the Mishnah and became part of mishnaic law. Negatively, in the sense that some mishnaic law is directed polemically against the teachings of pietists and sectarians.

An excellent example of a mishnaic law of pietist origin is the prohibition of moving certain kinds of implements on the Sabbath. Josephus reports the following about the Essenes (*Jewish War* 2.147):

> They are stricter than all Jews in abstaining from work on the seventh day; for not only do they prepare their food on the day before, so as not to kindle a fire on that one, but they do not even dare to move any implement or to defecate.

All Jews, says Josephus, abstain from work on the Sabbath; this is common Judaism. All Jews prepare their food a day ahead of time, that is, on Friday; indeed, in Jewish Greek, Friday came to be called *paraskeue*, "(the day of) preparation."[32] All Jews refrain from kindling a fire on the Sabbath. But the Essenes go farther than all other Jews in that they do not even dare to move any implement (or vessel, *skeuos* in Greek); since they do not move an implement on the Sabbath, they also do not defecate. (In the next sentences, Josephus goes on to describe the Essene process of defecation, which involves digging a hole with a shovel. Since a shovel is an implement, and since they do not move an implement on the Sabbath, they do not move their bowels either.)

No other text of the Second Temple Period attests the custom of not moving an implement on the Sabbath. Indeed, as Josephus says, in this regard the Essenes were exceptional, stricter than all other Jews. The Mishnah rejects the Essenes' blanket prohibition of moving any implement, but accepts the idea that some implements ought not to be moved. Such objects belong to the category called by the Talmud *mukzah*, "set aside (from use)." The opposite of *mukzah* is *mukhan*, "prepared." The mishnaic sages inherited the twin concepts of *mukhan* and *mukzah* from pietists of the Second Temple Period, but then developed these concepts in their own way, as I shall explain in the next section.

Pietistic rulings also influenced the Mishnah negatively; that is, the mishnaic sages sometimes rejected pietistic rulings. In one passage, the Mishnah records a series of debates between Pharisees and Sadducees; in other passages, the Mishnah acknowledges opposition to some rabbinic rulings from Boethusians, Sadducees, and anonymous others.[33] The historicity of these reports is unclear, but the Qumran scrolls show that pietistic groups did indeed dispute each other's rulings – in fact, two of the debates between the Pharisees and their opponents recorded by the Mishnah may recur in a Qumran document.[34] It is likely, therefore, that some rulings entered the Mishnah from pietistic circles, and that others were tacitly directed against pietistic rulings.[35]

7. THE CONTRIBUTION OF THE MISHNAIC SAGES

The six sources treated so far contributed many data points (laws, details, topics) to the Mishnah, but do not account for the Mishnah's distinctive concerns or turns of phrase. The Mishnah constructs legal categories, which often appear to be theoretical and abstruse, and then discusses, usually in great detail, the precise definitions and limits of those categories. It creates lists of analogous legal phenomena, and then proceeds to define and analyze every item on the list. It posits legal principles, and devotes much attention to those objects, cases, or times, which seem to be subject to more than one principle at once, or perhaps to none of the principles at all. These modes of thinking and writing, which can be characterized as *scholastic*, are endemic to the Mishnah, from one end to the other, and are not found in any pre-mishnaic Jewish document. Here we have come not to a source of mishnaic law but to the distinctive contribution of its creators.

Let us consider mishnaic law concerning the Sabbath. The Mishnah presents a list of thirty-nine prohibited labors, each of them called an *av melakhah*, which might be translated "archetypal category of labor." Anyone who accidentally performs a prohibited labor on the Sabbath is liable to a sin offering; anyone who accidentally performs a series of prohibited labors on the Sabbath is liable to a sin offering for each and every prohibited act. However, if the prohibited labors belong to a single archetypal category, the violator is liable to only a single sin offering. So, for example, plucking fruit, harvesting wheat, gathering grapes, collecting olives, cropping dates, garnering figs – all of these come under the single prohibited category of "harvesting" (T. Shabbat 9 [10]:17)."[36] The Mishnah assumes that these thirty-nine archetypal categories and all of the labors they subsume are prohibited under Torah law, notwithstanding the fact that the Torah says nothing about most of these thirty-nine, and knows nothing of the concept of archetypal categories. It is not just the Torah that knows nothing of these mishnaic ideas; this list of thirty-nine labors and this system of classification of archetypal labors and subordinate labors is unknown to Philo and all other pre-mishnaic documents.

The Mishnah argues that a violator of the prohibition of labor on the Sabbath is liable to punishment only if the prohibited labor is done a) in the manner in which the labor is normally performed; b) all at once, in a single act; c) by an individual;[37] d) with the intention of performing that labor and deriving benefit from the labor itself; e) sufficiently so as to exceed the legal minima of the prohibition.[38] If these and other like conditions are not met, the act in question is still prohibited (in the sense that a Torah-fearing Jew would not intentionally perform such an act on the Sabbath), but the actor is not liable for violating the prohibition. None of these subtle distinctions is attested in any pre-mishnaic document.

The Mishnah's treatment of the prohibition of "removing an item from one domain to another," in colloquial discourse called "the prohibition of carrying," is particularly rich and interesting. As I discussed in connection with Philo, this prohibition first appears not in the Torah but in Jeremiah 17:21–22 and Nehemiah 13:15, 19. Philo and his biblical predecessors conceive of this prohibition in terms of carrying a "burden."

In contrast, for the Mishnah, the legally determinative aspect of this prohibition is not whether the object that has been carried is a burden but rather whether it has been carried from one "domain" (*reshut*) to another. The Mishnah divides the landscape into "domains": the private domains of individual houses, the public domains of streets and markets, and shared areas like alleys and courtyards that are not quite public and not quite private. The prohibition of carrying is violated when one removes an object from one domain to another (M. Shabbat 1:1, 11:1; M. Eruvin passim). The Mishnah goes even further in eliminating the notion of "burden" from this prohibition. It declares that the prohibition is violated only if the object that has been carried is an object that people in general, or at least its carrier, value or use or keep; if it has no value or if it is too small to be used or if it is not worth keeping, then it is does not qualify as an "object" for the purposes of this prohibition. A Torah-fearing Jew would not remove even such a nonobject from one domain to another on the Sabbath, but incurs no liability for having done so (M. Shabbat 7:3–8:6, 9:5–10:1).

After investing enormous intellectual energy in defining domains and objects, the Mishnah invests even more intellectual energy in presenting a way to circumvent the whole prohibition. Through the process of *'eruv*, literally, "mixing," all the residents of a given block of private domains can link their properties together so as to permit carrying on the Sabbath from one domain (e.g., a house) to another and across the semiprivate domain (e.g., a courtyard) in between. Proper procedures, of course, must be followed for this *'eruv* to take effect, but wherever an *'eruv* is in operation one may ignore the prohibition of removing an object from one domain to another.[39]

Even within one's own domain certain objects may not be moved. These are *mukzah*, "set aside (from use)." Human intention is the key to the distinction between mukzah and non-mukzah objects. If an object has no permitted use on the Sabbath (e.g., a saw, a hammer); if on the eve of the Sabbath an object's owner could not have foreseen a use for it on the Sabbath and hence had no intention of using it; if an object did not yet exist or was not yet in one's possession on the eve of the Sabbath – any such object is said by the Talmud to be *mukzah*, "set aside (from use)" and may not be moved from one place to another, even within one's home. The Mishnah does not use the word *mukzah* in this sense, but certainly has the concept. The Mishnah devotes substantial attention to the laws of mukzah, in particular to the question of the portability of an item whose primary function is not permitted on the Sabbath but whose secondary function is permitted (e.g., may a hammer be picked up in order to smash the shell of a nut? [M. Shabbat 17–18; M. Betzah passim]). The opposite of *mukẓah* is *mukhan*, "prepared," is a category that is applied primarily, but not exclusively, to food. An item that was in one's possession on the eve of the Sabbath and that one intended to use on the Sabbath, or which, because of its very nature, is the sort of thing that a person might normally use on the Sabbath – such an object is mukhan and may be moved and used on the Sabbath (M. Shabbat 3:6, 17:1, and 24:4; also M. Betzah 3:4.). Food that is prepared before the Sabbath can be consumed on the Sabbath, provided that it meets the following two tests: first, at the moment that the Sabbath began the food was ready to be eaten; second, at the moment that the Sabbath began its owner intended – or can be assumed to have intended – to eat this food on the Sabbath.

I commented earlier that rabbinic *mukẓah* has its forerunner in the Essene refusal to move an implement on the Sabbath. A key difference between the Essene notion, as presented by Josephus, our sole source, and the rabbinic is that intention played no role whatever in the former but is central to the latter. For the Essenes, the prohibition of *mukẓah* is simple and absolute; for the mishnaic sages it is complicated and conditional. Similarly, the notion of *mukhan* has a forerunner in the literature of the Second Temple Period. *The Damascus Covenant* (10:22–23) records the following: "No man shall eat on the Sabbath day except that which is prepared (*mukhan*) and that which is lost in the field."

Here is a pre-rabbinic use of the term *mukhan* to refer to the food that may be consumed on the Sabbath, but note how the law of these pietists differs from the law of the mishnaic sages. For the pietists of the *Damascus Covenant*, the status of mukhan is simple and absolute; either food is ready to be eaten or it is not. Hence, fruit that is lying in a field is permitted on the Sabbath, since it is "prepared," that is, ready to be eaten.

For the sages, however, the status of mukhan is complicated and conditional; not all food that is ready to be eaten is mukhan. Fruit lying in a field is indeed ready to be eaten but nevertheless is not permitted to be eaten on the Sabbath, because it may have been attached to the tree on the eve of the Sabbath and no one could have possibly intended then to eat it on the Sabbath (since plucking fruit is prohibited).[40] By excluding intentionality, the Essene law of *mukẓah*, which prohibits moving any utensil or implement, is more severe than the mishnaic; by excluding intentionality, the *Damascus Covenant* law of *mukhan*, which permits the consumption of fruit that has fallen from a tree, is less severe than the mishnaic.

In sum, mishnaic Sabbath law is incredibly detailed and encyclopedic (thirty-nine prohibited categories, plus prohibitions subsumed under these categories, plus rabbinic extensions). It has a passion for cataloguing, classifying, and defining, (sometimes) basing its definitions not on real or empirical data, or for that matter on common sense, but on abstract principles and ideas (e.g., its definition of carrying on the Sabbath). It establishes minimal amounts or degrees that must be exceeded if the violator of a prohibition is to incur liability. It assigns great importance to human intention, with the result that identical acts by different actors can have different legal consequences, depending upon the actors' knowledge and intention.[41] It creates one legal theory (e.g., the prohibition of removing an item from one domain to another) only to counter it with another (e.g. *'eruv*).

Whence come laws of such complexity, categories of such abstraction, principles of such brilliance? Certainly not from Scripture; appeals to "the Oral Torah" cannot conceal the fact that nothing in the Torah points to the legislation, or even the kind of legislation, contained in Mishnah Shabbat. Nor from "common Judaism." Nor from priests, as far as we know. Nor pietists, who as a rule want simple categories with absolute answers. Certainly the pietists who wrote the *Damascus Covenant* and the Book of Jubilees did not develop Sabbath law in a manner akin to that of the Mishnah. Who then stands behind Mishnah Shabbat, and by extension all of mishnaic law? The obvious answer is the mishnaic sages themselves.

CONCLUSION: THE OLD AND THE NEW IN MISHNAIC LAW

The Mishnah is a compound of the old and the new, the traditional and the innovative. The Mishnah neither trumpets its oldness nor proclaims its newness. Not interested in its own origins, it says little about itself.

One obvious source for the Mishnah's laws is Scripture, the Torah in particular. We may be sure that virtually all ancient Jews who sought to find favor in God's eyes and to follow God's will studied the Torah in order to know what God expected of them. So it is no surprise that many laws of the Mishnah are derived from the Torah, and many tractates of the Mishnah are devoted to working out details of the Torah's legislation. Most of the time the Mishnah's relationship with Scripture is implicit, since the underlying verses are neither cited nor paraphrased. Sometimes the mishnaic law is the product of what might be called "simple exegesis," in which a surface reading of Scripture yields some obvious or almost obvious inferences. On other occasions the mishnaic law is the product of "complex exegesis," which involves the manipulation of Scriptural words, the application of hermeneutic rules, and deductions based on logical reasoning. The Talmud frequently explains the Mishnah by appeal to complex exegesis, but in most such cases it is hard to decide whether the exegesis precedes the law or the law precedes the exegesis.

In any case, since virtually all Jews with an interest in proper practice – lay preachers, priests, pietists, scribes – will have appealed to the Torah for support, the scriptural origins of mishnaic law will tell us nothing about the social group or groups from which the Mishnah derives. Nor can such derivation tell us whether a given law is a pre-mishnaic tradition or a mishnaic creation, since Jews read Scripture both before and after 70 c.e. If a mishnaic law can be shown to derive from a specific mode of reading Scripture, and if that mode of reading can be shown to derive from a specific group or a specific period, then of course the origins of that law would be established. But, as far as I know, convincing examples of this have yet to be adduced.[42]

Some bits and pieces of mishnaic law derive from the Second Temple Period, if not earlier. As we have seen, some laws of the Mishnah derive from the common practice of the ancient Near East or the common Judaism of Antiquity. Much of this material is scribal in character, concerning documentary formulas and the like, and we may assume that the scribes were the social medium by which these laws and practices were preserved and transmitted. We may assume, too, that the scribes of the Second Temple Period were the custodians of local case law, which in turn made its way into the Mishnah. Other laws have a priestly connection, either by dint of their subject matter or by their association with the Temple. We may assume that the Mishnah has drawn on the Torah of the priests and has accurately reported some of the rituals of the Temple. Perhaps the Mishnah contains some genuine historical reminiscences of other institutions of the Second Temple Period.

Last but not least in our survey of the sources of mishnaic law is the influence of the teachings of pietists and sectarians. The rabbis themselves are often said by modern scholars to have been the descendants of the Pharisees of Second Temple times; the evidence does not support a simple equation of the two, and in any case, the connections between (what is known of) pharisaic law and mishnaic law are neither numerous nor striking. But, as we have seen, there is a connection between the teachings of Second Temple pietists and mishnaic law. The twin concepts of *mukẓah* and *mukhan* entered the Mishnah from pietistic circles. Some mishnaic laws were formulated as responses to the teachings of one or another pietistic group.

Some mishnaic laws, then, derive from Second Temple times; does this fact imply that mishnaic law as a whole derives from Second Temple times? Some scholars have argued, or assumed, that this is so. In this conception, the mishnaic sages are primarily conservators, not innovators creating something new but traditionalists preserving something old. In this essay I have argued against this view, because what is striking about all the parallels between Second Temple sources and the Mishnah is that none of them parallels what is truly distinctive about the Mishnah. The mishnaic sages inherited this law, that practice, or that piece of information from their Second Temple Period predecessors, but they did not inherit the modes of argumentation, the dominant concerns, the logic, and the rhetoric that would come to characterize the Mishnah. These are conspicuously absent from Second Temple sources. The mishnaic sages were not conservators as much as they were innovators; mishnaic Judaism is a new and distinctive kind of Judaism.[43]

Notes

1. For discussion of these minimal and maximal views, see Halivni 1997. On the Mishnah as "Oral Torah," see Elizabeth Alexander's contribution to this volume. On the rabbinic "chain of tradition," see now Tropper 2004b.
2. Moses at Mount Sinai: M. Peah 2:6; Eduyot 8:7; Yadayim 4:3. At first they used to do *x*: Sheviit 4:1; Maaser Sheni 5:8; Bikkurim 3:7. Enactments: Rosh Hashanah 4:1–4; Gittin 4:3. (These lists of passages are representative, not exhaustive.)
3. This is the same method followed by Hayim Lapin in his excellent article (1995) (although, to be sure, Lapin also considers the Mishnah's attributions to named authorities).
4. See Steven Fraade's discussion of scriptural exegesis in these texts in the present volume.
5. The recitation of the *Shema* (Deuteronomy 6:4–9) may well have been part of "common Judaism" (see this essay, section 3), since it is referred to by Josephus, *Jewish Antiquities* 4.212. If we may trust M. Tamid 5:1, it was part of the Temple liturgy.
6. For a recent study of the Mishnaic citations of Scripture, see Samely 2002.
7. For a recent attempt to classify the various ways in which the Mishnah relates to the Torah, see Neusner 1999, 1–156.
8. M. Hagigah 1:8 has been much discussed; see, for example, Jaffee 2001, 85–87.

9. In general, see Greengus 1991; idem, "Law – Biblical and Ancient Near Eastern Law," *Anchor Bible Dictionary* 4.242–52, esp. 243–44; Gulak 1994.

10. The classic study is B. Levine 1968. See, too, Geller 1978, 237–40; Gulak 1994, 98–102; Levine 2002, 159–61.

11. *Discoveries in the Judaen Desert II* 1961, 243–47. By "documents discovered in the Judaean desert" I mean not the Qumran scrolls, also called the Dead Sea Scrolls, but rather the documents of the Bar Kokhba period found at Murabaat, Nahal Hever, and elsewhere. These documents are primarily nonliterary; they are marriage contracts, divorces, deeds of sale, and the like.

12. Greengus in *Anchor Bible Dictionary* 4.243; cf. Jeremiah 32:11.

13. Gulak 1994, 123.

14. The standard study in English is B. Cohen 1966. See, too, B. S. Jackson 1981, and Catherine Hezser, "The Codification of Legal Knowledge in Antiquity," in Schäfer 1998, 581–641.

15. The Mishnah also contains *ma'asim*, "anecdotes," which purport to describe the actions of real people. The historicity and historical utility of these reports are much debated. For discussion, see Shaye J. D. Cohen, "The Rabbis in Second Century Jewish Society," in Davies et al. 1999, Vol. 3, 922–90, esp. 961–71 and 980–87. For discussion of Talmudic *ma'asim*, see Hezser 1993.

16. Marriage contract formulas: P. Yadin 10 *in Judean Desert Studies: The Documents from the Bar-Kokhba Period in the Cave of Letters, Hebrew, Aramaic, and Nabatean-Aramaic Papyri* (Jerusalem: Israel Exploration Society, 2002), 118–41. *Discoveries in the Judaean Desert II*, 104–9 no. 19. Land sale formulas (the clause "and all that is in/on it"; cf. M. Bava Batra 4:9): *Discoveries in the Judaen Desert II*, 134–37 no. 25; *Discoveries in the Judaean Desert XXVII*, 34–37 no. 8a, and 123–29 no. 50.

17. See Sanders 1992, Part 2, esp. Chapters 11 and 12; see further Shaye J. D. Cohen, "'Common Judaism' in Greek and Latin Authors," *E. P. Sanders Festschrift* (forthcoming).

18. I have learned much from the following three studies: Doering 1999; Gilat 1992, 32–122, 249–61, and 301–62; Schiffman 1975, 84–133.

19. On the Sabbath in Greek and Latin writers, see R. Goldenberg 1979, and Schäfer 1997, 82–92.

20. Note, too, that four of Philo's five prohibitions are also stated by Jubilees 50:8–12 (lighting a fire, tilling a field, carrying a burden; Philo's prohibition of demanding the restoration of deposits seems to be included under Jubilees' prohibition of speaking of business matters).

21. Doering, 1999, 344, on Philo and burden. John 5:10 probably refers to carrying a burden; see Doering, 468–69.

22. M. Betzah 5:2 and Pesahim 6:2; T. Shabbat 16 (17):22. See Gilat 1992, 92, for a discussion of *shevut*. M. Sanhedrin 4:1 also assumes that judging is prohibited on the Sabbath.

23. *Covenant of Damascus* 10:17–19; cf. 4Q264a in *The Dead Sea Scrolls Reader: Part 1*, 178–79. For discussion, see Doering 1999, 138–43 and 345–46; Gilat 1992, 255–58.

24. Light lamps: M. Shabbat 2; Persius in M. Stern, *Greek and Latin Authors* no. 190; Seneca in Stern, *Authors* no. 188; Josephus, *Against Apion* 2.282. Sabbath limit: M. Eruvin (passim); Acts 1:12; perhaps Jubilees 50:12 (see Doering 1999, 87–94). Not to set out on a journey (?): Tibullus in Stern, *Authors* no. 126; Ovid in Stern, *Authors* no. 142; Doering, 288 n. 26. Circumcision: M. Shabbat 19; John 7:22. No healing: M. Shabbat 14:3–4; Mark 3:2 (and parallels).

25. Like the Mishnah, the *Temple Scroll*, too, is a utopian fantasy with its own calendar, Temple regulations, laws regarding the king, etc. For a comparison of the two, see Fraade 2003b, esp. 39–47.

26. M. Sukkah 5:5; Josephus, *Jewish War* 4.582; Doering 1999, 491 n. 63.

27. Gate of Nicanor: Josephus, *Jewish War* 5.201; M. Middot 1:4 (and elsewhere); Schürer 1979, 2.57 n. 170. Scare-raven on roof of the temple: M. Middot 4.6; Josephus, *Jewish War* 5.224; Lieberman 1950, 173.

28. Leviticus 15 requires only men to wash after sexual discharge; neither the menstruant nor the parturient needs to bathe in order to be purified. The only woman who is said by Leviticus to require washing is the woman who has had intercourse with a man (Leviticus 15:18). No document of the Second Temple Period attests the practice of immersion by a woman after menstruation. Nor does M. Niddah; the earliest reference to the immersion of menstruants is M. Mikvaot 8:1, 5.

29. But not impurity caused by direct contact with a human corpse, which requires sprinkling by a mixture of water and the ash of a red heifer (Numbers 19).

30. Sanders 1992 and 1990, 214–27.

31. See the full discussion in Sanders 1990. Sanders assumes that the two-pool *mikveh* is distinctively pharisaic. Since no evidence links the pre-70 Pharisees with the *mikveh*, a better formulation would be that the two-pool *mikveh* is "proto-rabbinic."

32. Matthew 27:62, 15:42; Luke 23:54; John 19:31, 42; and elsewhere.

33. Pharisees and Sadducees; M. Yadayim end. Boethusians: M. Menahot 10:3. Sadducees: M. Makkot 1:6, Parah 3:7. Others: M. Sukkah 4:9; M. Eruvin 3:2, 6:1. The Tosefta and the Talmudim expand this corpus.

34. Cf. M. Parah 3:7 with MMT 4Q394.13–6 in *The Dead Sea Scrolls Reader: Part 1*, 326–27; cf. M. Yadayim 4:7 with MMT 4Q394.55–58 in *The Dead Sea Scrolls Reader: Part 1*, 330–31.

35. E.g., M. Yoma 8:6 rules that the preservation of a life always takes precedence over the observance of the Sabbath. This ruling may have been directed against those who said that it did not; see Covenant of Damascus 11:16–17 and 4Q265 in *The Dead Sea Scrolls Reader: Part 1*, 322–23; Doering 1999, 201–4. Charlotte Fonrobert ingeniously conjectures that the rabbinic institution of 'eruv (see next section) was formulated as a response and an alternative to the Qumran practice of communal property; see Fonrobert 2004.

36. P. 40, ed. Lieberman 1955–88.

37. That is, if one person did half the labor and some other person did the other half, neither is liable.

38. a) M. Shabbat 10:3; b) M. Shabbat 10:2; c) M. Shabbat 1:1, 10:5; d) M. Shabbat 2:5; e) M. Shabbat 8, 9:5–7, 12:1–6, 13:1–4. Discussion in Gilat 1992, 48–62. See Neusner 1993, 15–30.
39. See the discussion in Fonrobert 2004.
40. On the prohibition of eating fallen fruit, see M. Pesahim 4:8 (opposition to the practice of "the men of Jericho"); Doering, *Schabbat* 156–58. The non-rabbinic usage of the term *mukhan* in the Covenant of Damascus encouraged modern scholars to emend the text; see Doering 1999, 155. For example, G. Vermes, *The Complete Dead Sea Scrolls in English* (Penguin Classics, 2004, rev. ed.), 139, translates, "No man shall eat on the Sabbath day except that which is already prepared. He shall eat nothing lying in the fields." The emendation on which this translation is based brings the Covenant of Damascus into conformity with rabbinic law.
41. Eilberg-Schwartz 1986.
42. The seven hermeneutical principles attributed to Hillel (T. Sanhedrin 7:11; *Sifra*, end of the introduction) and the thirteen attributed to R. Ishmael (*Sifra*, beginning of the introduction) have been studied many times in the Jewish scholarship of prior generations, but a new study is needed.
43. Lapin 1995 reaches a similar conclusion for the legislation of M. Bava Metzia.

7 Roman Law and Rabbinic Legal Composition

CATHERINE HEZSER

The discussion of legal issues and the creation and application of legal rulings was one of the main activities of both rabbis and Roman legal experts in Late Antiquity. In the course of this process, rabbis and jurists often dealt with similar topics, encountered similar problems, presented similar answers, and used similar literary forms to transmit their traditions to later generations. It is tempting to argue that such similarities concerning the form and/or content of their teachings point to direct influence of one set of scholars on the other. This is a temptation we should resist. Such tempting parallels need to be understood against the background of the rabbis' participation in a Late Antique cultural context dominated by Greco-Roman culture.

A comparative legal approach is interested in both similarities and differences in legal theory and practice. Similarities may point to shared social structures and moral concerns. Although rabbis and Roman jurists shared the Late Antique cultural context, their legal teachings were also based on their particular cultural heritages, the Hebrew Bible and ancient Roman legal traditions, respectively. When examining differences, legal scholars' indebtedness to these earlier bodies of material have to be taken into consideration as well.

The most appropriate issues of comparison to be discussed in more detail here are 1) the nature of Roman and rabbinic legal thinking, 2) the social setting of legal rulings and discussions, 3) the topics addressed in legal discourse, 4) the formulation and transmission of legal traditions, and 5) legal codification in Late Antiquity. An outline of the state of research on these matters will lead to a consideration of unanswered questions and further directions that comparative legal studies may take.

THE NATURE OF ROMAN AND RABBINIC LEGAL THINKING

Rabbinic texts are not easily accessible to modern readers with little exposure to classical rabbinic educations. Even a cursory glance will reveal the imposing compositional nature of these texts. Rather than finding carefully crafted introductions to legal topics and their details, readers confront more or less lengthy sequences of juxtaposed individual traditions whose topic, meaning, coherence, logic, and argumentation remain hidden from the uninitiated. The formulation of much of this material seems to follow a tacit code, lacking detail to the point of being elliptical and enigmatic. There is no obvious thematic focus to the argumentation, and logical principles, when adduced at all, seem idiosyncratic or counterintuitive. One case may be linked to another without being followed by general conclusions, principles, or rules. The editors of the collections seem to have refrained from imposing any systematic structure upon their received material. A coherent overall argument is difficult to identify within the amalgamation of attributed and unattributed traditions.

In the broader context of late Roman legal culture, however, the rabbinic writings are not quite as idiosyncratic as they might at first appear. The heterogeneous and polymorphic nature of rabbinic documents has its analogy in Roman legal writings. Scholars of Roman law have repeatedly emphasized that ancient Roman law was case law, and the essentially casuistic nature of ancient legal thinking is carried forward in rabbinic law as well.[1] Neither the rabbis nor the Roman jurists were interested in formulating legal principles and general rules. They rather focussed on the individual case and its possible solutions.

The entire legal discourse of the Roman jurists was casuistic and problem oriented rather than systematic and normative. The problems and conflicts of everyday life, rather than fixed legal norms, provided the basis of legal argumentation. It seems that ancient legal scholars – including rabbinic sages – were simply not interested in developing a unified, harmonious system. And they probably had no need for it since the casuistic legal practice served them well. Casuistic law had the advantage of being flexible, that is, adaptable to varying circumstances and easily changeable and expandable over time. Variants of case stories could be formulated in order to take different circumstances into account. On the basis of existing cases, hypothetical cases could be constructed and serve as the basis for further discussion. Additional details could be added or specific aspects subtracted to fit different situations.

This leads us to the question of fiction and reality in the formulation and transmission of case descriptions. If rabbis and Roman jurists created abstract versions of cases for transmissional purposes and formulated variants for further discussion, how can one distinguish between a real case and a fictional one, between theory and practice? The answer is that any clear-cut distinction is impossible in this regard, that in rabbinic and Roman case law reality and fiction are blurred. In all likelihood, neither the rabbis nor Roman legal experts were interested in such distinctions since they were not interested in historical accuracy. For legal problem solving, the question whether a case actually happened or merely could have happened is irrelevant.[2] The legal world becomes a separate onto-logical sphere governed by its own rules and distanced from simple social reality.

Certain rudiments of systematization are visible in the sources, especially at the later stage of codification: attempting to declare par-ticular opinions majority opinions, harmonizing traditions so that they support the same legal view, formulating rules on the basis of cases, insinuating legal principles. As M. Bretone (1992, 205) has pointed out, however, such attempts should be seen as mere "islands" within the sea of casuistry. The traditional material is never presented in a themat-ically coherent or deductively argued way. No clearly distinguishable set of legal rules is deducted from the cases. The material is, rather, presented topically and more or less loosely connected (sometimes by keyword association) to comprise a logical sequence that only the fellow legal scholar can follow.

Contradictions were tolerated as a necessary outcome of legal casu-istry. What mattered more than legal unity was the individual scholar's authority over ordinary people. Case law required the personal contact between litigant and legal advisor. So long as no theoretical legal sys-tem with fixed rulings existed, clients who required legal advice were personally dependent on the few who were knowledgeable of the legal traditions and able to apply them to new situations and circumstances. The scholars had undergone a long process of study and service them-selves. The ability to advise in legal matters and provide case decisions was handed down informally from teacher to student.[3] Accordingly, a small group of legal experts perpetuated themselves.

To support the authority and correctness of variant and sometimes contradictory rulings, rabbis declared all teachings the divinely inspired word of God. To cite but one example:

> A man might tell himself: "Since the House of Shammai declares unclean and the House of Hillel clean, person so-and-so prohibits, and person such-and-such permits, why should I henceforth learn Torah?" Scripture says: "Words . . . the words . . . These are the words . . . " [Deuteronomy 1:1]. All these words have been given by a single Shepherd, one God made them, one Provider gave them, the Lord of all deeds, blessed be He, has spoken it. (T. Sotah 7:12)

Such rabbinic legal thinking can only be properly understood when viewed against the larger background of casuistic law as practiced in the Roman Empire in Late Antiquity. When practicing case law, rabbis acted like other legal scholars of their time. To what extent they were familiar with Roman legal thinking cannot be defined precisely anymore. One may assume that rabbis who lived in or visited larger cities will have been aware of Roman jurisprudence to some extent. But no uniform rabbinic knowledge of foreign legal theory and practice can be identified.

THE SOCIAL SETTING OF RABBIS' AND ROMAN JURISTS' LEGAL PRACTICE

Rabbis and Roman jurists were both jurisprudents (scholars of the legal tradition) and legal advisors to the public. As jurisprudents, they were knowledgeable of the respective society's legal tradition and able to further develop existing law. As advisors to the public, they applied their legal knowledge to new circumstances occurring in daily life.

Roman civil law was created by jurists, rather than by the local or imperial government (Watson 1974, 102). These jurists were legal experts who often functioned informally, without the backing of a public office. On the basis of their expertise, they nevertheless possessed authority (*auctoritas*).[4] Besides being seen as personal representatives of the legal tradition and models of right conduct, they were able to provide authoritative legal advice (*consilium*) to all those who required it. Giving legal advice was seen as a duty as well as a privilege (*nobile officium*).

Until approximately 300 B.C.E. Roman legal science was in the hands of a group of priests administering the Roman state cult. In that period of time, sacred law and civil law were combined. With the shift from the priests to the aristocracy, sacred and civil law became separated, and civil law was increasingly treated in its own right. Although the upwardly mobile *homo novus* could theoretically become a legal scholar, he remained exceptional in both republican and imperial times.

Although Roman jurists were not organized in professional organizations, legal scholars would meet some of their colleagues on a more or less regular basis. In addition to collegial interaction, close teacher–student relationships developed. The giving of legal advice and the teaching of students could happen at one and the same time. Particular "school" traditions developed when former students transmitted their teachers' opinions to later generations. Such "schools" could also engage in disputes among one another.

Similarities between the social structure and function of Roman jurisprudence and rabbinic scholarship are immediately obvious. Like Roman jurists, rabbis functioned as intermediaries between an ancient body of legal traditions and the general populace unable to solve legal disputes on its own. Like Roman jurists, rabbis lacked a formal organizational structure and congregated informally.[5] They formed small clusters of colleague-friends who would meet more or less regularly to discuss issues of common interest. In addition, each individual rabbi had a circle of students who would live with him at home and accompany him in public. These students would learn from observing their master's practice, as well as participate in more theoretical study sessions. Once they had become rabbis themselves, they would transmit their teachers' views to later generations. Just like the profession of jurists, the rabbinical profession was a self-perpetuating entity.

Various aspects of comparison concerning the role and function of rabbis and Roman legal experts are worthy of further analysis. To what extent did Roman legal schools resemble Hellenistic philosophical schools that continued after the death of their founder, and to what extent did they resemble the informal disciple circles of rabbis? What was the relationship among legal experts, lawyers, and private and public law courts in the respective societies? Is the collegial interaction among Roman jurists comparable to that among rabbis, or was it more limited in nature? What would have been the difference between legal advice being given by members of the aristocracy (jurists) and by members of different social strata (rabbis)? Was the legal profession held in the same high esteem in Jewish as in Greco-Roman society? What were the social consequences of rabbis' assumed responsibility for both religious and civil law, in comparison with jurists' focus on civil law exclusively? Last but not least, did rabbis and jurists have similar authority within their respective societies?

The Roman legal system was very flexible and accommodated formal courts of arbitration as well as more informal types of legal agreement. Formal adjudication took place in courts and by judges officially recognized by the Roman government. Informal adjudication took place outside of such courts and without official Roman supervision, but its outcome was generally tolerated by the government authorities: "[T]he parties could agree on a respected individual, who would adjudicate the dispute – or some aspect of it – on the assumption that his verdict would be accepted."[6] Informal jurisdiction could involve negotiations among the litigants as well as the intervention by a mediator, and these two forms were complementary.

The Roman government will have been interested in solving disputes over issues of minor significance on a local and unofficial level, with a minimum amount of bureaucracy. Both rabbis and Roman jurists were involved in such settlements. In contrast to the judge whose decision is backed by the authority of the court, the informal adjudicator "must aim to reach agreement with the parties and may not impose his decision."[7] The parties must accept it of their own free will. This procedure puts a lot of weight on the personal relationship between the litigants and the legal expert. The litigants must be convinced of the legal expert's knowledge, good judgment, and impartiality. The legal expert himself must count on the litigants' acceptance of his judgment. If mutual trust is lacking, the judgment breaks down.

Roman jurists' function of *respondere*, of granting legal advice to all those who approached them, is very reminiscent of rabbis' role as halakhic advisors within the Jewish community. *Respondere* seems to have been the most important task of Roman jurists from the time of the Republic until the middle of the third century c.e., when classical jurisprudence came to an end and the legal system was bureaucratized (Bretone 1992, 116–17). The granting of legal advice could take place at the doorsteps of or inside a jurist's private house or in the public sphere of the forum or marketplace. Like the rabbi, the jurist had the role of an intermediary between the abstract and highly complicated legal tradition and the populace's legal problems. In the Hellenistic-Roman world, legal advice was considered a "divine good" by those who received it and an honor to those who were able to provide it (Bretone, 116).

At the time of Augustus, some jurists were granted the *ius respondendi*, the right to give *responsa* backed by the authority of the emperor (Digest 1.2.2, Pomponius). Augustus seems to have introduced this principle to bring order into the existing chaos by limiting the number of jurists who were officially legitimized to respond. While the ius respondendi bestowed special authority on some jurists, lawyers were not forced to accept their rulings and people could still use the services of other adjudicators who could not call themselves *iures consulti*.[8] Under Hadrian (117–38) the particularly authorized judges' responsa became obligatory, that is, lawyers were bound to follow them in case of unanimity. While Hadrian seems to have granted the ius respondendi to a larger and more diverse pool of candidates, including those from the equestrian order, the examples of Gaius and Pomponius show that even in the second century there were prominent legal experts who did not possess this right.[9]

The granting of legal advice seems to have also been one of the most important functions of rabbis in tannaitic and amoraic times.[10] While there is no evidence that any rabbi was granted the *ius respondendi*, a few rabbis seem to have been officially appointed as judges of municipal courts.[11] The large majority of rabbis, however, seem to have provided their contemporaries with legal advice unofficially.

Roman jurists' and rabbis' legal counsels were probably originally transmitted orally. According to Bretone (1992, 140), orality was one of the most significant characteristics of the *responsum*. Before codification, jurisprudence took the form of the orally formulated legal counsel, of discourse, discussion, dialogue. In private and public discourse, legal opinions would be discussed, compared, objected against, and changed. This discourse took the form of an agonistic competition in which the one with the superior argumentative skills was victorious. No system or dogmas or generalizations existed at that stage.

Eventually, written anthologies of responsa were created by the first century B.C.E.[12] They were called *Digesta, Quaestiones,* or *Responsa* and belonged to the so-called problematic or problem-oriented literature. These anthologies of individual solutions to legal problems probably constitute the earliest type of legal literature.[13] Their number decreases at the end of the classical period, that is, by the middle of the third century C.E. Although no direct evidence of collections of rabbinic case stories exists, this lack does not preclude the possibility that such collections circulated among rabbis.[14]

At the time when the responsum was given, no justification or explanation was necessary. The solving of the case in the presence of litigants could be followed by a discussion with students or colleagues, however, in which the case became a theoretical problem for which a variety of solutions were suggested (Bretone 1992, 143). This theoretical discussion constituted a further development, a second stage after the initial case decision. The case had now acquired a didactic function. The secondary expansion of the case, which could include variant versions as well as theoretical rules, could be included in responsa collections.

Rules may have sometimes emerged as generalizations of case stories. In accordance with the casuistic character of ancient jurisprudence, the case always took precedence over the rule. According to an often quoted principle transmitted in the name of the third-century C.E. jurist Paul, "*non ex regula ius sumatur, sed ex iure, quod est, regula fiat*": "one does not derive a [practical] decision out of a [theoretical] rule, but out of a [practical] decision a rule should be made" (Dig. 50.17.1). The term *ius* may refer to the entire body of legal experience here (Nörr 1972, 28 n. 32).

When they appeared, rules were always based on a limited number of cases and therefore had a limited validity.

THE TOPICS OF LEGAL DISCOURSE IN ROMAN AND JEWISH SOCIETY

Rabbinic *halakhah* deals with religious and ritual law as well as with civil and criminal law issues, to the exclusion of capital law, which was the domain of the Roman provincial government at that time. In rabbinic documents, no clear distinction is drawn between religious and civil law. It seems that rabbis considered civil law, which also comprised family law, religiously significant as well: Rabbinic *halakhah* concerned almost all aspects of everyday life. The Jewish religious concern with seemingly secular, worldly matters had its origin in the Torah: The Israelite's proper relationship to God, enacted in rituals and purity observance, would also be expressed in his proper moral conduct toward his fellow(wo)men.

The combination of religious, civil, and criminal law also existed in Roman law as long as jurisprudence was the domain of the priests. The *pontifices* not only dealt with issues concerning the divine sphere but had a monopoly on private law as well (Bretone 1992, 83). The Twelve Tables of the fifth century B.C.E. were mostly concerned with private law but also contained some criminal and sacral laws. A. Watson (1974, 180–81) explains that "between the time of the XII Tables and the beginning of the first century B.C., law itself had undergone a change. Whereas much of the private law of the earlier date was also sacral law, religion had virtually ceased to have any role in private law by the time of Quintus Mucius"; "private law had become secularized." Classical jurisprudence as it existed from the third and especially the first century B.C.E. to the third century C.E. was mainly concerned with private law. Public law was the responsibility of the emperors. The distinction among private, public, and sacral law was "probably the most fundamental legal distinction" undertaken in Roman society before the end of the Republic.[15]

The two great compilations of Roman-Byzantine times, the *Codex Theodosianus* and the *Corpus Iuris Civilis* of Justinian, contain both civil and imperial, private and public law. The legal compilations of Palestinian rabbis, that is, the Mishnah, Tosefta, and the Talmud Yerushalmi, on the other hand, deal with civil, criminal, and religious law only. This means that the rabbinic compilations are comparable with earlier Roman jurists' writings, such as Paul's *Sententiae* and Gaius's *Institutes*, and with Justinian's Digest, but not with the imperial laws of the *Codex Theodosianus* and the *Codex Justinianus*. Unlike the Digest, rabbinic documents contain religious law as well. The discussion of issues related to the Sabbath and festivals, purity rites, circumcision, and immersion has no equivalent in Roman civil law codes. Although Roman jurists used case stories and examples in their legal discussions, rabbinic works also incorporate nonlegal material, such as *chreiai*, anecdotes, exegetical texts, and historical notes.

Almost all of the central areas of Roman private law were dealt with by rabbis as well. Both rabbis and Roman jurists discussed issues of property law, inheritances and donations, the proper form of contracts and other types of agreements, family law (including marriage and divorce), regulations concerning slaves and free laborers, loans and rental agreements, and damages to another person's property. This basic similarity with regard to the topics of Roman and rabbinic legal discourse need not necessarily be based on direct influence, though. As already pointed out, rabbis and Roman jurists had a very similar function within their respective societies. As legal advisors to the public, they were confronted with similar problems.

With regard to the issue of slave law, for example, many of the same issues are discussed in both rabbinic and Roman legal writings. Both corpora draw a clear distinction between enslaved and free persons; provide detailed rulings on the ways in which slaves were to be enslaved and manumitted, bought and sold; discuss the usage of slaves as intermediaries in business transactions; regulate the master's punishment of slaves; and determine the status of slaves' children.[16] Regardless of the extent of slavery in the respective society, one can assume that Jewish and Roman slave owners were confronted with much the same problems in everyday life. Both rabbis and Roman jurists tried to provide slave owners with guidance.

It has been argued that Roman jurists who belonged to the upper classes acted on behalf of the slave-owning strata of society. Since rabbis' socioeconomic background was more diverse and not all rabbis will have been slave owners, one may expect to find more diverse opinions. On the other hand, the middle classes often imitated the upper classes and took over their values. Those whose social status was lower will have felt more need to distinguish themselves from slaves, especially from those who had prominent positions within wealthy masters' households, for example, the slaves of the patriarch and exilarch in Jewish and the emperor's slaves in Roman society.

The similarities between Roman and rabbinic slave law are striking:[17] Both Romans and rabbis viewed slaves as objects and types of property (cf. Gaius, Inst. 2.14a) Dig. 1.5; Genesis Rabbah 56:2). Only in the case of damages, when they were supposed to be held responsible for their actions, were they attributed reason. The enslavement of prisoners of war and the automatic slave status of the offspring of slave women were taken for granted in rabbinic and Roman society. Rabbis and Roman jurists discussed the obvious advantages of having oneself represented by one's slave in business dealings. Although slaves could not own property, they could use their master's property on his behalf and under certain circumstances benefit from it. Masters' absolute authority over their slaves became evident in their right to physically violate them as punishment for misbehavior.

Despite these general similarities, differences in rabbinic and Roman slave law seem to have existed as well. For example, in contrast to Roman society, where debt slavery and self-sale were strictly prohibited, rabbis allowed these practices under certain circumstances, namely, in the case of poverty. This difference may be due to the fact that debt slavery and self-sale are taken for granted in the Bible and/or because rabbis were more conscious of the plight of the poor than were upper-class jurists. Another difference in rabbinic and Roman slave law concerns the possibility of slave marriages, a phenomenon that Roman jurists opposed but which rabbis seem to have tolerated. In contrast to Roman law, neither biblical nor rabbinic law grants masters an unlimited power of life and death over their slaves. With regard to these and other differences, rabbis' indebtedness to the biblical tradition, as well as socioeconomic and religious-moral concerns, can be adduced as possible explanations.

For example, in both Roman and rabbinic law, the slave is seen as both chattel and human being, but no direct dependence of rabbinic on Roman law can be claimed in this regard. Rabbis do not explicity define slaves as things or *res mancipi* as Roman law does (cf., e.g., Gaius, Inst. 2.14a). But they do compare slaves to animals in general and to asses in particular (cf. Genesis Rabbah 56:2). Slaves' ambiguous status between objects and human beings not only found expression in legal texts but must also be viewed within the wider context of ancient Jewish and Greco-Roman society.[18]

THE FORMULATION AND TRANSMISSION OF LEGAL TRADITIONS IN RABBINIC AND GRECO-ROMAN SOCIETY

Precedent and legal ruling were the two most frequently used literary forms in which legal traditions were transmitted in rabbinic and

Roman society. Precedents or case stories had their *Sitz im Leben* in rabbis' and jurists' function of providing legal advice to all those who approached them (*respondere*), as explicated earlier. They were not exact records of these proceedings, however, but abstractions and sometimes entirely hypothetical creations formulated for the purposes of legal discussion and teaching. In rabbinic and Roman legal literature, they are usually combined with theoretical rulings and later rabbis' and jurists' comments, additions, explanations, and harmonizations.

Rabbinic and Roman case stories usually consisted of two or three parts: a brief description of the legally problematic situation (*casus*), the formulation of a question (*quaestio*), and the legal expert's solution to the problem at the end (*responsum*).[19] For example:

> [A = *casus*] Lucius Titius had bought estates in Germany on the other side of the Rhine and paid part of the price. When the heir of the buyer was sued for the rest of the amount, he posed a question saying that these possessions were partly expropriated through imperial precept [and] partly assigned to veterans as a gift.

> [B = *quaestio*] I ask [quaero] whether the danger of this matter can affect the seller.

> [C = *responsum*] Paul answered [*respondit*] that future cases of eviction after the contract of purchase do not affect the seller and therefore, according to that which has been reported, the price of the estates can be claimed. (Dig. 21.2.11)

The following rabbinic case story, which also concerns property law, has a similar structure:

> [A = *casus*] A young man sold his property.

> [B = *quaestio*] The case came before R. Hiyya b. Yosef and R. Yohanan.

> [C = *responsum*] R. Hiyya b. Yosef said: On the assumption that he was a reasonable person [i.e., an adult] they [the witnesses] signed [the document]. R. Yohanan said: Since he [the purchaser] took it upon himself to remove the property from the family, he must bring proof [for the validity of the purchase]. (Y. Bava Batra 9:6/8, 17a)

In the second part of rabbinic case stories, the question is usually not explicitly formulated. The legal problem is merely implied. Both rabbinic and Roman case stories are characterized by their conciseness

and concentration on the most important elements necessary for understanding the issue at hand. All embellishing details as well as the names
of the litigants are usually missing. The litigants remain anonymous
("a person") or are given stereotypical names (Lucius Titius, *Ploni*). The
anonymity of the litigants already indicates that the authors, transmitters, and editors of the stories were not interested in preserving historical
records of actual cases. They formulated the stories for easy memorization and transmission, that is, for didactic and discursive purposes.

At an early stage, case stories could be combined with theoretical
rules. They could be used as illustrations of such rules, if the rule preceded them, or the rule could be derived from one or more case stories,
if it followed the narrative texts. Stories and rules must not have been
formulated in direct relation to each other, however. They could also be
connected on the basis of keyword associations or thematic similarities
only. Rules and precedents are sometimes attributed to one and the same
legal authority, but they could be transmitted in the name of different
scholars or anonymously as well.[20]

Both rabbinic and Roman case stories are occasionally followed by
hypothetical expansions that vary the circumstances of the case and/or
offer different solutions to its problem.[21] The theoretical nature of the
variant versions is sometimes made evident by their introduction with
"if..." For example, Y. Bava Kamma 6:7, 5c transmits a story about
a tenant who had deposited a pound of gold. When the tenant and his
landlord died, their heirs fought with one another for the ownership of
the property. The first rabbi to whom the case was brought decided in
favor of the children of the landlord; after this rabbi's death, another
rabbi decided in favor of the children of the tenant. This second decision
is followed by a hypothetical expansion:

> What is the law, if the children of the tenant of Bar Ziza say to the
> children of Bar Ziza: Give us what you have received? They can
> say to them: What has been done by the court has been done.
> What is the law if the minor [children of Bar Ziza] say to the adult
> [children]: Let us share with you? They can say to them: We have
> found a find.

Details could be added to the description of the case or particular
aspects could be exchanged. Differences in the circumstances of the case
required different solutions. In these hypothetical additions to case stories, one can recognize a first step away from the individual case toward a
theoretical discussion interested in legal issues but not in what actually

happened. The theorizing was based on an initial case but took place in the unreal, fictitious world of legal discourse.

Case stories, precedents and rules, and case stories followed by hypothetical continuations could be transmitted in collections. The connections between the originally independent traditions would have been made by the editors of the collections, who also decided upon the principle on which the series would be based. Series of thematically related traditions would circulate, as well as series of traditions associated with one and the same authority (Bretone 1992, 187–89).

The existence of rabbinic story collections can be hypothesized only.[22] Sometimes thematic and/or formal connections exist between stories that are quoted successively in one and the same Talmudic *sugya'* (= thematic unit), or between stories in different *sugyot*, tractates, or rabbinic works.

The connections among case stories and between case stories and rulings have to be examined within the respective literary context in which they are found. They may be due to the editors' usage of preredactional collections, or they may be the editors' own work. If the connection between the traditions is based on a principle relevant to the present literary context, one may assume that the "final" editors can be considered responsible for the connection. If the connection is based on internal aspects of the traditions only, that is, if a second case story is quoted because it is attributed to the same rabbi as the first or transmits the same rabbi's case decision, or because it shares a keyword connection with the first story, then it is likely that the connection between the traditions existed at a preredactional level already. Yet even in the latter case, the "final" editors are responsible for choosing the respective traditions and for integrating them into a new literary context.

Another literary form besides case stories and rulings, in which legal knowledge was transmitted in both Jewish and Roman society, was the legal commentary. The classical Roman jurists published commentaries on earlier law that were used by the editors of Justinian's Digest. The earlier legal traditions that the jurists comment on are the *ius praetorium* or *ius honorarium* and the *ius civile*. The *ius civile* included all norms and regulations governing the Roman citizen's life. The Twelve Tables were the first official Roman compendium of civil law compiled in the middle of the fifth century B.C.E.[23] Since the rest of the civil law did not exist in codified form, the jurists had to rely on its literary renderings by Quintus Mucius Scaevola, *pontifex maximus* in the first century B.C.E., and by Massurius Sabinus and Plautius in the first century B.C.[24] The jurists Labeo and Gaius wrote commentaries on the Twelve Tables, Paul wrote a commentary on Plautius's *ius civile*, Pomponius on Quintus Mucius Scaevola and Sabinus. Sabinus's collection was also commented on by Paul and Ulpian.

The second body of earlier law on which the classical jurists commented was the Praetorian Edict.[25] The Praetorian Edict developed gradually through additions and innovations made to the existing edict (*edictum perpetuum*) by the new praetor (*edictum novum*). In the second century c.e., Hadrian commissioned the legal scholar Salvius Iulianus to edit the accumulated material and declared the *Edictum Hadrianum* unchangeable. Until the third century, governors were obliged to publish this edict in its authorized form. Commentaries on the Edict began to be written already by the first century b.c.e. (Servius = Sulpicius Rufus), and the commentary literature continued during the first three centuries c.e. (Labeo, Sabinus, Pomponius, Paul, Ulpian). The commentaries explained, supplemented, and critiqued the earlier rulings, they limited or extended their range of application, and they sometimes provided alternative solutions. For example:

> [A] The *praetor* says: Where any pome [*glandem*] falls from the premises of that one [your neighbor] upon yours, I forbid force to be employed to prevent him from gathering them, and carrying them away within the space of three days.
>
> [B] The term "pome" includes any kind of fruit. (Dig. 43.28.1)

Here, the meaning of a term is expanded in the commentary to make the Praetorian rule more widely applicable.

Neither the Praetorian Edict nor the collections of *ius civile* are extant today. They can be accessed only through the jurists' commentaries, which are transmitted in Justinian's Digest. The Digest is arranged according to the order of the Praetorian Edict. In the Digest, the jurists' comments usually follow the citation of passages from the Edict, introduced with "The praetor says: . . . " The comments may be brief or more detailed, consist of mere glosses on particular terms, or discuss the applicability of a rule. They can also refer to and discuss earlier jurists' comments on the Edict.

Roman jurists' commentaries on the Edict and *ius civile* are very reminiscent of amoraic rabbis' commentaries on tannaitic traditions. Like Justinian's Digest, the Palestinian Talmud transmits amoraic rabbis' commentaries on earlier *mishnayot* and *baraitot*. Like the jurists, rabbis gloss earlier traditions, explain certain terms, discuss the applicability of a ruling, expand cases, or provide alternative solutions. For example:

> [A] He who buries turnips or radishes under a vine, if some of its leaves were exposed, he does not fear [that he has transgressed] . . .
>
> [B] Hezekiah said: They taught [in the Mishnah that one might bury] only turnips and radishes, but not other things.
>
> [C] R. Yohanan said: It makes no difference whether it is turnips, radishes, or any other things. (Y. Kilayim 1:9, 27a)[26]

As in the Roman example, the meaning of the earlier ruling is expanded in R. Yochanan's commentary, whereas Hezekiah tries to maintain the more limited literal meaning of the words.

The particular forms in which the *mishnayot* and *baraitot* were available to the 'Amora'im are unknown. Whereas Saul Lieberman assumed that the entire Mishnah was published and circulated orally, it is more likely that rabbis had access to particular Mishnah tractates only and that such tractates also existed in writing, even if they continued to be recited from memory in the framework of oral teaching and discussion.[27]

It is also uncertain in what form amoraic commentaries on tannaitic traditions were transmitted in amoraic times. Roman jurists' comments were originally transmitted in written collections that were later taken apart by the editors of the Digest. Whether such written collections of particular rabbis' comments on the Mishnah existed we do not know.[28] In all likelihood, however, rabbis did not write such commentaries themselves. Although notes and notebooks are occasionally mentioned in rabbinic texts, rabbis' emphasis on oral teaching will have generally prevented them from recording their comments in writing.[29] It is possible, however, that students would memorize their teachers' sayings and later transmit them orally and/or compile them in written form.[30]

Detailed comparative studies of the various literary forms used by rabbis and Roman jurists – case stories, rules, commentaries – are necessary before any more definite conclusions concerning the respective legal scholars' use, adaptation, and transmission of these forms can be reached. Similarities in the occurrence of the forms in both rabbinic and Roman legal corpora may have been due to similarities in rabbis' and jurists' role within the respective societies, as indicated earlier. Case stories, rulings, and commentaries on earlier law would naturally evolve as the forms most suited for legal transmission. The phenomenon that both rabbinic and Roman law were casuistic will have been responsible for the formal similarities. Whether and to what extent rabbis were knowledgeable of the forms of Roman legal transmission remains an open question.

LEGAL CODIFICATION IN RABBINIC AND ROMAN SOCIETY

Although certain earlier prototypes existed, in both Roman and Jewish society the large-scale codification of legal knowledge was a phenomenon of late Roman-Byzantine times.[31] At the beginning of the fifth century C.E., imperial laws (*leges*) were codified in the Codex Theodosianus.[32] While Theodosius had already planned to create a Digest of jurists' law (*ius*), this project was not carried out before Justinian, a century later. Justinian's *Corpus Iuris* also comprised imperial law; therefore the Talmud is only really comparable to the Digest.

Legal scholars may have persuaded Justinian to compile earlier jurists' law, but the emperor was responsible for the initiation and organization of the project. In 530, Justinian set up a commission to compile a Digest of the writings of earlier jurists who held the *ius respondendi*. Unlike the Digest, the Talmud did not have a political authority's backing. In fact, nothing is directly known about its origins. One can only hypothesize that at some point, some rabbis considered it worthwhile or even necessary to create a compendium of earlier teachings that had accumulated over time.

The Digest was arranged according to the order of the Praetorian Edict. The order of the Praetorian Edict provided a kind of "external system," that is, a general topical arrangement of the material, but it did not lead to inner coherence and harmony. Similarly, the Talmud was arranged according to the order of the Mishnah. Just as the Digest cannot be considered a mere commentary on the Edict, the Talmud is much more than a commentary on the Mishnah. The Edict and the Mishnah merely provide broad structural models for the jurists' and rabbis' arrangement of material according to their own concerns.

Justinian gave the editors complete freedom with regard to omitting repetitions and superfluous passages and completing and harmonizing traditions (C. 1.17.1). Although the legal traditions already existed in written collections, the goal was not the mere quotation and literal preservation of earlier jurists' words. The editors were supposed to dismiss opinions that had fallen into disuse and to equally represent all those they decided to include. They had to fragment the earlier collections and to rearrange and combine them in a new way. The integration of traditions into new literary contexts would sometimes necessitate the reformulation, abbreviation, and harmonization of the earlier texts.[33]

The editors of the Talmud probably proceeded in a very similar way. They, too, had to start with collecting material and choosing the traditions they wanted to preserve. Unlike the Roman jurists, who had written collections at hand, they had to gather oral traditions which had been transmitted – and reformulated – for generations. They probably had to contact a large number of their colleagues for that purpose. Once collected, the traditions had to be put into writing. They could then be arranged together with material that may have been taken from written collections. Like the Romans, the rabbinic editors would have felt free to reformulate, abbreviate, expand, and harmonize their material to create a new whole.

The ways in which rabbinic and Roman legal documents were edited need to be examined and compared in detail. Such an examination would lead to a better understanding of the development of both Roman law codes and the Talmud. How do the editors use their earlier material and how do they connect it to create new meanings? What difference did the use of oral traditions make? What was the function of the discourse form in the two legal contexts? How and to what extent were traditional contradictions harmonized? What is the relationship between the attributed and anonymous portions of the text?

Both practical-pragmatic and political-ideological reasons seem to stand behind Justinian's codification project. Justinian seems to have hoped that the restoration of ancient law would also lead to political restoration and renewal. Classical jurisprudence represented the crown of Roman culture. Its codification could serve as the common denominator of a reunified Roman Empire (Wieacker 1961, 239). The jurists will have had their own reasons for supporting the codification project. It allowed the preservation and organization of a previously chaotic and diffuse body of legal traditions. Their motives will have been classicistic and antiquarian in nature. Similar motives may have guided rabbis in their endeavor to create a Talmud. They, too, were faced with a huge, contradictory, and difficult-to-access legal tradition. To preserve this material for later genererations of scholars will have been their primary goal. The codifications would, at the same time, foster rabbis' and jurists' own positions within the respective societies. The compilations were created by scholars for scholars and could not be properly accessed and understood without more experienced scholars' help. This would set in motion an ongoing process of study, explanation, and commentary, which still continues today.

BIBLIOGRAPHICAL EXCURSUS: KEY FIGURES
IN COMPARATIVE LEGAL STUDIES

The comparative approach to rabbinic law began at the end of the nineteenth century and was practiced by German-Jewish scholars who rejected the ahistorical systematic-halakhic approach of their predecessors.[34] David Farbstein's comparison of the rights of wage laborers in rabbinic and Roman law (1896), Jacob Neubauer's comparative approach to marriage law (1920), and Alexander Gulak's analysis of the use of documents in the Talmud, in papyri, and in Greco-Roman law (1935) can serve as examples for the early stages of this development. The comparative-legal approach reached its climax in the 1950s and 1960s with David Daube, Reuven Yaron, and Boas Cohen. David Daube's many comparative studies in biblical, Hellenistic, rabbinic, and Roman law are truly interdisciplinary and range from women's rights, witnesses, and court proceedings to legal terminology and legal forms. His students Reuven Yaron (1960) and Bernard Jackson (1975) carried on his approach. Yaron examined references to gifts in contemplation of death in Jewish and Roman law, and Jackson introduced new structural approaches.

Another prominent scholar of comparative *halakhah* to be mentioned in this regard is Boas Cohen (1966). His collection of articles is arranged according to the order of Gaius's Institutes (A. General Part; B. Law of Persons; C. Law of Things; D. Law of Actions), and the topics covered are taken over from Roman law (e.g., *peculium, contractio, antichresis, usufructus*). Some of them have direct analogies in rabbinic law (e.g., betrothal, divorce, oath); others do not. Roman law clearly provides the framework and starting point for Cohen's analysis. He stresses that the prerequisite for comparative studies is a broad knowledge of the respective legal traditions and of the languages in which the legal texts are written. Comparative legal study must always be based on a careful analysis of the original texts.

Since the 1960s, scholars have continued to conduct comparative legal studies, especially in the area of family law.[35] Yet many topics are still in need of (re)investigation, especially since the critical historical study of rabbinic texts is a relatively recent phenomenon. The older studies often lack proper distinctions between Palestinian and Babylonian, tannaitic and amoraic texts. They quote Babylonian next to Palestinian texts, for example, and try to elucidate them on the background of Greco-Roman law. Roman law may be considered the proper framework for examinations of the legal traditions transmitted in Palestinian documents only. For the Babylonian Talmud, Persian law has to be consulted, as Yaakov Elman has repeatedly emphasized. He has provided a number of practical examples of how such an approach can be conducted.[36]

The concept of intertextuality is particularly relevant with regard to comparative-legal studies. With Julia Kristeva (2002, 446), intertextuality is to be understood in a much broader sense than has previously been done: All texts are based on a multitude of prior texts or signifying practices that must not be mentioned directly and of which the author does not even need to be aware. The prehistory of a text should not be reconstructed in a positivistic way by claiming direct influence of one text on another. The text should, rather, be seen within the cultural context in which it was created. Its intertext is the entire surrounding culture in its literary, legal, religious, socioeconomic, and political manifestations.[37]

Notes

1. See Schulz 1954, 27–45, as well as Wieacker 1961, 80 and 142–3, and Bretone 1992, 201–7. See Catherine Hezser, "The Codification of Legal Knowledge in Late Antiquity: The Talmud Yerushalmi and Roman Law Codes" in Schäfer 1998, 629–31.
2. See also Wieacker 1961, 144.
3. See Hezser 1997, 332–46.
4. See Wieacker 1961, 130ff. Our brief presentation of Roman lawmaking draws from Wieacker, as well as Bretone 1992, Kunkel 1952, and Söllner 1980.
5. See Hezser 1997, 228–39.
6. Jill Harries, "Creating Legal Space: Settling Disputes in the Roman Empire," in Hezser 2003, 64–65.
7. Ibid., 67.
8. See Kunkel 1946, 457 n. 45.
9. See Söllner 1980, 103 (Gaius); Kunkel 1946, 444 (Pomponius).
10. See Hezser 1997, 354–86.
11. See ibid., 269–70.
12. See Bretone 1992, 142 and 189; Söllner 1980, 114.
13. See Schulz 1954, 33. On the transmission of precedents in Roman Egypt, see Katzoff 1972, 256–92.
14. See Goldberg 1974, 25; Hezser 1993, 269–82; Melamed 1977, 94 and 105–6; E. L. Segal 1979, 201, and 1990, 90ff.
15. See Schulz 1954, 18–23 and 179.
16. See Catherine Hezser, "Slaves and Slavery in Rabbinic and Roman Law," in Hezser 2003, 133ff.
17. See ibid. for a detailed discussion of the relevant texts.
18. See Hezser, "Slaves," 134–39.
19. See Hezser, "Codification," 588–91, with examples. On the form of case stories in rabbinic literature, see Hezser 1993, 292–303. On case stories in the Mishnah, see Goldberg 1974, 1ff.; on case stories in the Babylonian Talmud, see Segal 1979, 199ff., and 1990.

20. See Hezser, "Codification," 591–92, for examples.
21. See Bretone 1992, 143–45, with examples; Hezser, "Codification," 592–94.
22. See Goldberg 1974, 25; Hezser 1993, 269–82; Melamed 1977, 93–107; Yassif 1990, 103–45, on aggadic story collections.
23. On the Twelve Tables, see Bretone 1992, 62–63; Söllner 1980, 34–36.
24. On these see Söllner 1980, 82–3, and 113.
25. On the development of the Praetorian Edict, see Watson 1974, 31–58.
26. For further examples, see Hezser, "Codification," 597–600.
27. See Hezser 2001, 427–33, and 2002, 167–92.
28. Bokser 1980 assumes that a collection of Shmuel's teachings on the Mishnah existed, even if the comments were not formulated for that purpose but "originated individually in response to the Mishnah" (423).
29. See Hezser 2001, 95–104.
30. See also Bokser 1980, 420–50.
31. See Hezser, "Codification," 611–15.
32. On the Codex Theodosianus, see Harries and Wood 1993.
33. See Hezser, "Codification," 615–29, on this process.
34. See Catherine Hezser, "Introduction," in Hezser 2003, 1–3.
35. See especially the recent collection of articles by Lapin, Jackson, Elman, and Katzoff in Hezser 2003.
36. In addition to his essay in this volume, see, e.g., Elman, "Marriage," in Hezser 2003.
37. See Hezser, "Introduction," 11–13.

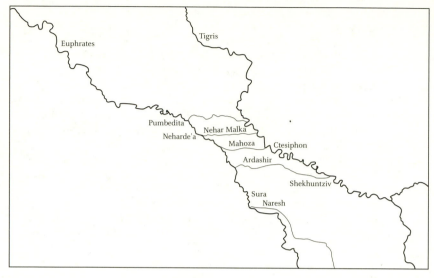

Jewish Babylonia in Talmudic Times

8 Middle Persian Culture and Babylonian Sages: Accommodation and Resistance in the Shaping of Rabbinic Legal Tradition

YAAKOV ELMAN

JEWS AND PERSIANS

Jews and Persians had coexisted in Mesopotamia, mostly peaceably, for some 750 years before the Sasanian dynasty took over from the Arcasids in 224 C.E.[1] They would continue to do so for more than another four centuries, including the entire amoraic period (220–500 C.E.).[2] As the late third-century R. Huna put it, the Babylonian "exiles" were at ease in Babylonia, as the other exiles – those in the Roman world – were not (B. Menahot 110a). The Persian emperor wanted it that way. Jews were a significant minority in a vital province; Mesopotamia was both the breadbasket of the empire and the province most vulnerable to Roman invasion;[3] unlike Christians, who might become a fifth column once Christianity became a tolerated religion in 313 C.E., the Jews would support the regime if they were left alone.

At the same time, the official religion of the Persian Empire, Zoroastrianism, was comfortable and even familiar to the Jews, with its theological doctrines of creation by the benevolent and omniscient Ohrmazd, the fight against evil, reward and punishment, heaven and hell, judgment, creation, the coming of three pivotal "messianic" figures, the ultimate defeat of evil, the resurrection of the dead, and the renewal of creation. This was true of its ethical system as well, with its emphasis on right thought, speech, and action, and its ritual system, with its stress on the avoidance of idolatry, its hatred of sorcery, "wasting of seed," and contact with menstruant women and dead bodies. Moreover, such staples of rabbinic thought as the importance of oral transmission of sacred texts and the authority of learned elites have striking analogues

To my teacher, friend and colleague, P. Oktor Skjoervø...an I ka mard ewag ān ī ka mard ēwag abāg did nē wēnēd bē nām ašnwēd...mihr ō rōz ēwag abāg did ō wēnišn rasēnd 100 and abzāyēd...*Denkard* VI; 242, ed. Shaked, p.94

among Zoroastrian thinkers. True, the operation of the sociological/psychological principle of the "narcissism of small differences" would have inspired leaders of both religions to stress their differences rather than similarities; but as the evidence preserved in the Babylonian Talmud indicates, Jewish acculturation to the Persian way of life, mores, and culture was high.

Nevertheless, despite the intensity of acculturation in early Sasanian times, it is becoming clear that this "golden age" lasted only a few centuries and that conditions changed in the fifth century, perhaps with the persecutions launched at the end of the reign of Yazdegird II (439–57 C.E.) but certainly with Peroz (459–84 C.E.), who issued even more severe anti-Jewish measures in 468 C.E.[4] The effect of this on the more acculturated elements of the community must have been traumatic. It is not surprising, therefore, that the attitude of the redactors of the Babylonian Talmud (second half of the fifth century C.E.) toward Sasanian law turns sharply negative.

RELIGIOUS FERMENT IN THE SASANIAN EMPIRE

By "Persian religion" we mean more than the official Zoroastrianism of the Sasanian state, for as Samuel N. C. Lieu recently put it:

> The Sassanian [sic] Empire was a meeting point of religions and cultures. Although the official religion of the ruling dynasty was Zoroastrianism, Judaeo-Christian sects and Semitic pagan cults jostled with each other in splendid confusion in Mesopotamia. To these was added a strong Jewish presence in Babylonia and Adiabene.... The victories of Shapur I brought large numbers of captive Romans to residence in the Sassanian Empire and many of them were Greek-speaking Christians from conquered cities like Antioch.[5]

Lieu describes a situation in which interreligious dialogue and polemic were the order of the day, with Judaeo-Christian sects like the Elchasaites, among whom the founder of Manichaeism, Mani, was raised, Christian sects such as the Marcionites, and, certainly, the Manichaeans and Nazarenes, jostling for converts, and perhaps the Mandeans as well.[6] In eastern parts of the empire, Buddhism and Hinduism were also factors. According to Pahlavi sources (albeit from the ninth century C.E.), Shapur II (309–79 C.E.) held religious disputations.[7] According to Manichaean accounts, at least, Shapur I (241–73) harbored Mani in his entourage, though his motives for doing so are unclear.[8] Indeed, if Shaul Shaked is correct, it was precisely the encounter with Judaism and

Christianity that turned Zoroastrianism into a more thoroughly dualistic religion.[9]

Generally, these religious groups did not exist in peaceful isolation from one another; some were persecuted severely at various times, especially the more Orthodox Christian sects that were looked upon as natural allies of the Roman enemy. In 341, the *catholicos*, Simeon bar Sabba'e, was martyred under Shapur II.[10] A century before that, Mani died in prison, martyred by Vahram I (273–76 C.E.) – but only after he had, apparently, enjoyed the protection of a succession of monarchs for thirty-five years. The intolerant Zoroastrian priest Kerdir, whose influence grew under Shapur I, eventually boasted (in his inscriptions) of persecuting "Jews and Buddhists and Hindus and Nazoraeanes and Christians and Baptists and Manichaeans."[11] He also claims to have smashed idols and converted shrines to Zoroastrian fire-temples, but there is no evidence that this affected the Jewish community.[12]

In spite of persecution, Mani's influence continued to grow, even in the Jewish community, as did that of the Sasanians' rejuvenated Zoroastrianism, as we shall see later. This was especially true of Mahoza, a suburb of Ctesiphon, capital of the empire and its cultural and religious center. It is hardly surprising that as a crossroads of (traveling) religions, Mahoza was home to many proselytes, and we may well expect a fair amount of interchange of a complex sort, not only the influence of one on another, or the borrowing of one element – legal, ritual, or even theological – from one group by another, but an atmosphere in which mutual borrowing, or mutual aversion *and* transformation, might take place. Already existing concepts or institutions may be modified by contact with their parallels in the neighboring culture. Rejection, partial or total, can be evidence of contact and "influence." As James Russell has observed, "influences from one quarter . . . do not preclude promiscuous intermingling with material from another tradition . . . ; influences need not be a graft, but can be also a stimulus that brings into prominence a feature that had been present previously, but not important."[13] H. W. Bailey surmised two generations ago, under the impact of Manichaean polemic against reliance on oral transmission, that the magi or Zoroastrian priests embarked on the massive task of producing a suitable alphabet for recording the *Avesta* – the Zoroastrian Bible – in written form, a task that was finally accomplished by the middle of the sixth century C.E, after nearly two millennia of oral transmission.[14] Originally transmitted orally with increasing incomprehension, the *Avesta* was supplied with a targum-cum-commentary, the *Zand*, the current version of which dates from the fourth to the sixth centuries C.E. It may be suggested that this polemic seems to have had its effect on the Jewish community as well.

The work of tracing these influences, counterinfluences, and mutual accommodation is just beginning. In this essay, we will begin to limn the relationship between rabbinic Judaism, on the one hand, and Zoroastrianism and Manichaeism, on the other. Detailed comparisons will have to await the completion of text-critical editions of crucial Middle Persian texts. The most important texts for us to work with are the Sasanian law book from the seventh century C.E. called the *Matakdan i Hazar Datistan* ("The Book of Thousand Judgments"),[15] as well as the *Dadestan i Denig* ("Religious Decisions"), a ninth-century collection of Zoroastrian responsa that often reflect earlier attitudes.[16] The comparisons offered in this essay, therefore, have to be understood as fragments toward a much larger enterprise.

ACCOMMODATION, RESISTANCE, AND THE SHAPING OF RABBINIC LEGAL CONCEPTIONS

A principal goal of this essay is to offer ways of assessing the mutual entanglements of rabbinic Jewish culture and the surrounding Persian milieu during the centuries that the legal institutions and conceptions of the Baylonian 'Amora'im were gaining their classic formulations in the traditions of the Babylonian Talmud. Since legal traditions are embedded in and part of more comprehensive cultural systems, we shall approach rabbinic legal formulations by contextualizing them within broader cultural settings discernable in Middle Persian texts, some of which may have been composed at that time.

Not all regions of Jewish settlement were equally open to the outside world, and degrees of acculturation seem to have varied, even in urban centers. For example, the aforementioned Jewish community of Mahoza was, as we might have expected, highly acculturated. This is especially apparent in statements preserved in the names of R. Nahman and Rava, prominent third- and fourth-generation authorities of the first half of the fourth century C.E., who can both clearly be described as "accommodators," that is, relatively open to Persian culture, to use terminology originally developed to describe contemporary American rabbis.[17] Fourth-century Babylonian Jewry was heir to more than 850 years of peaceful coexistence with its neighbors, and even towns farther from the capital than was Mahoza were open to Persian culture. Thus, in the first half of the third century, Rav and his son-in-law, R. Hannan b. Rava, both of Sura, as well as Samuel of Neharde^ca – both centers of rabbinic learning on the Euphrates – fall in the category of "accommodators." On the other hand, R. Yosef of Pumbedita on the Euphrates and 100 kilometers from the capital, could be described as a "resister." His opinions of Persians were distinctly negative, but he was nonetheless strongly influenced by at least one element of Zoroastrian thought and shows knowledge of others. Careful consideration of the intellectual *gestalt* of these rabbinic figures may thus provide a more nuanced understanding of the varying degrees of acculturation of the rabbinic elite, and perhaps the urban communities that accepted them as leaders. Given the density of Mesopotamian population, and its millennia-long heritage of urban culture, it is unlikely that the "rural" population differed greatly, at least in general terms. Indeed, given the rabbinic role as the conservators of tradition, it is unlikely that there were any large reservoirs of "fundamentalist resistance."

Despite this information, our knowledge of the differing degrees of acculturation in areas outside of Mahoza is indirect; only Rava and, to a smaller degree, R. Nahman have left substantive reflections on their community. In the concluding section of this chapter, an initial probe will be made to determine the extent of acculturation in various rabbinic centers. We shall examine important examples of acculturation that will enrich our understanding of this process and its consequences within the Babylonian Jewish community, especially that of the first half of the Sasanian era. We will then be in a position to analyze the process in terms of socioeconomic class and geographical location, and examine the major rabbinic centers documented in the Bavli, such as Sura, Neharde'a, Pumbedita, and Mahoza.

As noted, the second half of the Sasanian Period confronted the Sasanian regime with a number of challenges from within and without. These led to a restructuring and centralization that affected the minorities adversely. The resulting tensions may underlie the negative rabbinic view of the Persian regime, as manifested in the famous opening passage of B. Avodah Zarah 2b and elsewhere. It is likely that a good deal more of resister-like opinion will be found in the anonymous redactional layers than in the earlier attributed material. Nevertheless, despite some increase in anti-Jewish activities initiated by Peroz after Jewish messianic hopes were raised around 468 C.E. (400 years after the destruction of the Temple), Jewish relations with non-Jews continued. Babylonian rabbinic legislation against mingling was in general less restrictive than in Palestinian sources, for example, and Persian cultural influence continued on the community as a whole, as well as on the redactors.

THE RANGE OF ACCULTURATION

Let us provisionally outline a number of considerations that will help us to assess the Persian cultural presence within emerging

Babylonian rabbinic legal thought. We consider, *first*, a matter that precedes the issue of rabbinic law per se, the mostly anecdotal or fragmentary evidence of the lifestyles of rabbinic figures of various types, ranging from accommodators to resisters; the ordinary Babylonian Jew, especially women; the exilarch and the persianized aristocracy (including matters of language, dress, and the like); and, finally, associates of the rabbinic elite.

Our *second* focus moves more closely into legal territory by addressing rabbinic intellectual-theological engagement with Persian tradition regarding the authority and authenticity of rabbinic or Zoroastrian oral tradition, and the question of theodicy, a burning issue for nearly all Sasanian religions.

The *third* interpretive focus is ritual acculturation, especially the extent of stringencies regarding menstrual impurity; the ritual use of a belt; prospective and retrospective impurity and similar technical matters. In this area, we find a Zoroastrian codifier taking a rabbinic option into account, though ultimately rejecting it.

Fourth, we confront the issue of legal accommodation as rabbinic sages meet the challenge of Sasanian law and the government-sponsored law courts, adopt a Sasanian legal institution, and promulgate legal decisions that were untouched by such considerations but shed light on the common ambient culture.

Finally, we examine rabbinic cultural sensibility, as expressed in the attitude toward the efficiency in legal adjudication and toward cosmopolitanism. In our concluding remarks, we will briefly sketch the importance of considering local differences within the Babylonian rabbinic community. These factors will be taken up in sequence, though lifestyle will occupy center stage because of its importance as an indicator of acculturation.

INTIMATE LIFESTYLE ISSUES

Rabbinic attitudes toward sexuality seem to have been particularly susceptible to Iranian influence, though not when they contravened biblical norms. In his study of rabbinic norms of sexuality, Michael Satlow (1994b) observed that "Babylonian sources reflect much more complex, and conflicted, sexual assumptions than do Palestinian sources," but also a more positive one than do Palestinian sources. In particular,

> in Babylonian sources on sexual activity we might be observing a clash between Jewish law and its interpretation and the credos of

an honor-shame culture that most likely prevailed in Babylonia at that time. That is, the ideal co-exists uneasily with the realities of a society in which honor is achieved by acquiring the love of another man's woman. Unfortunately, in this as in so many areas we know so little about Sasanian Babylonia that it is impossible to test this thesis. (318–19)

With our current knowledge of Sasanian sexual mores and practices, we can be more certain of our ground. Middle Persian culture, at least as represented by Zoroastrian texts (as opposed to Manichaean and Christian texts), betrays a much more relaxed attitude toward sexual ethics than do Palestinian Jewish and Greco-Roman pagan and Christian texts. According to the seventh century Sasanian (law) *The Book of a Thousand Judgments,* adultery is not a capital crime for women (MHD 73:8–9 and 73:9–10 – a fine of 700 drachmas is levied for adultery and 500 for abduction), while deflowering a minor carries a penalty of 600 drachmas.[18] Further, if a male accompanying a female to study religious texts at a Zoroastrian school seduces her, especially in an area in which the husband's word carries weight, it is considered as though the man had done so under the husband's orders or his implicit permission![19]

With this in mind, we can better understand why two prominent rabbis contracted temporary marriages in accord with the Sasanian institution. Rav, the revered first-generation 'Amora', who brought a fresh infusion of Palestinian learning to Mesopotamia in the second quarter of the third century C.E., and R. Nahman, a prominent jurist of the early fourth century, disciple of Rav's colleague Samuel and teacher of the most influential authority in the Babylonian Talmud, Rava, contracted temporary marriages when away from home. The extent of the "Iranization" of the rabbis and redactors of the Bavli may be gauged from the fact that the Bavli contains not a hint of criticism or moral condemnation (B. Yevamot 37b, B. Yoma 18b). Temporary marriage cannot be separated from the issue of polygyny, which was certainly permitted by the most influential Babylonian rabbis, from Rav to Rava, though it was much less common, or approved of, in Palestine.[20]

> If the husband states that he intends to take another wife to test his potency [to beget children], [the Palestinian] R. Ammi ruled: He must in this case also divorce [his present wife] and pay her the amount of her *ketubah* [marriage contract]; for I maintain that whoever takes another wife in addition to his present one must divorce the former and pay her the amount of her *ketubah.*

> [The Babylonian] Rava said: A man may marry wives in
> addition to his first wife, provided only that he possesses the
> means to maintain them. (B. Yevamot 65a)

The following dictum attributed to Rav is also pertinent:

> [The Babylonian] Rav [said] to R. Assi: and don't marry two [wives,
> but] if you marry two, marry three. (B. Pesahim 113a)

The last comment reveals a good deal of the "battle of the sexes"
mentality found elsewhere in the Bavli. Rashi explains Rav's suggestion
as follows: Two wives will plot against their husband, but one of the
three will inform on the other two. It was thus expected that women
will plot against their husbands. R. Nahman quoted a popular proverb to
explain Abigail's forwardness in recommending herself to David when
her husband would be dead (I Samuel 25:29): "When a women talks,
she spins [webs of influence for her own benefit]" (B. Megillah 14b).
Similarly, advice attributed to the fourth-century Zoroastrian high priest
Ādurbād ī Mahraspandān is not to trust women with secrets. This puts
her in the company of "wrong-headed" men or "babblers" (Zaehner 1976,
101).

Of course, the effect of a polygynous marriage is that it puts the
wives in a permanently subordinate position. They are always "replace-
able," and *temporary* marriage merely adds insult to the injury. It should
be remembered that R. Akiva had long since permitted divorce for a reason as simple as the husband finding a more beautiful woman to marry
(M. Gittin 9:10).

It is also reported that R. Nahman would interchange his slaves'
sexual partners, in contrast to his master Samuel, who would attempt
to maintain the integrity of the slave couples (B. Niddah 47a). Here, too,
there is no discernable criticism of R. Nahman's practice. Elsewhere,
however, R. Nahman, and with him the rest of the "accomodationist"
"Persianized" Jewish aristocracy, were criticized by the "resisters" of
Pumbedita for allowing their womenfolk to mingle with men (B. Kiddushin 70a–b), and his daughters were accused of not attempting to
escape the danger of rape under conditions of captivity (B. Gittin 45a).

R. Nahman's disciple, Rava, permitted a husband to pretend to sell a
piece of land to his wife in order to determine whether she had illegally
hidden away money for herself; if she had, the land remained his (B. Bava
Metzia 51b).[21]

Rava's decision is thoroughly un-Iranian in its methods, since Iranian women certainly had rights to their own property, as when they

inherited from their fathers or were appointed supervisors over their deceased husbands' estates, for instance, as *sturs*, an Iranian institution according to which a man or woman – often the deceased husband's widow – was obliged to provide an heir for the deceased while in the meantime managing the estate. Alternatively, women, as seems often to have been the case, were partners in managing the family estates, as described in *The Book of a Thousand Decisions*. While this text dates from the first quarter of the seventh century C.E., judging from the kings mentioned in it, it may reflect conditions from the last century and a half of the Sasanian period, and even earlier.

Thus, it would seem that for Mahozan Jewish society, polygyny, temporary marriage, and the entrance of women into social relations are evidence of Iranian influence, while the rabbis drew the line at giving women property rights or allowing them Torah study. Even their view of women's strong sexual desires matched those of the neighboring Iranian culture.[22] Further, Rava's permissive stance in regard to daytime marital intercourse (B. Niddah 17a) had a Zoroastrian demonological belief at its base, as did the Bavli's suggestion that nail parings should be buried (B. Moed Katan 18a).[23]

Iranian attitudes predominated in more personal matters. For example, both R. Nahman and Rava had a fear of death – of the process of dying, which was considered painful (B. Moed Katan 28a). This is in line with the Zoroastrian: "The soul of the righteous undergoes much pain when it departs from the world; until it has passed through that frightful account, it laments." The talmudic anecdotes reflect an attitude to death on the part of rabbis very different from those attributed to the Palestinian sages R. Yehoshua b. Levi and R. Hanina b. Papa, who defy the Angel of Death and where R. Yehoshua b. Levi manages to outwit him and enter paradise bodily (B. Ketubot 77b).[24] Finally, R. Nahman is reported to have told his daughters: regarding the killing of lice, "Kill the hated ones and let me hear the sound!" (B. Shabbat 12a), quite like a Zoroastrian, for whom the killing of noxious beasts and insects was a *mizvah*, a *kirbag*.

THE *KULTURKAMPF:* MAHOZA AND PUMBEDITA

From the account of the Pumbeditan "resisters" of a confrontation between R. Yehuda, founder of the *yeshiva* in Pumbedita, and R. Nahman, who in the Babylonian Talmud represents the quintessential Persianized Mahozan Jewish aristocrat, it is clear what the controversial issues were. Thus, a story (in B. Kiddushin 70a–b) criticizes the latter for his elitist, persianized language (the use of such words as *atrunga* [citron] and *anbag* [spiced wine]), and his permitting freer social mixing of the sexes than the Pumbeditans thought desirable or permissible. In particular, R. Yehuda is depicted as objecting to being served by R. Nahman's minor daughter Donag, as well as to being asked to send a greeting to Yalta, generally presumed to be his wife, even through her husband. All this is attributed to Samuel, their common master, who surprisingly is otherwise known for his *accommodationist* tendencies, as demonstrated by his friendship with Shapur I. Samuel is famously known for his proclamation that "the [civil] law of the government is [valid] law [for Jewish courts]," a statement that is cited repeatedly throughout the Babylonian Talmud (B. Nedarim 28a, B. Gittin 10b, B. Bava Kamma 113a, and especially B. Bava Batra 54b). But there are less well-known indicators of his general accommodation of Persian culture, namely, his attendance at a *Be 'Abadan*, a Zoroastrian temple annex, apparently for what could be considered interdenominational discussions (B. Shabbat 116a). Despite this, Samuel's authority is mobilized as supporting a resisters' critique of the Mahozan elite. Perhaps this apparent contradiction can be explained by suggesting that Samuel was not iranized in his personal lifestyle. As noted earlier, R. Nahman is *not* criticized for contracting temporary marriages, a practice adopted by Samuel's colleague Rav – a precedent that may have protected R. Nahman from censure.

The criticisms of upper-class lifestyle, however, did not end with R. Nahman himself; they continued with his family, especially Yalta, who is described as high-handed and proud (B. Berakhot 51a), as well as timorous and desirous of her comfort (B. Betzah 25b). His daughters are depicted and condemned for not being particularly eager to be rescued from captivity among gentiles, with its concomitant danger of rape (B. Gittin 45a).

At the same time, the anonymous critic of upper-class Mahozan life in this text reveals a large amount of cultural and linguistic sophistication. He distinguishes three registers of Hebrew and Aramaic – rabbinic, popular, and elitist – and, as we have just noted, knows that *atrunga* and *anbag* are Middle Persian loanwords. Clearly, this was one of the defining issues of his world, as important to him as the question of the mingling of the sexes. It should be recalled that R. Papa knows the difference between names that are used by both Jews and non-Jews and names that are unambiguously non-Jewish – Hannez, Abudina, Bar Shibtai, Bar Qidri, Bati, Naqim, and Una (B. Gittin 11a). In other words, the Bavli knows its cultural landscape well!

This critique allows us to trace what may be considered a *Kulturkampf* within rabbinic circles in Babylonian Jewish society. The talmudic linguistic critique revealed here seems to echo a cultural condemnation, employing the stereotypes of national character and lifestyle. Though directed against R. Nahman, this critique is not primarily directed at Persian mores; if it were, we might expect an attack on *xwēdōdah*, the Zoroastrian next-of-kin marriage, which would have represented the nadir of depravity for the rabbis. Instead, the Bavli does associate both Persians (B. Shabbat 94a) and the Jewish persianized elite with "arrogance" (*ramut ruha*), a trope known from the Byzantine historians. It is, rather, a critique of a specific type of aristocratic adaptation to them, that is, the upper-class Mahozan. The critique is articulated in terms too general to represent merely personal pique, since it is effectuated by means of cultural stereotypes. As noted, it is also a carefully calibrated attack.

As in the case of R. Nahman, there are other reports of Rav's persianizing ways, but he is apparently immune from criticism: Not only is he reported to have been a close associate of Artavan V, the last Parthian king (B. Avodah Zarah 10b, 11a) upon whose death (ca. 225 C.E.) Rav is said to have exclaimed: "The bond is snapped." But he often cites typically Persian habits. Thus, he quotes elements of the Middle Persian theological determination that attributes essential elements of the good life, namely, wife and property (B. Sotah 2a), not to good works as one would have expected in rabbinic discourse, but to fate. Rav further advises not to travel by night out of fear of demons (B. Bava Kamma 60b), certainly a Zoroastrian belief.[25] Still, Rav may have seen this as a neutral element of the common Iranian-Mesopotamian culture, rather than as a specifically religious teaching. This may shed light on the pervasiveness of Jewish acculturation; even Zoroastrian theological teachings were transmuted into neutral "knowledge."

As to those associated with the rabbinic elite, we might point to the example of Rava having to inform his servant on how to estimate the start of twilight for "you who are not clear" (B. Shabbat 35b). From what class or social circle was this servant drawn? This exchange is especially interesting in that elsewhere in the Babylonian Talmud (B. Avodah Zarah 58a), it is a *Rav* Elyakim who is Rava's servant in Mahoza. Perhaps the servant mentioned in Shabbat was a menial one – a valet, so to speak – while R. Elyakim was a kind of secretary. On Rava himself and his community, we will have more to say later.

As to the nonelitist Babylonian Jews, we have at most anecdotal evidence in the Talmud, such as the report regarding the ordinary Babylonian Jewish *woman*. R. Zera reports that it was the "daughters of Israel" who had undertaken to be so strict with themselves as to wait seven [clean] days [after the appearance] of a drop of blood the size of a mustard seed [though biblically, they are required only to separate for seven days from the onset of regular menstruation]" (B. Berakhot 31a, Megillah 28b, Niddah 66a). Although medieval talmudic commentaries assume that this was a rabbinically inspired severity, it is clear from Rava's response to R. Papa (in B. Niddah 66a) that he considered this stringency to be a custom, and not a prohibition. The Babylonian Talmud itself testifies to the popular origin of this stringency – perhaps in response to a "holier than thou" attitude perceived by the populace as emanating from their Persian neighbors, a social pressure to which the rabbis themselves sometimes responded (e.g., B. Sanhedrin 37b). Surely, we must conclude that Babylonian Jewish women had internalized their Zoroastrian neighbors' critique of rabbinic Judaism's relatively "easygoing" ways in this regard; Jewish women did not have to remain isolated on spare rations in a windowless hut for up to nine days, as was prescribed for Zoroastrian menstruant women.

INTELLECTUAL-THEOLOGICAL ENGAGEMENT

1. Authority and Authenticity of Oral Tradition

The fourth-century rabbinic sage Rava faced theological challenges not only from Zoroastrianism, the state religion, but also from Manichaeism, a religion without state support. Here, the rabbis and the Zoroastrian magi were on the same side, both privileging oral transmission.

The situation that Rava faced may be delineated by the following three texts.

> Said Rava: How foolish are most people who rise [in respect] before a Torah scroll but not before a rabbinic scholar, for in a Torah scroll is written, "forty [strokes shall you give him and not more]" [Deuteronomy 25:3], and the Rabbis came and reduced it by one! [Thus they are due as much respect as a Torah scroll, if not more, since they control its interpretation, even when it goes against the plain meaning of the biblical text.] (B. Makkot 22b)

And again:

> Who is a heretic [of which the Mishnah states that he will have no portion in the World to Come]? . . . Said Rava: As those members of the household of Benjamin the Physician, who say: What use are the Rabbis to us? They never permitted the raven [which the Torah forbids], nor have they forbidden the dove [which the Torah allows; thus the Rabbis cannot undo what is written in the Torah]. When

[members] of the household of Benjamin the Physician would bring a [question regarding the permissibility for consumption of animals] with a fatal organic defect [which are ordinarily forbidden] before Rava, when he saw a reason to be lenient, he would say to them: See, I have permitted the raven for you! And when he saw a reason to be stringent, he would say to them: See, I have forbidden the dove to you! (B. Sanhedrin 99b–100a)

In this environment, we can well understand why Rava shows a deep sensitivity to the problems of rabbinic biblical exegesis. He is one of only two 'Amora'im to whom the principle that "a verse does not depart from its plain sense" is attributed;[26] he was sharply attentive to the problems involved in the study of *midrash halakhah*, some of which he learned from the 'Amora'im of Eretz Israel who preceded him, at least one from his father-in-law, R. Hisda, and some of which he pioneered himself.

The "household" – presumably, the sons, but perhaps even the grandsons – of Benjamin the Physician charged the rabbis with being ineffectual, since they could not permit what the Torah forbade, and vice versa. Note that the exchange focuses on the matter of biblical versus rabbinic authority. Rava, presumably on another occasion, pointed to the rabbis' power in limiting the forty stripes prescribed by Torah to thirty-nine. Elsewhere, Rava emphasizes the severity of violating rabbinic ordinances, even as against those of the Torah:

Rava expounded [in public]: What [is the meaning of the verse] that is written, "And of more than these, my son, take heed, the making of many books" [Ecclesiastes 12:12]. My son, take heed of the words of the Scribes more than the words of the Torah, for the words of the Torah contain positive and negative commandments, while as to the words of the Scribes, whoever transgresses the words of the Scribes is worthy of death: Perhaps you will say that if they have substance to them, why were they not written down? The verse [therefore] says: "Of the making of books there is no end" [Ecclesiastes 12:12]. (B. Eruvin 21b)

Thus, when Rava wished to emphasize the greater severity attendant upon the violation of rabbinic norms over biblical ones, he felt the need to deal with the question "if they are indeed valid, why are they not written?" Once again, we hear echoes of the family of Dr. Benjamin – or their Mahozan neighbors, the other "sharp-witted ones of Mahoza" (B. Berakhot 59b). Indeed, we hear even more distant echoes of theological controversies beyond the Jewish community, as we shall see.

Ideally, and to this Rava must agree, a written form is the proper venue for the transmission of law; why then is the law of the rabbis unwritten? Rava responds to this problem by quoting Ecclesiastes 12:12 "Of the making of books there is no end"; that is, rabbinic law is too voluminous to be reduced to writing. It is pertinent to recall at this point that the largest Middle Persian compilation known to us is the *Dēnkard*, a nine-book Zoroastrian encyclopedia that dates from the ninth century, and runs to only 169,000 words. In contrast, the Babylonian Talmud weighs in at about 1,836,000 words.[27] Based on the large, ancient, probably eighth-century fragment of B. Hullin 101–5 identified by Marc Bregman and published by Shamma Friedman a few years ago, which contained an average of 576 words per column, and assuming a Torah-size scroll as standard, about ten and a half scrolls of that size would have been needed for 2,522 columns.[28] Even if we assume that Rava's "words of the Scribes" in the fourth century ran to a third of the size of the Bavli, this would have been beyond the capabilities of Mesopotamian scribes of the mid–fourth century.

Aside from the technical problems, however, we must note that Rava's statement can be seen as a response to Mani's critique of oral transmission, the outcome of which, it has been suggested by H. W. Bailey, was the invention of the Avestan alphabet and the reduction to writing of the Avesta. Mani, in one of his surviving Middle Persian texts, claims the following:

> The religion that I [i.e., Mani] have chosen is in ten things above and better than the other, previous religions ... the former religions [existed] as long as they had the pure leaders, but when the pure leaders had been led upwards [i.e., had died], then their religions fell into disorder and became negligent in commandments and works.... [But my religion, because of] the living [books(?)], of the Teachers, the Bishops, the Elect and the Hearers, and of wisdom and works will stay on until the End. (Cited in Asmussen, *Manichean Literature*, 12)

As Jes Asmussen (16) commented,

> this immense confidence in the written tradition was something quite exceptional in the history of antiquity that never questioned the reliability and security of the oral tradition.... And, to take just one more example, the *Dēnkard* without hesitation states that the living spoken word is much more important than the written one.

If Rava's involvement with this challenge consisted merely of preachments and ironic comments, the results of our investigation would be interesting, but hardly compelling. These challenges induced him to undertake two major restructurings of rabbinic teachings, both of which influenced the eventual shape of the Bavli considerably. From the available data, Rava had already embarked on a systematic examination of the rabbinic approach to Scripture, an examination that stood him in good stead when confronted with the challenges of the household of Dr. Benjamin and the other "sharp-witted ones of Mahoza," among them "most people" (B. Makkot 22b), "the household of Dr. Benjamin" (B. Sanhedrin 99b–100a), and Yaakov the Heretic, with whom he debates a point of rabbinic legal exegesis (B. Hullin 84a).

R. Nahman, too, Rava's master, was faced with the challenge of dualists of some sort, presumably Jewish/Christian or Jewish-Christian Gnostics. He is reported as having warned that whoever can respond to the *minim* like R. Idit could, should respond; otherwise, he should not (B. Sanhedrin 38b). It may be that he considered himself one of those unfit to respond. Again, his comments about the absence of *minim* among non-Jews (B. Hullin 13a), while ambiguous, still conforms to the cosmopolitan nature of his surroundings. This statement is very provocative, certainly in the far more introspective view of the sixth-century redactors, and may well have raised eyebrows even in the fourth century. The question is, of course, what he meant by "minim." To render the term by the "neutral" heretic would be to assert that R. Nahman gave credibility to the "official" or established versions of each religion, and raises a large number of additional questions as well. Moreover, if S. Shaked is correct, there *was* no officially sanctioned Zoroastrian orthodoxy at this time, and the Zurvanite myth was not heretical (Shaked 1993, 18–19). Could R. Nahman have been taking a position on the status of Manichaeism as a Zoroastrian heresy? This is unlikely for the same reason. More likely is that he was referring to the various Judaeo-Christian-Mandean-Gnostic sects, such as the Elchasites of Mani's parents, and possibly the Marcionites, not to mention the mysterious Nazoreans or Nazarenes, who may have been Mandeans, Christians, or Jewish-Christians. Whatever his intent, this statement demonstrates the Jewish stake in the religious questions raised by the religiously innovative early Sasanian Middle Persian culture.

2. Theodicy
Rava's statements regarding the problem of theodicy also address a contemporary burning issue. Given the centrality of the problem of evil

in Zoroastrianism – indeed, in all the religions of Late Antiquity – it is easy to see why Rava was so concerned with it, and why R. Yosef in the previous generation devised a theology of divine anger. One of Rava's most radical statements on the topic fits perfectly within the context of the Middle Persian debate on "fate" and "works."[29] Rava attributes to the workings of fate – *mazal* – the three elements that we may see as components of individual contentment: "[length of] life, [surviving] children, and sustenance" (B. Moed Katan 28a). He asserts that these three aspects of human life are astrologically determined and are not dependent on religious merit.

This is not Rava's sole contribution to the matter, however; another example is that he further limits R. Yosef's statement on the limited utility of Torah study and the performance of mizvot as protection against sufferings (B. Sotah 21a); elsewhere he asserts that in some cases, one's merit may bring upon him yet more suffering, albeit "sufferings of love" (B. Berakhot 5a). All of these (the limited protection from the exigencies of human existence afforded by Torah study and the performance of commandments, humanity's own frail nature, and the "sufferings of love") contribute to the tragic dimensions of the human condition – a recognition that lies at the heart of Zoroastrianism's dualistic view of the universe.[30]

In the end, Rava's view of the astrological influences on the basics of human happiness were not universally accepted by the redactors of the Babylonian Talmud, who elsewhere transmit opinions that reject astrological influence as affecting Jews (see B. Shabbat 156a–b). However, Rava's saying fits extremely well within the context of Zoroastrian thought, where the theme of astrology versus merit, or "works," appears in many Middle Persian compilations. Thus, Rava's apparent citation of a Babylonian Aramaic proverb has a striking parallel in a Middle Persian one, and in other texts besides (Elman 1991).

RITUAL ACCULTURATION

We have already mentioned one significant example of the influence of Zoroastrian ritual norms on the Jewish Babylonian woman – and perforce, the Babylonian man – in the street, one that is especially revealing: the stringency adopted by Jewish women regarding menstrual impurity. This phenomenon indicates just how far acculturation had gone, just how much the values of the Other had been internalized into the rabbinic value system. More than that, the women apparently overcame their husbands' natural objections to a stringency that would almost double the time of prohibited marital relations per monthly cycle. Clearly, both sexes felt the force of the "holier than thou" argument.

Another indication typifies not only the persianized aristocracy but the rabbis as well. First, the exilarch Huna b. Nathan reports on an audience he had had with Yazdegird I (399–420 C.E.), who is remembered in Zoroastrian lore as the "Sinful One" for his tolerance of Jews and Christians:[31]

> R. Ashi said: [The Exilarch] Huna b. Nathan [once] said to me: Once I was standing before King Yazdegird [I], and my belt slipped upwards, whereupon he pulled it down, observing to me: It is written of you, "a kingdom of priests and a holy nation" [Exodus 19:6] [and so you must take care to wear your belt like a priest, and not so high]. When I came before Amemar, he said to me: [The verse in Isaiah 49:23] has been fulfilled regarding you: "Kings will be your nursemaids." (B. Zevahim 19a)

The exilarch, who had the status of a Persian nobleman (of minor status) clearly dressed the part, and wore a Zoroastrian belt, a *kustig*, a fact that explains Yazdegird's otherwise inexplicable use of the verse from Exodus. The kustig is untied and retied during Zoroastrian prayer, and is a component of Zoroastrian identity.[32] Clearly, the "belt" had a religious significance, but a discussion elsewhere in the Talmud indicates that the use of a belt was a general Babylonian Jewish custom:

> When is the beginning of eating [a meal so that if one has begun, we do not trouble him to interrupt his meal for the afternoon prayer]? Rav said: When one washes his hands; R. Hanina said: When one loosens his belt. However, they do not differ: one refers to ourselves [= Babylonians], and one refers to them [= Palestinians].
>
> R. Sheshet objected: Is it any trouble to remove the belt? Moreover, let him stand thus [unbelted] and pray? – Because it is said: "Prepare to meet your God, o Israel" [Amos 4:12]. [Girding one's loins oneself is a preparation for prayer.] (B. Shabbat 9b)

From this it is clear that even the rabbis, like their fellow Jews at large, wore belts, which their Palestinian coreligionists did not.

Commenting on this passage in his study on nonverbal elements in rabbinic prayer, Uri Ehrlich points to the Zoroastrian parallel of a kustig, but concludes that "it is difficult to suppose that Zoroastrian literature directly influenced the custom of putting on a belt in Jewish prayer, and therefore it may be that the influence penetrated through the general [Babylonian-Iranian] dress-code (that is, without a religious context)."[33] However, from the data cited here, it is clear that the custom's Zoroastrian origin would not have hindered its acceptance, nor was an acquaintanceship with Zoroastrian literature necessary, merely a knowledge of a neighbor's customary garb. Certainly the exilarch, and probably R. Ashi, would have been aware of its religious significance, or, perhaps, its religious significance did not motivate them to forgo its use.

When it comes to codification and analysis of ritual, we enter an even more complex area, one in which we may discern a welter of influences and counterinfluence in both directions. Some things are clear; for example, it has long been apparent that the Bavli's recommendation regarding the disposal of the aforementioned fingernail parings has a Zoroastrian origin.

Michael Satlow pointed out a decade ago that the rabbinic emphasis on the severity of the sin of emitting seed vainly (*hoza'at zera^c levatalah*) is due to the work of the editor and redactor of B. Niddah 13a–b, and does not appear in the earlier sources cited there at all. He suggests that "perhaps they adopted this concept from Zoroastrian notions, to which, we may assume, they were exposed."[34]

This brings us to perhaps the most potentially fruitful area of research, a comparison of the rabbinic and Zoroastrian system of purities. Unfortunately, detailed comparisons will only be possible upon the completion of scientific editions of crucial Middle Persian texts. In the meantime, however, some general observations are possible. The two systems, first of all, operate with similar basic concepts regarding human corpses (*tum'at met*), dead animals (*tum'at nevelah*, both *Nasā* in Middle Persian parlance), and a menstruant woman (*tum'at niddah, zan ī daštān*). Because the basic biological processes that both systems must deal with are identical, though their construction of impurity may be different, the resulting systems will be sufficiently close to warrant extended comparative work. This is particularly important because the Zoroastrian system, while employing an elliptical style similar to rabbinic texts, lacks the medieval commentarial and comprehensive works available for the elucidation of rabbinic halakhic discussions.

Both systems struggled, moreover, with the problem of defining the onset and limiting the extent to which impurity may be said to exist. Impurity held much weightier consequences for the Zoroastrians, since, theologically, impurity was a weapon of the Evil One, while for the rabbis, whatever its biblical origins, impurity is a strictly ritual category. Zoroastrian authorities rejected extensions of impurity in directions that rabbinic authorities allow. Thus, it is recorded in a code dating from the Parthian Period that Ohrmazd rejects extending impurity through mixture (the rabbinic *ta^{c}arovet*), as when a bird deposits dead matter that had already been eaten or digested, vomited out or defecated, and then deposited on a tree that was being used for firewood, "for if these corpses, namely, dog-borne, bird-borne, wolf-borne, wind-borne, and fly-borne, were to make a man guilty, right away my entire existence with bones...every soul would be shuddering [in anger and fear], every body would be forfeit, by the large amount of these corpses which lie dead upon this earth" (*Vīdēvdād* 5.4).

Thus, while many rules are common to both systems, the concept of retrospective impurity (*tum'ah lemafre^{c}a*), common in rabbinic parlance, is rejected in *Šāyast nē Šāyast* in regard to the impurity caused by dead matter, but not in regard to that caused by menstruation, as is evident in the following: "There is one who says: *tahag* is from the beginning, while other things [are impure] from the day she knows [about the onset of blood-flow]" (Pahlavī *Vīdēvdād* 16.2).[35] The author of the later *Šāyast nē Šāyast* also suggests that menstruant women transmit impurity by gaze because it is so much more severe (*Šāyast nē Šāyast* 3:39), which indicates the beginnings of the comparative analysis of purity subsystems in Zoroastrian ritual law, so common in the Babylonian Talmud. Most intriguing is the discussion of the colors of menstrual blood in the Pahlavi *Vīdēvdād* 16.14, a concern otherwise known only from Judaism.[36]

LEGAL ACCOMMODATION

1. Parallels and Convergences

The rabbinic category of the "rebellious wife," the *moredet* (B. Ketubot 62a–b), finds its exact counterpart in the Sasanian concept of *atarsagāyīh*, "insubordination," to which an entire chapter of *The Book of Thousand Judgments* is devoted, with similar definitions, such as refusal of marital relations, domestic "work" and personal spousal service, and penalties.[37] In this case, as in others, the differences are sometimes as illuminating as are the similarities, and historians of Jewish and Sasanian law ignore them at their peril.[38] The rabbinic concept of *'ona'ah*, "overreaching" in sales, may be paralleled by *Madayan* 37:2–10, with the same three-day period stipulated, but with a quarter rather than a sixth of the price (B. Bava Metzia 49b–51a, 69a). Then there is the institution of *me'un* ("refusal"), whereby an underage girl could be married off by her mother or brothers, but could, upon reaching her majority, leave her husband.[39] Such examples could be multiplied.

Some of these involve matters with which every legal system must deal, and are most likely the result of independent development. Similar conditions – economic, social, and religious – produce similar concerns. But studying each in isolation prevents us from gaining a complete picture of the conditions under which each system developed, and the way that each responded to common problems. Is it not likely that the rabbis and the Iranian jurisconsults were faced with a rash of fraudulent land sales, with people claiming to own land they did not, as evidenced by B. Bava Metzia 14a–b and MHDA 8:13–9:5? The hunger for arable land, certainly in short supply in the Persian Empire, would likely yield such a scheme in Jewish Babylonia (because of the density of population) and Iran (because of the arid conditions of its plateaus and mountains).

Such scattershot parallels need not detain us for long, since they are typical of any legal system. Moreover, programmatic studies examining the relation between rabbinic and Sasanian law that have appeared in the last two years, or are about to appear, indicate that the relationship between the two legal and ritual systems was more complex than a simplistic search for influences alone would show. There are more pertinent examples of the contact of halakhah with Sasanian law.

2. Land Tenure and Private "Eminent Domain"

Samuel's dictum, mentioned earlier, that "the [civil] law of the government is [valid] law" indicates that already early on in the Sasanian period, one of the greatest Babylonian rabbinic authorities was willing to come to terms with the new regime and its legal system. This attribution is confirmed by his ruling regarding land tenure along the river banks near Neharde^{c}a, his hometown.

Apparently, a stranger to the neighborhood had taken advantage of Persian law to take possession of a riverbank in order to either build a quay or plant a crop on the riverbank. Samuel was reluctant to remove him, but later on, perhaps generations later, when the stakes were higher and the Sasanian government was willing to give the interloper control of the adjacent riverbed as well, the rabbis were prepared to remove him. Although the legal and public policy issues are too complex to discuss here, it is clear that the rabbis were quite aware of Sasanian law and legal terminology and prepared to intervene to protect the local Jewish community's rights (Elman 2004b).

3. Conditional and Returnable Gifts

One of Samuel's disciples, the aristocratic R. Nahman, who, as noted, contracted temporary marriages when away from home, is also credited in both Talmuds with originating the rule of temporary or conditional "ownership" – that is, of adopting the Sasanian rule of conditional and temporary gifts both in his legal decisions (B. Bava Batra 137b) and in his personal life. This is especially noteworthy in the case of the set of "four species" that he lent his son on a temporary basis on Sukkot (see Leviticus 23:40), since according to tannaitic law, the one who "takes" these species must have absolute ownership of them.[40] But he applied this principle to other loans and transfers. In some places, his more famous disciple Rava is credited with the innovation, though he rejects the extreme use of the institution in every case (see B. Kiddushin 6b, B. Bava Batra 137b). R. Nahman's authorship is confirmed by the testimony of the Talmud Yerushalmi (Y. Sukkah 3:10, 54a) and conforms to our knowledge of R. Nahman's affinities; the principle was introduced by the master and not the disciple.

4. Meeting the Competition of Persian Courts

It is important to note that R. Nahman, who in the Bavli is universally considered an authority on Sasanian law, also modified the mishnaic rules regarding a gift made in contemplation of death (*donatio mortis causa*, in Roman jurisprudence) so as to make the abandoning of rabbinic law in favor of resort to a Persian court less advantageous (Yaron 1960, 85–89). In the Bavli, his explicit references to "Persian law" are always negative (B. Bava Batra 173a–b, Bava Kamma 58b, Shevuot 34b), but further analysis indicates that the negative views are those of the redactors and may date from a period more than a century later, as already mentioned, when Peroz and Yazdegird II promulgated anti-Jewish decrees and Babylonian Jewry's "golden age" had passed. Given our current appreciation for R. Nahman's acculturation, it is unlikely that he expressed these negative and inaccurate views. For example, it is clear that Persian law did not obligate a surety to pay the lender even when the borrower was solvent (as Bava Batra 173b would have it; see MHD 57:2–12), but also because no one would agree to be a surety under such circumstances, thus shutting off the flow of credit. Again, his modification of *donatio mortis causa* in B. Bava Batra 148b may indicate that he felt the competition of the Persian courts.

As R. Nahman was an acknowledged expert in Persian and rabbinic civil law, however, his comments on the Sasanian legal system would have carried considerable weight among the acculturated members of the Babylonian Jewish community, including those who might have resorted to the Persian courts when dissatisfied with the rabbinic courts, either in a particular decision, where they suspected that the case would go against them, or did go against them, or because of their low opinion of rabbinic versus Persian courts (e.g., B. Bava' Kamma' 58b, B. Bava Batra 153a–b). And the starkly negative manner of their depiction in the Bavli suggests that the rabbis were concerned about just such a danger. Thus, Persian law, like Roman or rabbinic law, does not obligate the guarantor to repay the debt even when the debtor is solvent (see MHD 57:2–12) or invalidate testimony when irrelevant circumstances are asserted (MHD 8:15–10:11), respectively. These rabbinic assertions seem to date from a time during which the rabbis were thoroughly alienated from the regime and ignorant of the Sasanian court system. Abaye's more nuanced comments regarding the Persian courts in B. Gittin 28b (before 338) are thus more accurate, as is his knowledge of Persian legal terminology.[41]

5. Keeping Estates Together

Study of Sasanian law may aid us in placing rabbinic legislation in its proper context in another sense. For example, J. A. Crook (1967, 118) observed that no fewer than eleven of the books of Justinian's Digest are devoted to questions of succession and inheritance. Likewise, a third of the folios of the Sasanian law book contain mentions of *stūrīh*, the Zoroastrian equivalent of the biblical levirate marriage, but its interest is devoted more to property settlements than levirate marriage per se. In contrast, only two chapters of the Mishnah's 530 are devoted to the subject of inheritance, and very little of the sixteen chapters of Tractate Yevamot ("levirate marriages") and the thirteen of Ketubot ("marriage contracts") deal with inheritance. Moreover, it is clear that the Mishnah's (and the Talmuds') attention are devoted to the smallish family farm run by a nuclear family along with temporary laborers hired for planting and harvest and not to the large Roman and Sasanian *latifundia*. The difference in social policy – and class interest – could not be more striking.

6. Nonaccommodation: Women's Property, Inheritance, and Other Civil Rights

An equally striking but more complicated contrast involves the improvement in women's legal rights over the latter part of the Sasanian period, as can be discerned from Madayan. The right of a married woman to hold, manage, and sell her own or her husband's property, and her right to inherit property from her parents or her husband, were never a universal given in the world of Late Antiquity. Nevertheless, when one examines these issues within the context of Roman, Sasanian, and rabbinic law, a striking difference emerges. Over time, women's rights to property increased in the first two legal systems, as marriage with tutelage or guardianship gave way to forms that allowed women more autonomy. The rabbinic system, on the other hand, retained many features of the earlier period. While this is undoubtedly due in part to the rabbinic view of the divine origin of biblical law, an examination of the relevant legislation indicates that in many areas, the legislation in question was recognized by the rabbis themselves as rabbinic in origin, and yet women's legal status remained static.

This may be explained by demographic and economic factors. A large number of cases in the Sasanian law book indicates that there was a severe shortage of upper-class males to run the family estates, and so females were drafted to replace them. On the other hand, several noteworthy cases indicate that there was also a shortage of aristocratic women of marriageable age. Two factors seem to account for this. One is the recurrence of outbreaks of the black plague, which reached Byzantium in 542, according to Procopius, and which continued for two centuries. Women, while more resistant on the whole, nevertheless succumbed to the plague, especially young women.[42] Adult men were less resistant to the plague bacillus than women; moreover, the continuous wars of the sixth century against Rome and the Hepthalites decimated upper-class males, from which the officer corps was drawn. The result was a demographic crisis that left upper-class women in charge of estates as female "levirs" or *stūr*s. As a result, they won the right to represent the estate in court and alienate estate property, and so on. This was the case even during their menstrual period, when, as good Zoroastrians, they should have been isolated in windowless huts. It would seem that while *Vīdēvdād* (in Chapter 16) portrays menstruant women as isolated from their families in fireless, windowless huts, other Zoroastrian texts, chiefly the Pahlavī *Hērbedestān* and *Nērangestān*, ponder the question of the relative worth of observing these rules or *caring for an estate* or *tending and worshipping the fire*.[43] This particular discussion mirrors the very dilemma brought on by the demographic crisis described here.

We have no evidence on the Jewish side, since the Babylonian Talmud was in all probability completed – except for episodic posttalmudic additions – before the black plague struck; plague hardly figures in the Bavli as a manifestation of divine wrath, unlike drought and famine. Indeed, the famine caused by the plague, as well as the subsequent shortage of agricultural workers, might have been expected to affect the Bavli, but there is no indication of that.[44] Since post-talmudic data are sparse for several centuries (perhaps *because* of the plague), we simply have no way of judging how the rabbis dealt with the problem of a shortage of adult males. In any case, since Jews did not serve in the army, the wars of the sixth century would not have affected them directly.[45] All this comes at the end of the talmudic era, however; the heyday of Jewish-Iranian symbiosis seems to have occurred during the *first* half of the Sasanian era, from the reigns of Shapur I (221–70/73) and Shapur II (309–79), or perhaps through that of Yazdegird I (399–420), and was certainly over by that of Xusro I (531–79).

While the case of retrospective impurity stems from a tannaitic source, this problem, and others like it, served to create a common universe of discourse, no less than the problem of destiny and works and theodicy or the question of the authority of an unwritten tradition. While the sociological law of the "narcissism of small differences" would apply to these neighboring societies as a whole, and mandate that the closer the similarities, the greater the attempt to keep them apart, the existence of these parallels indicates that this was not the whole story. Indeed, these ritual matters may well have been less divisive than theological questions that eventually turned on the irreconcilable issue of dualism. In regard to purities, the rabbis and Zoroastrian priests were on the same side, with Manichaeans and perhaps others – certainly Christians in regard to purities and the primacy of oral traditions – on the other. True, the narcissism of small differences would keep the priests and rabbis apart, despite the commonalities, and, indeed, exacerbate the conflict. But, as the reports of Samuel's friendship with Ibbalit suggest, such relationships were not unthinkable, and especially the example of Rava's approach to the problem of theodicy, as well as the consideration that *Šāyast nē Šāyast* gives to the possibility of retroactive impurity, indicate that some contacts and crossovers did occur.

RABBINIC CULTURAL SENSIBILITY

1. Judicial Efficiency

In a series of decisions, Rava opts for clear-cut definitions in part, it would appear, to avoid drawn-out legal cases. Thus, lost objects are the property of the finder even before the loser is aware of his loss and has given up hope of recovering it (B. Bava Metzia 21b–22b). Again, *edim zomemim* (witnesses giving false testimony, who are the subject of retaliation as per Deuteronomy 19:19) become invalid as witnesses only from the time of conviction, and not retrospectively (B. Sanhedrin 27a). It is interesting to note that the eventual decision went to Abaye. In another case, he decides, again in contrast to Abaye, that a lender may collect collateral on a defaulted loan only from the time of the default. That is, if the debtor had alienated the collateral in some way before the default, according to Abaye, the lender could still collect.

One issue that may underlie all three disputes is that of retrospective ownership or status. The lost object is retrospectively that of the finder from the time of the loss; the witnesses' testimony is invalid from the time of the original testimony and not merely from that of the time the second set of witnesses testified against them; and the collateral can be collected from the time of the default and not the time of the loan. The issue would seem to be one of applying the principle of retroactivity, which had hitherto been applied only in cases of ritual impurity, to other areas of rabbinic law. We might expect, then, that Rava, whose pioneering effort in applying conceptualization to rabbinic law has recently been documented by Leib Moscovitz (2002), would be "on the cutting edge," so to speak. But in actuality, he applies the principle in the first case only.

We may suggest that his motives seem to have been to ensure judicial efficiency, that his own law court and others in heavily populated Mahoza and surrounding Jewish communities not be burdened with the need to investigate cases of disputed ownership or status. Do we have to reconsider every case in which the invalid witnesses testified from the time that they gave the original, tainted testimony? Or must we determine the exact time of the loser's awareness of his loss? While the redactors of the amoraic discussions saw the issue as a matter of principle, of part of the process of progressive conceptualization of halakhic traditions, there was a practical side to much of this, a sort of urban halakha and not conceptualization. The alternative would be to reassign attributions in those cases that diverge from the expected norm of having Rava on the side of conceptualization.

Discussions of Sasanian law and ritual manifest a disinclination to depart very far from the practical, as in Ohrmazd's decision regarding mixtures of impurities, mentioned earlier. Still, the urban and cosmopolitan context of Rava's activities seem to have influenced the development of his thought, though rabbinic legal thought seems to have been more sophisticated than its Sasanian counterpart.

2. Cosmopolitanism

Rava, a citizen of Mahoza, a suburb of the capital with its varied religious and ethnic groups, disagrees with Abaye of Pumbedita on the question of whether the testimony of someone who eats forbidden foods as an act of religious rebellion can still be valid as a witness in civil matters. Disregard for ritual prohibitions does not necessarily lead to dishonesty in monetary matters (B. Sanhedrin 27a). R. Nahman went further: One suspected of forbidden sexual relations (adultery with a married woman, or incestuous relations) (*'arayot*) can nevertheless function as a witness, though his disciple Rava suggests that he would not allow such a man to give testimony in a case involving women's issues (B. Sanhedrin 26b). The heterogeneous population of the Mahoza-Ctesiphon area would have given Rava the experience and, in accord with his preference for psychological and experiential reasoning, would have encouraged such a decision. It should be noted that nowhere else in the rabbinic world of Late Antiquity do we find a rabbinic authority of the first rank in a major metropolis of an empire; R. Abbahu of Caesearia in Palestine may be a similar case, but he never overcame his status as a disciple of the overwhelming authority of his master R. Yohanan, and Caesaria Maritima could not compete with Mahoza-Ctesiphon, capital and cultural center of an empire more heterogeneous than its Roman sister.

CONCLUSION: DEGREES OF ACCULTURATION IN DIFFERENT COMMUNITIES

Having surveyed some of the elements by which degrees of acculturation may be measured, we are now in a position to make some observations regarding the differences among various Babylonian Jewish communities, and, to some extent, among various strata of rabbinic society. In the comments that follow, however, two factors should be kept in mind. First, our data is restricted to the Bavli, except for the magic bowls, which may date from a later time, and we are thus at the mercy of the redactors of that compilation and of the rabbinic class they represent and re-present. Second, it should always be kept in mind that, culturally speaking, *all* Babylonian Jews – accomodators and resisters alike – were, at the beginning of the Sasanian era, already the product of 750 years of coexistence with Iranian culture. In that time, Iranian languages had developed from Old Persian to Middle Iranian, and both Zoroastrianism and Judaism, both conservative religions, had nevertheless undergone an extended process of development while sharing common space.

Mahoza

Mahoza is the one community for which we have fairly detailed information, primarily because we have some of Rava's reflections and observations of his community. Its geographical situation dictated its cultural ambience. It was situated on the west bank of the River Tigris;

to the north and east, on the other bank and less than a mile away, was the Persian capital of Ctesiphon.[46]

Altogether, Mahoza was part of a huge *entrepot*, the most important metropolis of the entire Sasanian Empire, where the exilarch, the official head of the Jewish community who was a persianized aristocrat, had his seat, courts, and bureaucracy, as did, at least in the next century, the *catholicos*, the head of the Persian Christian Church. It thus had a heterogeneous population, with impressive churches, and Jews were the minority (B. Eruvin 40a), Persian soldiers were common, and some were billeted with Jewish families (B. Shabbat 47b, B. Pesahim 5b, B. Taanit 20b, 21a). Mahoza had a significant population of proselytes (B. Kiddushin 73a, Avodah Zarah 70a) and Christians (see B. Shabbat 88a and B. Hullin 84a), as did Ctesiphon, some of whom were originally Jews.[47] And, as we know from the Talmud[48] and later Islamic histories, there were at least two bridges joining Mahoza to Ctesiphon.

Mahozans had the reputation of being wealthy (B. Shabbat 59b), cosmopolitan, canny (B. Berakhot 59b), and skeptical of rabbinic authority, as we have seen (B. Sanhhedrin 99b–100a, Makkot 22b, Shabbat 133b), and even the intimates of the household of a rabbinic authority were not greatly informed of the intricacies of even everyday halakhah (B. Shabbat 35b). Mahozans were said to be perspicacious (B. Berakhot 59b) and delicate (B. Shabbat 109a); the women were pampered (B. Pesahim 50b) and idle (B. Shabbat 32b); the men pursued still more wealth (B. Gittin 6a, Bava Metzia 59a) and the good life (B. Rosh Hashannah 17a). It thus provides an illustration of Babylonian Jewish upper-class, or "upscale," life. From the nature of Rava's relationship to his community, it would seem that he himself was of middle-class origins (see his prayer for wealth in B. Moed Katan 28a) and responded to the various religious challenges because elements of his community forced him to do so. R. Nahman b. Yaakov, a relative of the exilarch (by marriage, or both by birth and marriage), was, as it were, to the manor born. It may be significant that both he and Rav, also of aristocratic birth, who became an in-law of the exilarch (B. Hullin 92a), contracted temporary marriages, while Rava did not. Rava also responded skeptically to his master's introduction of the Sasanian legal institution of returnable gifts into rabbinic law (see B. Bava Batra 137b and Kiddushin 6b).[49]

For the other rabbinic centers, we have few direct observations about the character of their inhabitants, and none of these really touch on aspects of acculturation, except insofar as the following rabbinic personalities represent a significant percentage of extremely influential rabbinical figures. This makes the question of how typical these rabbis are of their class as a whole less urgent; how typical they were of the population as whole is another story. However, since the entire community, its rabbinic elite included, had been settled in Mesopotamia for so long, it is noteworthy that one issue in contention was the persianizing cast to R. Nahman's Babylonian Aramaic; the question of the place of women in mixed society was probably an inevitable one. Again, the fact that temporary marriage seems *not* to have been a bone of contention is significant. Even within the ranks of the accomodationists, however, the question of attendance at a Be Abadan seems to have been an issue: Rav did not, Samuel and R. Yosef did or would, and Rava avoided doing so "with an excuse" (B. Shabbat 116a).

SAMUEL OF NEHARDE^CA

Little need be said of Samuel, since he has been long known as a rabbi with "liberal" tendencies (Hoffman 1873). As a slaveholder (B. Niddah 47a), he too was a member of the upper class. The question then arises: Why were so many members of this class influential as rabbis? Clearly, acculturation was no impediment to highly successful rabbinic careers, while wealth would have aided them. Some of the resisters may have been opposed to flagrant examples of persianizing acculturation, but not to acculturation per se. Those who were – if they existed – were apparently a powerless, negligible minority.

R. Yosef of Pumbedita

While Mahoza was particularly well situated – both in the geographical and socioeconomic sense – to absorb outside influences, Pumbedita, 100 kilometers away from the capital and on the Euphrates rather than the Tigris, was also part of a Babylonian Jewish community.

Nevertheless, distance from the capital was a factor, as in the following anecdote:

> [The Mahozan] Rava and [later a Pumbeditan and probably earlier also] R. Nahman b. Yitzhak were sitting together when R. Nahman b. Yaakov passed by in a gilt palanquin and wearing a purple cloak. Rava went to meet him, R. Nahman b. Yitzhak did not stir, for he said: "Perhaps this is one of the court of the Exilarch; Rava needs them but I do not. When he saw R. Nahman b. Yaakov approaching he bared his arm and said: The south wind is blowing [and it is dangerous to move around.]" (B. Gittin 31b)

Rabbinic attitudes to R. Nahman of Mahoza were ambivalent. On the one hand, he was a rabbi; on the other, he was a member of the persianized circle around the exilarch.

This ambiguity is captured by a story in B. Bava Kamma 58b, one that also indicates the presence of resisters even in Mahoza. A man first resorted to the exilarch's court but was dissatisfied with the decision. "What have I to do with an exilarch['s court] which decides according to Persian law?" he said, and went to R. Nahman. While the complaint was self-serving, it would seem to echo a sentiment expressed by others. It also indicates that even a man who would abandon the rabbinic courts for the exilarch's considered R. Nahman an exemplar of the first, not the latter. Ironically, R. Nahman decided the case the same way, and indeed, the codified law follows him in this, as in other cases of civil law. For our purposes, however, it is important to note that there were resisters even in Mahoza and that R. Nahman was not seen as a representative of the exilarch by some.

As to R. Yosef, while he consigned Persians to perdition (B. Berakhot 8b) and compared them to demons (B. Megillah 11a), his theology of divine anger owed much to Zoroastrian theological demonology. He would not pray during a time of divine anger (famine; see B. Ketubot 106a), and advised against praying (in private) at a time of divine judgment – even on Rosh Hashanah (B. Avodah Zarah 4b); his conception of the Destroying Angel of the Exodus was of a destructive being who, once unleashed, did not distinguish between the righteous and the wicked (B. Bava Kamma 60a). His condemnation of Zoroastrians itself shows an informed and acute knowledge of its theology. He terms Persians as "demons," that is, the armies of the Evil Spirit, and even describes them with the help of an Iranian *topos* as "demons with parted hair." Again, when expressing his confidence in going to disputations at a *Be 'Abadan*, he declares that "I am of them, and I have no fear of them!" (B. Shabbat 116a).[50] Could he then have been of Persian origin? This hypothesis raises another problem. How did the descendant of a Persian proselyte rise so high in Babylonian rabbinic ranks, in a community in which proper descent was so important? On the other hand, it may explain his reluctance to accept the post (B. Horayot 14a). Still, it illustrates that theodicy was a problem in Pumbedita, a center held out as a bastion of traditional values (at least compared to Mahoza) in B. Kiddushin 70a–b. It should be remembered that he placed limits on the efficacy of performing mizvot as protection against misfortune (B. Sotah 21a).

Rav of Sura

The great first-generation authority Rav, too, seems to have been thoroughly acculturated, but that does not mean that he did not adopt some resister-like positions. He was of aristocratic birth; his uncle R. Hiyya, a disciple of Rabbi Judah the Prince, called him "son of satraps";

and he was an in-law of the exilarch. Most indicative of his acculturation, he is reported to have contracted temporary marriages, and expresses a view of the nighttime and demons typical of the Zoroastrian view of the world, though one that was almost certainly more general (B. Bava Kamma 6ob). He also refers to two elements of the Zoroastrian pentad of "wife and property" as not being assigned by merit but announced by a heavenly echo forty days before the creation of the embryo (B. Sotah 2a). However, unlike Rava and the Middle Persian saying, he does not attribute the allotment of wife and property to astrological conjunction, in accord with his opinion that Jews are not susceptible to astrological influence (B. Shabbat 156a–b), similar to his son-in-law R. Hanan b. Rava regarding authority (B. Berakhot 58a), but unlike his great-grandson-in-law Rava (B. Moed Katan 28a). Likewise, Rav is quoted as expressing the view that anyone who learns something from a magus is worthy of death (B. Shabbat 75a).

Again, Rav refused to go to gatherings at which interdenominational religious discussions or disputations took place, though his colleague Samuel went to some of them (B. Shabbat 116a). Rav also engaged in antipagan polemics.[51] All in all, much more work must be done before we can clearly differentiate the resisters from the accommodators, but Rav's aristocratic origin and affiliations are clear.

Generally speaking, both historians of the period and Talmudists have accepted the view that, as Jacob Neusner put it: "Whatever the state of practice among the masses, the doctrines of competing cults made no impact whatever upon those of the Judaism known to us from the Talmud and cognate literature" (1965–70, 2:25). The evidence cited here, and more in the studies on which it is based, indicates otherwise. Middle Persian attitudes and doctrines made inroads in many areas of Babylonian rabbinic culture, in law, in theology, and in general cultural attitudes. This is all to be expected, not only because of their long, relatively peaceful sojourn in Mesopotamia but also because Zoroastrianism was, if anything, on the whole, a more benign presence than either Roman paganism or Christianity. Its theological and ritual structure was more in tune with that of rabbinic Judaism than Roman paganism was, and while it shared an expectation of a messianic advent with Judaism, that advent was in the future, and therefore not a subject for acrimonious debate as it was with Christianity. It is time for Talmudists and historians of Late Antiquity to integrate the Middle Persian cultural and religious factor into their understanding of the Babylonian Talmud and Babylonian Jewry and to reorient their curricula accordingly.

Notes

1. Oppenheimer, Isaac, and Lecker 1983, 179–235.
2. For a convenient overview of the period, see Frye 1983, 287–339 ("The Sasanians").
3. Neusner is careful not to give a figure for the Jewish population of Mesopotamia, or indeed, for the Persian Empire as a whole; see Neusner 1965–70, I:15, but he suggests that "the Jews formed minority communities in almost every city of the Euphrates Valley...and occupied large tracts of farmland outside of the major cities of Babylonia." Seth Schwartz accepts a figure of 500,000 for the Jews of Palestine. See Schwartz 2001a, 11, 41. We must posit a figure several times that for the Jews of Mesopotamia.
4. Neusner 1965–70, 5:60–69, but see Wiesehöfer 1996, 215–16.
5. Lieu 1994, 25.
6. On these various groups, the respective entries in the *Encyclopedia of Religion* (2005) should be consulted.
7. See Boyce 1979, 118, and Shaki 1981, 114–25, esp. 119.
8. Lieu 1985, 58–59; Neusner 1965–70, vol. 2, 16–18.
9. See S. Shaked 1993, 10–13, 22–26, especially his concluding comments on 26.
10. See Lieu, 1985, 39, and Klijn and Reinink 1973.
11. D. N. MacKenzie, ed., "Kerdir's Inscription," in *Iranische Denkmäler*, fasc. 13, "The Sasanian Rock Reliefs at Naqash-i Rustam," 42 (transcription), 54 (transliteration), and 58 (translation).
12. See Robert Brody, "Judaism in the Sasanian Empire: A Case Study in Religious Coexistence," in Shaked and Netzer 1982–2003, vol. 2, 52–62.
13. See now James R. Russell, "Ezekiel and Iran," in Shaked 1982–2003, vol. 5, 6.
14. See Bailey 1971, 172, but also the discussion on 159–76.
15. Das sasanidische Rechtsbuch "Matakdan i Hazar Datistann" (Teil II), cited as MHDA, and Rechtskasuistik und Gerichtspraxis zu Beginn des siebenten Jahrhunderts in Iran: Die Rechtssammlung des Farrohmard i Wahrāman, and Perikhanian, The Book of a Thousand Judgements. MHD is found in a single manuscript that was divided into two parts, which were published separately; they are usually abbreviated as MHD and MHDA (= MHD Anklesaria). The second deals with family law in the main, and was published by Macuch as a separate volume ("Teil II").
16. See Mahmoud Jaafari-Dehaghi, *Dādestān ī Dēnīg*, Part I, Transcription, Translation and Commentary, 78–79.
17. See Gurock 1985.
18. The *Dādestan ī Dēnig*, Chap. 78, by contrast, has severe things to say about adultery, but that is in a text that otherwise shows Islamic influence, which MHD does not. See for now the translation of E. W. West in *Sacred Books of the East*, Chap. 78, 227–32.
19. See in Firoze M. Kotwal and Philip Kreyenbroek, *The Hērbedestān and the Nērangestān*, §6.7, 44–45.

20. See Schremer 1997–2001, 181–223. It does seem that Babylonian Jewish rabbinic society was more enthusiastic about the practice than their Palestinian colleagues.
21. For the details, see "Marriage and Marital Property," in Hezser 2003, 235–36.
22. See "Marriage," 242–47.
23. See Elman forthcoming. And see Gafni (2002), 246.
24. See Elman 2004a, esp. 47–48.
25. On the prominence of demonological material in the Babylonian Talmud as evidence for its immersion in Middle Persian culture, see also I. Gafni, "Babylonian Rabbinic Culture," 2002, 244–46.
26. Mar b. Ravina (Rabbana) of the third generation to R. Kahana in B. Shabbat 63a, and Rava in B. Yevamot 24a; the third occurrence, in Yevamot 11b, is anonymous and probably redactional.
27. My thanks to Rabbi Dr. Jeremy Wieder for this figure. The figure for the Denkard comes from Carlo G. Cereti, *La Letteratura Pahlavi: Introduzione ai testi con riferimenti alla storia degli studi e alla tradizione manoscritta* (Milan: Mimesis, 2001), 41. The introductory constitution of Justinian's Digest of 534 C.E. states that Tribonian's committee had reduced some 200 books with 3,000,000 lines to altogether 150,000 lines.
28. See Friedman 1995 and Elman 1999, 69–70.
29. See Shaul Shaked 1993, 174–75, and see both Zaehner 1972, 400–18, and Shaked's notes for parallel texts.
30. See Elman 1991.
31. This information stems from al-Tabarī's history; see *The History of al-Tabarī (Ta'rikh al-rusul wa'l-muluk)*, Vol. 5, *The Sāsānids, the Byzantines, the Lachmids, and Yemen*, translated and annotated by C. F. Bosworth, 70.
32. See J. C. Tavadia, Šāyast nē Šāyast: *A Pahlavi Text on Religious Customs*, Chap. 4, 85–90.
33. Ehrlich 1999, 134, and see his discussion on 132–35.
34. See Satlow 1994b, 137–69; the suggestion appears on 168, with sources provided on 161, nn. 88–89.
35. My thanks to Dr. Mahnaz Moazami of the Center for Iranian Studies of Columbia University for providing me a copy of Chapter 16 of her as yet unpublished edition of the Pahlavi *Vīdēvdād*.
36. See Fonrobert 1999, 77 n. 10. Apparently, Samaritan and Karaite halakha also recognize different colors of menstrual blood.
37. See Perikhanian 1997, 252–59, Macuch, vol. 2, 25–29, 97–120.
38. See my "Marital Property in Rabbinic and Sasanian Law," in Hezser 2003.
39. M. Yevamot 13:1, 4, 7, and B. Yevamot 107a; for the parallel, see MHD 89:15–17.
40. See my "Returnable Gifts in Rabbinic and Sasanian Law," in Shaked 1982–2003, vol. 4.
41. *pursišn nāmag*; see B. Gittin 28b and MHD 34:6.
42. For the specific demographic effects of the plague, see the literature cited in "Marriage and Marital Property," 274 n. 129.

43. See Shai Secunda, "On the Importance of a Zoroastrian '*Sugya*': Sasanian Rabbinic and Zoroastrian Study," presented at the AJS Thirty-sixth Annual Convention, December 29, 2004.
44. Michael the Syrian records such famine; see Morony 2000, 3.
45. For all of this, see my "Marriage and Marital Property," 227–76 (see n. 20).
46. See Oppenheimer, Isaac, and Lecker 1983, 179–235, and the map on 233.
47. See Neusner 1965–70, vol. 3, 12–14, 20–29.
48. See B. Eruvin 57b, B. Moed Katan 25b, and Oppenheimer, Isaac, and Lecker 1983, 223–41, and map on 233. Mahoza and Ctesiphon were therefore considered one city as far as Sabbath laws were concerned. Since Mahoza was part of the suburb of Weh-Ardashir-Mahoza-Kohe, Mahozans would have been able to cross over to the capital even on the Sabbath.
49. See my "Returnable Gifts in Rabbinic and Sasanian Law," in Shaked 1982–2003, vol. 4, for details.
50. Current editions attribute this to Mar b. Rav Yosef, a colorless figure who is otherwise cited only in halakhic contexts and only as always transmitting statements of Rava. MS Munich 95 reads: R. Yosef. In this connection it is pertinent to note that in B. Berakhot 17b, R. Yosef calls the inhabitants of Guba (?) (Guebers, *guba'ei* in Aramaic) *avirei lev* – "stout-hearted," because no proselytes have ever come from them; on the name, see Sokoloff, *Dictionary of Jewish Babylonian Aramaic* (Tel Aviv: Bar Ilan University Press, Ramat Gan, 2002), 265a, s.v. *guba'a*.
51. See Neusner 1965–70, vol. 2, 74–76, 84–85.

9 Jewish Visionary Tradition in Rabbinic Literature

MICHAEL D. SWARTZ

Judaism in Late Antiquity encompassed a wide variety of ritual forms and ideological expressions rooted in the diversity of particular Jewish communities. Such eclecticism characterizes even apparently unified movements such as that of the rabbinic sages. Although we tend to associate rabbinic Judaism with the scholastic emphasis on the study of Torah and the observance of halakhah, there are distinct streams of Judaism in the rabbinic milieu that concentrate on visions of and communications with God and the heavenly retinue. Judaism, like other religions of the Greco-Roman world, encompassed within it not only legal, philosophical, and ritual traditions but also esoteric tendencies in which magical and visionary practices were put to use for the needs of individuals. Among the most unusual of these are the traditions in which human beings are said to travel to heaven and gaze at the figure of God on the divine throne or encounter angels and other supernatural beings, who endow them with extraordinary wisdom and memory. Evidence for these ideas can be found within the rabbinic canon and in a corpus of texts related in complex ways to the Talmuds and *midrashim*. This chapter will assess the evidence for visionary and mystical phenomena in rabbinic culture with an eye to understanding them in the context of the development of rabbinic Judaism, as well as the broader Greco-Roman religious environment.

VISIONS OF GOD

The authors of the Hebrew Bible believed that it was possible to see God directly in anthropomorphic form. Narratives of visions of the divine presence are well attested in biblical literature.[1] At Mt. Sinai, according to Exodus 24:9–11, Moses, Aaron, his sons, and the seventy elders of Israel ascended the mount and "saw the God of Israel; under His feet was a pavement of sapphire." The most foundational texts for the early Jewish visionary tradition are the visions in Isaiah, Chapter 6, and Ezekiel, Chapters 1–3. Isaiah sees God "seated on a high and lofty throne" (Isaiah 6:1) in the Temple. On seeing God's face in the Temple, Isaiah fears for his life, perhaps acquainted with the tradition in which God tells Moses, "no one may see Me and live" (Exodus 33:20). He is then purified by an attending angel. In the Book of Ezekiel, the prophet, who is on the banks of the River Chebar, sees God on a traveling throne borne by fiery beings. In Daniel 7, the prophet sees a vision of God, known as the Ancient of Days, in a dream seated on a fiery throne over a river of fire.

The throne of Ezekiel's vision is not given a special name in the Masoretic text. However, in 1 Chronicles 28:18, the structure formed by cherubs that frame the Ark of the Covenant is called "the figure of the Chariot" (*tavnit ha-merkavah*). The Second Temple priest and author Yeshua ben Sira (49:8) writes of Ezekiel that "he saw a vision, and described the different [creatures] of the chariot." Thus in post-biblical Jewish tradition, the heavenly throne came to be known as the Merkavah. At Qumran, descriptions of the Merkavah and the angelic liturgy surrounding it inspired several texts, including a liturgical cycle known as the "Songs for the Sabbath Sacrifice."[2]

Rabbinic sources by and large expressed little doubt that the ancient Israelites had seen God in this way. According to the Mekhilta of Rabbi Ishmael, all Israelites experienced a direct vision of God at the Red Sea: "A maidservant saw at the Red Sea what Isaiah and Ezekiel did not see."[3] An unusual tradition about a divine vision in the Temple occurs in the Babylonian Talmud:

> Rabbi Ishmael ben Elisha said: Once I entered [the Holy of Holies] to offer incense, and I saw Akhatriel, YH YHWH of Hosts sitting on a high and lofty throne. And He said to me, "Ishmael, my son, bless Me!" (B. Berakhot 6a)

This story concerns one of the leading rabbis of the second century, Ishmael ben Elisha. However, the story presents several problems for interpreters. One is the obvious historical anachronism; as Gershom Scholem points out, the real Rabbi Ishmael was but a boy when the Temple was destroyed.[4] The story implies as well that he was the High Priest, offering incense in the inner sanctum of the Temple on Yom Kippur in accordance with Leviticus 16:12–13. Nowhere else in rabbinic literature is he represented in this way.[5] The name for God given here, Akhatriel YH YHWH of hosts, is unique to this story in rabbinic literature although it does resemble names found in esoteric and magical Jewish texts from Late Antiquity. These may be indications that the story comes from outside the usual sources that the Talmud employs. Whatever its origins, its author and editor believed that it was possible to see God in the Temple.

Rabbinic literature often sees God as able to manifest Himself potentially in many forms, however. Elsewhere in the section of the Mekhilta quoted here, the *midrash* describes several of those forms:

> "YHWH is a warrior, YHWH is His name" [Exodus 15:3]. Why is this said? Because he was revealed at the sea as a hero making war, as it is said, "YHWH is a warrior"; but once [Israel] was redeemed, what does it say? "[And they saw the God of Israel; under His feet there was the likeness of a pavement of sapphire,] like the very sky for purity" [Exodus 24:10]; then it says, "As I looked, thrones were set in place [and the Ancient of Days took His seat, His garment was like white snow, and the hair of His head was like lambs' wool . . .]"; and it says, "A river of fire streamed forth from before Him" [Daniel 7:9–10]. In order not to give the nations of the world an excuse to say that there are two powers, [Scripture says], "YHWH is a warrior": It was He in Egypt, He at the sea, He in the past, and He in the time to come, He in this world, and He in the world to come.

The midrash stems from an apparent redundancy in the biblical verse: Why repeat the name of God?[6] The answer is that God appeared in different forms to Israel at different times. When He fought on their behalf at the Red Sea, He appeared as a young warrior, but once the nation was redeemed and He appeared as a lawgiver, He appeared as a wise old man.[7] The midrash further states that lest the argument be made by heathens that these are manifestations of two separate gods, Scripture states clearly, YHWH is His name – the same God that fought at the Red Sea appeared at Sinai.

THE VISIONARY TRADITION

In these biblical texts and later traditions, visions of God are initiated by God Himself and not the prophet. The individual makes no apparent attempt to incubate them nor does he express an explicit wish to see them. At what point did Jews think it was possible to ascend to heaven *at will* and see the heavenly hosts and the divine throne? This question is significant for the history of Jewish mysticism, for one essential element of Jewish mysticism is considered to be the human attempt to approach the sphere of the Divine.[8] Evidence for this idea from rabbinic literature itself is difficult to identify. The evidence most cited for it is a cryptic story in the Tosefta.

The second chapter of M. Hagigah identifies bodies of religious knowledge that may be imparted only in very exclusive circles of disciples. These include the laws governing incestuous sexual practices in Leviticus 18, the "work of creation" (*ma'aseh bere'shit*) as described in Genesis 1, and the vision of God described in Ezekiel 1–3, known as *ma'aseh merkavah*, the "work of the chariot." The Tosefta adds several details to these regulations, including a mysterious story about four famous Rabbis of the second century C.E.:

> Four entered the *Pardes*: Ben Azai, Ben Zoma, Aḥer,[9] and Rabbi Akiva. One glimpsed and died, one glimpsed and went mad,[10] one glimpsed and cut the shoots. And one went up safely and went down safely.
>
> Ben Azai glimpsed and died. About him Scripture says: "Precious in the eyes of the Lord is the death of His faithful ones" (Psalms 116:15). Ben Zoma glimpsed and went mad. About him Scripture says: "If you find honey, eat only what you need, [lest you be sated with it and vomit it]" [Proverbs 25:16]. Aḥer glimpsed and cut the shoots. About him Scripture says: "Do not let your mouth cause your body to sin" [Ecclesiastes 5:5]. Rabbi Akiva went up safely and went down safely. About him Scripture says: "Draw me after you, let us run; [the king has brought me to his chambers]" [Song of Songs 1:4].[11]

From the early centuries of the rabbinic period to the present day, this enigmatic story has served as a kind of *tabula rasa* for our understanding of mystical and visionary dimensions of rabbinic civilization. It has served as evidence that the early rabbis engaged in philosophical experimentation, methods of biblical hermeneutics, and mystical practice.[12] In recent decades, this story and its parallels in talmudic and cognate literatures have been the subject of several scholarly studies.[13] One of the suppositions of these studies has been that if we can decipher this story, we can determine if the early rabbis, the intellectuals responsible for the intricate legal systems that produced the Mishnah and Talmuds, were also mystics who cultivated visions of the divine throne and pursued ecstatic journeys through the heavens.[14] But the story provides precious few details.

A few facts are known to us. The word *pardes*, an early loanword from Persian, means "orchard." Each of the figures in the story is familiar from other rabbinic texts. Rabbi Akiva was one of the founders of the mishnaic tradition and a rabbinic hero, known by tradition as a "scholar, saint, and martyr."[15] His colleagues Ben Azai and Ben Zoma are the source of numerous teachings and stories. *Aher*, as we see from the subsequent expansion of the brief statement at the beginning, is a term meaning "the other one," for Elisha ben Abuya, who was notorious in rabbinic literature for having been a prominent rabbi who became a heretic.[16] However, the story itself yields little about its context and meaning. What is this *pardes* – a physical place, a metaphor of some sort, or a term for a spiritual state or supernatural location? What exactly did three of the four rabbis "glimpse?" Why did those three meet with tragic fates – assuming, on the basis of the quotation of Ecclesiastes 5:5 in the passage, that "cutting the shoots" means some form of transgression?

Subsequent rabbinic traditions do not clarify these questions. The Palestinian Talmud (Y. Hagigah 2:1, 77b) interprets the phrase "cut the shoots" to mean that Elisha ben Abuya "killed masters of Torah." The Tosefta and the Palestinian Talmud also relate a story whereby Ben Zoma's speculation about the nature of creation (*ma'aseh bere'shit*) drives him to madness and death.[17] The Tosefta follows the *pardes* story with a parable likening it to a king's orchard with a raised platform built over it; one is allowed to peek, but not to feast one's eyes on it. This parable may be alluding to the fact that Rabbi Akiba is not listed as having "glimpsed," but simply entered safely and departed safely. A second parallel likens the matter to a road flanked by two paths, one of fire and one of snow, so that one must walk in the middle. The only thing these stories indicate is that the Pardes, whether a real place or a metaphor for a kind of activity, is fraught with danger. At the same time, the story does not discourage the reader entirely from entering it. The story implies that if one is somehow like Rabbi Akiva, entry to the Pardes is possible.

The parables in the Tosefta and the stories in the Palestinian Talmud constitute the earliest commentaries to the passage. However, they do not support one particular interpretation. The parable of the king's orchard might lead the reader to think of the Pardes as a real, if supernatural, place, perhaps the precincts of the Divine presence. However, the story of Ben Zoma's madness might support the interpretation of the Pardes as a metaphor for exegetical speculation on the secrets of creation and cosmology. It should also be pointed out that the two notions are not mutually exclusive. Exegetical conclusions can serve as a basis for a mystical practice; conversely, mystical traditions often develop contemplative techniques of scriptural interpretation. All told, however, the early interpretations of the Pardes episode do not lead us to firm conclusions about visionary activity among the early rabbis. Indeed, the divergent streams of interpretation suggest that the meaning of the passage was lost even to the editors of the Tosefta.

A brief passage in the Babylonian Talmud (B. Hagigah 14b) leads us in a somewhat different direction. After quoting the Pardes story, the Talmud relates:

> Rabbi Akiba said to them, "When you arrive at the pure marble stones, do not say, 'water, water,' as it is said, 'He who speaks untruth shall not stand before my eyes.'" (Psalms 101:7)

It was Gershom Scholem, the founder of the modern academic study of Jewish mysticism, who brought the Pardes story to prominence by suggesting that it constituted valid historical evidence for early Jewish visionary practice.[18] Scholem related Rabbi Akiva's warning about the marble plates in the Babylonian Talmud to a similar passage found in another corpus of Hebrew texts from Late Antiquity, the so-called Hekhalot literature.

These remarkable texts remained in relative obscurity in manuscripts from medieval Germany until Scholem showed their relevance to rabbinic Judaism in Late Antiquity. They describe journeys undertaken by early rabbis, such as Rabbi Akiva and especially his contemporary Rabbi Ishmael, through seven layers of heaven, known as *hekhalot*, "palaces" or "temples," to the throne room of God. The rabbis travel from palace to palace, warding off hostile angelic guardians at each of the gates, and finally reach the divine throne room, where they see God Himself seated on his chariot-throne, the *Merkavah*.

Earlier generations of scholars had argued that this literature was written in the early Middle Ages, well after the close of the rabbinic canon, by marginal groups influenced by Islamic throne mysticism.[19] However, Scholem showed that the Hekhalot texts belonged to Late Antiquity. He further argued that this literature represents a window into the inner spiritual life of the central shapers of rabbinic Judaism. A text that has come to be known as *Hekhalot Zutarti* describes a moment when the traveler is invited to enter the sixth palace, whereupon it seems to him as if millions of waves of water are raining down on him. But those waves of water are an illusion and it is only the marble plates with which the palace was tessellated.[20] Scholem argued that this passage preserved the original meaning of Rabbi Akiva's warning in the Babylonian Talmud's version of the story, and that the term *pardes* stands for *paradise* or the inner chambers of heaven. The stories of ascent to heaven, in Scholem's view, were therefore pseudepigraphic records of visions cultivated by mystical circles within the rabbinic elite.

Scholem's arguments for the existence of an esoteric mystical tradition within the heart of early rabbinic Judaism have been debated. Most prominently, David J. Halperin (1980) argued on the basis of a form-critical study of rabbinic traditions about the Merkavah that talmudic literature does not support the thesis that visionary mysticism was practiced by the early rabbis. Halperin's conclusion has been challenged, in particular by C. R. A. Morray-Jones (2002), but his research has called into serious question the thesis that the rabbis practiced ecstatic visions of the Merkavah. For unambiguous expressions of the idea that human beings can travel at will to heaven, it is therefore necessary to look outside the conventional rabbinic canon to Hekhalot literature.

HEKHALOT LITERATURE

The Hekhalot texts appear in their most complete form in manuscripts transmitted from the fourteenth century to the sixteenth century by scribes associated with the German Jewish pietists known as the Ashkenazic Hasidim. Fragments of the texts also appear in the Cairo Genizah. Traces of the literature and the phenomena they represent can be found in Jewish magical literature, Talmud and midrash, and the Jewish controversial literature of the early Middle Ages. But although these texts are attributed to rabbis who lived in the second century c.e., they were almost certainly not written by those rabbis.

The major Hekhalot texts have been published in two indispensable synoptic editions by Peter Schäfer.[21] Schäfer's edition and his statements about the nature of the manuscript evidence indicate the problems faced by the scholar who wishes to approach them, especially as a single phenomenon. The manuscripts do not attest to individual texts that can be traced to a single original text (*urtext*) but show a complex network of smaller texts (what Schäfer calls microforms) that are organized in different ways into larger units (macroforms). This situation does not simply mean that reconstructing an original text is difficult; rather it challenges us to look at ancient Jewish literature in a new way.[22] Much as the variety of recensions of one liturgical unit attests to a mode of composition in which improvisation precedes codification,[23] each manuscript or recension of Hekhalot literature must be seen as a separate performance of a set of intermediate units that combine according to the needs of the scribe or community that edited it.

These texts, by the very nature of their transmission, cannot therefore constitute evidence of a single author recording his experiences and reporting them pseudepigraphically. Rather, the collective nature of the texts leads us to consider the array of literary forms, ritual practices, myths, and interpretations that led to the literature we have before us. This should make us more attuned to the separate streams, tensions, revisions, and interpolations that constitute Hekhalot literature.

With these considerations in mind, we can identify a few main streams of Hekhalot texts, or macroforms. The two main types are 1) ascent texts that describe how a rabbi traveled to the divine throne room, and 2) adjuration texts that provide instructions for conjuring an angel known as the Prince of the Torah (*Sar Torah*) or Prince of Wisdom (*Sar ha-Hokhmah*), who will grant the practitioner wisdom and skill in learning Torah. Related to the ascent texts are the *Shi'ur Komah* texts, which describe in graphic detail the measurements of God's body.

A. Narratives of Ascent

The organizing principle of the main macroforms in Hekhalot literature is the ascent to heaven of rabbinic heroes. However, the major ascent texts also include other subjects, such as the transformation of men into angels and the cultivation of the *Sar Torah*. The paradigmatic ascent text is *Hekhalot Rabbati* ("The Greater [Book of the] Palaces"). The text, as well as the literature as a whole, takes its name from a cosmological scheme whereby heaven is conceived as consisting of seven concentric chambers, each called a *hekhal*, meaning palace or temple. The seventh hekhal is the throne room of God, where He is seated on a glorious throne, the Merkavah, surrounded by angels who sing praises to Him. But standing at each gate are ferocious angels who guard that hekhal against intruders.

The premise of the text is that any qualified human being can ascend through those heavens to the Merkavah. The approach to the Merkavah is paradoxically called "descent" (*yeridah*) in *Hekhalot Rabbati* and a few other places in the literature. In *Hekhalot Rabbati*, the travelers to the throne are called *yordei merkavah*, "descenders to the chariot." It is not clear why this odd terminology is used. Among the most plausible suggestions advanced is that the term is analogous to the practice of going before the ark in the synagogue to lead prayers, an action that is called *yeridah lifnei ha-teva'*, "going down to the ark," in rabbinic sources;[24] another is that the term refers simply to the last phase of the journey, where the traveler, having ascended through the seven heavens, enters ("goes down to") the throne room itself.[25] The human traveler who wishes to ascend to the divine throne room must appease those angels and present the proper credentials.

Hekhalot Rabbati is one of the most comprehensive and complex macroforms in the literature, encompassing hymnology, ascent, a *Sar Torah* narrative, and apocalyptic materials.[26] The main ascent section of *Hekhalot Rabbati* is a continuous narrative from §198 to §277 as published in Schäfer's *Synopse zur Hekhalot-Literatur*. It is worth summarizing this section to understand how ascent is portrayed in the literature.

The ascent section begins with an introduction in which Rabbi Ishmael, the narrator of the text, tells that when Rabbi Neḥuniah ben ha-Kannah heard that Rome was planning to destroy the sages, he gathered a company of rabbis together to "reveal the nature (*middah*) of the secret of the world" (§198). This is most likely an allusion to the Apocalypse of the Ten Martrys, a widely disseminated narrative tradition about ten second-century rabbis put to death by the emperor Hadrian, a version of which appears elsewhere in *Hekhalot Rabbati* (§§107–21).[27] The passage also reflects a motif found frequently in Jewish literature that a crisis forced the sages or a given author to write down what had been an esoteric tradition handed down exclusively by oral transmission.[28] Rabbi Neḥuniah then employs a parable about the technique:

> To what can this technique [*middah*] be likened for the descenders
> to the chariot? It is like a man who has a ladder in his house
> and can go up and down on it, and no creature can prevent him.
> [Thus it is for] anyone who is pure and innocent of idolatry,
> sexual sin, bloodshed, libel, desecration of the divine name, and
> causeless hatred, and observes every positive and negative
> commandment...he may descend and gaze at the wondrous glory,
> extraordinary majesty, exalted glory, and radiant majesty that rush
> forth before His throne of glory three times a day. (§§199–200)

At this, Rabbi Ishmael reports, he despaired that there was no one on earth so virtuous. In response, Rabbi Neḥuniah instructs him to gather their colleagues so that he can reveal the secrets of creation that will allow anyone to make the journey.

The rest of the text (§§202–58) consists of the instructions, presumably given by Rabbi Neḥuniah, for ascending to heaven and descending to the *Merkavah*. There are at least two sets of instructions, the second set interrupted by several excurses and interpolations. The first set of instructions (§§204–18) describes the ascent through the *hekhalot*, culminating in a detailed description of the seventh *hekhal*. The second set (§§219–48) lists briefly the instructions for passing through the first hekhal through the fifth and proceeds to detailed descriptions of the sixth and seventh hekhalot, especially the process of descent at the final stage. These instructions are interrupted for two stories in which Rabbi Nehuniah clarifies a cryptic detail.

In the first ascent narrative, Rabbi Nehuniah explains the cosmology of the hekhalot:

> Rabbi Ishmael said: Thus said Rabbi Nehuniah ben ha-Kanah: TWTRWSY'Y YY, God of Israel dwells in seven *hekhalot*, a chamber inside a chamber, and at the gate of each *hekhal* there are eight guards of the doorway at the right side of the lintel. (§206)

In the subsequent descriptions, the names of the guardians of each gate are listed and marvelous angels, celestial horses, and rivers of fire at the seventh hekhal are described. Following a litany praising God as king, a testimony assures the reader that God (here known by the esoteric name TWTRWSY'Y YY, God of Israel)[29] awaits the *yordei merkavah* as much as He anticipates the redemption that is reserved for Israel:

> When will the *yordei merkavah* see the redemption on high? When will he hear the tidings of salvation [*qez yeshuah*]? When will he see what no eye has seen? When will he ascend and tell the seed of Abraham?

Here, as practically nowhere else in Hekhalot literature, the journey to the Merkavah is equated with redemption.[30] This is also a strikingly poignant expression of the idea that God desires the visit of the *yordei merkavah* to the divine court.

Despite God's wish to receive the visitors to His divine abode, the traveler encounters severe and frightening obstacles. At the gate to each palace stand fearsome angelic guards who are waiting to attack anyone who is not properly qualified to enter. The traveler succeeds in entering each palace by having in his possession elaborate divine names (sometimes known as "seals"), which he presents to the angelic guard, and by having esoteric knowledge of the heavenly topography and the names and characteristics of specific angels. One prevailing motif of the ascent narrative is the awe and terror that grips the traveler as he confronts the angels or witnesses the rivers of fire or vast chambers of the divine realm. At the same time, the adept is rewarded and assured if he does manage to gain admission to the next hekhal. A passage from the second ascent narrative in *Hekhalot Rabbati* illustrates this dynamic. The passage depicts the moment when a man who wishes to descend to the

Merkavah arrives at the gate of the seventh hekhal. He is met by the angel Anafiel, who opens the gate for him. However, when the *ḥayyot,* the holy creatures described in Ezekiel 1:5–12, cast their 512 eyes on him,

> he trembles, quakes, recoils, panics, and falls back fainting. But the angel Anafiel and the sixty-three guards of the seventh palace assist him and say, "Do not fear, son of the beloved seed! Enter and see the King in his beauty. Your eyes will see, you will not be slaughtered, and you will not be burned!" (§248)

The passage portrays the tension between the terror felt by the traveler when confronted with the angels and God's desire to receive him to the divine throne room. This tension recalls in a way the paradox of the Pardes narrative as well; the story warns of the danger but still holds out the possibility that under the right circumstances, the rewards of the journey can be acquired. Where this passage differs is in its depiction of the emotions of fear and hope that beset the individual who experiences the journey.

Not all macroforms in the Hekhalot corpus are organized around the journey through seven hekhalot, although most do presuppose such a journey. For example, *Ma'aseh Merkavah* is a text that consists mostly of prayers to be recited to achieve a vision of the divine throne or to conjure the *Sar Torah.*[31] In one passage Rabbi Akiva, the main informant in the narrative of the text, lists such images as the chariots of fire, the flames that go forth from them, and the doxologies they sing to God hekhal by hekhal. However, this scheme does not form the structure for the work as a whole. *Sefer Hekhalot* ("The Book of the Palaces)," also known as *3 Enoch,* is a late fusion of Hekhalot and apocalyptic narrative traditions. Although this text also presupposes a scheme of seven hekhalot, the bulk of the text concerns Enoch's narrative of how he ascended to heaven, and, having resisted the challenge of angelic guards of the divine presence, was transformed into Metatron, the archangel who stands at God's right hand.

B. Hymnology

Unusual hymns praising God and describing the celestial beings are inserted at crucial points in the ascent texts of *Hekhalot Rabbati.* Hymnology plays an important role in Hekhalot literature as a whole. When the seventh *hekhal* is described in the first set of ascent instructions, the description is followed by a litany of adjectives describing God as king:

Righteous king, faithful king, gentle king, humble king, compassionate king, holy king, pure king, blessed king, proud king, mighty king, gracious king, merciful king, the king of kings and lord of crowns. (§217, MS Munich 22)

This passage may have been placed at this strategic point in the narrative of *Hekhalot Rabbati* to illustrate the angelic liturgy in which the traveler participates. The repetition and profusion of synonyms in this passage are emblematic of one style of Hekhalot hymnology. Elsewhere, verbs of praise accumulate in series when describing the heavenly court. This is known to be a characteristic style of Hekhalot hymnology.[32]

This style is by no means the only one in Hekhalot literature, however. One distinctive type of hymn used extensively in separate sections of *Hekhalot Rabbati* follows a complex pattern and contains allusions to the *Yordei Merkavah* and the journey itself. These culminate in the recitation of the liturgical *kedushah*, the doxology sung by the angels in Isaiah 6:3. One such hymn addresses the angels directly:[33]

You who annul the decree, who dissolve the oath,
who repel wrath, who turn back jealousy,
who recount love, who array authority
before the magnificent splendor of the wondrous hekhal,
why is it that you sing praises, and at times you rejoice?
Why is it and you are fearful, and at times you recoil?
They said, "When the wheels of the divine glory darken,
we stand in great dread,
but when the radiance of the *Shekhinah*[34] gives light,
we are happy, very happy,"
as it is said, "Holy, Holy, Holy is the Lord of Hosts, the fullness of
    the earth is his glory" [Isaiah 6:3]. (§158, MS Munich 22)[35]

The mythic context of this striking composition seems to be a dialogue between a human visitor and the angels. The poem therefore presupposes that the speaker of the hymn is in heaven witnessing the angelic liturgy described in Isaiah 6. This would correspond well with the narrative of ascent in *Hekhalot Rabbati*. However, the particular premise of the dialogue – the idea that the wheels (*'ofanim*) of the divine throne sometimes darken and sometimes give light – does not figure in Hekhalot narrative.[36] This may be an indication that the hymns come from another source, perhaps within the same circles that produced the ascent narrative. Nonetheless, it is clear that one of the duties of the traveler to the Merkavah is to participate in the angelic praise of God.

Another major text, *Ma'aseh Merkavah*, consists largely of esoteric prayers framed by a narrative of the vision of the heavens and the cultivation of the *Sar Torah*. The hymns in this text draw from the earliest stage of post-biblical Hebrew liturgical poetry, called *piyyut*.[37] This style uses parallelism, the prevailing characteristic of biblical poetry, as well as a steady rhythm, usually of four feet, to convey the praise of God and the participation of both angels and humans in this praise. One hymn in *Ma'aseh Merkavah* expresses it this way:

> Be blessed, God, great, mighty, and strong,
> King, exalted in beauty, magnificent in glory.
> In glory You spoke and the world came into being;
> With the breath of Your lips You established the firmament,
> and Your great name is pure and exalted
> over all those above and all those below.
> Angels stand in heaven,
> and the righteous are sure in their remembrance of You,
> and Your name hovers over them all. (§587)[38]

This hymn begins with the theme of God's creation of heaven and earth. The parallelism counterpoises God's creation of heaven with the creation of earth and His sovereignty over "all those above and all those below." The hymn thus emphasizes that God (especially His divine name, which plays an important role in the text) transcends both the angelic community in heaven and the human worshippers (the "righteous"). This reinforces the idea prominent in the text that humans have the right to praise God in correspondence with the angelic liturgy. In the texts themselves, prayer and hymnology have several functions. For the ascent texts in *Ma'aseh Merkavah*, prayer actually causes the divine vision. Rabbi Akiva declares, "When I recited this prayer I saw 6,400,000,000 angels of glory facing the throne of glory" (§551).

C. The Shape of God

Visionary texts in Hekhalot literature are predicated on an anthropomorphic image of God. One distinctive genre within the corpus is the *Shi'ur Komah*, or "Measurement of the Body." The *Shi'ur Komah* consists of enumerations of the dimensions of the body of God. Each part of the divine body is given a specific measurement, given in *parsangs* (Persian miles), as well as an esoteric name:

> "The left ankle of the Creator is named 'TRQM, may he be blessed. It is 190,000,000 *parsangs* tall, which equals 43,250 *shekalim*. From his ankles to the knee of the Creator, may he be

blessed, is called GMGY, may he be blessed, and has a height of 600,000,080 *parsangs.*"[39]

It is explained that one of the divine parsangs equals 1,640,000,025,000 terrestrial *parsangs.* The text seems to have been written for the purpose of liturgical recitation and also contains several hymns. This text represents an extreme example of anthropomorphic tendencies prevalent in Hekhalot literature, as well as its tendency to ascribe gargantuan dimensions to heaven and its inhabitants.[40] However, with the exception of the passages quoted earlier in which God expresses his wish for human visitors, God rarely speaks directly to humans in Hekhalot ascent texts, even if they visit in his throne room. He is usually portrayed anthropomorphically but not anthropopathically, distinguishing this genre from apocalyptic literature, in which God initiates the encounter with the human who is snatched up to heaven, and delivers a message (by himself or through an angelic informant) concerning the secrets of history and the destiny of Israel. In Hekhalot literature, God simply radiates splendor from his throne. He is there to be worshipped by angels and humans.

D. Rituals and Incantations

The ascent narrative in *Hekhalot Rabbati* and those like it, however, comprise a small portion of the Hekhalot corpus as a whole. Another prominent genre within Hekhalot literature consists of rituals and incantations for more conventionally practical purposes, especially the cultivation of wisdom or skill in learning Torah by means of the conjuration of an angel, the Prince of the Torah or *Sar Torah.* These are closely allied with the Jewish magical tradition, but unlike magical texts from Late Antiquity and the early Middle Ages, they are framed by narratives in which Rabbi Ishmael and his colleagues learn and perform *Sar Torah* rituals and encounter the angels of wisdom and Torah. The narrative serves to introduce ritual instructions and to attest to the effectiveness of the ritual.

These instructions usually involve extensive rituals of preparation. The practitioner is instructed, sometimes by an informing angel, to purge himself of all traces of ritual impurity by elaborate rituals of seclusion, fasting, ablution, and avoidance of infinitesimal traces of menstrual impurity (*niddah*). These rituals go well beyond those prescribed in rabbinic law for ritual purity. The object of these rituals of purification is to prepare the individual for the encounter with the angel, who will tolerate no contamination in his presence. Another important feature is the recitation of prayers and incantations that include elaborate magical names. These, like the "seals" of the ascent texts, provide the assurance to the intermediaries that the practitioner's request carries with it divine authority.

When the angel does arrive and grant the practitioner the skill in learning that he desires, the narrative relates the miraculous transformation of the ordinary student into a great scholar. In a *Sar Torah* text appended to *Hekhalot Rabbati*, Rabbi Ishmael attests that "I did not believe [in the effectiveness of the incantation] until I brought a certain fool and he became equal to me" in learning (§305). In addition to these abilities, the practitioner acquires cosmic secrets and the specific esoteric knowledge transmitted by the magical tradition.

The relationship between the *Sar Torah* texts and the ascent texts is a complex one. Scholem considered them to be a secondary development to the ascent tradition, reflecting a later stage when Merkavah mysticism had degenerated into "magic, pure and simple."[41] Halperin considers the *Sar Torah* tradition to be an early development from midrashic elaborations of Moses' ascent to heaven to acquire the Torah at Sinai. The ascent tradition, by his account, would serve to validate the *Sar Torah* practice and recommend it to its audience. Peter Schäfer has pointed out that this position is simply a reversal of Scholem's and does not take the intricacies of the transmission of the literature into account.[42] Literary analysis of the texts in which the *Sar Torah* materials appear suggest that the tradition developed independently of the ascent materials and that they were appended to them later in the editing process. Whatever their place in the history of Hekhalot literature, these texts are an indication of the centrality of memorized knowledge in the scholastic society formed by rabbinic Judaism. At the same time, they draw on the extensive Jewish magical tradition, which preserves other rituals and incantations for the improvement of memory.

At the same time, these traditions bear directly on the cultivation of visions in ancient Judaism. Magical texts from Hekhalot literature and the Genizah preserve rituals in which a supernatural figure is supposed to appear to the practitioner. A unique text in Babylonian Aramaic preserved in Hekhalot, called "The Book of the Great Name," provides instructions for reciting the powerful names recorded in the book without being harmed. When the ritual is performed, the practitioner will see an apparition:

Any man who reads this book must go by himself to the river to a place that is concealed from human beings and from the spirits that go out into the world. There he will see a man, and he will survive by His mercy, and by his prayer he will be saved. (§495)[43]

Likewise, a Genizah fragment in the Adler collection of the Jewish Theological Seminary Library apparently comes from a manual for reciting magical names according to times of the year.[44] It includes a ritual in which the practitioner clothes himself, as it were, with the name of God. The text then describes the results of the ritual:

> When you perform all of these [procedures] you should go out to the trough and say many prayers and supplications, and ask that you not fail again. Then speak this glorious name in fear and trembling. If you see the image of a lion of fire in the trough, know that you have succeeded wearing this holy name. Then you shall take the golden plate[45] on which this holy name is engraved and tie it around your neck and on your heart. Take care not to become impure again when it is on you, lest you be punished. Then you may do anything and you will succeed.

In the course of this regimen, the practitioner is to "go out to the trough" – presumably for watering his cattle – where he is to pronounce the divine names, apparently provided by the text. Success is assured by the appearance of the image of a lion of fire in the water. The most likely association for this image is with the lions' heads that appeared on the cherubim in the vision of Ezekiel (Ezekiel 1:10). Indeed, this part of the ritual could be read as a kind of evocation of Ezekiel's vision, the trough standing for the body of water, an association that most likely informed the aforementioned "Book of the Great Name."

These rituals point up an interesting feature of ancient Jewish visionary literature. Fully formed rituals for achieving a vision or encountering a divine being occur not in the ascent texts in Hekhalot literature but in texts for bringing down an angel or other being to earth.

EXPERIENCE, LITERATURE, MYTH, AND RITUAL

Since Scholem brought the study of Hekhalot literature to the attention of the scholarly community, discussion of these texts has focused on two main issues: the relationship between this literature and rabbinic Judaism, and the experiential basis behind the literature. The first question depends on several factors, including the historical background of the passages from talmudic literature quoted at the beginning of this chapter and the internal evidence from Hekhalot literature for the social location of the authors. This question will be discussed later. The second question raises several methodological issues concerning the term *mysticism,* the relationship between literature and inner experience, and ritual.

Scholem maintained that key elements in Hekhalot literature were evidence that the texts reflected ecstatic visions of the divine world cultivated by a circle of mystical practitioners. By this account, the repetitive hymns in *Hekhalot Rabbati* and related texts served as a kind of mantra to be repeated, inducing a trance. Likewise, the elaborate rituals of fasting, social isolation, and ablutions also aided in cultivating a mystical state. This view of the purpose of Hekhalot literature has been challenged in several ways. David Halperin, in *The Faces of the Chariot* (1988, 376–83), argues that the purpose of the ascent texts was not to engender a mystical trance but to provide a mythic justification for the *Sar Torah* practices, which he considers to be the "center" of Hekhalot literature. Peter Schäfer (1992) also calls Scholem's understanding of the literature into question, emphasizing the liturgical function of the ascent. Martha Himmelfarb, assessing the implications of this scholarship, focuses on the ascent texts as narrative and argues that "the Hekhalot literature should be understood not as rites to be enacted but as stories to be repeated."[46]

Two texts were instrumental for Scholem in setting the paradigm of Hekhalot literature as ecstatic visionary practice. One was a responsum by the post-talmudic legal authority Hai Gaon (939–1038 C.E.), who, when asked about this literature, remarked that some people believed that a person could gaze at the chambers of heaven by fasting a certain number of days, putting his head between his knees, and whispering hymns to the ground. Scholem took this as a testimony to an active mystical praxis. Halperin (1984) showed that Hai's response seems to be based on a secondary reading of a brief passage in *Hekhalot Zutarti* that serves as a ritual for obtaining favor at the New Year.

Another influential text for the idea of an ecstatic visionary practice occurs in the ascent narrative in *Hekhalot Rabbati.* When Rabbi Neḥuniah decides to reveal the secrets of the journey, he instructs Rabbi Ishmael:

> Bring before me all the heroes of the fellowship and the eminences of the academy. Rabbi Ishmael then gathered the entire Great Sanhedrin and Lesser Sanhedrin to the third great entrance of the House of the Lord. He was sitting on a pure marble bench that my father Elisha gave me, from my mother's estate.... We sat before [Rabbi Neḥuniah] and all the colleagues stood on our feet. For we saw balls of fire and torches of light going between them and Rabbi

Neḥuniah ha-Kannah would arrange before them all the matters of the Merkavah, the descent and ascent, how one who descends can do so, and how one who ascends can do so.

The passage is set in the Temple. It depicts a context whereby the instructor is seated on a marble bench and recites his vision to his attending disciples, who record what he sees. The marble bench is used because it cannot contract impurity. Scholem and others have suggested that this passage depicts a social context for the ascent texts in which a mystic goes into a trance, and tells his vision, while a circle of initiates records that vision. The Hekhalot literature, in Scholem's view, would thus be a result of those experiences.

The literature is none too clear about the relationship between mind and body in the ascent, however. Another passage that depicts this scenario is an excursus in which the students need to bring Rabbi Neḥuniah down to earth to answer a question about the journey. They do so by means of an elaborate ritual by which they contaminate Rabbi Neḥuniah with a marginal degree of ritual impurity, thus casting him from heaven without violating earthly halakhah.[47] This passage is interesting from the phenomenological perspective. While it is clear that Rabbi Neḥuniah's body is on earth, what happens to that body affects him physically in heaven – that is, the impurity with which he is contaminated is enough to cast him from heaven. An equally curious detail is found in a Genizah text influenced by the narrative of *Hekhalot Rabbati*.[48] At the sixth *hekhal*, the angelic array and the roaring fires cause such a tumult that they could cause the traveler to faint. Therefore, he must dig his fingernails into the "ground of the firmament" and plug up his orifices so that his breath does not escape.[49] These details are probably an indication that the author did not distinguish sharply between body and soul. It is not only an immaterial soul that ascends to heaven in this narrative, but, somehow, some aspect of the physical person himself. Likewise, the author apparently thinks of heaven as a physically real place.

These curious details bear on how we should view this complex literature. As we have seen, Scholem and those who accept his interpretation argue that they are the results of visionary experiences; others argue that no such visions occurred. Both schools, however, focus on the inner experience of the authors, speculating on the presence or absence of mystical visions. However, it is agreed that this is a composite literature, composed of highly stereotyped formulae used by different scribes in different ways. The internal states of mind that engendered these texts in their present form are most likely irrecoverable. It may be more productive to analyze this literature as myth and ritual, uncovering the cultural and social factors that contributed to its creation. Whether or not the Hekhalot literature yields direct evidence for an ancient mystical practice, it deserves attention as a rich source of myths, rituals, and conceptions of the divine and human that vary in significant ways from the classical literature of rabbinic Judaism. They may be evidence of the influence of cultic and esoteric practices that are downplayed in the rabbinic canon. At the same time, they reflect the influence of rabbinic values and ideals on social circles beyond those that produced the Talmuds and midrashim.

JEWISH VISIONARY TRADITIONS IN CONTEXT

This survey of Hekhalot literature suggests some possibilities about the nature and setting of Jewish visionary traditions in Late Antiquity. There are several points of affinity between Hekhalot literature and rabbinic literature. The basic theological premise, that God is visible in anthropomorphic form, is a commonplace in rabbinic literature. The idea that the heavens consist of layers can be found in cosmologically oriented rabbinic texts, especially passages in Genesis Rabbah and related midrashim.[50] However, the specific idea that these seven layers are "palaces" guarded by fierce angels is not attested in the main texts of the rabbinic canon. As we have seen, early interpretations of the Pardes story do not constitute clear evidence that the Tanna'im believed that Rabbi Akiva and his colleagues ascended through the hekhalot. However, the Babylonian Talmud's interpretation makes it more likely that its editors were familiar with the Hekhalot tradition.

The influence of rabbinic literature on Hekhalot literature is easier to track. The authors of the texts looked upon the early rabbis as their heroes, holy men whose virtue and expertise in esoteric lore allowed them to ascend to the divine throne. In addition, the *Sar Torah* texts serve as a testimony to the influence of rabbinic scholastic values on social circles outside the rabbinic elite. Rabbinic *halakhah* seems to have influenced some of the purity regulations found in the texts, although they usually go beyond the boundaries of the *halakhah*.

Other cultural influences can be discerned, however. One of the most important of these influences is the Temple, its priesthood, and its sacrificial system, which had long been destroyed when the Hekhalot literature developed. The word *hekhal* can mean both palace and Temple, and it is likely that the hekhalot were considered to be the heavenly equivalent of the Temple, or more accurately its celestial prototype. Rabbi Ishmael's status as a priest, according to legend, seems to have had something to do with his selection as the principal hero in Hekhalot narrative. In subtle ways as well, patterns of ritual, purity, and world-view found in Hekhalot literature draw from the Temple cult. A case in point is the story described earlier of Rabbi Nehuniah's deposition from heaven in *Hekhalot Rabbati*. The story takes place in the Temple itself. Moreover, the premise of the story is that an extraordinary degree of purity is required for Rabbi Nehuniah to remain in the divine presence. Likewise, rituals for the conjuration of an angel stress purity above all other factors, warning the practitioner to stay away from any trace of menstrual impurity.

These affinities between Hekhalot literature and the Temple system are not fully developed; for example, the idea that angels make sacrifices in the heavenly Temple does not appear in Hekhalot, despite its appearance in rabbinic literature and strong precedents for this idea in the Angelic Liturgy from Qumran.[51] Nonetheless, this literature suggests that the priesthood and Temple enjoyed particular prestige among its authors. Moreover, the dynamics of danger and attraction that characterize Hekhalot narrative can be seen as reflections of how the approach to the presence of God was understood in the ancient Temple. As the cautionary tale of Aaron's sons in Leviticus 10:1–3 and other warnings attest, the divine presence could only be approached under the most precise ritual conditions. These extra-rabbinic influences and other factors suggest that the authors of this literature may be found not among the rabbinic elite or the lower classes but in circles of secondary elites, who drew upon rabbinic values and popular religious traditions alike.[52]

A larger question is how the Jewish visionary literature of the rabbinic period fits into the Greco-Roman cultural environment. Gershom Scholem, Morton Smith, and others have noticed affinities between the ascent texts and Greco-Roman mystery cults and other religious trends, especially Gnosticism. The ascent texts describe a human traveler (whether in bodily or spiritual form) ascending to heaven, encountering obstacles in the form of hostile supernatural guardians, and finally triumphing by entering a transcendent celestial sphere. This scheme can also describe one of the most common Gnostic myths. This affinity prompted Scholem to characterize Merkavah mysticism as a Jewish movement analogous to Gnosticism.[53] This description has been called into question, especially in light of the reevaluation of Gnosticism that has occurred in the last few decades.[54] Nonetheless, Scholem's explorations into these affinities have alerted scholars to the way in which Jewish visionary and magical traditions interacted with others of the ancient Mediterranean. One easily detectable sign of this interaction is the use of foreign words in magical texts. Greek words or names, usually in altered form, occur in Jewish magical and Hekhalot texts. Likewise, Hebrew divine names, ideal figures from Jewish scriptures, and elements of Jewish ritual appear in Greek magical texts.[55] In the ascent narrative of *Hekhalot Rabbati*, the traveler is greeted by the angel at the sixth *hekhal* with a mysterious phrase. Hans Lewy has shown that this phrase is a greeting in Greek transliterated into Hebrew.[56]

More substantially, both Jewish visionary texts and the literature of Greco-Roman magic and mystery religions attest to a cosmological climate in Late Antiquity where the boundaries between the earthly and otherworldly realms were seen as permeable. We have seen that *Sar Torah* texts and other rituals are meant to result in the apparition of an angelic figure or "man" who grants the practitioner extraordinary powers. Likewise, in a mysterious and complex ritual text known as the Mithras liturgy in the Great Magical Papyrus of Paris, a series of invocations results in the adept's being lifted up into midair and visited by various classes of deities, from divine "Pole Lords" to Helios himself.[57] In Late Antiquity as well, circles of theurgists sought to use rituals for direct contact with divine souls.

Jewish visionary traditions attest to considerable diversity within the cluster of social circles, worldviews, administrative systems, and ritual practices that constituted Judaism in Late Antiquity. While the rabbis stressed the value of observance of halakhah, the study of Torah, and patient preparation for the world to come, others imagined a more direct encounter with God and His intermediaries. After all, from time immemorial the Temple had been seen as the locus of contact between the realms of divine and human, and the rabbis themselves believed that their ancestors had seen God's presence and that it was possible to detect the presence of angels, dead spirits, and other supramundane beings. However, the authors of the Hekhalot literature and similar texts apparently believed that travel to the divine throne and direct apprehension of God were possible in their lifetimes. Their elaborate narratives, hymns, and rituals may have been intended to be used actively in visionary practices or simply as stories of their heroes. They were certainly meant to convey the idea that the distance between divine and human worlds could be traversed.

Notes

1. For a useful survey of biblical and rabbinic attitudes to visions of God, see Wolfson 1994, 13–51.
2. On the Merkavah in the Dead Sea Scrolls, see Schiffman 1994, 351–66, and Swartz 2001b. On the Songs of the Sabbath Sacrifice, see Newsom, *Songs of the Sabbath Sacrifice: A Critical Edition.*
3. Mekhilta de-Rabbi Ishmael *Shirata* 3 (ed. Horowitz and Rabin, 126).
4. Scholem 1961, 356 n. 3. On this passage, see Swartz 1996, 65.
5. Cf. T. Menahot 13:20, which refers to a "house of Elisha" as a priestly family.
6. On this passage, see Wolfson 1994, 33–34.
7. The purpose of the juxtaposition of Exodus 24:10 with Daniel 7:9–10 is to make this point. Exodus 24:10 does not indicate signs of old age, but only that He is seated on the throne. Daniel 7 describes His appearance as a white-haired elder while seated on the throne.
8. See Scholem 1961, 7–8.
9. Aḥer, literally "the Other One," is a reference to Elisha b. Abuyah, as we shall discuss later. See n. 16.
10. Literally, "was afflicted."
11. T. Hagigah 2:3 (ed. Lieberman).
12. On interpretations of this passage in the Middle Ages, see Idel 1995.
13. See, for example, Davila 1996, 457–78, and Morray-Jones 2002.
14. On the concepts of mysticism and mystical experience and how they have been applied with regard to rabbinic Judaism and its milieu, see Swartz 1996, 15–18.
15. This was the subtitle of Louis Finkelstein's 1936 biography of Akiba, Finkelstein 1970.
16. On legends of Elisha ben Abuya, see Y. Hagigah 2:1–2, 77a–c; B. Hagigah 15a–b; and Goshen-Gottstein 2000.
17. T. Hagigah 2:6; Y. Hagigah 2:1, 77a.
18. Scholem 1961, 52–53, and 1960, 14–19.
19. See Graetz 1859, 67–78, 103–18, 140–53.
20. The text from *Hekhalot Zutarti* appears in Peter Schäfer, *Synopse zur Hekhalot-Literatur*, §408. The passage was cited in connection with the Pardes story by the tenth-century rabbinic authority Hai be Sherira Gaon (B. Lewin [ed.], *'Otzar ha-Geonim*, vol. 4, Part II [Hagigah], p. 14); and by the eleventh-century talmudic commentator Hananel ben Hushiel's commentary to B. Hagigah 14b.
21. Schäfer 1983, *Synopse zur Hekhalot-Literatur*; Peter Schäfer, *Genizah-Fragmente zur Hekhalot-Literatur*. All passages from Hekhalot literature in this chapter will be cited from these editions with the exception of the *Shi'ur Komah*, which will be quoted from Martin Samuel Cohen, *The Shi'ur Qomah: Texts and Recensions.*
22. Schäfer has argued that this textual situation applies to the rest of rabbinic literature as well; Schäfer 1986a, and see Jaffee's discussion in this volume.

23. See Heinemann 1977.
24. Scholem 1960, 20 n. 1.
25. Wolfson 1993. For a survey of the evidence, see Kuyt 1995.
26. On *Hekhalot Rabbati*, see Smith 1963.
27. The story of the Ten Martrys has a long and complex history in Hebrew literature of Late Antiquity and the Middle Ages. For the principal text, see Gottfried Reeg, *Die Geschichte von den zehn Märtyrern*. On the version in *Hekhalot Rabbati*, its place in Hekhalot literature, and pseude-pigraphic and apocalyptic narratives in Hekhalot in general, see Boustan 2005.
28. A similar explanation is offered for the writing down of the Babylonian Talmud by the tenth-century authority Rav Sherira Gaon; see Strack and Stemberger 1992, 192–94.
29. This name seems to be derived from the Greek *tetras*, "four," as in the Tetragrammaton. On magical names in Hekhalot literature, see Scholem 1960, 75–83.
30. Another enigmatic passage that seems to reflect this idea appears in a Genizah text that is apparently influenced by the Hekhalot Rabbati tradition, a text called *Ḥotam ha-Merkavah*, "The Seal of the Merkavah" (MS Cambridge TS K1.21.95.C, published by Ithamar Gruenwald and Schäfer, in 1969, *Geniza-Fragmente* Text 8 [97–109]). In a testimony to the effectiveness of the praxis that he has just described, Rabbi Ishmael declares that on seeing the King in his beauty, "immediately the world was redeemed."
31. The text that appears in portions of *Ma'aseh Merkavah* was first published by Alexander Altmann in 1946. The text was then published in Scholem 1960, 101–17, and Schäfer, *Synopse*, §§544–96. For analyses of the text, see Swartz 1992 and Janowitz 1989.
32. See Scholem 1961, 57–63, and Swartz, 1992.
33. Schäfer, *Synopse* §158, according to MS Munich 22. This translation has drawn from Morton Smith's in Scholem 1960, 22.
34. The divine presence. In MS Oxford 1531, the word *merkavah* is inserted above the line.
35. This translation has been drawn from Morton Smith's in Scholem 1960, 22.
36. One important manuscript (MSS Munich 22 and Budapest 238) tradition does not mention the Merkavah by name, although it does mention the *hekhal*. However, other hymns in this section do mention the Merkavah.
37. For introductions to *piyyut*, see Yahalom 1987 and Swartz 2005, 1–15. The value of the *piyyut* for studying the impact of Byzantine culture in Palestine upon rabbinic Judaism is discussed in this volume by Seth Schwartz.
38. On this passage, see Swartz, 1992, 145–47, 171–84.
39. Cohen, *Shi'ur Komah: Texts and Recensions*, 30–31.
40. On anthropomorphism and the gargantuan proportions of the deity in the *Shi'ur Komah*, see Jackson 2005.
41. Scholem 1961, 78.
42. Schäfer 1992, 151–53.

43. For an English translation of the entire work, see Swartz 2001a.
44. MS JTSA ENA 6643.4. See Swartz 2005.
45. Heb. *ẓiẓ*, a word that also refers to the frontlet on the priest's forehead, according to Exodus 28:36.
46. Himmelfarb 1993, 109. This argument is spelled out in Himmelfarb 1988.
47. Lieberman 1980, 241–44.
48. *Hotam ha-Merkavah*, on which see note 30.
49. Schäfer, *Geniza-Fragmente*, Text 8 (p. 103), fol. 2a, lines 43–45.
50. On the affinities between Palestinian midrashim and esoteric cosmology, especially the *Baraita' de-Ma'aseh Bere'shit*, see Schäfer 2004.
51. Cf. Elior 2004, which argues that the primary forces behind the Hekhalot literature were circles of priests going back to the Second Temple era.
52. For this argument to the authors of the *Sar Torah* literature, see Swartz 1996. Recently, Davila 2001 has argued that the Hekhalot tradition is the product of a class of shamanistic practitioners.
53. See Scholem 1961, 44, 73–75, and 1960, 1–5.
54. On this problem, see P. S. Alexander 1984.
55. See Scholem 1960, 75–83.
56. Lewy 1960, 259–65.
57. PGM iv 475–829. For a translation and annotation of this text by Marvin Meyer, see Hans Dieter Betz (ed.), *The Greek Magical Papyri in Translation*, 48–54.

10 An Almost Invisible Presence: Multilingual Puns in Rabbinic Literature

GALIT HASAN-ROKEM

Scholars of rabbinic literature are increasingly aware of the various ways in which the emerging culture of the sages was deeply in conversation with surrounding cultural currents. The essays by Seth Schwartz, Yaakov Elman, and Catherine Hezser in this volume already have pointed readers in this direction. In the present contribution, I wish to continue this theme from the perspective of linguistics and folklore studies. In particular, I shall focus on the expression of cultural proximity, maybe even intimacy, of the Aramaic and Hebrew-speaking Jewish culture of the Greco-Roman and Byzantine period with the Greek-speaking culture of the same time and place. The evidence I shall call upon is found in hidden puns relating to the Greek language that underlie some Aramaic or Hebrew texts. These demonstrate a marked interlingual proficiency and creativity on the part of the authors, narrators, and even their audiences. The traversing of linguistic borders that seems to have been regarded with aesthetic pleasure and cultural appreciation offers yet more demonstration that cultural isolationism was hardly a dominant trait in the culture that we call ancient rabbinic.

The texts in which I have found these puns are from rabbinic works, shaped between the third and the sixth century, approximately, in Jewish Palestine, texts in which the Hebrew Bible serves as a constant point of reference and basis for interpretation. Remarkably, maybe one could even say paradoxically, one important literary context in which such puns appear is the midrashic account of the historical clash between Judah and Rome in Lamentations Rabbah, a text that surely emerges out of this period, although in its later formations it was strongly influenced by the Babylonian Talmud.

Hebrew literature has exerted dynamic interactions with other languages more or less throughout its history.[1] In the massive corpus of rabbinic literature, Hebrew and Aramaic interact and mingle constantly. In his book on Baroque Hebrew literary riddles created in Italy and Holland, Dan Pagis (1986) devoted considerable space to the documentation and analysis of the poetic device called by the Hebrew poets of Italy *lo'ez* (162–83). The use of *lo'ez* introduced into Hebrew poetic texture the words and meanings from the language of the majority linguistic community, in most cases discussed in the book in Italian, a language also spoken by the Jews who lived as a minority in the same culture. Pagis demonstrates with numerous examples that in the inventive poetics of the Hebrew poets of Italy, the *lo'ez* became a sophisticated and supple mode of expressing their identification with Italian culture and in inscribing their ownership of it, even while they wrote in Hebrew. In the context of the refined and highly cognizant poetics of their milieu, they practiced the use of other languages, mainly Italian and Latin, in their Hebrew poetry with great awareness and constant reflection.

More recently, the production of the authors of the Hebrew renaissance at the end of the nineteenth century was crafted in vital interaction with their Yiddish linguistic background.[2] The longtime existence of Hebrew as a part of complex linguistic and cultural polysystems, filling the needs of its speakers or writers only partially while many functions were filled by other languages, may have contributed to the active bilingual and multilingual creativity of authors in Hebrew.[3] Comparisons to similar phenomena in other languages are definitely beyond the scope of the present study. Explicit or implicit multilingual wordplays are extant in nonliterary uses of language as well. In most languages around the world nowadays, English – especially American English – is present in various forms of mass communication, particularly advertisement, and from there it spreads into private spheres of language as well as to literature.[4]

The focus of the present article is a specific case of multilingual punning between Hebrew and Aramaic texts referring to Greek. The presence of Greek in rabbinic texts, especially Palestinian ones, is a well-known fact and a relatively well-researched field.[5] The following passage from the Palestinian Talmud highlights the presence of Greek in expressive textual modes:

> Rabbi Jonathan of Bet Govrin said: Four languages are well suited for use in the world, and they are as follows: Greek for song (poetry), Latin for war, Syriac for wailing (laments), Hebrew for speech. And some add even Assyrian for writing. (Y. Megillah 1: 11, 71b)[6]

We should thus not be surprised to find echoes of Greek in poetic texts written predominantly in Aramaic and Hebrew. The examples that I shall analyze here are of the kind usually classified as folk literature.

Whereas the careful stylizing of the texts seems to suggest an "elite" literary sensibility, and thus obscures the theoretical division of folk literature from other domains of rabbinic literary creativity, the use of the term "folk literature" here is validated by the clear-cut reference of these texts to the genre system established in folk narrative research.[7] In my past work, short reference was made to the puns that will be discussed here but without further elaboration.[8] Following the lead of Pagis's insight about the role of punning in intercultural creativity, I shall propose that the Greek puns that will be shown to underlie Hebrew and Aramaic riddles, enigmatic tales and dream interpretations bear testimony to an intimate presence of the Greek language at least in some rabbis' creative minds as part and parcel of what they considered their *own culture.*

The first pun to be discussed is embedded in a tale of dream interpretation. The locus of the act of interpretation in this specific case is the house of learning, the *bet midrash.* The interpreter is no less than Rabbi Akiva, who is presented throughout the talmudic-midrashic corpus of texts as the most creative and influential shaper of the midrashic methodology itself. This methodology consisted of intricate and sophisticated methods of interpreting extensive meaning in the text of the Hebrew Bible in order to construct halakhic rules of religious and legal conduct, as well as to develop philosophical and narrative discourses of *'aggadah.*[9] The entirely explicit interlingual wordplay of the following tale is indeed located in Rabbi Akiva's academy:

> A man came to Rabbi Akiva, and said to him: I was shown in
> my dream "Go up to Qappadoqia[10] and you will find your
> father's holdings." He said to him: Did your father ever go up
> to Qappadoqia during his lifetime? [He said: No] He said to him:
> Get up and go count the beams, until the one at the head of ten
> [beams][11] and find your father's holdings. Rabbi Akiva learnt
> this from: *qappa* – beam [*kashurah*, Aramaic], *deqa*[12] – ten.
> (Lamentations Rabbah 1:1, ed. Buber, pp. 54–55)

The technique here applied by Rabbi Akiva combines *notarikon*, that is, dividing the word Cappadocia into two separate words, *qappa* and *deqa*, and attaching a separate meaning to each of the halves, and something similar to *gematria*, ascribing meaning to the numerical value of the letters.[13] The access to a bilingual or rather multilingual system of meanings complicates and enriches the interpretation. The point of departure is the place-name Cappadocia, a region in Asia Minor that in the fourth century C.E. was to become famous as the site for the life and work of some of the most creative and influential minds of the early Christian Church: Basil, Gregory of Nazianus, and Gregory of Nyssa, also known as the Cappadocian Fathers.

It may be useful to add some information on the context in which the tale is embedded. Lamentations Rabbah belongs to the genre of so-called exegetical midrash, characterized by an anthological structure that follows the order of biblical verses of the book it elaborates. Lamentations Rabbah includes homilies elaborating on the verses in their order in the biblical Book of Lamentations. The portion of the text to which this tale, and some of the tales discussed later belongs, refers to the first verse in the biblical Book of Lamentations, specifically the first two-thirds of verse: "How doth the city sit solitary, that was full of people [*rabbati 'am*]! How is she become as a widow! She that was great among the nations [*rabbati ba-goyyim*], and princess among the provinces, how is she become tributary!" (Lamentations 1:1). The interpretative elaboration addresses more exactly the seemingly superfluous doubling of *rabbati 'am* (full of people) – *rabbati ba-goyyim* (great among the nations). The parallelism is much more striking in the Hebrew original than the English translation reveals. In terms of biblical poetics, the parallelism does not constitute an exception; rather it is one of the standard conventions of biblical poetry,[14] and thus the recurring second part does not necessarily add information to the first part of the verse. However, rabbinic hermeneutic poetics – in other words *midrash* – presumes the opposite, that no letter of Scripture is void of "surplus meaning."[15] Thus, the seemingly repetitive *rabbati ba-goyyim* (the succinct Hebrew idiom is typically represented by a much longer English equivalent: "She that was great among the nations") is demonstrated to have a specific meaning:

> But *rabbati 'am* [that was full of people] was already mentioned, what are we to learn [*u-mah talmud lomar*] from *rabbati ba-goyyim* [that was great among the nations]? Indeed [we learn] *rabbati ba-de'ot* [great in knowledge]. (Lamentations Rabbah 1:1, ed. Buber, pp. 46)

The reading is based on the fact that the Hebrew parallelism is much more impressive phonetically and rhythmically than the English translation reveals, and the solution adheres to the same formula as the two parallel clauses from the biblical text. The direct expression for the surplus meaning derived from the parallel is crafted to demonstrate the principle borne out by another verse in the same biblical book: "The precious sons of Zion, comparable to fine gold" (Lamentations 4:2a),[16] understood to express the superior wisdom of Jerusalemites.

The intellectual preeminence of the Jerusalemites, according to the tales that then follow, seems to be an excellent adaptation to varying cultural environments and stimuli, rather than an insistence on the internal ethnic repertoire, as the texts in themselves embody such cultural competence. The puns, texts doubly encoded, inevitably create the impression that *someone along the line of the formation of the texts and their transmission has been able to shape these double encodings and some others have enjoyed them*, although we are today not capable of reconstructing exactly who, when, and where. However, for a large part of their audiences, these puns may have gone unnoticed.

The first cluster of texts in the section relating to the wisdom of the Jerusalemites includes eleven riddle tales, followed by a group of tales on the interpretation of dreams, and finally a short tale cycle describing Rabbi Joshua's wandering and search among the enigmas of age, gender, and history.[17] The riddle tales are largely unparalleled in rabbinic literature, which by and large is atypical of the corpus, usually characterized by intense cross-referencing of sources from various periods and various locations.[18] In later medieval and Renaissance collections, the tales were reproduced almost without alterations.[19] The riddle tales provide "solid proof" concerning the intellectual superiority of the Jerusalemites by being able to solve riddles that others fail in solving, or by being able to present riddles that others are unable to solve. The opposition *Jerusalemites/all the world* is achieved by effectively applying the hermeneutic rule of *a minori ad majus* (in Hebrew, *qal va-ḥomer*), by making the competitors Athenians: If they are able to prevail over the people of Athens, the uncontestable capital of wisdom in Antiquity, how much more then everyone else![20]

The rabbinic, talmudic-midrashic corpus is, as said before, marked by rich interreferencing and multiple distribution of parallels and versions of similar tales. Thus, the tales of dream interpretation, one of which was already quoted – the Cappadocia dream – have extensive parallels in the Palestinian Talmud (Y. Maaser Sheni 4:12, 55b–c) and in the "dream book" of the Babylonian Talmud (B. Berakhot 55a–57b), and fractional parallels in Genesis Rabbah. The enigmatic tale of Rabbi Joshua's journey is paralleled with small changes in the Babylonian Talmud (B. Eruvin 53b).

Let us now return to the Cappadocia dream tale to review the construction and semiotics of the Greek-Hebrew-Aramaic pun in its various manifestations in the different parallels and versions. As indicated earlier, the version of the tale in Lamentations Rabbah renders *qappa* as a synonym for *kashura*, the Aramaic word for "beam" selected by the narrator.[21] But whereas the Aramaic word is well known, we do not have good sources to explain the understanding of *qappa* as a beam.[22] The number ten of the recommended count is here derived from the slight transformation of the second half of the place-name, *doqia** → *deqa*, namely *deka*, ten in Greek.

The Babylonian Talmud has the following version of the tale:[23]

> He said to him: I saw [in a dream] that I was told: "Your father left for you possessions in Qappadoqia." He said [to me]: Do you have any possessions in Qappadoqia? He said: No. Did your father travel to Qappadoqia? He said: No. In that case: *qappa* – beam [*kashura*], *deqa* – ten. Go and examine the beam [*qappa*] until the one at the head of ten [beams], and you will find it full of *zuzim* [coins]. He went and found it full of *zuzim*. (B. Berakhot 56b)[24]

The division and the translation of the words are the same as in the Lamentations Rabbah version.[25] Yet another set of possibilities is demonstrated in the version of the Palestinian Talmud for the tale:[26]

> A man came to Rabbi Yose ben Halafta and said to him: I saw in my dream that I was being told: Go to Qappadoqia, and you will find your father's property. He said to him: Did that man's father ever go to Qappadoqia? He said to him: No. He said to him: Go count ten beams inside your house and you shall find your father's holdings. Ten beams [*qappa deqoria*]. (Y. Maaser Sheni 4:12, 55b)

The third version displays a different verbal technique for reaching more or less the same interpretation for a more or less similar dream. Here, the beam is glossed in Aramaic as *qoria*, to be compared with the Greek *keria* and the Hebrew *qora*.[27] The number ten is apparently derived from the letter *kappa*'s position as the tenth letter in the Greek alphabet, notwithstanding its numerical value being twenty, but rather according to the Hebrew where the numerical value of the tenth letter *yod* is indeed ten. This is thus the most "Greek" of all the versions quoted up to now; however, the Greek has been adapted to Hebrew and Aramaic concepts.

As mentioned, this dream also appears in the Palestinian aggadic midrash Genesis Rabbah. There, we see it elaborating on Genesis 28:12, which introduces Jacob's dream about the ladder: "And he dreamed, and behold a ladder set up on the earth, and the top of it reached to heaven: and behold the angels of God ascending and descending on it."

The midrashic elaboration including the tale is specifically linked to the first phrase "And he dreamed":

> "And he dreamed," said Rabbi Abbahu, dream matters neither improve nor harm: A man went to Rabbi Yose ben Halafta and said to him: It was said to "that man" [meaning himself] in a dream: Go and bring your father's holdings from Qappadoqia. He said to him: Did your father ever go to Qappadoqia? He said to him: No. He said to him: Go count twenty beams [*sharyin*] in the corner of your house and you shall find it. He said: There are not twenty [beams]. He told him: If there are not twenty, count them from first until last and from last to first and when you reach [number] twenty you will find it. He went and did so and found. And wherefrom did Rabbi Yose learn it? From Qappadoqia. (Genesis Rabbah 68:12, ed. Theodor and Albeck 2:784–85)

The passage opens in a strange manner, because attaching to patriarch Jacob's visionary dream about the angels of heaven the claim "dream matters neither improve nor harm" seems at least somewhat inappropriate. Even stranger is the fact that the narrative following the saying of Rabbi Abbahu completely belies his claim by reporting a dream that actually did improve the dreamer's situation. In addition, immediately after the narrative itself Bar Kappara claims the opposite: "There is no dream that has not a solution." Above all, this story lacks the linguistic key to the solution given by Rabbi Yose in the Yerushalmi version, creating the impression that the connection between the city of Cappadocia and counting ten beams to find a treasure is common knowledge in the circle surrounding the formulation of the Genesis Rabbah materials.[28] And indeed, one can guess that the numerical value of kappa, twenty, could be widely known through trade and other modes of everyday life. The mode of the dream interpretation itself, starting with a mistaken instruction to count more beams than there are in the house, first leads us to believe that the dream indeed confirms Rabbi Abbahu's disclaimer. The easy change from twenty to ten back and forth further adds to the slightly jocular tone of the tale. The Genesis Rabbah version may thus be the basic form of the story, constructed around a well-known interlingual piece of information in a multilingual society, namely, that the Greek letter kappa, audibly included in the first half of the name of the city Cappadocia, means twenty. The sophisticated elaborations playing with the various alternative words that could be found for "beam" were probably the pastime of literati inside the rabbinic academies or around them.

Solomon Buber, the editor of the Casanata manuscript edition of Lamentations Rabbah, was also impressed – or rather perplexed – by the linguistic variation of the different versions of the tale. He composed an extensive exposition that includes more or less everything that has been pointed at here[29] and quite clearly prefers the wording of the version in Lamentations Rabbah in the manuscript that he published.

On the basis of all the different versions, we may proceed to a systematic presentation of the full paradigm of the complex system of multilingual punning that emerges from the different versions. The complexity arises from the contemporaneous availability of a number of languages whose relationships are characterized by various kinds of overlaps and interchanges. Thus, at different instances in time, at least the following languages were available for the supposed authors and listeners/readers of the texts that are discussed here: Aramaic, Hebrew, Syriac, and Greek, and at a greater distance also Persian and a number of other languages extant in Mesopotamia and Asia Minor, as well as Arabic. This multilingual menu created a network of possibilities for playing with words that narrators and copiers in various locations and at different periods made the most of in order to please and stimulate their audiences.

Here are the basic components of the equation:

1. The name of the city mentioned in the dream: Cappadocia or, in its form in most of the rabbinic sources, *qapodqia*.
2. The beams of the house introduced by the interpreter of the dream: *qorah* in Hebrew; *kashura* in Syriac and Aramaic, *dokos* in Greek.
3. The number of beams, typically ten, once, however, twenty.

The combinatorial options are enabled by the resources of the midrashic techniques whose connections with the Greek language and the Hellenistic culture were demonstrated in detail by Saul Lieberman (1950, 68–82). One of these devices already mentioned is the *notarikon*, the division of a word into components whose separate meanings are raised from potential to manifest.[30] Here, the word that is divided is the name of the city, Cappadocia. Another device is translation, from one language to another, as well as from one culture to another.[31] The narrators quoted visibly translated the word designating "beam" from one language to another. A third device is loan words, the usage of one language's words in the other; thus, the number ten represented especially by the word *deka*, less so by the letter *kappa*, seems to have traversed quite easily the linguistic borders from Greek to the Semitic languages. The Greek number ten – deka – is derived either from the sound *ka* of the first half of the name of the city, or from the *docia* of its second half.

In this intricate "card game," the joker is the word referring to the beams, a necessary component of the plot as it has been transmitted by all the narrators and copiers. That is, the signified object of beams is an agreed element, yet its verbal signifier is surprisingly unstable and flexible. The signifier is possibly chosen according to the phonetic needs arising from the choice of word to represent the number of beams. The selection of the word for the number of the beams produces a choice of word for the beams themselves based on the part of the word Cappadocia that is left "free." If the word *deka* represents the number, then *kappa* is free to serve the beam word. However, if *kappa* represents the number, *docia* is left free for the beam. Or rather vice versa; since the number is derived from Greek in any case, and the two possibilities are more or less known, deka and kappa, then the choice of the word for beams ends up being the "joker," changeable according to linguistic and cultural preferences of each place and period.

Another element of cultural translation that seems to be of consequence is the import into the midrashic corpus of the internal Greek wordplay between deka (ten) and dokos (beam). This pun itself could constitute the kernel of the tale of the type "the hanged man's treasure": A person who is about to die leaves a will to his son whereby he orders him to hang himself on the beam of the house if he loses his property. This indeed happens, and the son is about to hang himself as he was told by his father, at which point the beam on which he should hang himself collapses and a treasure hidden there by the foresighted father is revealed.[32]

The second pun that I will analyze is also included in the tales on dream interpretation in Lamentations Rabbah, and the Greek word for beam, *dokos*, is a key element in it as well. The interlingual context is less manifest than in the first case, but it is relatively easily retrievable:

> A woman once came to Rabbi Eleazar. She said to him: "In my dream I saw the beam of the house breaking." He said to her: "That woman [meaning the dreamer] will bear a male child." And so she did. She came at another time and did not find him [R. Eleazar] there, but found his students. She said to them: "Where is your Master?" They said to her: "What do you want?" She said to them: "In my dream I saw the beam of the house breaking." They said to her: "That woman will bury her husband." When she left she heard that her husband was dead and she began to scream. R. Eleazar heard her voice and said to her: "What do you want?" His students said to him: "She came and asked us about a

dream." Said he to them: "And what did you tell her?" Said they: "We told her that that woman would bury her husband." Said he: "You have lost a human being. Is it not written that 'And it came to pass, as he interpreted to us, so it was'?" [Genesis 41:13]. (Lamentations Rabbah 1:1)[33]

The passage continues with a meta-interpretative comment and an almost desperate attempt to make things right again:

And Rabbi Yohanan said: The dream follows its interpretations, except for wine, for some drinking it means good, for some drinking it means bad, a scholar drinks and it means good, the illiterate drinks and it means bad. Their Master said to her: "Dreams neither improve nor harm." She came a second time and told him: "I saw in my dream that the [upper] floor of the house was breaking." He said: "That woman [meaning the dreamer] will bear a male child." And so she did. (Ibid.)

For this tale, too, there are textual variants: The beam is here termed in Aramaic *shrit, shrita* in Y. Ma'aser Sheni, and in Genesis Rabbah *tinita*.[34] The interlingual pun, consisting of a tacit presence of the almost total wordplay of *dokos* (beam) and *tokos* (birth), is not overtly reflected upon in the text itself, but may be conjectured with a rather high level of certainty.[35]

In an earlier analysis of the text (Hasan-Rokem 2000, 104–5), I attributed the dissimilarity between the interpretations of the rabbi and that of his disciples to the difference in maturity. The teacher fully understands that the process of pregnancy and birth involves a rupture of the woman's body, encoded in the dream as the breaking of the beam, whereas the disciples identify the beam somewhat simplistically as the "phallic" symbol of the husband, the patriarchal rafter of the household, whose breaking in their imagination can only mean death. The inability to see death and life, as well as masculinity and femininity, as continuities rather than oppositions brings about the disastrous interpretation of the students. But Rabbi Eleazar may have yet another source of knowledge that enables him to see the connection between beam and birth, namely, the knowledge of the Greek language, in which the connection is expressed exactly by the pun on the two words. The added episode, absent from the Y. Ma'aser Sheni version, seems hyperpointed, and may express the burning wish of one of the transmitters of the tale to reach a happy ending, against the earlier tendency to reflect the tragic outcome in its naked horror.

In this case, too, the Genesis Rabbah version seems to hold a key position, being attached to the verse that was repeated in its vicinity in the other versions as well, namely, the chief baker's confirmation in the ears of Pharaoh of the superb competence of Joseph as a dream interpreter: "And it came to pass, as he interpreted to us, so it was" (Genesis 41:13a):

> A woman went to Rabbi Eliezer and said to him: I saw in my dream that the beam of the house [*tiniata de-beita*] split open. He said to her: You are pregnant with a male child. She went her way and so it happened. She saw another time the same [dream]. She went to Rabbi Eliezer and told him, and he said: You are pregnant with a male child, and so it happened. She saw the third time, went to him and did not find him. She told his disciples: I saw in my dream that the beam of the house split open. They said to her: "That woman [she herself] buries her husband," and so it happened. Rabbi Eliezer heard a cry and said to them [his disciples]: What now? They told him the story, and he said to them: You killed a man, isn't it written: "And it came to pass, as he interpreted to us, so it was." Rabbi Yohanan said: All the dreams follow the mouth [i.e., oral interpretations], except for wine, for some drinking it means good, for some drinking it means bad, a scholar drinks and it means good, the illiterate drinks and it means bad. (Genesis Rabbah 89: 13, ed. Theodor and Albeck, 3:1095–97)

One may wonder about the frequency of rafters as dream images in rabbinic literature. Notably, this phenomenon is further substantiated by one of the most famous dreams of the ancient world, namely, Penelope's dream in the *Odyssey* (XIX, 273). In her dream, Penelope has seen a great bird, an eagle that flew down from the mountains and broke the necks of her twenty geese, leaving her crying. While she thus weeps the Achaian lasses with their beautiful tresses congregate around her. Surprisingly, the eagle returns and sits down on the rafter and turns to her in a human voice, explaining to her that the dream was a true vision, the geese being the suitors and the eagle her husband. Penelope then famously proceeds into a meta-hermeneutic discourse about dreams, true and false ones, incidentally rooted in punning relations between the various terms, gates of "ivory" and "untrue," gates of "horn" and "reality." Punning and dream interpretation are thus coupled from one of the earliest Greek instances of the two genres. The internal relationship between dreams and puns may also explain the abovementioned link between dreams and beams, a beam being in Greek *dokos*, a vision *doke*.[36] However, this indicates that the connection between dreaming and punning may well have served as a cultural interface between Greek culture and rabbinic literature.

The order of examples that I have chosen to present is from the more explicit to the less overt. The third example is thus much more subject to interpretation, and the interlingual pun in it will be more difficult to demonstrate persuasively. The text concerned is the first in the cycle of eleven riddle tales of Lamentations Rabbah:

There was a man from Jerusalem who went to Athens to stay with a friend for several days. His time came [to die] and he entrusted his belongings to the man he was staying with. He told him: Should my son come to you and desire these belongings, don't give them to him unless he does three wise acts [things]. They [the Athenians] had [an agreement] that none of them would point the way to another person's house for a traveler. The son heard [of his father's death] and went there, knowing the name of the man. He came and sat at the city gate, saw a man carrying a load of wood and said, "Are you selling that wood?" He said: "Yes." He said: "Take payment and go unload it [at so-and-so's house]." He followed him until they arrived at the man's house. He [the wood carrier] began calling for him. [The master of the house] looked through the window and asked: "What do you want?" Said he: "Come out and take the wood." He said to him: "Did I tell you to bring it to me?" He said: "It's not yours, but belongs to the one sitting behind it." He came down to ask who he was and said: "Who are you?" He said to him: "I am the son of the man from Jerusalem who died at your house." He took him in and prepared a meal for him. The man had a wife, two sons, and two daughters. They sat down to eat and they brought him five young fowl. He said to him: "Take them and serve." He said to him: "It is not my [role], since I am a guest." He said to him: "Give me the pleasure." He took one bird and set it before the master of the house and his wife, took another and set it before the two sons, took another and set it before the two daughters, and took two for himself. He said to him: "How have you served?" He said to him: "I said to you, did I not, that I am a guest and that it is not my [role], but I have served well in any case – you and your wife and the bird make three heads, your two sons and a bird make three heads, your two daughters and a bird make three heads, and I and two birds make three heads." In

the evening he prepared a feast for him and brought him one fowl.
He said to him: "Take it and serve." He said to him: "It is not my
[role], since I am a guest." He said to him: "Give me the pleasure."
He took the head and set it before the master of the house, took
the stomach and set it before his wife, took the legs and set them
before the two sons, took the wings and set them before the two
daughters, and took the body and all the rest for himself. He said to
him: "How have you served?" He said to him: "I told you, did I not,
that it is not my [role], but I have served well in any case. I gave you
the head because you are the head of the house, and the stomach
and entrails to your wife because these children came from her. I
gave the two legs to your two sons who are the pillars of your
house, I gave the two wings to your two daughters who will take
their marriage contracts and leave, and I took the body [shaped like
a boat] and the rest for myself, since I shall be leaving on a boat."
He said to him: "Go ahead and give me my father's belongings and
I will go my way." He went ahead and gave him his things and he
went away. (*Midrasch Echa Rabbati*, ed. Buber, pp. 46–47)[37]

The intercultural aspects of this tale are manifold, and I have discussed them in the context of an exposition of comparative methods
in folk narrative research.[38] The acting of the young (we may suppose
that he was relatively young, according to the plot) Jerusalemite at the
table, when asked to divide a number of fowl or to carve one, belongs
to a large category of narratives whose common theme is "strange and
inexplicable acts."

Here I elaborate on the interlingual pun emerging toward the end
of the narrative that was only mentioned briefly in the former work.[39]
The tale as a whole has rich international comparative material.[40] The
mathematical exercise of the first division of birds is an example of a
well-known favorite.[41] When supplying an explanation for his odd carving of the fowl, the Jerusalemite explains all the other stages by the
symbolical roles of the various family members, and the explanations
all make sense in terms of quite traditional and conventional symbols.[42]
The enigmatic explanation, however, regards the share that he takes
to himself in a seemingly gluttonous gesture. The explanation given is
encoded already in the term *a boat* (*ilpa*) that both the narrator and the
protagonist use to describe the part of the bird that he leaves for himself, namely, all of the body except for limbs, head, and intestines. The
form of a bird's body, especially a chicken's body, structurally resembles
a boat, and terminology concerning boats often consists of animisms,
including personifications. In many languages ships are feminine, even

in cases where an unequivocally gendered form is not demanded by the language itself.[43]

I would, however, suggest that the gesture and the sentence in which the Jerusalemite describes his future act as "leaving on a boat" are also connected by a pun. The pun is constructed upon the similarity of a word concerning a bird, on the one hand, and words that refer to boats and sailing, on the other hand. Such a pun does not exist in Hebrew or Aramaic,[44] but may be reconstructed in Greek, namely: *ploion*, a boat, and *peleia*, a kind of a dove. Moreover, these words also pun on the Aramaic word chosen for the boat, *ilpa* sharing with it the consonants *p* and *l*.[45] In addition, there are two verbs that are quite close in their meaning to the verb "leave" (the Aramaic *azeil*) in which the Jerusalemite describes his plans: *poleomai*, to go to and fro, and *pleo*, referring especially to a sea voyage.

The three examples that have been discussed here demonstrate the encoding of intercultural punning whereby Hebrew and Aramaic narrating seems to have enriched its cultural repertoire by including Greek puns tacitly in the background. Can we surmise how this process actually happened? Hardly, but some possibilities enter the mind:

1. The stories entered the Hebrew-Aramaic written corpus from sources written in Greek that have not been preserved, and the translated versions retain the punning of the originals.
2. The stories were told and/or written down by narrators who were multilingual enough so that their proficiency in Greek, in addition to their native Hebrew/Aramaic, enabled them to create the whole multilingual system of punning, possibly to amuse an equally multilingual audience.
3. The stories were extant in a Hebrew/Aramaic that was continuously impressed by Greek until they reached the narrators/editors of the rabbinic texts, who retained the form of the tales without being necessarily aware of the puns.

What is the effect of these puns from a foreign but yet known language that loom from the poetical texture of collectively authored texts related at once to the sacred and the quotidian? In the complex and chronologically drawn-out corpus of rabbinic texts, these riddles construct, deconstruct, and reconstruct the world as riddles mostly do.[46] They articulate a vast cognitive and emotional continuum of interrelations represented in the texts of the rabbis: Greek, Aramaic, and Hebrew; rabbis, disciples, and dreamers; men and women; mothers, husbands, fathers, sons and daughters, siblings; Athens, Jerusalem, and Cappadocia; numbers and letters; houses and boats. The porosity of identities in proximity is expressed here, not in neighborly relations and acts but in a purely discursive form.[47] Words that sound alike but have different meanings or words that sound different but mean the same may cause great perplexity in a world where strangers are liable to constitute threats. They may shake the foundations of signification and endanger the very discursive mode in which they are embedded. But they may also open up possibilities to acknowledge the foreign in the well known and the intimate in the unfamiliar; making a home in the heart of the *Unheimlich*, discovering the Other in oneself.

Notes

1. Weinreich 1974 treats the linguistic aspects of such interactions in a variety of languages. For Hebrew-Aramaic interlinguistic relations, especially in the first three centuries c.e.: Gluska 1999. S. Schwartz 1995 deals mainly with the Hebrew-Aramaic interface; however, the relationship of both with Greek is also mentioned, 32.
2. Shaked and Budick 2000; G. Shaked 1965.
3. Codde 2003; Even-Zohar 1990a and 1990b; Lachman 2000.
4. E.g., Ronny Somek, *Bloody Mary* (poetry; Hebrew), Tel-Aviv, 1984.
5. For a selection of works from various periods, see Krauss 1898–99; Lieberman 1994. See especially the article "Preliminary Indications of Greek Interacting with Hebrew and the Apocalypse and Exodus in the Hebrew Tradition," 88–100, in Hezser 2001. For Amaraic in particular, see Momigliano 1994, where he points to the sibylline texts as an intertextual encounter among Judaism, Christianity, and paganism.
6. This is the version of the best manuscript extant for the Palestinian Talmud: *Talmud Yerushalmi*, According to Ms. Or. 4720 (Scal. 3) of the Leiden University Library with Restorations and Corrections, Introduction by Y. Sussmann, Jerusalem, 2001, 748. In his article, S. Fraade quotes the passage that is of special consequence for the present work: "Rabbinic Views on the Practice of Targum, and Multilingualism in the Jewish Galilee of the Third–Sixth Centuries," in Levine 1992, 253–86.
7. I have elsewhere written extensively about the central position and special significance of riddles and other enigmatic modes, dream narratives and enigmatic tales, in Lamentations Rabbah: Hasan-Rokem 2000, especially 39–107, 191–201. Riddles in rabbinic literature have in the past been studied by B. Z. Bacher, J. Perles, S. Fraenkel, H. Schwarzbaum, and D. Noy. For a more detailed exposition of their work, see ibid., 219 note 36.
8. Hasan-Rokem 2000, 219 n. 37.
9. Lieberman 1950, 47–82. For more specific sources for the *middot*, and for the rabbis' legitimate "measures" according to which meanings may be derived on the basis of verbal elaboration and manipulation of the biblical: *Sifra on Leviticus*, ed. L. Finkelstein, vol. 2, pp. 3, 10–11; H. G. Enelow, *The Mishnah of Rabbi Eliezer or the Midrash of Thirty-Two Hermeneutic Rules*, 10–41.

10. I chose this unusual spelling to clarify the differences between *qof* (q) and *kaf* (k) in the Hebrew and Aramaic that may be important for the analysis.

11. This seems to be Buber's understanding of the term. Another possibility would be the head beams, the major beams that hold up the roof like "headstones."

12. The same reason as n. 10 for the strange spelling.

13. Solomon Buber, the editor of the Casanata MS edition of Lamentations Rabbah, *Midrasch Echa Rabbati,* pointed out the use of *notarikon* that takes into account the Greek meaning of the words.

14. Kugel 1981.

15. I borrow Paul Ricoeur's term, so suitable that it could have been invented to address the poetics of midrash.

16. Lamentations 4:2b: "how are they esteemed as earthen pitchers, the work of the hands of the potter!" Describing the traumatic "present" rather than the glorious past is temporarily suspended in the reading.

17. The three groupings of texts are discussed extensively in Hasan-Rokem 2000, respectively on 39–87, 88–107, 191–201.

18. The exceptions here: one tale of which there is a parallel version in B. Sanhedrin; a riddle to which there is a parallel in *Midrash Mishle* 1,1, edited by B. Visotzky, 4–5; and, finally, a genre parallel in B. Bekhorot 8b, where Rabbi Joshua B. Hanania competes with the elders of Athens in riddle solving in front of the [Roman] emperor.

19. E.g., *Sefer Zikhronot by Yerahmeel,* ed. E. Yassif, 336–45.

20. For Athens as symbol of wisdom, Momigliano op. cit.

21. M. Sokoloff, *A Dictionary of Jewish Palestinian Aramaic,* Ramat Gan, 1990, 270; ibid., *A Dictionary of Jewish Babylonian Aramaic,* Ramat Gan, 2002, 605, mentions the Akkadian *gushūru* and the Syrian *kashura* as background.

22. A slight possibility would be *kappa,* Sokoloff, *Jewish Babylonian Aramaic,* 594, for "shoulder," which may metaphorically stand for beam.

23. The tale is part of a long chain of dreams told by a Sadducean, in the versions Cuthean (= Samaritan), interpreted by Rabbi Ishmael, though the names are not explicitly mentioned in each specific instance.

24. I follow here the printed version. The text has many variations due to its ultimate position in the tractate.

25. The tales of Lamentations Rabbah have, in general, many parallels with the versions extant in the Babylonian Talmud. The eleventh-century Talmud exegete Rashi (Rabbi Shlomo Itzḥaqi) explains at this locus as follows: "The *qappa* that you were told is a *kashura* since in Persian and in Greek a *kashura* is called *qappa. Deqa* is ten, since in Greek ten is called *deqa* and thus you were told that there is money in the tenth beam." Alexander Kohut in his *Arukh Completum,* Vienna 1878 (repr.: Vienna 1926 and New York 1955) quotes seventeenth-century Amsterdam commentator Benyamin Mussafia, who contradicts Rashi's claim. I thank Professor Shaul Shaked for sharing his deep knowledge of Iranian languages and cultures to corroborate Mussafia's and Kohut's correction.

26. More or less identical to the Lamentations Rabbah Munich MS and printed edition.

27. Sokolov's suggestion to read *deqoria* as an adjectival form denoting "the tenth" seems to me less convincing.

28. This suggestion parallels the one we presented at the end of our article: Hasan-Rokem and Rokem 2000, 235, saying: "Did not Sophocles himself assume that all Athenians knew the famous riddle when he refrained from introducing it in the text of *Oedipus Tyrannos*?"

29. *Midrasch Echa Rabbati*, ed. Buber, 54–55 n. 149.

30. On the specific device of dividing a word into two in dream interpretation, ibid., 75.

31. Asad 1986. Although the translation from language to another is not among the explicitly mentioned "measures" of rabbinic interpretative practice, it serves them often; e.g., Leviticus Rabbah, 16, 1 (*Midrash Wayyikra Rabbah: A Critical Edition Based on Manuscripts and Genizah Fragments with Variants and Notes*, 346) grounds a reading of Lamentations 4:15 on a Greek word. There are numerous other examples grounding exegesis of Scripture on Greek, Syriac or Aramaic, Egyptian, Babylonian, Arabic, and Persian words.

32. Aarne and Thompson 1973, no. 910D, 314.

33. *Midrasch Echa Rabbati* ed. Buber, 55. The translation based upon that of Batya Stein in Hasan-Rokem 2000, 104.

34. In his commentary on Genesis Rabbah, *Midrash Bereshit Rabba*, vol. 3, 1095, Albeck suggests that *tinita* is the "second floor" of a house, going further and comparing the second floor to the husband on top of the "house" (the wife in common rabbinic parlance). This explanation hardly motivates Rabbi Eleazar's (here Rabbi Eliezer's) interpretation about the birth.

35. Possibly the more adequate meaning for the present text is "offspring." A compound such as *theotokos*, the attribute of the Virgin Mary following a dogma accepted at the Council of Ephesus in 431, also makes it possible for those with partial knowledge of Greek to assume a separate meaning of *tokos* as "mother."

36. A kind, anonymous reader of the Hebrew version of the essay made me aware of the fact that this meaning of δοκή is extremely rare.

37. The translation by Batya Stein in Hasan-Rokem 2000, 46–47.

38. Hasan-Rokem 2000, 67–87. I would now like to add the specific aspect of Roman meal culture that shows that having the Jerusalemite serve the food is a veiled attempt to gain control and superiority over him: Dunbabin 2003. On the *symposium* as a site of "actual and symbolic struggle," McClure 2003, 262.

39. Hasan-Rokem 2000, 219 n. 37.

40. Aarne and Thompson 1973, tale type no. 1533, "The Wise Carving of the Fowl."

41. A sexually more saucy example, where instead of birds a youth is supposed to divide eggs in a group consisting of women as well as men, *Peregrinaggio di Tre Giovani Figliuoli del re di Serendippo*, Venice: Michele Tramezzino (according to the bibliographical work by Marino Parenti,

Prime Edizioni Italiane, Milano, 1948); edited by Richard Fick and Alfons Hilka as *Die Reise der drei Söhne des Königs von Serendippo,* translated by Theodor Benfey, Folklore Fellows Communication no. 98, Helsinki: Academia Scientiarum 1932, 66–67. For an extensive discussion of the parallels between this book and the riddle tales of Lamentations Rabbah, see Hasan-Rokem 2000, 79–82, where this particular example is discussed on 81.

42. E.g., "The pillar of the family is the son." Euripides, "Ifigenia in Tauris," ll. 56–57, *Greek Tragedies,* edited by David Grene and Richard Lattimore, Chicago: University of Chicago Press, 1960, 117.

43. Swedish may provide the example here, too, a ship always being "hon."

44. The extant dictionaries for Aramaic all list for *ilpa* only Semitic cognates. Accordingly, the word is not mentioned in S. Krauss, 1898–99; repr.: Hildesheim 1964.

45. In Sokoloff, *Dictionary of Jewish Palestinian Aramaic,* 60, for the second meaning, "portion of a bird," there is only one reference, this tale; Sokoloff, *Dictionary of Jewish Babylonian Aramaic,* 116.

46. Abrahams 1980; Don Handelman, "Traps of Trans-formation: Theoretical Convergences," in Hasan-Rokem and Shulman 1996, 37–61; Dina Stein, "A King, a Queen and the Riddle Between," ibid., 125–47.

47. For neighborly relations in narrative dialogues of Jews and Christians, Romans and provincials, see Hasan-Rokem 2003.

Part III

*Hermeneutical Frames for Interpreting
Rabbinic Literature*

11 The "Other" in Rabbinic Literature

CHRISTINE HAYES

Group identity is a social and cultural construct that may be defined as a group's subjective sense of itself as being different from other groups. Since ancient times, the identity of Israel has been explored and constructed in opposition to gentile, or alien, others. But the self–other dyad is by no means stable or constant. Dramatic changes in the political and cultural conditions of Jewish life in Antiquity led inevitably to revision and renegotiation of the self–other dichotomy. Moreover, the self–other dichotomy can be differently constructed by different elements within a single ethnic or religious group, leading to internal conflict over the self-definition and boundaries of that group. These tensions may contribute to the formation of distinct sects espousing different views on the group's identity and the nature of the boundaries that serve to demarcate and preserve that identity. Identity construction is thus a complex task, as a group defines itself not only in contrast to other groups ("external others") but also in contrast to members of its group that would contest the group's identity or construct it in a different way ("internal others").

In rabbinic literature, reference is made to non-Israelites (gentiles of various descriptions). These "external others" often appear in rabbinic literature as mirror opposites of Israelites, and so sharpen the rabbis' definition of Israel.[1] However, insofar as this literature explores and develops a definition of the *rabbi* as the ideal Jew, reference is made to non-rabbinic Jews (of various descriptions). These "internal others" often appear in rabbinic literature as *mirror opposites of the rabbis* and so sharpen the rabbis' definition of their own class.

Yet theories of the other do more than prescribe and maintain group boundaries. They also serve as the means by which a group can explore its own internal ambiguities, experiment with alternative possibilities, embrace negativities, and "confront (even admire) what they themselves are *not*."[2] As we shall see, at times the "other" – both external and internal – is deployed in rabbinic literature not to facilitate but rather to complicate and even undermine attempts to construct a Jewish, or a rabbinic, self.

Two preliminary remarks are in order. First, it is increasingly evident that rabbinism in the first centuries of the common era was neither representative of nor widely and enthusiastically endorsed by the entire community of Jews in Palestine and, certainly, beyond. At some point in Palestine and in Babylonia, rabbis began to exert greater influence over the larger Jewish community, and rabbinic Judaism became more broadly disseminated (recent scholarship points toward the early fourth century in Palestine, though precision on this point is not possible). Nevertheless, this essay makes no claims regarding the actual beliefs and behaviors of the broader Jewish populace. Our focus is on the shifting representation and deployment of the other in texts produced by and for a religious elite. It is important to remember that this elite long occupied a marginal position even in Jewish society, so that even the most triumphant discourse of the other is rarely a discourse of *genuine* hegemony. It is more often a discourse from a position of disempowerment not only vis-à-vis the external other but, for an extended period of time, even vis-à-vis the internal other.

Second, rabbinic literature comprises many works of widely diverse genres. For the most part, we will assess the evidence of halakhic and aggadic texts separately, before seeking to characterize the composite whole that emerges from them in all its complexity (for in rabbinic texts many voices speak at once).[3] It must be remembered that rabbinic texts contain thousands of individual teachings and incidental remarks, which can be hyperbolical, polemical, idealistic, ironic. Such statements must be used with circumspection.

EXTERNAL OTHERS: GENTILES

Rabbinic literature shows little interest in gentiles *for their own sake*. For the most part, the gentile is considered, in halakhic literature at least, as a subject of practical legislation. Because Jews confronted gentiles on a regular basis in the land of Palestine, tannaitic rabbis saw a need to set forth rules that would govern Jewish–gentile interaction. These rules were elaborated upon by later generations of 'Amora'im. In this activity, the rabbis were no different from legal experts in any culture who struggle to define the rights, privileges, responsibilities, and obligations of noncitizens under the law.

The halakhic materials that pertain to gentiles are the product of a complex interaction of three factors.[4] First, the rabbis draw upon biblical concepts and terminology, even when anachronistic (e.g., Canaanite slave, resident alien). Second, the rabbis employ systematic halakhic thinking and abstraction in the generation and elaboration of rules relating to gentiles. Third, rabbinic rules are influenced by actual encounters with specific gentiles and a specific gentile culture.

The Gentile as Ethnic Other

In rabbinic *halakhah*, the gentile can be imagined as an ethnic other *or* as a religious other. As an ethnic other, the gentile is merely a non-Israelite or *goy* (member of a non-Israelite nation) to whom the laws of the Mosaic covenant do not apply. In tannaitic law, the gentile is seen in contrast to the Israelite, as one who does not observe the dietary laws, is not obligated by the ritual purity system, does not separate charitable contributions from his produce, does not contribute to the upkeep of the sanctuary, does not pay the half-shekel tax, and so on.

Not bound by Israel's covenant with the God of Abraham, the gentile is held to be generally ignorant of its terms. This presumed ignorance means that the Jew must be on guard against unintentional violations of the law in his interaction with a gentile. The tractate of the Mishnah that deals with Jewish–gentile interactions (M. Avodah Zarah) is best understood as a set of regulations that makes it possible to deal with gentiles with the confidence that one is not violating any religious prescriptions. For example, Chapter 2 contains a detailed list of gentile foods prohibited because of the possibility of mixture with, absorption of, or defilement by impure or forbidden substances, as well as a list of foods to which no such anxiety attaches.

This depiction of the ethnic other – as outside and ignorant of the covenant – is not as straightforward as it might appear. According to the Pentateuch, some of the terms of Israel's covenant apply even to non-Israelites who choose to take up residence among the nation of Israel as resident aliens (*ger*, pl. *gerim*). The pentateuchal model of peaceful coexistence, cooperation, and even limited integration of an ethnic other is realized in halakhot that exempt *but do not forbid* gentiles from observing certain laws. Thus, while gentiles are declared to be exempt from the various agricultural obligations incumbent upon Israel, they are not prohibited from separating *terumah* (heave offering) and tithes from their produce (M. Terumah 3:9). Similarly, although they are exempt from the requirements of the sacrificial system, tannaitic halakhah allows them to bring certain sacrificial offerings and donations to the sanctuary.[5]

The retention of the biblical model of coexistence and limited integration is not an obvious move. In rabbinic times, the term *ger* was no longer understood as referring to a resident alien but to a full-fledged convert. Thus, it required a special effort to read the resident alien (unconverted gentile) into the Torah, an effort the rabbis were prepared to make on occasion. Through creative exegesis, they found biblical warrant for gentile observance of some terms of the covenant. What actual gentiles may have done is beside the point. For our purposes, it is significant that rabbinic law constructs a difference between the Israelite self and non-Israelite other based on the observance of Torah law, and then undermines that very construction by imagining the possibility of a gentile's limited, voluntary observance of Torah law.

The Gentile as Religious Other

The gentile is also imagined as a *religious* other (*'oved 'avodah zarah*) who worships a deity or deities other than Israel's deity. The gentile as religious other falls under greater suspicion and is subject to more severe and at times hostile legislation than the gentile as ethnic other. Nevertheless, the rabbinic treatment of the idolater contains some interesting surprises best seen when contrasted with other ancient Jewish attitudes.

According to several biblical texts, the worship of gods other than YHWH is the proper, even divinely apportioned, mode of worship for foreign nations in their own lands (Deuteronomy 4:19). Only in YHWH's land is exclusive fidelity to YHWH required (Exodus 34:13–16; 2 Kings 17:24–41). For this reason, the Israelites are charged with the complete eradication of idolaters and idolatry from the land (Deuteronomy 7:1–5). While prophetic texts envisage a time when the sole divinity of YHWH is universally recognized, pentateuchal law does not extend the war against idolatry beyond the boundaries of YHWH's land.

The rabbis universalize the biblical ban against idolatry (limited in the Pentateuch to the Land of Israel) by including it in the so-called seven Noahide laws, which, according to rabbinic tradition, were imposed on all members of the human family in the time of Noah. Yet despite some expressions of deep hostility and intolerance toward paganism, *the Mishnah lacks any normative command to destroy pagans living in the Land of Israel.* M. Halbertal notes that "[t]he avoidance of such a command is interesting since the starting-point of biblical law is that coexistence is not allowed and that Israel ought to wage a total war against the pagans in the land of Israel" (1998, 163).

The rabbinic approach may be contrasted with that of the Hasmoneans, for example, "whose campaigns against Gentiles in the land of Israel included forced conversions and destructions of pagan temples and images" (Halbertal, 164) and with that of separatists who lived in voluntary self-exile until such time as the Lord of Israel would restore his people. How, we may ask, in an environment replete with pagan worshippers and symbols, did the rabbis negotiate the biblical zero tolerance policy for idolaters within the Land of Israel?

According to Halbertal, the tannaitic rabbis engaged in a war of passive resistance. Forced to accept the entanglement of Israelite and pagan society, they adopted a twofold strategy of 1) distancing themselves from pagans through various avoidance mechanisms and 2) creating a neutral space for legitimate interaction (165–66). As regards the first strategy, instead of destroying idolatry, Jews were to avoid either supporting or benefiting from pagan worship directly or indirectly (Halbertal, 164). Indeed, most of the prohibitions and regulations contained in tractate Avodah Zarah are motivated by the concern neither to benefit from nor to contribute to idolatry. M. Avodah Zarah 1:1 prohibits certain transactions in the days prior to an idolatrous festival lest one provide the means or motivation for idolatrous worship. M. Avodah Zarah 1:5 prohibits the sale to a gentile of specific items commonly known to be used in idolatrous worship. Libation wine is prohibited to an Israelite in M. Avodah Zarah 2:3. The fragments of images are prohibited in M. Avodah Zarah 3:2, as are any worshipped objects (B. Avodah Zarah 45b–47a). No benefit may be derived from an *asherah* – its shade (M. Avodah Zarah 3:13) or its wood (M. Avodah Zarah 3:14–15).[6]

The second strategy employed by the rabbis enabling existence in an environment saturated with pagan objects and idolatrous practices is that of neutralization (Halbertal, 166ff.). Through a variety of legal moves and distinctions, rabbinic law (re)described contemporary reality in a neutral way, opening the door for licit interactions. Thus, images need not be avoided if they are merely aesthetic rather than genuinely cultic. When asked how he could bathe in the bath of Aphrodite in light of the biblical ban on idolatry, Rabban Gamaliel is said to have responded that Aphrodite's statue serves a purely decorative and not a cultic function in the bathhouse (M. Avodah Zarah 3:4). Other rabbinic traditions note that gentiles use images as decoration on all sorts of items (such as household utensils) and that these images do not qualify as idols that Israelites are biblically commanded to destroy (M. Avodah Zarah 3:1, 3:4; T. Kelim Bava Metzia 4:8; Y. Avodah Zarah 3:1, 43c; B. Avodah Zarah 40b–41a, 44b). In short, only that which is *treated* (worshipped) as a deity falls under the biblical prohibition of idolatry. The Tanna'im even assert that an idolater can annul an idol or image (M. Avodah Zarah 4:4), thereby rendering it permitted for benefit by a Jew. Annulment occurs when a pagan performs some action on or with the idol, indicating its profane status in his eyes (e.g., damaging or defacing it). Annulment converts forbidden images and idols into cultically neutral objects that may legitimately be used by Israelites for various purposes. Other conceptual and legal distinctions create a neutral status or space in which Jews may interact with pagans and paganism.[7]

The rabbinic regulations concerning interaction between Jews and gentiles – as both ethnic and religious others – were not designed to prevent all interactions between Jews and gentiles or even to make such interaction difficult or cumbersome for Jews. Rather, these regulations were designed to prevent interaction *that would involve the observant Jew in a violation of the halakhah*. Setting out required standards and precautionary criteria, constructing legal distinctions and classifications, the rabbis negotiated a neutral space in which extensive commercial, business, and legal interactions – and even social contacts – between gentiles and halakhically observant Jews could occur.

Gentiles and Purity

That rabbinic texts dealing with gentiles should be characterized by negotiation and compromise ought to occasion no surprise, and recent scholars have pointed out how deeply embedded Palestinian rabbis were in their Greco-Roman context. Nevertheless, older assumptions persist – particularly the assumption that purity concerns would have mandated a policy of strict separation on the part of the rabbis. In outright contradiction to the testimony of biblical and rabbinic texts, scholars have long maintained that gentiles were considered by biblical Israelites and by pharisaic rabbis in Late Antiquity to be ritually impure either because they do not observe the biblical laws of ritual purity (Emil Schürer) or because of an intrinsic and permanent impurity that inheres in the gentile qua gentile (Gedalyah Alon).[8] Moreover, it was held that this impurity was the basis for a strict and burdensome policy of separation. Recently, however, Jonathan Klawans has demonstrated that gentiles are not deemed by biblical or tannaitic texts to bear an intrinsic ritual impurity transferable to Israelites, nor are they ritually impure due to a failure to observe the pentateuchal purity regulations. Klawans has concluded that it is an error to assume that a notion of gentile ritual impurity would have been an impediment to Jewish–Gentile interaction (1995, 288).

Klawans's work builds on the conceptual distinction between ritual and moral impurity. Ritual impurity is a highly contagious but impermanent condition resulting from an Israelite's primary or secondary contact with certain natural, and often unavoidable, processes and substances (corpses, genital flux, scale disease). Removed by rituals of purification, this impurity is not in itself sinful and implies only a state of cultic disqualification. Indeed, ritual impurity can arise from acts that are positively viewed, or even commanded, in the biblical context. There is nothing inherently sinful about being in a state of ritual impurity; sin arises only when the relevant rules and prohibitions are not observed. By contrast, moral impurity is a condition arising from the commission of certain heinous sins (murder, idolatry, and specified sexual sins). Moral impurity is said to defile the sinner himself, the land, and the sanctuary, leading eventually to severe divine punishment. Moral impurity is not associated with contact contagion (sinners are not ritually impure and, in some cases, they enter the sanctuary) and do not ritually defile those within their reach.[9]

All tannaitic and amoraic texts agree that the biblical laws of ritual purity are addressed to Israelites, and do not apply to gentiles (Sifra *Zavim* 1:1, Sifra *Tazri'a* 1:1; see also T. Zavim 2:1 and *beraitot* on B. Niddah 34a and B. Shabbat 83a). Gentiles neither contract nor communicate ritual impurity by means of scale disease and various genital fluxes (M. Negaim 3:1, 7:1, 11:1, 12:1; M. Niddah 4:3; cf. T. Niddah 5:5, M. Niddah 7:3, M. Mikvaot 8:3–4, M. Zavim 2:1, 2:3). The tannaitic conviction – apparently and remarkably unanimous – that gentiles are not ritually impure because of a failure to observe Israel's ritual purity legislation is axiomatic for the 'Amora'im. Neither are gentiles viewed as *intrinsically* ritually impure, as indicated by the fact that they may contact certain sancta.[10]

Nevertheless, despite the overwhelming evidence against an ancient principle of gentile ritual impurity, a few traditions describe a gentile ritual impurity *promulgated as a special rabbinic (not biblical) decree.* The decree was not incorporated in R. Judah's Mishnah, but appears in the Sifra, the Tosefta, and both Talmuds.[11] After noting that gentiles are biblically exempt from ritual impurity, these traditions state that "however, the rabbis decreed concerning them that they defile like *zavim* (persons with an abnormal genital flux) in every respect." The gentile is not decreed to *be a zav*, or to suffer from zav impurity, but to defile *like* a zav.[12] The zav defiles in very many different ways, such as by contact, carriage, shifting [*hesset*], bodily pressure [*madras*], impurity of being under certain objects [*maddaf*], sexual intercourse, and certain bodily fluids. Yet rabbinic texts explicitly exempt the genital fluxes of a gentile from impurity despite this decree. The analogy drawn between the gentile and the zav is therefore partial, and the most commonly encountered understanding of the decree is that the spittle and urine of a gentile defile like that of a zav (M. Zavim 5:7, M. Makkot 6:6).[13]

Scholars have assumed that the purpose of this decree – which appears to have had no widespread influence on legislation regulating interaction with gentiles – was to discourage sexual connections between Israelites and gentiles, but the explanation is implausible. The threat of a ritual impurity only one degree more severe than the impurity contracted in licit sexual relations with one's own spouse, and easily removed by rituals of purification, is hardly an effective deterrent for persons inclined to interethnic sexual relations.

Gentiles and Moral Impurity

The type of impurity most consistently applied to gentiles is moral impurity. All ancient Jewish sources – from the Bible to the Talmud – assert that gentiles no less than Israelites are capable of generating moral impurity through the commission of heinous deeds of idolatry and immorality (Leviticus 18:24–30, Psalms 106:38, Ezra 9:11). Immorality and the moral impurity it generates are not a function of ethnicity but of deeds. In the biblical view, gentiles qua idolaters engage in immoral deeds that generate a moral impurity that defiles the land. But gentiles who do not engage in idolatry and who observe the land's (moral) residency requirements do not generate a defiling impurity.

In rabbinic literature, a hostility to paganism as fundamentally immoral is found in a few laws that bespeak a general distrust of gentiles as dangerous and licentious. M. Avodah Zarah 2:1 prohibits the isolation of an Israelite woman with a non-Jew because the latter is suspected of sexual immorality, and M. Avodah Zarah 2:2 prohibits certain types of healing at the hands of a non-Jew (for fear that he will inflict harm or damage). Similar fears for life, limb, and property underlie the prohibition against patronizing a gentile barber in private (M. Avodah Zarah 2:2), against selling weapons or dangerous animals to a gentile (M. Avodah Zarah 1:7, T. Avodah Zarah 2:4), and against leaving an animal unsupervised in a gentile-owned stable (M. Avodah Zarah 2:1). In articulating these laws, the gentile is sometimes compared to a "dissolute Israelite" – since neither is constrained by the laws of the Torah to curb his base desires.

Is there not a contradiction in the rabbinic legislation pertaining to the gentile? We have seen a remarkable tendency not only to presume the trustworthiness of the gentile but also to create the very conditions for that trustworthiness (through strategies of "neutralization"). Yet here we see the opposite tendency: to presume in certain cases that the gentile is untrustworthy and dangerous. The explanation for this apparent contradiction has to do with the nature of law and the role of presumption in formulating general rules. The relevant consideration in rules pertaining to the gentile is the gravity of the consequence should the presumption of trustworthiness turn out to be wrong. Should an Israelite woman be left alone with a gentile man? The potential risk to the woman is too great, and so the law forbids – not because the rabbis believe every gentile man is depraved but because the law is designed to protect, and the failure to protect one woman in one instance would be failure absolute. Should a woman worry that her gentile neighbor entered her home and stirred her pot on the stove while she attended afternoon prayers? The potential risk – unintentional violation of the dietary laws – is of relatively minor importance, and so the meal in the pot is declared permitted (B. Avodah Zarah 38a–b). Permission is granted not because the rabbis believe gentile women never tend their neighbor's stoves but because the inconvenience and suspicion are unwarranted when so little is at stake.

There is no contradiction here – just legal strategizing around diverse risk factors. In cases of potential sexual assault, bestiality, and murder, the rabbis consistently prefer to err on the side of suspicion. In many other realms of life – commercial interactions, ritual purity, and other low-stakes areas – the rabbis consistently prefer to err on the side of trust. Moreover, the good opinion of their gentile neighbors played a part in the tendency toward leniency and trust. Maintaining peaceful relations with gentiles and avoiding their enmity are explicitly cited as relevant considerations in many legal rulings and determinations (Sifrei Devarim 344, T. Bava Kamma 10:15, Sifra *Behar* 9:2–3, B. Gittin 61a).[14] Thus, when the consequence of error is not grave, compromise and trust are the order of the day.

In one area, however, no compromise was considered possible. While rabbinic legislation envisages and even facilitates extensive interaction between Jews and gentiles, all sexual activity between Jews and (unconverted) gentiles is strictly prohibited, and the children of such a union are deemed illegitimate (*mamzerim*).

Interethnic Sexual Unions and Intermarriage
The rabbis maintain the pentateuchal view of intermarriage according to which 1) marriage to non-Israelites is *not* universally prohibited, and 2) Torah prohibitions of intermarriage to certain nations are based on the fear that intermarriage will lead to the Israelite's religious apostasy (Deuteronomy 7:25, 20:18; cf. Exodus 34:15–16, Leviticus 18:27–28, Numbers 33:50–56). In the period of the restoration, this picture

changes. A ban on intermarriage with *all* gentiles is promoted by Ezra and Nehemiah, and an entirely new rationale is advanced. Ezra is the first to define Jewish identity in almost exclusively genealogical terms. Elaborating on earlier pentateuchal and prophetic themes, Ezra advanced the novel argument that *all* Israel – not merely the priests – is a holy seed distinct from the profane seed of gentiles.

The word pair holy/profane must not be confused with the word pair pure/impure, for while the two pairs of terms are related, they are not identical. The term "impure" denotes a state of cultic disability and is the antonym of "pure." The term "holy" denotes that which has been consecrated and thus belongs to God and is the antonym of "profane," which designates ordinary nonholy entities. The default state for most entities is profane and pure. Something must happen to render a profane object holy – an act of consecration – or to render a pure object impure – an act of defilement. The holy must always be pure. If defiled, holy entities are automatically profaned or desecrated and must be purified before being reconsecrated. Thus, holiness and impurity, while not antonymic, are inimical states. According to Ezra, Israel as a nation has been consecrated to God, and only those of Israel's seed are holy. For Ezra, then, genealogical purity – required pentateuchally of the high priest only – is required of all Israelites in order to guard against "profanation" (desacralization) of the holy seed. When holy and profane seed cannot be mixed, intermarriage becomes impossible. As a desecration of holy property, it is a serious offense against YHWH. Assimilation of gentiles by any means is precluded, since one's genealogy – unlike one's religion – is not susceptible to alteration or conversion. At best, sympathetic gentiles form their own self-contained class of resident aliens (*gerim*) alongside native Israelites, without any possibility of "conversion" or assimilation through intermarriage.

The Ezran line is picked up and developed by such works as Jubilees, 4QMMT, and some Qumran writings, which, to varying degrees, understand all Jews to be a holy seed apart from the rest of humanity and the boundary between Jews and gentiles to be impermeable. In addition, through creative exegesis, these writings declare interethnic sexual unions to be a pentateuchally prohibited capital crime.

The rabbis seem eager to disassociate themselves from Ezran holy seed rhetoric and related Second Temple traditions that denounced even casual interethnic unions as capital crimes, subject to the vengeance of zealots. They rule that those who read a universal prohibition of intermarriage into the Bible are to be severely suppressed (M. Megillah 4:9). The rabbis' failure to take up Ezra's ban on foreign wives and their children – indeed, their very reversal of this program by allowing conversion – is all the more remarkable in light of the rabbis' general perception and presentation of themselves as Ezra's (indirect) successors.

Certainly, the rabbis do not approve of sexual relations – marital or nonmarital – with gentiles. Yet they are not prepared to follow Second Temple sources that vilify interethnic relations as a profanation of holy seed (Ezra), or a permanent moral defilement deserving of death (Jubilees, 4QMMT).[15] Such a view presupposes an inherent Israelite holiness that the rabbis explicitly reject. What else is left in their rhetorical toolbox to both characterize and vilify interethnic sexual relations? Only ritual impurity, which is by definition impermanent and of little real consequence. When placed within their proper historical and cultural context, the scattered references to a rabbinic decree of gentile ritual impurity may be seen for what they are – a resistance to, a contestation of, competing characterizations of gentiles and the dangers of intergroup unions that is striking in its very *leniency*. The primary cultural work accomplished by this decree is not the prevention of interethnic unions (as we have seen, rabbinic texts attest to and facilitate extensive interactions) but the articulation of the rabbinic position in a hotly debated, intra-Jewish controversy. Deterrence is effected through the threat of corporal punishment and personal status rulings that stigmatize the offspring of Jewish-gentile unions, not the threat of an impermanent and relatively mild ritual impurity.

Converts

The holy seed ideology of Ezra and related Second Temple sources precludes the possibility of both intermarriage and conversion. The rabbis reject Ezra's near-exclusive focus on genealogy, adopting a definition of Jewish identity that creates a permeable group boundary and the possibility of assimilation of converted foreigners. However, while the moral-religious element of Jewish identity takes center stage in rabbinic literature, genealogical considerations remain in play. Insofar as certain privileges or functions within Jewish society might be genealogically based, the convert (or non-native Jew) retains a distinctive identity within the larger group. Thus, despite the rabbinic declaration that a convert is a Jew in all respects, the convert remains in some ways a non-Israelite (i.e., an ethnic other). As a classic example, converts do not recite prayers that refer to various Israelite ancestors with the possessive pronoun (*our* fathers, *our* father Abraham, etc.).[16]

The ambiguity in the rabbinic conception of the convert is seen most markedly in laws concerning the marital rights of converts and their offspring.[17] The convert is permitted to marry a native-born Israelite or Levite; conversion has obviated the convert's foreign origin. However, in the cases of marriage to priests and marriage to persons prohibited to a native-born Jew, the convert's foreign origin is not obviated by conversion. Marriage to a priest (permitted to a native-born Jew) is prohibited to a convert, and marriage to a *mamzer, natin,* and the like (persons prohibited to a native-born Jew) is permitted. Conversion confers upon the convert some, but not all, of the marriage rights of a native-born Israelite.

The situation is even more complex than this summary might suggest. First, the Tosefta cites a dissenting view prohibiting converts from marrying persons prohibited to native-born Israelites (T. Kiddushin 5:1–2).[18] Second, despite the blanket prohibition of priest-convert intermarriage in M. Kiddushin 4:1, more detailed rabbinic statements make it clear that gender distinctions obtain. Thus, a male convert may marry a woman of priestly stock (T. Kiddushin 5:2; Y. Kiddushin 3:14, 64c; B. Kiddushin 72b).[19] As regards the female convert, most rabbinic statements follow the biblical requirement of endogamy for priests (Ezekiel 44:22) and state that the female convert is not permitted to marry a priest. However, the daughter of a convert or converts is the subject of some debate in M. Kiddushin 4:6–7 (see also M. Bikkurim 1:5). The most lenient view, attributed to R. Yosi, declares that the daughter of two converts is equal to a native-born Israelite and may marry a priest. Though wholly derived from foreign seed *in fact,* the daughter of two converts is not deemed to be so derived *in law.* For R. Yosi, conversion fully obviates the implications of a woman's foreign origin within just one generation.[20] Both Talmuds endorse the view of R. Yosi, with the result that a woman of entirely foreign descent may marry a priest (Y. Bikkurim 1:5, 64a–b; B. Kiddushin 78b).[21]

These texts are evidence of isolated attempts at a socially (or, more precisely, halakhically) constructed descent group into which the convert might be absorbed.[22] Similarly, some Palestinian authorities assert that the recitation accompanying the offering of first fruits that mentions God's oath to "our fathers" should be permitted to converts, since Abraham can be understood in a metaphorical sense to be the father of converts (Y. Bikkurim 1:4, 64a). Here also, the definition of the descent group "Israel" is socially constructed, rather than biologically determined.[23]

Halakhically, there is a tendency within rabbinic literature to remove the obstacles to full assimilation suffered by persons of foreign descent – a tendency stronger in Palestinian sources than in Babylonian sources where a concern for genealogy becomes more pronounced. Such legal maneuvers could not, however, remove the *social* stigma associated with foreign lineage. Narrative texts are marked by a more polarized ambivalence than the legal material, and contain views of converts that range from extremely negative to extremely positive.[24] Individual traditions express hostility to converts as a class, none as infamously as the statement attributed to R. Helbo that "converts are as difficult for Israel as a sore" (B. Yevamot 47b and parallels). Some rabbis doubt the sincerity of converts, suspecting ulterior motives, and the Bavli explicitly forbids conversion for the sake of marriage. Such views are countered, however, by numerous traditions of praise and blessing. Marc Hirshman has argued that traditions attributed to the school of R. Yishmael are particularly positive toward converts (2000, 110–12). The Mekhilta de-Rabbi Ishmael contains a paean to the convert,[25] and deems the divine covenant with converts to be superior to the covenant with David since the former is unconditional while the latter is not. Three things, the midrash declares, are eternal – the Torah, the divine covenant with Aaron, and the divine covenant with converts.

The rabbinic ambivalence about converts may account for the rabbis' general abstention from active proselytizing. There is some evidence for Jewish proselytism, particularly in the first century C.E.,[26] but rabbinic literature reflects little interest in or enthusiasm for this activity. "Let the left hand repel while the right hand draws near" (Mekhilta de-Rabbi Ishmael, *'Amalek* 3:160, ed. Lauterbach, 138) is a classic expression of the predominant rabbinic view of proselytizing. Rabbinic literature mentions just over two dozen cases of historically plausible conversion, and numerous conversions of a legendary quality, and in all cases, the rabbis do not represent themselves as missionizing. Rather, converts approach rabbis and ask to be converted.[27] The rabbinic attitude toward those who do convert is captured perfectly in the conversion ceremony outlined in B. Yevamot 47a–b. The ceremony assumes the initiative of the convert and an initial coolness on the part of the rabbinic authorities who interview him, in order to test the sincerity of his motives. Efforts are made to dissuade the potential convert by pointing out the many difficulties and disadvantages of life as a Jew. But should the convert persist, he is accepted, circumcised, and treated gently so as not to be overwhelmed by the challenge of life lived under the Torah.[28]

Fearers/Venerators of God/Heaven

Palestinian rabbinic sources employ the term "venerators of heaven" (*yir'ei shamayim*) in reference to gentile sympathizers of one sort or another.[29] Many scholars equate the rabbinic venerator of heaven with the "God-fearer/venerator" attested in Josephus, Acts, and various pagan and inscriptional sources.[30] While the rabbinic term *yir'ei shamayim* probably reflects some sort of historical reality, it is not entirely clear that the rabbis are referencing an identifiable group of "semi-Jews" known to us from extra-rabbinic sources.[31] However, our immediate concern is not to determine the historical identity of the rabbinic *yir'ei shamayim* but to describe how the God-venerator is represented in rabbinic texts and to consider the literary and cultural purposes that the God-venerator serves.

Palestinian rabbinic texts draw a clear distinction between full converts and venerators of heaven. In Mekilta de-Rabbi Ishmael, *yi'rei shamayim* are counted among the four categories of true worshippers of the God of Israel, the other three being sinless Israelites, full converts (the *ger zedek*) and repentant sinners.[32] The distinction appears to be one of degree, rather than kind. The God-venerator is viewed as a partial convert, rather than a full convert (Y. Megillah 3:4, 74a; Deuteronomy Rabbah 2:24; *Pesiqta Rabbati* 43), a difference marked by the presence or absence of circumcision.[33]

The depiction of gentile sympathizers of high station (king, senator, Roman *matrona'* [i.e., female Roman aristocrat]) is a literary topos in rabbinic narratives. There are tales that feature an elite gentile's admiration for Judaism and its rabbinic representatives, or a king's or governor's recognition of the power of Israel's God or the beauty of Israel's Torah.[34] In some cases, the dignitary in question is specifically said to be a venerator of heaven. A tradition attributed to the Palestinian 'amora' R. Eleazar states that the emperor Antoninus will head the line of *yir'ei shamayim* accepted as converts in the time of the messiah. Here again, the venerator of heaven is just steps away from conversion.

To claim sympathizers among the righteous elite of other nations is certainly a self-flattering move. Nevertheless, there are rabbinic stories that revolve around very ordinary gentiles whose righteousness is exemplary. A certain gentile named Dama bar Netina appears as the model of filial piety (Y. Peah 1:1, 15c; Y. Kiddushin 1:7, 61b; B. Kiddushin 31a; B. Avodah Zarah 23b–24a). Aware that loving treatment of and respect for one's parents are left to the individual conscience, the rabbis seek to inspire their fellow Jews with stories of this gentile who – though not even commanded to honor and revere his parents – exceeds all expectations with his righteous behavior.

Marc Hirshman (2000) has recently argued for a school of thought within second- and third-century rabbinic Judaism that welcomed gentile involvement in the Torah short of full conversion.[35] But even

Hirshman agrees that later rabbinic tradition favors an isolationist view, according to which the Torah was intended for Jews alone. A positive version of this view appears in the oft-repeated dicta "anyone who renounces idolatry acknowledges the entire Torah" and "anyone who renounces idolatry is called a Jew."[36] A negative version of isolationism appears in a few hyperbolic amoraic pronouncements decreeing death for a gentile who studies Torah (Y. Peah 4:2, 17a; B. Sanhedrin 59a) or who keeps the Sabbath (B. Sanhedrin 58b). In Exodus Rabbah 25:15, a gentile who observes the Sabbath is compared to an outsider who interrupts an intimate conversation between a king and a *matrona'*.

Shaye Cohen argues that the turn to isolationism is connected with the absence of any ideological need to convert gentiles to the "true faith" (1983, 40). Gentiles were obligated by the seven Noahide laws – seven commandments of universal application (unlike the 613 commandments that obligate only Israel). The earliest presentation of the seven Noahide laws is T. Avodah Zarah 8:4–6.[37] The list includes prohibitions of idolatry, blasphemy, homicide, illicit sexual relations, robbery, consumption of a limb from a live animal, and an injunction to establish courts of justice. Although the argument has been made that these laws were promulgated as guidelines for actual God-fearing gentiles in the process of conversion, David Novak argues persuasively against this view. There is no indication in rabbinic literature that these laws were viewed as legally operative in any enforceable way or that they ever served as the basis of any real adjudication.[38] On the contrary, the seven Noahide laws are a theoretical construct that hypothesizes a standard of gentile morality independent of the revelation of the Torah. Gentiles who renounce idolatry and live up to this standard are righteous gentiles, but there is nevertheless a decided lack of rabbinic interest in the righteous gentile's fate.[39] While some rabbis may have continued to hope for the universal adoption of the Torah and the conversion of the gentiles (a scenario increasingly assigned to the eschaton, or end-time), most did not. There was no rabbinic consensus on the question of the ultimate destiny of humankind, and in general it was held that until the eschaton, the nations "could simply be left alone to follow their own national habits; they would give their own accounting to the Creator in the Creator's own good time."[40]

INTERNAL OTHERS

Numerous internal others (non-rabbinic or nonobservant Jews of various types) populate the pages of rabbinic literature – far more than can be surveyed here. Keeping in mind that the rabbis constituted a textual community so that distance from literacy and textuality were "the principal determinants of otherness,"[41] we will confine our discussion to those non-rabbinic Jews whose connection to the textual tradition, so central to the rabbinic movement, is understood by the rabbis to be inadequate or inappropriate: Christians and heretics, holy men and wonder workers, and ignoramuses (the '*am ha'arez*).

Christians and Heretics

Early Christianity was a dissident Jewish movement among other Jewish movements. Only in the late first century do Christian writings begin to affirm Christianity *over and against Judaism*, a trend that increased rapidly in the second century. As rabbinic Judaism took firmer shape and gentile Christianity set itself off from Jews, the group referred to by scholars as Jewish Christians emerged in the middle.[42] The latter were followers of Jesus who, like Jesus and the apostles, kept the law of Moses.[43] In early rabbinic literature, Jews partaking of the Christian heresy fell under the classification of *min* (plural *minim*), an umbrella term that included not only Jewish Christians but also a variety of Jewish sectarian groups, such as Sadducees, Boethusians, Zealots, and Samaritans (but not in an early period in Palestine, gentiles).[44]

Minim are almost universally depicted as possessing a knowledge of Scripture, but differing from the rabbis in their interpretations of Scripture (some even mocking or criticizing it) and in their ensuing halakhic positions. Interpretations of Scripture that supported Christian, Gnostic, or other heretical views were a special threat to rabbinic interpretations of Scripture. Indeed, our sources give the impression that even idolaters are not considered to be as dangerous as various internal others (Bible-reading heretics and Jewish Christians) who, by virtue of their similarity to other Jews, exerted a powerful influence on the latter. Several stories hint at the attraction heretical teachings sometimes held even for rabbinic Jews.[45] In other stories, people are attracted to minim because of their skill as healers (T. Hullin 2:20–23; B. Avodah Zarah 27b; Y. Shabbat 14:4, 14d; Kohelet Rabbah 1:8) – a skill to which the rabbis vehemently object.[46]

Early Palestinian sources, in particular, urge rabbis and their families to avoid all contact with minim and Christians.[47] The most vehement set of proscriptions against minim is found in T. Hullin 2:20–21. Many of these prohibitions stand in explicit contrast to similar laws concerning gentiles and are remarkable for their severity. Various statutory designations indicate the special animosity reserved for the min: The animal slaughter performed by a min is equivalent to idolatry, his bread is like that of a Cuthean, his wine is classified as prohibited libation wine, his fruits are deemed untithed, his books are considered witchcraft, and his children are statutory bastards. One must not engage in any commercial interaction or even conversation with minim, teach their children a trade, or be healed by them.

Narratives depicting Palestinian rabbis engaged in Scriptural debates with minim appear primarily in the Babylonian Talmud (e.g., B. Berakhot 58a, B. Hullin 87a).[48] The use of literary conventions and stereotyping[49] supports Naomi Janowitz's assertion (1998, 459) that the min is employed in these stories not as a historical figure but as a literary foil for the rabbis' developing definition of orthodoxy. Because the min functions literarily as a "placeholder" for a heretical or non-rabbinic other, it should occasion no surprise that parallel or similar versions of a min story will replace the min with a Samaritan, a Sadducee, a Cuthean, a Roman, or, on occasion, a rebellious disciple of the sages. The actual identity of the rabbinic opponent is not important – the min is just one among many stock types in the literary representation of rabbis and their opponents.

The min appears in texts in which orthodoxy is being defined or created out of an earlier confusion or multiplicity of opinions. Minim are assigned whatever position has been singled out for rejection. And far from being a perverse form of heresy, in some cases, the position is well attested in Jewish, if not rabbinic, circles. By assigning the view to minim, rabbinic storytellers can distance themselves from it and, in the process, create an orthodoxy on the matter.[50]

Holy Men, Wonder Workers

Rabbinic literature contains numerous references to and stories about pious men known as "ḥasidim" or as "men of deeds." References to these charismatic holy men – in both halakhic and narrative texts – are deeply ambivalent. In later Babylonian sources, this ambivalence is sometimes resolved by a process of "rabbinization." Recasting men of charisma in a rabbinic mold, Babylonian rabbinic narrators blur the boundary between self and other and domesticate a potential threat to their power.

A classic example of the charismatic holy man is R. Hanina ben Dosa. Known as the last of the great men of deeds (M. Sotah 9:15), he is said to have taught that fear of sin and deeds of loving-kindness not only take precedence over the wisdom and learning so highly valued by the rabbinic sages, but also lead to closeness with God (M. Avot 3:1).[51] Holy men like R. Hanina b. Dosa are described as fully intentional when praying, so much so that "even if a king were to greet a hasid or a snake were crouched at his heel, he would not break off his prayer" (M. Berakhot 5:1).

The holy man's lack of sin opens a direct channel to God in prayer, and he speaks with God, directly and intimately, like a member of God's household on the most familiar terms. It is this intimacy that is the cause of such ambivalence – even jealousy – on the part of our rabbinic narrators, as is evident in the famous story of Honi the Circle Drawer, who sketches a circle and refuses to leave it until God grants his petition for rain. On the one hand, the rabbis acknowledge the holy man's privileged position and effectiveness as a petitioner to God and even join others in requesting the aid and intercession of the holy man in times of crises (Y. Berakhot 5:5, 9d; B. Berakhot 34b). On the other hand, their recognition of the holy man's effectiveness is grudging at best.[52]

The ambivalence that surrounds holy men and their controversial methods is sometimes partially resolved in later Babylonian sources. Thus, the too-familiar intimacy and arrogance that characterize Honi the Circle Drawer in the Mishnah are omitted in the Bavli's retelling of the story (B. Taanit 23a). His refusal to move from the circle is legitimated by the identification of a biblical precedent. Moreover, although Honi violates a halakhic norm by acceding to the people's demand that he pray for an end to the rain, he does so cautiously and reluctantly, citing the halakhah in good rabbinic fashion, and accompanying his prayer with a sacrificial offering as if in recognition of the extraordinary nature of his request. In this Babylonian retelling, Honi has been rabbinized – if not fully halakhically then at least in demeanor – in an effort to ease the tension between Torah and charisma.[53] Of course, some rabbinic texts ease this tension in another way. In many stories, rabbis are depicted as possessing the powers of holy men – killing with a glance or performing other wonders. Thus, by recasting holy men as rabbis and rabbis as holy men, rabbinic self and non-rabbinic other often blur together in intriguing and unsettling ways.

The 'Am Ha'arez

Rabbinic attitudes toward the common run of folk who do not share the rabbis' scholarly preoccupation with Torah are many and varied. The term *'am ha'arez* (lit., "people of the land") is used in our sources to refer to such non-rabbinic Jews. However, the characterization and evaluation of the 'am ha'arez shifts dramatically over the course of the rabbinic period and between Palestine and Babylonia.

In halakhic texts of the tannaitic period, 'am ha'arez is a technical term that stands in opposition to the term *haver*. The haver observes the laws of tithing and purity in a stringent manner while the 'am ha'areẓ does not (see T. Avodah Zarah 3:10). Insofar as the 'am ha'areẓ is unobservant or ignorant of Jewish law, the observant Jew (or ḥaver) must take certain precautions in dealing with him, so as not to be led into a violation of his own more stringent standards regarding purity and tithing.[54] Tannaitic sources do not refer to the 'am ha'areẓ with any particular disrespect or vituperation. Interaction with the 'am ha'areẓ is expected, though too much intimacy is discouraged.[55]

In a Babylonian baraita at B. Berakhot 47b, the 'am ha'areẓ is variously defined as one who does not don tefillin, one who does not have zizit (fringes) on his garment, one who does not affix a mezuzah to his door, one who does not dedicate his sons to Torah study, or – most remarkably – one who does not attend upon the sages despite having studied some Scripture and some Mishnah. As Jeffrey Rubenstein (2003, 125) notes, these definitions are tantamount to saying that an 'am ha'areẓ is any Jew who is not of the class of sages and their disciples.

Nevertheless, tannaitic and amoraic sources, both Palestinian and Babylonian, contain nothing like the hostile elitism that is found in the stammaitic layer of the Babylonian Talmud.[56] These materials express a degree of contempt and disgust for non-rabbis that is completely absent from other rabbinic works. This contempt is most apparent in a largely stammaitic discussion of marriage between rabbinic and 'am ha'areẓ families at B. Pesahim 49a–b. While earlier sources entertain but discourage such unions (because of the participants' diverse levels of observance), stammaitic sources vehemently denounce them on the basis of the almost subhuman nature of the 'am ha'areẓ. The female 'am ha'areẓ is likened to a beast and to vermin and the male 'am ha'areẓ is likened to a ravaging lion. The depiction of the 'am ha'areẓ as bestial in B. Pesahim 49a–b exceeds in its invective almost anything said in any rabbinic source about Gentiles, idolaters, or slaves.[57]

J. L. Rubenstein (2003, 124) rightly notes that it would be wrong to read these few hyperbolic texts as reflecting real social relations. The negative attitudes expressed in these late texts were probably intended for an audience of other sages and served as a means of self-definition and self-justification by contrasting the academic life of the sages with that of the outside world. The powerfully negative rhetoric against the 'am ha'areẓ may point to

> a growing sense of detachment that prevailed within the academy. The sages perhaps perceived their academic world of Torah study as increasingly professionalized, elitist, and isolated from the general population. As a result, nonrabbis outside of the academy

were viewed as "Others" and even included with other categories of "Others" – slaves, Gentiles and animals. (Rubenstein 2003, 141)

Richard Kalmin's work supports Rubenstein's tentative description of the later Babylonian rabbinic academy as relatively isolated and reclusive. According to Kalmin (1999, 27–50), comparison of Palestinian and Babylonian sources, early and late, suggests that the rabbinic movement in Palestine was relatively more open to penetration from the outside than was the case in Babylonia. Palestinian rabbis interact with non-rabbinic Jews and even attempt to win disciples from among the non-rabbinic population, while Babylonian rabbis tend to remain aloof from non-rabbis, interacting with them in primarily formal – and rarely informal – contexts. Reasons for this difference include 1) the relatively weak position of Palestinian rabbis in society as compared to Babylonian rabbis, and 2) the heightened concern for genealogical purity among later Babylonian rabbis (in keeping with Persian attitudes). According to Kalmin, Babylonian rabbis are wary of even casual relationships with non-rabbis lest they lead to more intimate relationships and eventually marriages that would compromise their highly prized purity of lineage (1999, 27). Palestinian rabbis are less concerned about marriage to non-rabbis, as we have seen, and some sources encourage the practice as a path to social, financial, and even heavenly reward. Differences between the two rabbinic communities may be a reflection of trends in the larger cultural environment as described by Kalmin (1999, 8–13). Non-Jewish Babylonian society was rigidly hierarchical, and purity of lineage was strongly emphasized. In Rome and throughout the empire, class structures were breaking down through the first few centuries c.e., and learning and scholarship became increasingly important paths to power. The advantages of pedigree were, if not eradicated, at least easily enough overcome by education and personal effort.

This is not to say, however, that there are no exceptions to the diverging tendencies described here. Dissenting voices are certainly present within the works produced by each of the two rabbinic communities.[58] These crosscurrents leave us with a richly conflicted corpus of materials in which only trends and tendencies, rather than hard and fast ideological positions, can be traced.

CONCLUSION

At the heart of the rabbinic self-understanding lies a text. A rabbi is one who devotes himself to this text and associated traditions of learning and practice as developed by the class of sages. Rabbinic literature imagines the alterity of persons who are not devoted to this text and its rabbinic elaboration. Some of these "others" – gentiles – are, by birth and culture, entirely distant from the text. Interaction with these persons must be negotiated and controlled. Yet the rabbis resist simple dichotomies and locate many gentiles along a spectrum of proximity, as seen in rabbinic discussions of the righteous gentile, the venerator of heaven and the convert. Some others – non-rabbinic Jews of various types – are, by birth and culture, heirs to the text but have neglected, distorted, or abandoned it in some way. Because they embody a genuine alternative – an alterity within – the *min*, the holy man, and the 'am ha'areẓ pose a unique threat to, and resource for, the rabbinic attempt to construct a stable self.

Notes

1. Porton 1994, 4.
2. Boon 1982, 232, as cited in Green 1985, 51.
3. See R. Goldenberg 1998, 98, for a characterization of the rabbinic materials on gentiles as multivoiced and complex.
4. For a similar, but not identical, threefold list of the sources of rabbinic rulings regarding gentiles, see Porton 1988, 285–87.
5. Sifra, *'Emor* 7:2 provides the biblical justification for this ruling, while M. Zevahim 4:5 and Menahot 5:3, 5:6, 6:1, and 9:8 all assume sacrifices by gentiles.
6. The treatise *De Idolatria* composed by Tertullian around 200 C.E. contains numerous parallels with tannaitic regulations in both substance and principle. A Christian must in no way benefit from or support idolatry.
7. Thus, for example, a Jewish construction worker employed in the construction of a pedestal for a pagan altar or a private bath need desist only upon reaching the cupola that houses the idol (M. Avodah Zarah 1:7). The building is understood to be religiously neutral; the cupola is not.
8. For details on the views of Schürer and Alon, see Hayes 2002, 4–5. A comprehensive discussion of the topic of this section can also be found in Hayes 2002.
9. For a full account of ritual and moral impurity see Klawans 2000, 21–42.
10. Tannaitic texts permit gentiles to offer *terumah*, tithes, and certain sacrifices if they so choose. Klawans 1995, 307, notes that the impurity of gentiles is not a concern in many mishnaic texts that depict Jewish-Gentile interaction: e.g., passages that assume commensality of Jews and Gentiles (M. Berakhot 7:1, M. Avodah Zarah 5:5), or collaboration between Jews and Gentiles with regard to wine production (M. Avodah Zarah 4:9–12).
11. The decree appears in Sifra *Zavim* 1:1, T. Zavim 2:1, T. Niddah 9:14, B. Niddah 34a, B. Niddah 69b. Although there is no explicit statement of the rabbinic decree of gentile ritual impurity in the Mishnah, it is assumed in certain rulings (e.g., M. Makkot 2:3).

12. A comparison with the case of a Samaritan woman is instructive in this regard. M. Niddah 4:1 states that Samaritan women are deemed to be menstruants (*benot kutim niddot*). The Samaritan woman is not deemed to defile *like* a menstruant. Rather, because she is subject to the Torah's laws of ritual impurity but does not follow the rabbinic interpretation of these laws, the Samaritan woman is suspected of bearing a genuine menstrual impurity at all times. The full text of the tradition is that Samaritan women are deemed to be menstruants from their cradles (*benot kutim niddot me'arisotan*). In other words, the status of menstruant due to doubt commences in infancy. Israelite women are also susceptible to the impurity of menstruation due to doubt from infancy (a weaker impurity than that arising from actual, or certain, menstruation). By contrast, the gentile is not suspected of suffering an impure genital flux from which he fails to purify himself. He bears no actual biblical impurity at all. Rather, he is to be treated *as if* he defiles in a manner analogous to the manner in which a *zav* defiles. See further Fonrobert 2001c.

13. Thus, M. Shekalim 8:1, Tohorot 5:8, and T. Tohorot 5:4 assume the impurity of a gentile's spittle, while M. Makkot 2:3, T. Tohorot 5:2, and T. Mikvaot 6:7 assume the impurity of gentile urine. For a full discussion, see Hayes 2002, 127–31.

14. For more on the role of such concerns – real or imagined – in the formulation of *halakhah*, see Hayes 1997, 148–53, 238 n. 46.

15. For a discussion of the influence of Ezran and sectarian holy seed thinking on Pauline and early Christian attitudes to "others," and to mixed (believer-unbeliever) marriages generally, see Hayes 2002, 92–103.

16. These include the recitations accompanying the presentation of first fruits and second tithe (M. Bikkurim 1:4; T. Bikkurim 1:2; Mekhilta de-Rabbi Ishmael, *Mishpatim* 20; Sifrei Devarim *Ki Tavo'*; Y. Bikkurim 1:4, 64a; B. Makkot 19a).

17. M. Kiddushin 4:1 lists converts as one of ten distinct genealogical classes. The list is comparable to Gaius's distinction in the *Institutes of Matrimony* between various classes of persons (Romans, Latins, foreigners, slaves, freedmen, etc.).

18. A compromise is struck in the Bavli when it is decided that marriage between a convert and a mamzer is prohibited after several generations (B. Kiddushin 75a). Normalization of the convert's status is attributed, however, to the desire to avoid the appearance of sin: After several generations, the convert background of a person will be forgotten, and if he marries someone prohibited in marriage to a full Israelite, he will be thought to be sinning.

19. The male convert's legal situation was truly anomalous. On the one hand, he could marry into the priesthood like a native-born Jew; on the other hand, he could marry a mamzer unlike a native-born Jew. R. Yosa (= R. Assi) is said to have analogized the convert to cotton: "A convert is comparable to cotton. If you want to weave it with wool it is permitted and with flax it is permitted" (Y. Kiddushin 3:14, 64c). The metaphor draws upon the law of *sha'atnez*, according to which flax and wool may not be woven together (Deuteronomy 22:11). In R.

Yosa's metaphor, the wool stands for the mamzer, the flax stands for the priest, and the cotton stands for the convert. Just as wool and flax must never be interwoven, priest and mamzer must never intermarry. However, just as cotton may be interwoven with either wool or flax, so the convert may intermarry with either a female mamzer or a woman of priestly stock. The convert, it is implied, is in an enviable position – one with maximum flexibility and minimum restriction. Compare this metaphor with that of 4QMMT, which speaks of foreigners and even lay Israelites as diverse seeds and intermarriage as *kilayim*, a prohibited mixture. In R. Yosa's tradition, foreigners and lay Israelites are diverse threads that *can* be interwoven – a metaphor of ability, not inability. Nevertheless, certain Babylonian rabbinic stories are sensitive to the fact that the anomalous legal situation of the convert might be cause for offense (B. Kiddushin 75a).

20. A *baraita* in both the Yerushalmi and the Bavli presents a fourth and even more extreme view that does not appear in the Mishnah. According to this *baraita* (Y. Kiddushin 4:6, 66a [= Y. Bikkurim 1:5]; B. Kiddushin 64a), R. Shimeon bar Yohai would waive the prohibition of a female convert herself under certain circumstances: "It was taught [likewise] in the name of R. Shimeon: 'A girl who converted at the age of less than three years and one day is valid for marriage into the priesthood.'"

21. Palestinian amoraic sources are inclined to be more lenient than Babylonian amoraic sources. A few early Palestinian authorities (R. Romanus, R. Joshua b. Levi) are even said to endorse the most radical view of R. Shimeon bar Yohai, permitting priestly marriage to a woman who converted in extreme youth. By contrast, Babylonian sages, more than their Palestinian colleagues, appear to approve priestly scrupulosity on this matter (B. Kiddushin 78b). Moreover, they object vehemently to reports of Palestinian authorities ruling in accordance with the lenient view of R. Shimeon b. Yohai and permitting marriage to a woman who converted as a very young girl.

22. Contra Porton 1994, 7, who asserts that there is no evidence that rabbinic law creates a socially constructed descent group to which converts could be fully assimilated.

23. For a discussion of the debate between the Mishnah and the Yerushalmi as a debate over the nature of the claim to possess Jewish fathers, see Cohen 1991, 421–22. For the Mishnah, the claim is historical and real, while for the Yerushalmi, the claim is metaphorical and mythic.

24. Goldenberg 1998, 93.

25. Perek *'Amalek* 3, ed. Lauterbach, 277–80.

26. Feldman 1993, 288–341, argues that Jews in the first centuries C.E. engaged in aggressive missionary activity that won large numbers of converts. But see the important and persuasive criticisms in Catherine Hezser's review in the *Journal of Theological Studies* 45 (1994), 2: 638–43.

27. Cohen 1983, 39–40.

28. For an insightful analysis of the rabbinic conversion ceremony, see Cohen 1990.

29. The term does not appear in the Mishnah. The seventeen occurrences in the Bavli refer to pious Jews, with one problematic exception in B. Sanhedrin 70b. See Feldman 1993, 353.
30. The Greek terms are *theosebeis, sebomenoi ton theon,* and *phobo-umenoi ton theon.* MacLennan and Kraabel 1986, 48, express strong "doubt that there ever was a large and broadly based group of Gentiles known as "god-fearers." Feldman concedes that the word "theosebes" may not refer to a special class or group of sympathizers; however, this does not mean that such a class did not exist. He adduces extensive and persuasive evidence from a wide range of pagan, Christian, inscriptional, and Jewish sources for the existence of a class of sympathizers at least in the first century C.E. and especially in the third century C.E. (see Feldman 1993, 342–82). Diatribes against Judaizing are produced by Christian clerics in the fourth and fifth century. Likewise, Gager 1986, 93, points to the extensive literary evidence for gentiles attracted to Judaism and for various forms of participation in Diaspora synagogues.
31. Nor is it clear that Josephus, Acts, pagan sources, and inscriptions all attest to one and the same phenomenon among themselves, or mean the same thing when they use terms like theosebes. As a mark of righteousness and piety, the term *theosebes* can be applied to anyone, even Jews. In inscriptions it may be used to signal gentile patrons or benefactors who have no personal or special interest in Jewish belief or practice whatsoever. Feldman 1993, 344, concludes: "The term G-d [*sic*] fearers or sympathizers apparently refers to an 'umbrella group,' embracing many different levels of interest in and commitment to Judaism, ranging from people who supported synagogues financially (perhaps to get the political support of the Jews) to people who accepted the Jewish view of G-d [*sic*] in pure or modified form to people who observed certain distinctively Jewish practices, notably the Sabbath. For some this was an end in itself; for others it was a step leading ultimately to full conversion to Judaism."
32. Perek *Nezikin* 18. See also Numbers Rabba' 8:2; Leviticus Rabba 3:2.
33. Feldman 1993, 354. Other texts also imagine gradations of sympathizers. Y. Yevamot 8:1, 8d, contains a debate over the definition of a *ger toshav* (the biblical term with the greatest affinity to the rabbinic "venerator of heaven"), with positions ranging from one who abstains from idol worship to one who observes nearly all of the obligations of the Torah.
34. For a bibliography on many of these stories, see Cohen 1999, 146 n. 17.
35. In the *Mekhilta d'Arayot* to Lev 18:5, for example, R. Yirmia praises the gentile who "does" Torah (fulfills the commandments) by equating him with the high priest.
36. Y. Nedarim 3:4, 38a; B. Megillah 13a; B. Nedarim 25a; B. Hullin 5a; B. Shevuot 29a; B. Kiddushin 40a; Sifrei BaMidbar 1.111; Sifrei Devarim 54.
37. Full lists appear also at Genesis Rabba 16:16, Song of Songs Rabba 1:16, and in the extensive discussion at B. Sanhedrin 56a–60a. According to Novak 1978, 309, there is no convincing evidence that the doctrine of the Noahide laws is pre-tannaitic.
38. Ibid.

39. Whether the righteous gentile will enter the world to come is the subject of a single brief tannaitic dispute (T. Sanhedrin 13:2), a dispute cited just once, without resolution, in B. Sanhedrin 105a.

40. Goldenberg 1998, 87–88.

41. See Green 1985, 58, for a list of titles designating those whom the rabbis could not trust or whose presence they could not abide, including the blasphemer, Sabbath violater, seducer, sorcerer, Samaritan, denier of resurrection, denier of Torah's divine origin, Epicurean, apostate, informer, heretic, 'am ha'areẓ, and so on.

42. That this group would not have adopted such a label for themselves is self-evident. Depending on the specifics, such persons might have called themselves Jews while being called by their opponents either heretics or Christians.

43. P. J. Tomson, "The Wars against Rome, the Rise of Rabbinic Judaism and of Apostolic Gentile Christianity, and the Judaeo-Christians: Elements for a Synthesis," in Tomson and Lambers-Petry 2003, 5–8.

44. See Sussman 1990a, 54 n. 176. Rabbinic references to *minim* are often unclear as to the kind of Jewish heresy that is intended. In some cases, it can be shown that the minim referred to are Jewish-Christians. In M. Berakhot 9:5, a *min* is one who fails to believe in the world to come (Sadducees and Epicureans being prime examples). In M. Rosh haShannah 2:1, minim dispute the calendar of the Pharisees (this would include Boethusians and Essenes). In M. Hullin 2:9, the minim are said to believe in many powers in heaven, and in M. Hullin 2:9 and M. Yadayim 4:8, a min adopts idolatrous practices or gentile customs. See further Boyarin 2004, 52–56.

45. In a story in B. Avodah Zarah 16b–17a, R. Eliezer attributes his arrest and trial by the Romans to the fact that he once heard a word in the name of Yeshua ben Pantiri (Jesus) that pleased him. For the convergence and mutual attractions of Judaism and Christianity (to risk anachronism) in Late Antiquity, see Boyarin 2004, passim, and especially 221 on R. Eliezer's attraction to *minut*. R. L. Kalmin 1999, 68, states that the message of R. Eliezer's story is that even when minim offer teachings that suit rabbinic tastes, they are to be avoided. Their words are persuasive and can lead to sin.

46. In T. Hullin 2:20–23 and B. Avodah Zarah 27b, R. Yishmael rejoices that his ailing nephew died before he could accept healing in the name of Jesus by one Yaakov ish Kefar Sekhanya. See further the discussion of these and related texts in Boyarin 1999, 34–41.

47. Kalmin 1994a, 160.

48. Kalmin 1994a, 166. See G. Bohak, "Magical Means for Handling Minim in Rabbinic Literature," in Tomson and Lambers-Petry 2003, 267–76, for an analysis of dispute stories in which rabbis resort to curses and magic to harm the minim who pester them. Kalmin argues that since Bible-reading heretics like Christians were prevalent in the Roman world and all but nonexistent in Persian Babylonia, these stories are almost certainly literary fabrications (166). To this, Adam Becker objects that "the massive corpus of Syriac Christian literature composed in the same milieu as

the Talmud" attests to a complex relationship between fourth-century Jewish and Christian communities in the East and so stands as a serious challenge to this claim. See Becker, "Beyond the Spatial and Temporal *Limes*," in Becker and Reed 2003, 373–92, esp. 382. Boyarin adopts a middle position: While Christians were certainly present in the Sasanian environs of the Babylonian rabbis, they were no longer an internal threat. With the borders between Judaism and Christianity clearly established, the latter "was no longer considered a subversive danger for believing Jews" (Boyarin 2004, 223–24). As the heretical internal other became less of a threat, the term *min* came to mean gentile and especially gentile Christians in the Babylonian Talmud (223).

49. Kalmin, ibid., 163–65.
50. Janowitz 1998, 457–60. At times, however, rabbinic authors introduce minim and other non-rabbis as a mask, rather than foil, in order to voice and grapple with their own ambivalence and radical doubt on a matter of some debate. An example is found in the lengthy sugya at B. Sanhedrin 90b–91a. See the full discussion of the displacement of a thoroughly rabbinic anxiety in Hayes 1998. Other scholars working in related areas have noted similar displacements from rabbinic or Jewish characters to non-rabbinic or non-Jewish characters (though the work of censors, beginning with the Basle edition of 1578–81, complicates our ability to identify such displacements with confidence). Miller 1993, 396–97 notes that B. Berakhot 56b, in which R. Ishmael interprets the sinful dreams of a certain min, is dependent on Palestinian stories in which the sinful dreams are attributed to a Jew. Ilan 1994 argues that the Roman matron depicted in dialogue with rabbis was originally a Jewish woman named Matrona who was transformed into a pagan figure in later, especially Babylonian, material. Miller also shows that in later Babylonian polemics, the min functions as a literary convention or gentile foil to the rabbis; see Miller 1993, 385, 394–99.
51. These ideas are not alien to normative *halakhah*, as we shall see. Nevertheless, they so thoroughly infuse the traditions concerning hasidim and "men of deeds" (see, for example, the traditions of R. Pinhas ben Yair in Y. Sotah 9:15, 24b; Y. Shabbat 1:3, 3c) that we are justified in thinking of them as typically pietistic ideas.
52. Indeed, the Mishnah readily incorporates the hasidic ideal of intentional prayer into the normative halakhah at M. Berakhot 5:1. However, later sources contain and limit the application of this practice. Ordinary persons are not expected to pray with such complete intentionality and should not endanger themselves before kings and snakes as the hasidim do. The ideal of intentional prayer is just that – an ideal that should be set aside when danger (physical or spiritual) threatens.
53. For the Bavli redactors' tendency to rabbinize characters and events that were originally non-rabbinic in character (including Hanina b. Dosa and Honi the Circle Drawer), see Rubenstein 2003, 23–28.
54. Thus, the home of an 'am ha'arez is considered a likely source of impurity as are his garments, since he is presumed to be lax about laundering after seminal emission or gonnorheic flux (M. Pe'ah 2:3, M. Demai 2:3,

B. Shabbat 15a). The ḥaver should not be a guest in the home of an 'am ha'areẓ for fear that he will unwittingly partake of untithed or impure foods. Moist produce is susceptible to impurity, and thus a ḥaver should buy only dry produce from the 'am ha'areẓ (ibid.). In addition, the ḥaver should not jeopardize produce by selling any that is untithed to an 'am ha'areẓ (ibid.). There are several regulations that place limits on association with an 'am ha'areẓ lest one end up assisting the 'am ha'areẓ in defiling some item (M. Shekalim 5:9, M. Demai 6:6, B. Hagigah 22a). A baraita on B. Nedarim 20a states: "Do not make a practice of vowing for ultimately you will trespass in the matter of oaths and do not frequent an 'am ha'areẓ for eventually he will give you untithed produce." However, this particular stricture is debated in M. Demai 2:2: "If a man has taken upon himself to be trustworthy (ne'eman), he must tithe whatever he eats and whatever he sells and whatever he buys and he may not be the guest of an 'am ha'areẓ R. Judah says: 'a man who is the guest of an 'am ha'areẓ may still be considered trustworthy.' But they said to him: 'if he is not trustworthy in respect of himself, how can he be considered trustworthy in respect of others?'"

55. Rubenstein 2003, 124.
56. Indeed, some are explicitly favorable. Rubenstein points to two in particular in ibid., 135. In Y. Bikkurim 3:3, 65c, R. Meir shows respect for an elderly 'am ha'areẓ on the assumption that his long life must be a sign of piety. In Bereshit Rabba 78:12, R. Hoshaya is so taken with a midrash told to him by an 'am ha'areẓ that he promises to repeat it in public in the man's name.
57. See Rubenstein 2003, 124–31.
58. Thus, the Babylonian Talmud contains narratives critical of both the premium placed on purity of lineage and the dominant trend toward isolationism (see the traditions at B. Kiddushin 71a–72b). Other traditions appear to celebrate scholars who are descended from 'ammei ha'areẓ or converts (B. Yevamot 45b, B. Yoma 71b).

12 Regulating the Human Body: Rabbinic Legal Discourse and the Making of Jewish Gender

CHARLOTTE ELISHEVA FONROBERT

The study of the cultural constructions of gender in rabbinic literature is a relatively young field, certainly compared to other literatures.
Although already in the seventies Jewish feminist critics joined their
colleagues in different religious contexts to critique the encrusted patriarchal traditions of Judaism, serious analyses of the workings of gender
in the literature produced by the Late Antique rabbis began only in the
nineties of the past century. Influenced by Michel Foucault's work as
well as academic feminist theory, scholars started to move beyond the
somewhat one-dimensional analytic and critical categories of "sexism,"
"misogyny," and "patriarchy" that had inspired the earlier feminist critics. Now, Jewish "sexuality" as encoded by rabbinic texts came to have
a history and cultural context (Daniel Boyarin, Michael Satlow), as did
the Jewish "body," both male and female (Boyarin, Charlotte Fonrobert).
Rabbinic "work" (that is, descriptions of productive labor and laborers)
became gendered (Miriam Peskowitz), as did rabbinic thinking about
"space" (Cynthia Baker).

Moreover, as gender – defined here as knowledge about sexual difference – has evolved as an analytic category, rabbinic texts have come
to be viewed as riddled with tensions and ruptures in gender perspectives. This lends a new dynamic quality to the rabbinic literature. No
longer do these texts merely reflect the gender economy of the supposed
sociohistoric reality from which they emerge, but they have come to
be viewed as actively engaging the various gender possibilities in their
cultural universe, favoring some, rejecting others, which however may
leave traces within a text.

Rabbinic thinking about and representations of the body have played
a central role in all of this work. But as of yet, no systematic account
exists as to how the body is represented, especially in rabbinic legal
texts. Clearly, to the degree that Jewish cultures have been shaped by
the halakhic perspectives of their rabbinic elites, such an account is
crucial in order to understand how gender works in Jewish cultures in

general. Rabbinic legal thinking, which provides much of the structural framework of subsequent Jewish cultures, aims first and foremost at instituting a rather pronounced dual gender grid, imposed on the social organization of Jewish society as the rabbis envisioned it. Most of the individual laws of rabbinic halakhah apply to either men or women. Differently put, in rabbinic legal thinking it is almost always important whether the halakhic agent is a man or a woman. The same is true, of course, for other ancient legal systems. If, as the historian of Roman law Jane F. Gardner claims, "determining the sex of individuals is a legal as well as social necessity" in general (1998, 136), our observation may indeed be a moot point, if not banal. At the same time, I would insist, legal cultures differ significantly from one another not only with respect to the specific gender roles and legal capacities they assign to each sex. Rather, they differ also with respect to the effort they invest in establishing and maintaining more or less stable sexual identities that support the attempt to regulate gender norms. The more the existence of men and women is taken for granted as a biological fact, the more a system of role distribution is rendered invisible and, therefore, persuasive.

Representations of the body are an important means for grounding gender, and for justifying the distribution of legal privileges and disadvantages. As theorists of gender have come to recognize, representations of the body often serve the aim of naturalizing and therefore legitimizing legal privilege. Hence, so the theory goes, almost everyone may agree now that gender differences are cultural constructs. Gender is variable, and gender differences are scripted differently in different social and cultural contexts. But the fact that gender differences exist to begin with is traditionally considered to be based in biological fact. Nature – or biology – has made bodies different, male and female, and different cultures only inscribe this reality with their specific ways of differentiating between genders. In the rabbinic case, this translates, for instance, into the prohibition of cross-dressing, inherited from biblical law (Deuteronomy 22:5), in order to uphold the clear distinction between the sexes. Or it famously translates into the general positioning of men as always "obligated" by Jewish law, while women are only sometimes obligated and mostly "exempt" (M. Kiddushin 1:7), a legal rhetoric that already early feminists have recognized as a way of privileging the male position in Jewish law.

At the same time, scholars in various fields have come to recognize that the claim for the transhistorical or prediscursive character of biology, and specifically of the category of sexual identity, cannot be upheld. Biology and sex, so the theory goes, are just as much socially and historically determined constructs as are their supposed cultural interpretations.[1] The most radical consequence to be drawn from this recognition has, of course, been Judith Butler's famous claim that the differentiation between the sexes is only a "copy without original." That is, she – along with those who have followed her lead – have insisted on collapsing the category of sex and gender altogether. The biological differentiation of the sexes is to be regarded as only a product of the preexisting *social* differentiation between genders, not a pregiven *natural* order. Much is at stake for those who take this approach: Without the possibility of taking recourse to a "natural" differentiation between the sexes, any insistence on the rootedness of a cultural gender differentiation in nature will lose its hold, as does what Butler regards as the heterosexual imperative in the social order.

The political implications of this discussion hardly apply to the case of rabbinic legal thinking, since the rabbis do not legitimate their overt gender dimorphism by taking recourse to nature. Butler's critique works first and foremost in the context of the European philosophical and sociopolitical tradition, inherited from Plato and Aristotle. The rabbis, on the other hand, draw on the precedent of biblical law and its gender dimorphism, established by divine authority. Hence, while the legitimization of gender hierarchies and the traditional heterosexual imperative in Western societies may be undone by unmasking nature as culture, rabbinic legal discourse takes recourse to "tradition," a cultural construct to begin with, albeit one with divine authority.

What, then, is to be learned from the theoretical discourse of the body we have briefly mapped? First and foremost, this calls for a thoroughgoing account of how indeed the rabbis did represent the body in their legal discourse and what it took to be recognized as male or female in their view. In this effort, figures such as the dual-sexed hermaphrodite (Hebr. *androginos*) and his parallel, the nonsexed or not-yet sexed person (Hebr. *tumtum*) ought to be given much more space than they have so far. Far from being marginal figures, they pervade the legal discussions as early as the Mishnah. At the very least, the prominence of these figures in rabbinic texts, especially the early rabbinic legal texts, demands some explanation. Why do the rabbis talk so much about them? What effect does foregrounding the category of the hermaphrodite have for the rabbinic legal thinking about gender as a whole? Does he undermine the overall halakhic insistence on the sexual differentiation into man and woman? Does the androginos inhabit a stable "sexual identity" as a third possibility, next to men and women, or as the exception to the rule, or does the very presence of a "neither-nor"[2] or "both this and that" category in the legal system suggest a hint of instability in the legislative effort of stabilizing sexual identities? Are they constructs, even more, born from fantasy? Are they aberrations? I would point out further that the relative variability of bodies in rabbinic legal thinking is particularly noteworthy in view of Butler's critique of Western presumptions of prediscursive sexual differentiation into male and female bodies. The following can only be understood as a preliminary reflection on some of these questions.

The early rabbinic texts provide us with what can be viewed as a centralized effort to take on the problem of the hermaphrodite:

> [As far as] the *androginos* [is concerned]:
> there are with regard to him [grammatical gender] ways in which
> he is similar to men, and there are ways with regard to him in
> which he is similar to women, and there are ways with regard to
> him in which he is similar to both men and women, and there
> are ways in which he is dissimilar from both men and women.
> (T. Bikkurim 2:3)[3]

While generally the early compendia of rabbinic literature organize their collection of legal materials by contents, we can find various attempts to organize individual commandments in lists grouped according to some overarching principle, such as gender or age.[4] Our paragraph introduces such a list of commandments, most of which can be found in different contexts in tannaitic literature. "The ways in which the androginos is similar" to either men or women are not conceived abstractly. Rather, they are explored by means of gender-specific laws and the way they apply to the androginos as a basic conceptual paradox: the person who, while designated by a masculine noun in rabbinic Hebrew, has both male and female sets of genitalia.

For instance, the biblical prohibitions of rounding the corners of the hair of one's head and of marring the corners of one's beard (Leviticus 19:27) apply to the androginos, as it would to men. But were he to have a menstrual discharge, would the biblical laws of impurity (Leviticus 15) apply to him accordingly, as they would were he to have a seminal discharge? This particular collection of laws under the previous paragraph might signal that the rabbinic editors here make an attempt to collate those widely strewn laws as a concentrated reflection on the issue of gender and law by means of the hybrid category of the androginos.[5]

Finally, the fact that the rabbis choose a Greek loanword to designate the hybrid category signals their engagement – however limited – with the Greco-Roman culture, both legal and social, in which the production of early legal rabbinic literature was embedded. As we shall see, sexual and gender ambiguity was a phenomenon widely discussed by Roman lawmakers. It also made its mark in various other cultural contexts, in the literature and oratory especially of what is known as the Second Sophistic, a Greek cultural movement of the second and third century C.E., not to mention art, such as sculptures of hermaphrodites that were dispersed throughout the Roman world. The relevance of this material for the making of rabbinic law and legal thinking has only recently begun to be entertained.[6]

In what follows, we will first sketch out some of the particular ways in which the human body is represented in early legal rabbinic texts. This will aid us in our pursuit of an answer to the questions of how the rabbis establish the identity of their category of "men" and "women," and how much ambiguity their legal thinking tolerates. Secondly, we will discuss the embeddedness of this particular aspect of rabbinic thinking about gender, and particularly sexual ambiguities, in its Greco-Roman context. A focus on earlier rabbinic literature is advisable, since this allows for a somewhat firmer historical grounding of our attempt to draw out the connections of rabbinic legal thinking with its Roman counterpart and Greek cultural echoes.

THE BODY IN RABBINIC LEGAL DISCOURSE

In her article on "imperfect men in Roman law," Jane F. Gardner has argued that in Roman law, the basic classification as men or women was "biological." She elaborates that in contradistinction to the variety of approaches in current medical science, the only method to determine sex in the ancient world "was the visual – simply looking at the external appearance of the genitalia" (1998, 137).[7] At first glance, this would seem to be the case for the legal discourse of the rabbis. True, the Mishnah never spells out explicitly what it is that determines the difference between the sexes, but the Tosefta contains a statement according to which "one circumcises the baby at the place from which it can be recognized whether he [the baby] is male or female ['*im zakhar 'im nekevah*']" (T. Shabbat 15:9), cited in the Babylonian Talmud (B. Shabbat 108a), and drawn on in midrashic literature (Genesis Rabbah 46:5, 46:13) glossing Abraham's circumcision. This remark clearly assumes that it is the morphology of the external genitalia that determines sexual identity. When the Mishnah raises the question of what the difference between a man and a woman is, as it does once explicitly (M. Sotah 3:8), it answers with a list of the distinct legal capacities attributed to both, not with an abstract determination of biological or anthropological differences.

At the same time, the Mishnah itself is replete with references to the human body. Generally, the early rabbinic legal texts have much more to say about the female body. They trace its surface as well as construct its internal structure in ways that do not apply to the male body. Two texts stand out specifically with their overt rhetorical strategy of metaphorical representation of the body.

According to the first text:

> The sages made a simile [*mashal mashelu*] with regard to the woman: the chamber, the antechamber and the upper chamber. Blood from the chamber establishes ritual impurity. If it is located in the antechamber, there is a doubt whether it establishes ritual impurity, since the assumption is that it stems from the source. (M. Niddah 2:5)

This first cluster of metaphors has its context in the discussion of which kind of genital blood is to be considered menstrual and therefore a potential source of ritual impurity and, by implication, reason to prohibit marital sex. The specifics of the priestly system of ritual purity in biblical law, about which much has been written, need not deter us here. Suffice it to say that the concept of ritual purity lacks moral connotations in rabbinic thinking. As a temporary physiological condition, a status of ritual impurity, brought about by genital discharges, prohibited one from participation in the Temple cult. By the time of the rabbinic editing of their texts, these laws took on a somewhat antiquarian character, as the Temple no longer existed. They had lost their practical functionality. This is not to say that the theoretical, or antiquarian, discussion of the laws of ritual impurity did not have an effect on how Jews would think about the body and especially the female body in later times, even today. Indeed, the concept of impurity, once it became detached from its cultic context in the Temple operations, came to serve a variety of ideological and theological purposes, among them ways to conceptualize the body as well as ethnic boundaries.[8] This is especially true with regard to menstrual impurity, since the parallel prohibition of marital sex during the wife's menstrual period (Leviticus 18 and 20) is articulated as an absolute prohibition, not dependent on the historical existence of the Temple. The sexual prohibition continues to be effective even today.

Be that as it may, the three rooms here refer to a woman's internal organs, most likely reproductive but perhaps also the bladder. As I have argued elsewhere, this text is a part of the tannaitic project to represent the female body linguistically in terms of domestic architecture.[9] Accordingly, this project may function, if not be designed, to underwrite the social agenda of the rabbis, which is to strengthen the association of woman and the domestic scene, thereby further keeping her away from the institution most valued and defended by rabbinic culture, namely, the institution of learning.[10] The representation of woman as house may further tend to enforce a fundamental, albeit not exclusive understanding of womanhood as motherhood.[11]

The second text can be found in the midst of the attempt to determine the legal status of a girl with respect to her father, based on her age:

> The sages made a simile [*mashal mashelu*] with regard to the woman: the green fig, the almost-ready-to-pick fig, and the almost-too-ripe fig [*pagah, bohal ve-ẓemel*]. *Pagah* – she is still a young child. *Bohal* – these are the days of her "youth." For both of these her father has the rights to what she finds, to the work of her hands, and to undoing her vows. *Tsemel* – since she already matured, her father has no longer any authority over her. (M. Niddah 5:7)

Here, the rabbis distinguish between three different phases in a girl's life with the help of the metaphor of the fig in its various stages of ripening: her status as absolute minor, an in-between status, and her status of having reached legal majority. Even though rabbinic Hebrew provides specific terms for each stage of the fig's ripening, corresponding to the three legal stages of maidenhood, the translation suggested here appropriately captures the connection between fruit and girlhood, her transition from connection to her father's house to her availability to another man. Food metaphors of matters involving eros and sex are, of course, hardly a rabbinic invention, considering that biblical literature is replete with them,[12] to name but one relevant precedent with regard to the rabbinic texts. The text that follows makes the link to the woman's ripening body explicit and, I think, underlines the eroticism of this cluster of metaphors:

> What are her signs [i.e., of the almost too-ripe fig]? Rabbi Yosi ha-Galili says: From the point that a wrinkle is formed under her breast. Rabbi Akiva says: From the time that her breasts start to hang. Ben Azzai says: From the time that her nipple [*pitomet*]

darkens. Rabbi Yosi says: So that one can put one's hand on the nipple [*okez*], push it in and it does not emerge right away. (M. Niddah 5:8)[13]

The cluster of fruit metaphors is extended, as the various terms for nipple and areola are used for the peduncle and the blossom end of the fruit as well. The (heterosexual) eroticism of the male gaze can hardly escape the reader, especially since the association of female breast with fruit evokes the rich poetic language of the Song of Songs (e.g., 7:7–9). Can one read this discussion "neutrally," as an attempt to develop legal precision in the effort to determine legal majority by physical maturity? I would think hardly, especially if we assume an all-male audience of various age groups in the early rabbinic study circles – as well as in the later study halls – whose imagination and desire may variously get fired up. Eros takes hold of the law, and – we may surmise – of those who gather around their teacher sage to study law.

As some early feminist readers of this passage have noted, the stripping of the female body and the exposure of its breasts by the legal imagination here stands in marked contrast to the overall rabbinic valuation of female modesty and the care taken to cloak the female body.[14] The only other imagined exposure of a woman's breast happens in fact in a punitive context, as the editors of the Mishnah describe what is to happen to a woman suspected of adultery, namely, a public humiliation staged in the Temple, exposing her to the gaze of everyone:

> A priest seizes her garments. If they are rent, they are rent, and if they become unstitched they are unstitched until he uncovers her bosom, and he undoes her hair. R. Yehudah says: If her bosom was beautiful he does not uncover it, and if her hair was beautiful he does not undo it. If she was clothed in white, he clothes her in black; if she wore golden ornaments and necklaces, ear-rings and finger-rings, they remove them from her in order to make her repulsive. After that [the priest] takes a common rope, and binds it over her breasts. Whoever wishes to look upon her comes to look with the exception of her male and female slaves, because her heart is made defiant through them. (M. Sotah 1:5–6)[15]

In our legal context, however, the text does not advocate or make a gesture toward actual exposure of the breast. When the Babylonian Talmud does consider this as a potential practical consequence of our mishnaic text, in the form of an examination of exposed breasts to verify the various rabbinic suggestions, it does so only to immediately reject this option as inappropriate.[16] But the female breast remains an object of the legal discourse, and as such it reveals the (heterosexual) eroticism involved in such an act. It becomes a tool of shaping the heterosexual desire of the male student of Jewish law.

Both set of texts read together, then, the female body as house and fruit, confront us with an attempt to make the female body an object of legal discourse. And, we can add now, more so and differently so than the male body. The explicit effort to represent the female body through metaphors ("with respect to the woman, the sages made a simile") and the creation of clusters of metaphors to represent the female body in the Mishnah are notable. One way to understand the phenomenon would be that as much as this rhetorical strategy construes the woman as object of law via her body, it also underlines the difference between male and female body – men and women are as different as their bodies are made out to be and, perhaps even more importantly, as different as the way the rabbinic sages and their disciples talk about their bodies.

This is not to say that male bodies are not objectified or that men are not embodied by the legal imagination. Not at all. There are contexts in which male physiology finds its place in the legal discussions. Male genital fluids, for instance, receive just as much attention as menstrual blood, at least in the early rabbinic texts. The Mishnah devotes a whole tractate to ritual impurity due to male genital fluids. Another context would be the prohibition for priests to eat sacrificial meat after having had an orgasm: "If he was eating from the heave-offering and feels his limb beginning to shake [as in sexual arousal], he should take hold of his member, and swallow the heave-offering [before he ejaculates]" (M. Niddah 5:2). Far from this having only antiquarian relevance for Temple-related matters, the concern about the impact of sexual arousal and ejaculation is applied to what are considered the sancta of rabbinic law, such as, significantly, prayer (e.g., M. Berakhot 3:1–2) and study and recitation of the Torah (e.g., T. Berakhot 2:12). The "ejaculant" (*ba'al keri*) fragmentizes the male legal subject position just as much as does the "menstruant" (*niddah*). Finally, in later talmudic narratives, to name but one other example, male bodies are subjected to fantastic and grotesque representations.[17] Thus, one may postulate a certain discursive parallelism between male and female in matters of embodiment. Still, we must insist, the male body does not engender the same kind of creative energy for *metaphoric* representation as does the female body.

On the contrary! A different dynamic comes into play in the rabbinic thinking about the male body, in contexts that at first sight do not seem to be entirely relevant. This dynamic is one where the male body comes to be represented as the human body ('*adam*), something which never applies to the female body. Let me illustrate this point before clarifying further. The Mishnah famously provides a map of the human body, by way of listing the limbs of '*adam*, of a human being. This list can be found in the context of an explication of which kind of human body parts would convey a ritual status of impurity of the dead, if one were in close proximity to them, either in the same room or even just touched by the shadow of the structure that houses them. Generally, it is the human corpse as a whole that conveys this most severe kind of ritual impurity, which requires an elaborate Temple ritual for purification. Indeed, this kind of impurity is so strong that it can be transferred by the least tangible way spelled out here. A part of the corpse has the same effect as the corpse and stands in for the whole. Accordingly, our list enumerates 248 primary parts or limbs of a human being ('*adam*) that fulfill that function.[18] '*Adam* here can actually not clearly be read as "man," rather than human being. That is, read as a map of the human body, the list remains somewhat ambiguous as to its sexual identity. Although it does mention five apertures (*neqavim*) as a part of the number 248, the term for apertures remains ambiguous as it can refer to the openings of the digestive or the reproductive system without marking them as either male or female.[19] The ambiguity notwithstanding, the term '*adam* here suggests the male body, and I would argue assumes '*adam* to be male. A contemporary tradition cited in the Babylonian Talmud uses our Mishnah to argue that contrary to the 248 limbs of '*adam* cited in the Mishnah, women have four additional parts of the body, based on empirical evidence provided in that text.[20] It does not suggest that the number 248 is wrong, but just claims that women have more limbs, the implication being that the body of '*adam* in our Mishnah is understood to be equated with male.[21] These sources, then, clearly read the map of the human body to be equated with the male body. Are these simply later readings of the Mishnah? Perhaps, but other mishnaic texts equally and more explicitly equate human with male.[22]

What, then, is to be made from these observations? Let us summarize our findings in the following way: '*adam*, the term for human, can come to be represented by the male body, but never by the female body. Perhaps this is due to the influence of Genesis 2 on the rabbinic thinking in this case. The fact is that the body of '*adam* can be human or male specifically, in relation to which the female body [always woman, *'ishah*] inevitably occupies a position of difference. Additionally, the male body is less overtly "constructed" than the metaphorized female body. Hence, while overtly the rhetoric of the legal texts might appear to cast an objective perspective, we have traced various strategies of disguising male as human. The legal language of the body is one that casts a predominantly male perspective, that is, of those who look at the female body, and who inhabit it. Rabbinic overt objectivity in its representation of the body then masks a deeply masculine conception of the nature and purposes of sexuality. Such a rhetorical strategy, we may further claim, cements the heterosexual norm of rabbinic culture in that the female body is written into rabbinic law as the body to be desired, desired by the implied (male) subject of lawmaking, which includes, of course, only those who are its students.

Here we must pause, however. This general picture seems to be disrupted by the repeated appearances of ambiguous bodies in the legal literature that form a rather noticeable thread woven into the early rabbinic legal discussions in which sexual identity matters. This is where the androginos and his counterpart, the tumtum, the one that has no visible or visibly identifiable genitalia, come into play. There are other legal categories having to do with sexual identity that are instituted by the early rabbinic texts, namely, the eunuch (*saris*) and the masculine woman (*aylonit*), both of which have much more to do with the legal determination of an inability to reproduce than with differentiating between sexual identities. Space will not allow us to deal with all these categories in conjunction. Instead, we will focus on the hermaphrodite. If male versus female body are the main characters of early rabbinic legal literature in matters of constructing sexual identity, and are assigned the role of underwriting the heterosexual economy of its culture, then the representation of ambiguous bodies might suggest the possible instability of that economy. Let us return, then, to the androginos.

AMBIGUOUS BODIES

Just as we have observed with the male and female body, the Mishnah does not provide an explicit morphological description of the hermaphrodite. In fact, one possibility inherent in the term might have been what has been called the vertical hermaphrodite, the one who has male genitalia but female breasts. Such is the convention of the hermaphrodite's representation in classic and late ancient sculpture.[23] This possibility is indeed not entirely unknown to the rabbis, since in the list of the blemishes disqualifying the priest from service at the altar in the Temple, one is that "his breasts are hanging like those of a woman" (M. Bekhorot 7:5).[24] Nonetheless, such an anatomical constellation does not turn the male priest into a hermaphrodite or androginos.

Rather, the rabbinic texts clearly have in mind a person who has both genitalia. This emerges from various rules regarding the androginos, such as, for instance, rendering him subject to the rules of ritual impurity by genital discharges, either white or red (T. Bikkurim 2:4–5). However, contrary to the first impression of this list as a zero sum game, the presence of both genitalia are weighted in different ways. Most crucially, our list of laws refers to an (anonymous) law cited from another context in the Mishnah that the hermaphrodite may marry a woman, but may not be married by a man.[25] It would appear, then, that the presence of a penis has greater defining power than the vagina, so much so that when it comes down to making a decision in terms of establishing social order qua marriage, the hermaphrodite should take on the position of the male. Similarly, he is prohibited from dressing and cutting his hair according to women's fashions,[26] most likely to preserve the appearance of a normally dual-sexed world, in which clarity of who may pursue whom rules the day. Accordingly, the default legal sex assigned to the hermaphrodite would simply be male.

But is this indeed all that simple? In the original context of the law, the Mishnah cites a disagreeing opinion attributed to Rabbi Eliezer that "with regard to a hermaphrodite one contracts the death penalty of stoning, as in the case of a male." This enigmatic articulation has a slightly different formulation in the Tosefta:

> Rabbi El'azar[27] said: I have heard with regard to the *androginos* that one contracts the death penalty of stoning when having sex [*'al mishkavo*] with him as in the case of a male. To what does this refer? To the instance when one has sex with the hermaphrodite [*she-ba' 'alav*] by way of his [the hermaphrodite's] *zakhrut*. If one does not have sex with him by way of his *zakhrut* one is exempt [from the death penalty]. (T. Yevamot 10:2)

Accordingly, a man would be exempt from capital punishment for having sex with an androginos if both men restrict themselves to the hermaphrodite's vaginal area. *Derekh zakhrut*, literally, "by way of his masculinity," must then refer to anal intercourse.[28] It is the rabbinic parallel to the biblical idiom *mishkav zakhar*, or "the lying down of a male," which – as Saul Olyan has convincingly demonstrated[29] – refers to male vaginal penetration. But performed with a man, therefore, anal penetration would be the – prohibited – equivalent.[30] The concern behind the rabbinic legal thinking presented here seems to lie with the possibility of male–male penetration, while the problem of potential infertility of the connection never enters the discourse.

Be that as it may, this discussion raises some interesting questions. First of all, the permission for a hermaphrodite to marry a woman remains uncontested. It is only the sexual connection between a hermaphrodite and a man that engenders legal disagreement. According to one opinion (Rabbi El'azar in the Tosefta), a man can have sex with a hermaphrodite by way of his female genitalia, or at the very least in that case, he would be exempt from capital punishment. By implication, the prior anonymous opinion (prohibiting marriage of a hermaphrodite to a man) holds that a man cannot have sex with a hermaphrodite at all. If this is only implied in the earlier legal opinions, later amoraic statements in the talmudic discussion of our passage explicate that "with respect to [sex with] a hermaphrodite one contracts the death penalty of stoning for [sex by way of] either of the places" (B. Yevamot 83b).[31] The latter would seem to follow a logic in which the presence of a penis never becomes insignificant, so as to render sex with him permissible. Rabbi El'azar's opinion, on the other hand, would indeed maintain the hybridity of the sexual identity of the hermaphrodite as a valid legal subject position, and – although this is never explicated – allow for a relative choice on behalf of the hermaphrodite: He can choose to marry a woman, or he can choose to have sex with a man "by way of his femininity." Should he, however, choose to have sex with another man "by way of his masculinity," the law should treat him just like any other man having sex with a man.

Let us do some accounting of these tensions and try to sketch out the bigger picture: If rabbinic law had just contented itself with categorizing the hermaphrodite as "a creature in its own right," as one minority opinion would have it in our list of laws concerning the hermaphrodite,[32] the taxonomy of sexual identities would have remained neat and clean. In this case, the rabbinic legislators would have denied the hermaphrodite any legal subject position ("and the sages could not decide whether he was a man or a woman"), which requires an unequivocal sexual identity. We may think here of the Roman equivalent of this logic, which was to consider him a freak creature with the respective consequences this entailed, such as drowning the baby in the earlier Republican period, or – according to Pliny – considering him as a figure of entertainment.[33] But it is with the attempt to fit the hermaphrodite into the dual-sex grid holding rabbinic legal thinking in a tight grip that the question of his sexual identity is rendered unresolved and unresolvable. Contrary to what one might think at first, the tensions that this produces do not just target the sexual identity of the hermaphrodite himself. Rather, they equally concern the logic of the legal system as a whole, namely, the question of how much sexual identity or, rather, transparency of sexual identity matters. Naturally, this is central to the effort of regulating sexual relations that goes to the very core of the body politic, especially in a culture such as the rabbinic that attributes high value to appropriate sexual relations and their respective offspring, based on ethnic, ritual, and social status.

It is also remarkable that although in the context of regulating sexual relations the rabbinic texts generally bend the identity of the hermaphrodite in the direction of the masculine pole (with the exception of Rabbi El'azar), this does not amount to an effort of entirely disambiguating his identity. By contrast, Ulpian (d. 228 C.E.) – the Roman jurist contemporary to the rabbis who produced the Mishnah – attempts to do just that. He simply assumes that one of the sexes will be the prevalent one and that is the determining one, as we shall see instantly. Rather, in the rabbinic texts, especially those addressing matters of sexual relations, the inherent ambiguities remain foregrounded.

Let us consider one last example from a context that has nothing to do with regulating sexual relations, to illustrate this point. This context is peculiar to rabbinic ritual culture. The question considered is which kind of actions connected to circumcision are allowed or prohibited on the Sabbath. While circumcision itself is unquestionably permitted on the Sabbath, since the eighth day is explicitly fixed in biblical law as the day of circumcision (Leviticus 12:3), subsidiary actions connected to circumcision might still raise a problem. In general, the rabbinic thinking is quite liberal when it comes to caring for the well-being of the baby and its wound. Here, the following disagreement is introduced: "If there is a doubt [that the baby will live]³⁴ or he is an *androginos*, one does not profane the Sabbath because of him. Rabbi Yehudah rendered it permissible with an *androginos*" (M. Shabbat 19:3). The legal logic seems to be that there must be sufficient reason for permitting something as grave as profaning the Sabbath. Therefore, if the baby will most likely die due to premature birth, for instance, there is – according to this logic – not enough reason to perform the circumcision on the eighth day that is a Sabbath, rather than, for instance, waiting a day. The same is applied to the hermaphrodite, by way of the category of certainty: Yes, he does have a penis that should be circumcised, but that in and by itself is not sufficient to profane the Sabbath. In the words of an early midrashic commentary: "[The biblical phrase: 'And on the eighth day the flesh of] 'his foreskin' [shall be circumcised' (Leviticus 12:3) implies that] one who falls in the category of *certain* supersedes the [laws of the] Sabbath, but a hermaphrodite does not supersede the Sabbath" (my emphasis).[35] True, "certain" here is first and foremost understood as a legal category, rather than an anatomical category; that is, only he who is "certainly" obligated to fulfill a commandment, or for whom certainly a commandment applies, has enough legal weight to have the Sabbath profaned on his behalf. Still, the rhetorical effect is that the hermaphrodite's "commandedness," that is, his legal position as male, is not certain enough to justify superseding the laws of the Sabbath.[36] Differently put, he is not man enough to justify superseding the laws of the Sabbath.

Before arriving at general conclusions, though, let us briefly consider the Roman context of the rabbinic legal interest that we have traced here in broad strokes.

THE RABBINIC HERMAPHRODITE AND ITS ROMAN CONTEXT

Let us begin with the term *androginos* itself, a rabbinic neologism and obviously a loanword from Greek, most likely via its latinized form. Loanwords do not just have linguistic significance, as to the development of a language, but carry with them a semantic baggage of cultural associations. As Amram Tropper has argued in a different context: "By means of a loanword from Greek or Latin, the author of a rabbinic text may have alluded to a specific setting or institution well known to his audience" (2005, 207). Whether the audience was aware of the loanword's original context, as Tropper claims, perhaps is questionable and not the point here. More important is the suggestion that loanwords may indicate the rabbinic awareness, at least to some degree, of how the terms operated in the cultural context from which they are taken. There may also not just have been one context in which a term operated, as is the case with the term *androginos*, so that the question becomes the context or contexts with which the rabbinic authors may have been familiar. In fact, it seems that everyone talked and thought about the figure of the hermaphrodite.

Of special interest here is Pliny's remark that his contemporaries now call *hermaphroditi* what formerly was called *androgyni* (*Naturalis Historia* 7.3.34). Indeed, Roman legal texts, such as remarks by Ulpian and Paulus (both of third century C.E.) generally use the term *hermaphroditus*, while rabbinic texts use the term *androginos* exclusively.

Ulpian, for instance, remarks that a hermaphrodite (hermaphroditus) should be classified as belonging to that sex which is the most prevalent one (Dig. 1.5.10).[37] In the Digest, there are various legal contexts in which the *hermaphroditus* is discussed, namely, those where legal rights are restricted to men. Thus, Ulpian suggests that "a hermaphrodite, obviously, if male characteristics (*virilia*) prevail in him, will be capable of instituting a posthumous heir" (Dig. 28.2.6.2).[38] It is not entirely clear what he means by "prevail" and how such prevalence is to be demonstrated. According to a remark by Paulus, although only men could serve as witness to a will, a hermaphrodite could do so as well "if he exhibits the ability of his sex to warm up" (Dig. 22.5.15.1 *Paulus iii sententiarum*).[39] That is, the hermaphrodite needs to demonstrate his ability "to function as a man" in order to acquire male legal rights in this context.

Even with such few examples, the commonalities with rabbinic legal thinking are obvious here. It is true that the rabbis do not discuss the nature of the hermaphrodite in terms of what sex prevails, at least not explicitly. But they do seem to assume that the penis has greater signifying power than the presence of a vaginal opening. More significantly, however, the hermaphrodite appears in legal contexts where *male* legal rights are discussed and where the problem of ambiguous *masculinity* matters. We could have a case, then, where institutional associations – namely, law – are imported via the loanword that either the rabbis only knew in its Greek form, or deliberately translated into the Greek form in order to avoid the mythological associations inherent in the Latin term. Hermaphroditus is, after all, the son of Hermes and Aphrodite.[40] One would be hard pressed to construe an antiquarian tendency among the rabbis, who might for some reason insist on the term *androginos* rather than *hermaphroditus*, along the lines of Pliny's remark. Pliny does not provide us with reasons for the linguistic change, which makes it next to impossible to make more of this remark.

There is yet another cultural setting of the term *androginos*, this time in its Greek form, with which the early rabbis might have been familiar in some form, and which potentially enlarges the semantic range of the rabbinic understanding of it. The (linguistically) Greek context approximately contemporary to the early rabbinic texts in which the *androgynos* is rather prominent is the literature and performance culture of the Second Sophistic and its preoccupation with gender identity. The movement that is referred to as the Second Sophistic[41] consisted predominantly of male orators who traveled around the late ancient world with a fan club in tow and attracted huge crowds who delighted in the mud-slinging combat by words performed on stage. Who is to say whether perhaps a rabbinic sage sat in the audience of one of these orators! Of the speeches some survive, especially some by Marcus Antonius Polemon of Laodicaea (died 145 c.e.). Polemo's colorful polemics against his much-detested colleague Favorinus have been rendered beautifully accessible for those who study the history of gender by Maud Gleason's analysis.[42]

In the context of the Second Sophistic and its politics of self-presentation, the term *androgyne* came to be deployed toward ends rather different from the rabbinic ones. Polemo inherits the term from the physiognomic tradition in which surface appearances are analyzed for hidden realities. Often, in this tradition, appearances take on the valence of lies. Thus, the physiognomic tradition defines *androgynoi* as "people who are unable to keep their eyelids straight or their eyebrows level but tremble slightly there while their gaze keep shifting." That is, androgynoi are people "who are forcing themselves to be men,"[43] even though they are really not. An anatomical notion may indeed adhere to the term in this tradition, but the interest of the physiognomists consists in the fact that these people are deceptive as to creating a masculine appearance, that is, "those who are by nature (*physei*) *androgynoi* but mold themselves on the masculine pattern" (Gleason 1998, 79). A well-trained physiognomist, however, will easily detect their true nature. So also with Polemo, the early rabbis' contemporary. For Polemo, *androgynoi* is a term to denote male impostors, and he clearly stages himself as an experienced physiognomist: "You may recognize the *androgynos* by his provocatively melting glance and by the rapid movement of his intensely staring eyes. . . . He minces his hands with palms turned upward. He has a shifting gaze, and his voice is thin, weepy, shrill and drawling" (1998, 63), all of which, of course, applies to his enemy Favorinus. Physiognomic imaginative polemic develops entire catalogues of signs by which the expert can detect gender deviance. Maud Gleason has argued that the physical sense of the word *androgynos* as referring to sexual ambiguity is not the one that the physiognomists, including Polemo, draw on. Rather, she points out, it has become synonymous, perhaps even indistinguishable, from the word *cinaedus*, which "describes sexual deviance, in its most specific sense referring to males who prefer to play a 'feminine' (receptive) role in intercourse with other men."[44] Both terms, then, are used to "describe men of effeminate appearance and behavior" (1998, 64). *Androgynos* in this context, then, is the equivalent of effeminacy.

The differences from the rabbinic use of the term, as we have discussed it, could not be more pronounced. In fact, the situation here is the reverse of the parallels with the Roman legal traditions: While the term is linguistically the same, and the rabbinic loanword stems from the Greek, the institutional context is quite different. One is situated in the oratorical performance culture of the Second Sophistic and its polemics, which draw on gender stereotypes, while the second is situated in a legal, definitional context. While the sophists use the term in order to discuss *gender* deviance, the rabbinic sages discuss *sexual* ambiguity. Sexual deviance is possible in the rabbinic case, as articulated by Rabbi Eliezer (mYevamot 8:6) or Rabbi El'azar (tYevamot 10:2), discussed earlier, but the rabbinic texts do not denounce the person or character of the androginos. Rather, the devil lies in the sexual act itself, which can be avoided even by the androginos. Hence, to the rabbis, the hermaphrodite remains a strictly morphological category, an ambiguous one, and a potentially problematic one, should he make the wrong choices. But then, any "regular" man or woman could do exactly the same thing.

How do we account for the overlaps and differences? Is it that law – as a genre – has its discursive limits, as Jane Gardner put it with regard to Roman law: "There is little room within the rules of Roman law for the kind of explicit gender-stereotyping, reflecting ordinary social attitudes, found in literary sources"?[45] Does this mean that the rabbis took the term simply out of its Greek context, to use it toward their own ends and genre purposes, namely, lawmaking? Or did they purposefully use the term differently, translate it in such a way as to completely obliterate the preoccupation with effeminacy on the Greek side, turning it into a preoccupation with the gender workings of their own legal system? Or do the rabbis learn the concept of the hermaphrodite as a Roman legal term and then whitewash the mythological background of the Roman figure while otherwise copying their occupiers' categories and ways of legal thinking? I do not think that we can answer these questions with any degree of certainty. What we can observe, however, is that there is a significant amount of pressure on the rabbis in the Greco-Roman world to consider the possibility of sexual ambiguity in the figure of the hermaphrodite. Everyone talks about him, everyone discusses him, and so did the rabbis.

There may, in fact, be two reasons other than the historical-cultural context why the rabbis of the early legal literature discuss the hermaphrodite so extensively. Thus, one could assume that their interest in the hermaphrodite arises out of empirical evidence. Surely, in their occupation with husbandry they would have come about sexual ambiguities. Similarly, contemporary activists on behalf of what is now called intersexuality claim that the statistic occurrence of human sexual ambiguity is much higher than is "commonsensically" assumed.[46]

But even if this is true, and was true for the rabbinic period, empirical evidence in and by itself does not explain entirely what emerges into discourse and what does not.

A different reason may be the internal logic of the early rabbinic system. Thus, one might think that any legal system that insists on the strict divisions of gender, and bases legal privileges thereon, diverges to hybrid categories in order to examine and most likely reinforce its normatively dual system. For instance, the rabbis invent hybrid categories in other dual systems, such as the *koi*, an animal that is neither domesticated nor wild.[47] Accordingly, the preoccupation with the hybrid category is not a specifically historical phenomenon, or one to be historicized, rather than a logical phenomenon. Other systems, entirely unrelated to the rabbis by geography or historical period, such as is the case with Buddhism, do in fact enter into similar discussions.[48] In such a case, one should choose more of a comparative than historical approach.

The path we are choosing here, however, is more of a historical one. That is not to claim that the preceding two reasons are invalid. In fact, they may not be exclusive of each other. However, the historical relationship between rabbinic literature and the Greco-Roman material is in my mind undeniable in this instance. More than that, the Greco-Roman hermaphrodite provides an important anchor, and trying to untangle the relationships can only add an important layer to our understanding of how the rabbis think legally about gender.

CONCLUSION

Rabbinic thinking about the body as articulated in the early discussions of a legal nature can be summarized in this way, then: Predominantly, the rabbinic sages project an assumption of the existence of two kinds of human bodies as far as their sex is concerned, male and female. At the same time, rabbinic legal thinking admits to a greater variability of human bodies. There are male and female bodies, bodies that are both, and others that are neither, to name those that we have discussed here. To expand the list a bit more, there are eunuchs and their female counterparts, whom we did not discuss here.

The question remains why the rabbinic sages devoted so much space to discuss the legal repercussions of sexual ambiguity in the figure of the hermaphrodite. If this were simply a sign of their anxiety about the stability of the dual-gender grid of their lawmaking, it might have been easier for them to simply ignore this figure and go about their ways. Perhaps this was not an option, due to the omnipresence of the hermaphrodite in all kinds of discursive contexts. At the very least, we are confronted with an interesting constellation, especially in view of the feminist theoretical argument mapped in the beginning of this essay. The rabbinic sages admit to a significant degree of sexual variability. This hardly amounts to the scale of sexual identities that contemporary advocates for intersexuality point to, where human bodies and their sexual identity are considered to be as variable as can possibly be imagined along the scale of "intersexuality." Still, contrary to the situation theorized by Judith Butler, where the duality of genders in a "heterosexualist" economy of gender is rooted in a promotion of a two-sex system, the rabbis' legal thinking did indeed allow for a variety of sexual ambiguities. In fact, we have to take note that the rabbis maintain a legal system with a dual-gender grid in spite of ambiguous bodies. And they did not consider these as external to the system they crafted, but they integrated them into the system. Hence, hermaphrodites are not only human but also Jews, something that must be emphasized in view of the cultural alternatives also available in the Roman world. They are to be circumcised (if not on the Sabbath), and they can marry.

Contrary to the sophists, the rabbinic sages hardly ever deploy the hermaphrodite as a term to designate effeminacy, of deceptive masculinity, a masculinity that only pretends to be one but really is not. Such patterns of thought the rabbinic sages refuse. The baby may not be considered male enough to justify something as severe as transgression of the Sabbath for his circumcision, but in the end, this is more a question of whether the biblical law that explicates "male" applies to him as it does to a male baby than of whether he is really "male enough."

There is a stark juxtaposition between the variability of bodies, admitted into legal consideration, and the absolute insistence of the gender duality of law. Sex is variable but gender is not. In the end, perhaps, it only makes sense that the hermaphrodite could not be considered "a creature in its own right" by the rabbinic sages. It was much more important to demonstrate that the Torah, in the form of law or halakhah, could absorb everything under its mantle. Thus, the repeated insistence on fitting the hermaphrodite into the legal conditions as instituted by the rabbinic sages could only serve to demonstrate the viability of their law.

Notes

1. Such an approach is by definition built on Michel Foucault's work, developed especially in *The History of Sexuality*, as well as the work of Judith Butler, who has argued against the possibility of ever having access to the body as such, in Butler 1990. See also Peskowitz 1997, 8–9.
2. The neither-nor category is more appropriately represented by the *tumtum*, the counterpiece to the *androginos*, in that he is the person who

does not have visible genitalia at all. It seems, however, that in most of the rabbinic discussions, such a person can eventually be disambiguated by surgical means, and in most cases the anxiety is that he might turn out to be a man, and based on this anxiety he should be treated accordingly in the meantime. This essay will focus on the androginos, mostly for reasons of space, but also because he is a category more relevant for the argument to be advanced here.

3. This list appears not only in the Tosefta but can also be found in most English translations of the Mishnah as M. Bikkurim 4 with a number of differences, where it was placed already in the *editio princeps* of Naples (1492). For the most important text critical question, consult Saul Lieberman's critical edition of the Tosefta with commentary, *Tosefta Ki-Fshuta.*

4. The Mishnah time and again produces such lists, e.g., M. Sotah 3:8 ("what is the difference between a man and a woman?"), M. Niddah 5 (on both gender and age), M. Shabbat 7:2 ("the main labors prohibited on the Sabbath are forty minus one"), M. Bekhorot 6 (blemishes of a firstborn animal disqualifying it from being sacrificed in the Temple), and M. Bekhorot 7 (blemishes of a priest disqualifying him from serving in the Temple). On the penchant for such academic list making as a Hellenistic phenomenon, see Cohen 2000, as well as Jaffee 2001. On M. Bekhorot 6 and 7, see Rosen-Zvi forthcoming.

5. The androginos is by no means a singular phenomenon of hybrid categories in rabbinic legal thinking. A parallel phenomenon, relevant in this context, would be the *koi*, a (nonexisting) creature, who is both a domesticated and wild animal and is discussed in the Tosefta immediately preceding our list of commandments concerning the androginos.

6. Sarra Lev, *Genital Trouble: On the Innovations of Tannaitic Thought Regarding Damaged Genitals and Eunuchs* (Ph.D. diss., New York University, 2004), which, however, focuses on the legal figure of the eunuch, Hebr. *saris*. See also Rosen-Zvi forthcoming.

7. However, it should be mentioned that in current terminology, this would suggest a morphological approach rather than a biological approach in the strict sense of the word. On these distinct approaches, see Fausto-Sterling 2000.

8. Klawans 2000, Hayes 2002, and the latter's contribution to the present volume.

9. On this, see "The Woman as House: Conceptions of Women's Corporeality in Talmudic Literature," in Fonrobert 2000, as well as Baker 2002. The range of metaphors around this cluster is expanded significantly, in that we can add doors, hinges, a door bolt, and more from other texts.

10. On the institutional setting of rabbinic texts, see Jeffrey Rubenstein's essay earlier in this volume.

11. See Baker 2002, who emphasizes that "the edified body is not identical with the pregnant or maternal body" but notes that it is still related to "rabbinic concerns about the reproduction of Jewish bodies and rabbinic culture," 57.

12. In matters of the female body prominently, of course, the Song of Songs. See Marilyn Yalom, *A History of the Breast* (Ballantine Books, 1998), 22–26.

13. Cf. the corresponding text in T. Niddah 6:4 (Zuckermandel), which provides more opinions about different ways to describe the development of the breast.

14. E.g., Rachel Biale, *Women and Jewish Law: The Essential Texts, Their History and Their Relevance for Today* (1984; reprint, New York: Schocken, 1995). This has led some to read this passage as a form of rabbinic pornography.

15. For a careful discussion of the transformation of the biblical ritual, described in Numbers 5, in early rabbinic literature, see Ishay Rosen-Zvi, *The Ritual of the Suspected Adulteress (Sotah) in Tannaitic Literature: Textual and Theoretical Perspectives* (Ph.D. diss., Tel Aviv University, 2004).

16. The rabbinic authority in question is Samuel, an early student of our mishnaic text, who takes one of his slave women to examine the mishnaic opinions about the female breast. Of course, one might argue that the description implies the necessity of an examination of the girl in case legal question arise. It should be noted, however, that later Jewish law gave preference to chronological age, rather than physical maturity, as a way to determine legal majority.

17. See Boyarin 1993, Chapter 7 "(Re)producing Men: Constructing the Rabbinic Male Body," 197–227.

18. The Tosefta explains the mishnaic term for limbs ('*ever*) to refer to limbs that contain bones with some flesh (sinews) attached; see T. Ahilot 1:7. Recently, Meir Bar Ilan has argued that the list should be read as a scientific description, which has an origin in a different source than the mishnaic chapter ("Medicine in Israel in the First Centuries of the Common Era," *Kathedra* 91, 1999, 31–78 [Hebrew]).

19. In his translation of *The Mishnah* (New Haven, Conn. and London: Yale University Press, 1988), Jacob Neusner claims that this refers to the genitalia, "five [vertebrae] in the genitals" (951). An early tradition cited in the Babylonian Talmud uses the term to refer both to the urinal and seminal ducts in the penis (B. Bekhorot 44b). This text again uses '*adam* to refer to the male body. To me, the ambiguity in the text points much more to an assumed male identity of this representation of the body than to my friend and colleague Ishay Rosen-Zvi, who understands this mishnah as refusing to distinguish between men and women.

20. I.e., two doors and two hinges, presumably referring to the genital area (B. Bekhorot 45a). See my discussion in Fonrobert 2000, esp. 40–68. For a critical discussion of this reading, see Baker 2002, 48–59.

21. In the ensuing talmudic discussion, one of the early readers of this mishnah, Rav, suggests that even if women were to have four more limbs, these do not need to be considered in the original list of 248, as these do not convey ritual impurity. He draws on a midrashic reading of Numbers 19:14: "'This is the rule regarding the person ['*adam*] who dies in a tent' – [impurity of the dead can be conveyed] only by a matter that is

shared by *all human beings* [*'adam*]," B. Bekhorot 45a (my emphasis). His suggestion does not reject in principle the difference of women from the body of 'adam either.

22. See, for instance, another kind of map of the body, this one of potential blemishes of the priest's body. Again the list is introduced as referring to *'adam*, not *'ish* (man): "these are the blemishes with regard to a person [*'adam*] [that disqualify him from service in the Temple]" (M. Bekhorot 7:1). In this case, the body is clearly sexed, since blemishes may occur in the male genitalia (M. Bekhorot 7:5). For an important extended discussion of this list, see Ishay Rosen-Zvi forthcoming.

23. Among the most famous sculptures is the reclining hermaphrodite attributed to Polycles of Athens in the second century B.C.E. The figure is lying on a couch in such a way as to expose both his breasts and his male genitalia. This figure was copied multiple times in the ancient world. The most famous, a Roman copy of the 2nd century C.E., is housed in the Louvre. Another example, albeit not contemporary to the rabbis, is the vase painting of Hermaphroditos chasing a hare, from around 340 B.C.E., in the Museum of Art, Rhode Island School of Design, Museum Catalogue # RIDS 1986.158.

24. Significantly, breasts are not included in the list of signs indicating that a man might be a *saris*, or eunuch (T. Yevamot 10:6, B. Yevamot 80b), rendering him unable to reproduce.

25. Perhaps citing M. Yevamot 8:6. In that context, the Mishnah further lists an opinion attributed to two Tanna'im, Rabbi Yosi and Rabbi Shime'on, that "if a priest who was a hermaphrodite (*androginos kohen*) married the daughter of an Israelite, he confers upon her the right to eat heave-offering," the ultimate ritual theory of validating a marriage. It should be mentioned here that all the cognate verbs of marriage in rabbinic Hebrew are grammatically active for the man, but passive for the woman. Thus, the passive verb ("being married to") would indicate that the hermaphrodite cannot be put in the subject position of wife-to-be. On this point, see Michael Satlow 1994a, 18.

26. If Lieberman's comment on the commandment is correct, see his critical edition of the Toseftan text. For the biblical prohibition of cross-dressing, see Deuteronomy 22:5.

27. Note that this is not Rabbi Eliezer of the Mishnah, which has significant consequences for the discussions of this law in the Babylonian Talmud. Both names are attested well in the manuscript traditions for the respective texts.

28. The idiom appears nowhere else in tannaitic literature. The Mishnah, in fact, never uses the abstract noun *zakhrut*. Elsewhere in rabbinic literature, *zakhrut* by itself clearly refers to the penis or phallus (B. Avodah Zarah 44a). Once in the Babylonian Talmud it may actually refer to sexual identity in toto, rather than merely the organ itself (B. Shabbat 108a). The Palestinian Talmud uses the expression "the side of masculinity" (Y. Yevamot 8:6, 9d).

29. Saul M. Olyan 1994, 184, with reference to Numbers 31:17–18 and 35; Judges 21:11–12.

30. Indeed, in the rabbinic idiom, *mishkav zakhor* has turned into a technical term for male-to-male anal penetration. See also Daniel Boyarin in his programmatic article "Are There Any Jews in 'The History of Sexuality'?" (1995), 336 with reference to B. Niddah 13b.

31. The Babylonian Talmud attributes this opinion to Rav, an early Amora, and strengthens that opinion further by drawing on a tannaitic tradition, where a Rabbi Simai supposedly holds the same opinion. However, that tannaitic tradition, for various reasons that cannot be expanded on here, seems to be pseudepigraphic, so to speak, and not a genuine early legal tradition. For a discussion of such a phenomenon, see Judith Hauptman 1988.

32. So according to Rabbi Yosi in T. Bikkurim 2:7. This statement is cited in the Babylonian Talmud B. Yevamot 83a to point out a contradiction with an opinion attributed to the same Rabbi Yosi in the Mishnah that the hermaphrodite priest bestows upon his wife the right of eating the heave-offering. The Talmud suggests various ways to harmonize this tension, one of which is to suggest that Rabbi Yosi changed his mind.

33. "Persons are also born of both sexes combined – what we call hermaphrodites, once called *androgyni* and classed as prodigies [*prodigiis*], but now as entertainments [*deliciis*]" (*Naturalis Historia* 7.3.34). As far as the earlier Roman custom of drowning hermaphrodite babies is concerned, see Brisson 2002, and the sources cited in his section on "An Ominous Prodigy," 8–31.

34. So according to the talmudic interpretation of this law, see B. Shabbat 135a. Rabbinic literature assumes that a baby that is born in the eighth month of pregnancy will not live, but a baby that is born in the seventh will live. In this context, this means that if there is a doubt whether the baby was born in the seventh or eighth month, he should not be circumcised on the Sabbath.

35. *Sifra Tazria*, Par. 1, Chap. 1, also cited in the Babylonian Talmud B. Shabbat 134b–135a.

36. It should be mentioned here that this contradicts one of the rules listed in the collection of laws concerning the hermaphrodite, namely, that "he is obligated to all the commandments mentioned in the Torah, like men" (T. Bikkurim 2:4), a rule not mentioned elsewhere in tannaitic literature.

37. Cited by Gardner 1998, 138: Quaeritur: hermaphroditum cui comparamus? Et magis puto eius sexus aestimandum qui in eo praevalet.

38. I am citing Gardner's translation here. It should be mentioned that *virilia* often connotes the penis specifically. See Lewis and Short, *A Latin-English Dictionary*.

39. Gardner's paraphrase, 139, does not capture the language here, although she does comment on this remark that "Paulus' colorful language (*incalescentis*) suggests not, perhaps, that a prospective witness challenged as hermaphrodite might be asked on the spot to demonstrate his essential physical virility by achieving an erection, but perhaps that that criterion was used where sexual re-assignment of a grown person was being considered," 148 n. 12.

40. See Ovid, *Metamorphoses* 4:380–86, and especially the discussion by Williams 1999, 128.
41. The term itself is coined by Philostratus (ca. 170–ca. 247 C.E.) who catalogued and celebrated the most famous of the orators in his *Lives of the Sophists.*
42. Gleason 1998. On the physiognomic tradition of the Second Sophistic and its gender politics, see also Barton 1994, esp. 115–19.
43. Gleason 1998, 78. She cites Adamantius, a fourth-century sophist who paraphrased Polemo's text.
44. Gleason notes that, "the second-century lexicographer Pollux considered the words *androgynous* and *cinaedus* synonyms"; ibid., 65.
45. Gardner 1998, 136. The gender stereotypes developed by the orators of the Second Sophistic would represent such literary sources, I assume. Gardner does not cite any.
46. On this, see Fausto-Sterling 2000, Chapters 1–3.
47. And it is not by chance that the list of laws concerning the androginos is immediately following the discussion of the koi (T. Bikkurim 2:1–2), rather than being located in a more suggestive context.
48. See Gyatso 2003. I thank Jonathan Schofer for calling my attention to this informative article.

13 Rabbinic Historiography and Representations of the Past

ISAIAH GAFNI

At the very conclusion of his monumental *Antiquities of the Jews*, the noted Jewish historian Josephus, sensing that what he had just achieved was the exception, rather than the rule, among Jewish intellectuals of his day, indulges in a measure of self-adulation. Singularly among the learned men of his day, he claims, he alone has succeeded in bridging the gulf between Greek learning, apparently a sine qua non for the historiographical achievement embodied in the *Antiquities*, and a curriculum that was far more revered among his Jewish compatriots: "For our people ... give credit for wisdom to those alone who have an exact knowledge of the law and who have the capability of interpreting the holy writings."[1] This hierarchy of Jewish knowledge, he seems to be saying, relegated historiographical undertakings of the Hellenistic-Roman model to a somewhat neglected status, and while he does not chastise his fellow Jews for this neglect, one might conclude that those who did devote themselves to the study of the law and its interpretation felt no pangs of remorse for not embracing a pursuit of the past in the critical manner of their Greco-Roman counterparts.

Indeed, the variegated corpus of rabbinic literature did not preserve any work that might point to an effort on the part of the rabbis at producing a systematic and critical study of the past.[2] To be sure, the biblical past was at the center of much of their deliberations, but this "past" was for them already laid out in its fullest detail, thereby providing the basis for an ongoing search of its religious significance, and hardly requiring any compilation and examination of sources in a Thucydidean-type search for "truth" and "accuracy."

The events of the Bible were known to all, and it was their meaning and moral implications that would be taken up by the rabbis. The apparent lack of a concerted historiographical agenda on their part has attracted much attention among modern scholars, with no lack of explanations preferred. Arnaldo Momigliano, for example, suggests that history simply lost out to what was perceived as a higher calling: "History had nothing to explain and little to reveal to the man who meditated the Law day and night" (1990, 23). Yosef Yerushalmi goes one step further, claiming that with the Bible "they already knew of history what they needed to know," inasmuch as "the Bible was not only a repository of past history, but a revealed pattern of the whole of history" (1989, 21). Jacob Neusner maintains that rabbinic Judaism (as well as early Christianity) read Scripture's words as "paradigms of an enduring present," and thus for the rabbis, past, present, and future were all rolled up into a single framework. Meaning for all historical events was derived from atemporal models of thought that obviated any distinctions between past and present, thereby eliminating any inclination to resort to historical undertakings of the classical mode (1997 and 2004). Others have suggested that the belief in an eternally sanctioned legal system not subject to the vicissitudes of history removed any need for (or interest in) a study of the changes in human events that lie at the core of the historian's curiosity.[3] Not only might the sages have felt their sole control of the oral law challenged by the notion that changing historical realities also contributed to this legal system,[4] but a community embracing the notion that "whatever an established disciple will teach in the future...was already told to Moses at Sinai"[5] would certainly be prone to an ahistorical mind-set, with the important issues of life well established beyond the influences of time or place. Yet another frequently posited solution links the abandonment of historiographical activity on the part of the rabbis to the removal, in their day, of Jews from the political frameworks that normally encouraged such an enterprise.[6]

In fact, one rabbinic story actually appears to comment on the removal of Israel from the ebb and flow of historical processes. Jacob's ladder, we are informed, and the angels ascending and descending, are in fact a portrayal of the rise and fall of the nations of the world: "He [God] showed him [Jacob] the prince of Babylonia ascending and descending, and the prince of Media...and the prince of Greece...and the prince of Edom.... He [Jacob] said to Him: Just as these have descended I too will descend? God told him: Fear not, go up, for you will ascend but not descend! Nevertheless he feared and did not ascend" (Leviticus Rabbah 29:2). The author of this *midrash* actually indicts Israel for choosing to remain outside the historical process, notwithstanding God's promise that if it does "ascend" it would not be subject to the natural laws and forces that otherwise govern that process. Rather than a denial of history, there is a sense here of the irrelevancy of its laws and their ultimate subordination in favor of an ideal Jewish reality, with only a lack of faith on the part of Jacob (= Israel) causing the nation to be overwhelmed by the political process.

This Judaeo-centric context provided the rabbis with all they needed to know when addressing the events of world history, and whereas classical historians, beginning with Thucydides, searched for a natural causality that determined the flow of history, the rabbis applied a totally different system of reasoning. World powers rose and fell regardless of the natural or social conditions governing their behavior, but solely on the basis of moral criteria, and their practical application toward Israel:

> Rome is destined to fall to Persia, *a minori* [*kal va-ḥomer*]: If in the case of the First Temple, built by the Semites [i.e., Israelites], it was destroyed by the Babylonians, and the Babylonians fell to the Persians, [and] the Second Temple was built by the Persians and destroyed by the Romans, is it not fitting that the Romans fall to the Persians? (B. Yoma 10a)

While there is no denial of historical causality in such reasoning, the underpinning of the process is derived from a framework of moral virtue or culpability, wherein destroyers are punished and builders rewarded. But this behavior takes on meaning only when assessed by its practical application toward Israel, thereby supplying the rabbis with the theodicic principles required for any appraisal of historical processes. Needless to say, this mind-set would hardly be conducive to the espousal of a historical agenda fashioned after the Greco-Roman model of classical antiquity.

To be sure, the rabbis were certainly in possession of traditions relating to historical events or central figures and institutions that functioned during the centuries that preceded them. A significant number of parallel sources can be found in the writings of Josephus and rabbinic literature,[7] but despite the few ambitious attempts in early modern times to reconstruct Second Temple history based on these traditions,[8] it is clear that the sages had little critical control over what they received, and incorporated these sources into their deliberations primarily for halakhic reasons, or to underscore the moral lessons do be derived from these stories.[9]

Indeed, not only did the rabbis refrain from producing historiographical literature; they seem to have consciously steered away from seeking support for a historical agenda even in those scriptures that, at first glance, might have provided for an active encouragement of one. The biblical exhortation to "ask now concerning the days that are past, that were before you, ever since God created man on earth" (Deuteronomy 4:32) not only does not serve as the underpinning of a rabbinic commitment to a study of the past, but is primarily employed as a proof text for the tannaitic prohibition of any inquiry into the earliest days of cosmic existence.[10] Similarly, the sweeping biblical requirement to "remember the days of old, consider the years of ages past" (Deuteronomy 32:7) is reduced by the sages to specific events and people: "Remember what I have done to the people of the generation of the flood . . . to the people of the generation of the dispersion [*dor ha-pelaga*] . . . to the people of Sodom" (Sifre Devarim 310). Remembering "days of old" and "years of ages past" was thus steered away from any contemplation of all that transpired "before our time," and interpreted instead as a mere refocusing on those events that were already "known," not through any process of examination (*historia* in Greek) but by revealed tradition. For some sages, even this exegesis may have seemed redundant, and so they redirected it entirely toward the future: "Remind yourselves of all the good things and consolations that He will give you in the world-to-come" (Sifre Devarim 310).

Once the shackles of strict adherence to a factual history were removed, the rabbis were free to retell the biblical past in a manner that might reflect their own values and mores, even at the risk of blatant anachronism. King Ahab, clearly a biblical example of the wicked Israelite monarch, was nevertheless granted a prolonged reign because he provided "sages" (*talmidei hakhamim*) with financial sustenance (B. Sanhedrin 102b). Similarly, when the pregnant Rebecca passed near "synagogues and houses of study" (*batei knesiyot ubatei midrashot*), we are informed that Jacob tried to leave the womb. The authors of the *midrash* had no problem with this obvious rabbinization of the biblical narrative, notwithstanding the fact that just a few lines later, in the very same midrash, after stating that Rebecca went to seek help at Shem's academy, they immediately revert to a sober historical awareness and declare: "But did synagogues and schools exist in the days of Rebecca?"![11]

This last example is noteworthy, for it suggests that a recasting of the past, whether for pedagogical or polemical reasons, need not always reflect a systematic disdain or subversion of the notion that a factual past does exist, and must at times be addressed. Nevertheless, scholars have frequently searched for evidence of just such a rabbinic downplaying of the legitimacy involved in historical inquiry, and one common argument for this position has been to cite the talmudic aphorism "what happened – happened." The phrase itself appears in fourteen Babylonian Talmud passages,[12] and has been cited by Moshe Herr and others as a clear expression of rabbinic disregard for the past, a "lack of interest in questions that bear only 'archaeological' or historical significance."[13]

This blanket conclusion, however, warrants a reexamination. To begin with, almost all the occurrences of the phrase "what happened – happened" are unattributed to named sages, and appear in the reflections of later redactors. What these *stamma'im* (as Halivni would call them) appear to be asking is: What are questions couched in the language of historical contemplation doing in our Talmud, whose agenda was clearly shaped by other endeavors, primarily the explication of Scripture and the legal details derived from them?

A perfect example of this is the brief and anonymous discussion in B.Yoma 5b, addressing the installation of Aaron and his sons as priests:

> How [i.e., in what order] did he [Moses] dress them? What happened – happened!
>
> Rather: In the [messianic] future how will he dress them? In the future? – When Aaron and his sons come, Moses [will also be] with them!
>
> Rather: [The question] "How did he dress them?" – [is intended] to explain [conflicting] Scriptures.
>
> The sons of R. Hiyya and R. Yohanan disagree on this: One says Aaron and then his sons, the other says Aaron and his sons at the same time.

The structure of this passage represents one of the most succinct summaries of why people – and rabbis – either do or don't "do" history. The discussion opens with a question that at first glance seems to be asking how things were in the past ("wie es eigentlich gewesen ist"). This is the question of the antiquarian scholar, but the anonymous response, rather than providing an answer, deflects it by the categorization that "this is history," and, as Rashi explicates: "why should we even ask?" The imagined questioner, however, persists by introducing into the discussion the one factor that might possibly justify such a question, for it addresses the "practical" aspect of knowledge of the past, namely, its application in future situations.[14] This category, "the uses of history," is not a modern concept, and the greatest of medieval Jewish thinkers, in his famous attack on the reading of history books (and other literary genre) as "a sheer waste of time" explains that these works contain "neither wisdom nor physical usefulness" (*'ayn hokhmah bahem ve-lo' to'elet gashmit*).[15]

Nevertheless, our talmudic editor refuses to accept practicality as a sufficient justification for this departure from common rabbinic discourse, and responds with a humorous put-down of any such attempt, as if to say: Don't lose too much sleep over how Aaron and his sons will be dressed in any future Temple restoration; should Aaron and his sons reappear, they will surely be accompanied by a knowledgeable Moses!

Only in the final stage of the *sugya'* does our editor steer us back to familiar territory. The question, he explains, derives from contradictory Scriptures: Whereas Exodus 29:6–9 seems to suggest that Aaron and his sons were dressed at one and the same time, Leviticus 8:1–13 describes a sequential process: first Aaron, then his sons.

The implied message of this literary talmudic construct is thereby far more sophisticated than might appear at first glance. It is fully aware of the reasons that might lead some to inquire of the past, whether to satisfy an intellectual curiosity or to gain some practical advantage. It does not necessarily dismiss these desires as frivolous, and even the flippant reference to Moses solving halakhic problems does not imply a rabbinic rejection of a belief in, and contemplation of, an idealized future. What the passage is arguing is that these inquiries are not characteristic of talmudic discourse, which is committed primarily to an explication of Scripture,[16] and the exegetical, legal, and didactic consequences of these interpretations. "What happened – happened" is in essence a sort of signpost warning of a potential distraction, a divergence into uncharted waters, rather than a consciously stated opposition in principle to any contemplation of the past.

All this notwithstanding, it is just as obvious that the rabbis possessed a definite sensitivity to differences between past and present, through which they were able to cultivate their own unique historical consciousness. Indeed, one expression of just such an awareness that things today are not what they once were also drew the attention of the anonymous talmudic redactors, who – as in the previous case cited – wondered why this reference is even necessary, for "what happened – happened." The case centers on the mishnaic requirement that virgins be married on Wednesdays, "because the courts sit in the towns twice a week, on Mondays and on Thursdays, so that if he (= the husband) lodges a suit concerning her virginity, he may straightaway go to the court in the morning."[17] To this tannaitic statement a fourth-century 'Amora', R. Shmuel b. Yitzhak, adds the following observation: "This [practice] was only taught following the ordinance of Ezra [who established] that courts [should] sit regularly on Mondays and Thursdays, but before the ordinance of Ezra, when courts sat every day, the marriage could take place every day." Once again the anonymous talmudic redactors wonder why an 'Amora' would go out of his way to comment on the historical basis for past and present halakhic practice, for "what happened – happened"! Their solution is telling, for they claim that his intentions were relevant to the *present*, rather than merely bent on supplying us with information on the transitory nature of past Jewish behavior, concluding that "if courts *today* sat as they did prior to the days of Ezra, a woman could marry on any day" (B. Ketubbot 3a) (author's emphasis). As in the previous example, here, too, the redactors evince their own sensitivity to the talmudic agenda, which they feel should be aimed at some practical purpose, either in resolving contradictions between Scriptures or supplying us with halakhic information that bears some useful significance.

While later redactors, however, were on guard lest rabbinic discourse appear to be stepping beyond the bounds of proper rabbinic contemplation, some rabbis nevertheless were caught up with notions of past and present. In fact, expressions of how the present differs from the past appear throughout rabbinic literature, and are introduced for a wide variety of reasons. One frequent context for deliberations of this nature was the obvious disparity, noted by the rabbis, between religious or legal requirements stipulated in the Bible and contemporary practices that evince a totally different reality. Explaining these changes provided the lead into far wider discussions of how things "today" are not what they used to be. One excellent example of this process appears at the end of Tractate Sotah of the Mishnah. Chapter 9 of that tractate describes in detail the laws relating to "the breaking of the heifer's neck" (*'eglah 'arufah*), whereby the Bible (Deuteronomy 21:1–9) prescribes requisite communal behavior when a dead body is discovered and the guilty party remains unknown. After a lengthy exposition of the details prescribed in the Bible (M. Sotah 9:1–8), M. Sotah 9:9 states: "When murderers increased in numbers, the rite of *'eglah 'arufah* was abolished." This provided the perfect introduction to a far broader observation, relevant to the entire tractate: "When adulterers increased in number, the administration of the bitter water ceased, and Rabban Yohanan ben Zakkai abolished them." These two statements are significant, for they declare that the two changes in legal behavior just noted were not merely examples of a whole range of practices that were abolished – for obvious reasons – with the destruction of the Temple, but in fact were changes consciously instituted because of a perceived change in historical reality.

Having thus established the link between a fluidity in social behavior and the practical application of biblical law, the Mishnah created a platform for presenting a wide range of consequences deriving from historical change, with a bearing not only on legal practice but also on natural phenomena, behavioral patterns, and even emotional sensitivities: "From the time the Sanhedrin was abolished, singing was discontinued from banquet halls.... When the Temple was destroyed the *shamir*[18] and the honey of Zofim [apparently the choicest honey] ceased, and men of faith ceased to exist.... [F]rom the day the Temple was destroyed there is not a day without its curse, and the dew has not fallen in blessing, and the fruits have lost their flavor" (M. Sotah 9). Now the rabbis had no way of knowing how honey or fruits tasted two hundred years before their own day, and apparently their sensitivity to practical change over time was easily grafted upon their propensity for imagining an ideal past in contradistinction to a diminished present. Consequently, the Talmud attached to this mishnah a long list of contemporary moral deficiencies, citing the past causes that led to them.[19] This in itself should not be taken as a sign of historical awareness, but rather as a literary construct conjuring up an imagined past as a means of expressing dissatisfaction with current realities. But the knowledge that, in fact, the past once was different and had evolved over time, thereby effecting changes of a legal nature, created a suitable context for idealizing the past as well.

In fact, rabbinic literature is replete with phrases that suggest change. The most common of these is the phrase "at first" (bari'shonah), which frequently designates a state of religious practice or legal behavior that existed prior to a later one, or prior to the one known to us today.[20] This formula "at first ... but when such-and-such ensued it was ordained [tiknu; hitkinu] ..." or variations thereof appear quite frequently in the Mishnah, Tosefta, and the Talmuds. To be sure, the various examples can be subdivided into smaller categories, based on the nature of the causes for change (behavioral, political, the destruction of the Temple, and more), as well as the nature of the changes themselves. What is apparent at first glance is that the changes introduced into legal/religious behavior, for whatever reasons, are frequently referred to as takkanot, that is, ordinances. These ordinances never actually clash with an earlier halakhah, the rabbis felt, but rather redirected the behavior of the halakhah's practitioners to meet some new reality. This dialectic, to be sure, is the natural consequence of the challenge that practical change posed to the cardinal belief among the rabbis, that the halakhah itself was normative and unchanging from the days of Moses to their own time. Indeed, this was the clear message to be drawn from the first mishnah of tractate Avot, which lays out the chain of transmission from Sinai to contemporary rabbinic times.[21]

The belief in a normative, unchanging halakhah, however, need not assume a concomitant blanket denial of change and historical processes. Phrases such as bari'shonah, as well as other terms (batehilah, i.e., in the beginning ... but later), and in particular the designation "nowadays" (ba-zman ha-zeh), in contrast to either some earlier reality or a possible future one, clearly reflect an awareness of change, in most cases between past and present. The question is: Were the sages convinced, as the examples of Mishnah Sotah mentioned here seem to suggest, that the present is always a reduced and inauspicious reality when compared to a glorious past, or might there possibly be exceptions to this linear regression that argue for an improved and superior present when compared to the past?

One possible answer goes to the heart of rabbinic self-imagery, and may have weighed heavily on the sages' perception of the past, or, conversely, how they wished to project it. The rabbis were certainly conscious of the fact that the prophetic age of biblical times no longer exists.[22] The watershed, at least according to *Seder Olam*, was the early Hellenistic period: "He is Alexander of Macedon who ruled for twelve years; until that time the prophets prophesied through the Holy Spirit, from then on bend your ear and hear [or: heed] the words of the sages" (*Seder Olam* 30). Not only is this a clear allusion to a difference between past and present, but it may subtly even raise the question of whether the linear movement of our world is necessarily on a downward slope. The Babylonian Talmud (B. Bava Batra 12a), quoting Rav Amemar, actually proclaims that "a sage takes precedence over a prophet," while another sage, Rav Avdimi, maintains that "from the day the Temple was destroyed prophecy was taken from the prophets and given to the sages."[23] The Palestinian Talmud, in the same spirit, states that "the words of the sages are stricter [*hamurin*] than the words of the prophets," and in an explanatory parable clearly embraces the primacy of the sages:

> A prophet and a sage – to what may they be compared? To a king who sent two of his senators to a province. Concerning one he wrote: "If he does not show you my seal and signet, do not believe him," and about the other he wrote: "Even if he does not show you my seal and my signet believe him." So with the prophet it is written: "[If a prophet arises among you] ... and shows you a sign or a wonder" [Deuteronomy 13:1]. Whereas here [regarding a sage]: "According to the instruction they give you" [Deuteronomy 17:11]. (Y. Avodah Zarah 2:7, 41c)

The preference of sages to their *immediate* predecessors as leaders of Israel is even more blatant. Rabbinic literature is replete with references to the corrupt priesthood of the Late Second Temple Period,[24] and actually goes out of its way to compare the misdeeds of the "sons of Aaron" with the proper behavior of the sages, who in effect are "the disciples of Aaron."[25]

In light of such comparisons, we might certainly wonder whether the rabbis indeed suffered from a perennial inferiority complex when dealing with the past, or possibly thought that the present bears definite advantages as well. Both possibilities, we shall see presently, played major roles in the rabbinic projection of earlier Jewish history.

Indeed, one might argue for a clear rabbinic preference (at least in some circles) for the post-Temple reforms and adaptations of religious expression, when compared with a Temple cult that fell short of expectations. The somewhat enigmatic statement attributed to the third-century sage R. Eleazar – "From the day the Temple was destroyed a wall of iron separates [or: was removed; *nifsekah*] between Israel and their Father in heaven" (B. Berakhot 32b) – has been rather convincingly shown by the late Baruch Bokser to have been misunderstood, and in fact refers to the removal – rather than the establishment – of a barrier between God and the Jewish nation. R. Eleazar's statement appears within a larger treatment of the potency of prayer, and significantly, the same sage is quoted as saying that "Prayer is greater than all the sacrifices" (B. Berakhot 32b). Prayer in rabbinic eyes, however, was not just a means for petitioning God, but – together with the other major component of rabbinic Judaism, namely, the study of Torah, came to assume an alternative (and possibly higher) manifestation of worship. Bokser not only concludes that in R. Eleazar's eyes, "the post-Temple period offered more direct and greater access to God," but elsewhere maintains that by the talmudic period, the sages no longer considered their innovations as alternatives intended to fill a post-Temple vacuum, but in fact believed that "past institutions [were] superseded by the present ones and the latter are superior to the former" (Bokser 1983, 61). The degree of supersession embraced by different rabbis varies, as they all appear to be searching for its precise articulation. While some rabbis might claim that "whoever occupies himself with the law of sin-offering is regarded as if he offered a sin-offering," others, such as Rava, seem to be taking a more extreme position by claiming that "whoever occupies himself with the study of Torah *needs no* burnt-offering nor sin-offering, no meal offering nor guilt-offering".[26] It is but a small step from there to the conclusion that surely God from the outset designed these superior post-Temple rites and ideals, in which case the practices of the past were destined to be transitory all along (Bokser 1983, 57).

If, indeed, we can assume that the contemporary rabbinic Judaism espoused by certain talmudic sages held up favorably when compared with earlier expressions of the faith, issues of past and present no longer suggest a one-directional regression from the glories of the past. With this in mind, we might better understand a well-documented phenomenon in rabbinic midrash, namely, the "rabbinization of the past."

By rabbinization, I refer to the representation of earlier figures or institutions of Jewish history – primarily biblical but quite a few post-biblical ones as well[27] – in the image of the rabbinic world in which the sages functioned.

The process is evident even on the basis of a casual reading of Midrash Genesis Rabbah. The rabbinic ideal of "Talmud Torah" as the driving force in Jewish religious behavior is projected as a constant factor in the lives of the patriarchs: The children of the patriarchs study in the *batei midrash* of Shem and 'Ever;[28] Jacob strives to establish "a house of Talmud where he might teach Torah" in Egypt (Genesis Rabbah 95:3); Abraham was well versed in the prohibition of carrying on Shabbat without an *'eruv;*[29] Joseph kept the Sabbath in Egypt, and therefore prepared his Sabbath needs on Friday (Genesis Rabbah 92:4); he and his father Jacob even studied Torah together before they were separated, and because both remembered the last chapter they had covered together, it could serve as a sign through which Joseph made himself known to his father (Genesis Rabbah 94:4).[30] Indeed, once a Judaizing process brought even Adam into the Jewish fold, to the extent that he required burial in a "Jewish" cemetery,[31] we hear that he, too, was devoted to "Talmud Torah" (Sifre Devarim 41; Pirkei de-Rabbi Eliezer 12), offered sacrifices on Passover (Pirkei de-Rabbi Eliezer 21), was fastidious about keeping the Sabbath (Genesis Rabbah 16:5), and even recited Psalm 92: "*Mizmor shir le-yom ha-Shabbat*" (Genesis Rabbah 22:13). Adam's task in the Garden of Eden, "to work it and to keep it" (Genesis 2:15), was thereby easily understood as the requirement to study Torah therein (for, the rabbis ask, what physical labor or sacrificial worship was there in that distant past?) (Sifrei Devarim 41).[32] Other midrashim inform us that the three patriarchs instituted the three daily prayers, with King David establishing four prayers for the Day of Atonement (Midrash to Psalms 55:2). Yet another midrash finds Aaron teaching the ignorant how to pray and recite "*keriyat shema*" (Seder Eliyahu Rabbah 14, ed. Friedman, p. 63). In light of the rabbinic preference for prayer over sacrifices noted here, it is noteworthy that one of the outstanding features of the rabbinization of the past is not only a heightened stress on Torah study but also the attention paid by a wide range of biblical figures to prayer as well.

The phenomenon of rabbinization has been noted by numerous scholars, with the most succint and cogent discussion being that of Izḥak Heinemann (1940, 35–39), as in so many other aspects of aggadic literature. Heinemann notes that the very same rabbis who impose their contemporary rabbinic ideals on the biblical figures also express a keen awareness of this anachronistic approach. To his mind, these seemingly opposite approaches do not suggest two opposing schools of thought, but rather the tension created by the dual goals of attempting, on the one hand, to describe the heroes of the past in historical terms while simultaneously searching for the timeless truths of their acts and words, on the other.

Beyond this and other explanations,[33] there might have been an even greater stimulus for portraying the past in rabbinic terms. For those sages who, as we have seen, the Jewish religious expression of their own day had achieved a spirituality superior to earlier forms, the surest way of expressing reverence for a glorious past would be to paint that past in rabbinic tones. We have no reason to assume that the sages questioned the legitimacy of their own lifestyle, certainly not the 'Amora'im who were the major practitioners of rabbinization, and who had inherited a post-Temple reality that by their day had accrued a 150-year pedigree of acceptance. Rather, if any group in the collective Jewish memory lacked such impeccable credentials, it would be the ancients, who had not been privy to those loftier expressions of Jewish behavior embraced by the rabbis. And yet if those earlier generations were blessed by God, as the Bible seems to make evident, and consequently merit our veneration, surely they must have been party to that knowledge that would ultimately serve as the permanent guideline for proper Jewish behavior.

Moreover, the converse situation seems to prove this mind-set. When were various leaders of past generations punished or given to a variety of harsh decrees? Precisely when they did *not* adhere to the very principles that constitute the core of rabbinic Judaism. Thus, we are informed that "Jerusalem was only destroyed because of the sin of *bitul Torah* [neglect of Torah]";[34] "Jerusalem was only destroyed because the recitation of *shema* morning and evening was neglected"; "Jerusalem was only destroyed because they [abandoned the teaching] of schoolchildren"; and the most telling example claims that Jerusalem was destroyed because "they showed disrespect for sages" (B. Shabbat 119b = Lamentation Rabbah 1). Disrespect for *talmidei ḥakhamim* was not limited to the Second Temple Period, and the Babylonian Talmud had no difficulty making the following projection from present to past: "Why was our Patriarch Abraham punished and his sons enslaved in Egypt for 210 years? Because he enforced *angaria* [military service] on *talmidei ḥakhamim*, as it is written: 'He armed his dedicated servants'" [Genesis 14:14] (B. Nedarim 32a). What we appear to confront in these cases is a "de-rabbinization" of a "rabbinized" past, that is, a situation where ancient figures who ought to be behaving in proper rabbinic fashion somehow fall short and are therefore punished. But not only do bad things happen to good people in the rabbinic reshaping of the past. The converse also transpires, and those who appear to us as evil are actually rewarded for the respect they reportedly evinced toward rabbis and Torah learning:

> R.Yohanan said: Why did Ahab warrant a reign of twenty-two years? Because he respected the Torah that was given in twenty-two letters.... Ahab was willing to part with his money, and because he supported *talmidei ḥakhamim* from his wealth, half [of his sins] were forgiven. (B. Sanhedrin 102b)[35]

How interesting that the outstanding sins of the past, as well as the unknown good deeds of otherwise evil people, were precisely those aspects that constituted the essence of rabbinic Judaism.

Indeed, some scholars have taken this rabbinic manipulation of the past a step further, suggesting that the rabbinic treatment of biblical figures, by imposing upon them otherwise unattested misbehavior or, conversely, attributing laudatory practices to seemingly unworthy individuals, was actually a way of dealing with *post-biblical* Jewish personalities and communal leaders. V. Aptowitzer was convinced that rabbinic statements of either support or opposition to King David were, in essence, the masked residue of Second Temple political alliances that either supported or opposed the Hasmonean monarchy.[36] More recent scholars have suggested that rabbinic treatment of the sons of Moses or Eli were, in fact, a means of voicing criticism of contemporary rabbinic tendencies toward nepotism.[37] But while the past may have served as a prop for addressing more recent social tensions,[38] pointing to specific cases remains a decidedly speculative exercise at best, and frequently reflects more on the agenda-driven imagination of later writers than on original rabbinic motives.[39]

Nevertheless, the tendency to "rabbinize" the past obviously contributed to a clouding of delineation between past and present, and consequently we, as readers of rabbinic literature, come away not only with a sense of anachronism but also a total disregard for historical processes and changes in the rabbinic mind. The truth, however, might be somewhat more complex. The rabbis may have been acutely aware of the changes that ensued throughout Jewish history, and especially cognizant of what they considered a heightened spiritual status for Jewish behavior in its rabbinic image. But in contradistinction to Christian historiography that raised the supersession of present religious understanding as taught by the Church, when compared to earlier contexts, to theological heights, the rabbis were not willing to relegate the past to the status of a *praeparatio evangelica*. The path chosen to ensure an untarnished past, notwithstanding their conviction that a sage takes precedence over a prophet and that prayer is more effective than sacrifice, was the process of rabbinizing the past. And thus, while Eusebius in the introduction to his *Ecclesiastical History* (Chapter 4) is convinced that Abraham and his contemporaries did *not* keep the Sabbath or abstain from certain foods, "nor regard other injunctions which Moses subsequently delivered to be observed," the rabbis would embark on a totally different path. To be sure, the sages were not the originators of the idea that the commandments were already known – and to a major degree observed – by Adam and Abraham, as this was already one of the central themes in the Book of Jubilees.[40] But, as noted earlier, the Sifre and other midrashim seem to have gone beyond Jubilees. While Genesis Rabbah (16:5) does suggest that Adam offered sacrifices (as does Jubilees), the Sifre Devarim (41) already suggests that the study of Torah has supplanted, or at least is equal to, sacrifice as the true interpretation of the commandment to Adam to "work" the Garden of Eden (*le-'abdah*).[41]

With the advent of the Church and its teachings, the significance of Adam's offering sacrifices or keeping the Sabbath according to the rabbis took on new meaning, and is seen by some as a rabbinic response to the antinomian claims based on Adam's ignorance and nonobservance of these *mitzvot*.[42] But while the practical observation of the Law by pre-Sinaitic figures predates the rabbis, the more thorough rabbinization of the past by endowing it with a more focused stress on uniquely post-Destruction religious and social categories was clearly the work of talmudic sages, emerging primarily in amoraic (and not tannaitic) literature. The rabbis may have been motivated, at least in part, by a wish to avoid the type of supersession imagery embraced by the Church. However, in fact they were, to a certain degree, doing precisely what the Fathers had done, namely, applying to the patriarchs a more spiritualized behavior in manifesting their Jewish identity. This process, however, was not accompanied with a removal of the Jubilees phenomena that projected the ancients as performing the commandments, in contradistinction to those Church Fathers who were careful to project Adam and Abraham as *not* having kept practical commandments and thus serving as ideal prototypes for the contemporary Church. Both communities, it would seem, share a model of an idealized past, corrupted just prior to their own appearance (so in the rabbinic version; the Church dated the corruption much earlier), which then ushered in a superior model – which must have been the divinely fashioned one that rendered all previous religious expression tentative and transitory. While not "history," the past now assumed enormous importance in the religious constructs of both communities. One can only wonder to what degree proximity of time and place indeed contributed to these radically different – and yet in certain cases quite similar – fashionings of the past by both groups of religious leaders.

Notes

1. *Antiquities* 20:264. This passage has recently been subjected to a detailed analysis in Milikowsky 2002; Milikowsky suggests that the two terms cited by Josephus, "knowledge of the law" and "interpretation of the holy writings" are the precise equivalents of the rabbinic categories of "*mishnah*" and "*midrash*."

2. The idiosyncratic midrash known as "Seder Olam," while evincing an antiquarian curiosity, is not really an investigation of the past in the manner of classical historiography, but instead is a close reading of the biblical narrative, aimed at enhancing our understanding of the events by drawing on certain chronological connections implicit in the text itself. Milikowsky has produced a critical edition of Seder Olam together with a comprehensive introduction not only to the work itself but to the entire question of Jewish historiographical efforts in the classical era. The work is scheduled to be published by the Israel Academy of Sciences; see for now: Milikowsky 1985.

3. D. R. Schwartz 1999.

4. B. Lewis 1975, 19; Lewis points to a similar fear of historiography in Shi'ite Islam (ibid., 23–25).

5. Y. Peah 2:6, 17a and parallels; Schwartz (1999, 46 n. 6) cites this tension and sees it as the determining factor in removing the parameter of time from rabbinic thinking, "for if what is destined to transpire already existed from the beginning, there is no place for significant change through time."

6. Kochan 1977, 1–6; Meyer 1987, 13.

7. Cf. S. J. D. Cohen 1985; curiously, and as yet unexplained satisfactorily by modern scholars, many of these parallels found their way into the Babylonian Talmud, rather than into rabbinic sources of Palestinian provenance.

8. Cf. J. Derenbourg 1867; for a recent attempt at enlisting rabbinic sources for the study of Second Temple social history, see Baumgarten 1995.

9. Kalmin 2002.

10. Cf. M. Hagigah 2:1, T. Hagigah 2:7, Genesis Rabbah 1:10.

11. Genesis Rabbah 63:6; A succinct and cogent discussion of this phenomenon, citing the example of Rebecca, is that of Heinemann 1940, 35–39; Yerushalmi 1989, 123 n. 21, obviously follows Heinemann here.

12. For a list of these passages, and a discussion of the phrase and its implications, see Gafni 1996, 29–32 and n. 34.

13. Herr 1977; cf. Urbach 1976. Urbach maintains that in certain cases, the phrase seems to imply that events that have transpired cannot be changed

(fait accompli), and this, he maintains, might qualify the decidedly ahistorical tendency read into the phrase by most scholars.

14. See, for example, Tosh 1991, 27: "Society expects an interpretation of the past which is relevant to the present and a basis for formulating decisions about the future."

15. Maimonides, Commentary to the Mishnah, Sanhedrin 10:1, following the translation of Rabbi Joseph Kafah, Jerusalem 1964, 210. For the most detailed analysis of Maimonides' position, see Baron 1934–35; see also Schachter 1998–99, 252 n. 10.

16. See Milikowsky 1985: "For the rabbis the all-important pivot was the Bible.... The study of the past was not an independent value but directly derived from the crucial significance of the biblical text" (119–20).

17. M. Ketubot 1:1; the sages frowned on Sunday weddings, which might cause a desecration of the Sabbath, and so the Wednesday option was the only other acceptable one.

18. The *shamir*, according to talmudic legend, was a worm that was able to cut through the hardest of surfaces, and was therefore used by King Solomon to hew the building stones for the Temple.

19. B. Sotah 47b: "When hedonists (*ba'alei hana'ah*) multiplied justice became perverted, conduct deteriorated, and there is no satisfaction [to God] in the world.... When they who draw out their spittle [Rashi: a sign of arrogance] multiplied, the arrogant increased, disciples diminished, and Torah went about looking for them who would study it. When the arrogant multiplied, the daughters of Israel began to marry arrogant men, because our generation looks only to outward appearance.... [W]hen there multiplied they who accepted charity from gentiles, Israel became on top and they below, Israel went forward and they backward" (a euphemistic reverse of what actually transpired; for the historical context of this last statement, see Urbach 1951). Inasmuch as the practical moral implications of these references to the past were explicit, it is not surprising that the anonymous redactors refrained from commenting "What happened – happened."

20. See, for example, M. Bikkurim 3:7.

21. I take issue here with Urbach (1976), who maintains that "the well-known chain of tradition in the first Mishnah of Avot testifies to a historical consciousness." More recently, A. Tropper has argued that the chain of rabbinic tradition in Avot is modeled after the contrived intellectual pedigrees produced within certain Greek circles at the time, namely, those of the Second Sophistic. See Tropper 2004a and 2004b.

22. See Urbach 1946; also Milikowsky 1994.

23. Milikowsky 1994, 90 n. 34, notes the inconsistency between these statements as a sign of their obvious tendentiousness; he considers contrary statements attributed to other sages, such as R. Yohanan's famous pronouncement that with the destruction of the Temple prophecy was granted "to fools and children" (B. Bava Batra 12b), to be responses to the position espoused by R. Avdimi.

24. E.g. T. Menahot 13:20 and B.Pesahim 57a ("Woe is me of the House of Ishmael ben Phiabi, woe is me of their fists; for they are High Priests,

and their sons are treasurers, and their sons-in-law are trustees and their servants beat the people with sticks"). Murder in the Temple among the priests was also cited by the sages; cf. T. Kippurim 1:12.

25. B.Yoma 71b; see Urbach 1975, 575; recent scholarship has posited a continued role and vital communal position for the priests even after the destruction of the Second Temple, in which case rabbinic aspersions on past priests might not be devoid of a more immediate polemical agenda. For a list of recent work on priesthood following the Destruction, see Kalmin 2002, 50 n. 107.

26. B. Menahot 110a; cf. Urbach 1975, 610–11.

27. Cf. S. J. D. Cohen 1985, 11–12; by comparing the limited rabbinic references to certain leaders of the Second Temple Period with the information on them supplied by Josephus, Cohen maintains that the sages rabbinized priests such as Joshua ben Gamla and Simon the Righteous, as well as Babylonian Jews who found their way to Roman Judaea, such as the residents of "Bathyra," to no less a degree than they did biblical figures, with the classic example from the Bible being Moses, "our rabbi."

28. E.g., Genesis Rabbah 63:10 (Jacob sat in "tents" [Genesis 25:27] – signifying two "tents," i.e., "the *bet midrash* of Shem and the *bet midrash* of Ever"); cf. Kugel 1990, 101. See also Genesis Rabbah 56:11, where Isaac is sent to Ever to study Torah after surviving the *'akedah*.

29. Specifically an *'eruv hazerot*. Bereshit Rabbah 49:2; in Bereshit Rabbah 95:3, he was also careful about *'eruv tavshilin*. For Abraham as the prototype of the Torah sage see I. Jacobs 1995, 79–94.

30. Cf. Kugel 1990, 102–3.

31. For the removal of Adam's gravesite from Jerusalem to Hebron, see I. Gafni 1987.

32. Cf. S. Fraade 1991, 89–92.

33. Yerushalmi 1989, 18, likewise stresses that the nature of the rabbinic enterprise dictated their anachronistic representation of the past; rather than adhering to "what really happened," "they were engrossed in an ongoing exploration of the meaning of the history bequeathed to them, striving to interpret it in living terms for their own and later generations"; a more recent comment on the phenomenon, by R. Kalmin, suggests that the preponderance of rabbinization in the Babylonian Talmud reflects the greater insularity of Babylonian sages, who, he claims, interacted primarily with other rabbis rather than with non-rabbinic circles; cf. R. Kalmin 2002, 17, 50–52, and R. L. Kalmin 1999, 101–9.

34. Ekhah Rabbah, ed. Buber, 1 (= Avot de-R. Nathan, vers. B, chap. 5).

35. See also B. Sanhedrin 103b, for Ahab's comprehensive study of Leviticus.

36. Aptowitzer 1927; Aptowitzer assumed that pro-Davidic rabbinic statements, even covering up his obvious transgressions, were intended to underscore their dissatisfaction with the usurpation of the Davidic role by the Hasmoneans. Anti-Davidic sentiment, on the other hand, was a way of legitimizating the appropriation of the monarchy by the Hasmoneans.

37. Cf. Beer 1976 and 1977.

38. See the recent studies of Kalmin 1999, 83–93 (King David), 94–100 (Moses).

39. A case in point is the oft-repeated claim that the rabbis "ignored the battles of the Maccabees in favor of the cruse of oil that burned for eight days," Yerushalmi 1989, 25; this statement of "fact," which began to assume currency among early modern Jewish scholars who took for granted a rabbinic spiritualizing and subsequent reshaping of history, simply does not stand up to a comprehensive examination of all the rabbinic references to the Hasmonean episode; cf. Gafni 1995.

40. See the references in Ginzberg 2003, 259 n. 275.

41. See the citations in Fraade 1991, 240 nn. 72 and 73.

42. Cf. Ginzberg 2003, vol. 5, 93 n. 55.

14 Rabbinical Ethical Formation and the Formation of Rabbinic Ethical Compilations

JONATHAN WYN SCHOFER

In the rabbinic communities of Late Antiquity, the study of texts was framed as not only a process of mastering information but also an intrinsic element in the development of the disciple's character. The student was to shape desires and impulses through the guidance of teachers, and the teacher's role, in turn, was to convey, represent, and embody the models of inspiring sages from the past. The material was performed in a context of teaching and learning – spoken, heard, read, and written – where its internalization and creative appropriation could be a key element in the transformation of a student into a cultivated member of the rabbinic movement. Most all of rabbinic literature has ethical or moral dimensions, but some texts reveal a particular focus upon ideal comportment and internal states of mind and sentiment.

A prominent feature of rabbinic ethical literature is that it is not only descriptive but also prescriptive. The sources portray the workings of emotions and desires as well as the details of sagacious behavior, and they also address the reader directly and convey values. Studying the textual sources that are central to the formation of rabbinic character, then, requires us to attend closely to the genres and styles of expression in the literature. This essay will begin with an overview of key themes in rabbinic ethics, but the bulk of the discussion concerns various forms of rabbinic instruction imbedded in the literature. After summarizing features of the distinctly ethical anthologies, I will present exemplary cases illustrating a few of the many ways that ethical teaching emerges and develops through maxims, exegesis, parables, and narratives.

ETHICAL THEMES AND CONCERNS

As with terms such as "rabbinic" and "literature" discussed in the Introduction, there is no classical rabbinic term equivalent to "ethics." Rather, ethics is a contemporary category that we can employ in order to arrange, identify, and exposit clusters of themes that are present but not named as such in the material. Rabbinic ethical instruction is not systematic but, rather, consists of distinct teachings that are edited, arranged, and commented upon in innumerable combinations and variations. Any definition of "rabbinic ethics," then, will not illuminate a comprehensive, unified ethic but instead will be a pragmatic starting point for thinking about particular teachings and their arrangements, connections, and contrasts.

The word "ethics" has its roots in an ancient Greek term with a range of meanings that include custom, disposition, and character. This sense of ethics was prevalent in the Hellenistic philosophical schools that preceded and, to some degree, overlapped with the late ancient rabbis, and more generally these schools saw philosophy as central to an art of living that encompassed multiple aspects of a person's development. The scope of ethics, however, has narrowed significantly in European and North American philosophical discussions of modernity. Today, many ethical debates concern not character in a broad sense but procedures of reasoning that lead to a given action: for example, asking what rules should guide behavior, or how one can generate the greatest positive consequences. Still, certain modern and postmodern approaches to ethics, such as "virtue ethics" and study of the "subject" and its formation, have defined ethics in an expansive sense drawing from ancient usages.[1] The specific contents and features of late ancient rabbinic ethical instruction call for a definition of ethics that concerns character as developed through study and practice of the Torah. My starting point draws from contemporary work on virtue ethics and subject formation, adapting their approaches in light of rabbinic thought, to set out three key elements.

First, rabbis were concerned with describing the emotions and desires in their spontaneous or unreformed states. Accounts of human nature address the raw material that is to be channeled through cultural processes of transformation. As with other aspects of rabbinic culture, embodied existence is a crucial presupposition, and this body is generally presumed to be male with heterosexual desires that are often of great concern. Numerous ethical teachings also emphasize the finitude of the body and its end in dust, worms, and maggot.[2] Specific bodily functions – including those related to consumption and excretion – are often the focus of attention in guidelines for behavior. Emotions and desires tend to be located in specific organs, most notably the heart (which often is the seat of thought as well) but also the kidneys and liver. Perhaps the most important category that rabbis employ to describe instincts and inclinations is the *yezer*, a word that is based on the root for "formation" and denotes the impulses that are formed by the heart. As I will discuss in detail, many teachings set out a duality of two impulses, a "bad" one that is chaotic, uncultured, or even actively transgressive, and a "good" one that guides and regulates according to the instructions of Torah and divine precepts (perhaps the closest analogues to these constructs in today's terminology are the psychoanalytic "id" and "superego").

Second, rabbinic ethical sources set out ideal actions and states of character, the ultimate goal or *telos* of self-cultivation. The perfected rabbi is a sage, a wise man whose desires are fully shaped by the wisdom of Torah and the practices that it sets out. The virtues associated with Torah are sometimes characterized through lists, the longest of which includes forty-eight qualities (Avot 6:5). Often ideals are portrayed through narratives in which sages and biblical characters display correct behavior, whether in the course of instruction, or through encountering various tests of their characters, or through their interactions with one another. Other stories (particularly in Babylonian sources) present flawed or conflicted heroes, reflecting upon virtues by showing the failures of rabbis in attaining them. Ethical cultivation is not separated from worldly and spiritual benefits, in part because of the theological belief that God rewards right action. If all is right in the world, a perfected sage would receive both wealth and mystical experience, such as death through a kiss from God, as divine response to his life's course.[3] However, at least some teachings emphasize that one should not be motivated by desire for such reward, but rather out of love and reverence (*'ahavah* and *yir'ah*) for the deity.

The third element of rabbinic ethics, which in many ways encompasses the first two, is the path that one takes to attain the ideal: the process of transformation from the initial, natural state to the perfected, cultivated character. In rabbinic ethics, this transformation centers on study and practice of Torah, as well as the appropriate worship of the God of Israel. Rather than competing with the observance of law, rabbinic ethics frames legal guidance as central to self-cultivation. Individual passages vary, though, as to whether they concern halakhic observance as such (addressing all observant Jews) or a more full immersion in a community of disciples centered on a sagely teacher. The ethical anthologies taken as a whole, though, tend to have overarching scholastic concerns.

When describing the changes from a natural state to the ideal, such as the shaping of bad impulses in relation to the good, the texts use a range of metaphors to describe the students' relations to the sages, to the Torah that they practice, and to the God whose commandments they observe. One set of images centers on nourishment and growth: The sages' words may be water that quenches thirst, or Torah may be food that strengthens the body, or Torah may grow within the self. Other motifs have more harsh tones, as when the student submits to his tradition as a farm animal to a yoke, or as metal to fire, or as a subject to a king. In these cases, religious authority is portrayed as more powerful than the disciple, but ultimately the student forms himself through that power and internalizes some of it in his development.

ETHICAL ANTHOLOGIES

Recent scholars have drawn much attention to the anthological nature of rabbinic sources, such as the Talmuds and the midrashic collections.[4] Ethical instruction appears throughout those compilations in a variety of ways, and in addition, some rabbinic circles produced anthologies specifically focusing on the development of ideal character and action. The most distinctive rhetorical form in these anthologies is the short maxim or saying: dense, compact words of wisdom, often attributed to a particular sage and often presented in imperatives that address the reader or listener directly. These expressions may be developed through commentary in which the entire maxim, or distinct elements, become points of discussion, elaboration, and emendation. In these materials, the widespread rabbinic concern with instruction of the student is particularly prominent, and a key scholarly challenge is to envision how the text was conveyed through the voices of actual sages and responded to by students who would appropriate the teachings in their decision making and character development.

Ethical literature tends to appear in the form of tannaitic sources: written in Hebrew and naming early sages as speakers of sayings and as characters in narratives. The texts were probably very fluid throughout Late Antiquity, often circulating in parts, likely growing by accretion through numerous editorial hands, with their final composition sometime after that of the Babylonian Talmud. We cannot define a single date of their composition, then, but rather a timeline that includes the formation of many maxims and narratives in the first centuries C.E., the creation of anthologies perhaps in the sixth through eighth centuries, and the earliest surviving manuscripts written several centuries later in the Middle Ages. The dating of any specific passage, though, has to be carried out on a case-by-case basis.[5]

The most commented upon and prominently located of the ethical texts is known as Avot, a title that is generally translated as "Fathers" and understood as referring to the early sages named in the text. The word *'avot* also has the overtone of basic principles or primary categories – such as *'avot mela'khah* (classes of work prohibited on the Sabbath) and *'avot nezikim* (primary types of injury or damage)[6] – which may characterize the contents of the maxims. Tractate Avot was a late addition to the Mishnah, and it also came to be studied on the Sabbath in Jewish communities starting in Gaonic times, which led to its circulation in prayer books.[7] Over the course of later Jewish tradition, Avot became a center point of ethical reflection and generated innumerable commentaries. The first of these, which began to develop alongside the composition of Avot itself, is Avot de-Rabbi Natan (*The Fathers According to Rabbi Nathan*). This great compilation develops the maxims of Avot through *midrash* and narrative, and it also includes many additional sayings. The text has been preserved in two major versions, each of which has distinct features, which are labeled as "A" and "B."

Two other key texts are Derekh Erez Rabbah and Derekh Erez Zuta: the "large" and "small" collections concerning *derekh 'erez*. This phrase literally means "way of the land," and in rabbinic sources it appears with a number of quite divergent senses, including worldly or business matters, sexual activity, etiquette, and supererogatory activity (actions beyond what is required by basic legal or ethical guidelines). These collections tend to focus on manners, the details of students' behavior during study as well as in everyday life, and certain emotional ideals. Both are anthologies of smaller manuals that likely circulated independently in Late Antiquity as guides for conduct, and researchers have often studied and translated the parts in discreet units. Commentary to large portions of the Derekh Erez texts appears now in Kallah Rabbati ("the large text concerning brides"). Kallah Rabbati differs from The Fathers According to Rabbi Nathan in that the exegesis of the maxims employs much Aramaic and is closer in style to that of the Babylonian Talmud. Derekh Erez Zuta has also been associated in both themes and content with a large and quite beautifully written ethical midrash entitled Tanna Devei Eliyahu ("the teachings of the School of Elijah," also known as Seder Eliyahu Rabbah and Zuta).[8]

These ethical collections appear to have circulated in a variety of literary and material contexts, for we now have them preserved in several different arrangements. For printed editions of the Babylonian Talmud, many of the ethical texts were collected and located among the extracanonical tractates: Avot de-Rabbi Natan Version A, Derekh Erez Rabbah and Zuta, and Kallah Rabbati. Other combinations have existed, as manuscripts contain ethical sources in groups with midrashic sources and other materials. One particularly interesting early modern (1600 C.E.) handbook is now in the library of the Jewish Theological Seminary: It groups together biblical writings attributed to Solomon (Proverbs and the Song of Songs) with portions of the *Derekh Erez* material, all in Hebrew with Judeo-Persian translation (MS L 433, Adler 428). This compilation may have been some form of a conduct manual, with biblical and rabbinic wisdom gathered in a compact package that includes both sacred language and vernacular. Over the centuries, then, ethical texts have been incorporated into the larger matrix of the Bavli in a somewhat ancillary position, and they have also had an independent life, sometimes disseminated in forms whose structure implies a distinct concern for instruction and guidance.

The social setting presented and presumed by the ethical anthologies is a scholastic community in which the purpose of study is twofold: It is an intellectual activity, and it sets out a way of life that distinguishes the participants from the broader society.[9] Ethical materials often reveal a strong concern with the dynamics of this setting – the comportment that teachers should have toward students, students toward teachers, and students with other students. For example, teachers are instructed to "raise up many students" and to "be careful" with their words in their teaching of Torah (Avot 1:1, 1:11). Students are told, "Let your house be a meeting place for the sages, sit in the very dust of their feet, and drink with thirst their words" (Avot 1:4). One commentary to this maxim specifies the student's relation to the sage as one of subordination to an authoritative figure: "For every word that emerges from your mouth, let him receive it upon himself in awe, fear, trembling, and shaking." Elsewhere in the same text, this fourfold emotional response describes Moses' state when receiving the Torah at Sinai (Avot de-Rabbi Natan *A*, Chaps. 1, 6; ed. Schechter, p. 1, 27).[10]

Teachings often address day-to-day concerns of students. A crucial maxim instructs, "Appoint for yourself a teacher, acquire for yourself a fellow [*ḥaver*], and judge every man with the scales weighted in his favor" (Avot 1:6). The word "fellow" (*ḥaver*) has a range of meanings centering on sharing and friendship, including the sense of a "fellow" in maintaining piety, righteousness, purity, or Torah study. Commentary upon the saying, moreover, emphasizes that fellows should eat together, worship together, read together, and, if they are unmarried, sleep together (Avot de-Rabbi Natan *A*, chap. 8; ed. Schechter, p. 36). Other ethical maxims address students' relations with one another and with teachers in their everyday lives – at the dining table, when walking between houses, when entering others' houses, in the bathhouse, and at the toilet (Derekh Ereẓ Rabbah, Chaps. 4–10). All social space, not only the study house, becomes pedagogical – offering the opportunity and responsibility for learning behavior appropriate for the students of the sages.

In the rest of this survey, I set out exemplary cases of rabbinic ethical instruction. Each illustrates a range of themes and a set of rhetorical forms. Two of them show how distinctly ethical sources relate to or are incorporated into other rabbinic materials. I begin with a prominent saying and its commentary.

A MAXIM AND ETHICAL EXEGESIS: "MAKE A FENCE FOR THE TORAH"

The first maxim in Avot is attributed to the Great Assembly, a legendary group that would have existed sometime in the Second Temple Period before the second century B.C.E.:[11] "Be patient in judgment, raise up many disciples, and make a fence for the Torah" ('Avot 1:1). What does the last imperative mean?[12] The rabbinic exegesis in Avot de-Rabbi Natan does not try to fix a singular meaning to the "fence" but, rather, offers a multiplicity of interpretations:

> *Make a fence for the Torah.*
> And make a fence for your words, in the way that The Holy One,
>   blessed be He, made a fence for His words,
> and the first Adam made a fence for his words.
> Torah made a fence for her words.
> Moses made a fence for his words.
> So too, Job as well as the Prophets, the Writings, and the Sages – all
>   of them made a fence for their words. (Avot de-Rabbi Natan *A*,
>   Chap. 1; ed. Schechter, p. 3)

The commentary first makes a significant shift, glossing "Torah" as "your words," and the instruction becomes "Make a fence for your words." Implicit in this change is a strong link between Torah as teaching that is performed verbally and the words of instruction that circulate in a scholastic setting: Torah is oral, and speech in the disciple circle is Torah. The text then lists eight different "fences," each of which is discussed at length later.

Of the eight fences that are discussed, the one that is conceptually most basic is not the first but the last, the fence of the sages. The key point, which appears with some variations in several other rabbinic sources as well, is that one should follow a stricter standard than explicitly stated in the Bible in order to avoid transgressing divine law. The specific example in Avot de-Rabbi Natan is the latest time that one can say the evening *Shema*. The legal boundary is dawn, but the sages counsel that one should do the ritual by midnight or earlier in order to ensure that one does not fall asleep and fail entirely (Avot de-Rabbi Natan *A*, Chap. 2; ed. Schechter, p. 14).[13]

In four of the fences – those attributed to Torah, Moses, Job, and the Writings – this legal hermeneutic is extended into the realm of ethics, particularly self-control. For each case, the fence is found within the Bible itself – one scriptural verse is taken to be the fence for a rule stated in another verse. For example, the fence of the Torah is based upon two passages in the Book of Leviticus that command "do not come near" a woman. The first centers on the law prohibiting a man from having intercourse with a menstruating woman, in Leviticus 18:

> Which fence did the Torah make around her words? It says, "To a women in her time of menstrual impurity, do not come near to uncover her nakedness" [Leviticus 18:19].
>
> Could he hug her, kiss her, and speak idle chatter with her? Scripture says, "Do not come near."
>
> Could he sleep with her, when she wears her clothes, upon a bed? Scripture says, "Do not come near."
>
> Could she wash her face, or color her eyes? Scripture says, "Concerning the woman who is unwell [*ha-davah*] in her menstrual impurity . . . " [Leviticus 15:33]. All the days that she is in menstrual impurity [*she-beniddah*], she shall be in isolation [*beniddui*].
>
> From this they say: For any woman who disfigures herself in the days of menstrual impurity, the spirit of the sages is satisfied with her. For any woman who adorns herself in her days of impurity, the spirit of the sages is not satisfied with her. (Avot de-Rabbi Natan *A*, Chap. 2; ed. Schechter, pp. 8–9)[14]

This passage is built upon the intersection of two different passages in Leviticus that concern a man's relations with a menstruating woman. In Leviticus 18, intercourse with a woman during her menstrual period is named as a prohibited sexual relation, along with such practices as incest and bestiality. Their punishment is *karet*, or "extirpation," which rabbis understood as premature death through divine judgment. Leviticus 15 presents the matter in a very different way, with menstruation bringing a state of impurity upon a woman that can be transmitted to her husband if he touches or has intercourse with her. One who becomes unclean in this way must carry out rituals of purification and bring an offering to the Temple. In much of rabbinic literature, these two ways of conceptualizing menstruation are combined. The laws of purity in relation to the Temple ritual are no longer in effect, and the expression "I am impure" is used to say "I am menstruating, and therefore sexually prohibited."[15]

In this passage, however, a different and very specific relation is found between the two passages. The laws of purity in Leviticus 15:19–24 are taken to be the base law, stating that a man who is in a pure state should not touch a woman during her menstrual period. For Leviticus 18:19, the midrash interprets the command "do not come near" in hyperliteral terms: The biblical euphemism for intercourse becomes an instruction not to approach a woman in any way while she is menstruating. Then the exegesis proscribes any action that could lead to the arousal of sexual desire – hugging, kissing, speaking flirtatiously, or sleeping in the same bed while clothed. A man is told both to restrain himself and to keep women distant. The ethical teaching also says that a woman must make herself unattractive to men in order to limit their desire, and this point is reinforced through emphasizing a biblical verse in which a word meaning "sick" or "unwell" is used for a menstruant (*ha-davah*).

The second case of rabbis portraying the Torah as establishing a fence around its own laws is Leviticus 18:6, which states that one should not "come near" a close relative "to uncover nakedness." The implicit law inside the fence here is incest, and again the ethical instruction seizes upon the call for distance and interprets it in an expansive way:

> Thus it says, "For all men: to one of his own flesh, do not come near . . . " [Leviticus 18:6].
>
> From here they say, a man should not join with any of the women at an inn, even with his sister or his daughter, because of public opinion.
>
> He should not tell stories with a woman in the market, even if she is his wife – and needless to say, with another woman – because of public suspicion. (Avot de-Rabbi Natan *A*, Chap. 2; ed. Schechter, pp. 8–9)

The exegesis generalizes a concern with incest in two respects. First, the focus shifts from the actual act to appearances (*mar'it ha-'ayin*): The man should not only avoid transgression but also avoid generating public suspicion of transgression. Second, even though the biblical verses concern family members, the ethical instruction becomes far more comprehensive, calling for distance from any woman.

These passages, then, teach two distinct forms of boundary marking through the biblical command "do not come near" – one case concerning a man and a menstruating woman in private, and the other concerning a man and any woman in public. The editors, then, derives a more general principle that is expressed through two ethical maxims:

> It is said here [Leviticus 18:19], "do not come near," and it is said there, [Leviticus 18:6], "do not come near." To anything that brings one to the hands of transgression, do not come near. Distance yourself from that which is hideous and that which resembles something hideous. Therefore, the Sages said: Distance yourself from a minor sin lest it bring you to a major sin. Run to fulfill a minor commandment, for it will bring you to a great commandment. (Avot de-Rabbi Natan *A*, Chap. 2; ed. Schechter, pp. 8–9)

The biblical commands "do not come near" are framed as specific instances of the ideal of maintaining "distance" from whatever is hideous or improper (a similar maxim appears independently in Derekh Erez Zuta 1:13). Then, this entire discussion becomes the support for an instruction to develop proper habits in observance, since sin leads to more sin and observance to more observance (compare Avot 4:2).

The broad statement about distance that concludes the Torah's fence appears at the opening of a different account of hedging, Job's fence (even though the latter discussion does not follow immediately upon the former). God states that Job is constantly "turning from wrong" (Job 1:8), and the interpretation of this spatial metaphor is that "Job distanced himself from anything that may bring him to transgression, from that which is hideous and that which resembles something hideous." What is Job's specific way of preserving this distance? The Ten Commandments prohibit both adultery and coveting another man's wife, and Job makes a fence for these laws:

> Thus it says, "I made a covenant with my eyes, lest I gaze at a virgin" [Job 31:1]. This teaches that Job was strict with himself and did not even look [*nistakkel*] at a virgin.
>
> Thus we reason from the minor case to the major: If with a virgin – whom if he wanted he could marry for himself, or to his son, or to his brothers, or to his cousin – Job was strict with himself and did not look [*nistakkel*] at her; how much the more so with a man's wife!

Why was Job strict with himself and would not even look [*nistakkel*] at a virgin? Because Job thought: Perhaps I will stare ['*estakkel*] today, and tomorrow another man will come and marry her. Then it will be found that I was looking [*mistakkel*] at another man's wife. (Avot de-Rabbi Natan *A*, Chap. 2; ed. Schechter, pp. 12–13)

The "virgin" of Job 31:1 is interpreted as being any woman eligible for marriage. Job's "covenant" not to gaze at such a woman is developed through verbs with the root *s-k-l* (*nistakkel, mistakkel*), which have senses of both vision and contemplation. Strictness regarding the gaze is a way of both setting limits on his own desire and maintaining separation from women. Why is this necessary? The justification is elaborate: If he lusts after an unmarried woman, in the future another man may marry her, and Job would retroactively be guilty of lusting after another man's wife (note that the concern here is not with the impact upon the woman but upon her future husband). The standard is high: A man should suppress desire not only for other men's wives but for any woman who could become another man's wife (compare Matt. 5:27–30).

The fences of Torah and Job are only two of the four ethical fences, but they exemplify central thematic issues. The legal hermeneutic of setting out guidelines that are stricter than those in Scripture is elaborated with a focus upon self-control. The motifs of distance and limitation are developed in complex ways: Male sexual craving is framed as problematic, and an aspiring sage fences out women and sin in general, and fences in his own desire and gaze. The tropes, then, become a way of orienting toward the law and understanding its relation to one's own desires and impulses. This all occurred in a context where rabbis were relatively immersed in broader social relations. The ethical literature presumes that they will be in the markets and inns, among other things interacting with women. In these contexts and through this exegesis, the Great Assembly's fence becomes a discursive, figurative way of maintaining separation from external stimuli and of controlling internal impulses that inspire improper action.

A MAXIM AND ITS TRAVELS

In the fence of Job presented in Avot de-Rabbi Natan, we saw rabbinic concern with limiting a man's desire to look at a woman, and the key term for this dangerous looking was *mistakkel*. In the Mishnah and the amoraic midrashic collection Genesis Rabbah, which are earlier sources, the same term is used in a prohibition related to mystical or philosophical matters. The forbidden objects of *mistakkel* here are "what is above, what is below, what is before, and what is after" (M. Hagigah 2:1; Genesis Rabbah 1:10). A highly influential maxim in Avot, by contrast, sets out certain points of focus that one should attend to (*histakkel*) in order to avoid sin:

> Akavya ben Mahalalel says: Attend to [*histakkel*] three things, and you will not come into the hands of transgression. Know from where you come, to where you go, and before whom in the future you will give reckoning.
>
> From where you come: from a putrid drop.
>
> To where you go: to a place of dust, worm, and maggot.
>
> Before whom in the future you will give reckoning: before the King of the kings of kings, the Holy One, blessed be He. (Avot 3:1)[16]

The direction of focus is dual. On one end is the human body in its temporal extremes: past in a drop of semen and end in decay.[17] On the other end is God as king, highlighted in the role of dispensing judgment. By focusing on the contrast between human finitude and divine power, particularly as located in the future, the sage states that one "will not come into the hands of transgression."

In the commentary of Avot de-Rabbi Natan to a variant of this maxim, a parable expands upon the link between human embodiment and humility before God:

> Rabbi Simeon ben Eleazar says: I will tell you a parable. To what can this matter be compared? To a king who built a great palace and lived in it. A tannery pipe passes through its midst and empties upon the opening. Every passerby says, "How beautiful and praiseworthy would this palace be, were a tannery pipe not to pass through it." So too, a human is similar. While now, a filthy stream issues from his bowels, and he exalts himself over the other creatures – if a stream of fine oil, balsam, and ointment did so, how much the more that he would exalt himself over the other creatures! (Avot de-Rabbi Natan A, Chap. 19; ed. Schechter, p. 70)

Again the body is invoked for pedagogical purposes, but here the focus is not upon the end of the lifespan but upon the end of the alimentary canal. The bowels and their excretions constantly serve as reminders of the differences between the human and the divine. People may try to beautify themselves, but their "filthy stream" flows throughout a lifetime as in all other animals.

A similar instruction, with different focus, appears earlier in Avot among a series of teachings attributed to R. Yehudah ha-Nasi. Again there is a spotlight on corporeality, but here attention is upon God's body:

> Attend to [*histakkel*] three things, and you will not come into the hands of transgression. Know what is above you: an eye sees, an ear hears, and all of your deeds are written in a book. (Avot 2:1; also Avot de-Rabbi Natan *B*, chap. 32; ed. Schechter, p. 70)

God's perception and memory of all actions are conveyed through the anthropomorphic images of an eye, an ear, and an implied hand writing in a book. The scene conveys a sense of hierarchical observation: The deity sees and hears from on high, and awareness of this constant surveillance leads one to avoid improper action.

Akavya ben Mahalalel's teaching also made its way to midrashic collections, where it was set in relation to Leviticus 15:2 and the highly evocative imagery of Ecclesiastes 12:1–7. The combination makes for a creative set of reflections on old age, death, and divine justice. In Leviticus Rabbah 18:1, a homiletic midrash opens by drawing together its three key elements:

> "When any man has a discharge from his body, he is in the status of impurity" [Leviticus 15:2].
>
> "Remember your Creator [*bvr'yk*][18] in the days of your youth" [Ecclesiastes 12:1].
>
> We learn, Akavya ben Mahalalel says: Attend to three things and you will not come into the hands of transgression.
>
> Know from where you come: from a putrid secretion.
>
> And to where you go: to worm and maggot.
>
> And before whom you in the future will give reckoning: before the King of the kings of kings, the Holy One, blessed be He.
>
> Rabbi Abba bar Kahana in the name of R. Pappi, and R. Yehoshua of Siknin in the name of R. Levi: Akavya interpreted all three of them from one phrase: "Remember your Creator [*bvr'yk*]." Remember your origin [*b'yrk*], your pit [*bvrk*], and your Creator [*bvr'k*]."
>
> Remember your origin: This is a putrid secretion.
>
> Your pit: This is worm and maggot.
>
> Your creator: This is the King of the kings of kings, the Holy one, blessed be He, who in the future will give reckoning.
> (Leviticus Rabbah 18:1; ed. Margulies, pp. 389–90)[19]

The commentator opens by citing Ecclesiastes 12:1, which is spatially and conceptually distant from the verse in the Pentateuch, Leviticus 15:2. The maxim of Akavya ben Mahalalel triangulates the two biblical sources, being linked with Leviticus 15:2 by a concern with that which flows from a penis (the "discharge" of Leviticus is reinterpreted as the "putrid secretion" that all humans come from), and with Ecclesiastes 12:1 by way of a complex midrash. Ecclesiastes 12:1 begins by saying "Remember your *bvr'yk*." The word for what is to be remembered is problematic, as the letters *v*, ', and *y* (*vav*, *'alef*, and *yod*) in combination pose difficulties for explanation and interpretation. This ambiguity provides the opportunity for a threefold exegesis, that calls for remembrance of one's *bvr'* or Creator, one's *b'yr* or spring/origin, and one's *bvr* or pit/cistern. Rabbis find all of Akavya ben Mahalalel's teaching embedded in this one word with superfluous consonants.

The bulk of the ensuing unit exposits Ecclesiastes 12:1–7, which is a beautifully written poem about the body's decline through age that has many challenging metaphors. The presence of the ethical maxim means that the ideal of constant focus upon "where you go" in the future is infused into the sequence, while the midrash adds subtlety to the maxim by integrating a graphic exposition of the body's aging with the attention to death. I will consider three examples of this rich literary unit, the first two of which develop Ecclesiastes 12:2. This verse specifies that one should remember one's Creator "before the sun darkens, and the light, and the moon and stars, and the clouds return after the rain." The cosmic imagery is framed as describing the body's decline:

> "Before the sun darkens." This is the brightness of the face.
> "And the light." This is the forehead.
> "And the moon." This is the nose.
> "And the stars." These are the cheekbones. (Leviticus Rabbah 18:1;
>   ed. Margulies, p. 391)

We see here a part of a motif that appears in more developed forms elsewhere in rabbinic sources: The human body, or part of it, is a microcosm of the larger world.[20] The particular associations in this midrash may be derived from the idea that light reflects off these parts of the face, and the association between the moon (*yareah*) and the nose could be inspired by a pun with the word for smell (*reyah*).[21] The darkening of the celestial bodies becomes reinterpreted as the darkening or fading of vitality in the face as the body weakens.

One tension that runs through the midrashic unit, and rabbinic thought more broadly, is whether aging affects everyone regardless of their ethical cultivation (for all people, the light of the face ultimately darkens), or whether a sagely life transforms even this aspect of life. In the exegesis of the last part of Ecclesiastes 12:2, a midrash distinguishes the followers of the rabbis from others:

> "And the clouds return after the rains." R. Levi said: two [interpretations], one for fellow disciples and one for uncultivated people. One for fellow disciples: He is about to cry, and tears flow from his eyes. One for uncultivated people: He goes to urinate, and balls [of excrement] come first. (Leviticus Rabbah 18:1; ed. Margulies, p. 391)

Developing the ominous image of clouds returning after rainfall, R. Levi contrasts the aging of rabbis with that of others. The cultivated person becomes increasingly emotionally sensitive with age, such that his eyes flow with tears before he begins to cry (after the initial "rain," then the "clouds" of full weeping come on). The ordinary person simply becomes unable to control bodily functions. The point is made in quite graphic terms, with striking oppositions: disciple/uncultivated, cry/urinate, tears/excrement. In more general terms, the disciple is characterized as emotionally sensitive in contrast with the others' physical incontinence, and most bluntly, the first is characterized through his face and the other by way of his genitals and anus.

The central contrast in the maxim of Akavya ben Mahalalel is between the ultimate death and decay for all people and God's reward for the righteous. In part of the midrash to Ecclesiastes 12:5, this point is developed vividly through exegesis and a parable. The verse states that each person "goes to his eternal home." The Hebrew can be read hyper-literally as "house of his eternity," which inspires the interpretation that each person is judged individually by God after death:

> "For the man goes to the house of his eternity [*bet 'olamo*]." R. Simeon ben Lakish: This teaches that each and every righteous man has an eternity of his own.
>
> [This can be compared to] a king who enters a capital city, and with him are commanders, governors, and soldiers. Even though they all enter through one gateway, each one of them dwells according to his honor. So too, even though everyone tastes the taste of death, each and every righteous man has an eternity of his own.
>
> "And the mourners surround the market." These are the worms. (Leviticus Rabbah 18:1; ed. Margulies, pp. 396–7)

The phrase "eternal home" (*bet 'olam*) is an ancient Semitic expression for a grave.[22] The midrash plays on the complex spatio-temporal term *'olam*, which can mean the entire world or a very long duration of time.[23] More specifically, since the biblical text literally says that a person goes to "his *'olam*," the midrash highlights that each person goes to a distinct long-lasting world after death, based on divine assessment of deeds and character traits. While all people ultimately die and are consumed by worms, afterwards each person dwells according to ranking in a divinely established system of honor.[24]

These examples show us how an ethical maxim can be developed through midrash to intensify and make more vivid the instruction. Akavya ben Mahalalel instructs one to focus upon the mortal body as a way of emphasizing the decisive nature of divine judgment. The threat of judgment, then, gives motivation for action in accord with the norms set out by divine prescriptions. This basic instruction and set of themes are then developed through an extended exegetical discussion of embodiment, portraying in strong dramatic terms the changes of bodies late in life, the processes of death and decay, and the relation between these somatic elements of existence and normative assessment of humans by the deity.

The combination is an ethical instruction that highlights divine justice favoring those who act in accord with divine ideals, but whose picture gains nuance through subtle reflections upon the weakening, death, and decay of people's bodies. The text maintains the standard rabbinic dichotomy between the righteous and the wicked but integrates that with vivid attention to features of embodied existence that even ethical action before a just God cannot deter. This midrash is the most expansive example of rabbinic reception, development, and modification of Akavya ben Mahalalel's teaching. These ethical instructions address a person with a mortal body and call for attention in every moment, during the course of everyday study and practice, to the workings of divine power. The goal is to rid oneself of transgressive tendencies and to steer away from sin.

A CONCEPT AND ITS DEVELOPMENT

The *yezer* is perhaps the most important concept that rabbis employ for reflection on the nature of the psyche and on the ways that an aspiring sage addresses his emotions and desires. I noted earlier that this Hebrew word denotes impulses that are formed by the heart, though often rabbinic sources go further than that, presenting the *yezer* as a distinct entity – a part of the self, or perhaps even an independent being that a person must confront. Some teachings portray the yeẓer as a singular presence, while others set out a binary relation of good (*tov*) and bad (*ra'*) impulses. Often the *yeẓer ha-ra'* is rendered in English as "the evil impulse," but I prefer to translate *ra'* as "bad," since rarely do rabbinic sources present human inclinations as "evil" in the strong sense of taking pleasure in doing what is wrong or harmful.

The *yeẓer* is an exegetical creation. The idea that the human heart has negative impulses appears in two verses framing the account of the flood in the Book of Genesis. Both state that the yeẓer of the heart (*lev*) of human beings is bad (*ra'*): The first verse justifies the destruction of the human race, and the other appears after the Flood, stating that God accepts human imperfection and will not curse the earth again (Genesis 6:5 and 8:21). The notion of there being two inclinations, one good and one bad, is linked with Adam's creation, where the verb has an unusual repetition of the letter *yod* (*y*): "The Lord God formed [*vayyiẓer*] the human [*ha-'adam*], dust from the earth" (Genesis 2:7). In Genesis Rabbah, this doubling inspires a discussion of various dualities that condition human existence: Some elements of the human are beastly and others angelic, humans have bad and good impulses, and also humans face life in this world and in the world to come.[25] Another important verse for the construct of *yeẓer* is the command of the *Shema*: You should love God "with all of your heart [*levavekha*]" (Deuteronomy 6:5). The doubled consonants (*levav* rather than *lev*) are interpreted in a number of ways, and one of them is that they indicate two tendencies in the heart, both of which should be directed toward the Divine. You should love God, then, "with good *yeẓer* and bad *yeẓer*."[26]

Rabbinic sources offer differing accounts concerning the nature and functioning of the yeẓer. The key issues can be summarized in three groups of questions to ask of any given passage. First, what impulses constitute or are generated by the yeẓer? Is it an impulse toward transgression, or is it raw desire that may lead to virtue or vice?[27] Second, can the yeẓer be transformed in one's lifetime, or does one only struggle with it, ultimately to be judged after one dies? Third, what aspects of rabbinic culture are central to the transformation or removal of the yeẓer: Does a given passage highlight study and practice of Torah, prayer to God, eschatological divine judgment, or some other process? Let us now turn to two compilations of material concerning the yeẓer, each of which presents a distinct constellation of responses to these three concerns.

The first anthology appears near the end of Babylonian Talmud Sukkah (B. Sukkah 51b–52b). Chapter 5 of Mishnah Sukkah describes a great celebration at the Temple, and the memory of this event includes lights, music, dancing, and generally the ultimate experience of joyousness. M. Sukkah 5:2 includes a brief mention of a "great enactment" (*tikkun gadol*) that was made in the court of the women, but it does not spell out exactly what was enacted or why it was needed. The Babylonian compilers exposit this point by describing a separation of men and women, and the underlying issue appears to be the danger of sexual impropriety in a time of merriment.

The discussion develops through juxtaposing two topics – the messiah and the yeẓer. This may seem to be a strange combination. Presumed here is a long-standing link between Sukkot and God's ultimate redemption (see, for example, Zechariah 14:16–18, and note that verses from Zechariah 12 appear near the start of the sugya'), and this redemption includes freedom from negative impulses. A teaching early in the sugya', attributed to R. Yehudah, develops the motif that the bad yeẓer will be eliminated:

> In the future to come, the Holy One, blessed be He, will bring out the bad *yeẓer* and slaughter it in front of the righteous and the wicked.
>
> For the righteous it will appear as a towering mountain, and to the wicked it will appear as a thread of hair. Both will cry.
>
> The righteous will cry and say, "How were we able to conquer this towering mountain?"
>
> The wicked will cry and say, "How were we not able to conquer this thread of hair."
>
> So too, the Holy One, blessed be He will be astonished along with them, as it is written: "Thus says the Lord of Hosts, 'Though it will seem impossible to the remnant of this people, shall it also be impossible to me?'" [Zechariah 8:6]. (B. Sukkah 52a)

Both the righteous and the wicked experience their lives of facing the bad yeẓer as "impossible," but for opposite reasons: The righteous are amazed that they could overcome it, the wicked that they could not. What can we infer about the nature of the impulses that God slaughters? At least two interpretations are possible. One emphasizes that the righteous have a mountainous yeẓer, which implies that the impulses can inspire good as well as bad. The other focuses on the point that the difference in size is a matter of appearance, implying not that the yeẓer inspires goodness but only that the righteous are more aware of their wayward tendencies than are the wicked.[28]

The tension between these two views runs through the rest of the sugya'. Some teachings portray the yeẓer as bringing disaster, from self-annihilation to the destruction of the Temple in Jerusalem, and we even read that God regrets creating it. A person must struggle with this presence, or try to destroy it by going to the study house, but ultimately the decisive action will be taken by the deity in the next world. Other passages present a more ambivalent picture: The yeẓer brings not only transgressive tendencies but also the energy that animates great intellects, spiritual development, and emotional cultivation. Sexual desire is apparently a key manifestation of this raw passion, which is exemplified in a story of a Babylonian sage, Abaye. He saw a couple walking off alone and followed behind, thinking that they were going to have a sexual liaison, in order to stop them. The couple spoke in a friendly manner and parted company. Abaye realized that he was projecting his own desire onto them, and that if he were walking alone with a woman in the meadows, he could not have restrained himself. But, he was comforted by the saying of an old man: "Whoever is greater than his fellow, his *yeẓer* is also greater."[29]

While the Babylonian sugya' focuses upon God destroying the yeẓer, an exposition of Avot de-Rabbi Natan emphasizes the role of Torah in transforming desire (a point that appears but is not emphasized in the talmudic sequence). Chapter 16 of version A comments upon a maxim of R. Yehoshua: "The malicious eye, the bad *yeẓer*, and hatred of creatures cast a man out from the world" (Avot 2:11).[30] What is this formation that casts a person away? The commentary begins:

> They said: The bad *yeẓer* is thirteen years older than the good *yeẓer*. From the belly of a person's mother it grows and comes with him.
>
> If he begins to desecrate the Sabbath, nothing in him protests.
> If he begins to commit murder, nothing in him protests.
> If he goes to do an act of transgression, nothing in him protests.
> After thirteen years, the good *yeẓer* is born.
> When he begins to desecrate Sabbaths, it says to him, "You idiot! Look, it says, 'The one who desecrates it will surely die!'" [Exodus 31:14].
> When he goes to commit murder, it says to him, "You idiot! Look, it says, 'If a man spills the blood of another man, his blood will be spilled'" [Genesis 9:6].
> When he goes to do an act of sexual transgression, it says to him, "You idiot! Look, it says, 'the adulterer and the adultress will surely die'" [Leviticus 20:10] (Avot de-Rabbi Natan *A*, chap. 16; ed. Schechter, pp. 62–3)

The passage elaborates the relations between good and bad inclinations. The bad is primordial, appearing in the infant while still in the womb.

It manifests itself as an impulse to violate rabbinic law and inspire the paradigmatic sins of rabbinic Judaism – breaking the Sabbath, murder, and adultery – which are extreme forms of religious, misanthropic, and sexual transgressions. The good impulse is a receptor of Torah that enables one to internalize verses from the Bible and remember them at crucial times, and it is also an inner monitoring faculty that prevents action contrary to Scripture. The psychological dualism, then, contrasts innate tendencies to transgress and the guidance of the tradition. The emergence of self-regulation crystallizes at age thirteen, which is an approximation of adolescence and linked with an intensification of immersion in halakhic practice (see, for example, Avot 5:21 and B. Ketubbot 50a).

The rest of the unit includes nine more passages that develop the account of the yeẓer with tremendous subtlety and psychological insight. One passage portrays in vivid terms the self-destructive capacities of humans, attributing those to the bad impulses, and another says that the yeẓer wants the body to perish not only in this world but in the world to come. God is not at the forefront of the material to the same degree as in Bavli Sukkah, though passages mention divine judgment upon the yeẓer and call for divine compassion upon those who cannot adequately transform themselves. The material consistently presents Torah as the way to channel and respond to these internal forces. Sages quote biblical verses to overcome their fears and sexual desires, or they recite the Mishnah when facing temptation. The most explicit picture of tradition reforming the bad yeẓer is a teaching that builds from a metaphor of metalwork:

> Rabbi Simeon ben Eleazar says: I will tell you a parable – to what can this matter be compared?
>
> The bad *yeẓer* can be compared to iron that is placed in a flame. All the time that it is in the midst of the flame, people can make from it all the utensils that they want.
>
> So too, the bad *yeẓer*: its only means of reform are the words of Torah, for they are like fire, as it is written, "If your enemy is hungry, feed him bread, and if he is thirsty, give him water to drink; for you pile up coal upon his head, and the Lord will repay you [*yeshallem lakh*]" [Proverbs 25:21–22]. Do not read "will repay you [*yeshallem lakh*]" but "will put him at peace with you [*yashlimennu lakh*]." (Avot de-Rabbi Natan *A*, Chap. 16; ed. Schechter, p. 64)

The metaphors convey a gloomy view of innate tendencies. The bad yeẓer, being metal, resists change while in its natural state. This pessimism is accompanied by an intensely positive sense of Torah's transforming influence, for when immersed in the flames of Torah, parts of the self that are otherwise unchangeable become responsive: Negative tendencies and energies become useful. One should then "pile up coal" of Torah upon the "head" of one's transgressive tendencies, in order to transform and come to peace with them.

While both the sugya' of Bavli Sukkot and the chapter of Avot de-Rabbi Natan embrace study and observance of divine commands in self-cultivation, the two works differ in their emphases. The first highlights a struggle with the yeẓer that culminates in God's judgment at a messianic or eschatological time, while the second calls for the shaping and reworking of desires during one's lifetime through engagement with Torah. Comparing the two of them helps us see the range of ways that rabbis employ this concept and also shows how ethical instruction can be interwoven both into commentaries upon maxims and into talmudic debate.

CONCLUSION

Rabbinic ethical cultivation is not a solitary endeavor, but rather a communal activity that is embedded within a scholastic context. Ethical literature is studied with fellow disciples under the guidance of a teacher, and it presumes immersion in the tradition of Torah and observance of the divine commandments. The genres of rabbinic literature reflect that context: presenting sagely instructions through pithy sayings, presenting sagely behavior through narrative, and presenting the authority of tradition through midrashic development of Scripture. By attending to the intertwining of literary form with the contents of the ethical instruction, we can gain a glimpse into the ways that our written sources preserve what once was a textually conditioned social world: a world in which pedagogy weaves through the texts and the texts presume pedagogy.

Notes

1. Two useful starting points are Yearley 1990 and Davidson 1994. A recent and important study of Hellenistic philosophical schools is Nussbaum 1994.
2. On "dust, worm, and maggot," see M. Avot 3:1 and parallels, which I will discuss later. For other perspectives on "the body" in rabbinic literature,

especially the "gendered body," see Charlotte Fonrobert's contribution to this volume.

3. On the motif of a kiss from God in ethical literature, see Schofer 2005, 138–41 and notes; a full treatment of the image appears in Fishbane 1994.

4. See D. Stern 2004 and Jaffee's contribution to this volume.

5. For an overview of these sources, see M. B. Lerner, "The External Tractates" in Safrai 1987, 367–403. Sperber 1990 offers important reflections on their transmission.

6. See, for example, M. Shabbat 7:2, M. Bava Kamma 1:1, and also M. Kelim 1:1.

7. For discussions of this custom, and its variations from location to location, see the articles listed in Tropper 2004b, 1.

8. This last point has been made by Shmuel Safrai in a number of writings, though the relations between the two texts have not been fully worked out; in English, see Safrai 1994b.

9. Anthony Saldarini discusses the scholastic ethos of Avot de-Rabbi Natan in Saldarini 1982b.

10. Solomon Schechter and Menahem Kister, Avoth de-Rabbi Natan: Solomon Schechter Edition.

11. See Ira J. Schiffer, 237–73, esp. 270.

12. Key works on the fence motif are Stein 1979 and Goldin 1988, 3–25.

13. See also Avot de-Rabbi Natan *B*, chap. 3; B. Berakhot 4a; Mekhilta de-Rabbi Ishmael to Exodus 12:8; the value of the final deadline being dawn and not midnight is highlighted in M. Berakhot 1:1.

14. This translated excerpt and most others from Avot de-Rabbi Nathan appear in Schofer 2005, though the analyses and some formatting have been completely redone for this setting.

15. For a full discussion of these issues, see Fonrobert 2000, esp. 20–29.

16. Three recent treatments of Akavya ben Mahalalel's maxim and related materials are Saldarini 1982a, Steinmetz 2002, and Schofer 2003b.

17. The specific triad of dust, worm, and maggot probably emerges from biblical verses such as Genesis 2:7, 3:19; Isaiah 14:11; Job 25:6; and Ecclesiastes 12:7.

18. In my discussion of this passage, I only transliterate the consonants of the key words, so that the midrashic moves made by the rabbinic exegesis will stand out clearly.

19. Mordecai Margulies, *Midrash Wayyikra Rabbah*.

20. See especially Avot de-Rabbi Natan *A*, Chap. 31; this passage includes correspondences between the sun and the forehead (combining images that are separate in Leviticus Rabbah 18:1), as well as the stars and the cheeks. For another form of correspondence, see Derekh Erez Zuta 9:13.

21. In the parallel passage of Koheleth Rabbah 12:2, however, the correlations are light/nose and moon/forehead, and so the pun would not be a factor.

22. See C. L. Seow, *Ecclesiastes: A New Translation with Introduction and Commentary*, 364; Fox 1999, 328–29.

23. On *'olam*, see Fox 1999, 210–211. Both senses are combined in the notion of the future and enduring "world to come."

24. This aspect of the exegesis is implicit here but explicit in other witnesses of this text, as well as in Koheleth Rabbah 12:5; see the discussions in Margulies, Midrash Wayyikra Rabbah, 396, and Theodor and Albeck, eds., *Midrash Bereshit Rabba*, 1237.

25. For key examples, see Genesis Rabbah 14 to Genesis 2:7 (Theodore and Albeck, 126–29); Genesis Rabbah 34 to Genesis 8:21 (Theodor and Albeck, 320–21) and parallels listed there. These features of rabbinic thought led F. C. Porter to write more than a century ago, "In order to understand the Jewish doctrine of the *yeçer* we must remember that it is not at all a speculative but wholly an exegetical product"; 1901, 108.

26. See Sifre Devarim 32; Louis Finkelstein, ed., *Sifre on Deuteronomy*, 55; and note that here the definite article does not appear; also M. Berakhot 9:5; Fishbane 1994, 3–8.

27. This question is inspired by Daniel Boyarin's distinction between "monistic" and "dualistic" rabbinic psychologies. See Boyarin 1993, 64, and generally 61–76.

28. My analysis draws from Elizabeth Shanks Alexander's careful study concerning the opening passages of this sugya, E. S. Alexander 2002, 125–31.

29. D. Boyarin discusses the story of Abaye as a key example of rabbinic monistic psychology; 1993, 64–67.

30. For a full treatment of this literary unit, see Schofer 2003a.

15 Hellenism in Jewish Babylonia

DANIEL BOYARIN

The great doxographer of the Sophists, Philostratus, relates the following legend about one of his heroes:

> When this Leon came on an embassy to Athens, the city had long been disturbed by factions and was being governed in defiance of established customs. When he came before the assembly he excited universal laughter, since he was fat and had a prominent paunch, but he was not at all embarrassed by the laughter. "Why," said he, "do ye laugh, Athenians? Is it because I am so stout and so big? I have a wife at home who is much stouter than I, and when we agree the bed is large enough for us both, but when we quarrel not even the house is large enough."

Those familiar with the Babylonian Talmud will be reminded of the following anecdote:

> When Rabbi Ishmael the son of Yose and Rabbi Elazar the son of Rabbi Shimon used to meet each other, an ox could walk between them [under the arch formed by their bellies] and not touch them.
> A certain matron said to them, "Your children are not yours."
> They said, "Theirs [our wives' bellies] are bigger than ours."
> "If that is the case, even more so!"
> There are those who say that thus they said to her: "As the man, so is his virility." And there are those who say that thus did they say to her: "Love compresses the flesh." (B. Baba Metzia 84a)[1]

To the memory of my father, Sidney Boyarin, z"l (d. 10 Kislev).

I wish to thank Adam Becker, Jonathan Boyarin, Charlotte Fonrobert, Richard Kalmin, Derek Krueger, Ronald Reissberg, Dina Stein, and Samuel Thrope for extremely helpful comments to this paper.

These narratives are strikingly similar: A sophist/sage is made fun of owing to his avoirdupois. In both cases, the response is that his/their wives are even fatter than they are. In the talmudic version, the sexual slur is made directly, while in Philostratus it is only alluded to, but in both cases, the response is that where there is love, there is room in the bed! It is hardly necessary, I think, to argue further that the talmudic story is a version of the wandering Hellenistic narrative told about various sophists, but if further conviction is necessary, let me offer the following. The retort of the sophist Leon that his wife's stomach is bigger than his is clever, as well as his witty explanation; the retort of the rabbis that their wives' stomachs are bigger than theirs is witless, for since she had accused them of not being able to have intercourse with their wives owing to their obesity, retorting that their wives are even more obese seems distinctly counterproductive, as the Matrona immediately grasps.[2]

This minor but genuine ungrammaticality of the narrative (thematized within the narrative itself) makes most sense if the original retort is an artifact of an earlier version of the story from elsewhere, an elsewhere that we have before us in this instance. Moreover, as Derek Krueger has reminded me, the form of this narrative as a *chreia* in both its Greek and Jewish guises is also highly suggestive of a common Hellenistic origin.[3] What is significant here, or at least heuristically stimulating, is that to the best of my knowledge, this anecdote only appears within rabbinic literature as part of a late legend cycle in the Babylonian Talmud. One cannot certainly prove that it did not circulate among Jews and even rabbis earlier than this, which would be an argument *ex silentio*, but at least as an initial provocation, it seems defensible to see this as a parallel specifically between a Hellenistic topos and a latish Babylonian story, one that suggests that Hellenism and Babylonian rabbinism are hardly as far from each other as generally surmised.[4] Note that, while in this case, I am claiming a particular direction of influence, from an earlier (second-century) Greco-Roman narrative to a later and secondary talmudic version (fifth century or so), this is not the general burden of my thesis here, suggesting as I am, rather, a shared cultural milieu within which cultural innovation and productivity take place.[5] I use this example as an instance with which to demonstrate the plausibility of such a shared world between Hellenistic and Christian traditions and those of the Babylonian rabbis.

It is commonly held among scholars and learned lay folk alike that while the Palestinian rabbis were in dialogue (and dispute) with

Christians and other Hellenists, the rabbis of Babylonia only contended with such secondarily through the medium of their interaction with Palestinian rabbis and their literature and traditions.[6] Thus, in a recent essay, Shaye Cohen points to the great scholarship of the twentieth century (especially of David Daube [1949] and Saul Lieberman [1950]) that sought Hellenism in Palestinian Judaism, and while Cohen himself is searching for Hellenism in unexpected (ostensibly anti-Hellenistic) places, all of those places are, nevertheless, within the obviously Hellenistic (Roman) ambit of Palestine.[7] Cohen completes his argument with the keen formulation that "through it all, Jews remained Jews, and Judaism remained Judaism, but even in their non-Hellenism they were hellenized" (2000, 237). Just so.

In this chapter, I would like to begin to show how we might need to revise significantly our understanding of the role of both Christianity and Hellenism more generally in the formation of the Babylonian rabbinism of the Sasanian realm. This is especially so with respect to matters not known from Palestinian rabbinic traditions and which, at least arguably, only enter the rabbinic textual world at a period and in a stratum of the Babylonian Talmud in which impact from Palestine is considerably less likely than interaction with the local milieu of trans-Euphratian Christian Hellenism.[8] In another very important discussion, Shaye Cohen himself has pointed to the Hellenism in Jewish Babylonia, noting that the very structure of the rabbinic academies there, resembling the Hellenistic philosophical schools with their successions of "heads," is not to be found in rabbinic Palestine, and, therefore, "perhaps then the parallels between patriarchs and scholars tell us more about the Hellenization of Babylonian Jewry in the fourth and fifth centuries than about the Hellenization of Palestinian Jewry in the second."[9] Most recently, Catherine Hezser has doubted Cohen's suggestion, claiming that "however, especially in cases such as this, where no Palestinian evidence exists, one can also reckon with the possibility of a merely fictional construction or with an independent development of certain general institutional patterns in different cultural contexts. It is not necessary to assume a Hellenistic influence on Babylonian Jewish life."[10] Consistent with this position, when she considers "the extent of their knowledge of and ways of adapting Graeco-Roman philosophy"[11] it is only "the rabbis of Roman Palestine" that she considers in this regard. The argument of this chapter will tend to support the position of Shaye Cohen fairly vigorously, albeit not in terms of Hellenistic "influence," nor even yet in terms of "hellenization," so much as of Babylonian Jewish culture as itself a Hellenism.

DATING THE TALMUD: THE STAMMAITIC HYPOTHESIS

The recent convergence of a number of disparate but related directions in talmudic scholarship is increasingly leading us to look closely at Babylonian rabbinism and especially the period just after the amoraic period when the Babylonian Talmud was being redacted as the locus of some far-reaching changes and developments within the Babylonian rabbinic culture, changes and developments, indeed, that are so significant that they have simply given rise to the very features that we usually take as characteristic of rabbinic Judaism.[12] Several scholars have been investigating this hypothesized period – now dubbed by these scholars the period of the Stamma'im – in the wake of David Halivni's and Shamma Friedman's pioneering textual archaeologies, as one of the most formative and crucially determinative moments in the history of Judaism. Of course, it must be emphasized that there was not, to the best of anyone's knowledge, any group that ever were named the *Stamma'im* either by themselves or by anyone in Jewish history until the last three decades.[13] The term is a conceit, a shorthand name for a hypothesis to the effect that the bulk of the crucial redactorial work, that which makes the Babylonian Talmud the Talmud, was actually done at the end of the period of the cited authorities, that is, in the immediate post-amoraic period.[14] This is, in short, a historical hypothesis to account for the aspect, literary and thematic, of the Talmud that speaks, as it were, as a voice from no one, and has accordingly been dubbed in the tradition for centuries the *Stamma*, the anonymous voice (hence, the new coinage *Stamma'im*), or even more tellingly, just *The Talmud*. Seeing that this layer or voice in the text is independent of and later than the textual citations within it allows us to perform several operations on it. One is to place the production of the voice, the voice that gives us the Talmud itself (both structure and content), into an at-least-hypothesized historical, cultural context. The second is to inquire into the role that that voice plays in the history of rabbinic Judaism and the production of its most characteristic forms of thought.

There is, to be sure, another historical approach to the "anonymous" voice in the Talmud, which would see this voice as constantly developing throughout the amoraic period itself, with each Stamma representing the contemporaneous view of the 'Amora' in question, rendered anonymously because all agreed! Halivni explicitly points to the famous letter of Rav Sherira Gaon (fl. ca. 906–1006) as the major source of this pious account.[15] It is increasingly being recognized how this nearly unique source for the institutional history of the talmudic period is prone to

systematic distortion via anachronism, that is, simply projecting backward (nearly five hundred years) institutions of its own time to the
talmudic past. Much of our progress in the historiography of the talmudic period consists of critical work on the positions occasioned by
this source. Richard Kalmin has produced some of the most painstaking
work that has been done to disprove this traditional view and establish
a new hypothesis in his 1989 monograph devoted to the subject.[16] In
this book he has made clear the distinctions between the major extant
views:

> This difference of opinion concerning the redaction of the Talmud
> is in large part a dispute over who authored the stam, the anony-
> mous layer of the Talmud. In the anonymous layer, the Tannaitic
> and Amoraic portions of the Talmud are analyzed, explicated, and
> when necessary, emended and completed. In other words, this
> Tannaitic and Amoraic material was edited by the stam. According
> to the theory of Saboraic redaction, the Saboraim authored the
> stam, while according to the theory of continuous redaction, the
> stam derived from all Amoraic generations. According to the
> theory of stammaitic redaction, the bulk of the stam was produced
> by the stammaim, sages whose names have not survived within
> the Talmud itself.[17]

What Kalmin successfully shows is that the anonymous voice nearly
always – if not always – comments on the named utterances of even the
latest of 'Amora'im, and the opposite is never the case, and, moreover,
the anonymous voice frequently misunderstands or even wilfully dis-
torts the meaning of earlier named utterances in its drive for a coherent
literary/logical structure, the *sugya'*. This suggests strongly, if, I will
confess, not entirely ineluctably, that the work of Stamma'im (here to
be understood simply as the producers of the *Stam*) was done after the
production of the various chronological layers of named tradents had,
as it were, had their say.[18] For the purposes of my argument here, the
only important assumption is that the essential work of redaction was
in the post-amoraic late fifth–sixth centuries or later and that it was so
substantial as to make the term "redaction" a misnomer. The Talmud
and its major discursive peculiarities – the very traits that make rabbinic Judaism what it is, that we so often think of when we talk about
rabbinic Judaism – are the product of a time beginning in the late fifth
century and continuing perhaps for decades or longer.[19] These points
seem to me well established, inter alia, by Kalmin's own work in that
monograph.

Kalmin himself remains "unable to account for the advent of a new era, characterized by anonymous editorial activity, coming after the conclusion of the Amoraic period." He rejects with good reason the traditional explanation offered by Rav Sherira Gaon that in 469, the 'Amora'im ceased their activities owing to a persecution on the part of Yazdigird,[20] as well as its modern variants as yet another iteration of the discredited "lachrymose" theory of Jewish history, concluding only that "we have no choice but to acknowledge our ignorance regarding the critical issue of the transition from attributed to unattributed discourse."[21]

What needs to be added to this point is that Rav Sherira's opinion is of a piece with other aspects of his entire picture of the development of the Talmud. He retrojects into the amoraic period the types of institutions that he knows from his own time and the preceding centuries, namely, the existence of large, formally constituted *yeshivot*, which are administered and led by a succession of leaders. In the context of such an institution, it is just about possible (but I think even then hardly plausible) to imagine that the work of a particular given "generation" – whatever that might quite mean – is redacted and entered into a developing schooltext, which is then handed on and added to by another generation of named scholars who are then redacted once again. Moreover, if there was no great institutional change that took place between amoraic and later times, the necessity for an external explanation of such a discursive shift as the cessation of this process becomes, as well, vitally necessary. In a book written three decades ago, the importance of which, I think, the measure has not yet been wholly taken, David Goodblatt demonstrated that the great institutional *yeshivah* is a product of the post-talmudic period, while study in the amoraic period was characterized by ad hoc study circles centered around individual teachers.[22] Both Rav Sherira's account of continuous creation and his "lachrymose" explanation for its end become obviated by the lack of an institution in which such literary activity could take place, and we require a different kind of historical explanation for both institutional and discursive shifts.

The work I am doing here provides, I think, such an alternative historical hypothesis to that traditional one. A conjecture that I have begun developing elsewhere links three highly significant historical and cultural developments and locates them in the late fifth and sixth centuries. These are 1) the foundation of the great talmudic academies or yeshivot, which Goodblatt showed to be post-amoraic and Isaiah Gafni showed to be highly comparable in structure and tone to the great Christian (East Syrian) school in Nisibis = institution;[23] 2) the actual redaction of the Talmud together with its constitutive stammaitic layer = curriculum; and finally 3) the production of the Yavneh myth, a grand myth of origins for rabbinic Judaism = founding legend[24] – comparable at least in part to the story of the alleged School of the Persians at Edessa as the origin for the School of Nisibis.[25] The new institution and the new form of study as well as the new text all hang together on this theory. The hypothesization of the crucial role of the late redactors, these anonymous "Stamma'im," in forming the rhetorical structures of the Talmud, when put together with their increasingly appreciated role in shaping the talmudic legends (especially about Yavneh)[26] and the historical insight that the institutional yeshivah is also a product of this period, provides us with a powerful historical hypothesis and an attractive historical context for the formation of major structures of rabbinic Judaism in the late fifth and sixth centuries: Institution (yeshivah), founding text and curriculum of study (Talmud), theological innovation (indeterminacy of meaning and halakhic argument), and practice (endless study as worship in and of itself) all come together at this time to produce the rabbinic Judaism familiar to us until this day.

We have to stop, I think, speaking of the *redaction* of the Talmud, as if there were a Talmud already to be redacted (or even several to be combined, selected from, and redacted) and talk instead about the *production* of the Talmud in this period. The Stamma'im who produced the Talmud were so successful in "hiding" themselves that they were able to retroject those patterns and make it seem as if they were a product of a "real" Yavneh of the first century.[27] As David Halivni makes richly clear, it is at least a likely hypothesis that the vast bulk, if not all, of the characteristic Babylonian talmudic dialectic practice is to be attributed to the anonymous voice.[28] He writes that "all we have is what we see before our eyes which comes out of the Talmud itself. In the Talmud the anonymous portions constitute the spinal cord of the *sugya*: they object and they answer, they build and tear down and come to conclusions. . . . The stammaim created the *sugya*."[29] To the extent that it is this redactorial level and voice that contribute so much to that which makes the Talmud unique and meaningful (as appears in such common usages as "The Talmud says" referring to the anonymous layer), it is justifiable to investigate this voice in its *hypothesized* historical context of the late fifth and sixth centuries (and even perhaps extending later than that), which will enable us, presently, to hazard a way through Kalmin's aporia. The importance of the painstaking work that scholars have done on "redaction" and the critical separation of literary layers in the Babylonian Talmud now comes into its own as providing a new set of historical and cultural contexts for perceiving, analyzing, and synthesizing the determining cultural work that constitutes the Talmud and, hence, its culture as a culture.

BETWEEN THE TALMUDS

Zecharia Frankel's classic observation in the nineteenth century that "the Yerushalmi will frequently raise questions or objections and never supply an answer to them. This phenomenon is extremely rare in the Bavli"[30] requires some reframing in my view. Frankel surely meant to indicate a certain defect in the Yerushalmi, an apparent willingness to abandon discussions in midstream. When looked at, however, from a non-Bavliocentric point of view, this translates as the willingness of the Yerushalmi to declare that one opinion is wrong and another right, while the Bavli's practice of refusal of such closure discloses the stranger and more surprising epistemology.[31] It is a key feature of the Babylonian Talmud that its dialectic seems most often to be there for its own sake, that even the attempt to achieve truth through logical procedure has been abandoned (or transcended) in favor of the pure spiritual pleasure of the logic chopping.[32] I would place the two Talmuds clearly in diachronic relation. The Palestinian Talmud was redacted on all accounts in the third quarter of the fourth century or so, while the Babylonian Talmud is some century and a half or two centuries later. Rather than presenting the practice of the Palestinian Talmud as a deviation, a "rejection," I would prefer to imagine that it was the practice of the Babylonian Talmud that was constituted through a renunciation of the desire for "certain knowledge." The making of decisions is, after all, the more obvious telos of an intellectual endeavor, while the "the chaos of speculation" and "plurality of possibilities," the endless deferral of decision that characterizes the Babylonian Talmud, is more of an innovation.[33]

The work of Christine Hayes is also very instructive in this regard. Hayes (1997) articulates the distinction between two modes of understanding the differences between the Talmuds as an "external" approach that sees these differences as being the product of "cultural, regional, historical factors," versus an "internal" approach that sees the differences as "textual, exegetical/hermeneutical, dialectical, redactorial," but also then as "the natural evolution of a complex and fertile core tradition." I am exploring here a third option, one that deconstructs the very opposition between "external" and "internal" approaches, namely, positing that precisely the textual, exegetical/hermeneutical, dialectical, redactorial factors are themselves bound up with complex historical, cultural interactions between the rabbis, respectively, of Palestine and Mesopotamia and the other communities in which they were embedded. To put this another way, Hayes considers that a "reductive historical approach" "posits historical and contextual reasons for halakhic differences between the two Talmuds...that ignore the textual, hermeneutical, and dialectical characteristics of the sources in question" (1997, 3–4), but she does not seem to inquire into the historical and extratextual reasons for precisely those different "characteristics of the sources in question," which is the project of this current work of mine. Hayes explicitly allows us to see "historical" factors only when the respective exegetical methodologies of the two Talmuds are "muted, compromised, or distorted" (1997, 8), whereas I am seeking the history made precisely in and by the formation of those distinct exegetical methodologies and discursive practices more generally.

The diachronic difference between the two Talmuds adds up to a significant epistemic shift between the earlier and the later stages of rabbinic thought.[34] In that shift, within rabbinic Judaism, the Logos, one of the central theological entities of the common Judeo-Christian heritage of Judaism and Christianity, is shattered, with the notion of determinate meaning giving way to a notion of truth not as unitary and univocal but as plural and indeterminate, like the sparks struck by a hammer from a rock.[35]

The Palestinian Talmud seems to consider determination of the correctness of one of the views of paramount importance, whereas for the Babylonian, it is most often the case that such an apparent proof of one view is considered a difficulty (*kushi'a*) requiring a resolution that, in fact, shows that there is no resolution, for "These and these are the words of the Living God." David Kraemer writes: "This contrast in overall compositional preferences may be the most important difference between the Bavli [Babylonian Talmud] and the Yerushalmi [Palestinian Talmud]" (1990, 95). When seen, as it traditionally is, from the point of view of the Bavli – after all, the hegemonic work for rabbinic Judaism – the practice of the Yerushalmi can seem as strange and even defective. This crucial, if not determinitive, epistemic shift within Babylonian rabbinism that comes, on my hypothesis, fairly late in the day should be, I now suggest, read in the context of a late ancient Mediterranean culture in general.

I would like to explore here this development as one case for a conjectured growing interaction between Mesopotamian Jews and a Hellenism promoted in the East by its Christian connections. I begin by reconsidering and elaborating on a fascinating development within Greek culture, especially but not only Christian, during the relevant period. In his historical account of the drive of the orthodox Church toward *homonoia*, single-mindedness, and of the fate of disputation in the formation of Christian orthodoxy, Richard Lim (1994) provides a crucial context for reading the history of disputation and its theological place in the formation of rabbinic Judaism, as well. As Lim demonstrates extensively, the notion of homonoia, the notion that Christian truth must be one, immutable, and *undebatable*, was a long time developing.[36] Its development coincides, moreover, as argued especially by Virginia Burrus, with the displacement of the Logos theology of ante-Nicene Christianity.[37] One possible context for that development could be, of course, the shift of Christianity from embattled sect to state religion of the empire.

Lim points out that in Origen's mid–third century, we find "the use of public debate as a means for restoring social order and discipline within divided Christian communities" (1994, 17). As paraphrased by Lim, the *acta* of one such a debate present a "prevailing tone" that is "of a friendly conversation: the sincere goodwill demonstrated by Origen and his respondents recalls the intimate collegiality of Plutarch's dialogues" (1994, 19), and indeed, upon being caught by Origen in a reductio ad absurdum, his disputant concedes defeat and agrees never to express Christological opinions again.[38]

What is important here is the emphasis on rationality and dispute as modes for arriving at agreement. This pattern is more or less characteristic of the Palestinian Talmud, roughly contemporary in time and exactly coterminous in the space of its production with Origen's own Palestinian activity.[39] Within that earlier Talmud, reasoned argumentation not infrequently results in one or another of opposing views being discredited. Origen, likewise, insists that Christians were not "of one mind," not as a concession,[40] but rather as part of a refutation of Celsus's imputation that Christianity has become degenerate as it has grown in numbers:

> From the outset there were disagreements among the believers about the interpretation of the books regarded as divine. At least, when the apostles were preaching and the eyewitnesses of Jesus were teaching his precepts, no minor dispute in the Church took place among the Jewish believers about those of the Gentiles who were converted to the faith; the question was whether they ought to keep the Jewish customs, or if the burden of clean and unclean meats ought to be taken away so that it would not be a load upon those Gentiles who abandoned their traditional customs and believed in Jesus.[41]

Origen goes on to cite Paul's disputes with other Christians about the nature of the resurrection and even Timothy's refutation of "the gnosis which is falsely so-called" as other examples of the differentiations in views between "believers" at even the earliest beginnings of the Jesus movement, as indeed had Justin before him.

Origen's practice in his *dialektoi* suggests that in spite of the endemic nature of disagreement among Christians, he believes that there is finally truth and that it can be discovered through rational means and via disputation:

> The man who is qualified in medicine is he who is trained in the various sects and who after examining the several schools of thought with an open mind chooses the best; and a man who is well advanced in philosophy is he who by having known about several schools of thought is trained in them and follows the doctrine which has convinced him. So also I would say that a man who looks carefully into the sects of Judaism and Christianity becomes a very wise Christian.[42]

In the end, for Origen, "Christ gave to the Church, whom He had gathered in from the prostitution of many philosophical doctrines, pledges of future perfection, and put this necklace of obedience on her neck."[43] but the Christian attains to this perfection only after thoroughly studying philosophy, which is, for Origen, "cosmetics for the soul" through which "the vanity of the world is discovered and the deceitful marvels of perishable things are rejected."[44] Orthodoxy itself, for Origen, is not so much a fideistic gesture as the carefully derived product of right reasoning and right dialectic from right principles.

Lim very carefully documents the political and social shifts in a late Roman Christian society that transformed it from one in which controlled dissensus was not a threat but a resource to one of "simplicity," the notion that there is and always had been only one truth and the social ideal is homonoia, total agreement without discussion or dispute. These shifts in the modes of discourse were central in the transformation of the classical world into the world of the Byzantine culture:

> An intensified advocacy for apophatic simplicity as a paradigmatic virtue was but one of many results of this confluence of competing interests. Many individuals and groups sought to domesticate the perceived threat of dissensus in public disputing, choosing from various ideological strategies and cultural values to mobilize hierarchical forms of authority against a culture that validated individualistic claims and rational argumentation. (Lim 1994, 20)

With the close interaction between Syriac and Greek Christian think-ing, beginning at least with Efrem, the kataphatic/apophatic distinction, preferring the latter, pushes its way eastward, ever gathering strength. Evagrius of Ponticus's spirituality has a powerful influence on Isaac of Nineveh, a figure "who represents the culmination of East-Syrian monastic spirituality."[45] This development extends, moreover, beyond the confines of Christian intellectual culture, as we shall yet see.

This is precisely the historical context within which the classical rabbinic literature came into being, as well. However, while equally transformed within this period in its ideals of discourse, rabbinic Judaism went in what seems *at first glance* the opposite direction from orthodox Christianity. Since rabbinic Judaism has been interpreted by scholars more as an essence than as a historical and historically shift-ing cultural form, it is not surprising that it has not been much studied in the context of the histories of the developing discourses about dis-course within the late Roman cultural world. While early Palestinian rabbinism manifests a version of the dispute pattern, however, later and especially Babylonian rabbinism defeated dialectic instead by promot-ing a sensibility of the ultimate contingency of all truth claims. Thus, while dialectic is, of course, the very stuff of the Babylonian Talmud, it almost never issues in agreement. The Babylonian talmudic text elabo-rates a third term in the paradigm, neither dialectic toward agreement nor the rejection of dialectic, as the Christians had, but rather dialectic without telos: Without ever reaching agreement or even seeking to do so, *dispute that cannot ever be resolved as both holy rabbis are always already right even when they directly contradict each other.* The prac-tice of dialectic is, then, a pseudodialectical practice, a devotional – or even liturgical[46] – act (known as "enlarging the Torah and making it wonderful") and not truly an intellectual one. Better put, perhaps, it is a devotional (as opposed to teleological) use of the intellect. In the earlier Palestinian rabbinic imagination, presumably sufficient investigation could discover the original truth, whether Hillel's or Shammai's, simi-larly in this respect to the earlier dispute pattern described by Lim for ante-Nicene Christianity; by the latter stratum, the contradictory views of the disciples of both of these sages are being declared equally the words of the Living God in direct contravention of the original model of decline from an original situation of truth and homophony. The (hypothesized) Stamma'im have moved beyond a notion of rational discovery of truth (or at least the securing of agreement) through dialectic into a realm in which the words of the Living God are paradoxical, self-contradictory, undecidable, and undiscoverable and talk goes on forever.

DIALECTIC AND DIVINATION

A remarkable story in the Talmud is a product, I reckon, of this epistemic shift:

> Rabbi Yehudah said that Rav said: In the hour that Moses ascended on high, he found the Holy Blessed One sitting and tying crowns for the letters. He said before him: "Master of the Universe, What [lit., who] holds you back?" He said, "There is one man who will be after several generations, and Akiva the son of Joseph is his name, who will derive from each and every stroke hills and hills of halakhot." He said before him: "Master of the Universe, show him to me." He said to him: "Turn around!" He went and sat at the back of eight rows [in the study house of Rabbi Akiva], and he didn't understand what they were saying. His strength became weak. When they reached a certain issue, the disciples said to him [to Akiva], "From whence do you know this?" He said to them: "It is a halakhah given to Moses at Sinai." [Moses'] spirit became settled.
>
> He returned and came before the Holy Blessed One. He said to him: "Master of the Universe, You have such a one and yet You give the Torah by my hand?!" He [God] said to him: "Be silent! That is what has transpired in My thought." (B. Menahot 29b)

It is, to be sure, difficult to assert positively a late date for this narrative, given its attribution to Rav Yehudah in the name of Rav, but, in any case, it is clearly of Babylonian provenence and at the earliest a product of the early fourth century, even if this attribution be deemed reliable.

In this talmudic story, knowledge is thoroughly opaque in its form; no one, not even Moses himself, could possibly know what Rabbi Akiva knows nor contest rationally his interpretive assertions. The latter's mode of interpretation of the Torah could be fairly characterized as divination clothed in the language of tradition. Rabbi Akiva's "divination" – if I may call it that – seems to involve something like contemplation of the serifs of the letters to divine their meanings. Rabbi Akiva seems to be dangerously innovating using virtually divinatory methods, but the tradition (Moses) is mollified (at least somewhat) when he describes the contents of his divination as having been transmitted (only to him?) from Moses at Sinai. It will be seen that something like apostolic authority is being promulgated here. The only way that such knowledge could be achieved, moreover, is via access to the traditions of the particular community. Who but an Akiva could know what is meant by jots, tit-tles, and decorations on letters? And how could we know other than by being his disciples? Moses would represent on this account a more ratio-nal, logically based reading of the Torah, while Rabbi Akiva represents almost a postrational account.

I would like to suggest that this story represents a conflictual moment in the historical development of Babylonian rabbinism, one in which earlier dialectical methods for discovering truth were begin-ning to be replaced by divinatory and traditionalist ones, while at the same time the act of study was made an end in itself, not requiring any results to achieve its religious purpose, the notion that becomes, inci-dentally, determinative within later rabbinic Judaism as the concept of Torah for its own sake (*torah lishmah*). This is, itself, strikingly akin to the place of dialectic and study within the East Syrian school of Nisibis as described by Becker and bespeaks some kind of cultural interaction between the two communities, without asking for or even imagining the validity of inquiry into or a model of a specific historical account of influence in one direction or the other.[47] Indeed, the time has come, I think, to cease thinking in terms of influence and think, rather, of shared and overlapping cultures imbricated on each other and partly simply just the same culture in different variants.[48] In the face of Moses' demand, as it were, for rational understanding of Rabbi Akiva's discourse, he is told, in effect, to be silent and have faith. Moses' faith is, however, to be tested even more severely, for

> He said to Him: "Master of the Universe: You have shown me
> his Torah, show me his reward." He said to him: "Turn around!"
> He turned around and saw that they were weighing the flesh of
> Rabbi Akiva in the market [after his martyrdom]. He said to Him:
> "Master of the Universe, this is the Torah and this is its reward?!"
> He said to him: "Be silent! That is what has transpired in My
> thought."

This silence is redolent of the silence of the apophatic moment in Chris-tian theology, as well. Without determining lines or directions of influ-ence, indeed denying, as I do, the significance and even possibility of such determination, I would nevertheless submit that such comparisons bespeak a common intellectual, discursive, spiritual millieu between patristic Christianity and Babylonian rabbinic Judaism.[49] I think we are witness in this text to a distinctive turn to both fideism and apophati-cism in Babylonian rabbinic circles that answers to similar develop-ments within patristic Christianity both Western and Eastern.

The significance of the argument does not rest, however, in the theorization of a particular Christian/Jewish milieu within which the institutions of rabbinic Judaism and the Church of the East developed together. More than that, I am suggesting that we look in general at the Greek intellectual culture of Late Antiquity in its various manifestations as an important aspect of the context within which Babylonian rabbinic Judaism developed even in its phases that are independent of further Palestinian input, subsequent, that is, to the end of vigorous literary creativity in Palestine.[50] The Church of the East (and other Syriac-speaking Christians) provide then a pendant on which to hang – by analogy – the plausibility of claims for Hellenism in Jewish Babylonia as much, or more, than as a vehicle for transmission. The extent to which the post-amoraic rabbinic community in Babylonia seems to have been open to the scholasticism of the Nisibene foundation renders the notion of a hermetically sealed, exclusively inner-directed community less and less convincing.[51] In addition to the Persian connections discovered by such scholars as E. S. Rosenthal and Shaul Shaked and increasingly being exposed by Yaakov Elman,[52] we certainly need, I would suggest, to be looking to the West and the Greco-Roman Christian world as well in order to understand the culture of the Babylonian Talmud.

We can use the evidence of such specific connections to reconstruct a *shared* cultural millieu. Once again, the sophistical doxographers have something to contribute here, for I think that the Kulturkampf being dramatized in the narrative about Rabbi Akiva manifests itself as well in a story that we find in Eunapius. This legend manifests the rivalry between dialectical discussions, on the one hand, and thaumaturgy and divination, on the other, in the latter part of the fourth century (during Julian's reign, the same Julian whom the Christians call "the apostate" and Eunapius "the holy").

In this narrative we are told that a certain Aedesius, a great sophist, had two pupils in the latter fourth century, Chrysanthius and Eusebius. Eusebius remained entirely loyal to the old rule of dialectic and logic, while Chrysanthius became particularly attached to the newfangled doctrines of Maximus: "Now Chrysanthius had a soul akin to that of Maximus, and like him was passionately absorbed in working marvels, and he withdrew himself in the study of the science of divination." Eusebius, it seems, was somewhat in awe of this Maximus, for

> when Maximus was present, [he] used to avoid precise and exact divisions of a disputation and dialectical devices and subtleties; though when Maximus was not there he would shine out like a bright star, with a light like the sun's; such was the facility and

charm that flowered in his discourses. . . . Julian actually reverenced Eusebius. At the close of his exposition Eusebius would add that these [dialectical discussions, trans.] are the only true realities, whereas the impostures of withcraft and magic that cheat the senses are the works of conjurors who are insane men led astray into the exercise of earthly and material powers.

"The sainted Julian" was puzzled by this peroration that he regularly heard and asked Eusebius what he meant, whereupon the latter said:

Maximus is one of the older and more learned students, who, because of his lofty genius and superabundant eloquence scored all logical proof in these subjects and impetuously resorted to the acts of a madman. . . . But you must not marvel at any of these things, even as I marvel not, but rather believe that the thing of the highest importance is that purification of the soul which is attained by reason.

Eusebius receives something of a surprise, for "when the sainted Julian heard this, he said: 'Nay, farewell and devote yourself to your books. You have shown me the man I was in search of'"[53] (much like, even verbally, the "You have shown me his Torah" of the talmudic text).[54]

The earlier, traditional commitment to dialectical investigation and surety that logic would provide answers has been rejected, and by no less, it seems, than the sainted Julian, in favor of thaumaturgy and divination. But not without conflict – a conflict, I think demonstrated also in the narrative about Rabbi Akiva. Lim's account of the downfall of dialectic can be extended both further east and outside of Christian circles as well (not, I hasten to add, that Lim had ever said or implied that it was a singularly Christian, or Western, phenomenon).

RABBI ELIEZER AT NICAEA: RUFINUS AT YAVNEH

Normally, however, the Babylonian Talmud is characterized by both traditional and critical scholars as the very repository of rational, dialectical discourse.[55] My thesis seems, then, to produce a paradox, arguing for a breakdown of dialectic precisely at a moment of its seemingly most vigorous development. We may be able to gain some further insight into this development within rabbinic discourse via comparison with seemingly very different shifts in the patterns of Christian discourse and, in particular, by reading a very familiar (redacted in the stammaitic period)[56] talmudic story about Yavneh in the context of an equally powerful fifth-century and therefore contemporary legend about Nicaea. The rabbinic narrative will be seen to be full of paradox itself.

Lim argues that the exigency of articulating an opposition to dialectical discourse in Christian theology comes, in a sense, in the wake of the success of that very dialectic. He describes a situation in which: "[i]n a language game that allowed for the clear articulation of nuances, people pressured each other to profess their beliefs in the middle of a controversial minefield, the features and contours of which were just beginning to be mapped" (1994, 153–54). This pressure led to the conclusion that the endemic dissension of the Christian Church had arisen precisely because of "vain disputes and questionings,"[57] even among some who had been trained as highly skilled practitioners of this discursive modality. One solution to this "problem" was the turn to a mystical and apophatic theology, as most fully expressed in the writings of Pseudo-Dionysius and Evagrius of Pontus, the latter of which had, as suggested earlier, a major impact precisely on the propensity toward the apophatic (and subordination of the kataphatic to it) in the East Syrian Church. Related to this was the demand, on the part of such a centrally located theological authority as Gregory Nazianzus, to avoid dialectic and engage in Christian practice. One of the responses that Gregory articulated to Christian theological argumentativeness was the catechism.

The climax of Lim's narrative is his account of the effects of the Council of Nicaea in the century immediately following the time of the great Cappadocians. The centerpiece of Lim's argument in his chapter on Nicaea and its discursive afterlife is the analysis of a legendary encounter between a confessor and a philosopher at Nicaea, as preserved in the Christian historians' writings of the late fourth and fifth centuries. Because these legends are more similar in genre to the only type of "historiographical" text preserved within rabbinic literature at this precise period, they provide us a particularly interesting basis for comparison of discursive movements within the two formations at the time: "These legends about Nicaea are inherently interesting to the modern historian, not because accurate information can be mined from them but because they tell us much about the period in which they arose and circulated"(Lim 1994, 187).

According to the version in Rufinus of Aquileia's *Church History*:

> Now we may learn how much power there is in simplicity of faith from what is reported to have happened there. For when the zeal of the religious emperor had brought together priests of God from all over the earth, rumor of the event gathered as well philosophers

and dialecticians of great renown and fame. One of them who was celebrated for his ability in dialectic used to hold ardent debates each day with our bishops, men likewise by no means unskilled in the art of disputation, and there resulted a magnificent display for the learned and educated men who gathered to listen. Nor could the philosopher be cornered or trapped in any way by anyone, for he met the questions proposed with such rhetorical skill that whenever he seemed most firmly trapped, he escaped like a slippery snake. But that God might show that the kingdom of God is based upon power rather than speech, one of the confessors, a man of the simplest character who knew only Christ Jesus and him crucified, was present with the other bishops in attendance. When he saw the philosopher insulting our people and proudly displaying his skill in dialectic, he asked for a chance to exchange a few words with the philosopher. But our people, who knew only the man's simplicity and lack of skill in speech, feared that they might be put to shame in case his holy simplicity became a source of laughter to the clever. But the elder insisted, and he began his discourse in this way: "In the name of Jesus Christ, O philosopher," he said, "listen to the truth. There is one God who made heaven and earth, who gave breath to man whom he had formed from the mud of the earth, and who created everything, what is seen and what is not seen, with the power of his word and established it with the sanctification of his spirit. This word and wisdom, whom we call 'Son,' took pity on the errors of humankind, was born of a virgin, by suffering death freed us from everlasting death, and by his resurrection conferred upon us eternal life. Him we await as the judge to come of all we do. Do you believe this is so, O philosopher?" But he, as though he had nothing whatever that he could say in opposition to this, so astonished was he at the power of what had been said, could only reply to it all that he thought that it was so, and that what had been said was the only truth.... The philosopher, turning to his disciples and to those who had gathered to listen, said, "Listen O learned men: so long as it was words with which I had to deal, I set words against words and what was said I refuted with my rhetoric. But when power rather than words came out of the mouth of the speaker, words could not withstand power, nor could man oppose God."[58]

What is stunning about this story, of course, and well analyzed by Lim, is its staging of an opposition between the power of human reason and rhetoric and the simplicity of faith in which – of course – "nor could man oppose God."

This staging can serve, as well, as the setting for an interpretation of some of the best known of Yavneh legends from the Babylonian Talmud that may be implicated in the same historical changes and discursive contexts that informed the developments that Lim has laid bare, even if not necessarily responding to them in precisely the same fashion. The most palpable of comparisons would seem to be with the story of Rabbi Eliezer's controversy with the sages, in the tale of the proverbial "Stove of Akhnai," a controversy in which he was unable to convince the sages via dialectical reasoning after arguing the entire day to support his traditions from his teachers, and even direct divine interventions on his side did not win the day, and not, of course, because his interlocutors doubted the divinity of the intervenor but because God, too, is only a participant in the dialectic.[59] As we have seen with respect to the *chreiai*, here too there are sufficient points of similarity between the plots of these two narratives to suggest some kind of cultural connection between them. Perhaps the best would be to conceive of them in the manner of folklorists as *oikotypes* (local variants) of a single oral tale type.

The talmudic tale, perhaps more written about than any other narrative in the Talmud, can be seen in an entirely different light when compared with Rufinus's roughly contemporaneous production:

> On that day,[60] Rabbi Eliezer used every imaginable argument [refutation], but they did not accept it from him. He said: If the law is as I say, this carob will prove it. The carob was uprooted from its place one hundred feet. Some report four hundred feet. They said to him: One does not quote a carob as proof. He further said to them: If the law is as I say, the water pipe will prove it. The water began to flow backwards. They said to him: One may not quote a water pipe as proof. Again, he said to them: If the law is as I say, the walls of the house of study will prove it. The walls of the house of study leaned over to fall. Rabbi Yehoshua rebuked them, saying to them, If the disciples of the wise are striving with each other for the law, what have you to do with it? They did not fall because of the honor of Rabbi Yehoshua, and did not stand straight for the honor of Rabbi Eliezer. He said to them, if the law is as I say, let it be proven from heaven. A voice came from heaven and announced: The law is in accordance with the view of Rabbi Eli'ezer. Rabbi Yehoshua stood on his feet and said "it [the Torah] is not in heaven." (B. Bava Metzia 59a)

On the original halakhic question, Rabbi Eliezer initially tried to support his position using the "normal" rabbinic modes of rabbinic dialectic, the very modes of argument [*teshuvot*, lit., refutations] that might be said to define rabbinic rationality. When that failed, however, he didn't accept defeat, but rather turned to another source of authority: miracles and heavenly oracles. The parallels with the Nicaea tale are obvious: Dialectic (for an entire day, or longer) fails to produce agreement, and resolution is, in the end, achieved by some other means entirely. This brief sequence out of the longer narrative of Rabbi Eliezer accordingly represents something like a close narrative parallel of Rufinus's story of the old Christian and the philosopher.

At first glance, it seems (and so it did for me in previous publications) to be a sort of inversion, for in Rufinus's text, of course, it is the miracle workers and divine voice that win the day, defeating the dialecticians, while in the Talmud, at first glance it would seem that the dialecticians defeat the miracles and the voice of God. We shall see, however, that the plot is yet thicker than that. Rufinus is "altogether reluctant to report debates" and legitimizes his account of the Council of Nicaea via the power of faith of the simple confessor,[61] as expressed in his legendary narrative cited here. For the rabbinic legend of the same moment, it is precisely the debate that is the crux of the religious life, and the reporting of debates becomes the very stuff of rabbinic textuality. God himself and his miracles cannot interfere with this holy dialectic, this sacred polyphony: "If the disciples of the wise are striving with each other for the law, what have you to do with it?"

Paradoxically then, while on the one hand, the story seems to be the opposite of Rufinus's tale, since divine knowledge seems to be excluded as a source of authority, on second look it is more similar than different, owing to the crucial fact that Rabbi Eliezer's apparently cogent dialectical arguments are not successful in achieving agreement any more than are those of rhetors of Nicaea. Dialectic is predicated on the validity of arguments to command assent (not to establish "absolute truth," whatever that might mean, but rather to move people from one position to another), which neither the Babylonian Talmud nor the post-Nicene Church seem prepared to endorse. For all their dissimilarity, then, the story of Rufinus and the talmudic story are also in some significant ways both comparable and compatible. In a way that seems at first to be entirely different but in the end achieves – at least negatively – the same result, Rabbi Yehoshua also rejects the notion of dialectic. Rabbi Yehoshua's statement, frequently taken as an instance of a sort of protodeconstruction, in this Babylonian version, represents an instance of a complete collapse in credence in dialectic to produce truth or even assent. The device of the majority vote, while more democratic perhaps than other possible solutions, is just as indicative of this collapse as any other in Babylonian rabbinic Judaism and thus represents a particular episteme of power/knowledge different even from that of earlier Palestinian Judaism. In the face of the perceived failure of dialectic to produce consensus, a perceived failure that I wish to suggest was endemic around the fourth-century Mediterranean and later, the Jewish text seeks to effect a transfer of authority and of control over discourse from heaven – which now can be seen to mean, at least sometimes, reasoned argument – to earth, the allegedly God-given authority of the majority of rabbis, while the Christian text transfers such authority to an equally unquestionable "apostolic" authority, the Council of the Fathers. Both communities turn from reasoned and reasonable attempts to persuade those with whom they disagree to the use of "power" against them. Rabbi Eliezer, possessor of the capacity to provide refutations for an entire day, is very severely punished by excommunication and exile from the House of Study for his refusal to accept the conclusions of the majority, failure to accept the will of the majority thus having consequences as dire as dissent from Christian orthodoxy from the fourth century on.[62]

Even Julian, losing faith in the power of dialectic, turns to the magician Maximus as an alternate source of authority, yielding yet a third variation on the pattern. The pattern of the Babylonian Talmud, in which endless and bootless dialectic finally only receives conclusion via arbitrary rules for deciding the law, would be, on this hypothesis, only a reflection of the general collapse of faith in dialectic characteristic of the latter part of Late Antiquity in the West and in the East, as well (according to this conjecture). Apophatic dialectic proves remarkably similar, in this sense, to apophatic simplicity. Difference between the patterns remains, of course, as significant as semblance. Note that I am not claiming that one group or text influenced the others, but rather that there was a common Mediterranean episteme, perhaps especially eastern Mediterranean episteme, within which these mutations in patterns of discourse and theories of knowledge took place.

The East Syrian connection, demonstrated so clearly by Gafni, provides the historical scene upon which a drama can be played with characters as seemingly incongruous as Cappadocian Fathers and Babylonian rabbis. As Becker has shown, all of the intellectual developments that took place among Nicene Christians, and in their world became transferred to the Syriac realm as well, and then translated further east with the founding of the school in Nisibis. Shouldn't we consider, at least as a possibility, the notion that increased interaction between Aramaic-speaking rabbis and Aramaic-speaking Christians, interaction that has been shown to have had enormous institutional impact on the rabbis and the East Syrian Church in the very founding of their most characteristic institutions – the post-amoraic yeshivah and the school at Nisibis – also makes plausible significant imbrication in the ways that these two scholastic communities thought and spoke?

The Talmud itself would seem to want to deny such a connection:

Rabbi Abbahu used to praise Rav Safra [a Babylonian immigrant to Caesarea Maritima] to the minim that he was a great man [i.e., a great scholar]. They released him from excise taxes for thirteen years.

One day they met him. They said to him: "It is written: Only you have I known from all of the families of the earth; therefore I will tax you with all of your sins" [Amos 3:2]. One who is enraged,[63] does he punish his lover?

He was silent, and didn't say anything to them. They threw a scarf on him and were mocking him.

Rabbi Abbahu came and found them.

He said to them: "Why are you mocking him?"

They said to him: "Didn't you say that he is a great man, and he could not even tell us the interpretation of this verse!"

He said to them: "That which I said to you has to do with mishnah, but with respect to the Scripture, I didn't say anything."

They said to him: "What is it different with respect to you that you know [Scripture also]?"

He said to them: "We who are located in your midst, take it upon ourselves and we study, but they do not study." (B. Avodah Zarah 4a)

We find the Talmud here explicitly denying that in Babylonia the Rabbis were "located in the midst" of Christians. In general, in the scholarly tradition this has been taken as straightforward evidence that the rabbis of Babylonia had no Christians with whom to contend,[64] but now I would see its rhetorical function as quite different from that straightforward reading, indeed almost as evidence for the opposite conclusion. Just as the sites in which the most avid disavowal of Hellenism are very Hellenistic sites, as Cohen showed in his essay, so might we argue vis-à-vis the Babylonians and Christianity. The very overstatement and vehemence of that denial, the palpably false claim that there are no Christians in the midst of the Babylonian rabbis, can (at least) be defensibly read in the wake of Cohen's work as manifesting the effort of the Babylonian Talmud to disavow any connection with, intercourse with, and influence of Christians, just as the Qumran folk and the Hasmoneans wish to present themselves as the very opposite of hellenized Jews.

Richard Kalmin (1994a) has demonstrated that contrary to what might be expected from the Talmud's own self-representation, it is in the Babylonian Talmud that we find a much greater instance of confrontations with early Christians narrated. Although to be sure, most of these narratives are about Palestinian sages, this phenomenon of increased narrative of such confrontations can best be explained in my view by assuming that Christians and Christianity were important dialogue partners (or polemic partners) in fourth-century Mesopotamia and later.[65] As Becker has argued with respect to other similar interactions: "In the process [of polemicizing], these intellectuals ironically developed a common ground in which their disputation could occur. The fact that teachers and students could come from different religious backgrounds and even engage in polemic with each others' faiths, yet could still maintain their academic relationships, demonstrates the proximate intellectual space that they shared" (Becker and Reed 2003, 390).[66] Could we not say the same for our rabbis and East Syrian schoolmen?

Be that as it may, it seems hardly implausible to consider even the rabbis of the eastern Mediterranean, even as late as the end of Late Antiquity, as part and parcel of the Hellenistic world. As Becker, once again, sharply put it, "Our assumptions about the lack of any interrelationship between the Jewish and Christian communities in late antique Mesopotamia have too often limited our capability of imagining how to use our wealth of textual evidence in new ways" (2003, 392). The transition into a Gaonic period (eighth to eleventh centuries) in which Babylonian rabbinism was deeply and explicitly involved in Greek thought will seem much less abrupt and sudden on this account, and it would be the overall developments of thought in late ancient eastern Hellenism, including Syriac Christianity, and not only the Muslim conquest that would have brought about such transition.

Notes

1. For longer discussion of this passage in its context, see Boyarin 1993, 200–206.
2. To the point that in my earlier writing on this text, I assumed that there had been an elaborate charade of misunderstandings.
3. See, on this most recently, Hezser 1996 and 2000, 167–69.

4. Note that even Henry Fischel, who most expansively considered the presence of *epicurea* and *rhetorica* in rabbinic literature and especially the role of the *chreia*, explicitly only considered it for Palestinian literature; Fischel 1973, xi, writes: "It is fortunate that at this stage of scholarship no further defense has to be made for the assumption that Greco-Roman situations were well-known to the creators of the Midrash, i.e., the literature that modifies the word and the world of Scripture by interpretation, explicitly or implicitly. Rather the problem is how far this knowledge went, how much of Greco-Roman academic procedure and philosophical quest was used in that on-going process in which the culmination of the tannaitic culture, c. 200 C.E. (the codification of the Mishnah) and that of Palestinian amoraic culture, c. 400 (Jerusalem Talmud) were important stages." For Fischel, it seems, the "Near East" for these purposes extends as far as Palestine and Asia Minor but no farther (Fischel 1973, 2–3). For Fischel on the *chreia*, see especially 86.

5. I thus disagree very slightly with Catherine Hezser's suggestion that "[t]he influence question, which occupied scholars for many decades, is a question which can never be answered in a satisfactory way," (2000, 162). In total agreement with Hezser's overall strictures, and even more importantly, with her alternative models for thinking about shared materials and those of others, I do think, nevertheless, that occasionally, as here, one can determine the direction of a certain flow.

6. A very recent exception is Richard Kalmin, who, in a forthcoming book, will explicitly treat other aspects of Western connections for Babylonian rabbinism. It should be mentioned that Kalmin has indeed been making an impressive case for profound textual/literary *influences* on the Babylonian 'Amora'im, i.e., for the actual importation of Palestinian texts in the fourth century, which, if correct, would only partly vitiate the present argument, for I am looking at developments that seem to have taken place *after* the demise of Palestinian rabbinic culture sometime around the late fourth century. The argument presented herein is particularly valid, I think, if we consider precisely those developments, such as the loss of trust (as I argue) in dialectic as a means for producing consensus, that are not to be found in Palestinian texts and traditions.

7. Cohen 2000. The last of his examples is ambiguous on this point; he writes of a Babylonian talmudic passage that has partial parallels in Palestinian sources. This would suggest that this is an example of a Palestinian topos that had migrated eastward. In any case, Cohen declines to consider the differences between the Palestinian and Babylonian versions, so from my perspective, some more work (beyond the scope of the present essay) is required on that text.

8. In a parallel discussion, Adam Becker has argued that most scholars, including the present writer in the past, have regarded the question of "partings of the ways" (or not, as the case may be) as largely an issue confined to the Roman West; "Beyond the Spatial and Temporal *Limes*: Questioning the 'Parting of the Ways' Outside the Roman Empire," in Becker and Reed 2003, 373.

9. Cohen 1981, 85. Further, Abraham Wasserstein has, at least, adumbrated such a result, arguing: "The Jews were as susceptible to the lure and influence of Hellenism as their gentile neighbours. This is no less true of the Aramaic-speaking Jews in Palestine and Babylonia than of those of their co-religionists who, living in Asia Minor or in Egypt, or in Greek-speaking cities in Palestine and Syria, had either adopted Greek speech or inherited it from their forebearers" (1994, 223). I thank Shamma Boyarin for bringing this essay to my attention. It is important to point out that Wasserstein emphasizes as well the common Hellenistic world of the Rabbis and of Syriac-writing Christians (ibid.). I would only, of course, wish to emend here the language of "influence," which seems to imply that Hellenism is a substance free of the actual actors, necessarily not only imported by Greeks (for otherwise it wouldn't be Hellenism but Hellenicity!) For which term and concept, see Hall 2002.

10. Hezser 2000, 164.

11. Ibid., 186.

12. This is the conclusion of my "The Yavneh-Cycle of the Stammaim and the Invention of the Rabbis." in J. L. Rubenstein 2005, 256–309. See also Schremer, "Stammaitic Historiography," ibid., esp. 226, making very similar points.

13. To the best of my knowledge, the term was introduced by David Halivni 1982.

14. For an excellent discussion of various approaches to the stammaitic question, see Schremer, "Stammaitic Historiography."

15. Halivni, "Aspects," 76.

16. Kalmin 1989.

17. Ibid., 51.

18. See now too Schremer 2005 and Halivni, "Aspects," 74, distinguishing clearly between two quite distinct literary projects and thence (in my view, precisely on Ockham's razor!) between two groups of redactors.

19. Halivni, "Aspects," 73. While I am less than fully comfortable with certain positivistic aspects of Halivni's argument, namely, the assumption of bounded and named periods, functions, and functionaries, I think he is absolutely right to hypothesize that the redactorial activity that produced the Talmud was lengthy and uneven (Halivni, "Aspects," 75). If there were no other evidence at all, the witness of a Gaonic work, *The She'iltot of Rab Ahai Gaon* (fl. ca, 650–782) would provide sufficient reason for this view, as the author of that work is clearly working from a significantly different version of the Talmud, one that is the product of other Stamma'im than the ones in the Talmud that has come down to us (on this point Halivni, "Aspects," 90–91). The work of the Stamma'im may very well have still been going on during the seventh and into the eighth centuries, in accord with Halivni's latest position. If Halivni's position stands, it will be necessary to rethink the nexus between the Talmud and the beginnings of Islam and the Karaite movement in the wake of this very late dating.

20. *Iggeret Rav Sherira Ga'on*, 96–97, although Yazdigird II was no longer shah then, having been succeeded in 459 by Peroz.

21. Kalmin 1989, 93–94.
22. Goodblatt 1975, esp. 267.
23. Isaiah Gafni, "Nestorian Literature," 567–76. It is important, however, to caution that I am *not* arguing for a direct influence causation relationship here. Becker has well demonstrated that the founding of the school of Nisibis entailed itself a transition from study circle to institutional corporate structure (2006, 62), similar to the transition from amoraic study circles to institutional yeshivah exposed by Goodblatt. One could as easily, perhaps, hypothesize influence in reverse. I prefer, as usual, to think of shared universes of discourse. See, too, Becker 2006, 167.
24. Boyarin, "The Yavneh-Cycle."
25. For the destabilization of that Syriac myth, see Becker 2006, 41–61. See also his important comments at 71.
26. Rubenstein 2002.
27. See fascinating discussion of Halivni, "Aspects," 94–97, on the anonymity of the Stamma'im. His explanation (that their names were not given in order to protect the authority of Rav Ashi) is not incompatible with mine that they hid themselves in order to project their own activity as the activity of the Tanna'im and Amora'im themselves, a kind of pseudepigraphy, the authors of which, by definition, remain anonymous.
28. Halivni, "Aspects," 76.
29. Halivni, "Aspects," 95–96.
30. As paraphrased in ibid., 96.
31. Cf. also ibid., 123–24, for related observations.
32. This characteristic has been known historically on more than one moment to deteriorate into a logic chopping empty even of spiritual passion and devotion and to become the virtual equivalent of a chess match. This is less often so, however, than enlightened enemies of the Talmud would have us believe.
33. Neusner 1991, 110–11. For an exhaustive discussion of these characteristics of the Babylonian Talmud, also dating them to the redactional level of the text but presented in a somewhat different explanatory framework, see Kraemer with many examples as well.
34. For extensive argument that this shift is, indeed, a shift within the history of rabbinic Judaism, see Boyarin 2004, 159–63, 190–92, making use, inter alia, of the work of Shlomo Naeh and of my own student, Azzan Yadin. Cf. the explanations offered by Kraemer 1990, 114–21. See Neusner 1995a, 103–6, for a rich characterization of the Bavli that I believe is compatible with the aspect that I am exploring here, as well). See also 94–95.
35. In an earlier stage of my thinking, I took this formulation very literally, more literally than I do now, as representing the enormous impact of a theological decision on other areas of textual practice, thus that the rabbinic rejection of Logos theology gave rise to midrash and Talmud in its Babylonian sense. I am less committed to actual cause and effect now, seeing the relationship between theology and textuality as more heuristic than necessarily historical (and the theological shift as less decisive than before, as well); see Boyarin 2007.
36. See also Martin 1995, 38–47.

37. Burrus 2000, 56–59.
38. As described by Lim, the tone seems remarkably similar to that of Justin's Dialogue with Trypho. See also on this question in general the very subtle and nuanced Lyman 2003.
39. Urbach 1971; Kimelman 1980.
40. Contrary to Lim 1994, 20.
41. Henry Chadwick, trans. and ed., *Origen: Contra Celsum*, 134–35.
42. Ibid., 136.
43. Origen, *The Song of Songs: Commentary and Homilies*, trans. R. P. Lawson, 148.
44. Origen, *Song*, 73.
45. Adam Becker, personal communication, Aug. 22, 2005.
46. My evidence for this would be moments in the Babylonian Talmud in which we find rabbis refraining from communal prayer, arguing essentially: "They do their thing and we do ours."
47. This is a moment to illustrate the compatibilities and differences between my approach and that of Hayes (Hayes 1997, 18–19). Thus, while elegantly (and convincingly) interpreting the passage as being about rabbinic anxiety and also self-confidence in respect of their hermeneutic positions vis-à-vis the Bible, she does not even consider the question of why this particular narrative was told, when and where it was told, and what may have generated this particular reflection at that time.
48. "In contrast to most prior research I advise against the positivistic search for 'influences' when dealing with similarities" (Hezser 2000, 162). I couldn't agree more, in spite of my modest modification of Hezser's position in n. 6.
49. See too Richard Kalmin, who in the introduction to his forthcoming book, writes: "Rather, it is my contention that the Jewish and Christian developments in the region during the fourth century, continuing until the advent of Islam in the seventh century, may be closely related, and that processes accelerated by Shapur's dramatic conquests of the third century may have had pronounced literary and practical consequences in Babylonia and surrounding territories." I thank Prof. Kalmin for letting me see this material prior to publication.
50. As Hayes informs us, the doyenne of Palestinian Talmud studies in our time, Prof. Y. Sussman of the Hebrew University regards the end of Palestinian amoraic activity to have been in the third quarter of the fourth century, while the Babylonians went on for centuries more elaborating and producing their Talmud.
51. Although, to be sure, as Richard Kalmin (1994b) has shown, precisely this openness to cultural impact from the surrounding Sasanian world promoted another kind of insularity among the Babylonian rabbis, insulation from contact with or power over and among their fellow, non-rabbinic Jews.
52. Yaakov Elman, "Middle Persian Culture and Babylonian Sages: Accommodation and Resistance in the Shaping of Rabbinic Legal Traditions," in this volume.

53. Philostratus, Eunapius, and Wright, *Philostratus: The Lives of the Sophists, Eunapius: Lives of the Philosophers*, 433–35.
54. I wish to thank Ronald Reissberg for pointing this out to me.
55. See notably Fisch 1997, an important work on which I have commented extensively elsewhere.
56. Note that my argument here is not crucially dependent on one particular determination of when that was so long as it is after (or even at the end of) the fourth century.
57. The *Vita Dianielis* 90, cited Lim 1994, 156 n. 35. See also McLynn 1992. Particularly striking and amusing in our present sociocultural context is the description by Gregory Nazianzen of dialecticians as being analogous to the wrestlers of the World Wrestling Federation and not even genuine athletes, apud Lim 1994, 162.
58. Rufinus, *The Church History of Rufinus of Aquileia, Books 10 and 11*, trans. Philip R. Amidon, 10–11. Compare somewhat different version of Lim, *Public Disputation*, 192.
59. For recent readings of this much-read story, see Rubenstein 1999, 34–64, and Fonrobert 2001b.
60. According to the Babylonian Talmud itself, "on that day" always refers to the crucial day of decision at Yavneh when the characteristic forms of Babylonian talmudic rabbinism were set in stone.
61. Lim 1994, 196.
62. Burrus 1995. Although, as Charlotte Fonrobert reminds me, it is not insignificant that his main tormentor, Rabban Gamaliel, is "killed" by talmudic legend in the end as punishment for his high-handedness, so nothing is quite simple.
63. Trans. following Rashi ad loc.
64. See now too Schremer, "Stammaitic Historiography," 223–24, critiquing the usual position.
65. For a related point, Becker, "Beyond the Spatial and Temporal *Limes*," 382 n. 39.
66. This formulation is quite similar to my own notion of smuggled "wheelbarrows," as developed in Boyarin 2004, 1–5.

Bibliography

Primary Sources

al-Tabarī. *The History of Al-Tabarī (Ta'rikh Al-Rusul Wa'l-Muluk)*. Translated by C. F. Bosworth. Vol. 5: *The Sāsānids, the Byzantines, the Lachmids, and Yemen*. Albany: SUNY Press (Bibliotheca Persica), 1999.

Altmann, Alexander. "Shirei kedushah be-sifrut ha-hekhalot ha-kedumah." *Melilah* 2 (1946), 1–24.

Asmussen, Jes P. *Manichean Literature: Representative Texts, Chiefly from Middle Persian and Parthian Writings*. Delmar, N.Y.: Scholars' Facsimiles and Reprints, 1975.

ben Asher ha-Levi, El'azar. *Sefer ha-zikhronot: hu divrei ha-yamim li-Yerahmi'el: mahadurah bikortit*. Edited by Eli Yasif. Ramat-Gan, Tel Aviv: Tel Aviv University Press, 2001.

Benoit, P., J. T. Milik, and R. de Vaux. *Discoveries in the Judaen Desert II: Les Grottes De Murabba'at*. Oxford: Clarendon Press, 1961.

Betz, Hans Dieter, ed. *The Greek Magical Papyri in Translation*. Chicago: University of Chicago Press, 1986.

Book of Jubilees, The. Translated by James C. VanderKam. Louvain: Peeters, 1989.

Brooke, George, et al., eds. *Qumran Cave 4. XVII: Parabiblical Texts, Part 3*. Oxford: Clarendon Press. 1996.

Buber, Solomon. *Midrasch Echa Rabbati*. Vilna: Widow and Brothers Rom, 1899.

Charlesworth, James H., ed. *The Old Testament Pseudepigrapha. Volume 1: Apocalyptic Literature and Testaments*. Garden City, NY: Doubleday, 1983.

Cohen, M. *The Shi'ur Qomah: Texts and Recensions*. Tübingen: Mohr, 1985.

Cotton, Hannah, and Ada Yardeni. *Discoveries in the Judaean Desert XXVII: Aramaic, Hebrew and Greek Documentary Texts from Nahal Hever*. Oxford: Clarendon Press, 1997.

Das Sasanidische Rechtsbuch "Matakdan I Hazar Datistan" (Teil II). Wiesbaden: Deutsche Morgenländische Gesellschaft/Kommissionsverlag Franz Steiner, 1981.

Ēmētān, A., ed. *The Wisdom of the Sasanian Sages*. Boulder, Colo.: Westview Press, 1979.

Enelow, Hyman G. *The Mishnah of Rabbi Eliezer or the Midrash of Thirty-Two Hermeneutic Rules*. New York: Bloch, 1933.

Finkelstein, Louis, ed. *Sifre on Deuteronomy*. New York: Jewish Theological Seminary, 1993.

Finkelstein, Louis, ed. *Sifra on Leviticus*. 5 vols. New York: Jewish Theological Seminary, 1983.

Flusin, Bernard. *Saint Anastase le Perse et l'histoire de la Palestine au début du VIIe Siècle*. 2 vols. Paris: Editions du Centre National de la Recherche Scientifique, 1992.

Gardner, Iain, and Samuel N. C. Lieu, eds. *Manichaean Texts from the Roman Empire*. Cambridge: Cambridge University Press, 2004.

Gruenwald, Ithamar. "Keta'im ḥadashim mi-sifrut ha-hekhalot." *Tarbiz̲* 38 (1969), 300–19.

Hayward, C. T. R. *Saint Jerome's Hebrew Questions on Genesis: Translated with an Introduction and Commentary*. Oxford: Clarendon Press, 1995.

Jaafari-Dehaghi, Mahmoud. *Dādestān I Dēnīg, Part I, Transcription, Translation and Commentary, Studiea Iranica, 20*. Paris: Association pour L'Avancement des Études Iraniennes, 1998.

Kasher, M. M. *Torah Shelemah*. Jerusalem: Beth Torah Shelemah, 1985.

Kern-Ulmer, Rivka. *A Synoptic Edition of Pesiqta Rabbati Based Upon All Extant Manuscripts and the Editio Princeps*. 3 vols. Atlanta: Scholars Press, 1997–2002.

Kotwal, Firoze M., and Philip Kreyenbroek. *The Hērbedestān and the Nērangestān*. Vol. 1: *Hērbedestān*. Paris: Association pour l'Avancement des Études Iraniennes, 1992.

Lauterbach, J. Z. *Mekilta de-Rabbi Ishmael: A Critical Edition on the Basis of the Manuscripts and Early Editions, with an English Translation, Introduction and Notes*. Philadelphia: JPS, reprint 1933–35, n.d. 1976.

Liddel, H. G., and R. Scott. *A Greek–English Lexicon*. Oxford: Clarendon Press, 1940.

Lieberman, Saul. *Tosefta Ki-Fshuta*. New York: Jewish Theological Seminary, 1955–88.

Margulies, Mordecai. *Midrash Wayyikra Rabbah*. New York: Jewish Theological Seminary, 1993.

Midrash Wayyikra Rabbah: A Critical Edition Based on Manuscripts and Genizah Fragments with Variants and Notes. Jerusalem: Wahrmann Books, 1972.

Mishnah, The. Translated by Jacob Neusner. New Haven, Conn., and London: Yale University Press, 1988.

Newsom, Carol. *Songs of the Sabbath Sacrifice: A Critical Edition*. Atlanta: Scholars Press, 1985.

Origen. *Origen: Contra Celsum*. Translated and edited by Henry Chadwick. Cambridge: Cambridge University Press, 1965.

Origen. *The Song of Songs: Commentary and Homilies*. Translated by R. P. Lawson. Wesminster, Md.: Newman Press, 1957.

Parry, Donald, and Emanuel Tov, eds. *The Dead Sea Scrolls Reader*. Part 1: *Texts Concerned with Religious Law*. Leiden: Brill, 2004.

Perikhanian, Anahit, ed. *The Book of a Thousand Judgments*. Costa Mesa, Ca.: Mazda Publishers in association with Bibliotheca Persica, 1997.

Philostratus, Eunapius, and Wilmer Cave France Wright. *Philostratus: The Lives of the Sophists, Eunapius: Lives of the Philosophers.* Translated by Wilmer Cave France Wright. Cambridge, Mass.: Harvard University Press, 1998.

Rechtskasuistik und Gerichtspraxis zu Beginn des siebenten Jahrhunderts in Iran: Die Rechtssammlung des Farrohmard I Wahrāman. Wiesbaden: Harrassowitz, 1993.

Reeg, Gottfried. *Die Geschichte von den zehn Märtyrern: Synoptische Edition mit Übersetzung und Einleitung.* Tübingen: Mohr Publishers, 1985.

Rick, Richard, and Alfons Hilka, eds. *Die Reise der drei Söhne des Königs von Serendippo.* Helsinki: Academia Scientiarum, 1932.

Rufinus. *The Church History of Rufinus of Aquileia, Books 10 and 11.* Translated by Philip R. Amidon. New York: Oxford University Press, 1997.

Sacred Books of the East. Translated by E. W. West. Delhi: Motilal Banarsidass, 1994.

Schäfer, Peter. *Genizah-Fragmente zur Hekhalot Literatur.* Tübingen: Mohr Publishers, 1984.

Schäfer, Peter. *Synopse zur Hekhalot-Literatur.* Tübingen: Mohr Publishers, 1981.

Schechter, Solomon, and Menahem Kister, eds. *Avoth De-Rabbi Nathan: Solomon Schechter Edition.* New York: Jewish Theological Seminary, 1997.

Seow, C. L. *Ecclesiastes: A New Translation with Introduction and Commentary.* New York: Doubleday, 1997.

Sifre: A Tannaitic Commentary on the Book of Deuteronomy. Translated by Reuven Hammer. New Haven, Conn.: Yale University Press, 1986.

Stern, M. *Greek and Latin Authors on Jews and Judaism.* 3 vols. Jerusalem: Israel Academy of Sciences, 1974–84.

Tavadia, J. C. *Šāyast Nē Šāyast: A Pahlavi Text on Religious Customs.* Hamburg: Friederichsen, de Gruyter & Co.,1930.

Theodor, J., and Hanokh Albeck, eds. *Midrash Bereshit Rabba.* Jerusalem: Shalem Books, 1996.

Visotzky, Burton L. *Midrash Mishle.* New York: Jewish Theological Seminary, 1990.

Yassif, E., ed. *Sefer Zikhronot by Yerahmeel.* Tel Aviv, 2001.

Secondary Sources

Aarne, A., and S. Thompson. *The Types of the Folktale.* Helsinki: Academia Scietiarum Fennica, 1973.

Abrahams, R. *Between the Living and the Dead.* Helsinki: Academia Scientiarum Fennica, 1980.

Abramson, S. "Writing the Mishnah (According to the Geonim and Rishonim) (Hebrew)." In E. A. Ben-Sasson (ed.), *Culture and Society in Medieval Jewry: Studies Dedicated to the Memory of Haim Hillel Ben Sasson.* Jerusalem: Merkaz Zalman Shazar, 1989.

Ackroyd, P., and C. F. Evans (eds.). *The Cambridge History of the Bible I: From the Beginnings to Jerome.* Cambridge: Cambridge University Press, 1970.

Albeck, H. *Mavo' latalmudim.* Tel Aviv: Devir, 1969.

Alexander, E. S. "The Fixing of the Oral Mishnah." *Oral Tradition* 14 (1999), 100–39.

Alexander, E. S. "Art, Argument and Ambiguity in the Talmud: Conflicting Conceptions of the Evil Impulse in *B. Sukkah* 51b–52a." *HUCA* 73 (2002), 97–132.

Alexander, E. S. *Transmitting Mishnah: The Shaping Influence of Oral Tradition.* Cambridge: Cambridge University Press, 2006.

Alexander, L. "Paul and the Hellenistic Schools: The Evidence of Galen." In T. Engberg-Pedersen (ed.), *Paul in His Hellenistic Context.* Edinburgh: T. & T. Clark, 1994, 60–83.

Alexander, L. "Ipse Dixit: Citation of Authority in Paul and in the Jewish and Hellenistic Schools." In T. Engberg-Pedersen (ed.), *Paul Beyond the Judaism/Hellenism Divide.* Louisville, Ky.: Westminster John Knox Press 2001, 103–29.

Alexander, P. S. "Comparing Merkavah Mysticism and Gnosticism: An Essay in Method." *JJS* 35 (1984), 1–18.

Alexander, P. S. "Retelling the Old Testament." In D. A. Carson and H. G. M. Williamson (eds.), *It Is Written: Scripture Citing Scripture: Essays in Honor of Barnabas Lindars.* Cambridge, Cambridge University Press, 1988, 99–121.

Alexander, P. S. "'The Parting of the Ways' from the Perspective of Rabbinic Judaism." In J. D. G. Dunn (ed.), *Jews and Christians: The Parting of the Ways* A.D. 70 to 135. Tübingen: Mohr Siebeck, 1992, 1–26.

Alexander, P. S. "Hillel, Jesus and the Golden Rule." In J. H. Charlesworth and L. L. Johns (eds.), *Hillel and Jesus: Comparative Studies of Two Major Religious Leaders.* Minneapolis: Fortress Press, 1997, 363–88.

Alexander, P. S. "Jewish Christianity in Early Rabbinic Literature (2nd–5th Centuries CE)." In O. Skarsaune (ed.), *Jewish Believers in Jesus.* Peabody, Mass.: Hendricksen, forthcoming.

Alon, G. *Toldot ha-yehudim be-'eretz yisra'el bi-tekufat ha-mishnah veha-talmud.* Tel Aviv: Ha-kibbutz Ha-me'uḥad, 1952–61.

Alon, G. *Jews, Judaism and the Classical World: Studies in Jewish History in the Times of the Second Temple and Talmud.* Jerusalem: Magnes Press, 1977.

Alon, G. *The Jews in Their Land in the Talmudic Age.* Cambridge, Mass.: Harvard University Press, 1989.

Aptowitzer, V. *Parteipolitik der Hasmonaerzeit im rabbinischen und pseudoepigraphischen Schrifttum.* Vienna: Verlag der Kohut Foundation, 1927.

Asad, T. "The Concept of Cultural Translation." In J. Clifford and G. E. Marcus (eds.), *Writing Culture: The Poetics and Politics of Ethnography.* Berkeley: University of California Press, 1986, 141–64.

Aune, D. E. *Prophecy in Early Christianity and the Ancient Mediterranean World.* Grand Rapids, Mich.: Eerdmans, 1983.

Avigad, N. *Beth Shearim.* Jerusalem: IES-Mossad Bialik, 1971.

Avi-Yonah, M. *Art in Ancient Palestine.* Jerusalem: Magnes Press, 1981.

Bailey, H. W. *Zoroastrian Problems in the Ninth-Century Books: Ratanbai Katrak Lectures.* Oxford: Clarendon Press, 1971.

Baker, C. *Rebuilding the House of Israel: Architectures of Gender in Jewish Antiquity.* Stanford, Calif.: Stanford University Press, 2002.

Baras, Z. E. A. (ed.). *Eretz Israel from the Destruction of the Second Temple to the Muslim Conquest.* Jerusalem: Yad Ben Zvi, 1982–84.

Bar Ilan, M. "Medicine in Israel in the First Centuries of the Common Era (Hebrew)." *Kathedra* 91 (1999), 31–78.

Baron, S. "The Historical Outlook of Maimonides." *PAAJR* 6 (1934–35), 5–113.

Barth, F. *Ethnic Groups and Boundaries: The Social Organization of Cultural Difference.* Boston: Little, Brown, 1969.

Barthélemy, D. *Les devanciers d'aquila.* Leiden: Brill, 1963.

Barton, T. S. *Power and Knowledge: Astrology, Physiognomics, and Medicine under the Roman Empire.* Ann Arbor: University of Michigan Press, 1994.

Baskin, J. R. *Pharaoh's Counsellors: Job, Jethro and Balaam in Rabbinic and Patristic Tradition.* Chico, Calif.: Scholars Press, 1983.

Baumgarten, A. I. "Rabbinic Literature as a Source for the History of Jewish Sectarianism in the Second Temple Period." *DSD* 2 (1995), 14–51.

Becker, A. H. *The School of Nisibis and the Development of Scholastic Culture in Late Antique Mesopotamia.* Philadelphia: University of Pennsylvania Press, 2006.

Becker, A. H., and A. Y. Reed (eds.). *The Ways That Never Parted.* Tübingen: Mohr Siebeck, 2003.

Beckwith, R. *The Old Testament Canon of the New Testament Church and Its Background in Early Judaism.* Grand Rapids, Mich.: Eerdmans, 1985.

Beer, M. *The Babylonian Exilarchate in the Arsacid and Sasanian Periods.* Tel Aviv: Dvir, 1970.

Beer, M. "The Sons of Moses in Rabbinic Legend." *Bar-Ilan* 13 (1976), 149–57.

Beer, M. "The Sons of Eli in Rabbinic Legend." *Bar-Ilan* 14–15 (1977), 79–93.

Belkin, S. *Philo and the Oral Law: The Philonic Interpretation of Biblical Law in Relation to the Palestinian Halakah.* Cambridge, Mass.: Harvard University Press, 1940.

Bernstein, M. J. "4Q252: From Re-Written Bible to Biblical Commentary." *JJS* 45 (1994), 1–27.

Bernstein, M. J. "The Contribution of the Qumran Discoveries to the History of Early Biblical Interpretation." In H. Najman and J. H. Newman (eds.), *The Idea of Biblical Interpretation: Essays in Honor of James L. Kugel.* Leiden: Brill, 2004.

Bernstein, M. J. "'Rewritten Bible': A Generic Category Which Has Outlived in Usefulness?" *Text* 22 (2005), 169–96.

Biale, D. *Cultures of the Jews: A New History.* New York: Schocken Books, 2002.

Biale, R. *Women and Jewish Law: The Essential Texts, Their History and Their Relevance for Today.* New York: Schocken Books, 1995.

Bokser, B. M. "Justin Martyr and the Jews." *JQR* 44 (1973–74), 97–121.

Bokser, B. M. *Post-Mishnaic Judaism in Transition: Samuel on Berakhot and the Beginnings of Gemara.* Chico, Calif.: Scholars Press, 1980.

Bokser, B. M. "The Wall Separating God and Israel." *JQR* 73 (1983), 349–74.

Bokser, B. M. "Rabbinic Responses to Catastrophe: From Continuity to Discontinuity." *PAAJR* 50 (1995), 37–61.

Bonsirven, J. *Exégèse Patristique Et Rabbinique.* Paris: Beauchesne, 1939.

Boon, J. A. *Other Tribes, Other Scribes: Symbolic Anthropology in the Comparative Study of Cutlures, Histories, Religions and Texts.* Cambridge: Cambridge University Press, 1982.

Bori, P. C. *The Golden Calf and the Origins of the Anti-Jewish Controversy.* Atlanta: Scholars Press, 1982.

Boustan, R. A. *From Martyr to Mystic: The Story of the Ten Martyrs, Hekhalot Rabbati, and the Making of Merkavah Mysticism.* Tübingen: Mohr, 2005.

Bowersock, G. W. *Hellenism in Late Antiquity.* Ann Arbor: University of Michigan Press, 1990.

Boyarin, D. *Carnal Israel: Reading Sex in Talmudic Culture.* Berkeley: University of California Press, 1993.

Boyarin, D. "Are There Any Jews in 'the History of Sexuality'?" *JHS* 5:3 (1995), 333–55.

Boyarin, D. *Dying for God: Martyrdom and the Making of Christianity and Judaism.* Stanford, Calif.: Stanford University Press, 1999.

Boyarin, D. *Border Lines: The Partition of Judaeo-Christianity.* Philadelphia: University of Pennsylvania Press, 2004.

Boyarin, D. "Another Coming of the Son of Man: How [I Think] I Do the History of Rabbinic Judaism." *Henoch*, forthcoming.

Boyce, M. *Zoroastrians: Their Religious Beliefs and Practices.* London: Routledge, 1979.

Bregman, M. "Pseudepigraphy in Rabbinic Literature." In E. G. Chazon and M. Stone (eds.), *Pseudepigraphic Perspectives: The Apocrypha and Pseudepigrapha in Light of the Dead Sea Scroll.* Leiden: Brill, 1999, 27–42.

Bregman, M. *The Tanhuma-Yelammedenu Literature: Studies in the Evolutions of the Versions.* Piscataway, N.J.: Gorgias Press, 2003.

Bretone, M. *Geschichte des römischen Rechts: Von den Anfängen bis zu Justinian.* Munich: C. H. Beck, 1992.

Brisson, L. *Sexual Ambivalence: Androgyny and Hermaphroditism in Graeco-Roman Antiquity.* Berkeley: University of California Press, 2002.

Brock, S. P. "Jewish Traditions in Syriac Sources." *JJS* 30 (1979), 212–32.

Brody, R. *The Geonim of Babylonia and the Shaping of Medieval Jewish Culture.* New Haven, Conn.: Yale University Press, 1998.

Brown, D. *Vir Trilinguis: A Study of the Biblical Exegesis of Saint Jerome.* Kampen: Kok Pharos, 1992.

Bultmann, R. *The History of the Synoptic Tradition.* Oxford: Blackwell, 1972.

Burrus, V. *The Making of a Heretic: Gender, Authority, and the Priscillanist Controvery.* Berkeley: University of California Press, 1995.

Burrus, V. *'Begotten, Not Made': Conceiving Manhood in Late Antiquity.* Stanford, Calif.: Stanford University Press, 2000.

Butler, J. *Gender Trouble: Feminism and the Subversion of Identity.* New York: Routledge, 1990.

Byrskog, S. *Jesus the Only Teacher: Didactic Authority and Transmission in Ancient Israel, Ancient Judaism and the Matthean Community.* Stockholm: Almqvist & Wiksell, 1994.

Calinescu, M. "Orality in Literacy: Some Historical Paradoxes of Reading." *Yale Journal of Criticism* 6 (1993), 175–90.

Cereti, C. G. *La letteratura pahlavi: Introduzione ai testi con riferimenti alla storia degli sStudi e alla tradizione manoscritta.* Milan: Mimesis, 2001.

Codde, P. "Polysystem Theory Revisited: A New Comparative Introduction." *Poetics Today* 24 (2003), 91–126.

Cohen, B. *Jewish and Roman Law: A Comparative Study*. New York: Gaunt, 1966.

Cohen, M. S. *The Shi'ur Qomah: Texts and Recensions*. Tübingen: Mohr Siebeck, 1985.

Cohen, S. J. D. "Patriarchs and Scholarchs." *PAAJR* 48 (1981), 57–85.

Cohen, S. J. D. "Epigraphical Rabbis." *JQR* 72 (1981–82), 1–17.

Cohen, S. J. D. "Conversion to Judaism in Historical Perspective: From Biblical Israel to Postbiblical Judaism." *Conservative Judaism* 36:4 (1983), 31–45.

Cohen, S. J. D. "The Significance of Yavneh: Pharisees, Rabbis, and the End of Jewish Sectarianism." *HUCA* 55 (1984), 27–53.

Cohen, S. J. D. "Parallel Traditions in Josephus and Rabbinic Literature." In *Proceedings of the Ninth World Congress of Jewish Studies*. Jerusalem: World Union of Jewish Studies, 1985, 7–14.

Cohen, S. J. D. "The Rabbinic Conversion Ceremony." *JJS* 41 (1990), 177–203.

Cohen, S. J. D. "Can a Convert to Judaism Say 'God of Our Fathers'?" *Judaism* 40 (1991), 419–28.

Cohen, S. J. D. *The Beginnings of Jewishness*. Berkeley: University of California Press, 1999.

Cohen, S. J. D. "Hellenism in Unexpected Places." In J. J. Collins and G. E. Sterling (eds.). *Hellenism in the Land of Israel*. Notre Dame, Ind.: University of Notre Dame Press, 2001, 216–43.

Crook, J. A. *Law and Life of Rome, 90 B.C.–A.D. 212*. Ithaca, N.Y.: Cornell University Press, 1967.

Daube, D. "Rabbinic Methods of Interpretation and Hellenistic Rhetoric." *HUCA* 22 (1949), 239–64.

Daube, D. *The New Testament and Rabbinic Judaism*. London: Athlone Press, 1956.

Daube, D. *Collected Works*. Berkeley: University of California Press, 1992.

Davidson, A. "Ethics as Ascetics: Foucault, the History of Ethics, and Ancient Thought." In J. Goldstein (ed.), *Foucault and the Writing of History*. Cambridge, Mass.: Basil Blackwell, 1994, 115–40.

Davies, W. D. *Paul and Rabbinic Judaism: Some Rabbinic Elements in Pauline Theology*. London: SPCK, 1970.

Davies, W. D., L. Finkelstein, W. Horbury, and J. Sturdy (eds.). *The Cambridge History of Judaism*. New York: Cambridge University Press, 1999.

Davila, J. R. "The *Hodayot* Hymnist and the Four Who Entered Paradise." *Revue de Qumran* 17 (1996), 457–78.

Davila, J. R. *Descenders to the Chariot: The People Behind the Hekhalot Literature*. Leiden: Brill, 2001.

de Lange, N. *Origen and the Jews: Studies in Jewish-Christian Relations in Third-Century Palestine*. Cambridge: Cambridge University Press, 1976.

Derenbourg, J. *Essai sur l'histoire et la geographie de la Palestine d'apres les Thalmuds et les autres sources rabbiniques*. Paris, 1867.

Dinur, B. Z. *Yisrael Ba-Golah*. Tel Aviv: Mossad Bialik, 1958.

Dinur, B. Z. *Israel and the Diaspora*. Philadelphia: Jewish Publication Society, 1969.

Doering, L. *Schabbat: Sabbat-halacha und -praxis im antiken Judentum*. Tübingen: Mohr Siebeck, 1999.

Dohrmann, N. B. "Reading as Rhetoric in Halakhic Texts." In C. A. Evans (ed.), *Of Scribes and Sages: Early Jewish Interpretation and Transmission of Scripture.* London: T. & T. Clark, 2004, 90–114.

Dunbabin, K. M. D. "The Waiting Servant in Later Roman Art." *American Journal of Philology* 124 (2003), 443–68.

Ehrlich, U. *'All My Bones Declare': Non-Verbal Elements in Prayer (Hebrew).* Jerusalem: Magnes Press, 1999.

Eilberg-Schwartz, H. *The Human Will in Judaism: The Mishnah's Philosophy of Intention.* Atlanta: Scholars Press, 1986.

Elior, R. *The Three Temples: On the Emergence of Jewish Mysticism.* Portland, Oreg.: Littman Library of Jewish Civilization 2004.

Elman, Y. "Righteousness as Its Own Reward: An Inquiry into the Theologies of the Stam." *PAAJR* 57 (1991), 35–67.

Elman, Y. "Orality and the Redaction of the Babylonian Talmud." *Oral Tradition* 14 (1999), 52–99.

Elman, Y. "Acculturation to Elite Persian Norms in Amoraic Babylonia." In E. B. Halivni, Z. A. Steinfeld, and Y. Elman (eds.), *Neti'ot David.* Jerusalem: Orhot, 2004a, 31–56.

Elman, Y. "'Up to the Ears' in Horses' Necks: On Sasanian Agricultural Policy and Private 'Eminent Domain.'" *JSIJ* 3 (2004b), 95–149.

Elman, Y. "He in His Cloak and She in Her Cloak: Conflicting Images of Sexuality in Sasanian Mesopotamia." In R. Kern-Ulmer (ed.), *Discussing Cultural Influences: Text, Context, and Non-Text in Rabbinic Judaism: Proceedings of a Conference on Rabbinic Judaism at Bucknell University.* University Press of America, forthcoming.

Epstein, J. N. *Introduction to the Text of the Mishnah (Hebrew).* Jerusalem and Tel Aviv: Magnes Press and Dvir, 2000.

Even-Shoshan (ed.). *The Even-Shoshan Dictionary: Revised and Updated for the Twenty-first Century.* Vols. 1–6. Israel: The New Dictionary, Inc., 2003.

Even-Zohar, I. "Aspects of the Hebrew-Yiddish Polysystem: A Case of Multilingual Polysystem." *Poetics Today* 11 (1990a), 121–30.

Even-Zohar, I. "Russian and Hebrew: The Case of a Dependent Polysystem." *Poetics Today* 11 (1990b), 97–110.

Farbstein, D. *Recht der unfreien und freien Arbeiter nach jüdisch-talmudischem Recht verglichen mit dem antiken speciell mit dem römischen Recht.* Bern, 1896.

Faur, J. *Golden Doves with Silver Dots: Semiotics and Textuality in Rabbinic Tradition.* Bloomington: Indiana University Press, 1986.

Faur, J. "Oral Recitation and Its Influence on the Style and Thought of the Mishnah." *'Asufot* 4 (1990), 27–34.

Fausto-Sterling, A. *Sexing the Body: Gender Politics and the Construction of Sexuality.* New York: Basic Books, 2000.

Feldman, L. *Jew and Gentile in the Ancient World.* Princeton, N.J.: Princeton University Press, 1993.

Finkelstein, L. *Akiba: Scholar, Saint and Martyr.* New York: Atheneum, 1970.

Finnegan, R. H. *Oral Poetry: Its Nature, Significance, and Social Context.* Bloomington: Indiana University Press, 1992.

Fisch, M. *Rational Rabbis: Science and Talmudic Culture*. Bloomington: Indiana University Press, 1997.

Fischel, H. A. *Rabbinic Literature and Greco-Roman Philosophy: A Study of Epicurea and Rhetorica in Early Midrashic Writings*. Leiden: Brill, 1973.

Fishbane, M. *Biblical Intepretation in Ancient Israel*. Oxford: Oxford University Press, 1985.

Fishbane, M. *The Kiss of God: Spiritual and Mystical Death in Judaism*. Seattle: University of Washigton Press, 1994.

Flusin, B. *Saint Anastase le Perse et l'histoire de la Palestine au début du viie siècle*. Paris: Editions du Centre National de la Recherche Scientifique, 1992.

Fonrobert, C. E. "Yalta's Ruse: Resistance against Rabbinic Menstrual Authority in Rabbinic Literature." In R. Wasserfall (ed.), *Women and Water: Menstruation in Jewish Life and Law*. Hanover, N.H.: University Press of New England, 1999, 60–82.

Fonrobert, C. E. *Menstrual Purity: Rabbinic and Christian Reconstructions of Biblical Gender*. Stanford, Calif: Stanford University Press, 2000.

Fonrobert, C. E. "The Didascalia Apostolorum: A Mishnah for the Disciples of Jesus." *Journal of Early Christian Studies* 9 (2001a), 483–509.

Fonrobert, C. E. "When the Rabbi Weeps: On Reading Gender in Talmudic Aggada." *Nashim: A Journal of Jewish Women's Studies and Gender Issues* 4 (2001b), 56–83.

Fonrobert, C. E. "When Women Walk in the Ways of Their Fathers: On Gendering the Rabbinic Claim for Authority." *JHS* 10:3/4 (2001c), 398–415.

Fonrobert, C. E. "From Separatism to Urbanism: The Dead Sea Scrolls and the Origins of the Rabbinic *Eruv*." *DSD* p. 11 (2004), 43–71.

Fonrobert, C. E. "Semiotics of the Sexed Body in Early Halakhic Discourse." In M. Kraus (ed.), *How Should Rabbinic Literature Be Read in the Modern World?* Piscataway, N.J.: Gorgias Press, 2006, 79–105.

Foster, L. *The Poet's Tongues: Multilingualism in Literature*. London: Cambridge University Press, 1970.

Foucault, M. "What Is an Author?" In P. Rabinow (ed.), *The Foucault Reader*. New York: Pantheon, 1984.

Fox, H., and T. Meacham (eds.). *Introducing Tosefta: Textual, Intratextual, and Intertextual Studies*. Hoboken, N.J.: KTAV, 1999.

Fox, M. *A Time to Tear Down and a Time to Build Up: A Rereading of Ecclesiastes*. Grand Rapids, Mich.: Eerdmans, 1999.

Fraade, S. D. "Sifre Deuteronomy 26 (ad Deut. 3:23): How Conscious the Composition?" *HUCA* 54 (1983), 245–301.

Fraade, S. D. *From Tradition to Commentary: Torah and Its Interpretation in the Midrash Sifre to Deuteronomy*. Albany: SUNY Press, 1991.

Fraade, S. D. "Interpretive Authority in the Studying Community at Qumran." *JJS* 44 (1993), 46–69.

Fraade, S. D. "'Comparative Midrash' Revisited: The Case of the Dead Sea Scrolls and Rabbinic Midrash." In M. L. Raphael (ed.), *Agendas for the Study of Midrash in the Twenty-First Century*. Williamsburg, Va.: Department of Religion, The College of William and Mary, 1999a, 4–17.

Fraade, S. D. "Literary Composition and Oral Performance in Early Midrashim." *Oral Tradition* 14:1 (1999b), 33–51.

Fraade, S. D. "Midrashim." In L. H. Schiffman and J. C. Vanderkam (eds.), *Encyclopedia of the Dead Sea Scrolls*. Vol.1. Oxford: Oxford University Press, 2000, 549–52.

Fraade, S. D. "Rhetoric and Hermeneutics in Miqsat Ma'ase Ha-Torah (4QMMT): The Case of the Blessings and Curses." *DSD* 10 (2003a), 150–61.

Fraade, S. D. "The Torah of the King (Deut. 17:14–20) in the Temple Scroll and Early Rabbinic Law." In J. R. Davila, *The Dead Sea Scrolls as Background to Postbiblical Judaism and Early Christianity*. Leiden: Brill, 2003b, 25–60.

Fraade, S. D. "*Mabbathdash 'al ha-midrash ha-hashva'ati: Megillot yam ha-melah umidreshe hazal*." In Y. Elbaum, G. Hasan-Rokem, and J. Levinson (eds.), *Minchat Yonah: Festschrift for Prof. Yonah Fraenkel*. Jerusalem: Magnes Press, forthcoming.

Fraade, S. D. "Rewritten Bible and Rabbinic Midrash as Commentary." In C. Bakhos (ed.), *Major Trends in the Study of Midrash*. Leiden: Brill, 2006, 59–78.

Fraade, S. D., and A. Shemesh (eds.). *Rabbinical Perspectives: Rabbinic Literature and the Dead Sea Scrolls*. Leiden: Brill, 2006.

Freeman, D. N. (ed.). *The Anchor Bible Dictionary*. New York: Doubleday, 1992.

Friedman, S. Y. "An Ancient Scroll Fragment (Bhul 101a–105a) and the Rediscovery of the Babylonian Branch of Tannaitic Hebrew." *JQR* 86 (1995), 9–50.

Froehlich, K. *Biblical Interpretation in the Early Church*. Philadelphia: Fortress Press, 1984.

Frye, R. N. *The History of Ancient Iran*. Munich: C. H. Beck'sche Verlagsbuchhandlung, 1983.

Gafni, I. "Nestorian Literature as a Source for the History of the Babylonian Yeshivot." *Tarbiz* 51 (1981–82), 567–76.

Gafni, I. "Court-Tales in the Babylonian Talmud: Literary Formations and Historical Projections (Hebrew)." *PAAJR* 49 (1982), 23–40.

Gafni, I. "Pre-Histories of Jerusalem in Hellenistic, Jewish and Christian Literature." *Journal for the Study of the Pseudepigrapha* 1 (1987), 5–22.

Gafni, I. *The Jews of Babylonia in the Talmudic Era: A Social and Cultural History (Hebrew)*. Jerusalem: Mercaz Zalman Shazar, 1990.

Gafni, I. "The Hasmoneans in Rabbinic Literature (Hebrew)." Jerusalem: Yemei Beit Hashmonai, 1995, 261–76.

Gafni, I. "Concepts of Periodization and Causality in Talmudic Literature." *Jewish History* 10 (1996), 21–38.

Gafni, I. "Babylonian Rabbinic Culture." David Biale ed. in (*Cultures of the Jews*), New York: Schocken Books, 2002, 223–67.

Gager, J. "Jews, Gentiles, and Synagogues in the Book of Acts." *HTR* 79:1–3 (1986), 91–99.

Gamble, H. Y. *Books and Readers in the Early Church*. Philadelphia: Fortress Press, 1984.

Gardner, J. F. "Sexing a Roman: Imperfect Men in Roman Law." In L. Foxhall and J. Salmon (eds.), *When Men Were Men: Masculinity, Power and Identity in Classical Antiquity*. London and New York: Routledge, 1992, 136–52.

Geller, M. "New Sources for the Origins of the Rabbinic Ketubah." *HUCA* 49 (1978), 227–45.

Gerhardsson, B. *Memory and Manuscript.* Lund: Gleerup, 1964.

Gil, M. *A History of Palestine, 634–1099 A.D.* Cambridge: Cambridge University Press, 1992.

Gilat, Y. *Studies in the Development of the Halakha (Hebrew).* Ramat-Gan: Bar Ilan University Press, 1992.

Ginzberg, L. "Die Haggada bei den Kirchenvätern und in der apokryphischen Literatur." *Monatsschrift für Geschichte und Wissenschaft des Judentums* 6–7 (1898–99), 6:537–50; 7:17–22, 61–75, 117–25, 149–59, 217–31, 292–303, 409–16, 461–70, 485–504, 529–47.

Ginzberg, L. *Legends of the Jews.* Philadelphia: Jewish Publication Society of America, 2003.

Gleason, M. *Making Men: Sophists and Self-Presentation in Ancient Rome.* Princeton, N.J.: Princeton University Press, 1998.

Gluska, Y. *Hebrew and Aramaic Contact in the Tannaitic Period: A Sociolinguistic View.* Tel Aviv: Papyrus, 1999.

Goldberg, A. "Form und Funktion der Ma'ase in der Mischna." *FJB* 2 (1974), 1–38.

Goldblatt, D. M. *Rabbinic Instruction in Sasanian Babylonia.* Leiden: Brill, 1975.

Goldenberg, R. "The Jewish Sabbath in the Roman World." In H. Temporini (ed.), *Aufstieg und Niedergang der römischen Welt, Vol. 19.* New York: de Gruyter, 1979, 414–47.

Goldenberg, R. *The Nations That Know Thee Not: Ancient Jewish Attitudes toward Other Religions.* New York: New York University Press, 1998.

Goldenberg, R. G. "The Spirituality of Talmudic Law." In A. Green (ed.), *Jewish Spirituality: From the Bible to the Middle Ages.* New York: Crossroad, 1987, 232–53.

Goldenberg, R. G. "Is 'the Talmud' a Document?" In S. J. D. Cohen (ed.), *The Synoptic Problem in Rabbinic Literature.* Providence, R.I.: Brown Judaic Studies, 2000, 3–10.

Goldin, J. *Studies in Midrash and Related Literature.* Philadelphia: Jewish Publication Society, 1988.

Goodblatt, D. "Towards the Rehabilitation of Talmudic History." In B. M. Bokser (ed.), *History of Judaism: The Next Ten Years.* Chico, Calif.: Scholars Press, 1980, 31–44.

Goodblatt, D. *The Monarchic Principle: Studies in Jewish Self-Government in Antiquity.* Tübingen: Mohr Siebeck, 1994.

Goodenough, E. *Jewish Symbols in the Greco-Roman Period.* Princeton, N.J.: Princeton University Press, 1953–67.

Goodman, M. "The Roman State and the Jewish Patriarch in the Third Century." In L. I. Levine (ed.), *The Galilee in Late Antiquity.* New York: Jewish Theological Seminary, 1992, 127–39.

Goodman, M. *State and Society in Roman Galilee, AD 132–212.* Totowa, N.J.: Roman and Allanheld, 1993.

Goshen-Gottstein, A. *The Sinner and the Amnesiac: The Rabbinic Invention of Elisha Ben Abuya and Eleazar Ben Arach.* Stanford, Calif.: Stanford University Press, 2000.

Graetz, H. "Haggadische Elemente bei den Kirchenvätern." *Monatsschrift für Geschichte und Wissenschaft des Judentums* 3–4 (1854–55), 3:311–19, 352–55, 381–87, 428–31; 4:186–92.

Graetz, H. "Die Mystische Literatur in der Gaonischen Epoche." *Monatsschrift für Geschichte und Wissenschaft des Judentums* 8 (1859), 67–78, 103–18, 140–53.

Graetz, H. *Geschichte der Juden.* Leipzig: Oskar Leiner, 1897.

Green, W. S. "What's in a Name? The Problematic of Rabbinic Biography." In W. S. Green (ed.), *Approaches to Ancient Judaism: Theory and Practice.* Missoula, Mont.: Scholars Press, 1978, 77–96.

Green, W. S. "Otherness Within: Towards a Theory of Difference in Rabbinic Judaism." In E. S. Frerichs and J. Neusner (eds.), *To See Ourselves as Others See Us: Christians, Jews, 'Others' in Late Antiquity.* Chico, Calif.: Scholars Press, 1985, 49–70.

Greengus, S. "Filling Gaps: Laws Found in Babylonia and in the Mishna but Absent in the Hebrew Bible." *Maarav* 7 (1991), 149–71.

Grene, D., and R. Lattimore (eds.). *Greek Tragedies.* Chicago: University of Chicago Press, 1960.

Gulak, A. *Das Urkundenwesen im Talmud im Lichte der Griechisch-Ägyptischen Papyri und des Griechischen und Römischen Rechts.* Jerusalem: Rubin Mass, 1935.

Gulak, A. *Legal Documents in the Talmud (Hebrew).* Jerusalem: Magnes Press, 1994.

Gurock, J. (ed.). *The American Rabbinate: A Century of Continuity and Change, 1883–1983.* New York: KTAV, 1985.

Gyatso, J. "One Plus One Makes Three: Buddhist Gender, Monasticism, and the Law of the Non-Excluded Middle." *History of Religions* 43 (2003), 89–118.

Halbertal, M. "Coexisting with the Enemy: Jews and Pagans in the Mishnah." In G. N. Stanton and G. G. Stroumsa (eds.), *Tolerance and Intolerance in Early Judaism and Christianity.* New York: Cambridge University Press, 1998, 159–72.

Halevy, E. E. *Amoraic Aggadot: The Biographical Aggadah of the Palestinian and Babylonian 'Amora'im in the Light of Greek and Latin Sources (Hebrew).* Tel Aviv: A. Armoni and Tel Aviv University Press, 1976.

Halivni, D. W. *Midrash, Mishnah, and Gemara: The Jewish Predilection for Justified Law.* Cambridge, Mass.: Harvard University Press, 1986.

Halivni, D. W. *Revelation Restored: Divine Writ and Critical Responses.* Boulder, Colo.: Westview Press, 1997.

Halivni, D. W. "Aspects of the Formation of the Talmud." In J. Rubenstein (ed.), *Creation and Composition: The Contribution of the Bavli Redactors (Stammaim) to the Aggada.* Tübingen: Mohr Siebeck, 2005, 339–61.

Hall, J. M. *Hellenicity: Between Ethnicity and Culture.* Chicago: University of Chicago Press, 2002.

Halperin, D. J. *The Merkabah in Rabbinic Literature.* New Haven, Conn.: American Oriental Society, 1980.

Halperin, D. J. "A New Edition of Hekhalot Literature." *JAOS* 104 (1984), 543–52.

Halperin, D. J. *The Faces of the Chariot: Early Jewish Responses to Ezekiel's Vision.* Tübingen: Mohr Siebeck, 1988.

Handelman, S. "The 'Torah' of Criticism and the Criticism of Torah: Recuperating the Pedagogical Moment." *Journal of Religion* 74 (1994), 356–71.

Harries, J., and I. Wood (eds.), *The Theodosian Code: Studies in the Imperial Law of Late Antiquity.* Ithaca, N.Y.: Cornell University Press, 1993.

Harris, J. M. *How Do We Know This? Midrash and the Fragmentation of Modern Judaism.* Albany: SUNY Press, 1986.

Hasan-Rokem, G. *The Web of Life: Folklore and Midrash in Rabbinic Literature.* Stanford, Calif.: Stanford University Press, 2000.

Hasan-Rokem, G. *Tales of the Neighborhood: Jewish Narrative Dialogues in Late Antiquity.* Berkeley: University of California Press. 2003.

Hasan-Rokem, G., and F. Rokem. "Oedipal Sub/Versions: A Dramaturgical and Folkloristic Analysis." In M. Vasenkari, P. Enges, and A.-L. Siikala (eds.), *Telling, Remembering, Interpreting, Guessing: A Festschrift for Prof. Annikki Kaivola-Bregenhøj.* Joensuu: Suomen Kasantietouden Tutkijain Seura, 2000, 226–35.

Hasan-Rokem, G., and D. Shulman (eds.). *Untying the Knot: On Riddles and Other Enigmatic Modes.* New York: Oxford University Press, 1996.

Hauptman, J. *Development of the Talmudic Sugya: Relationship between Tannaitic and Amoraic Sources.* Lanham, Md.: University Press of America, 1988.

Hayes, C. *Between the Babylonian and Palestinian Talmuds: Accounting for Halakhic Difference in Tractate Avodah Zarah.* New York: Oxford University Press, 1997.

Hayes, C. "Displaced Self-Perceptions: The Deployment of Minim and Romans in Bavli Sanhedrin 90b–91a." In H. Lapin (ed.), *Religious and Ethnic Communities in Later Roman Palestine.* College Park: University of Maryland Press, 1998, 249–89.

Hayes, C. *Gentile Impurities and Jewish Identities: Intermarraige and Conversion from the Bible to the Talmud.* New York: Oxford University Press, 2002.

Hayward, C. T. R. *Saint Jerome's Hebrew Questions on Genesis: Translated with an Introduction and Commentary.* Oxford: Clarendon Press, 1995.

Heinemann, J. *Darkei ha-'aggadah.* Jerusalem: Magnes Press (of the Hebrew University), 1940.

Heinemann, J. *Prayer in the Talmud.* New York: de Gruyter, 1977.

Henze, M. (ed.). *Biblical Interpretation at Qumran.* Grand Rapids, Mich.: Eerdmans, 2005.

Herford, R. T. *Christianity in Talmud and Midrash.* London: Williams & Norgate, 1903.

Herman, G. "The Relations between Rav Huna and Rav Hisda." *Zion* 61 (1996), 263–79.

Herman, G. *The Story of Rav Kahana (Bt Baba Qamma 117a–B) in Light of Armeno-Persian Sources.* Forthcoming.

Herr, M. D. "The Conception of History among the Sages." In *Proceedings of the Sixth World Congress of Jewish Studies.* Vol. 3. Jerusalem: World Union of Jewish Studies, 1977, 129–42.

Hezser, C. *Form, Function, and Historical Significance of the Rabbinic Story in Yerushalmi Neziqin.* Tübingen: Mohr Siebeck, 1993.

Hezser, C. "Die Verwendung der hellenistischen Gattung Chrie im frühen Christentum und Judentum." *JSJ* 27 (1996), 371–439.

Hezser, C. *The Social Structure of the Rabbinic Movement.* Tübingen: Mohr Siebeck, 1997.

Hezser, C. "Interfaces between Rabbinic Literature and Graeco-Roman Philosophy." In P. Schäfer and C. Hezser (eds.), *The Talmud Yerushalmi and Graeco-Roman Culture II.* Tübingen: Mohr Siebeck, 2000, 161–88.

Hezser, C. *Jewish Literacy in Roman Palestine*. Tübingen: Mohr Siebeck, 2001.

Hezser, C. "The Mishnah and Ancient Book Production." In A. Avery-Peck and J. Neusner (eds.), *The Mishnah in Contemporary Perspective: Part One*. Leiden: Brill, 2002, 167–92.

Hezser, C. (ed.). *Rabbinic Law in Its Roman and near Eastern Context*. Tübingen: Mohr Siebeck, 2003.

Hill, D. *New Testament Prophecy*. London: Marshall, 1979.

Himmelfarb, M. "Heavenly Ascent and the Relationship of the Apocalypses to Hekhalot Literature." *HUCA* 59 (1988), 73–100.

Himmelfarb, M. *Ascent to Heaven in Jewish and Christian Apocalypses*. New York: Oxford University Press, 1993.

Hirshman, M. *A Rivalry of Genius: Jewish and Christian Biblical Interpretation in Late Antiquity*. Albany: SUNY Press, 1996.

Hirshman, M. "Rabbinic Universalism in the Second and Third Centuries." *HTR* 93 (2000), 101–15.

Hoffman, D. Z. *Mar Samuel: Rector der jüdischen Akademie zu Nehardea in Baylonien: Lebensbild eines talmudischen Weisen der ersten Hälfte des dritten Jahrhunderts nach den Quellen dargestellt*. Leipzig: O. Leiner, 1873.

Horbury, W. "Jews and Christians on the Bible: Demarcation and Convergence." In J. Van Oort and U. Wickert (eds.), *Christliche Exegese zwischen Nicaea und Chalcedon*. Kampen: Kok Pharos, 1992, 325–451.

Horowitz, S., and I. A. Rabin (eds.). *Mekhilta de-Rabbi Ishmael*. Jerusalem: Sifre Vahrman, 1970.

Huettenmeister, F. G. "Synagogue and Beth Ha-Midrash and Their Relationship (Hebrew)." *Cathedra* 18 (1981), 37–44.

Idel, M. "Pardes: Some Reflections on Kabbalistic Hermeneutics." In J. J. Collins and M. Fishbane (eds.), *Death, Ecstasy, and Other Worldly Journeys*. Albany: SUNY Press, 1995, 249–68.

Ilan, T. "Matrona and Rabbi Jose – an Alternative Interpretation." *JSJ* 25 (1994), 18–51.

Jackson, B. S. *Essays in Jewish and Comparative Legal History*. Leiden: Brill, 1975.

Jackson, B. S. "On the Problem of Roman Influence on the Halakah and Normative Self-Definition in Judaism." In E. P. Sanders (ed.), *Jewish and Christian Self-Definition*. Vol. 2. *Aspects of Judaism in the Greco-Roman Period*. Philadelphia: Fortress Press, 1981, 157–203.

Jackson, H. M. "The Origins and Development of *Shi'ur Qomah* Revelation in Jewish Mysticism." *JSJ* 31 (2005), 373–415.

Jacobs, I. *The Midrashic Process*. Cambridge: Cambridge University Press, 1995.

Jaffee, M. S. "Oral Tradition in the Writings of Rabbinic Oral Torah: On Theorizing Rabbinic Orality." *Oral Tradition* 14 (1999), 3–32.

Jaffee, M. S. *Torah in the Mouth: Writing and Oral Tradition in Palestinian Judaism, 200 BCE–400 CE*. New York: Oxford University Press, 2001.

Jaffee, M. S. "What Difference Does the 'Orality' of Rabbinic Writing Make for the Interpretation of Rabbinic Writings?" In S. Krauss (ed.), *New Approaches to Rabbinic Hermeneutics*. Piscataway, N.J.: Gorgias Press, 2006, 11–33.

Janowitz, N. *The Poetics of Ascent: Theories of Language in a Rabbinic Ascent Text*. Albany: SUNY Press, 1989.

Janowitz, N. "Rabbis and Their Opponents: The Construction of the 'Min' in Rabbinic Anecdotes." *Journal of Early Christian Studies* 6:3 (1998), 449–462.

Judge, E. A. "The Early Christians as a Scholastic Community." *Journal of Religious History* 1 (1960–61), 125–37.

Kalmin R. *The Redaction of the Babylonian Talmud: Amoraic or Saboraic?* Cincinnati: Hebrew Union College Press, 1989.

Kalmin, R. "Christians and Heretics in Rabbinic Literature of Late Antiquity." *HTR* 87 (1994a), 155–69.

Kalmin, R. *Sages, Stories, Authors, and Editors in Rabbinic Babylonia.* Atlanta: Scholars Press, 1994b.

Kalmin, R. L. *The Sage in Jewish Society of Late Antiquity.* New York: Routledge, 1999.

Kalmin, R. "Jewish Sources of the Second Temple Period in Rabbinic Compilations of Late Antiquity." In P. Schäfer and C. Hezser (eds.), *The Talmud Yerushalmi and Graeco-Roman Culture, Vol. III.* Tübingen: Mohr Siebeck, 2002, 17–54.

Kalmin, R. *Jewish Babylonia Between Persia and Roman* Palestine. Oxford: Oxford University Press, 2006.

Kalmin, R. "Persian Persecution of the Jews: A Reconsideration of the Talmudic Evidence," in Shaked forthcoming.

Kalmin, R., and S. Schwartz (eds.). *Jewish Culture and Society under the Christian Roman Empire.* Leuven: Peeters, 2003.

Kamesar, A. *Jerome, Greek Scholarship, and the Hebrew Bible.* Oxford: Clarendon Press, 1993.

Kamesar, A. "The Evaluation of the Narrative Aggada in Greek and Latin Patristic Literature." *JTS* 45 (1994), 31–71.

Katzoff, R. "Precedents in the Courts of Roman Egypt." *ZSS* 89 (1972), 256–92.

Kellman, S. G. *The Translingual Imagination.* Lincoln: University of Nebraska Press, 2000.

Kelly, C. *Ruling the Later Roman Empire.* Cambridge, Mass.: Harvard University Press, 2004.

Kessler, E. *Bound by the Bible: Jews, Christians and the Sacrifice of Isaac.* Cambridge: Cambridge University Press, 2004.

Kimelman, R. "R. Yoh'anan and Origen on the Song of Songs: A Third Century Jewish-Christian Disputation." *HTR* 73 (1980), 567–95.

Klawans, J. "Notions of Gentile Impurity in Ancient Judaism." *AJS Review* 20 (1995), 285–312.

Klawans, J. *Impurity and Sin in Ancient Judaism.* New York: Oxford University Press, 2000.

Klijn, A. F. J., and G. J. Reinink. *Patristic Evidence for Jewish Christian Sects.* Leiden: Brill, 1973.

Kochan, L. *The Jew and His History.* New York: Schocken Books, 1977.

Koltun-Fromm, N. "Aphrahat and the Rabbis on Noah's Righteousness in the Light of the Jewish-Christian Polemic." In J. Frishman and L. V. Rompay (eds.), *The Book of Genesis in Jewish and Oriental Christian Interpretation: A Collection of Essays.* Leuven: Peeters, 1997, 57–71.

Kraemer, D. C. *The Mind of the Talmud: An Intellectual History of the Bavli.* New York: Oxford University Press, 1990.

Krauss, S. "The Jews in the Works of the Church Fathers." *JQR* 5–6 (1892–93), 122–57, 225–62.

Krauss, S. *Griechische und Lateinische Lehnwörter in Talmud, Midrasch und Targum*. Berlin: S. Calvary, 1898–99, repr. 1964.

Krauss, S., and W. Horbury. *The Jewish-Christian Controversy: From the Earliest Times to 1789*. Tübingen: Mohr Siebeck, 1995.

Kristeva, J. "Intimate Revolt." In K. Oliver (ed.), *The Portable Kristeva*. New York: Columbia University Press, 2002.

Kronholm, T. *Motifs from Genesis 1–11 in the Genuine Hymns of Ephrem the Syrian with Particular Reference to the Influence of the Jewish Exegetical Tradition*. Lund: Gleerup, 1978.

Kugel, J. *The Idea of Biblical Poetry: Parallelism and Its History*. New Haven, Conn.: Yale University Press, 1981.

Kugel, J. *In Potiphar's House: The Interpretive Life of Biblical Texts*. San Francisco: Harper Collins, 1990.

Kugel, J. "Reuben's Sin with Bilhah in the Testament of Reuben." In D. P. Wright, D. N. Freedman, and A. Hurvitz (eds.), *Pomegranates and Golden Bells: Studies in Biblical, Jewish, and Near Eastern Ritual, Law, and Literature in Honor of Jacob Milgrom*. Winona Lake, Ind.: Eisenbrauns, 1995, 525–54.

Kugel, J. *Traditions of the Bible: A Guide to the Bible as It Was at the Start of the Common Era*. Cambridge, Mass.: Harvard University Press, 1999.

Kunkel, W. "Das Wesen des Ius Respondendi." *ZSS* 66 (1946), 423–57.

Kunkel, W. *Herkunft und Soziale Stellung der Römischen Juristen*. Weimar: Hermann Böhlaus Nachfolger, 1952.

Kuyt, A. *The 'Descent' to the Chariot: Towards a Description of the Terminology, Place, Function, and Nature of the Yeridah in Hekhalot Literature*. Tübingen: Mohr, 1995.

Lachman, L. "'I Manured the Land with My Mother's Letters': Avot Yeshurun and the Question of Avant-Garde." *Poetics Today* 21 (2000), 61–93.

Lampe, G. W. H. (ed.). *The Cambridge History of the Bible II: The West from the Fathers to the Reformation*. Cambridge: Cambridge University Press, 1969.

Lapin, H. "Early Rabbinic Civil Law and the Literature of the Second Temple Period." *JSQ* 2 (1995), 149–83.

Lapin, H. "Jewish and Christian Academies in Roman Palestine: Some Preliminary Observations." In A. Raban and K. G. Holum (eds.), *Caesarea Maritima: A Retrospective after Two Millennia*. Leiden: Brill, 1996.

Lapin, H. "Rabbis and Cities in Later Roman Palestine: The Literary Evidence." *JJS* 50 (1999), 187–207.

Lapin, H. *Economy, Geography, and Provincial History in Later Roman Palestine*. Tübingen: Mohr Siebeck, 2001.

Le Cornu, H., and J. Shulam. *A Commentary on the Jewish Roots of Acts*. Jerusalem: Academon, 2003.

Leiman, S. Z. *The Canon and Masorah of the Hebrew Bible*. New York: Ktav, 1974.

Leiman, S. Z. *The Canonization of Hebrew Scripture: The Talmudic and Midrashic Evidence*. Hamden, Conn.: Archon Books, 1976.

Le Roux, P. "La Romanisation en Question." *Annales: Histoire, sciences socialies* 59 (2004), 287–311.

Levene, A. *The Early Syrian Fathers on Genesis from a Syriac Ms on the Pentateuch in the Mingana Collection.* London: Taylor's Foreign Press, 1951.

Levine, B. "Mulugu/Melug: The Origins of a Talmudic Legal Institution." *Journal of the American Oriental Soceity* 88 (1968), 271–85.

Levine, B. "On the Role of Aramaic in Transmitting Syro-Mesopotamian Legal Traditions." In A. Panaino and G. Pettinato (eds.), *Melammu Symposia III: Ideologies as Intercultural Phenomena.* Milan: Universita di Bologna Press, 2002, 157–67.

Levine, L. I. *The Rabbinic Class of Roman Palestine in Late Antiquity.* New York: Jewish Theological Seminary, 1989.

Levine, L. I. "The Status of the Patriarch in the Third and Fourth Century: Sources and Methodology." *JJS* 47 (1996), 1–32.

Levine, L. I. *The Ancient Synagogue: The First Thousand Years.* New Haven, Conn.: Yale University Press, 2000.

Levine, L. I. *Continuity and Renewal: Jews and Judaism in Byzantine-Christian Palestine.* Jeursalem: Yad Ben Zvi-Merkaz Dinur, 2004.

Levine, L. I. (ed.). *The Galilee in Late Antiquity.* New York: Jewish Theological Seminary of America, 1992.

Levy, J. *Chaldäisches Wörterbuch über die Targumim und einen grossen Theil des Rabbinischen Schriftthums.* Leipzig, 1878.

Lewin, B. M. (ed.). *Iggeret Rav Sherira Gaon: The Spanish Text and the French Text.* Haifa: Itzokofsky, 1921.

Lewis, B. *History – Remembered, Recovered, Invented.* Princeton, N.J.: Princeton University Press, 1975.

Lewis, J. P. *A Study of the Interpretation of Noah and the Flood in Jewish and Christian Literature.* Leiden: Brill, 1968.

Lewy, Y. *'Olamot nifgashim: meḥkarim 'al ma'amadah shel ha-yahadut ba-'olam ha-yevani-ha-roma'i.* Jerusalem: Mossad Bialik, 1960.

Lieberman, S. *Hellenism in Jewish Palestine.* New York: Jewish Theological Seminary of America, 1950.

Lieberman, S. "The Knowledge of *Halakha* by the Author (or Authors) of the *Heikhaloth.*" In I. Gruenwald (ed.), *Apocalyptic and Merkavah Mysticism.* Leiden: Brill, 1980, 240–44.

Lieberman, S. *Greek in Jewish Palestine.* New York: Jewish Theological Seminary of America, 1994.

Lieberman, S. J. "A Mesopotamian Background for the So-Called *Aggadic* 'Measures' of Biblical Hermeneutics." *HUCA* 58 (1987), 157–225.

Liebeschuetz, W. "The End of the Ancient City." In J. Rich (ed.), *The City in Late Antiquity.* London: Routledge, 1992, 1–50.

Lieu, S. N. C. *Manichaeism in the Later Roman Empire and Medieval China: A Historical Survey.* Manchester: Manchester University Press, 1985.

Lieu, S. N. C. *Manichaeism in Mesopotamia and the Roman East.* Leiden: Brill, 1994.

Lim, R. *Public Disputation, Power, and Social Order in Late Antiquity.* Berkeley: University of California Press, 1994.

Lim, T. H. *Pesharim*. Companion to the Qumran Scrolls. London: Sheffield Academic Press, 2002.

Linder, A. *The Jews in Roman Imperial Legislation*. Detroit: Wayne State University Press, 1987.

Lord, A. B. *The Singer of Tales*. Cambridge, Mass.: Harvard University Press, 2000.

Lyman, J. R. "The Politics of Passing: Justin Martyr's Conversion as a Problem of 'Hellenization.'" In A. Grafton and K. Mills (eds.), *Conversion in Late Antiquity and the Early Middle Ages: Seeing and Believing*. Rochester, N.Y.: University of Rochester Press, 2003, 36–60.

Mac Lennan, R. S., and A. T. Kraabel. "The God-Fearers: A Literary and Theological Invention." *BAR* 12 (1986), 46–53.

Mandel, P. "Between Byzantium and Islam: The Transmission of the Jewish Book in the Byzantine and Early Islamic Periods." In Y. Elman and I. Gershoni (eds.), *Transmitting Jewish Traditions: Orality, Textuality and Cultural Diffusion*. New Haven, Conn.: Yale University Press, 2000, 74–106.

Mandel, P. "Midrashic Exegesis and Its Precedents in the Dead Sea Scrolls." *DSD* 8 (2001), 149–68.

Martin, D. *The Corinthian Body*. New Haven, Conn.: Yale University Press, 1995.

Mason, S. *Flavius Josephus on the Pharisees: A Composition-Critical Study*. Leiden: Brill, 2001.

Matthews, J. F. *Laying Down the Law: A Study of the Theodosian Code*. New Haven, Conn.: Yale University Press, 2000.

McClure, L. "Subversive Laughter: The Sayings of Courtesans in Book 13 of Athenaeus' *Deipnosophista*." *American Journal of Philology* 124:2 (2003), 259–94.

McLynn, N. "Christian Controversy and Violence in the Fourth Century." *Kodai* 3 (1992), 15–44.

Melamed, E. Z. "Maasim Collections of Tannaim (Hebrew)." *PWCJS* 7 (1977), 93–107.

Meyer, M. A. *Ideas of Jewish History*. Detroit: Wayne State University Press, 1987.

Mihaly, E. "A Rabbinic Defense of the Election of Israel: An Analysis of Sifre Deuteronomy 32:9, Pisqa 312." *HUCA* 35 (1964), 103–43.

Milikowsky, C. "Seder 'Olam and Jewish Chronography in the Hellenistic and Roman Periods." *PAAJR* 52 (1985), 115–39.

Milikowsky, C. "The Status Quaestionis of Research in Rabbinic Literature." *JJS* 39 (1988), 201–11.

Milikowsky, C. "The End of Prophecy and the Closure of the Bible in Judaism of Late Antiquity (Hebrew)." *Sidra* 10 (1994), 83–94.

Milikowsky, C. "Josephus between Rabbinic Culture and Hellenistic Historiography." In J. L. Kugel (ed.), *Shem in the Tents of Japhet*. Leiden: Brill, 2002.

Miller, S. "The *Minim* of Sepphoris Reconsidered." *HTR* 86 (1993), 377–402.

Momigliano, A. *The Classical Foundations of Modern Historiography*. Berkeley: University of California Press, 1990.

Momigliano, A. *Essays on Ancient and Modern Judaism*. Chicago: University of Chicago Press, 1994.

Morony, M. "Michael the Syrian as a Source for Economic History." *Hugoye: Journal of Syriac Studies* 3:2 (2000). http://syrcom.cua.edu/Hugoye.

Morray-Jones, C. R. A. *A Transparent Illusion: The Dangerous Vision of Water in Hekhalot Mysticism. A Source-Critical and Tradition-Historical Inquiry.* Leiden: Brill, 2002.

Moscovitz, L. *Talmudic Reasoning: From Casuistics to Conceptualization.* Tübingen: Mohr Siebeck, 2002.

Most, G. W. (ed.). *Commentaries – Kommentare.* Göttingen: Vandenhoeck & Ruprecht, 1999.

Mulder, M. M. (ed.). *Miqra: Text, Translation, Reading and Interpretation of the Hebrew Bible in Ancient Judaism and Early Christianity.* Philadelphia: Fortress, 1988.

Müller, M. *The First Bible of the Church: A Plea for the Septuagint.* Sheffield: Sheffield Academic Press, 1996.

Murray, R. *Symbols of Church and Kingdom.* Piscataway, N.J.: Gorgias Press, 2004.

Naeh, S. "Structure and Division of the Midrash Torat Kohanim (a): Scrolls." *Tarbiz* 66 (1997), 483–515.

Najman, H. *Seconding Sinai: The Development of Mosaic Discourse in Second Temple Judaism.* Leiden: Brill, 2003.

Naveh, J., and S. Shaked. *Amulets and Magic Bowls: Aramaic Incantations of Late Antiquity.* Jerusalem: Magnes Press, 1985.

Naveh, J., and S. Shaked. *Magic Spells and Formulae: Aramaic Incantations of Late Antiquity.* Jerusalem: Magnes Press, 1993.

Nelson, W. D. "Oral Orthography: Early Rabbinic Oral and Written Transmission of Parallel Midrashic Tradition in the Mekhilta of Rabbi Shimon B. Yohai and the Mekhilta of Rabbi Ishmael." *AJS Review* 29 (2005), 1–32.

Neubauer, A. *Mediaeval Hebrew Chronicles.* Oxford, 1887–95.

Neubauer, J. *Geschichte des Biblisch-Talmudischen Eheschliessungsrechts. Eine Rechtsvergleichend-Historische Studie.* Leipzig: J. C. Hinrichs'sche Buchhandlung, 1920.

Neusner, J. "Notes on Goodenough's Jewish Symbols." *Conservative Judaism* 17 (1963), 77–92.

Neusner, J. *A History of the Jews in Babylonia.* Leiden: Brill, 1965–70.

Neusner, J. "The Rabbi and the Jewish Community." In J. Neusner (ed.), *Religions in Antiquity: Essays in Memory of Erwin Ramsdell Goodenough.* Leiden: Brill, 1968.

Neusner, J. *Development of a Legend: Studies on the Traditions Concerning Yohanan Ben Zakkai.* Leiden: Brill, 1970.

Neusner, J. *Aphrahat and Judaism.* Leiden: Brill, 1971a.

Neusner, J. *Rabbinic Traditions About the Pharisees before 70.* Leiden: Brill, 1971b.

Neusner, J. *Eliezer Ben Hyrcanus.* Leiden: Brill, 1973.

Neusner, J. *A History of the Mishnaic Law of Purities: The Redactiona and Formulation of the Order of Purities in Mishnah and Tosefta.* Leiden: Brill, 1977.

Neusner, J. *Form-Analysis and Exegesis: A Fresh Approach to the Interpretation of Mishnah.* Minneapolis: University of Minnesota Press, 1980.

Neusner, J. *Judaism: The Evidence of the Mishnah.* Chicago: University of Chicago Press, 1981.

Neusner, J. *Formative Judaism: Religious, Historical, and Literary Studies.* Chico, Calif.: Scholars Press, 1982.

Neusner, J. *Judaism in Society: The Evidence of the Yerushalmi: Toward the Natural History of a Religion.* Chicago: University of Chicago Press, 1983.

Neusner, J. *Invitation to the Talmud: A Teaching Book.* New York: Harper and Row, 1984.

Neusner, J. *The Memorized Torah: The Mnemonic System of the Mishnah.* Chico, Calif.: Scholars Press, 1985.

Neusner, J. *The Religious Study of Judaism: Description, Analysis, and Interpretation.* Lanham, Md.: University Press of America, 1986.

Neusner, J. *Judaism and Christianity in the Age of Constantine: History, Messiah, Israel and the Initial Confrontation.* Chicago: University of Chicago Press, 1987a.

Neusner, J. *Oral Tradition in Judaism.* New York: Garland Publishing, 1987b.

Neusner, J. *The Systemic Analysis of Judaism.* Atlanta: Scholars Press, 1988.

Neusner, J. *Making the Classics in Judaism: The Three Stages of Literary Formation.* Atlanta: Scholars Press, 1989.

Neusner, J. *The Talmud: A Close Encounter.* Minneapolis: Fortress Press, 1991.

Neusner, J. *The Judaism Behind the Texts.* Atlanta: Scholars Press, 1993.

Neusner, J. *The Documentary Foundation of Rabbinic Culture: Mopping up after Debates with Gerald L. Bruns, S. J. D. Cohen, Arnold Maria Goldberg, Susan Handelman, Christine Hayes, James Kugel, Peter Schaefer, Eliezer Segal, E. P. Sanders, and Lawrence H. Schiffman.* Atlanta: Scholars Press, 1995a.

Neusner, J. *Introduction to Rabbinic Literature.* New York: Doubleday, 1995b.

Neusner, J. "Paradigmatic Versus Historical Thinking: The Case of Rabbinic Judaism." *History and Theory* 36 (1997), 353–77.

Neusner, J. *The Mishnah: Religious Perspectives.* Leiden: Brill, 1999.

Neusner, J. *The Emergence of Judaism: Jewish Religion in Response to the Critical Issues of the First Six Centuries.* Lanham, Md.: University Press of America, 2000.

Neusner, J. *The Idea of History in Rabbinic Judaism.* Leiden: Brill, 2004.

Nörr, D. "Spruchregel und Generalisierung." *ZSS* 89 (1972), 18–93.

Neymeyer, U. *Die christlichen Lehrer im zweiten Jahrhundert.* Leiden: Brill, 1989.

Novak, D. "The Origin of the Noahide Laws." In W. Kelman and A. A. Chiel (eds.), *Perspectives on Jews and Judaism.* New York: Rabbinical Assembly, 1978, 301–10.

Noy, D. "Riddles at a Wedding-Banquet (Hebrew)." *Mahanayim* 83 (1963), 64–71.

Nussbaum, M. *The Therapy of Desire: Theory and Practice in Hellenistic Ethics.* Princeton, N.J.: Princeton University Press, 1994.

O'Donnell, J. J. *Avatars of the Word: From Papyrus to Cyberspace.* Cambridge, Mass.: Harvard University Press, 1998.

Olsson, B., and M. Zetterholm (eds.). *The Ancient Synagogue: From Its Origins until 200 C.E.* Stockholm: Almqvist & Wiksell International, 2003.

Olyan, S. M. "And with a Male You Shall Not Lie the Lying Down of a Woman: On the Meaning and Significance of Leviticus 18:22 and 20:13." *JHS* 5:2 (1994), 179–206.

Ong, W. J. *Orality and Literacy: The Technologizing of the Word.* New York: Methuen, 1982.

Oppenheimer, A. *Ha-galil bi-tekufat ha-mishnah.* Jerusalm: Merkaz Zalman Shazar, 1991.

Oppenheimer, A., B. H. Isaac, and M. Lecker (eds.). *Babylonia Judaica in the Talmudic Period.* Wiesbaden: Ludwig Reichart Verlag, 1983.

Pagis, D. *A Secret Sealed: Hebrew Baroque Emblem Riddles from Italy and Holland (Hebrew).* Jerusalem: Magnes Press, 1986.

Perikhanian, A. *The Book of a Thousand Judgments.* Costa Mesa, Calif.: Mazda Publishers in association with Bibliotheca Persica, 1997.

Peskowitz, M. *Spinning Fantasies: Rabbis, Gender, and History.* Berkeley: University of California Press, 1997.

Porter, F. C. "The Yeçer Hara: A Study in the Jewish Doctrine of Sin." In *Biblical and Semitic Studies: Yale Historical and Critical Contributions to Biblical Studies.* New York: Charles Scribner's Sons, 1901, 93–156.

Porton, G. G. *Goyim: Gentiles and Israelites in Mishnah-Tosefta.* Atlanta: Scholars Press, 1988.

Porton, G. G. *The Stranger within Your Gates: Converts and Conversion in Rabbinic Literature.* Chicago: University of Chicago Press, 1994.

Rosenfeld, B.-Z. *Lod ve-ḥakhameha bi-yemei ha-mishnah veha-talmud.* Jerusalem: Yad Ben Zvi, 1997.

Rosen-Zvi, I. "The Ritual of the Suspected Adulteress (Sotah) in Tannaitic Literature: Textual and Theoretical Perspectives." Ph.D. dissertation, Tel Aviv University, 2004.

Rosen-Zvi, I. "Bilhah the Inner Temptress: *The Testament of Reuben* and 'the Birth of Sexuality.'" *JQR* 96:1 (2005), 65–94.

Rosen-Zvi, I. "The Body and the Book: The List of Blemishes in Mishnah Tractate Bekhorot and the Place for the Temple and Its Worship in the Tannaitic Beit Ha-Midrash." *Mada'ei ha-yahadut*, forthcoming.

Rubenstein, J. L. *Talmudic Stories: Narrative Art, Composition and Culture.* Baltimore: Johns Hopkins University Press, 1999.

Rubenstein, J. L. "The Thematization of Dialectics in Bavli Aggada." *JJS* 53 (2002), 1–14.

Rubenstein, J. L. *The Culture of the Babylonian Talmud.* Baltimore: Johns Hopkins University Press, 2003.

Rubenstein, J. L. (ed.). *Creation and Composition: The Contribution of the Bavli Redactors (Stammaim) to the Aggada.* Tübingen: Mohr Siebeck, 2005.

Safrai, S. "Education and the Study of the Torah." In S. Safrai and M. Stern (eds.), *The Jewish People in the First Century, Vol. 2.* Amsterdam: Van Gorcum, 1976.

Sæbø, M. (ed.). *Hebrew Bible/Old Testament: The History of Its Interpretation.* Vol. 1: *From the Beginnings to the Middle Ages (until 1300). Part 1: Antiquity.* Göttingen: Vandenhoeck & Ruprecht, 1996.

Safrai, S. *The Economy of Roman Palestine.* London: Routledge, 1994a.

Safrai, S. "Jesus and the Hasidim." *Jerusalem Perspective* 42–44 (1994b), 1–22.

Safrai, S. (ed.) *The Literature of the Sages.* Philadelphia: Fortress Press, 1987.

Safrai, Z. E. *The Jewish Community in the Talmudic Period (Hebrew)*. Jerusalem: Merkaz Zalman Shazar, 1995.

Saldarini, A. "The Adoption of a Dissident: Akavya Ben Mahalaleel in Rabbinic Tradition." *JJS* 33 (1982a), 547–56.

Saldarini, A. *Scholastic Rabbinism: A Literary Study of the Fathers According to Rabbi Nathan*. Chico, Calif.: Scholars Press, 1982b.

Saldarini, A. *Pharisees, Scribes and Sadducees in Palestinian Society: A Sociological Approach* Grand Rapids, Mich.: Eerdmans, 2001.

Salvesen, A. *Symmachus in the Pentateuch*. Manchester: Manchester University Press, 1992.

Salvesen, A. (ed.). *Origen's Hexapla and Fragments*. Tübingen: Mohr Siebeck, 1997.

Samely, A. *Rabbinic Interpretation of Scripture in the Mishnah*. New York: Oxford University Press, 2002.

Sanders, E. P. *Jewish Law from Jesus to the Mishnah*. London: SCM Press, 1990.

Sanders, E. P. *Judaism Practice and Belief 63 BCE–66 CE*. Philadelphia: Trinity Press, 1992.

Satlow, M. "They Abused Him Like a Woman." *JHS* 5 (1994a), 1–25.

Satlow, M. "'Wasted Seed,' the History of a Rabbinic Idea." *HUCA* 65 (1994b), 137–69.

Satlow, M. L. *Tasting the Dish: Rabbinic Rhetorics of Sexuality*. Atlanta: Scholars Press, 1995.

Schachter, J. J. "Facing the Truths of History." *The Torah U-Madda Journal* 8 (1998–99), 200–77.

Schäfer, P. "Die Termini 'Heiliger Geist' and 'Geist der Prophetie' in den Targumim." *Vetus Testamentum* 20 (1970), 304–14.

Schäfer, P. *Die Vorstellung vom Heiligen Geist in der rabbinischen Literatur*. Munich: Kösel, 1972.

Schäfer, P. "Tradition and Redaction in Hekhalot Literature." *JSJ* 14 (1983), 172–81.

Schäfer, P. "Research into Rabbinic Literature: An Attempt to Define the Status Quaestionis." *JJS* 37 (1986), 139–52.

Schäfer, P. "Once Again the Status Quaestionis of Research in Rabbinic Literature: An Answer to Chaim Milikowsky." *JJS* 40 (1989), 89–94.

Schäfer, P. *The Hidden and Manifest God: Some Major Themes in Early Jewish Mysticism*. Albany: SUNY Press, 1992.

Schäfer, P. *Judeophobia*. Cambridge, Mass.: Harvard University Press, 1997.

Schäfer, P. "In Heaven as It Is in Hell: The Cosmology of Seder Rabbah Di-Bereshit." In R. A. Boustan and A. Y. Reed (eds.), *Heavenly Realms and Earthly Realities in Late Antique Religions*. Cambridge: Cambridge University Press, 2004, 233–75.

Schäfer, P. (ed.). *The Talmud Yerushalmi and Graeco-Roman Culture*. Tübingen: Mohr Siebeck, 1998.

Schiffer, I. J. "The Men of the Great Assembly." In William S. Green (ed.) *Persons and Institutions in Early Rabbinic Judaism*. Missoula, Mont.: Scholars Press, 1977, 237–73.

Schiffman, L. *The Halakhah at Qumran*. Leiden: Brill, 1975.

Schiffman, L. H. *Reclaiming the Dead Sea Scrolls: The History of Judaism, the Background of Christianity, and the Lost Library of Qumran.* Philadelphia: Jewish Publication Society, 1994.

Schiffman, L. H. "Dead Sea Scrolls, Biblical Interpretation." In J. Neusner and A. J. Avery-Peck (eds.), *Encyclopedia of Midrash: Biblical Interpretation in Formative Judaism.* Leiden: Brill, 2005.

Schiffman, L. H., and J. C. Vanderkam (eds.). *Encyclopedia of the Dead Sea Scrolls.* New York: Oxford University Press, 2000.

Schirmann, H. "Hebrew Liturgical Poetry and Christian Hymnology." *JQR* 44 (1953), 123–61.

Schofer, J. "The Redaction of Desire: Structure and Editing of Rabbinic Teachings Concerning Yezer ('Inclination')." *Journal of Jewish Thought and Philosophy* 12 (2003a), 19–53.

Schofer, J. "Spiritual Exercises in Rabbinic Culture." *AJS Review* 27 (2003b), 203–26.

Schofer, J. *The Making of a Sage.* Madison: University of Wisconsin Press, 2005.

Scholem, G. *Jewish Gnosticism, Merkabah Mysticism and Talmudic Tradition.* New York: Jewish Theological Seminary, 1960.

Scholem, G. *Major Trends in Jewish Mysticism.* New York: Schocken Books, 1961.

Schremer, A. "How Much Jewish Polygyny in Roman Palestine." *PAAJR* 63 (1997–2001), 181–223.

Schremer, A. *Male and Female He Created Them: Jewish Marriage in the Late Second Temple, Mishnah and Talmud Periods.* Jerusalem: Merkaz Zalman Shazar, 2003.

Schremer, A. "Stammaitic Historiography." In J. Rubenstein (ed.), *Creation and Composition: The Contribution of the Bavli Redactors (Stammaim) to the Aggada.* Tübingen: Mohr Siebeck, 2005, 219–37.

Schulz, F. *Prinzipien des Römischen Rechts.* München: Duncker & Humbolt, 1954.

Schürer, E. *History of the Jewish People in the Age of Jesus Christ.* Edinburgh: T. & T. Clark, 1979.

Schwartz, D. R. "From Alexandria to Rabbinic Literature to Zion: The Jews' Departure from History, and Who It Is Who Returns to It." In S. N. Eisenstadt and M. Lissak (eds.), *Zionism and the Return to History: A Reappraisal (Hebrew).* Jerusalem: Yad Yitshak ben-Tsevi, 1999, 40–55.

Schwartz, J. *Jewish Settlement in Southern Judaea from the Bar Kokhba Revolt to the Muslim Conquest.* Jerusalem: Magnes Press, 1986.

Schwartz, J. *Lod (Lydda), Israel: From Its Origins through the Byzantine Period.* Oxford: Tempus Peparatum, 1991.

Schwartz, S. *Josephus and Judaean Politics.* Leiden: Brill, 1990.

Schwartz, S. "Language, Power and Identity in Ancient Palestine." *Past and Present* 148 (1995), 3–47.

Schwartz, S. "The Patriarchs and the Diaspora." *JJS* 50 (1999), 208–22.

Schwartz, S. *Imperialism and Jewish Society, 200 B.C.E. to 640 C.E.* Princeton, N.J.: Princeton University Press, 2001a.

Schwartz, S. "The Rabbi in Aphrodite's Bath: Palestinian Society and Jewish Identity in the High Roman Empire." In S. Goldhill (ed.), *Being Greek under Rome:*

Cultural Identity, the Second Sophistic, and the Development of Empire. Cambridge: Cambridge University Press, 2001b, 335–62.

Schwartz, S. (2002) "Historiography on the Jews in the 'Talmudic Period.'" In M. Goodman (ed.), *Oxford Handbook of Jewish Studies.* Oxford: Oxford University Press, 2002, 79–114.

Segal, A. F. *Two Powers in Heaven: Early Rabbinic Reports About Christianity and Gnosticism.* Leiden: Brill, 1977.

Segal, E. L. "The Use of the Formula *Ki Ha D'* in the Citation of Cases in the Babylonian Talmud." *HUCA* 50 (1979), 199–218.

Segal, E. L. *Case Citation in the Babylonian Talmud: The Evidence of Tractate Neziqin.* Atlanta: Brown Judaic Studies, 1990.

Segal, M. "4q Reworked Pentateuch or 4q Pentateuch?" In L. H. Schiffman, E. Tov, J. C. Vanderkam (eds.), *The Dead Sea Scrolls Fifty Years after Their Discovery: Proceedings of the Jerusalem Congress, July 20–25, 1997.* Jerusalem: Israel Exploration Society and the Shrine of the Book, 2000, 391–99.

Segal, M. "The Relationship between the Legal and Narrative Passages in Jubilees (Reuben and Bilhah/Judah and Tamar)." In D. Dimant and E. G. Chazon (eds.), *Rewriting the Bible: Proceedings of the Seventh International Conference of The Orion Center for the Study of the Dead Sea Scrolls and Associated Literature.* Leiden: Brill, forthcoming.

Setzer, C. *Jewish Responses to Early Christianity: History and Polemics, 30–150 CE.* Minneapolis: Fortress Press, 1994.

Shaked, G. *Between Laughter and Tears: A Study of Mendele Mokher Sfarim's Works.* Tel Aviv: Masadah (Hebr.), 1965.

Shaked, G., and E. M. Budick. *Modern Hebrew Fiction.* Bloomington: Indiana University Press, 2000.

Shaked, S. *Dualism in Transformation: Varieties of Religion in Sasanian Iran.* London: School of Oriental and African Studies, University of London, 1993.

Shaked, S., and A. Netzer (eds.). *Irano-Judaica: Studies Relating to Jewish Contacts with Persian Culture Throughout the Ages.* 5 vols. Jerusalem: Makhon Ben Zvi, 1982–2003, Vol. 6 forthcoming.

Shaki, M. "The Denkard Account of the History of the Zoroastrian Scriptures." *Archiv Orientaln,* 49 (1981), 114–25.

Shemesh, A. "Scriptural Interpretation in the Damascus Document and Their Parallels in Rabbinic Midrash." In J. M. Baumgarten et al. (eds.), *The Damascus Document: A Centennial of Discovery.* Leiden, Boston, and Cologne: Brill, 2000, 161–75.

Shinan, A., and Y. Zakovitch. *The Story of Reuben and Bilhah: Genesis 35:21–26 in the Bible, the Old Versions and the Ancient Jewish Literature (Hebrew).* Jerusalem: Hebrew University Press, 1983.

Simon, M. *Verus Israel: A Study of the Relations between Christians and Jews in the Roman Empire (135–425).* Oxford: Oxford University Press, 1986.

Skarsaune, O. *The Proof from Prophecy: A Study of Justin Martyr's Proof-Text Tradition: Text-Type, Provenance, Theological Profile.* Leiden: Brill, 1987.

Smith, M. "Observations on Hekhalot Rabbati." In A. Altmann (ed.), *Biblical and Other Studies.* Cambridge, Mass.: Harvard University Press, 1963, 142–60.

Smith, M. "Goodenough's Jewish Symbols in Retrospect." *JBL* 86 (1967), 53–68.

Snaith, J. G. "Aphrahat and the Jews." In J. A. Emerton and S. Reif (eds.), *Interpreting the Hebrew Bible: Essays in Honour of E. I. J. Rosenthal.* Cambridge: Cambridge University Press, 1982.

Snyder, H. G. *Teachers and Texts in the Ancient World: Philosophers, Jews and Christians.* New York: Routledge, 2000.

Söllner, A. *Einführung in die römische Rechtsgeschichte.* Munich: C. H. Beck, 1980.

Sperber, D. *Roman Palestine, 200–400, Money and Prices.* Ramat Gan: Bar Ilan University Press, 1974.

Sperber, D. *Roman Palestine, 200–400, the Land: Crisis and Change in Agrarian Society as Reflected in Rabbinic Sources.* Ramat Gan: Bar Ilan University Press, 1978.

Sperber, D. "Manuals of Rabbinic Conduct." In L. Landman (ed.), *Scholars and Scholarship.* New York: Yeshiva University Press, 1990, 9–26.

Stein, S. "The Concept of the 'Fence': Observations on Its Origin and Development." In S. Stein and R. Loewe (eds.), *Studies in Jewish Religious and Intellectual History: Presented to Alexander Altmann on the Occasion of His Seventieth Birthday.* University, Ala.: University of Alabma Press, 1979, 301–29.

Steinfeld, Z. A. *'Am levaded yishkon.* Forthcoming.

Steinmetz, D. "Distancing and Bringing Near: A New Look at Mishnah Tractates Eduyyot and Abot." *HUCA* 83 (2002), 49–96.

Stern, D. (ed.). *The Anthology in Jewish Literature.* New York: Oxford University Press, 2004.

Stern, S. "The Concept of Authorship in the Babylonian Talmud." *JJS* 46 (1995), 28–51.

Stern, Y. S. "Images in Jewish Law in the Period of the Mishnah and the Talmud." *Zion* 61 (1996), 397–419.

Stock, B. *The Implications of Literacy: Written Language and Models of Interpretation in the Eleventh and Twelfth Centuries.* Princeton, N.J.: Princeton University Press, 1983.

Stone, M. E. (ed.). *Jewish Writings of the Second Temple Period: Apocrypha, Pseudepigrapha, Qumran Sectarian Writings, Philo, Josephus.* Philadelphia: Fortress Press, 1984.

Stone, M. E., and T. A. Bergren (eds.). *Biblical Figures Outside the Bible.* Harrisville, Penn.: Trinity Press International, 1998.

Stone, M. E., and E. G. Chazon (eds.). *Biblical Perspectives: Early Use and Interpretation of the Bible in Light of the Dead Sea Scrolls.* Leiden: Brill, 1998.

Strack, H. L. & Billerbeck, P. (1924–8). *Kommentar zum Neuen Testament aus Talmud und Midrasch,* München, C. H. Beck.

Strack, H. L., and G. Stemberger. *Introduction to the Talmud and Midrash.* Minneapolis: Fortress Press, 1992.

Strobel, K. "Jüdisches Patriarchat, Rabbinentum, und Priesterdynastie von Emesa: Historische Phänomene innerhalb des Imperium Romanum der Kaiserzeit." *Ktema* 14 (1989), 29–77.

Stroumsa, G. G., and B. Visotzky, B. *Fathers of the World: Essays in Rabbinic and Patristic Literatures.* Tübingen: Mohr Siebeck, 1995.

Sundberg, A. C. *The Old Testament in the Early Church*. Cambridge, Mass.: Harvard University Press, 1964.

Sussmann, Y. "The History of Halakha and the Dead Sea Scrolls: Preliminary Observations on Miqsat Ma'ase Ha-Torah (4qmmt)." *Tarbiz* 59 (1990a), 11–76.

Sussmann, Y. "Ve-shuv li-yerushalmi nezikin." In Y. Sussmann and D. Rosenthal (eds.), *Mehqerei Talmud*. Jerusalem: Magnes Press, 1990b, 55–130.

Swartz, M. D. *Mystical Prayer in Ancient Judaism: An Analysis of Ma'aseh Merkavah*. Tübingen: Mohr Siebeck, 1992.

Swartz, M. D. *Scholastic Magic: Ritual and Revelation in Early Jewish Mysticism*. Princeton, N.J.: Princeton University Press, 1996.

Swartz, M. D. "The Book of the Great Name." In L. Fine (ed.), *Judaism in Practice*. Princeton, N.J.: Princeton University Press, 2001a.

Swartz, M. D. "The Dead Sea Scrolls and Later Jewish Magic and Mysticism." *DSD* 8 (2001b), 1–12.

Swartz, M. D. "Understanding Ritual in Jewish Magic: Perspectives from the Cairo Genizah and Other Sources." In M. J. Geller (ed.), *Officina Magica: The Workings of Magic*. Leiden: Brill, 2005.

Swartz, M. D., and J. Yaholom (eds.). *Avodah: Ancient Poems for Yom Kippur*. University Park: Pennsylvania State University Press, 2005.

Swete, H. B. *The Holy Spirit in the Ancient Church: A Study of Christian Teaching in the Age of the Fathers*. London: Macmillan, 1912.

Thomas, R. *Literacy and Orality in Ancient Greece*. Cambridge: Cambridge University Press, 1992.

Tomson, P. J., and D. Lambers-Petry (eds.). *The Image of the Judaeo-Christians in Ancient Jewish and Christian Literature*. Tübingen: Mohr Siebeck, 2003.

Tosh, J. *The Pursuit of History*. New York: Longman, 1991.

Tov, E. (ed.). *The Texts from the Judaean Desert: Indices and an Introduction to the Discoveries in the Judaean Desert Series*. Oxford: Clarendon Press, 2002.

Tropper, A. "The Fate of Jewish Historiography after the Bible: A New Interpretation." *History and Theory* 43 (2004a), 179–97.

Tropper, A. *Wisdom, Politics, and Historiography: Tractate Avot in the Context of the Graeco-Roman Near East*. Oxford: Oxford University Press, 2004b.

Tropper, A. "Roman Context in Jewish Texts: On Diatagma and Prostagma in Rabbinic Literature." *JQR* 95:2 (2005), 207–22.

Urbach, E. E. "When Did Prophecy Cease [Hebrew]?" *Tarbiz* 17 (1946), 1–11.

Urbach, E. E. "Political and Social Tendencies in Talmudic Concepts of Charity (Hebrew)." *Zion*, (1951) 1–27.

Urbach, E. E. "The Rabbinical Laws of Idolatry in the Second and Third Centuries in the Light of Archaeological and Historical Facts." *IEJ* 9 (1959), 149–65, 229–45.

Urbach, E. E. "The Homiletical Interpreations of the Sages and the Exposition of Origen on Canticles, and the Jewish-Christian Disputation." *Scripta Hierosolymitana* 22 (1971), 247–75.

Urbach, E. E. *The Sages – Their Concepts and Beliefs*. Jerusalem, 1975; repr.: Boston: Harvard University Press, 1987.

Urbach, E. E. "Halakhah and History." In R. Hammerton-Kelley and R. Scroggs (eds.), *Jews, Greeks and Christians: Essays in Honor of W. D. Davies.* Leiden: Brill, 1976, 112–28.

Urbach, E. E. *Collected Writings in Jewish Studies.* Jerusalem: Magnes Press, 1999.

Urman, D. "The House of Assembly and House of Study: Are They One and the Same? (Hebrew)." *JJS* 44 (1993), 236–57.

Vanderkam, J. C. "Sinai Revisited." In M. Henze (ed.), *Biblical Interpretation at Qumran.* Grand Rapids, Mich.: Eerdmans, 2005, 44–60.

Vermes, G. *Scripture and Tradition: Haggadic Studies.* Leiden: Brill, 1973.

Vermes, G. "The Decalogue and the Minim." In G. Vermes (ed.), *Post-Biblical Jewish Studies.* Leiden: Brill, 1975.

Visotzky, B. L. "Anti-Christian Polemic in Leviticus Rabbah." *PAAJR* 56 (1989), 83–100.

Visotzky, B. L. *Fathers of the World: Essays in Rabbinic and Patristic Literatures.* Tübingen: Mohr Siebeck, 1995.

Walzer, R. *Galen on Jews and Christians.* London: Oxford University Press, 1949.

Wasserstein, A. "Greek Language and Philosophy in the Early Rabbinic Academies." In G. Abramson (ed.), *Jewish Education and Learning Published in Honour of Dr. David Patterson on the Occasion of His Seventieth Birthday.* Langhorne, Penn.: Harwood Academic Publishers, 1994.

Watson, A. *Law Making in the Later Roman Republic.* Oxford: Oxford University Press, 1974.

Weinreich, U. *Languages in Contact: Findings and Problems.* The Hague: Mouton, 1974.

Weitzman, M. P. *The Syriac Version of the Old Testament: An Introduction.* Cambridge: Cambridge University Press, 1999.

West, E. W. *Sacred Books of the East.* New Delhi: Motilal Banarsidass, 1994.

Whittow, M. "Ruling the Late Roman and Early Byzantine City: A Continuous History." *Past & Present* 129 (1990), 3–29.

Wieacker *Vom römischen Recht. Zehn Versuche.* 2d ed. Stuttgart: Kohler, 1961.

Wiesehöfer, J. *Ancient Persia: From 550 BC to 650 AD.* London: I. B. Tauris, 1996.

Wilken, R. L. *Judaism and the Early Christian Mind: A Study of Cyril of Alexandria's Exegesis and Theology.* New Haven, Conn.: Yale University Press, 1971.

Wilken, R. L. *The Land Called Holy: Palestine in Christian History and Thought.* New Haven, Conn.: Yale University Press, 1992.

Williams, C. A. *Roman Homosexuality: Ideologies of Masculinity in Classical Antiquity.* New York: Oxford University Press, 1999.

Wingren, G. *Man and Incarnation: A Study of the Biblical Theology of Irenaeus.* London: Oliver & Boyd, 1959.

Wolfson, E. "*Yeridah la-Merkavah*: Typology of Ecstasy and Enthronement in Ancient Jewish Mysticism." In R. A. Herrera (ed.), *Mystics of the Book: Themes, Topics, and Typologies.* New York: Peter Lang, 1993, 13–44.

Wolfson, E. *Through a Speculum That Shines: Vision and Imagination in Medieval Jewish Mysticism.* Princeton, N.J.: Princeton University Press, 1994.

Wolfson, H. *Philo: Foundations of Religious Philosophy in Judaism, Christianity, and Islam.* Cambridge, Mass.: Harvard University Press, 1947.

Yadin, A. *Scripture as Logos: Rabbi Ishmael and the Origins of Midrash.* Philadelphia: University of Pennsylvania Press, 2004.

Yahalom, J. *"Piyyut as Poetry."* In L. I. Levine (ed.), *The Synagogue in Late Antiquity.* New York: Jewish Theological Seminary of America, 1987.

Yahalom, J. *Poetry and Society in Jewish Galilee of Late Antiquity.* Tel Aviv: Ha-Kibbutz Ha-Me'uhad, 1999.

Yalom, M. *A History of the Breast.* New York: Ballatine Books, 1998.

Yaron, R. *Gifts in Contemplation of Death in Jewish and Roman Law.* Oxford: Clarendon Press, 1960.

Yarshater, E. (ed.). *Cambridge History of Iran.* Cambridge: Cambridge University Press, 1983.

Yassif, E. "The Cycle of Tales in Rabbinic Literature (Hebrew)." *JSHL* 12 (1990), 103–45.

Yassif, E. *The Hebrew Folktale: History, Genre, Meaning.* Bloomington: Indiana University Press, 1999.

Yearley, L. "Recent Work on Virtue." *Religious Studies Review* 16 (1990), 1–9.

Yerushalmi, Y. H. *Zakhor: Jewish History and Jewish Memory.* Seattle: University of Washington Press, 1989.

Zaehner, R. C. *Zurvanism: A Zoroastrian Dilemma.* New York: Biblio and Tannen, 1972.

Zaehner, R. C. *The Teachings of the Magi.* New York: Oxford University Press, 1976.

Zussman, J., and D. Rozental (eds.). *Talmudic Studies: Collected Studies in Talmud and Related Fields Dedicated to the Memory of Prof. Ephraim E. Urbach.* Jerusalem: Magnes Press, 2005.

Index

Source Index

Other titles in the series (*continued from page iii*)